Palgrave Studies on Leadership and Learning
in Teacher Education

Series Editors
Maria Assunção Flores
Institute of Education
University of Minho
Braga, Portugal

Thuwayba Al Barwani
College of Education
Sultan Qaboos University
Al Khod, Muscat, Oman

The series focuses on original and research-informed writing related to teachers and leaders' work as it addresses teacher education in the 21st century. The editors of this series adopt a more comprehensive definition of Teacher Education to include pre-service, induction, and continuing professional development. The contributions will deal with the challenges and opportunities of learning and leading in teacher education in a globalized era. It includes the dimensions of practice, policy, research, and university school partnership. The distinctiveness of this book series lies in the comprehensive and interconnected ways in which learning and leading in teacher education are understood. In the face of global challenges and local contexts, it is important to address leadership and learning in teacher education as it relates to different levels of education as well as opportunities for teacher candidates, teacher educators, education leaders, and other stakeholders to learn and develop. The book series draws upon a wide range of methodological approaches and epistemological stances and covers topics including teacher education, professionalism, leadership, and teacher identity.

More information about this series at
http://www.palgrave.com/gp/series/16190

Otherine Johnson Neisler
Editor

The Palgrave Handbook of Academic Professional Development Centers

palgrave
macmillan

Editor
Otherine Johnson Neisler 🄳
Center for Excellence in Teaching and Learning
Sultan Qaboos University
Muscat, Oman

ISSN 2524-7069 ISSN 2524-7077 (electronic)
Palgrave Studies on Leadership and Learning in Teacher Education
ISBN 978-3-030-80966-9 ISBN 978-3-030-80967-6 (eBook)
https://doi.org/10.1007/978-3-030-80967-6

© The Editor(s) (if applicable) and The Author(s), under exclusive licence to Springer Nature Switzerland AG 202
This work is subject to copyright. All rights are solely and exclusively licensed by the Publisher, whether t
whole or part of the material is concerned, specifically the rights of translation, reprinting, reuse of illustration
recitation, broadcasting, reproduction on microfilms or in any other physical way, and transmission
information storage and retrieval, electronic adaptation, computer software, or by similar or dissimi
methodology now known or hereafter developed.
The use of general descriptive names, registered names, trademarks, service marks, etc. in this publication do
not imply, even in the absence of a specific statement, that such names are exempt from the relevant protecti
laws and regulations and therefore free for general use.
The publisher, the authors, and the editors are safe to assume that the advice and information in this book
believed to be true and accurate at the date of publication. Neither the publisher nor the authors or the edit
give a warranty, expressed or implied, with respect to the material contained herein or for any errors or omissi
that may have been made. The publisher remains neutral with regard to jurisdictional claims in published m
and institutional affiliations.

Cover illustration: © CSA images / gettys.com

This Palgrave Macmillan imprint is published by the registered company Springer Nature Switzerland AG.
The registered company address is: Gewerbestrasse 11, 6330 Cham, Switzerland

This book would not have been possible without the many contributions of various local, national, and international organizations, including those listed below, and is dedicated to their founders and leadership who over many decades have contributed to the field of academic professional development:

The Professional and Organizational Development (POD) Network
Advance HE, previously the Higher Education Academy
The International Society for the Scholarship of Teaching
and Learning (ISSOTL)
The International Consortium for Educational Development (ICED)
The International Council on Education for Teaching (ICET)

Foreword: The Urgent Need for Different and Better Ways of Teaching

Introduction

There are two macro-changes occurring in our current era of the 21st century that have major implications for the educational needs of society and of individuals. The first is the greatly increased use of information technology. This has made the world more connected.[1] People, ideas, products, and problems are moving from one region of the globe to another much more frequently than previously. The second is the increased rate of change of multiple global characteristics. This refers to parameters such as urbanization, carbon emission, use of electricity, the evolution of new diseases, the development of new medicines, the sale of arms and weapons, climate change, desertification, destruction of the rainforests, ocean pollution, extinction of species, and so on.

These two macro-changes have some major benefits, but they also make the social and environmental systems that support us more complicated, complex, and problematic. As a result, all societies need citizens with a high level of education to solve the continual stream of new and challenging problems—and, in turn, individual people need a high level of education to "thrive and survive" in this new, rapidly changing, more complicated world. Some have argued that, as a result of these changes, the critical level of education needed now, in all societies, is not primary or even secondary education, but tertiary education; that is, university-level education.[2]

However, it is not enough just to have more people attending and graduating from universities. The universities themselves need to provide new and better kinds of learning. Preparing students to pass tests on disciplinary knowledge is clearly not sufficient to prepare them to deal with the personal, professional, and societal challenges they will face in this new world. Students do need to acquire a certain level of disciplinary knowledge, but they also need to develop strong capabilities for critical thinking, problem-solving, identifying the interaction between different kinds of knowledge, the ability to work with others—especially those different from themselves—and, perhaps most importantly, the ability to know how to engage in focused, independent learning throughout their personal, professional, and civic lives.

And how will students acquire these new and better kinds of learning? If we want big changes and improvements in student learning, we clearly need big changes and improvements in university-level teaching. And this means professors need to be educated about how to provide these new and better kinds of teaching.

The Need for Universal Faculty Development[3]

There are two major challenges that must be met, if we want better kinds of teaching in higher education. The first comes from the worldwide practice of hiring people to be university professors based on their having acquired a graduate degree (e.g., a masters or doctoral degree) in some subject matter. The problem is that the graduate programs for these advanced degrees focus almost exclusively on how to do research in that subject; they seldom include any formal preparation for university-level teaching. Hence, new professors have extensive training in how to do *research* in their areas of specialization, but no training on how to *teach* courses in that subject. The second challenge is that the graduate programs that provide these advanced degrees have not shown any widespread readiness to start including preparation for university-level teaching in their programs for graduate students. As a result of not having any formal preparation for teaching, the vast majority of beginner university teachers in all countries "teach the way they were taught." Consequently, they are not prepared to provide the new and different kinds of learning urgently needed by students in today's world.

What is the solution to this situation? If teachers are going to develop new and better ways of teaching, they will have to learn the ideas they need *after* they start teaching. That is, the universities that hire new professors need to provide their own, campus-based faculty development programs. These programs need to be capable of offering workshops and consulting services that can help new professors learn the ideas they need to educate students in a new and better way. Fortunately, there are two pieces of "good news" that can help universities do this.

Good News #1: New and Better Ideas about Teaching Are Available

During the 1970s and 1980s, there were not many books with major ideas on how to teach well. And the books that did exist were focused mainly on how to lecture more effectively; that is, they urged teachers to do such things as move around more, use facial expressions when talking, and establish eye contact with students. But, for various reasons, this all began to change starting in 1991. That was when the first books on *active learning* appeared. These books started a whole new line of thinking about good teaching. They said that good teaching involves more than what the *teacher* does; it involves what teachers have the *students* do.

Since that time, there has been an outpouring each year of books with major new ideas about university-level teaching. Here is a short list of some of the topics of these books:

* How students learn
* Learning-centered teaching
* Designing learning experiences
* Identifying *what* students might learn
* Using active learning
* Using small groups
* Assessing student learning
* Motivating and enabling students to learn
* Using powerful teaching strategies
* Teaching large classes
* Using instructional technology
* Evaluating teaching
* Having students reflect on their own learning processes.

By now, there has been research and informal observations on the use of these ideas, and the results are clear: professors who use these ideas effectively in their teaching are able to generate greater student engagement and better student learning than they did before. This leaves us with a new challenge: *How can we get more professors learning about and using these ideas?*

Good News #2: New Models of Faculty Development Are Available

Some countries have begun to recognize the significance of having high-quality teaching in their universities. Therefore, they have instituted national policies that have increased the proportion of their professors who are learning about and using these ideas and hence are teaching in a more effective way. I have collected some information about these policies and have identified four different levels of faculty development at the national level.[4] Here is a brief description of these four levels, starting with the lowest level first.

Level 1: Little or no Faculty Development Activity

This is the current situation in most regions of the world, for example Asia, the Middle East, Africa, and Latin America. In these regions, a few institutions have started such programs, but the percentage of all institutions doing this is very low.

Level 2: A Substantial Minority of Institutions Have Faculty Development Activities, but Faculty Participation Is Voluntary

This is the situation in countries such as the USA, Germany, and Thailand. In the USA, for example, approximately 35–40% of all institutions of higher education have a faculty development program. Within most of these institutions, only 20–35% of all professors participate at a substantial level each year.

Level 3: Nearly Universal Availability of Programs, and Participation Is Mandated for New Teachers

This is the situation in British Commonwealth countries (i.e., Canada, England, South Africa, Sri Lanka, Australia, and New Zealand) and several countries in Northern Europe. Nearly all universities have their own faculty development programs and education authorities have mandated participation at a certain level of faculty development; for example, 175–200 hours of formal learning about teaching is required for new professors before they can be considered for promotion.

Level 4: Continuous Faculty Development Is Expected of All Professors

This is rare, but I do know of one example that is doing an excellent job in this regard: the Faculty of Engineering at Lund University in Sweden. They have a Centre for Engineering Education that has put together a combination of activities for their professors that has two purposes: (1) to introduce all professors to new ideas about teaching and learning, and (2) to support a culture in which professors talk about pedagogical information and ideas with each other, both formally and informally. The center's activities include over a dozen different courses offered each year on different aspects of teaching; 200 hours of mandated training for junior professors (as described in Level 3 above); an annual conference on teaching and learning offered for all professors; and a special activity for experienced professors—the Pedagogical Academy.

Senior professors can apply for membership in the academy by submitting a portfolio in which they document their long-term interest and activity in being a reflective practitioner, being aware of the scholarship of teaching and learning, incorporating ideas from this scholarship into their own teaching, and sharing their experiences with others, such that everyone's teaching benefits from a faculty-wide culture of learning and talking about the topic of high-quality teaching. The university provides two financial incentives for the Pedagogical Academy: (1) an increase in salary for all professors who earn membership in it, and (2) a funding supplement for every department that has a professor who earns membership.

What are the results of all these activities? First, they have succeeded in getting a high percentage of all professors involved in continually learning about teaching. The director of the center reports that approximately 20% of all senior professors have earned membership in the Pedagogical Academy, and at least 80% of all professors, junior and senior, participate in some substantial activity on an annual basis.[5] Second, the benefit of this high participation in several activities has revealed itself in student ratings of the quality of courses across the whole faculty. There has been a continuing, discernible increase in the average combined student ratings of all courses in the faculty every year[6] since the full set of the center's activities became available in 2001.

Concluding Comments

What is needed at this time, worldwide, is for national and university leaders in each country to do two things:

1. Recognize that their educational programs will be inadequate to meet the educational needs of the current century until their universities have teachers who have learned how to create good curricula and teach more effectively
2. Search for and create policies that will ensure that all professors who teach—not just beginning teachers, but *everyone* who teaches—will continuously learn about and use the best teaching practices available in their own classrooms.

This book offers in-depth information about the models, mission, funding, and structure of different kinds of faculty development programs. This information can be immensely useful in helping institutional and program leaders generate high-impact educational programs in their institutions. Consequently, these institutions can then start graduating students who have achieved the several kinds of learning desperately needed in this century, both by the students themselves and by the societies in which their students will live, work, and serve.

Norman, OK, USA

L. Dee Fink

Notes

1. Friedman, T. L. (2005). *The World Is Flat: A Brief History of the Twenty-firs. Century*. Farrar, Straus, and Giroux.
2. Ibid., p. 289.
3. I use the term "faculty development" here as this is the phrase commonly use in the USA. However, in many countries, this same concept is referre to as "educational development" or "academic development."
4. Fink, L. D. (2013). The current status of faculty development internationall *International Journal for the Scholarship of Teaching and Learning, 7*(2), 4.
5. Torgny Roxå, personal communication, December 15 and 16, 2018.
6. Lund University (2018). *Self-assessment* (pp. 47–49). Centre for Engineeri Education, Lund University.

Preface

This book emerged from communications with academic professional development center (ADC) directors and related professionals whose work I referenced as I began the proposal for the Center for Excellence in Teaching and Learning at Sultan Qaboos University in Oman. Luckily, *A Guide to Faculty Development: Second Edition* (Gillespie & Robertson, 2010) became my foundational reference. *The Palgrave Handbook of Academic Professional Development Centers* presents case studies of ADCs whose missions, structures, programming, and evaluation reflect the theories and practices explained by Gillespie and colleagues, as well as those of the Professional and Organizational Development (POD) Network in the field of higher education (POD Network, n.d.).

The purpose of this book is to share experiences across different contexts and cultures and to provide models for those who are starting new centers as well as those seeking to change and improve existing centers. The global audience includes higher education faculty professional developers, administrators, and individual faculty members who are interested in a comparison of programs in various academic, cultural, governmental, and economic contexts.

To meet the needs of this international audience, 36 case studies were selected from over 239 submissions based on contributions to the field and to meet purposeful, stratified sampling criteria. These criteria included the Quacquarelli Symonds (QS) and Center for World University Rankings stratification systems, public/private control, mission, size, and geographic location. Overall, 10 of the centers described in the 36 case studies are housed within the QS world's top 100 universities, with almost all of those being within the top 10 in their respective countries. The rest of the ADCs span the ranking levels, except for 11 that represent national or regional rankings in niche categories. While these rankings were considered during the selection

xiv   Preface

process to ensure diversity, they are not reported herein. The university statistics shown in Appendix A are a more useful documentation of diversity for ADC strategic planning.

Part I: Regional Academic Development Historical Perspectives

This volume opens with four international country/geographic overviews: Australia, South America, China, and Africa, with a focus on Kenya. Overviews of the history of ADCs in the USA and the UK have been published previously (Crawford, 2008; Fink, 2013; Advance HE, n.d.; European Commission, n.d.). Summaries of the status of university teaching include those by Hunt and Chalmers (2008) and Lane and Lake (2015).

Part II: One Conceptual Model from the Field

Chapter 5 provides a conceptualization of a model center. Nilson's model is an excellent starting point for either the design of a new center or the foundation for planning a needs analysis for an existing center.

Parts III to XI: Case Studies of Specific ADCs

These history and concept-oriented chapters are followed by case studies of 36 specific ADCs. The titles of these ADCs reflect their diverse purposes, including but not limited to Centers for Excellence in Teaching, Centers for Teaching and Learning, Faculty Development Centers, Centers for Higher Education Pedagogy, Offices of Instruction and Assessment, Center for Student Engagement, and Centers for Mentoring and Academic Innovation. While their names may vary, the focus is on centers with a mission toward the development of excellence in research-based teaching in higher education. In this volume, *academics* include faculty, staff, and students. The term *professional development* refers to planned programming designed to support teaching and learning in the institution.

In general, each case study includes information regarding the:

* History of the center
* Political context of the center within the university

* Organizational structure of the center
* Relationships with other campus centers
* Influence of the center on administrative decision-making
* Administrative changes as a result of the center's operations
* Physical space of the center
* The center's champion and approval process
* Mission, vision, and goals
* Theoretical foundations
* Activities of the center
* Impact and evaluation procedures.

Each case study might then focus on one or more of the following:

* Effective workshops/training models/educational experiences for faculty
* Evidence of the impact of the center
* Surprises encountered or unintended outcomes
* Faculty participation and support
* Evidence of changes in teaching and learning
* Research about status of teaching (benchmark data, needs assessment data, change data, etc.)
* The center's research projects
* Faculty narratives, reflections, or comments
* Faculty voice in the center's decision-making
* Role of scholarship of teaching and learning (SoTL)
* Successes, challenges, and failures encountered.

Nine Major Themes

Nine themes emerged from the analysis of the original chapter proposals. These themes were then used as part of the final chapter selection process. They also served as organizing factors for the structure of the book and are reflected in the titles of Parts III through XI. Below is a brief explanation of each part. A more detailed explanation introduces each section.

Part III: Mission Differences Lead to Structural Differences

This section describes five centers with very different missions, each of which required divergent structures to accomplish its goals.

xvi   Preface

Part IV: Differences in Theoretical Foundations

Different theoretical foundations are mentioned even when mission and goals are similar. The three case studies highlight how ADC structure evolves from specific theories and missions.

Across the interactions of mission, theory, and structure, holistic academic development emerges within these cases. Some centers purposefully plan holistic professional development for academics, including examples of values development, spiritual development, and wellness. To further explore these mission-related themes, see the following indexing terms: "Values," "Ethical Education," "Theological," "Theoretical Foundations of ADCs," and "Theoretical Foundations of Teaching and Learning," along with Appendix A.

Several models, both centralized and dispersed, have been implemented, though the majority report to the academic affairs officer of their respective colleges or universities. There are interesting cases of changes from a centralized to decentralized structure or vice versa in response to changing faculty dynamics. Search within the indexing topic "ADC Structure."

Changes in ADC mission, foundational theories, and structure are required as institutional strategic goals and plans change. But the ADC must also change in response to dynamics such as changing faculty and student needs, new leadership, funding sources, available facilities, classroom research, and accreditation standards. For additional examples, explore such indexing terms as "Change and Transition" and "Innovation."

Part V: Differences in ADC Governance and Funding

There is no standard expectation for funding sources for ADC operations. Funding options vary from government and university funding to grants and even faculty payroll deduction. Both ADC governance and funding are interrelated. For those interested, please refer to indexing topics such as "ADC Funding," "ADC Structure," and "ADC Management," and to Appendix A.

Part VI: Student Focus and/or Student Involvement Is a Major Focus

One major recent trend in best practices concerning pedagogy and SoTL is the importance of involving students as partners in the teaching and learning process. This section focuses on several ADCs in which student engagement, partnerships, and success are prioritized. See such indexing terms as "Students as Partners," "Satisfaction," "Student Learning," and "Engagement/Participation."

Part VII: ADCs Based on Partnerships and Collaboration

Much of the faculty development conducted by several ADCs would not have been possible without the partnerships and collaborative relationships formed between different institutions, disciplines, and administrative entities, and even across international borders. Search for the indexing topics "Partnership," "Collaboration," "Intercultural," "Partner Universities," and "Networking."

Part VIII: Strategies for Building Community

Many ADCs place focus on facilitating the formation of communities of practice for geographically dispersed and local faculty members, as well as partnerships across campuses and institutions. Explore various indexing topics such as "Institutional Interrelationships," "Community of Practice," "Faculty Fellows," "Community-Engaged Learning," "Faculty-Centered Initiatives," and "New Faculty Orientation."

Part IX: Certification Program Examples

At least one-third of the case studies discuss some type of faculty teaching certification initiative. The options include voluntary, mandatory, in-house, partnership, face-to-face, and/or online modalities. However, faculty participation is a constant concern even for centers in which some type of ADC-sponsored certification is required. Search for the indexing topics "Certification in Higher Education Teaching and Learning" and "ADC Faculty Incentives" for guides to understanding the impact of various options used by centers.

Part X: ADC and Faculty Research About Teaching and Learning

The selected research studies use data such as mid-term student feedback, classroom and peer observations, and SoTL projects to better understand how to maximize student learning. See indexing topics "Evaluation of Learning," "Quality in Higher Education," "Scholarship of Teaching and Learning," "Assessment of Learning," "Assessment of Teaching," and "Research."

Part XI: Examples of ADC Impact Research

Centers are going beyond satisfaction surveys to gauge the impact of their work. Case studies in this section share research that investigates and documents the impact of ADC programs. Studies include investigation of the correlation between participation in ADC programs and course evaluation scores, instructional change, faculty perceptions, and key performance indicators. See the indexing terms "Impact of ADC," "Needs Assessment," "Quality in Higher Education," "Assessment of ADC," and "Research."

Summary

The research in this volume can be used in four main ways. First, it serves as an introductory text to understanding the international development of ADCs. Second, case study data in Parts III through XI can be analyzed for a comparison of design alternatives or for solutions to a specific problem, such as funding, organization, or structural change. Third, information can be accessed using the table in Appendix A (see Chart A.1) to discern which case studies best match a particular institutional/campus/center environment. Fourth, the index highlights important topics, authors, and references to enable readers to navigate to those sections of most interest to them.

Lastly, it has been a pleasure to work with such a knowledgeable, generous, and diverse group of colleagues. It is my honor to have been entrusted with the dissemination of their work.

Muscat, Oman

Otherine Johnson Neisler

References

Advance HE. (2019). *UK Professional Standards Framework (UKPSF)*. Advance HE. https://www.advance-he.ac.uk/knowledge-hub/uk-professional-standards-framework-ukpsf

Crawford, K. (2008). Continuing professional development in higher education: the academic perspective. *International Journal for Academic Development, 13*(2), 141–146.

European Commission. (2021). *Continuing professional development for academic staff working in higher education*. Eurydice Network. https://eacea.ec.europa.eu/national-policies/eurydice/content/continuing-professional-development-academic-staff-working-higher-education-65_sr

Fink, L. D. (2013). The current status of faculty development internationally. *International Journal for the Scholarship of Teaching and Learning, 7*(2), 4.

Gillespie, K., & Robertson, D. (2010). *A guide to faculty development* (2nd ed.). Jossey-Bass.

Hunt, L., & Chalmers, D. (Eds.). (2013). *University teaching in focus*. Routledge.

Lane, P., & Lake, P. (Eds.). (2015). *Global innovation of teaching and learning in higher education: transgressing boundaries*. Springer.

Professional and Organizational Development (POD) Network. (n.d.). *What is educational development?* POD Network. https://podnetwork.org/about/what-is-educational-development/

Contents

Notes on Contributors	xxvii
Abbreviations	li
List of Figures	lvii
List of Tables	lix

Part I Regional Academic Development Historical Perspectives   1

1 Australian Academic Professional Development Centers: 60 Years of Evolution   3
Denise Chalmers and Kym Fraser

2 Perspectives on Faculty Development in Latin American Universities: The Emergence of Academic Professional Development Centers   23
Fadia Khouri

3 The Past, Present, and Future of Faculty Development in China: Based on Multiple Scholarship for Cultivating Creative Talent   41
Yihong Fan

xxii   Contents

4   Africa: The Evolution of Faculty Development in East
     Africa—A Tale of Three Transformation Stories   59
     Charles Kingsbury, Mike Calvert, and Mary Omingo

Part II   One Conceptual Model for the Field   75

5   Imagining the Ideal Academic Professional Development
     Center: An Attainable, Fact-Based Vision   77
     Linda B. Nilson

Part III   Mission Differences Lead to Structural Differences   93

6   Assessment Work in an Academic Professional Development
     Center   97
     Ingrid Novodvorsky, Elaine Marchello, and Lisa Elfring

7   Implementing Academic Professional Development Strategies
     to Support Spiritual and Values-Based Engagement   109
     Sandra Sgoutas-Emch

8   Needs Analysis Leads to Sustainability: Development of a
     Medical Education and Informatics Department in the
     College of Medicine and Health Sciences, Sultan Qaboos
     University   123
     Nadia Mohammed Al Wardy and Rashid Al Abri

9   Tectonic Plates of American Higher Education: Yale
     University's Poorvu Center and a Multiplicity of Missions   139
     Kyle Sebastian Vitale and Nancy S. Niemi

10   Structural Changes Over Three Years: Evolution of Three
     Models to Support Learning and Teaching in a Large
     Research-Intensive University   151
     Tammy R. Smith, Kirsten Schliephake, and Barb Macfarlan

Contents   xxiii

Part IV   Differences in Theoretical Foundations   167

**11   Student Learning: A Framework for Designing Study
Programs to Stimulate Deep Learning**   171
Hester Glasbeek

**12   Theoretical Foundations for Online and Hybrid Faculty
Development Initiatives**   185
*Bridgette Atkins, Caroline Ferguson, Jeanette Oliveira, Sarah Stokes,
and Susan L. Forbes*

13   Mission-Aligned Teaching Center Initiative   201
Annie Soisson

Part V   Differences in ADC Governance and Funding   217

**14   At the Heart of the Campus: A Faculty-Led Teaching and
Learning Center**   221
Gwendolyn Mettetal and Carolyn A. Schult

**15   A Member-Driven, Donor-Supported Academic Professional
Development Center: The New Mexico State University
Teaching Academy**   235
Tara Gray, Laura Madson, and Morgan Iommi

**16   Faculty Leadership in Academic Professional Development
Centers: Building a Case for a Three-Director, Faculty-Led
Model**   251
Emily R. Smith and Carol Ann Davis

**Part VI   Student Focus and/or Student Involvement Is a Major
Focus**   265

**17   The Centre for Student Engagement: A Research and
Development Center for Students, Faculty, and Staff at the
University of Winchester**   269
Tom Lowe

xxiv   Contents

18   **Partnerships Between Undergraduate Students and Faculty in the Assessment of Teaching and Learning: A Program Design Model**   283
Adriana Signorini, Cathy A. Pohan, and James Zimmerman

19   **A Holistic Approach to Student and Faculty Success: Integrating Careers, Advising, and Teaching**   299
Heather Keith, Christina Fabrey, and Serena Eddy

Part VII   ADCs Based on Partnerships and Collaboration   313

20   **Creating Through International Partnership: A Faculty Development Center at a Pakistani University**   317
Asif Khan, Michele A. Parker, and Patricia Pashby

21   **Quality, Teaching, and Learning: A Networked Approach Across Pakistan and East Africa**   331
Tashmin Khamis and Zeenar Salim

22   **Using Student Research Data to Shape the Teaching and Learning Activities of a New Academic Development Center in Turkey**   351
Elif Bengu and Fatma Nevra Seggie

23   **Collaborative Faculty Development**   363
Jordan Cofer, Denise Domizi, Marina Smitherman, Jesse Bishop, and Rod McRae

24   **The Making of the Learning, Teaching, and Innovative Technologies Center: Building Upon an Internal Partnership**   379
Barbara Draude, Thomas Brinthaupt, and Sheila Otto

Part VIII   Strategies for Building Community   391

25   **Building Community: From Faculty Development to Pedagogical Innovation and Beyond**   393
Linda C. Hodges and Patrice McDermott

Contents **xxv**

26 A Holistic Vision of Faculty Excellence: Creating Sustainable Programming That Expands Community, Infrastructure, and Capacity 405
Jennifer Keys and Abiódún "G-P" Gòkè-Pariolá

27 Promoting a Culture of Teaching Excellence in a Chinese Research University 419
Yihong Qiu

28 Building Community and Supporting Mentors in a Dispersed College for Adults: A Case Study 433
Shantih E. Clemans

29 Virtual Faculty Learning Communities 445
Angela Atwell and Cristina Cottom

30 Planting Seeds for a Campus-Wide Conversation on Teaching and Learning in Oman: The Faculty Fellows Program at the Center for Excellence in Teaching and Learning, Sultan Qaboos University 457
Thuwayba Al Barwani and Otherine Neisler

Part IX Certification Program Examples 475

31 Achieving Certification and Innovation Simultaneously: Educational Leadership for Senior Faculty at a Research University in the Netherlands 479
Joyce Brouwer and Rachna in't Veld

32 Higher Education Faculty Certificate Program: Foundations of Reflective Teaching 495
Christopher E. Garrett and Christine A. Draper

33 Preparing Future Faculty: Developing Inclusive, Future-Focused Educators and an Adaptive Program 511
Shamini Dias

34 Diversity and Coherence: The Continuum of Staff Development Actions Around a Common Core 527
Dominique Verpoorten, Françoise Jérôme, Laurent Leduc, Catherine Delfosse, and Pascal Detroz

xxvi   Contents

Part X   ADC and Faculty Research About Teaching and Learning   543

35   Needs Analysis Research Leads to Specialized Faculty Development Programs   545
Pang Haishao and Zhang Yeye

36   Critical Reflection on Organizational Practice at a UK University Through Scholarship of Teaching and Learning   557
Aysha Divan, Paul Taylor, Andrea Jackson, and Rafe Hallett

37   Systematic Changes: Impact of Double-Helix Collaboration Toward Innovation in Faculty Development and Student-Centered Teaching and Learning   571
Yihong Fan

Part XI   Examples of ADC Impact Research   587

38   Change in Practice: Achieving a Cultural Shift in Teaching and Learning Through a Theory of Change   591
Grahame T. Bilbow

39   Developing Beginner University Teachers' Pedagogical Competencies Through a Professional Development Program   613
Roman Švaříček, Ingrid Procházková, Jeffrey A. Vanderziel, and Klára Šeďová

40   From Workshops to Impact Evaluation: The Case of a Chilean Center for Teaching Development and Innovation   629
Ricardo García, Héctor Turra, and Beatriz Moya

41   Extending International Collaboration to Certify High-Quality Online Teaching in Higher Education   641
Yan Ding and Yaping Gao

Appendix   657

Author Index   661

Subject Index   677

Notes on Contributors

Rashid Al Abri is the Head of the Medical Education and Informatics Department in the College of Medicine and Health Sciences (CMHS), Sultan Qaboos University (SQU), Oman. He is also Senior Consultant of Ear, Nose, and Throat and Associate Professor in the Department of Surgery, CMHS, SQU.

Thuwayba Al Barwani is a professor of Curriculum and Instruction at the College of Education as well as the Director of the Center for Excellence in Teaching and Learning (CETL) at Sultan Qaboos University (SQU), Oman. She has served as Board Member, Oman Academic Accreditation Authority; Member, The State Council, Oman; founder and member of the Board of Trustees of A'Sharqiya Private University; and Undersecretary of the Ministry of Social Development, and is the former Dean of the College of Education. Her funded research includes professional development in higher education; teacher quality and standards; school effectiveness and improvement; English language teaching; literacy; and gender and family studies. She is a recipient of His Majesty Sultan Qaboos Second-Class Honor for Culture and the Sciences, the Gulf Cooperation Council Women's Leadership Award, and the Middle East Award for Special Olympics.

Nadia Mohammed Al Wardy is an associate professor in the Department of Biochemistry, College of Medicine and Health Sciences (CMHS), Sultan Qaboos University (SQU), Oman. She obtained a PhD in Biochemistry from the University of Glasgow, Scotland, UK, and a Postgraduate Diploma in Medical Education from the University of Dundee, Scotland. In 2006, she established the CMHS Medical Education Unit, which she headed until 2015. In addition, she initiated a faculty development program to certify faculty in health professions education and was instrumental in developing a

xxviii   Notes on Contributors

new assessment policy for SQU and the new CMHS curriculum implemented in 2008. She chairs the College Examinations Committee. Al Wardy won the World Academy of Science Arab Regional Prize in 2011 for "the Development of Scientific Educational Material." She served as the CMHS Assistant Dean for Pre-Clinical Affairs and was a member of the State Council of Oman from 2007 to 2015.

Bridgette Atkins is a faculty development officer with the Teaching and Learning Centre of the University of Ontario Institute of Technology (Ontario Tech), Oshawa, Canada. Atkins played a role in the development of the updated Certificate in University Teaching program and continues to facilitate the program with her colleagues at the Teaching and Learning Centre. She also supports members of the university teaching community through course development projects, one-on-one instructional consultations, and workshops focused on the development of teaching strategies. She holds a Bachelor of Education and Master of Arts in Education from Ontario Tech.

Angela Atwell is a faculty developer for the Rothwell Center for Teaching and Learning Excellence (CTLE) at Embry-Riddle Aeronautical University-Worldwide where she works with faculty to explore pedagogy and best practices. She has diverse experience as a student, teacher, and developer in various modalities. She believes the most important component of a successful classroom is an engaged instructor and knows teachers can learn so much from each other.

Elif Bengü is an assistant professor in the Faculty of Educational Sciences, Abdullah Gül University (AGU), Kayseri, Turkey. Bengü received her BSc in Measurement and Evaluation in Education from Hacettepe University and her MSc and EdD from the University of Cincinnati. After graduation, she worked as a student affairs advisor at the International Office at the University of Kentucky. In 2016, she joined AGU and was appointed Coordinator of the Center for the Enhancement of Learning and Teaching (CELT). As part of the Erasmus+ teaching exchange program, Bengü taught various courses on faculty development, communicative competence, and cross-cultural communication. At AGU, she teaches graduate-level courses on faculty development and creative drama for engineering students and focuses on teacher relevance and self-efficacy in the classroom, rapport in the cross-cultural classroom setting, and the use of maker-spaces for mechanical engineering education, a project for which she received a research fund from AGU.

Grahame T. Bilbow has been Director of the Centre for the Enhancement of Teaching and Learning (CETL) at the University of Hong Kong since

2013. Prior to this, he was an assistant director of the Higher Education Academy (now Advance HE) in the UK, with responsibility for the arts and humanities. In recent years, his interests have centered on the quest for quality in teaching and learning in higher education internationally, which he believes is achievable through a process of managed change.

Jesse Bishop is Dean of Planning, Assessment, Accreditation, and Research at Georgia Highlands College, USA. He researches and writes about writing pedagogies, social media, and poetry and film.

Thomas Brinthaupt is a professor of Psychology at Middle Tennessee State University (MTSU), USA and has served as the Director of Faculty Development for the Learning, Teaching, and Innovative Technologies Center (LT&ITC) since 2010. He has published numerous papers related to the topics of teaching with instructional technologies, online learning, and faculty development. During his time at MTSU, he has received several awards, including the MTSU John T. Bragg, Sr. Distinguished Service Award, the Tennessee Board of Regents Award of Excellence for Online Teaching and Learning, the MTSU Distinguished Educator Award in Distance Learning, and the MTSU Foundation Outstanding Achievement in Instructional Technology Award.

Joyce Brouwer is an educational advisor and program leader with 25 years of experience in the educational field. She is part of the Learn! Academy at Vrije Universiteit Amsterdam (VUA) in the Netherlands and is a partner of Reflect Academy, an independent group focused on innovation in higher education, teacher training, and the development of leadership. In her work, Brouwer empowers teachers and supports them to create sustainable positive learning and teaching, not only based on educational insights but also inspired by her background in social psychology. In her advisory role at several universities of the arts in the Netherlands, she creates a space for learning and teacher development together with the teaching staff. In negotiating the context of higher education, she strives toward an honest dialogue about what kind of teaching fosters real learning for an increasingly complex world.

Mike Calvert has been involved in education throughout his career, first as a teacher of modern languages, then as teacher trainer and university lecturer. He worked at York and Sheffield Universities, UK, involving himself in international programs involving pedagogy. He developed expertise in faculty development and for 15 years, during his time at York St. John University, was involved in a number of capacity-building projects in universities in Africa, mainly in Kenya but also in other Sub-Saharan countries.

xxx **Notes on Contributors**

Denise Chalmers is Professor Emeritus in the field of higher education teaching and learning at the University of Western Australia, and was awarded an Office of Learning and Teaching (OLT) National Senior Teaching Fellowship in recognizing and rewarding university teaching in 2015 and an Australian Award for University Teaching: Citation for Outstanding Contributions to Student Learning in 2014. In 2017, she was awarded lifetime membership to the Higher Education Research and Development Society of Australasia (HERDSA). Over the past 25 years, Chalmers has demonstrated leadership in higher education, leading two university Centres of Teaching and Learning as Director, and was Foundation Director of the Carrick Institute (later the Australian Learning and Teaching Council) with responsibility for awards, fellowships, and international links. She served as President, and then Vice President, of the Council of Australian Directors of Academic Development (CADAD) from 2008 to 2014. She has initiated and led several institutional, national, and international initiatives and projects, including developing and embedding teaching quality criteria and indicators, and promoting the use of teaching and learning performance indicators to guide decision-making and resource allocation.

Shantih E. Clemans is an associate professor and Director of the Center for Mentoring, Learning, and Academic Innovation, State University of New York (SUNY) Empire State College, an experimental college for adult students with a dispersed model comprising 34 locations across New York State, USA. Clemans has extensive experience in teaching, mentoring, and faculty development. Thanks to her prior career in social work, specifically in the areas of trauma and group work, Clemans has offered many studies to community and human services students. She has published and presented on various topics, including group work with survivors of trauma, vicarious traumatization of social workers, staff supervision, cultural competency, and, more recently, the complexity, nuances, and rewards of teaching and mentoring adult students. Clemans also writes a monthly blog titled *Mentoring Moments: Reflections of love, listening and learning.*

Jordan Cofer is the Associate Provost for Transformative Learning Experiences and Professor of English at Georgia College, USA. He is the author of *The Gospel According to Flannery O'Connor* and co-author of *Writing the Nation: A Concise Introduction to American Literature.*

Cristina Cottom is the Research Specialist for the Rothwell Center for Teaching and Learning Excellence CTLE at Embry-Riddle Aeronautical University-Worldwide. She has diverse experience as an educator, advisor, and college instructor. Her strengths include teacher education, online course development, integration of research-based teaching and learning, active learning strategies, and collaborative learning environments.

Carol Ann Davis is a poet, essayist, and Professor of English at Fairfield University, USA, as well as Director of Curriculum Development at the Center for Academic Excellence. Her work has appeared in *Image*, *Agni*, and the *Journal of Adolescent and Adult Literature*.

Catherine Delfosse is a senior pedagogical advisor at the Institute for Training and Research in Higher Education (IFRES), University of Liège, Belgium. She has authored over 72 publications, including 32 journal articles, and has contributed to two books. Her research topics of interest include hybrid teaching, e-learning, incorporating physical activity into education, and reflection.

Pascal Detroz is a senior lecturer in Learning Sciences at the Institute for Training and Research in Higher Education (IFRES), University of Liège, Belgium. He has authored over 205 publications, including 28 journal articles, and has contributed to 21 books. His topics of interest include learning analytics, remote feedback/assessment, students' emotions in a learning context, and the evaluation of complex educational objectives in science, technology, engineering, and mathematics (STEM) fields.

Shamini Dias is an educator, artist, and scholar. She has directed the Preparing Future Faculty program at Claremont Graduate University, USA, since 2013, when she pioneered the program. Dias's scholarship integrates pedagogy across the ages; complexity and design thinking; the role of imagination, story, emotion, and the arts; and contemplative and reflective practices in teaching and leadership. She is fascinated with the ways in which metaphors and stories inform epistemological frameworks, particularly as this applies to educational research and practice. As part of her scholarly practice, she explores the nature and importance of transdisciplinary praxis in addressing educational issues. Her scholarly work is deeply informed by her work as an educator and teaching artist in K-12 and higher education settings, as well as in business. Dias received her first three degrees from the National University of Singapore in English Literature and Linguistics, and her PhD in Education from Claremont Graduate University.

Yan Ding is an associate professor at the Research Institute for Higher Education and Deputy Director of the Center for Faculty Development, Fudan University, China. She obtained her master's and PhD in Educational

xxxii   Notes on Contributors

Development from Nagoya University, Japan. Ding is one of the most sought-after experts in the field of faculty development research and practice in China. Her research interests include faculty development, evaluation of teaching and learning, and human resource management in higher education. She has authored four books and published 30 papers in Chinese, Japanese, and English journals. Ding has led project teams to develop various faculty training programs, including the Quality Matters (QM) Online Course Quality Rubric and learning-centered curriculum design. She is a core member of the team that won the 2017 Global Impact Award, the Fifth National Education Reform and Innovation Special Award, and the 2018 Shanghai Municipal Teaching Achievement Award of Higher Education.

Aysha Divan is an associate professor and Director of Student Education at the Faculty of Biological Sciences, University of Leeds, UK. Her main pedagogic and leadership activities include curriculum development and professional development. Divan has been involved in establishing the institution-wide Collaborative Writing Group initiative at Leeds Institute for Teaching Excellence (LITE).

Denise Domizi is the Director of Faculty Development for the University System of Georgia (USG), USA, and Co-Director of the USG Scholarship of Teaching and Learning (SoTL) Fellows Program. She works to promote and support innovation and research in teaching and learning at the system level.

Christine A. Draper is an instructional designer at Nevada State College, USA, where she is a passionate advocate for engaging and innovative curriculum and supports both full- and part-time faculty in professional development, course design, and finding amazing literature they can utilize in their classrooms. Draper was formerly an associate professor of Education at Georgia Southern University where she taught future and current teachers reading and language arts methods, integrated curriculum, young adult literature, and more.

Barbara Draude is the Assistant Vice President for Academic and Instructional Technologies for the Information Technology Division of Middle Tennessee State University (MTSU), USA, and co-directs the Learning, Teaching, and Innovative Technologies Center (LT&ITC). She is responsible for the areas of academic programming, statistical consultation, and technology integration into teaching and learning. She is also an assistant professor at the MTSU School of Nursing, where she was recognized in 1999 with the MTSU Foundation Award for Outstanding Achievement in Instructional Technology. She conducts faculty development seminars and workshops to assist faculty in developing technology-enhanced course materials and web-based courses. She has presented locally and nationally on instructional technology topics.

Serena Eddy is the Academic Director at Mansfield Hall in Burlington, Vermont, USA. She enjoys providing students with thoughtful guidance as they acquire skills, gain confidence, embrace new opportunities, and achieve their individual goals. Prior to working at Mansfield Hall, her work included advocating for individuals with disabilities, mobilizing volunteers, and empowering students in the career services offices of Green Mountain College, Harvard Law School, and Boston College Law School.

Lisa Elfring is Assistant Vice Provost of Instruction and Assessment for the University of Arizona (UArizona), USA, heading up the Office of Instruction and Assessment (OIA). Her departmental affiliation is Associate Specialist in Biology Education in Molecular and Cellular Biology. She received her BA in Biology and PhD in Molecular, Cellular, and Developmental Biology from the University of California, Santa Cruz. In over 20 years at UArizona, she has taught a wide variety of courses for well over 5,000 biology majors, graduate students, teachers-in-training, working K-12 teachers, and medical students. Her teaching and advising have been recognized by awards from UArizona's College of Science and Honors College. Her research focuses on developing programs to support instructors as they use evidence-based teaching strategies in science, technology, engineering, and mathematics classrooms, and she is a fellow for the Partnership for Undergraduate Life Sciences Education.

Christina Fabrey was the Associate Dean of Advising and Academic Achievement at Prescott College in Arizona, USA. Previously, she served as the Director for the Center of Advising and Achievement at Green Mountain College. She is a certified life and attention deficit hyperactivity disorder coach, and is also a certified mentor coach through the International Coach Federation. She received the Emerging Professional Award from the Vermont Women in Higher Education program for her work with coaching in the college setting, and is a contributing author of *Becoming Self-Determined: Creating Thoughtful Learners in a Standards-Driven, Admissions-Frenzied Culture.*

Yihong Fan is a professor of the Academic Affairs Office, Southwest Jiaotong University, and Professor Emeritus with the Institute of Education, Xiamen University, in China. He has an EdD in Education Policy and Leadership and a PhD from the College of Education, University of Massachusetts, Amherst, USA. His research areas include holistic education, faculty development, multiple scholarship, systematic organizational change, innovative teaching and learning, and comparative education.

xxxiv Notes on Contributors

Caroline Ferguson is a faculty development officer with the Teaching and Learning Centre of the University of Ontario Institute of Technology (Ontario Tech), Oshawa, Canada. She offers educational support to the teaching community in the areas of course development, general teaching strategies, and educational training and support. Ferguson is also a sessional instructor in the Faculty of Health Sciences as well as the Faculty of Science at Ontario Tech. Previously, she worked as a senior math and chemistry teacher as well as a physics and engineering specialist. Ferguson holds a PhD in Materials Science and Engineering from the University of Toronto as well as a Bachelor of Education from Ontario Tech.

Susan L. Forbes is the Manager of the Teaching and Learning Centre of the University of Ontario Institute of Technology (Ontario Tech), Oshawa, Canada, as well as a sessional instructor and adjunct professor in the Faculty of Health Sciences at Ontario Tech. Forbes has a PhD from the University of Western Ontario, an MA from Wilfrid Laurier University, and a BA from the University of Calgary. She has over 25 years of classroom-based experience, as well as being a highly published researcher.

Kym Fraser has worked in academic development and management roles in the tertiary education sector in Australia, the UK, Hong Kong, and the USA. She is the editor of several books, including *The Future of Learning and Teaching in Next Generation Learning Spaces* and *Education Development and Leadership in Higher Education*, former editor of the Higher Education Research and Development Society of Australasia (HERDSA) Green and Gold Guide Series, and author of *Studying for Continuing Professional Development in Health* and *Student Centred Teaching*. Fraser is a senior fellow of Advance HE, UK, and has served as an executive member of the Council of Australasian University Leaders in Learning and Teaching for many years. In 2016, she was awarded and led the Office of Learning and Teaching (OLT)-funded fellowship titled "A national, open-access learning and teaching induction program for staff new to teaching," which was a collaboration between 11 Australian universities. The massive open online course (MOOC) "Contemporary Approaches to Learning and Teaching" was launched in January 2018. Thousands of colleagues from over 50 countries have enrolled, a dozen universities from five countries have incorporated the MOOC into their learning management systems, and it is being translated into Mandarin, Spanish, and Portuguese.

Yaping Gao is the Senior Academic Director of Quality Matters, USA, and has over 25 years' experience in higher education both in China and the USA as faculty, instructional designer, learning management system administrator, and online education administrator. She received her PhD from Baylor University, Texas, and her master's and bachelor's degrees from Shanghai International Studies University, Shanghai, China. With a concentration on instructional design and educational technology, Gao believes quality course and program design supported by research facilitates effective instruction, promotes student engagement and active learning, and lays the foundation for student success and institutional advancement. In her position, Gao oversees and leads member services and external partnerships with a focus on international outreach and initiatives.

Ricardo García is the Director of the Center for Teaching Development and Innovation at the Universidad Católica (UC) de Temuco, Chile. He has led various initiatives of faculty development in the institution and has directed a Chilean Ministry of Education project on faculty development programs.

Christopher E. Garrett is an associate professor of Education and serves as Director of the Center for Excellence in Teaching and Learning at Nevada State College, USA. In addition to overseeing faculty development programming across the campus, he also teaches education and literature courses to undergraduate students. Several of his research interests include discussion-based learning, mentoring faculty, and leadership development in higher education

Hester Glasbeek is a senior educator, program leader, and educational advisor at the Learn! Academy of Vrije Universiteit, Amsterdam, Netherlands. Her mission is to contribute to a positive learning and teaching culture at the university by supporting and empowering teachers and students, thinking along with them, combining all relevant perspectives, and using every opportunity to connect people and their initiatives to improve education.

Abiódún "G-P" Gòkè-Pariolá is Provost and Vice President for Academic Affairs at North Central College and a professor of English with over 40 years of teaching and administrative experience at universities abroad and in the USA. His prior experience includes positions as the Provost/Vice President of Academic Affairs (VPAA) at Queens University of Charlotte, North Carolina; Provost/VPAA at Otterbein University, Ohio; Dean of the Evans School of Humanities and Social Sciences at Berry College, Georgia; Assistant VPAA at Georgia Southern University; and American Council on Education (ACE) Fellow and Assistant to the President, Illinois State University. He is the author of over 30 scholarly articles and a book on sociolinguistics and the political sociology of language.

xxxvi   Notes on Contributors

Tara Gray became the first Director of the Teaching Academy at New Mexico State University, USA, in January 2003; her tenure home is criminal justice. Gray sets the direction of the Teaching Academy in terms of programming, leads one-time and multi-session workshops, hosts outside speakers, builds spirit among academy staff, manages the budget, and fundraises. She studies scholarly writing, directing effective teaching centers, active learning, and collaborative faculty development programs. She has published 40 academic articles and book chapters as well as four books, including *Publish & Flourish: Become a Prolific Scholar.* Gray has won 10 awards for teaching, scholarship, and service, both on campus and nationally. She has presented workshops to more than 10,000 educators in 120 venues, 35 states, and seven countries.

Pang Haishao is a professor and doctoral supervisor of Higher Education at the School of Humanities and Social Sciences, Beijing Institute of Technology, China. She is the Director of the Center for Enhanced Learning and Teaching (CELT) and Secretary-General of the Chinese Association for Suzhi Education. Haishao is a visiting scholar at Columbia University and the Chinese University of Hong Kong. Her research concerns general education and *suzhi* education, college faculty development, scholarship of teaching and learning, and higher education management.

Rafe Hallett is a professor of Educational Innovation at Keele University, UK, and the Director of the Keele Institute for Innovation and Teaching Excellence. Hallet was formerly an associate professor of History at the University of Leeds and the former Director of the Leeds Institute for Teaching Excellence (LITE).

Linda C. Hodges is Associate Vice Provost for Faculty Affairs and Director of the Faculty Development Center at the University of Maryland Baltimore County (UMBC), USA. Before relocating to Maryland, she was Director of the Harold W. McGraw Jr. Center for Teaching and Learning at Princeton University. Hodges holds a PhD in Biochemistry from the University of Kentucky and was a faculty member for over 20 years before transitioning into faculty development and learning sciences. In 1999, Hodges was one of 28 faculty chosen nationally to study and assess new pedagogical approaches as a scholar of the Carnegie Foundation for the Advancement of Teaching. She has published widely on her work in faculty development, engaged student learning, and effective teaching practices, including the book *Teaching Undergraduate Science: A Guide to Overcoming Obstacles to Student Learning.* Her special interests include pedagogies of engagement and the scholarship of teaching and learning.

Rachna in't Veld is a senior advisor and co-founder of Reflect Academy, an independent group and frequent collaborator with the Learn! Academy at Vrije Universiteit Amsterdam (VUA) in the Netherlands which is focused on innovation in higher education, teacher training, and the development of leadership. She is specialized in leadership, change, and learning in the academic context. In working with leaders and teachers, in't Veld focuses her attention on creating conditions that allow for teachers to bring out the best in themselves and in students. With an academic background in social psychology, practical training in coaching, and over 15 years of experience in academia, she is not only able to steer her way through delicate innovation processes, but also to transfer this knowledge to others through the development of leadership programs.

Morgan Iommi was the Associate Director for Teaching and Learning of the Teaching Academy at New Mexico State University, USA. Iommi led one-time and multi-session workshops at the academy, and mentored faculty who led their own events. She also worked with the Director to coordinate and strategize about the focus for programming and university-wide initiatives related to teaching. In collaboration with other departments, she coordinated the training for and the use of the campus's technology-enabled active learning classroom. Iommi's scholarship focuses on the motivational factors influencing instructors' participation in faculty development programming.

Andrea Jackson is a professor of Student Education and Engagement at the University of Leeds, UK, and coordinates the Leeds Institute for Teaching Excellence (LITE) mentoring scheme. Her pedagogic research interests include the challenges presented by the transition of students from school to university and factors influencing student engagement. Jackson is a senior fellow and National Teaching Fellow of the Higher Education Academy (HEA).

Françoise Jérôme is a senior pedagogical advisor at the Institute for Training and Research in Higher Education (IFRES), University of Liège, Belgium. He has authored over 35 publications. His research topics of interest include blended learning, video learning, e-learning, effective scholarship of teaching and learning (SoTL) counseling, and personalized learning/individualized training.

Heather Keith is the Executive Director of Faculty Development and a professor of Philosophy at Radford University in Radford, Virginia, USA. Previously, she served as Associate Dean of Teaching and Learning at Green Mountain College. She is the co-author of *Intellectual Disability: Ethics, Dehumanization, and a New Moral Community* as well as *Lives and Legacies of*

xxxviii   Notes on Contributors

People with Intellectual Disability, and the co-editor of *Pragmatist and American Philosophical Perspectives on Resilience*. Her research and teaching interests also include American philosophy, feminist theory, Asian and comparative philosophy, environmental ethics, the philosophy of pop culture, and faculty development.

Jennifer Keys is the Assistant Provost for Teaching and Learning and Director of the Center for the Advancement of Faculty Excellence (CAFÉ) at North Central College, USA. She works collaboratively to ensure that faculty have enriching and holistic professional development opportunities and the support they need to achieve their highest aspirations as teacher-scholars. As a professor of Sociology, Keys teaches courses on Power-Based Personal Violence, Protest and Change, Families and Intimate Relationships, and Qualitative Methods. She is also an active scholar; her most recent publication is the second edition of *Abortion in the United States: A Reference Handbook* published in 2018.

Tashmin Khamis is the founding Director of the Network of Quality Assurance and Improvement and Network of Teaching and Learning at Aga Khan University (AKU), Pakistan. She has served as the most recent past President of the East African Quality Assurance Network (EAQAN) and board member of the International Network of Quality Assurance Agencies in Higher Education. As Associate Vice Provost, Khamis oversaw the accreditation of AKU faculty by the Higher Education Academy (HEA), UK, and the establishment of the AKU Teacher's Academy as the first such interdisciplinary teaching academy in the developing world. She is a principal fellow of the HEA, has been appointed to the HEA Quality Advisory Board, and is a judge for the Advance HE prestigious Global Teaching Excellence Award.

Asif Khan is Associate Dean of the Faculty of Arts and Humanities, Karakoram International University (KIU), Gilgit, Pakistan. Furthermore, for the last two years, Khan has worked as the Director of the Center for Faculty and Staff Development at KIU. He is a Fulbright Scholar who received his PhD in Education from the University of Pittsburgh, USA. He has published and presented a number of research papers in various international and national forums on such topics as international educational assistance, school leadership, teacher education, teaching practices at the tertiary level, and faculty development.

Fadia Khouri is the Director of the *Centro para la Excelencia Docente Uninorte* (Center for Teaching Excellence of Universidad Del Norte), Colombia. She holds a bachelor's degree in Psychology from Universidad del

Norte and received her Master of Educational Studies with a major in leadership from the University of Queensland, Australia. During her master's degree, she participated in the creation and development of a faculty learning community to support the 'Students as Partners' initiative of the Institute for Teaching and Learning Innovation. She previously held other academic-administrative positions at Universidad del Norte, where she coordinated and supported different institutional programs and initiatives related to accreditation, student evaluation of teaching, strategic planning of academic units, and the institutional assessment system. Her academic interests include building leadership capacity for educational change, support of innovation in teaching and learning, and education policy.

Charles "Chip" Edward Kingsbury was born in Washington D.C., USA. He grew up in Rockville, Maryland, attending public schools in the area. He received a bachelor's degree from William Jewell College, Liberty, Missouri, graduating magna cum laude in 1979. He also graduated the same year from Full Faith Church of Love Bible College, Shawnee, Kansas, with a diploma in Bible. In 1980, he was appointed a missionary with Elim Fellowship, Lima, New York, and stationed in Nyeri, Kenya. From 1980 until 1988, he conducted a Theological Education by Extension program for the Pentecostal Evangelistic Fellowship of Africa, an indigenous denomination in Kenya. In January 1984, he was ordained to the ministry by Full Faith Church of Love. From 1988 to 1989, he attended Wheaton College Graduate School, Wheaton, Illinois. He graduated in 1989 with an MA in Intercultural Studies. He returned to Kenya the same year. From 1989 to 1993, he became increasingly involved in the training of teachers for programs of ministry formation in East Africa. Interested in engaging in this on a full-time basis, he returned to the USA in 1993 to pursue a doctoral program in Adult Education at Florida State University (FSU). After completing his course work, he returned to Kenya in 1997 where he joined the faculty of Daystar University, an independent evangelical Christian university. He was appointed the coordinator of the Outpost Training program, the extension education arm of Daystar University. It was while working in this capacity that he conducted the research that formed the basis of his dissertation. He was awarded a PhD in Adult Education from FSU in the fall semester of 2002. In January 2001, he was appointed to direct the Center for Excellence in Teaching and Learning, the faculty development program of the university. He continues to serve as missionary faculty for the university. He has been the Chairperson of the Association for Faculty Enrichment in Learning and Teaching (AFELT) since its inception in 2014.

Laurent Leduc is a senior lecturer in Learning Sciences at the Institute for Training and Research in Higher Education (IFRES), University of Liège, Belgium. He has authored over 76 publications, including nine journal articles, and has contributed to four books. His research topics of interest include remedial systems, course/lesson planning, formative feedback, automated evaluation systems, and the importance of writing an effective syllabus.

Tom Lowe is the Manager of the Centre for Student Engagement at the University of Winchester, UK, and secretary for the international Researching, Advancing and Inspiring Student Engagement network. He is also the program leader for the Postgraduate Certificate in Student Engagement in Higher Education as a means of enhancing the student experience. Lowe is an expert in the practicalities surrounding student engagement/involvement in university processes and has experience working with over 20 higher education institutions across the UK. Before August 2017, he was the Higher Education Funding Council for England-funded Realising Engagement through Active Culture Transformation (REACT) Project Manager and facilitated collaborative development between 16 universities. Prior to REACT, Lowe was Vice President for Education at Winchester Student Union, during which time he gained a passion for enhancing student engagement across the university and started up the Winchester Student Fellows Scheme.

Barb Macfarlan has a Master of Education specializing in learning theories applied to sociolinguistics and over 18 years' experience as a teacher and learning designer using the affordances of ubiquitous technology to engage 21st-century learners. She is a senior education designer at Monash University, Australia, attached to the Faculty of Science. In this role, she is part of a team of faculty-based education designers that is engaged in transforming learning and teaching across a multidisciplinary faculty in the constantly changing education landscape.

Laura Madson received her PhD in Social Psychology from Iowa State University, USA, and joined the faculty of the New Mexico State University (NMSU) Psychology Department in August 1996. The NMSU Teaching Academy was one of her first stops upon arrival and it remains her favorite place to be on campus. Madson was recognized as a Fellow of the Teaching Academy in 2017 for her frequent contributions. In the Psychology Department, she specializes in teaching the Introduction to Psychology course using team-based learning. At the other end of the pedagogical continuum, Madson teaches a graduate course called Teaching of Psychology and directs the graduate program. Her scholarship focuses on helping instructors adopt team-based learning. When not working, she spends time with her husband, Keith, and sons (Ian, age 12, and Erik, age 10), or reads, runs, knits, or crochets, often with a nice pint of beer.

Elaine Marchello completed her PhD in Animal Sciences at the University of Arizona (UArizona), USA, in 1992. After teaching for eight years at Pima Community College, she went back to UArizona as a professor of Practice in the Department of Veterinary Science and Microbiology. Marchello added Assistant Dean to her title and moved into a more administrative position in the Office of Career and Academic Services at the College of Agriculture and Life Sciences. Along with teaching, she took on curriculum and assessment duties for the college. In 2015, Marchello moved from teaching and administrative work into UArizona's Office of Instruction and Assessment (OIA). As the Assistant Director of Assessment, she assists faculty with building and maintaining assessment plans for their programs. She also works with the General Education Program.

Patrice McDermott is Vice Provost for Faculty Affairs at the University of Maryland Baltimore County (UMBC), USA. McDermott joined the American Studies Department of UMBC in 1993 where she served as chair before joining the campus administration in 2007 to work on a series of institutional change initiatives, expanding the purview of the UMBC Faculty Development Center. She was the recipient of the National Women's Studies Association Book Award and UMBC Presidential Women's Achievement Award and is a senior scholar for the Association of American Colleges and Universities (AAC&U) on projects related to recruiting, advancing, and retaining women faculty and historically under-represented minority students in science, technology, engineering, and mathematics (STEM). McDermott serves as a member of the Board of Directors of the Society for STEM Women of Color, the Howard Hughes Medical Institute Inclusive Excellence Commission, and as a senior advisor to the National STEM Gender Equity Coalition.

Rod McRae is the Director of the Center for Teaching and Learning and a lecturer in English at the University of West Georgia, USA. His research focuses on transparent pedagogies, and he teaches first-year seminars, composition, and American and British literature.

Gwendolyn Mettetal is Chancellor's Professor Emerita of Psychology and Education at Indiana University (IU) South Bend, USA. She was the founding Director of the University Center for Excellence in Teaching from 1998 to 2001 and returned to that position from 2013 to 2018. Mettetal was a

xlii   Notes on Contributors

co-founder of the *Journal of the Scholarship of Teaching and Learning*. She holds a number of teaching awards including the IU South Bend Distinguished Teaching Award, the all-IU Frederic Bachman Lieber Award for Teaching Excellence, and membership in the all-IU Faculty Academy for Excellence in Teaching. She received a PhD in Developmental Psychology from the University of Illinois at Champaign-Urbana. Her early research interest was social development, but she focuses on faculty development topics such as mentoring and scholarship of teaching and learning.

Beatriz Moya is a faculty consultant for the Centre for Teaching Development and Innovation at the Universidad Católica (UC) de Temuco, Chile. She developed the School of Student Learning Assistants (SLAs) and directed a Chilean Ministry of Education project regarding the institutionalization of SLAs.

Otherine Neisler received a BA from Brandeis University, USA, before working at IBM. Subsequently, she received an MA from Fairfield University, and a PhD from Syracuse University where she began her work in faculty development, managing an IBM Interactive Teaching Laboratory. From 1994 to 2009 she taught at Boston College, and Yale University. A USA-Middle East Partnership Initiative grant led to her move to Sultan Qaboos University, Oman, in 2009. As Associate Professor of Curriculum and Instruction, she worked on National Council for Accreditation of Teacher Education accreditation and faculty grant writing. After designing and founding the Center for Excellence in Teaching and Learning (CETL), she was appointed Deputy Director and developed the Certificate in Higher Education Teaching and Learning. Neisler's grant-funded research includes university readiness, critical thinking in Omani higher education, and accreditation data analysis. Her keynotes focus on the achievement of standards-based student learning outcomes in HyFlex learning environments.

Nancy S. Niemi was the inaugural Director of Faculty Teaching Initiatives at Yale University's Poorvu Center for Teaching and Learning, USA. Niemi has held past positions as Professor and Chair of the Education Department at the University of New Haven, as well as being an elected school board member and middle school English teacher. Her professional interests focus on the intersections of social equity and higher education. Niemi is the author of *Degrees of Difference: Women, Men, and the Value of Higher Education* (2017) and co-author of the *International Handbook of Gender Equity in Higher Education* (2020). She also serves a reviewer for the *International Journal of Scholarship on Teaching and Learning* and *Gender & Education* and program reviewer for the

Massachusetts State Board of Higher Education. Niemi is the Past President of the American Association of the Colleges of Teacher Education.

Linda B. Nilson is Director Emerita of the Office of Teaching Effectiveness and Innovation at Clemson University, USA, and author of *Teaching at Its Best*, now in its fourth edition. She also wrote *The Graphic Syllabus and the Outcomes Map: Communicating Your Course, Creating Self-Regulated Learners*, and *Specifications Grading: Restoring Rigor, Motivating Students, and Saving Faculty Time*. Her latest books are *Online Teaching at Its Best* with Ludwika A. Goodson and *Creating Engaging Discussions* with Jennifer H. Herman. In addition, she co-edited *Enhancing Learning with Laptops in the Classroom* and volumes 25–28 of *To Improve the Academy*, the major publication of the Professional and Organizational Development (POD) Network in Higher Education. Nilson's career as a full-time faculty development director spanned over 25 years at three research universities. She has given over 500 keynotes, webinars, and live workshops at conferences, colleges, and universities, both nationally and internationally, on dozens of topics related to college teaching and scholarly productivity.

Ingrid Novodvorsky serves as the Director of Teaching, Learning, and Assessment at the Office of Instruction and Assessment (OIA) at the University of Arizona (UArizona), USA. She completed all of her degrees at the University of Arizona, including a Bachelor of Science in Physics & Math, a Master of Education, and a PhD in Secondary Education. After teaching high school science and math for 12 years, she returned to UArizona as one of the founding faculty members of the College of Science Teacher Preparation Program. In 2012, she moved to the OIA to work in assessment and faculty development. She leads the Faculty and Future Development team, which includes six faculty developers and a full-time member of the assessment team. In her time at OIA, she has worked with almost every unit on campus, supporting their work in improving teaching and assessing student learning.

Jeanette Oliveira is a faculty development coordinator with the Teaching and Learning Centre of the University of Ontario Institute of Technology (Ontario Tech), Oshawa, Canada. Oliveira holds a BA (Hons) degree from the University of Toronto and a Master of Education from Ontario Tech. She has worked at Ontario Tech since 2010 and brings a wide range of expertise in educational technology and pedagogical approaches. Her research interests include education and digital technologies and e-learning. In her role, she is accountable for a number of responsibilities, including university-wide course evaluations, faculty workshops, new faculty and teaching assistant (TA) orientations, educational technologies training (Blackboard, Turnitin, Adobe Connect, Turning Point, and Google Tools), newsletter coordination, and the Certificate of University Teaching for faculty and TAs.

Mary Omingo is an educational consultant in higher education in areas of curriculum development and course redesign and adjunct faculty at Strathmore University, Kenya. She is a founder member of the Association for Faculty Enrichment in Learning and Teaching (AFELT). She has worked as a faculty developer at Strathmore University and Aga Khan University. She is a fellow and senior fellow of Advance Higher Education (UK).

Sheila Otto is an associate professor of English at Middle Tennessee State University (MTSU), USA. She also serves as Director of Teaching Excellence in the MTSU Learning, Teaching, and Innovative Technologies Center (LT&ITC). She has held various positions at the university, including Director of General Education and Coordinator of Retention, Graduation, and Assessment for the College of Liberal Arts.

Michele A. Parker is a professor at the University of North Carolina, Wilmington, USA. Her doctorate is in Educational Research, Statistics, and Evaluation from the University of Virginia. Parker teaches research and evaluation courses as well as courses on college teaching. In 2020, she received the Chancellor's Teaching Excellence Award. Her co-authored book, *Taking Flight: Making your Center for Teaching and Learning Soar*, synthesizes research and best practices for strategic initiatives. The book guides personnel in applying their knowledge and skills to play a pivotal role in translating visionary strategies into meaningful actions.

Patricia Pashby teaches in the Language Teaching Studies MA Program at the University of Oregon, USA, and serves as Coordinator of English Resources for international graduate students at the American English Institute. She has taught English as a second/foreign language in higher education for over 30 years. Pashby holds a PhD in International and Multicultural Education from the University of San Francisco and an MA in Teaching English to Speakers of Other Languages from San Francisco State University. She has conducted numerous faculty development workshops in the USA, South Korea, Taiwan, Japan, Pakistan, Egypt, and Colombia. Her interests include pronunciation instruction, English medium instruction, teacher education, and testing/training international teaching assistants.

Cathy A. Pohan is the Associate Director of the Center for Engaged Teaching and Learning at the University of California, Merced (UCM), USA. She holds a PhD in Educational Psychology with an emphasis on learning and cognition. Prior to accepting this position at UCM, she served as a professor of Teacher Education for 24 years at four different institutions and had the privilege of collaborating with educators in Chile as a Fulbright Scholar.

Ingrid Procházková is an associate professor in the Department of Educational Sciences, Faculty of Arts, Masaryk University (MUNI) in Brno, Czech Republic. She also works as a project administrator at the Pedagogical Competence Development Centre (CERPEK) at MUNI. At CERPEK, she supervises the organization, preparation, and evaluation of professional development courses for new teachers. Her research interests include the voice of secondary school students in the context of the traditions and ideas of the grammar school, student boredom at grammar schools, and teachers' professional development.

Yihong Qiu is an associate professor at the Center for Teaching and Learning Development (CTLD) of Shanghai Jiao Tong University (SJTU), China. She obtained her PhD in Dynamics from the University of Glasgow, UK. She worked at the School of Biomedical Engineering of SJTU for about 10 years and published about 30 journal papers before joining the CTLD. Her research interests include teaching development, assessment for learning, and engineering education.

Zeenar Salim is a Fulbright Scholar pursuing her PhD in Instructional Design, Development, and Evaluation from Syracuse University, New York, USA. She has worked as a faculty developer with the Network of Teaching and Learning, Aga Khan University, and serves as a graduate assistant at the Faculty Center for Teaching and Learning, School of Information Management, Syracuse University. She is a fellow of the Higher Education Academy (HEA), UK.

Kirsten Schliephake is an experienced educational designer with a history of working in the higher education industry. A senior education designer in the Faculty of Medicine, Nursing and Health Sciences at Monash University, Australia, Schliephake is skilled in curriculum development and evaluation, communication, change management, and quality assurance. She has a background in environmental sciences with project management experience across environmental, energy, water, and waste industry sectors. Her research interests include scholarship of teaching and learning (SoTL), learning with technology, and authentic assessment.

xlvi   Notes on Contributors

Carolyn A. Schult is a professor of Psychology and the Director of the University Center for Excellence in Teaching at Indiana University (IU) South Bend, USA. Schult has been awarded several teaching awards, including the IU President's Award for Distinguished Teaching, the IU South Bend Distinguished Teaching Award, the IU South Bend Alumni Association Faculty Legacy Award, the Trustees' Teaching Award, and membership in the all-IU Faculty Academy for Excellence in Teaching. She received a PhD in Developmental Psychology from the University of Michigan. Her research interests include students' transition to college and the effectiveness of high-impact practices such as the 'Reacting to the Past' pedagogy.

Klára Šed'ová is an associate professor in the Department of Educational Sciences, Faculty of Arts, Masaryk University (MUNI) in Brno, Czech Republic. Her research centers on classroom discourse, the relationship between language and learning, and teachers' professional development in the area of dialogic teaching. She has published in numerous scholarly journals, including *Learning and Instruction, Teaching and Teacher Education, Learning, Culture and Social Interaction*, and the *International Journal of Educational Research*. She leads a Classroom Dialogue and Interaction Laboratory based on the principle that classroom dialogue can be used as a tool to improve students' learning and intellectual development.

Fatma Nevra Seggie is an associate professor of Educational Administration at the Department of Educational Sciences, Boğaziçi University, in Istanbul, Turkey. She received her PhD from Michigan State University in 2007. Seggie's main research and teaching interests are higher education policy analysis and higher education governance and administration. She has published articles in journals such as *Comparative Education, Higher Education, Race, Ethnicity and Education*, and the *Journal of College Student Development*. In addition, she is the author of *Religion and the State in Turkish Universities: The Headscarf Ban* published by Palgrave Macmillan in 2011. She also works on projects to develop curriculum and teaching and learning models for higher education institutions using action research as the research method and participatory methods as data collection techniques.

Sandra Sgoutas-Emch is a professor in the Department of Psychological Sciences and the Director of the Center for Educational Excellence (CEE) at the University of San Diego (USD), USA. She received her undergraduate degree in Psychology from Emory University and her PhD from the University of Georgia. She completed a two-year National Institutes of Health postdoctoral fellowship in Psychoneuroimmunology at Ohio State University until she was hired by the USD Psychology Department. She was one of the first faculty mentors for community service learning at USD. Sgoutas-Emch has several publications in the areas of faculty development, inclusion and diversity, and community engagement. Her awards include Woman of Impact and the Experiential Education Award. In addition, she was a 2015 finalist for the Thomas Ehrlich Civically Engaged Faculty Award and a Faculty Fellow for the California Campus Compact-Carnegie Foundation Award for service-learning for political engagement. In 2018, she served as scholar-in-residence for Campus Compact.

Adriana Signorini coordinates the Students Assessing Teaching and Learning (SATAL) program at the Center for Engaged Teaching and Learning at the University of California, Merced (UCM), USA. She holds master's degrees in Teaching English as a Foreign Language and in Applied Linguistics with an emphasis on language teaching and evaluation from the University of Reading, UK. Before coming to UCM, Signorini co-founded and directed an English-language school in her hometown of Rafaela, Argentina.

Emily R. Smith is associate professor of English Education in the Department of Educational Studies & Teacher Preparation and Director of Mentoring for the Center for Academic Excellence at Fairfield University, USA. Her research focuses on mentoring for faculty and beginning teachers.

Tammy R. Smith has qualifications and experience in education, health, and management and began her career as a primary school teacher. She has taught at all levels from junior primary school through to clinical practice and postgraduate, and is also a critical care nurse and educator with a drive to instill confidence and build capacity in others. Her passion is working in the area of intercultural communication to assist collaboration. Smith completed a PhD in Education (Research) at the University of Melbourne, Australia, in 2012. Her thesis was an ethnographic study exploring positionality in short-term volunteerism, emphasizing the critical role that reciprocity plays in enabling successful intercultural encounters.

Marina Smitherman is a professor of Biology and Chair of Life Sciences at Dalton State College, USA. She has directed faculty development since 2014 and chaired the Georgia Consortium of Teaching and Learning Directors. She is co-author of *Taking Flight: Making your Teaching and Learning Center Soar*.

Annie Soisson has helped grow the Center for the Enhancement of Learning and Teaching (CELT) at Tufts University, USA, into a well-respected center whose programs are frequented by faculty and have shifted the culture toward

xlviii   Notes on Contributors

one that is more learner-centered and focused on research-based strategies. Soisson was the principal investigator for a three-year grant from the Davis Educational Foundation, which has had a continuing effect on teaching and learning through an Inclusive Learning Institute, continuing programming, and a website with teaching resources. Soisson received a Multicultural Service Award for her work in defining Tufts University as a multicultural institution. She is actively engaged in teaching and a member of various local, national, and international professional development organizations. As Vice President of the Board of the New England Faculty Development Consortium, Soisson has been invited nationally and internationally to consult on center development and conduct faculty development workshops.

Sarah Stokes is a learning facilitator with the Office of Learning Innovation at the University of Ontario Institute of Technology, Oshawa, Canada. Her role provides project management support for institutional projects and initiatives related to teaching and learning, faculty engagement, and student success. Stokes also plays a role in institutional advocacy for experiential learning and open educational resources. She holds a master's degree in Educational Technology from the University of British Columbia.

Roman Švaříček is an associate professor of Education in the Department of Educational Sciences, Faculty of Arts, Masaryk University (MUNI) in Brno, Czech Republic. His research interests include classroom discourse, dialogic teaching, teacher identity, and teacher professional development. He is a member of the working group of the Pedagogical Competence Development Centre (CERPEK) at MUNI. As a member of the Research Ethics Committee, he focuses on quality of empirical research at MUNI, and as a member of the Executive Board of the Experimental Humanities Laboratory (HUME Lab), he participates in the development of an innovative research facility aimed at increasing our understanding of human interaction.

Paul Taylor is Pro-Dean for Student Education in the Faculty of Mathematics and Physical Sciences, University of Leeds, UK. His main pedagogic activities concern leadership of undergraduate research, including opportunities for undergraduates to disseminate their findings through undergraduate journals and conferences. Taylor's scientific research interests focus primarily on cancer research.

Héctor Turra is a faculty consultant for the Centre for Teaching Development and Innovation at the Universidad Católica (UC) de Temuco, Chile. He has worked with School of Engineering faculty and authorities and directed a

Chilean Ministry of Education project on science, technology, engineering, and mathematics (STEM) innovation.

Jeffrey A. Vanderziel is the academic guarantor for and Director of the Pedagogical Competence Development Centre (CERPEK) at Masaryk University (MUNI) in Brno, Czech Republic, where he is responsible for the coordination of CERPEK activities. He is also a lecturer in the Department of English and American Studies, Faculty of Arts, MUNI, where he was department head for 15 years. His area of expertise and research focus is on minorities in the USA and Canada, particularly indigenous peoples, African Americans, and the LGBTQ+ community. He is particularly interested in the use of stereotypes in popular culture.

Dominique Verpoorten is a senior lecturer in Learning Sciences at the Institute for Training and Research in Higher Education (IFRES), University of Liège, Belgium. He has authored over 164 publications, including 28 journal articles, and has contributed to nine books. His research topics of interest include blended learning, gamification of training activities, metacognition, e-learning, and reflective practice.

Kyle Sebastian Vitale is the former Assistant Director for Faculty Teaching Initiatives at Yale University's Poorvu Center for Teaching and Learning, USA. He received his PhD in Early English Drama from the University of Delaware, after which he taught for many years in rhetoric and composition, British literature, and world literature. Before coming to Yale, Vitale managed a National Endowment for the Humanities teaching grant at the Folger Shakespeare Library which funded new physical and digital approaches to teaching Shakespeare and created new accessible teaching resources. Vitale writes and publishes on strategies for teaching, form and meaning in Shakespeare, and interpersonal issues in academia. He is co-editing the collection *Shakespeare and Digital Pedagogy* and his writing has appeared in the *Edinburgh History of Reading, Religion and Literature, Notes & Queries, Christianity and Literature, Pedagogy, Chronicle for Higher Education, Inside Higher Ed*, and *Patheos*.

Zhang Yeye is a member of staff of the Center for Enhanced Learning and Teaching (CELT) at Beijing Institute of Technology, China. She received her BSc (2000) and MSc (2004) from Wuhan University, where she majored in software engineering. Yeye has worked as a teaching secretary for eight years and has valuable experience in teaching management. She has also participated in several teaching reform projects.

Notes on Contributors

James Zimmerman has a PhD from the University of Michigan, USA. He currently serves as the Associate Vice Provost for Teaching and Learning at the University of California, Merced (UCM). A nuclear scientist with a deep passion for learning and teaching, Zimmerman has participated in faculty professional development activities at the local, national, and international level. These activities have included developing a theory-based integrative model for learning and motivation in higher education, and designing assessment protocols for multi-campus initiatives. His scholarly agenda includes program, project, and classroom assessment, pedagogies for student success, and traditional faculty development.

Abbreviations

AAC&U	American Association of Colleges and Universities
AAO	Academic Affairs Office
ACC	Assessment Coordinating Council
AD L&T	Associate Dean of Learning and Teaching
AD	Academic Development
ADAC	Academic Development Advisory Committee
ADC	Academic Professional Development Center
ADE	Associate Dean of Education
ADU	Academic Development Unit
AFELT	Association for Faculty Enrichment in Learning and Teaching
AKDN	Aga Khan Development Network
AKU	Aga Khan University
ALTC	Australian Learning and Teaching Council
AMEEMR	Association for Medical Education in the Eastern Mediterranean Region
APR	Academic Program Review
AQF	Australian Qualification Framework
AQUA	Australian Universities Quality Agency
ASDP	Academic Staff Development Program
AUTC	Australian Universities Teaching Committee
AWB	Academics Without Borders
BCUR	British Conference of Undergraduate Research
BIT	Beijing Institute of Technology
BMS	Biomedical Science
BOPPPS	Bridge-In, Objectives, Pre-Assessment, Participatory Learning, Post-Assessment, and Summary
C&E	Change and Engagement
CAA	Center for Advising and Achievement

lii Abbreviations

CADAD	Council of Australian Directors of Academic Development
CAFÉ	Center for the Advancement of Faculty Excellence
CAT	Careers, Advising, and Teaching
CCS	Center for Christian Spirituality
CCTC	Center for Catholic Culture and Thought
CDO	Career Development Office
CeDID	Center for Teaching Development and Innovation
CEE	Center for Educational Excellence
CEL	Community-Engaged Learning
CELT	Center for Enhanced Learning and Teaching
CELT	Center for the Enhancement of Learning and Teaching
CEQ	Course Experience Questionnaire
CERPEK	Pedagogical Competence Development Centre
CETL	Center for Engaged Teaching and Learning
CETL	Center for Excellence in Teaching and Learning
CETL	Centre for the Enhancement of Teaching and Learning
CFD	Center for Faculty Development
CGU	Claremont Graduate University
CHED	Chinese Higher Education Development
CHETL	Certificate of Higher Education Teaching and Learning
CHPE	Certificate Course in Health Professions Education
CHRD	Center for Human Resource Development
CIDePES	Certificate of Pedagogical Development in Higher Education
CIE	Center for Individualized Education
CMHS	College of Medicine and Health Sciences
CML	Center for Mentoring and Learning
CMLAI	Center for Mentoring, Learning, and Academic Innovation
COE	College of Education
CoHE	Council of Higher Education
CoP	Community of Practice
COPUS	Classroom Observation Protocol for Undergraduate STEM
CPALM	College Professor of Adult Learning and Mentoring
CPD	Continuous Professional Development
CPS	Center for Preparatory Studies
CQAHE	Committee for Quality Assurance in Higher Education
CRT	Critical Reflective Thought
CSJ	Catholic Social Justice
CST	Catholic Social Teaching
CTL	Center for Teaching and Learning
CTLD	Center for Teaching and Learning Development
CTLE	Center for Teaching and Learning Excellence
CTLE-W	Center for Teaching and Learning Excellence-Worldwide
CTLHE	Certificate in Teaching and Learning in Higher Education

CUT	Certificate in University Teaching
CWG	Collaborative Writing Group
CWR	Center for Writing and Rhetoric
D/PVC L&T	Deputy or Pro-Vice Chancellor of Learning and Teaching
DFW	D Grade, Fail, or Withdraw
DVC	Deputy Vice Chancellor
ED	Educational Designer
EHON	Expertise Network Higher Education
EQA	Evaluation and Quality Assessment
ERAU-W	Embry-Riddle Aeronautical University-Worldwide
ETC	Educational Technology Center
FACET	Faculty Colloquium for Excellence in Teaching
FD	Faculty Development
FDC	Faculty Development Center
FDEC	Faculty Development and Evaluation Committee
FD-QM	Fudan University/Faculty Development-Quality Matters
FD-QM Alliance	Fudan University/Faculty Development-Quality Matters Online Course Quality Rubric Standard Alliance
FDRC	Faculty Development and Recognition Committee
FDU	Faculty Development Unit
FF	Faculty Fellow
FGD	Focus Group Discussion
FLC	Faculty Learning Community
FSS	Faculty Satisfaction Survey
FTDC	Faculty Teaching Development Center
FTE	Full-Time-Equivalent
FTI	Faculty Teaching Initiative
GA	Graduate Assistant
GA-CTL	Georgia Consortium on Teaching and Learning
GCC	Gulf Cooperation Council
GER	Gross Enrollment Rate
GET	General Education Teaching
GMC	Green Mountain College
GS	General Standard
GTA	Graduate Teaching Assistant
HE	Higher Education
HEA	Higher Education Academy
HEI	Higher Education Institution
HERDSA	Higher Education Research and Development Society of Australasia
HIP	High-Impact Practice
HKU	University of Hong Kong
ICT	Information and Communication Technology

liv   Abbreviations

ICWG	International Collaborative Writing Group
IDEA	Individual Development and Educational Assessment
IDEAL	International Databases for Enhanced Assessments and Learning
IDP	Individual Development Plan
IFRES	Institute for Research and Training in Higher Education
IMTL	Institute on Mentoring, Teaching and Learning
IRF	Invited Research Fellow
iSAP	Integrating Science and Practice
ISW	Instructional Skills Workshop
IT	Information Technology
IU	Indiana University
IUCEA	Inter-University Council for East Africa
KIU	Karakorum International University
LD	Lower Division
LGFD	Leading Group for Faculty Development
LITE	Leeds Institute for Teaching Excellence
LMS	Learning Management System
LT	Learning Transformation
LT&ITC	Learning, Teaching, and Innovative Technologies Center
LTB	Learning and Teaching Building
LTPF	Learning and Teaching Performance Fund
MD	Medical Degree
MEID	Medical Education and Informatics Department
MEIU	Medical Education and Informatics Unit
MEU	Medical Education Unit
MNHS	Medicine, Nursing, and Health Sciences
MOE	Ministry of Education
MOOC	Massive Open Online Course
MSF	Midterm Student Feedback
MTSU	Middle Tennessee State University
MUNI	Masaryk University
MU-OLT	Monash University Office of Learning and Teaching
NCC	North Central College
NEA	National Education Association
NIC	Network and Information Center
NMSU	New Mexico State University
NPM	New Public Management
NSF	National Science Foundation
NTNU	Norwegian University of Science and Technology
OBE	Outcome-Based Education
OCPD	Office of Career and Personal Development
OIA	Office of Instruction and Assessment

Abbreviations lv

Ontario Tech	University of Ontario Institute of Technology
OVPLT	Office of the Vice Provost, Teaching and Learning
PCAP	Postgraduate Certificate of Academic Practice
PCTLHE	Professional Certificate in Teaching and Learning in Higher Education
PD	Professional Development
PEFA	Pentecostal Evangelistic Fellowship of Africa
PFF	Preparing Future Faculty
POD	Professional and Organizational Development
PTCYT	Promoting Teaching Competencies for Young Teachers
QA	Quality Assurance
QAI_net	Network for Quality Assurance and Improvement
QEP	Quality Enhancement Plan
QM	Quality Matters
QS	Quacquarelli Symonds
QTL	Quality Assurance, Teaching, and Learning
QTL_net	Networks of Quality, Teaching, and Learning
REACT	Realising Engagement through Active Culture Transformation
REDCAD	Red Nacional de Centros de Apoyo a la Docencia
RMO	Risk Management Office
RTT	Rethinking Teaching Workshop
SaP	Students as Partners
SATAL	Students Assessing Teaching and Learning
SAW	Student Assessment Workshop
SDT	Self-Determination Theory
SET	Student Evaluation of Teaching
SGID	Small Group Instructional Diagnosis
SIE	Systemic Innovation in Education
SJTU	Shanghai Jiao Tong University
SLA	Student Learning Assistant
SoTL	Scholarship of Teaching and Learning
SQU	Sultan Qaboos University
SQUH	Sultan Qaboos University Hospital
SRS	Specific Review Standard
STEM	Science, Technology, Engineering, and Mathematics
STQ	Senior Teaching Qualification
SUNY	State University of New York
SWJTU	Southwest Jiaotong University
TA	Teaching Assistant
TCpNT	Training and Consultation Program for Novice Teachers
TEACH	Teaching Enhancement Accredited Certification of the Higher Education Academy
TEF	Teaching Excellence Framework

lvi   Abbreviations

TEP	Teaching Engagement Program
TEQSA	Tertiary Education Quality and Standards Agency
TESCEA	Transforming Employability for Social Change in East Africa
TILT	Transparency in Learning and Teaching
TL_net	Network of Teaching and Learning
TLC	Teaching and Learning Centre
TLEW	Teaching Learning Enhancement Workshop
UArizona	University of Arizona
UC Temuco	Universidad Católica de Temuco
UCET	University Center for Excellence in Teaching
UCM	University of California, Merced
UD	Upper Division
UDL	Universal Design for Learning
UE	Unit Enhancement
UGC	University Grants Committee
UKPSF	UK Professional Standards Framework
UMBC	University of Maryland Baltimore County
UO	University of Oregon
UPT	Unit of Pedagogical Training
UR	Undergraduate Research
USD	University of San Diego
USG	University System of Georgia
VC	Vice Chancellor
VERSE	Visiting and Early Research Scholar Experience
V-FLC	Virtual Faculty Learning Community
VPAA	Vice President of Academic Affairs
VUA	Vrije Universiteit Amsterdam
WFME	World Federation for Medical Education

List of Figures

Fig. 3.1	Extended mission of higher education in correlation with a multiple scholarship model	44
Fig. 3.2	Four-dimensional FD model	44
Fig. 3.3	Multiple scholarship model combined with four-dimensional FD model	45
Fig. 3.4	Organizational chart of the FDC of Renmin University, China	49
Fig. 6.1	OIA organizational chart	99
Fig. 8.1	Administrative structure and staffing of the MEID	128
Fig. 10.1	Model one—initial method of engagement with faculties (2014–2015)	156
Fig. 10.2	Model two—revision of the initial engagement method (June 2015–December 2017)	162
Fig. 10.3	Model three—addition of centrally located EDs (July 2017–present)	163
Fig. 12.1	Organizational structure of the TLC, Ontario Tech	187
Fig. 13.1	Correlation between course evaluation scores* and participation in CELT programming	209
Fig. 14.1	Organizational reporting and structure of UCET	224
Fig. 14.2	UCET visits by faculty rank 2017–2018	231
Fig. 15.1	Organizational chart* for NMSU Teaching Academy. *Accurate as of Spring 2020	238
Fig. 16.1	Reporting structure of the Center for Academic Excellence	253
Fig. 17.1	Reporting structure for the Centre for Student Engagement	273
Fig. 17.2	Placement in the organization of the Centre for Student Engagement	273
Fig. 18.1	CETL reporting and organizational chart	284
Fig. 21.1	Immediate satisfaction with QTL initiatives among participants	339

lviii   List of Figures

Fig. 21.2	Impact of QTL initiatives on knowledge and conceptions of teaching and learning after 1 to 3 years	340
Fig. 21.3	Comparison of teaching practices according to QTL_net program attendance after 5 years	341
Fig. 24.1	Organizational chart of the LT&ITC	382
Fig. 25.1	FDC organizational chart	396
Fig. 26.1	Diagram of the reporting structure of the CAFÉ	408
Fig. 27.1	SJTU CTLD organization chart	421
Fig. 28.1	Organizational reporting and structure of the CMLAI	437
Fig. 29.1	Reporting structure for CTLE-W	447
Fig. 29.2	V-FLC framework steps	451
Fig. 30.1	CETL organizational chart	460
Fig. 31.1	Reporting structure of the VUA in connection to Learn! Academy	481
Fig. 31.2	Diagram of the SIE model depicting crucial moments in the innovation process	488
Fig. 32.1	Reporting structure of the CTLE, Nevada State College	499
Fig. 33.1	The five mindsets for inclusive future-focused pedagogy	515
Fig. 33.2	Evolution of the PFF program over time	519
Fig. 34.1	Staff and hierarchy of the IFRES	529
Fig. 34.2	Continuum of pedagogical development designed by the IFRES	531
Fig. 35.1	CELT development path	546
Fig. 35.2	Mission and attributes of the CELT	547
Fig. 36.1	The organization of reflection based on Vince and Reynolds (2010) framework	558
Fig. 36.2	Structure of affiliation of the LITE	560
Fig. 37.1	Support system at SWJTU for FD and innovation in teaching and learning	573
Fig. 37.2	A student-designed logo for the interdisciplinary course 'Sports, Science, Technology, and Wise Life' (Figure reproduced with permission)	584
Fig. 38.1	Cynefin network (Figure reproduced with permission from Kurtz and Snowden, 2003)	597
Fig. 38.2	The Cynefin and Standard+Case approach (Figure reproduced with permission from England, 2013)	599
Fig. 38.3	CETL's decision-making model based on the combined Cynefin network and Standard+Case model (Figure reproduced with permission from England, 2013)	601
Fig. 40.1	Current faculty development programs at the CeDID	631
Fig. 41.1	Distribution of Chinese HEIs with established ADCs by province in 2017. Data source: *Report of the Network Training Center* (MOE, 2018)	643
Fig. 41.2	Learning process and outcomes of the FD-QM Online Course Quality Rubric Faculty Training Program	652

List of Tables

Table 3.1	Employer-demanded traits for Chinese university graduates 2015–2017	55
Table 5.1	Model ADC functions and services by the means to achieve/deliver them	84
Table 12.1	Offerings of the TLC and their modalities	189
Table 12.2	Lessons learned in faculty development programming and next steps to address them	198
Table 22.1	Interview protocol	356
Table 24.1	Sampling of services provided by the LT&ITC in 2017–2018	388
Table 30.1	CHETL content modules	466
Table 30.2	Types of activities conducted by FFs at the college/center/university levels	468
Table 30.3	CETL activities that the FFs found most useful	469
Table 30.4	Obstacles encountered by the FFs	470
Table 31.1	Connection between teaching levels, qualification structure, and teaching and learning products for qualification at each level	482
Table 35.1	Description of the component modules of the Honghu School pre-post training program	550
Table 38.1	CETL's logframe for change	603
Table 40.1	Example of the CeDID's impact evaluation framework	636
Table 40.2	Difference in students' pre-post results	637
Chart A.1	Case study summary chart	658

Part I

Regional Academic Development Historical Perspectives

Much has already been published about academic professional development in North America and in Europe (Crawford, 2008; Fink, 2013; Lane & Lake, 2015; Advance HE, n.d.; European Commission, n.d.). The four chapters in Part I provide new overviews of the status of academic professional development in four specific locations: Australia, Latin America, China, and Africa/Kenya.

Chapters in Part I

Chapter 1: Australian Academic Professional Development Centers: 60 Years of Evolution. Denise Chalmers, University of Western Australia, Crawley, WA, Perth, Australia, and Kym Fraser, Swinburne University of Technology, Hawthorn, VIC, Melbourne, Australia.

The 60-year history of academic professional development in Australia is characterized by fluctuating cycles in government funding, centralized/distributed structure, and foci on quality teaching, student learning, graduate employment, communities of learning, and student satisfaction.

Chapter 2: Perspectives on Faculty Development in Latin American Universities: The Emergence of Academic Professional Development Centers. Fadia Khouri, Centro para la Excelencia Docente / Center for Teaching Excellence, Universidad Del Norte, Barranquilla, Atlántico, Colombia.

2   Regional Academic Development Historical Perspectives

This report analyzes the extent to which 308 universities in 20 Latin American countries are engaged in continuous improvement in teaching and learning using assessment technologies and models focused on student-centered learning.

Chapter 3: The Past, Present, and Future of Faculty Development in China: Based on Multiple Scholarship for Cultivating Creative Talent. Yihong Fan, Southwest Jiaotong University Chengdu, Sichuan Province, and Xiamen University, Xiamen, Fujian Province, China.

The history of academic professional development in China since the 1980 reflects responses to government efforts toward mass higher education with an emphasis on innovation. An emerging trend away from teacher training to multiple scholarship: teaching, discovery, application, and integration is introduced.

Chapter 4: Africa: The Evolution of Faculty Development in East Africa—A Tale of Three Transformation Stories. Charles Kingsbury, Daystar University, Aithi River Kenya, Mike Calvert, York St. John University, York, UK, and Mary Omingo, Strathmore University, Nairobi, Kenya.

The history of academic professional development in Kenya has been grassroots faculty-driven within the context of cross-institutional and international partnerships.

References

Advance HE. (2019). *UK Professional Standards Framework (UKPSF)*. Advance HE. https://www.advance-he.ac.uk/knowledge-hub/uk-professional-standards-framework-ukpsf

Crawford, K. (2008). Continuing professional development in higher education: The academic perspective. *International Journal for Academic Development, 13*(2), 141–146.

European Commission (2021). *Continuing professional development for academic staff working in higher education*. Eurydice Network. https://eacea.ec.europa.eu/national-policies/eurydice/content/continuing-professional-development-academic-staff-working-higher-education-65_sr

Fink, L. D. (2013). The current status of faculty development internationally. *International Journal for the Scholarship of Teaching and Learning, 7*(2), 4.

Lane, P., & Lake, P. (Eds.). (2015). *Global innovation of teaching and learning in higher education: transgressing boundaries*. Springer.

1

Australian Academic Professional Development Centers: 60 Years of Evolution

Denise Chalmers and Kym Fraser

Introduction

In this chapter, we focus on the evolution and growth of Australian academic professional development centers (ADCs) in universities, providing a brief overview of key changes over a 60-year period. ADCs evolved from small units focused on individual academics to larger, strategic arms of institutional policy and strategy. This has taken place in a context of increased government regulation and oversight of higher education provision, as student participation has moved from an opportunity available only to the elite to a universal prerogative. As a consequence, the role of ADCs changed from being teacher- and learner-focused to include institutional and sector focus.

While it is possible to identify an overall trend of changes in ADCs when viewed from a 60-year perspective, it has not been a direct, untroubled, or singular trajectory. Centers within Australian universities have experienced expansion, contraction, mergers, and disestablishment amid periods of stability in which they made significant contributions to institutions and the broader

---

D. Chalmers (✉)
University of Western Australia, Crawley, Perth, WA, Australia
e-mail: denise.chalmers@uwa.edu.au

K. Fraser
Swinburne University of Technology, Hawthorn, Melbourne, VIC, Australia
e-mail: kfraser@swin.edu.au

© The Author(s), under exclusive license to Springer Nature Switzerland AG 2023
O. J. Neisler (ed.), *The Palgrave Handbook of Academic Professional Development Centers*,
Palgrave Studies on Leadership and Learning in Teacher Education,
https://doi.org/10.1007/978-3-030-80967-6_1

4 D. Chalmers and K. Fraser

field of higher education. These periods of stability and contribution largely resulted due to the Australian government's provision of significant funding for enhancing the quality of teaching and learning in universities over a 20-year period. However, with the demise of that funding and a national change in focus on quality assurance processes and performance reporting rather than quality enhancement, the strategic and operational role of ADCs in their universities has diminished. With the Australian government's proposed reintroduction of a national performance fund, we look forward with interest to see if this will lead to a resurgence of interest in academic development.

The Origins of ADCs and Academic Developers in Australia

Barbara Falk, from the University of Melbourne, is credited with initiating the first Australian ADC in the 1960s: "It was … my experience of attending lectures that made me realise that university teaching required a lot of improvement" (Lee et al., 2008, 25). Falk set up a teaching course for engineering academics and went on to become the head of the University Teaching Project Office in 1962, and the inaugural chair of the university's Centre for the Study of Higher Education in 1968. In the following years, ADCs were instituted in Australian universities in piecemeal and idiosyncratic fashion (Ryan & Fraser, 2010).

Ten years after Falk led the first ADC, the Australian academic development community formed the Higher Education Research and Development Society of Australasia (HERDSA), which continues to serve the interests of its members today. HERDSA was developed as an umbrella organization for those interested in higher education teaching, teaching research, and teaching development. From 1975, the organization conducted an annual conference. In 1982, the highly regarded journal, *Higher Education Research and Development*, was established, and, from 1984, members wrote research informed guides, such as *Supervising Postgraduate Students* and *Improving Student Writing*, written in an easy-to-read style for academics interested in improving specific aspects of their teaching.

Factors Influencing the Directions and Roles of ADCs: 1962–1999

In the 1960s and 1970s, the typical ADC was a centrally based unit, focused on the individual teacher (Ling, 2009). ADCs often operated with a 'shopfront' approach that taught generic, not discipline-specific, workshops and courses, all the while hoping for individual academics interested in teaching to come through their doors seeking support (Ryan & Fraser, 2010). The focus was on 'remediation'—improving the teaching of those who were identified, or who self-identified, as teaching 'poorly' (Lee et al., 2008). A pioneering example of accredited training for university teaching was the graduate diploma of tertiary education at the University of Southern Queensland in the late 1970s. In 1991, the University of New South Wales developed a graduate certificate in tertiary teaching, a trend that would increase into the next century.

Research

In the 1980s and 1990s, the ADC approach broadened to include a 'learner focus', as well as the established teacher focus (Ling, 2009). The phenomenographic research of Marton et al. (1984) captured the academic development community's collective interest in the improvement of students' learning. In the words of Prebble et al., "A deeper understanding of this interplay of teacher, context, student and curriculum … led to the development of more integrated conceptual models of teaching and learning that now play a major role in shaping the efforts of academic developers" (Prebble et al., 2004, 12–13).

While the purpose of these early ADCs was to improve university teaching, primarily by working with individual academics, by the 1980s several ADCs undertook research, bolstering and legitimizing the centers' academic credentials. Examples include: the impact of higher education on adult students at Monash University (West & Hore, 1989); postgraduate supervision at University of Sydney (Moses, 1984); and student evaluation at University of Queensland (Roe & McDonald, 1983). These research-oriented centers led the way in establishing the scholarly status of ADCs and higher education as a field of study, producing analyses and research on teaching and learning in higher education that had wide influence beyond Australia. At the same time, academic development was gaining credibility and prestige within universities not just for their scholarly work but for their capacity to inform quality enhancement and demonstrate quality assurance to reassure the Australian

6   D. Chalmers and K. Fraser

Government that their investment in higher education was delivering on expectations. This newly found influence provided ADCs with the opportunity to engage at the strategic level of the university.

National Initiatives and Influences

Discipline Reviews and Teaching and Learning Indicators

Universities were influenced by successive Australian governments taking an active role in quality assurance in universities from the 1980s, when there was a perceived need for universities to improve their efficiency, effectiveness, and public accountability, particularly in relation to teaching. The first direct quality initiative was to conduct discipline reviews across the sector from 1985 to 1991. These were carried out to determine standards and to improve quality and efficiency in major fields of study such as Engineering, Law, and Computing. In 1989, the government commissioned a team led by Professor Russell Linke to find performance indicators to assess the quality of higher education. Their report suggested that judgments regarding the quality of teaching must flow from the analysis of multiple characteristics and involve a range of procedures, including qualitative peer evaluation and student evaluation (Linke, 1991).

Three categories of indicators on teaching and learning were identified: quality of teaching, student progress and achievement, and graduate employment. These indicators became increasingly influential and were informed to a large extent by the work of notable scholars in ADCs. For example, the Course Experience Questionnaire (CEQ, n.d.) was designed and validated by Paul Ramsden and colleagues from the Centre for the Study of Higher Education at the University of Melbourne (Ramsden, 1991; Wilson et al., 1997). In 1993, the CEQ was sent to all Australian graduating students, and continues to be administered to all graduating students to this day. The CEQ is largely reflected in the Student Experience Survey, also designed by Ramsden and colleagues some 20 years later, a similar questionnaire which is completed by all final-year university students in the UK.

Institutional Audits

In 1992, trends in quality assurance moved from a focus on a specific discipline to a 'whole-of-institution' approach, with the Australian Government establishing the Committee for Quality Assurance in Higher Education

1 Australian Academic Professional Development Centers: 60 Years... 7

(CQAHE) to conduct independent audits of institutional quality assurance policies and procedures, and to advise the government on funding allocations. A significant amount of funding was allocated to universities that could "demonstrate effective quality assurance practices and excellent outcomes" (CQAHE, 1995, 26). Institutions received different levels of funding depending on their performance in annual reviews conducted from 1993 to 1995. Following these quality reviews, there was a brief lull in quality assurance initiatives from the Australian Government, other than the requirement for universities to submit an annual institutional report and plan from 1998 onward.

Learning and Teaching Funding

Concurrent with these quality assurance activities, the Australian Government established successive competitive funding initiatives that institutional or cross-institutional teams could apply for to support professional development activities, predominately focused on teaching enhancement, and, for the first time, competitive funding was provided for projects that were national in scope. The national funding agencies included the Commonwealth Staff Development Fund, established in 1990, the Committee for Australian University Teaching in 1992, and the Committee for University Teaching and Staff Development in 1997; in addition, national university teaching awards were introduced in 1997. Over the succeeding years, these iterations of national funding agencies grew in scope and available budget until the end of the first decade of the new century. During this period, a number of universities established internal funding for learning and teaching projects, while others as a collective, such as the Australian Technology Network, established competitive learning and teaching funding for universities in their network.

While the national funding agencies adopted different strategies for promoting and enabling change in teaching and learning, each was based on three premises:

* That change needed to be stimulated by a central agent, such as a national body, which could offer funding incentives;
* That brokering was a multilevel process, with the national agency acting as the original broker while encouraging individual institutions to act as brokers as a way to conduct their projects;
* And, finally, that funding for the projects was to be viewed as seed money, available only for the duration of the project and with the expectation that

the universities would continue to fund and/or embed the projects into their systems and practices thereafter (Borden et al., 2003).

While we will revisit this type of initiative later in this chapter, this initial national funding initiative, with its focus on teaching quality, facilitated a change in the direction and roles of ADCs. This was evident with ADCs being active participants in university-wide initiatives, and in many cases the lead applicants for this funding, contributing their expertise in organizational change and knowledge of research and its application in higher education.

Both national quality assurance and teaching development initiatives contributed to the growth and development of ADCs in universities. Universities that had not yet established ADCs scrambled to do so in order to demonstrate their quality assurance processes and practices, as well as to improve their success in winning grants.

Changing Models and Roles of ADCs

By the turn of the century, academic development work in Australia could be categorized into four different models:

* A central model (a shop front, generic approach);
* A dispersed model focused on discipline activities within the faculties;
* A mixed model of central and dispersed staff, often with little coordination between the center and the faculties;
* And an integrative model involving systematic collaboration between these two bodies (Hicks, 1999).

The effectiveness of dispersed versus central models was debated vigorously in the literature (Brew, 1995; Johnston, 1997; Blackmore et al., 1999), with most, if not all, present-day universities opting for a distributed model involving both central and faculty-based staff (i.e. a hub-and-spoke model), whose roles are concerned with both the development of teaching and the environments in which teaching occurs (Ling, 2009).

By the end of the century, the breadth and depth of Australian academic development would have surprised early ADC proponents. Chalmers and O'Brien (2005) summarized the scope of ADCs, which had expanded to include:

1. Maintaining a corporate memory of, and sustained engagement in, issues and innovations related to teaching in higher education;
2. Engaging in comprehensive and systematic implementation of teaching and learning initiatives;
3. Creating and facilitating communities of learning involved in the iterative and dynamic top-down/bottom-up engagement and management of educational initiatives;
4. And investigating, articulating, and disseminating scholarship in (and on) teaching, learning, and education development (Chalmers & O'Brien, 2005, 51).

But further change was to come as, after 15 years of free tertiary education in Australia, the move toward massification of the sector saw the gradual reintroduction of student fees from 1989 onward. By the end of the century, those changes brought the marked and sustained attention of successive Australian governments to the quality of teaching in universities, largely influenced by the quality assurance mechanisms of New Public Management (NPM), a term coined to describe an approach to management focused on proving performance across all public services (Hood & Peters, 2004). NPM was extended to higher education, with a proliferation of national policies and quality assurance agencies established by governments to maintain a national oversight role in regard to public expenditure (Lewis, 2004).

The First Decade of the New Century (2000–2010)

The beginning of the new century heralded unprecedented government regulation to assure university teaching quality, along with the funding of teaching projects of national priority, particularly those that incorporated new digital technologies as the government wished to explore possible cost-savings through the use of technology (Ryan, 2011). These changes significantly influenced the role of ADCs to further reinforce their focus on both the organization and sector. Universities became more managerial and business-oriented, with a concomitant determination to be "efficient and effective" (Coaldrake & Stedman, 1998), and responded to the government imperatives by introducing new layers of senior executives and managers, distributing learning and teaching leadership more broadly.

National Initiatives and Influences

Australian Universities Quality Agency

In 2000, the Australian Government established the Australian Universities Quality Agency (AQUA), an independent body responsible for promoting, auditing, and reporting on quality assurance in Australian higher education (AUQA Annual Report, 2002). AUQA's primary responsibility was to audit the effectiveness of an institution's quality assurance system every five years. The process involved an institutional self-evaluation, a site visit by a review team, and publication of the results of the review along with commendations and recognition of good practice and recommendations identifying areas for improvement. Institutions subsequently provided interim reports to AUQA on their progress in implementing these recommendations (Chalmers, 2007).

One focus of AQUA was on the quality of the programs taught in universities. While ADCs had for decades designed and run student evaluations of units/subjects and graduate student satisfaction surveys of programs, the focus shifted to the changes being implemented in response to student and employer feedback. Subject and program review documentation reflected that change, with the inclusion of specific requirements to document changes made and the rationale behind the changes. Another modification that the AQUA audits generated with regards to the role of ADCs was that, to be effective, they needed to work with program teams on their curriculum, rather than with individuals and their subjects. This 'whole-of-program' focus also facilitated the involvement of academic developers in explicitly embedding the learning and teaching elements of the university's strategic plan (a requirement of the Learning and Teaching Performance Fund [LTPF], as discussed below), which included curriculum design elements such as embedding graduate attributes. The AQUA focus on systematic professional development provision to improve the quality of teaching contributed to more Australian universities designing and teaching their own accredited Graduate Certificates of University Teaching, though most universities did not require even new academics to enroll in such programs (Fraser, 2005).

National Funding Initiatives for University Teaching

Simultaneously, by establishing AQUA to monitor university quality in 2000, the Australian Government revived its national funding of teaching by establishing a succession of organizations with different programs and priorities, influenced by the policies and priorities of the government of the day. The Australian Universities Teaching Committee (AUTC) was established in 2000, which, with revised priorities and programs, became the Carrick Institute of Learning and Teaching in 2006 and, subsequently, the Australian Learning and Teaching Council (ALTC) in 2008. The AUTC's remit was to promote quality and excellence in university learning and teaching in two ways:

1. By providing small competitive grants to identify and support effective methods of teaching and learning, and promoting the dissemination and adoption of these methods;
2. By administering the selection process for the Australian Awards for University Teaching.

The AUTC aimed to foster national collaboration and was one of the first of the Australian Government's national university teaching agencies to explicitly recognize brokering as an integral part of the role of the project team through their rejection of individual institutional projects and adoption of brokered national projects. It did this in two ways—through identifying projects that focused on the dissemination of good practice rather than the innovation or development of new practice, and in the project terms of reference, where dissemination was a specific focus that had to be described in the processes and budget. It also appointed a reference group to each project to ensure the project leaders retained their original focus and informed the AUTC of their issues and progress (Borden et al., 2003). What this meant for ADCs was that, for arguably the first time, the more strategic centers collaborated with each other to develop applications which focused on the implementation of good teaching practice across the sector (e.g., large class teaching and sessional staff development). ADCs' original focus on faculty-based academics through workshops and individual development changed to concentrating on the whole of the curriculum, university strategy, and national engagement with teaching and learning projects and their dissemination.

Learning and Teaching Performance Fund

In 2003, the Australian Government established the LTPF as part of their *Our Universities: Backing Australia's Future* scheme in order to "reward institutions that best demonstrate excellence in learning and teaching and, in doing this, enhance the quality of learning and teaching in Australian higher education" (Marks & Coates, 2007, viii). Funding of $54.4 million in 2006, $83 million in 2007, and over $83 million in 2008 was allocated as part of the government's renewed focus on teaching quality in Australian universities. The rationale for the LTPF was to promote the overall quality of the sector and place excellence in learning and teaching alongside research excellence as a valued contribution to Australia's knowledge systems. The scheme included two stages. In order to access the LTPF's significant funds, universities were required to show evidence in their policies and on their websites that they had:

* Learning and teaching strategic plans;
* Systematic support for professional development in learning and teaching for sessional and full-time academic staff;
* Systematic student evaluations of teaching and subjects that informed probation and promotion decisions for academic positions;
* And student evaluations of subjects that were publicly available.

Much of this work fell to each university's ADC, with many universities revising their policies and systems in relation to the systematic student evaluation of teaching and their provision of professional development activities for full- and part-time academics and tutors. The second stage determined the allocation of funding and was quite controversial, with anecdotal reports that some in the sector believed that the universities that missed out on funding were exactly those that most needed it in order to bring their systems, professional development provision, and learning and teaching strategies up to standard.

With the introduction of initiatives such as the LTPF, commissioned national teaching projects, and AQUA audits, ADC directors were called upon to provide strategic leadership to senior executive managers and university councils. Reporting lines of the centers were typically to a senior university executive, and many directors were members of influential university committees. It was also in these early years of the new century that ADCs began to be perceived by academics to be a tool of management (Fraser & Ryan, 2012).

With greater attention on teaching quality and reporting requirements by governments and AUQA to demonstrate systemic policy development and implementation, universities began to institute new layers of leadership with explicit responsibility for teaching and learning, something that had largely been left to discipline leaders in specific faculties.

New Leadership and Management Roles in Teaching and Learning

While the directors and staff of ADCs initially provided strategic leadership in teaching and learning, this was not sustainable as universities sought to address the new government quality assurance and funding agenda systemically across each institution. In the second half of the decade, a new level of learning and teaching leadership and management was established in universities—that of the deputy or pro-vice chancellor of learning and teaching (D/PVC L&T). Universities argued that this new management role allowed them to demonstrate that teaching was as important as research, as DVC research roles had been available for many years prior. Amongst other duties, the D/PVC L&T was responsible for responding to and implementing the requirements of AQUA audit reports, overseeing professional development opportunities, providing academic development support for programs and curriculum review, and incorporating technological advances into teaching practice. This resulted in ADC directors now reporting to the PVC L&T rather than the DVC L&T with, in isolated cases, the PVC L&T also being the ADC director. The PVC L&T also had a second, but not direct, line of management to support his/her work—the faculty Associate Dean of Learning and Teaching (AD L&T).

Initially, the responsibilities of this new faculty role were defined quite differently both between and within specific universities. In response to the AQUA imperative, some, if not many, ADs L&T were required to chair program reviews and accreditation processes in their faculty (Kift, 2004), and expected to implement the university's strategic learning and teaching goals into their faculty strategies. By 2010, those goals often included incorporating online teaching and learning elements into each unit or subject, embedding graduate attributes into the curriculum and broadening the types of assessment tasks used in programs. The ADC director and staff worked closely with ADs L&T, whose direct responsibility was to their faculty deans.

Council of Australian Directors of Academic Development

From 1977, ADC directors informally met as a group to discuss their work and roles (Dr. Robert Cannon, personal communication, November 15, 2019). These meetings would take place just before the annual HERDSA conference. In 2006, ADC directors decided to create the Council of Australian Directors of Academic Development (CADAD), a formal organization to represent and support the work of directors of academic development in Australia. It is clear that, at that time, national initiatives were a high priority for ADC directors, as the agenda of the inaugural meeting included the "examination of models for working with [the] Carrick [Institute] initiatives, including workload and opportunities" (Solomonides, 2016, 1).

In its first 10 years, CADAD significantly supported ADC directors in various ways: developing benchmarks for the performance of ADCs, providing academic development project seed funding, scheduling twice-yearly meetings for members to network and learn from each other, and building resources for use by the sector. Anecdotally, new directors found CADAD to be particularly relevant and useful as they embarked upon a steep learning curve of understanding their role as a director.

Current Status: 2011 to the Present Day

Over the past decade, several national initiatives have had a significant impact on ADCs, and ultimately contributed to the demise of many centers.

Change in Approach to Quality Assurance

The AUQA quality assurance processes were not seen as being sufficiently robust by a government that liked to keep the levers of funding and regulation under its own control. In 2011, AUQA was disestablished and replaced by the Tertiary Education Quality and Standards Agency (TEQSA). TEQSA's brief extended beyond universities to encompass all institutions (both public and private) that provided postsecondary education at the degree level as defined by the Australian Qualification Framework (AQF) (AQF, 2013). In addition, the AQF itself was significantly expanded in 2011 to encompass all tertiary qualifications, from initial vocational training through to doctoral degrees. While all institutional registration and accreditation determinations were consolidated under the TEQSA, the process of review became more risk-orientated, and a great deal of the work once carried out during site visits became primarily desktop audits. Under this model of quality assurance, with the focus being on risk minimization and demonstrating compliance with the Higher Education Standards Framework (2015), reporting was consolidated under, and prepared by, the corporate services of the university administration, and the contribution of ADCs became less relevant.

1 Australian Academic Professional Development Centers: 60 Years... 15

The standardization of approaches and data collection that had taken place throughout the first decade as a result of the increased requirements of quality assurance, have facilitated the capacity of the government to make the information publicly available as performance indicators of teaching quality. The indicators include the aggregated CEQ and Graduate Destinations data, student attrition, retention, and progression, and Student Experience Survey data—all indicators identified in the 1990s by the committee led by Professor Linke. Additionally, the government reports regularly on institutional funding, staffing numbers, and facilities, as well as on equity outcomes for staff and students, and this too is available publicly.

The search for performance indicators of quality teaching has long been sought by institutions and governments. There have been many reports that have strongly argued that we have more than enough performance indicators at the national, sectoral, and institutional levels to make sound determinations of quality (Chalmers, 2007, 2008, 2010). Unfortunately, these cannot be neatly packaged into a single score—the preferred solution of governments and a number of university executives. The change in focusing on quality assurance processes and performance reporting rather than quality enhancement has had an impact on the role of ADCs in their institutions. The provision of professional development of teaching practice through programs and workshops is no longer a significant part of quality assurance reporting, with the focus now being on curriculum design and assessment and the integration of technology-enabled learning. The individuals deemed best able to provide that support to teachers are identified, often as professional staff engaged in online resource and instructional design (Fraser & Ling, 2014). The need for academic staff with expertise in academic development to fill those roles is increasingly being questioned. ADCs with a 30-year history or more of contributions to their universities are now being closed down to make way for centers of technology, innovation, and curriculum design, largely staffed by professional staff to support curriculum development and learning technologies. This is not to disparage the contribution and quality of the work of these staff—they are needed, and provide excellent support to the academics and institutions they serve—but it raises the question: *Where in the institution does expertise in, and knowledge of, research in higher education teaching and learning and its application in universities, now reside?* To begin to answer this question, we need to return to the national funding initiatives begun a decade earlier.

The Unintended Impact of National Grants, Fellowships, Awards, and Networks

National awards for university teaching were first introduced in 1997. Although fellowships for noted scholars to fund their work on a significant project were established earlier, they were not consistently awarded until 2006, with substantial numbers subsequently being awarded through to 2016. While there had been changes to the criteria and number of awards and fellowships bestowed, this program resulted in a large pool of academic and professional staff recognized for their teaching excellence and expertise. Similarly, the grants awarded through competitive selection processes of teaching initiatives within institutions and across the sector supported not only the development of the projects, but the people engaged in their implementation. The projects were typically funded for one to three years in the recognition that establishing and implementing a project and achieving changes in practice took time. As a consequence of these various programs for funding, a significant number of academics engaged in and contributed to the research and evaluation of university teaching projects.

Universities keen to maximize opportunities for further funding, as well as to receive kudos for having nationally awarded teachers, ensured that staff in the ADCs would facilitate the writing of applications, identification of suitable projects, and brokering of connections between individuals, disciplines, and across institutions to maximize the likelihood of success and the impact of the project once funded. A significant number of the projects involved academics from the ADCs, either as leaders or as members of the team, as they had expertise with the relevant literature, as well as with strategies for implementing change and evaluations. For many ADCs, this was a 'golden' period, as they were well supported by their institutions, recognized for their expertise, and actively involved in projects within and across institutions.

This engagement across the sector and between disciplines was further supported with funding allocated to support preexisting networks to promote and disseminate the outcomes of various projects and to promote further implementation, research, and evaluation. Networks such as HERDSA, CADAD, and the Australian Learning and Teaching Fellows, as well as other regional networks, received funding to enable them to share resources and offer workshops and conferences enabling collaboration on projects and activities, and where award-winning teachers could present their practices.

In 2016, the Australian Government discontinued all new program funding and closed the Office of Learning and Teaching, the last organization following the ALTC. Few objections arose from the leadership in the universities, in stark contrast to the distressed feedback from the recipients of the awards and grants and the community of scholars who had participated and engaged in these developments, under the good faith that their contribution to teaching was valued and supported by their institutions and government, in part mirroring the support and esteem provided to research activities and researchers.

The response from institutions was relatively swift, characterized by the nonrenewal of contract positions primarily, but not exclusively, supporting applications for awards and grants. Reviews of ADCs were commissioned, with recommendations to focus on curriculum design and the integration of learning technologies being a common outcome. Academic positions in many centers were removed, and the heads of these units were subsequently appointed into professional positions or demoted to a lower academic level.

Changes in Academic Career Profiles

As the national focus on supporting teaching enhancement diminished, universities began to reframe academic profiles and career paths, explicitly establishing teaching-focused academic positions with workload allocations for teaching, but not research. The growth of these positions has been exponential (Probert, 2013), growing as much as 300% year on year.

While the majority of Australian institutions have created clear criteria, standards, and expectations for these teacher-focused academic levels—all the way from lecturer through to professor—with established promotion policies and processes, more work is needed to align the appointment, performance review, and promotion processes for these positions (Chalmers, 2019). Furthermore, more work is needed to ensure that promotion committees are trained and supported in their decision-making when the focus of applications is on teaching quality.

Counterintuitively, the growth of these teaching-focused positions and the development of criteria and expectations that invariably require evidence of, and contribution to, the scholarship of teaching and learning (SoTL) have not been supported by universities with regards to the provision of more professional development and access to expertise in SoTL, services traditionally provided by the ADCs. We posit that part of the explanation for this may be as a result of the people who have been appointed to these teaching-focused positions. Many have been recipients of awards and/or involved in grants and projects and been active members of the networks that formed for specific projects and regions. Many are early-career staff, who do not have a developed research profile. Others are mid-career academics, considered to be underperforming in research, and/or been active in teaching their discipline or engaging in teaching leadership. Typically, these people are assumed to have a strong theoretical understanding of their teaching practice. While some do, a good number have a rudimentary grasp of the educational basis of their practice, an understanding which is not tested until they apply for a promotion, at which point they are found wanting. Moreover, the capacity of supervisors and managers to appoint and then mentor and manage the performance of their staff in teaching with a view toward their promotion is largely absent. Leadership recognition that the development of teachers, but, more importantly, their supervisors and promotion committees, is needed is not widely evident. Teaching-focused academics are not well served by their supervisors and their institutional leadership, largely because the gap in their understanding of teaching is not recognized by the leaders of teaching and learning, such as their DVCs L&T. In particular, ADs L&T often have a rudimentary knowledge at best of the higher education learning and teaching literature, a dilemma which, because of a return to valuing teacher practice over teaching and learning research and evidence-informed teaching, is growing.

Conclusion

While we have presented a rather gloomy picture of the current state of academic development in Australia, we are optimistic that the tide will turn. Ultimately, we need teams of professional staff and academic developers to support the development of their colleagues in all aspects of their roles, including teaching, research, and service. In the meantime, national networks and organizations such as HERDSA and CADAD, now renamed the Council of Australasian Leaders in Learning and Teaching, continue to serve their members and representatives.

In 2020, the government planned to introduce a performance fund that unsurprisingly draws on many of its original performance indicators, including quality of teaching, student satisfaction and engagement, and retention and progression of students. It was hoped that universities would refocus their attention on ways in which they can maximize their access to these funds and will lead to a resurgence of interest in academic development. This raises the question as to who might fill these academic development roles, as not just an understanding of SoTL is required, but also an understanding and capacity to carry out organizational change and sophisticated brokering to develop individuals, teams, and disciplines at multiple levels in the organization.

References

Australian Qualifications Framework (AQF). (2013). *Australian Qualifications Framework*, 2nd edition. Adelaide: Australian qualifications framework council. https://www.aqf.edu.au/sites/aqf/files/aqf-2nd-edition-january-2013.pdf

Australian University Quality Agency. (2002). *Australian Universities Quality Agency annual report*. Melbourne: Australian Universities Quality Agency. https://www.voced.edu.au/content/ngv%3A79651

Blackmore, P., Gibbs, G., & Shrives, L. (1999). *Supporting staff development within departments*. Oxford Centre for Learning Development, Oxford Brookes University.

Borden, V., Chalmers, D., Olsen, M., & Scott, I. (2003). International perspectives on brokerage in higher education. In N. Jackson (Ed.), *Engaging and changing higher education through brokerage: Monitoring change in education series* (pp. 215–242). Ashgate Publishers.

Brew, A. (1995). *Directions in staff development*. Society for Research in Higher Education and Open University Press.

Chalmers, D. (2007). *A review of Australian and international quality systems and indicators of learning and teaching. V1.2*. Carrick Institute.

Chalmers, D. (2008). *Indicators of university teaching and learning quality*. Carrick Institute.

Chalmers, D. (2010). *National teaching quality indicators project: Final report. Rewarding and recognising quality teaching in higher education through systematic implementation of indicators and metrics on teaching and teacher effectiveness*. Australian Learning and Teaching Council.

Chalmers, D. (2019). *Recognising and rewarding teaching. Final report on Senior National Teaching Fellowship program*. Australian Government Department of Education & Training.

Chalmers, D., & O'Brien, M. (2005). Education development units and the enhancement of university teaching. In K. Fraser (Ed.), *Educational development in the higher education sector: Context, structure, processes and strategies*. Routledge Falmer.

Coaldrake, P., & Stedman, L. (1998). *On the brink: Australia's universities confronting their future*. University of Queensland Press.

Committee for the Quality Assurance in Higher Education (CQAHE). (1995). *Report on the 1994 quality reviews*. Australian Government Publishing Service.

Course Experience Questionnaire (CEQ). (n.d.). *Course Experience Questionnaire*. Australian Learning and Teaching Council. https://docs.education.gov.au/system/files/doc/other/australian_learning_and_teaching_council.pdf

Fraser, K. (2005). Education development: The role of graduate university teaching programmes. In K. Fraser (Ed.), *Education development and leadership in higher education*. Abingdon.

Fraser, K., & Ling, P. (2014). How academic is academic development? *International Journal for Academic Development, 16*(1), 226–241.

Fraser, K., & Ryan, Y. (2012). Director turnover: An Australian academic development study. *International Journal for Academic Development, 17*(2), 135–147.

Hicks, O. (1999). Integration of central and departmental development – Reflections from Australian universities. *International Journal for Academic Development, 4*(1), 43–55.

Higher Education Standards Framework (Threshold Standards). (2015). *Tertiary Education Quality and Standards Agency Act 2011: Higher Education Standards Framework*. Australian Government Federal Register of Legislation. https://www.legislation.gov.au/Details/F2015L01639

Hood, C., & Peters, G. (2004). The middle aging of new public management: Into the age of paradox? *Journal of Public Administration Research and Theory, 14*(3), 267–282.

Johnston, S. (1997). Educational development units: Aiming for a balanced approach to supporting teaching. *Higher Education Research and Development, 16*(3), 331–342.

Kift, S. (2004). Between a rock and several hard places: Where does a faculty learning & teaching sub-dean sit and what is that role? *Higher Education and Development Society of Australasia News, 26*(3), 8–11.

Lee, A., Manathunga, C., & Kandlbinder, P. (2008). *Making a place*. HERDSA.

Lewis, R. (2004). Ten years of international quality assurance. In *Ten years on: Changing higher education in a changing world*. Centre for Higher Education Research and Information, Open University.

Ling, P. (2009). *Development of academics and higher education futures. Vol. 1. Report to the Council of Australian Directors of Academic Development*. Council of Australian Directors of Academic Development. https://www.voced.edu.au/content/ngv:64806

Linke, R. D. (1991). *Performance indicators in higher education: Report of a trial evaluation study, 1*. Department of Employment, Education and Training.

Marks, G., & Coates, H. (2007). *Refinement of the learning and teaching performance fund adjustment process. Report to the Department of Education and Training*. Australian Council for Educational Research.

Marton, F., Hounsell, D., & Entwistle, N. (1984). *The experience of learning*. Scottish Academic Press.

Moses, I. (1984). Supervision of higher degree students – Problem areas and possible solutions. *Higher Education Research and Development, 3*(2), 153–165.

Prebble, T., Hargraves, H., Leach, L., Naidoo, K., Suddaby, G., & Zepke, N. (2004). *Impact of student support services and academic development programmes on student outcomes in undergraduate tertiary study: A synthesis of the research*. Ministry of Education.

Probert, B. (2013). *Teaching-focused academic appointments in Australian universities: Recognition, specialisation, or stratification? Commissioned Report for the Australian Learning and Teaching Council.* Australian Learning and Teaching Council.

Ramsden, P. (1991). A performance indicator of teaching quality in higher education: The Course Experience Questionnaire. *Studies in Higher Education, 16*(2), 129–150.

Roe, E., & McDonald, R. (1983). *Informed professional judgement: A guide to evaluation in post-secondary education.* University of Queensland Press.

Ryan, Y. (2011). An elephant's lifetime, the patience of Job. In L. Burge, C. Campbell Gibson, & T. Gibson (Eds.), *Flexible pedagogy, flexible practice: Notes from the trenches of distance education* (pp. 175–186). Athabasca University Press.

Ryan, Y., & Fraser, K. (2010). Education development in higher education. *International Encyclopedia of Education, 4,* 411–418.

Solomonides, I. (2016). *Council of Australasian Directors of Academic Development annual report.* Council of Australasian Directors of Academic Development.

West, L. H. T., & Hore, T. (1989). The impact of higher education on adult students in Australia. *Higher Education, 18*(3), 341–352.

Wilson, K., Lizzio, A., & Ramsden, P. (1997). The development, validation and application of the Course Experience Questionnaire. *Studies in Higher Education, 22*(1), 33–53.

2

Perspectives on Faculty Development in Latin American Universities: The Emergence of Academic Professional Development Centers

Fadia Khouri

Introduction

High-quality teachers are considered a necessary condition for the overall quality of universities and for the educational processes that take place within them (Sorcinelli et al., 2006). This high quality of teaching includes not only the expected and necessary disciplinary expertise of university teachers but also their ability to create student-centered learning environments (Sorcinelli et al., 2006). To achieve this purpose, universities have established strategies and programs to support faculty development.

However, the emergence and consolidation of programs for faculty development has varied worldwide. Some authors have described the different waves in which educational development has taken place in the past (Beach et al., 2016; Sorcinelli et al., 2006). In fact, before 1970, in countries such as the USA, these programs were mainly focused on the development of the disciplinary expertise of teachers in order to consolidate their research profile and consequently increase their intellectual production. Beginning with the student rights movements that took place in the 1960s, a reconceptualization of the role of university teachers began, and support started to be offered to

F. Khouri (✉)
Centro para la Excelencia Docente / Center for Teaching Excellence,
Universidad Del Norte, Barranquilla, Atlántico, Colombia
e-mail: khourif@uninorte.edu.co

© The Author(s), under exclusive license to Springer Nature Switzerland AG 2023
O. J. Neisler (ed.), *The Palgrave Handbook of Academic Professional Development Centers*,
Palgrave Studies on Leadership and Learning in Teacher Education,
https://doi.org/10.1007/978-3-030-80967-6_2

improve faculty pedagogical skills (Beach et al., 2016; Sorcinelli et al., 2006). The trend was later consolidated in the so-called *Age of the Learner* in the 1990s, in which student learning became the cornerstone of teacher development.

A similar shift toward supporting the pedagogical development of faculty is also found in countries such as Australia and the UK (Beach et al., 2016). According to an analysis carried out by Fink (2013), commonwealth countries (such as South Africa, Sri Lanka, and New Zealand) as well as Nordic countries (Finland, Norway, Sweden, and Denmark) and the Netherlands similarly have a long history of teacher development, with this being compulsory for new faculty. On the other hand, Fink (2013) found that, for countries in Latin America, Africa, Asia, and Eastern and Southern Europe, very few teacher development programs have been implemented.

A deeper analysis of the situation in Latin America shows that, before 1995, there was an interest on the part of multilateral and/or regional organizations to promote pedagogy and educational innovation within universities. Some documents, such as *Pedagogía universitaria en América Latina: Antecedentes y Perspectivas* [University pedagogy in Latin America: History and perspectives] (Centro Interuniversitario de Desarrollo [CINDA], 1984) and *Innovación en la educación universitaria en América latina: Modelos y casos* [Innovation in Latin American higher education: Models and cases] (CINDA, 1993), serve to illustrate this focus. However, in the late 1990s, access to education and graduation began to be emphasized. Indeed, until a few years ago, the documents produced by these multilateral and/or regional organizations related to the development of Latin American higher education rarely included faculty and their pedagogical work as an axis of analysis and action (Gazzola & Didriksson, 2008). In those documents in which teaching quality is considered, most of the variables refer to hiring or advanced studies at the disciplinary level of faculty (i.e., masters and doctorates) (Brunner & Ferrada Hurtado, 2011; Brunner & Miranda, 2016).

Latin American higher education has faced a myriad of challenges, including access, quality assurance, funding, and regional political instability (Gazzola & Didriksson, 2008; United Nations Educational, Scientific and Cultural Organization, 2013). These factors, paired with the preeminence given to international rankings, research output, and funding oriented toward disciplinary research, have influenced Latin American universities toward disciplinary training that limits faculty teaching and learning development.

Despite these local and international pressures, the pedagogical component of faculty profiles has not been completely neglected over the last several decades. Diverse initiatives and institutional programs for educational development have existed since the beginning of the 1990s (CINDA, 1991, 1993). However, an analysis of these initiatives reveals that they are usually isolated and disjointed actions that do not count as institutional primacy.

Indeed, the approach that has traditionally been used in these programs is that of generic pedagogical training, with lecture-based classes and a focus on theory rather than practice which has been widely challenged. Some of the main criticisms are the disconnect with faculty interests and needs (Hénard & Roseveare, 2012), and its limited effects on authentic and lasting curriculum transformation, particularly faculty teaching methodologies (Jayaram et al., 2012). Further, pedagogical training often generates faculty resistance. As mentioned by Zabalza (2013), the faculty are characterized by high disciplinary training, have great autonomy in their work, and are expected to be critical. It is therefore very difficult for them to accept a pedagogical training approach in which they are told how to do their job (Zabalza, 2013).

In addition to this scenario, global conditions such as the diversification of student profiles, emphasis on learning outcomes, and the rapid development of technologies—factors that influence students' interests, as well as create new demands for universities (Sorcinelli et al., 2006)—are challenging the current role of universities, and therefore of faculty. These conditions have forced Latin American universities to rethink their work and the traditional methods that have been used for faculty development.

New Approaches Toward Continuous Improvement and Accompaniment

The above-mentioned forces have resulted in the development of new approaches in which continuous improvement in teaching and learning, the use of technologies for learning, and models aligned with student-centered learning are fundamental.

These concerns have been addressed through a greater emphasis on faculty teaching profile. In particular, some universities have recently opted to create centers for teaching-learning or academic professional development centers (ADCs) that emphasize pedagogical work but through a different approach: from generic theoretical training toward guidance, support, and accompaniment (i.e., a shared journey). As proposed in a national policy meeting in 2013:

> It is necessary to redefine policies and lines of action for faculty development, starting by understanding them less as "training" (from the ideas of external

experts) and more as actions to support the educational development of degrees and their teaching teams (from their specific experiences and challenges). (Patricio, 2013, 499)

This new approach is supported by the findings of Chism et al. (2012). Their review suggests that faculty learning communities and consultations have more long-lasting and deeper effects on teachers' beliefs and practices compared to short workshops, courses, and grants.

In order to have a broad overview of such centers, a search was carried out between March 2018 and 2019 of the webpages of 308 Latin American universities, including universities from Argentina, Bolivia, Brazil, Chile, Colombia, Costa Rica, Cuba, the Dominican Republic, Ecuador, El Salvador, Guatemala, Honduras, Mexico, Nicaragua, Panama, Paraguay, Peru, Puerto Rico, Uruguay, and Venezuela. Each of the pages was navigated to identify possible programs, centers, or units for educational or faculty development and/or teaching and learning innovation.

Additionally, to have a deeper understanding and to characterize the new centers for teaching and learning or, as referred to in this volume, the ADCs that have been established in some Latin American universities, a survey was sent to the universities in which some faculty development strategies were identified. Fourteen universities answered the survey. Eight centers in which an important development was identified were also chosen to conduct semistructured, online interviews of approximately 40 minutes with their directors. Additionally, the personal experience of the author (the director of the *Centro para la Excelencia Docente Uninorte* [Center for Teaching Excellence of Universidad del Norte]) was included in the analysis for a total of nine study cases. These centers were located in Argentina (1), Chile (4), Colombia (2), Mexico (1), and Peru (1). Consistent with the research purpose, the interview questions were focused on the establishment, approach, and structure of the centers. Questions about impact, challenges, and recommendations for other centers were also included.

The Latin American Landscape of Faculty Development

An initial search of the Latin American universities' web pages suggested that most of these universities do not yet have a formally constituted ADC (unless such information has not been published online). Indeed, in 65% of cases, no strategy for faculty development was found. In the remaining 35%, faculty development initiatives and even complete units were found; however, in most cases, these were isolated strategies, with an important emphasis still on offering a menu of isolated courses or just a teaching certificate. Nonetheless, several cases of developing or well-developed ADCs that are based on the new philosophy of pedagogical accompaniment or guidance also emerged.

Considering the interviewees' responses, survey results, and online search, it seems that Chile is the country that initiated the movement to create ADCs in Latin America. Most Chilean centers started between 2006 and 2010. They have a network of centers under the Red Nacional de Centros de Apoyo a la Docencia (REDCAD) [National Network of Teaching Support Centers], a network created in 2012 that includes more than 35 universities (REDCAD, n.d.). According to an interviewee, the provision of funds granted by the Chilean Government in 2001 to create these types of centers fostered this trend. Between 2011 and 2013, some of the top universities in Colombia began to create ADCs, and this trend has increased since then. In fact, in 2016, a national network of ADCs (RedCrea) also emerged to foster collaboration between Colombian centers. According to the information provided by one of the interviewees, there was an important boom in Argentina before 2010 in public universities, which then stopped for a few years. Today, it seems that the center creation movement is resurfacing. In Peru, there is also important interest in the development of these centers. For the remaining countries, data has not yet been obtained.

As mentioned previously, eight interviews were conducted to gain a deeper understanding of these new ADCs in Latin America. An analysis of the interviews shows that these centers have a similar approach as well as common characteristics and challenges.

An Analysis of Latin American ADCs

Student Learning, Reflection, and Innovation: The Cornerstones of Latin American ADCs

It is clear that the ultimate aim of these centers is the learning of students. Although most work only with teachers, the basic idea is to guide faculty in their teaching to improve student learning. Most of the directors mentioned that the main goal of the centers they lead is supporting faculty to create effective, innovative, and meaningful learning experiences that are engaging for their students and contribute to the achievement of expected learning outcomes. As mentioned by some participants:

28   F. Khouri

> We collaborate with our faculty through accompaniment, advice and faculty training, within the framework of a university teaching model focused on student learning … for the development of an innovative teaching, contextualized, linked to the environment, which generates a significant impact on the quality of student learning. (Interviewee, University V, Chile)

> The role of the center is to strengthen the role of the faculty members so that their students achieve deeper and more significant learning in all its students, that the faculty members strengthen their teaching so that the students at the end obtains more and better learning. (Interviewee, University CC, Chile)

Although each center has different programs and strategies, the accompaniment of faculty is mainly based on promoting reflection and innovation in their own practice. For these centers, action is a key objective. In the words of a collaborator from an Argentinean university: "We try to be catalysts of pedagogical reflection and experimentation" (Interviewee, University SA, Argentina). Similar comments were made during the interview with the Peruvian university:

> I believe that many faculty maintain a concern about what they teach, but it is important to make these beliefs and concerns also associated with being a better teacher and that is our role to make faculty more aware, strategic and empowered with respect to their teaching … to do so in such a way that it is not only a discourse but also becomes a real practice of faculty in the classroom. (Interviewee, University CP, Peru)

To some extent, these results are similar to those obtained by Beach et al. (2016) in a survey of directors of ADCs in North America. In their study, the researchers found that creating or sustaining a culture of teaching excellence and advancing new initiatives in teaching and learning were the most common answers to the question concerning the goals of the ADC.

Based on Wright et al.'s (2018) analysis, it can also be concluded that the Latin American ADCs that participated in the present study have made the shift from a teaching paradigm to a learning paradigm. However, the most recent approach of a decentered educational environment in which more reciprocal relationships between teachers, students, and resources exist (Wright et al., 2018) has not yet been promoted by these centers. If one considers that these centers are a new trend in the region it is understandable that the first goal is to promote a student-centered learning approach among faculty.

Structure, Areas, and Services of Latin American ADCs

Similar to findings reported by Sorcinelli et al. (2006), most of the study case centers (eight out of nine) in this analysis can be described as having a single, centralized structure, the most common approach in research and comprehensive universities, such as those chosen for the interviews. All these centers report to the vice provost or vice president for teaching or academic affairs, an aspect that can be considered an indicator of the strategic position that they have within the universities. A reporting line to academic affairs is, in fact, highly desirable because it grants easier access to institutional leaders and facilitates alignment with academic mission and strategic goals (Lee, 2010). The ninth center was part of an academic school or division; however, having a specialized center is understandable in this case, given the large number of professors and students at this particular university. In some cases, the centers are for both faculty and students; however, the most common approach is to have separate centers.

As opposed to a well-developed ADC, it was found that, based on the surveys and website analysis, in universities that do not have an ADC but offer some strategies for educational training and development, the services are led by people or offices that report to mid-level leaders or are offered by the School of Education. As mentioned by Smith and Hudson (2017), leaders' passive acceptance or active discouragement of faculty development can become an important barrier to improving teaching. Therefore, lines of report to and support from high-level leaders is important.

Regarding the units of action, well-developed Latin America centers usually have the following areas: instructional development, didactic use of technologies, curriculum development, evaluation of learning, and design of educational materials. Few universities include a research unit. This area may have different emphases: classroom research, research on teaching-learning methodologies, and/or research on the management of the center. In fact, although known about by the directors, the scholarship of teaching and learning (SoTL) or classroom action-research has not been widely promoted by the centers. Like the international trend (Schwartz & Haynie, 2013), SoTL has recently started to be a topic of discussion, with some initiatives to create and promote a Latin American SoTL network since it started in August 2019. It is worth highlighting that, regardless of the areas and particularities of the centers, pedagogical and learning-centered livelihoods appear to be the cross-cutting element.

Within each area, there is a great diversity of programs and services, but they are the usual ones that the literature suggests (Lee, 2010). The following are examples: video recordings of classes, grants and calls for innovation, support in the development of academic programs or curricular innovation, appropriation of information communication technology, and faculty learning communities, among others. It was consistently found that almost all of these programs and services are voluntary. Usually the only program that is mandatory is an induction of or orientation for new faculty, especially those with no teaching experience or education background.

Making Things Happen: ADC Teams in Latin American Universities

All the ADCs consulted are characterized by the creation of interdisciplinary teams. As a result, a wide diversity of professionals and profiles, including students, come together. Although psychologists and pedagogues are found in all teams, part of the richness of these centers is the diversity of perspectives. In fact, all of the directors suggested that it is undesirable to hire just teachers or educators because "they tend to over-pedagogize education, and that doesn't work" (Interviewee, University C, Chile). Furthermore, the interdisciplinary nature of the teams facilitates innovation and diversity of programs and services as well as dialogue with faculty from different areas:

> I would like to clarify that the group is interdisciplinary; that is to say, we try to have a balance that precisely appeals to the fact that the teaching within the university is enhanced by these multiple views. (Interviewee, University CP, Peru)

> I wanted to dispel the notion that the center consists of only pure teachers or pedagogues, I simply believe that, as interlocutors of the community it serves, they come from different perspectives, and that they are people who teach courses and are more or less experts in their area, then I have a historian, I have two psychologists, an engineer, and I, myself, am an economist. (Interviewee, University A, Chile)

In terms of the size of the centers, they range from three employees to more than 60 in some cases. The most common was to find teams of between 7 and 14 collaborators. In some cases, the direction and coordination of these centers is carried out by administrative staff (some of whom teach some courses); in other cases, faculty with assignments or bonuses perform these leadership functions.

It is important to emphasize that—beyond the professional faculty profile, characteristics, and expertise—it was highlighted in all of the interviews that the collaborators of these centers are passionate about what they do and have a deep conviction about their work. In addition, they are characterized by an inherent curiosity that leads them to be constantly deepening their own teaching and learning approaches and to innovate in the work of the center:

> Here, sin is not "not knowing", sin here is "not wanting to learn" and here kids are constantly being challenged by what may come. (Interviewee, University C, Chile)

Further, it was found that staff in these centers are very open and willing to form ADC networks, partnerships, or collaborations to share good practices, offer recommendations, and carry out joint innovations and exchanges of collaborators. It was also highlighted that the teams of these centers maintain very close and warm relations with the faculty and present an attitude of service that facilitates the expected relationship of support and accompaniment of the faculty. As mentioned by Smith and Hudson (2017), faculty members need supportive spaces when they are exposed to new pedagogies that challenge their beliefs and practices. Otherwise, it is likely that they stop innovating once they come to face the first obstacles.

Based on the experience of the author and some ADC case studies (Cook, 2011), responsiveness and kindness are common features of ADCs around the world. Indeed, almost every person who attends the conferences of the Professional and Organizational Development (POD) Network can be considered a great exemplar of the service orientation and warmth that characterizes ADCs. However, these human-based features are not usually included in the analysis of ADCs, although they can make the difference between a good center and an extraordinary one.

Other Special Considerations

The directors implicitly express that the ADCs have a positive image of faculty and positive approach to working with faculty members. The faculty member is seen as an expert who is interested and wants to continually improve his/her teaching process. Therefore, what it requires are resources and colleagues or peers who can accompany and guide it in the process. This implies that the centers start from the needs and interests of faculty, and not from the preconceptions that schools and academic departments have of what the faculty members should be doing. This also means that the ADCs have to be very flexible and diverse in terms of the programs, services, and resources they offer in order to cater precisely to the diversity of faculty member profiles.

Although in some of these centers the faculty are evaluated, in no case are they remedial centers or focused on faculty who obtained low scores in their teaching or performance. On the contrary, there is an important emphasis on working with all faculty (regardless of age, area, expertise, etc.), reflecting on their pedagogical practice and constantly innovating:

> I could not continue with the idea that the center was an "urgent care clinic" where poorly evaluated faculty were rehabilitated. Nor is it a hospice for "terminally ill" faculty, and in contrast we encourage teaching to be seen in an attractive and reflective way. (Interviewee, University CP, Peru)

> The other great challenge, I believe, is this balance that one has to establish between institutional needs and the closeness that one has with faculty … one of our roles is based on teaching evaluations, and when they do not have good teaching evaluations, their academic units refer them to work with us, but that's something you have to be careful not to look like the bad guys in the movies … it's based on the fact that they're successful professionals in their fields, but they may not necessarily have the requisite teaching skills, so it's something that they can develop over time as well. (Interviewee, University AI, Chile)

In addition, faculty are encouraged to enjoy the activities they carry out in the center as well as their teaching. In fact, Zabalza (2013) argues that teacher development should include not only technical but also emotional elements:

> What interests us … from my point of view, consolidating in the university feelings among faculty for a "taste for teaching", because it is not always given in advance that a professor at the university enjoys teaching. There are good researchers, there are good connoisseurs in general. But being a good researcher at an institution does not necessarily equate to being a good teacher. (Interviewee, University CP, Peru)

> Then the challenge is how to hook them naturally [the faculty], so that they can enjoy it [programs and activities] and so that this exercise is enjoyed by all, including the center's team, and that it is an interesting experience from which we all learn. (Interviewee, University A, Colombia)

In summary, ADC staff generally view the faculty as experts in their field who want to know about teaching and that the activities of the ADC should be engaging and motivating, as well as informative.

Challenges That Can Become Opportunities

From the interviews, it was possible to identify three major challenges common to all of the centers. First, given the transformation processes generated by these centers at the level of the faculty, students, and the institution itself, measuring impact was consistently mentioned as one of the main challenges. Indeed, models that can guide the measurement of impact in the processes of pedagogical accompaniment of faculty are still incipient (Chalmers & Gardiner, 2015). In addition, it is clear that student learning responds to several variables, which generates difficulties when correlating the impact of the center with the results of such learning. Hence, all of the centers consulted still have very indirect evaluations and, at the most, basic levels of impact (i.e., coverage, satisfaction, etc.). It is important to mention that this challenge is presented not only by the inherent need to continually improve teacher development programs (Patricio, 2013) but also by the emphasis on higher education accountability (Beach et al., 2016).

Another major challenge for these centers is the struggle to maintain the necessary balance between institutional demands and the relationship with the teachers. It is sometimes contradictory to expect faculty to follow very structured institutional lines of action when they are required to be experts in their field, autonomous, and creative in their work. However, at some universities, leaders can expect these centers to be the very ones to make faculty follow institutional guidelines. To do so would entail a loss of closeness and trust in the relationship with faculty due to a lack of knowledge of their nature and role. The opposite is not desirable either; responding only to the particular interests of faculty can lead to the development of a large number of innovations and projects that do not have a central axis and can therefore culminate in a series of isolated experiences with low impact:

> Something that I think is essential is that we are a very important support for faculty, and I think we are making a difference because we give personalized attention … attention to faculty and the chair of the department to help in the needs that they may have, however, should be focused on the [name of the university] university model and the strategy of the institution. (Interviewee, University MD, Mexico)

Therefore, as mentioned by Hénard and Roseveare (2012), the centers should be the result of collaboration and reflection on the quality of teaching and learning that harmonizes the values, identity, and educational project of the institution with the expectations, interests, and needs of the faculty.

Thirdly, the long-term sustainability of the centers is another major challenge. These centers cannot be understood as a passing initiative for the faculty or for the institution. On the contrary, the work of the centers must generate a sustained impact over time and the work must be directed toward lasting changes. As mentioned by Jerez and Silva (2017), the centers' actions are long-term processes that are not reduced to a single moment, but rather to a constant and continuous development in time that requires time, effort, and resources. This, in turn, implies that the centers must have deep interest and capacity to be constantly rethinking and innovating:

> We have to be reviewing the strategies and changing them, we have to learn to take away the fear of facing new things, to define ourselves again to start over … recognizing everything we bring and what we know, but also without losing sight of the ultimate objective. (Interviewee, Universidad de los Andes, Colombia)

> The centers must always be exploring beyond what they are doing day by day … Undoubtedly some are going to turn out, others are not, that has to be something constant now, for that to turn out to be important that the people at the center have to be in tune with that perspective. (Interviewee, Universidad Adolfo Ibáñez, Chile)

This staff member reiterates that the learning and continuous development of the members of the center are as essential to sustainability as the relationship with faculty and good programming.

Some Final Remarks and Recommendations

It is clear that these centers are having a significant impact on the pedagogical work of faculty and thus, it would be expected, on student learning. Therefore, the main recommendation is that Latin American universities support the creation and consolidation of such centers. However, for them to really have the impact that is expected, some conditions are required.

Recommendations for Institutional Leaders

First, as mentioned by all interviewees, there is a need for strong institutional support, backing, and leadership. This includes not only a deep conviction among university leaders of the importance of teaching and the role of these centers but also support at the level of resources, spaces, and opportunities. Therefore, at the organizational level, the suggestion is that ADCs depend directly on the provost or vice provost in order to eliminate possible barriers and "open roads" more easily. This institutional support also implies a clear recognition of teaching.

Likewise, teaching activities should be included within the institutional schemes and goals, and should not become additional burdens for faculty. As mentioned by Hénard and Roseveare (2012), clear institutional support means that faculty are not the only ones concerned with teaching, but that deans, chairs of department, and other leaders also consider this to be a priority in their management, thus ensuring a collective commitment to teaching:

> The first recommendation is that, at the institutional level, it be an important standard and that it be lowered from the leaders so that it has a weight, in addition to being aligned with the model that each institution has. (Interviewee, University M, Mexico)

> We also recognize the idea that change is costly and difficult and that it has to be accompanied by incentives; it is a matter of motivation, it is a matter of academic career, it is a matter of infrastructure, it is a curricular matter, and a matter of leadership. (Interviewee, University A, Chile)

In the same vein, institutions must ensure that these centers are not associated with remedial or sanctioning functions. On the contrary, a more aspirational vision of continuous improvement should be encouraged in which the center is a strategic ally. Hence, any initiatives that relate the center to underperforming faculty, or that compromise the relationship of trust between the ADC and faculty, should be avoided. Likewise, it is not recommended to conduct summative evaluations of teaching effectiveness at these centers.

Thirdly, these centers must have opportunities to experiment and "go wrong" from time to time; it is part of the innovation process:

> It has always been conveyed to the team that we are not only a center for faculty development, but also a center for pedagogical innovation and, as such, we have the right to experiment with things; it is key for us to keep trying. (Interviewee, University CC, Chile)

Equally, staff must understand that not all faculty are going to participate, nor are changes going to be immediate.

Recommendations for ADC Leaders

At the center level, it is also important to consider the following recommendations. The work of the centers cannot focus solely on bringing about immediate or superficial change. On the contrary, the objective should always be to generate long-lasting impact and to foster a culture of reflection and pedagogical innovation that in fact transcends the work of the teacher:

> I believe that making innovation a transforming process, and assuming it as a cultural change, that is, not a fad or passing event ... Our greatest challenge is with the professors, our commitment is not only the transformation of courses and programs, but also of conceptions and pedagogical practices. (Interviewee, University A, Colombia)

> The main role is to change culture, it is not to do training, that is the tool. The error of the centers falls only within the scope of its trainers' abilities; the point is to change cultures. (Interviewee, University C, Chile)

To achieve this goal, ongoing opportunities should be offered to teachers. These programs and strategies should be practice-based and job-embedded and take into consideration faculty needs and interests. The teaching and learning methodologies used by faculty developers should also model the activities and learning strategies that we expect teachers to use with their students (Smith & Hudson, 2017).

The work of the center should impact leadership and institutional decisions and policy related to teaching-learning processes. Therefore, these centers must understand their task and mission as a slow, long-term process. Likewise, understanding and helping faculty to understand that the process of reflection on one's own practice, as well as the innovations that may result, require time, conviction, and motivation (Hénard & Roseveare, 2012). It might be necessary to:

> Make it clear to the teacher that what is being done is not short term, it requires work, commitment, and the results are not seen overnight and know that if the first semester or first time it did work or did not work, it is important to keep trying and if you see that the teaching evaluations are going down and not up, then it is part of the process to convey to the teacher that improvement is not immediate and requires a long-term commitment. (Interviewee, University CC, Chile)

Understanding the diversity of areas of knowledge and the interests and needs of faculty and academic units must be evident in the accompaniment offered. As mentioned by Hénard and Roseveare (2012), initiatives cannot be given from the top-down, as they will meet greater resistance on the part of faculty because they read it as an intrusion to their autonomy and a disregard for their own expertise.

Although few centers presented a strong area of classroom research, the literature suggests that SoTL and action-research projects by faculty are two "of the professional development strategies that best fit the purpose of transforming conceptions and beliefs about teaching and learning and overcoming intrinsic barriers in innovation and improvement processes" (Patricio, 2013, 497).

The centers must also be coherent and therefore model the ideas they promote. In this sense, the selection of people who will work hand in hand with the faculty is fundamental. They should be passionate about teaching and learning processes, innovative, and able to show through their attitudes and actions what is expected of the educational process and the teacher-student relationship.

Finally, beyond involving students as part of the center, it is interesting that in none of the interviews were specific strategies found to promote the necessary active role of students in their learning process, or to capitalize on the expertise they can offer in educational changes and innovations in the classroom. Therefore, if there are centers for students in universities, it is important to make alliances that allow for discourse and joint strategies with faculty.

Acknowledgments I would like to thank Dr. Alberto Roa Varelo for his encouragement to undertake this study and the insights he provided; the Centro para la Excelencia Docente Uninorte team for their invaluable help with the webpage search; and the centers' directors for their openness and collaborative attitude during the interviews.

References

Beach, A. L., Sorcinelli, M. D., Austin, A. E., & Rivard, J. K. (2016). *Faculty development in the age of evidence: Current practices, future imperatives*. Stylus Press.

Brunner, J. J., & Ferrada Hurtado, R. (2011). *Educación superior en Iberoamérica: informe 2011 – CINDA*. RIL Editores.

Brunner, J. J., & Miranda, D. A. (2016). *Educación superior en Iberoamérica: informe 2016 – CINDA*. RIL Editores.

Chalmers, D., & Gardiner, D. (2015). The measurement and impact of university teacher development programs. *Educare, 51*(1), 53–80.

Chism, N. V. N., Holley, M., & Harris, C. J. (2012). Researching the impact of educational development: Basis for informed practice. *To Improve the Academy, 31*(1), 129–145.

Centro Interuniversitario de Desarrollo (CINDA). (1984). *Pedagogía universitaria en América Latina: Antecedentes y perspectivas.* Alfabeta Impresores.

Centro Interuniversitario de Desarrollo (CINDA). (1991). *Docencia universitaria en América Latina: ciclos básicos y evaluación. Estudio de casos.* Santiago.

Centro Interuniversitario de Desarrollo (CINDA). (1993). *Innovación en la educación universitaria en America Latina: modelos y casos.* Alfabeta Impresores.

Cook, C. E. (2011). Introduction: CRLT and its role at the University of Michigan. In C. E. Cook & M. Kaplan (Eds.), *Advancing the culture of teaching on campus: How a teaching center can make a difference.* Stylus Press.

Fink, L. D. (2013). The current status of faculty development internationally. *International Journal for the Scholarship of Teaching and Learning, 7*(2), 1–9.

Gazzola, A. L., & Didriksson, A. (Eds.). (2008). *Trends in higher education in Latin America and the Caribbean.* United Nations Educational, Scientific and Cultural Organization International Institute for Higher Education in Latin America and the Caribbean. http://unesdoc.unesco.org/images/0016/001620/162075e.pdf

Hénard, F., & Roseveare, D. (2012). *Fostering quality teaching in higher education: Policies and practices. An IMHE guide for higher education institutions.* Organisation for Economic Co-operation and Development Institutional Management in Higher Education. https://www.oecd.org/education/imhe/QT%20policies%20 and%20practices.pdf

Jayaram, K., Moffit, A., & Scott, D. (2012). *Breaking the habit of ineffective professional development for teachers.* McKinsey & Company. https://www.mckinsey.com/industries/social-sector/our-insights/breaking-the-habit-of-ineffective-professional-development-for-teachers

Jerez, O., & Silva, C. (2017). *Innovando en la educación superior: Experiencias claves en Latinoamerica y el Caribe 2016–2017* (Volumen 1: Gestión curricular y desarrollo de la docencia). Universidad de Chile.

Lee, V. S. (2010). Program types and prototypes. In K. H. Gillespie & D. L. Robertson (Eds.), *A guide to faculty development* (2nd ed., pp. 21–33). Jossey-Bass.

Patricio, J. (2013). ¿Repensar la formación del profesorado? ¿Por qué habríamos de hacer tal cosa? *Revista de Docencia Universitaria, 11*(3), 495–500.

Red Nacional de Centros de Apoyo a la Docencia (REDCAD). (n.d.). *Quienes somos.* REDCAD. http://redcad.cl/portal/quienes-somos/

Schwartz, B. M., & Haynie, A. (2013). Faculty development centers and the role of SoTL. *New Directions for Teaching and Learning, 2013*(136), 101–111.

Smith, C., & Hudson, K. E. (2017). *Faculty development in developing countries: Improving teaching quality in higher education.* Routledge.

Sorcinelli, M. D., Austin, A. E., Eddy, P. L., & Beach, A. L. (2006). *Creating the future of faculty development: Learning from the past, understanding the present.* Anker Publishing.

United Nations Educational, Scientific and Cultural Organization (UNESCO). (2013). Educación superior. In *Situación educativa de América Latina y el Caribe: hacia la educación de calidad para todos al 2015.* UNESCO Regional Bureau for Education in Latin America and the Caribbean. http://www.unesco.org/new/fileadmin/MULTIMEDIA/FIELD/Santiago/images/SITIED-espanol.pdf

Wright, M. C., Lohe, D. R., & Little, D. (2018). The role of a center for teaching and learning in a de-centered educational world. *Change: The Magazine of Higher Education, 50*(6), 38–44.

Zabalza, M. A. (2013). Editorial: la formación del profesorado universitario. Better teachers means better universities. *Revista de Docencia Universitaria, 11*(3), 11–14.

3

The Past, Present, and Future of Faculty Development in China: Based on Multiple Scholarship for Cultivating Creative Talent

Yihong Fan

Introduction

This chapter introduces the context and evolution of faculty development (FD) work in China from a three-tier tertiary teacher training system to more diversified FD modes being established all over China. Besides this brief introduction, the chapter is divided into five parts: (1) the theoretical underpinnings of FD work in China; (2) the context, evolution, and development of past FD work in China; (3) present FD work, including structure, mission, programs, and exemplary cases; (4) a look forward to the future in terms of further needs, challenges, and trends; and (5) conclusion.

From the mid-1980s to the mid-1990s, the three-tier tertiary teacher training system in China functioned very well. Subsequently, higher education in China began to witness dramatic changes, first with various reforms in the mid-1990s, and then with enrollment expansion in 1999. Chinese higher education entered a phase of mass higher education in 2003, before the national government called for the development of an innovative nation in 2006. The year 2012 witnessed a turning point, wherein 30 national exemplar FD centers (FDCs) were sponsored by the Ministry of Education (MOE),

---

Y. Fan (✉)
Southwest Jiaotong University, Chengdu, Sichuan Province, China

Xiamen University, Xiamen, Fujian Province, China
e-mail: 1400201046@qq.com; fanyihong@aliyun.com

© The Author(s), under exclusive license to Springer Nature Switzerland AG 2023
O. J. Neisler (ed.), *The Palgrave Handbook of Academic Professional Development Centers*,
Palgrave Studies on Leadership and Learning in Teacher Education,
https://doi.org/10.1007/978-3-030-80967-6_3

with certain requirements being set for these centers' mission, structure, and operation, and so on. Since 2012, FDCs have flourished all over China, with some being sponsored provincially, some municipally, and some with university funding.

As both global and national faculty development needs have changed dramatically in recent decades, the missions of universities have also expanded from three- to four-dimensional—namely, teaching, research, service, and leading innovation. Thus, in order to cultivate creative and innovative talent, the underpinning concept for FD needs to extend from scholarship of teaching and learning (SoTL) to multiple scholarship, including scholarship of teaching, scholarship of discovery, scholarship of application, and scholarship of integration (Boyer, 1990). With this lens in mind, the past, present, and emerging future of FD in China is clearly presented, as well as a case analysis of best practices at selected Chinese universities.

The Theoretical Underpinnings of FD Work in China

The underpinning concept and analytical lens of this study is threefold: (1) in order to cultivate creative talent, the underpinning concept for FD needs to be extended from SoTL to multiple scholarship, namely "scholarship of teaching, of discovery, of application and of integration" (Boyer, 1990; Fan & Tan, 2009); (2) in order for FD to achieve its full potential, we need all four dimensions of FD, namely personal development, academic development, professional development, and organizational development as asserted by the National Education Association (NEA) (NEA, 1992); and (3) in order to ensure FD work, a learning organization scheme is required, given that an FDC does not operate alone and FDC staff need to cooperate and collaborate with various units both on and beyond campus (Senge, 1990). With these underlying thoughts in mind, we can see how the extension of the mission of higher education needs multiple scholarship.

Extension of the Mission of Higher Education Needs Multiple Scholarship

Since the former Chinese president, Jiang Zemin, put out a call underlining the need for the country to become an innovative nation in 2006, the mission of universities has extended from three dimensions to four dimensions as *teaching, research, service, and leading innovation.* In the author's opinion, the four-dimensional university mission corresponds very well with the model of multiple scholarship advocated by the educator Ernest Boyer (Boyer, 1990); as such, it makes sense that multiple scholarship should be incorporated when designing FD programs (Fan, 2011, 2013; Fan & Tan, 2009). Moreover, I would argue that SoTL can only deal with the dichotomy between teaching and research; it is not sufficient to contribute to the needs of cultivating creative and innovative talent. In particular, Boyer suggests that faculty "feel the need to move beyond traditional disciplinary boundaries, communicate with colleagues in other fields, and discover patterns that connect" (Boyer, 1990, 20).

Boyer's proposition was verified by Julie Feilberg, prorector of the Norwegian University of Science and Technology (NTNU), when I interviewed her for the cooperative book, *Assuring University Learning Quality: Cross-Boundary Collaboration*, compiled by myself and colleagues at NTNU. During our interview, when I asked her how NTNU had been able to carry out all of their innovative (interdisciplinary educational) programs, Feilberg's reply was:

> I always believe that new ideas are created when you bring people from different backgrounds to work together, to communicate with each other and to share experiences, because they have different thinking and different perspectives. When they collaborate on certain projects, they will cross-fertilize and these efforts will result in new ideas. (Feilberg, in Feilberg & Fan, 2006, 295)

How the concepts of multiple scholarship correlate with the extended missions of higher education and then to FD needs are clearly illustrated in Fig. 3.1 (Fan, 2011).

Braskamp and Ory (1994) regard Boyer's call to expand the domains of scholarship as imperative to achieving the mission and responsibilities of colleges and universities, as this achievement largely depends on acknowledgment of the complexity of the academic work. I believe that only with a full range of Boyer's multiple scholarship model could academic work encompass such complexity.

Four-Dimensional FD Framework

As per the model proposed by the NEA (1992), a full range of FD also contains four dimensions, as shown in Fig. 3.2.

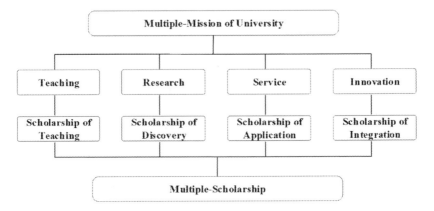

Fig. 3.1 Extended mission of higher education in correlation with a multiple scholarship model

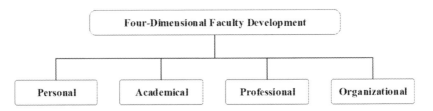

Fig. 3.2 Four-dimensional FD model

In turn, Fig. 3.3 displays what happens when we combine multiple domains of scholarship with the four-dimensional FD model.

Thus, we have a clear underpinning concept for FD that gears toward the extended mission of the colleges and universities to teach, to perform research, to engage in service for the community and society, and to lead innovation. And to achieve this vision, we need to facilitate the academic and professional development of faculty and promote the personal development of faculty and the organizational development of the university (as will be illustrated later in Chap. 37). I believe that only when we arrive at clear concept of all those dimensions and how they interact with each other can we design programs that have far-reaching impact.

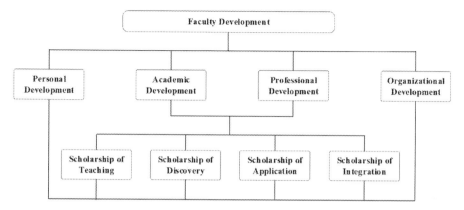

Fig. 3.3 Multiple scholarship model combined with four-dimensional FD model

The Past: Context, Evolution, and Development of FD Work in China

In China, tertiary teacher training refers to teacher training for all kinds of higher education institutions (HEIs) in the country, including universities, colleges, and higher professional or vocational schools. In the early years after the founding of the People's Republic of China, teachers' development used to be the responsibility of the Teaching Research Section of each department where teachers would gather once a week to discuss program plans, course plans, and pedagogical development. Young teachers' development usually took the form of an apprenticeship approach, in which some senior faculty acted as mentors for younger ones.

In 1985, educational reform in China was promulgated by the *Decision of the Central Committee of the Communist Party of China on the Reform of the Educational System*. In addition to requirements related to the reform of teaching content, teaching methods, the teaching system, and improving the quality of higher education, it emphasized that efforts should be made to improve the teaching competencies and academic capabilities of tertiary teachers.

In the same year, the State Education Commission of the People's Republic of China started the three-tier tertiary teacher training system, responding to the developmental needs of the Seventh Five-Year Plan of the country and of the FD of HEIs (Chen & Fan, 2013).

The Three-Tier Tertiary Teacher Training System from the Mid-1980s

In the mid-1980s, the three-tier tertiary teacher training system was set up, consisting of two national centers, one being the Beijing Center and the other the Wuhan Center for Tertiary Teacher Training and Exchange, six regional centers, and about 70 provincial centers. This system functioned very well from the mid-1980s to the turn of the 21st century with its well-established structure and clear reporting line: the national centers provided policies, guidelines, and training plans for the regional centers, the regional centers supervised the provincial centers to form specific plans, and the provincial centers operated various tertiary teacher training programs.

One of the most prominent programs offered by these tertiary teacher training centers was for university-entry teachers. All entry teachers were required to go through two to three weeks of intensive training revolving around four texts: *Educational Law and Regulation, Higher Education Pedagogy, Psychology of College Youths*, and *Moral and Ethics Education for College Teachers*. The training programs were centrally designed and required, without much consideration of the developmental needs of each specific HEI. The programs were mainly carried out in lecture format, and each individual was assessed by open examination (Fan, 2011).

Over the years there have also been other programs, such as a visiting scholar program which involved sending teachers from smaller, less famous universities to selected top universities in order to learn frontier ideas for research and teaching. There were also training programs for leading teachers to keep abreast of new trends of learning in specific disciplinary areas. The well-structured tertiary teacher training program operated very well in its first 15 years. But, at the turn of the 21st century, tremendous changes had taken place in Chinese higher education; hence, FD in China also needed significant changes.

The Context of Significant Changes in Chinese Higher Education

The higher education reforms in the mid-1990s and the higher education enrollment expansion in 1999 presented major challenges to higher education in China. In June 1999, the Central Government of China made a decision to expand higher education, which resulted in an unprecedented increase in enrollment. The gross enrollment rate (GER) of the college age cohort (i.e., those aged 18–22 years) increased from 6.8% in 1998 to 17% in 2003. Only four years after the enrollment expansion, Chinese higher education changed from a system of elite higher education to a system of mass higher education (Trow, 1973). In 2006, the central government called for the development of an innovative nation. In 2007, the GER further increased to 23%, almost four times that of 1998. The number of students in Chinese HEIs increased from 6.43 million in 1998 to 27 million in 2007; similarly, the number of staff and teachers increased from 1.02 million in 1998 to 1.945 million in 2007 (Fan, 2011; Lin, 2013).

Emerging FDCs at Different Universities in China

As the result of the higher education reform, research and comprehensive universities were granted the autonomy to develop their own strategic planning. These universities therefore needed university-based FD to meet the changing needs of both the faculty and the university. Tsinghua University was the first to establish an FDC in 1998, known as the Center for Teaching Research and Faculty Training (Fan, 2011); thereafter, Southwest Jiaotong University (SWJTU) established their Center for Faculty Training in 2001 and Ocean University of China set up their Center for Teaching and Learning Support in 2007, to name just a few.

The first International Conference on Faculty Development was organized at the Institute of Education, Xiamen University, in October 2006, as a joint cooperative effort between three universities: Xiamen University, China; Norwegian University of Science and Technology, Norway; and Kaunas University of Technology, Lithuania. This conference attracted about 300 participants from both home and abroad and first brought the theme of FD into open academic discussion in China. The conference generated two published proceedings, one in Chinese and the other in English, entitled *Key to University Quality Assurance: Faculty/Staff Development in Global Context* (Pan et al., 2007). By 2011, quite a number of universities had established their own FDCs.

MOE-Sponsored National Exemplary Faculty Teaching Development Centers

The year 2012 marked a turning point for FD work in China, with the MOE granting the title of national exemplary faculty teaching development centers

(FTDCs) to 30 FDCs, with MOE funding and specific requirements for the mission, structure, operation, and so on, of these designated centers (MOE, 2012). After 2012, FDCs flourished all over China, with some being sponsored provincially, some municipally, and some with university funding.

Although the three-tiered system remains in place, the national centers no longer function as a central planning and guiding entity; however, they have started to offer certain training programs to meet new trends and needs. The regional centers merged with the Schools of Education of the universities they were originally associated with. The provincial centers are still carrying out the entry teacher training programs as required by national higher education policy.

The Present: Structure, Mission, Programs, and Exemplary Cases

The MOE has stated clearly that their goal in supporting the 30 FTDCs is to focus on improving the professional level and teaching competencies of young and middle-aged teachers and basic course teachers in colleges and universities.

The Structure, Mission, and Programs of FTDCs in Current-Day China

In 2012, when the MOE first started to sponsor the 30 FTDCs, it sent out a very strong government policy signal for FD work, one that was very focused on developing faculty teaching competencies. However, judging from the actual name of each FDC, the structure and mission of these centers actually vary from institution to institution, as 23 are referred to as FTDCs, five as FDCs, and two as faculty development and learning support centers. Thus, we can see that some of the centers have a broader mission than others, which marks an emerging trend of FD work in China.

Structure

Based on the centers' introduction on each of the FTDCs' websites, we learn that 16 of the 30 MOE-sponsored FTDCs report directly to the vice president of their associated universities, five to the head of the Academic Affairs

3 The Past, Present, and Future of Faculty Development in China...   49

Office (AAO), and nine have directors who are solely responsible for FD work on campus. Structurally, the FDC of Renmin University of China illustrates how FDCs in mainland China actively explore an innovative organizational structure.

In order to build a contingent of faculty with sufficient levels of academic innovation, Renmin University of China decided to develop an FDC in 2014, on the basis of the FTDC that was set up in 2011, by adding five more sections, each responsible for a specific area. In this way, the FDC realized their goal of providing integrated resources across the whole university to promote the all-round development of all faculty.

The broadened FDC currently operates under the guidance of a Leading Group for Faculty Development (LGFD), headed by the Secretary of the Party Committee and the president of the university. The LGFD has 12 members. The new FDC is comprised of six sections dedicated to career development, pedagogical development (which functions as an FTDC), research development, promoting undergraduate/graduate study, information and communication technology (ICT)-enhanced teaching and learning, and overall support for faculty. Each section corresponds to a specific unit of the university, such as the Human Resource Department, Academic Affairs Department, Research Department, Graduate Study Section and Undergraduate Study Section, the Trade Union and the ICT Support Center. Six working groups have been set up in seven departments to take on the responsibility of supporting FD work on campus. The organizational chart of the broadened FDC is illustrated in Fig. 3.4.

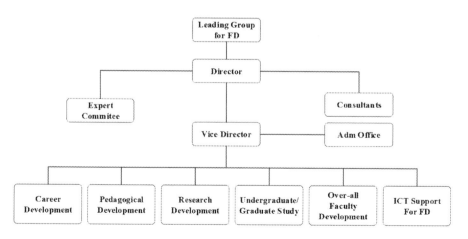

Fig. 3.4 Organizational chart of the FDC of Renmin University, China

50   Y. Fan

Judging from the structure of the FDC of Renmin University of China, we learn that it develops a broader vision and mission of FD work, extending from pedagogical development, clearly connecting with both undergraduate and graduate teaching and learning on campus, and seeking to cover the overall development of the faculty.

Mission

Most of the FTDCs operate as service organizations that aim to promote teachers' academic and professional development and integrate training, consultation, and research. The centers follow the natural paths of teachers' development, integrate high-quality resources both inside and outside the university, provide services, offer continuous support for teachers' career development, and strive to promote the organic unity of teachers' growth and university development.

Functional Tasks

The functional tasks of the FTDCs cover six dimensions:

1. *Training* to improve the teachers' development system, offer professional development, and improve teachers' ideological understandings and pedagogical competences
2. *Consulting* to meet the growth needs of the teachers while alleviating teachers' development confusion and stimulating teachers' development potential
3. *Exchange* to follow the development strategy of the university and build a platform for teachers to exchange ideas, interact, and create a robust academic environment
4. *Resource coordination* to build an allocation and sharing mechanism of teachers' development resources and promote joint efforts of various institutions on campus for FD purposes
5. *Quality evaluation* to conduct teaching and learning quality evaluations, give feedback to teachers and departments, and offer suggestions for improvement
6. *Regional leadership* to take leadership and promote FD work beyond the campus and extend it to the entire region.

Programs

Most of the FTDCs focus on the development of new teachers, young teachers, and leading teachers in each field, by designing various programs to support their development needs. The programs are carried out in various formats or consist of various activities such as courses, workshops, lectures, salons, and practices. The themes covered include teachers' ethics, student-centered teaching and learning, pedagogical competencies, teaching innovation, academic research, action research, project-based learning, outcome-based learning, course design, interdisciplinary course development, curriculum design, graduate teaching assistant training, and organizational leadership, among others.

Cases of Good Practice

After eight years of progress, FD work in China has taken on diverse development modes and shapes. This section offers an illustration of the exemplar practices of some outstanding programs which are unique in certain aspects.

The Teaching Assistant Development Program at Shanghai Jiao Tong University

Since June 2012, the Center for Teaching and Learning Development (CTLD) of Shanghai Jiao Tong University started a Teaching Assistant Development Program with the goal of improving the quality of teaching assistant (TA) work. At Shanghai Jiao Tong University, TA positions are mostly held by master's and doctoral students and a small number of outstanding senior undergraduates. The mission of the TA development program is to help the TAs accomplish their tasks well.

Excellent Teaching Assistant Award

At the beginning of each semester, CTLD staff organize an opening ceremony to start the TA program for the semester. During the ceremony, awards are granted to excellent TAs from the previous semester. During the ceremony, the former TAs who have won the Excellent Teaching Assistant Award share their experiences in the program and encourage new TAs to work conscientiously and take full responsibility. New TAs are able to learn from these events as the excellent TAs share their successful experiences in assisting teaching.

Modules

In the weeks following the opening ceremony, the CTLD organize several modules of training for the new TAs. TA training components and methods include workshops, discussions, exchange of experience, teamwork, and so on. The training modules include effective communication, how to review homework and grade papers, organization of classroom discussions, construction and maintenance of the course website, strategies for accomplishing group micro-teaching exercises, and so on. The trainees must complete three modules before they can become a qualified TA and obtain the TA certificate issued by the CTLD.

TA Training Manual

In addition to training, the CTLD also prepares a detailed TA manual for new TAs. This handbook covers the most typical cases in TA work, including preparation for a new semester, communication with students, organization of classroom discussions, exercise classes, experiment classes, homework review, and use of the curriculum center website, and so on.

The TAs benefit a great deal from this well-designed program, and are very much inspired by their peers who received awards last year. The CTLD of Shanghai Jiao Tong University also offers other well-developed FD programs. For details, please see Chap. 27.

Promoting Research on Teaching and Learning Innovation at Fudan University

The CTLD of Fudan University takes a prominent role in promoting research on teaching and learning innovation at Chinese universities. Since 2012, the CTLD has organized an Annual Conference on Teaching and Learning Innovation. They also publish a journal, the *Journal on Teaching and Learning*, to promote the development of innovative teaching and learning practice on the basis of theoretical and practical research.

The Annual Conference on Teaching and Learning Innovation has made this imperative theme a focus of attention of researchers and teachers

3 The Past, Present, and Future of Faculty Development in China... 53

throughout the Chinese mainland. Through presentation and discussion at the annual conference, many researchers and teachers gain an understanding of new teaching and learning methods and characteristics so as to better apply them in practice. The *Journal on Teaching and Learning* integrates many up-to-date research ideas related to FD, teaching and learning innovation, promoting interaction between researchers and teachers, and providing theoretical guidance for front-line teachers.

Systematic FD Work Results in Innovative Teaching and Learning at SWJTU

The FDC of SWJTU, in close collaboration with the AAO, has systematically designed FD programs based on the multiple scholarship model and organizational learning principles. By changing the organizational scheme related to participation in FD programs from a demand to an invitation, the program has triggered participants' inner willingness to join the program. The FDC's programming components varies from lectures to workshops, seminars, saloons, and forums, thus stimulating the teachers' intrinsic motivation and their interests in participatory teaching and learning innovation. The FDC has established a shared vision for fostering both teachers' and students' all-round development, used system thinking to change the faculty's mental models of teacher-centered teaching to student-centered learning, helped the faculty achieve personal mastery of new ways of teaching and learning, and gone one step further by facilitating teamwork among teachers in designing and implementing innovative courses that tap into the potential and creativity of both the teachers and their students.

Just taking the interdisciplinary courses as an example, the FDC has joined force with the AAO to help teachers design and implement 64 interdisciplinary courses over four years, and helped groups of teachers teaching in innovative approaches. As a result, both teachers and students have discovered their own potential, elevated their self-confidence and creativity, and increased their overall development and growth. For more details, please turn to Chap. 37 of this book.

Full-Cycle FD Program at Yunnan University, China

The CTLD of Yunnan University has set a goal of improving young faculty's teaching competencies as a top priority. To meet this goal, the CTLD has planned a full cycle of FD programs in a three-year rotation, in which all associate and assistant professors are required to participate (Fan et al., 2017, Zhang & Wang, 2013).

University Policy Support

In 2012, the full-cycle FD plan became a part of the teacher evaluation and promotion policy of Yunnan University; therefore, teachers are required to have this FD program certificate in order to be eligible for promotion. In other words, the CTLD designed the program, while the university senior leadership supported relevant policies, funding, space, and so on. The university vice president and the head of the AAO were named directors of the center. The university also set up a special FDC operating fund of ¥ 200,000 each year to implement the FD program.

Modules

The full-cycle FD program has four modules:

1. Module 1: Higher education pedagogy, didactics, and approaches to professional development (2–4 hours)
2. Module 2: Teaching methods and techniques (2–4 hours)
3. Module 3: Course development strategies (8–12 hours)
4. Module 4: Innovative teaching and application practice (4–8 hours).

These modules are offered in order and each has a number of sub-sessions or activities. Faculty members choose sessions and activities according to their own interests. They need to complete 20-hour credits of the full-cycle FD program to be granted the FD certificate required for promotion.

From 2011 to 2014, 13 rounds of the program were offered, with participation of 1,300 faculty members. Each round was accompanied by action research carried out by the CTLD staff, in line with the design-act-observe-reflect-redesign cycle (Zhang & Wang, 2013).

Summary

In summary, as FTDCs have now been established across China, many universities have been promoting teaching and learning innovation. They are

3 The Past, Present, and Future of Faculty Development in China...

helping faculty achieve a paradigm shift from teacher-centered to student-centered learning and teaching. They have made many new developments with regards to concept, organization, management systems, incentive mechanisms, and program offerings. The gradual spread of these new initiatives has improved the quality of teaching and learning practices.

Looking Ahead: Further Needs, Challenges, and Emerging Trends

In line with revolutionary global changes in ICT, artificial intelligence, and students' learning styles, higher education also has need of tremendous changes, especially in terms of teaching and learning approaches. The human resource needs of employers have also undergone major changes. According to employment data from SWJTU graduates, the traits deemed most in demand for graduates are listed in Table 3.1.

When we look back at university teaching in China, we can see that not enough focus has been placed on these generic competencies and qualities. Thus, we understand clearly that using only discipline-oriented, classroom-confined learning is not adequate for developing the necessary overall competencies, quality, and characteristics of the students. Teaching and learning in colleges and universities need fundamental changes. We need to clearly understand the further needs, challenges, and trends of FD work. Only in this way will we be able to meet these needs, deal with these challenges, and lead these trends.

Table 3.1 Employer-demanded traits for Chinese university graduates 2015–2017[a]

Trait	2015	2016	2017	Order
Communication	3	5	4	1
Oral Expression	2	4	6	2
Self-confidence	7	1		3
Creative Spirit	1	8	5	4
Written Skills	8	6	1	5
Organizational Management	6	7	3	6
Humanism	4	10		7
Technical Skills	5	2	14	8
Self-management	10	3	11	9
Cooperation	9	11	10	10

[a]Data source: Employment Quality Report of Graduates of Southwest Jiaotong University from 2015 to 2017

Further Needs and Challenges for FD Work in China

Currently, China is facing two important challenges for higher education: one is to cultivate creative talent and the other is to develop new academic programs. In particular, the latter refers to new engineering programs, medical programs, and agricultural programs, as advocated by Wu Yan, director of the Higher Education Section of the MOE. Both challenges call for innovative teaching and learning which is more student-centered, practice-oriented, and integrated or interdisciplinary-oriented. To return to the theoretical underpinnings described in a previous section of this chapter, this is why SoTL is not considered broad enough for directing future FD work; as Boyer advocated, we need to incorporate all four domains of the multiple scholarship model (Boyer, 1990; Fan, 2011, 2013; Fan & Tan, 2009).

In order to cultivate creative talent, teaching and learning needs to go beyond the four bounds of college classroom study, namely, "time-bound, space-bound, role-bound and efficiency bound" (O'Banion, 1997). To achieve these fundamental changes, organizational changes are required, including changes in the teaching and learning evaluation system (quality assurance), faculty incentives and awards for university teaching, FD program design, academic and disciplinary program design, interdisciplinary programs, and innovative course design and implementation, as well as an education quality assurance scheme.

Emerging Trends: Organizational Learning and Cross-Boundary Collaboration

Teaching and learning innovation is not the task of an FDC alone. It calls for cross-boundary collaboration between various units in the university. Only through organizational learning can the leaders, administrators, and teachers on campus achieve a shared vision; a support system is needed to facilitate the fundamental change of mental models, or a paradigm shift of the teachers. Teachers have to gain personal mastery and learn to work as a team. This means that all five principles espoused in Senge's (1990) concept of learning organization should be used to systematically facilitate organizational learning and systematic changes.

In China, the SWJTU has already attempted the systematic development of FD work that has resulted in pedagogical innovation for the deep learning and holistic development of students and teachers on campus. For details, please read the relevant section in Chap. 37 which specifically illustrates a case representing this emerging trend in FD work and its impact on innovative learning experience.

Conclusion

To quote from my prior work, *From Integrative World View to Holistic Education*:

> In the present world, most people go through formal education until their early twenties. If we want a world of peace and people of profound understanding of life, society, nature and the world, we have to offer a holistic education where self and others; inner world and outer world; rational intelligence and other intelligence; subjects and real-life experiences; theory and practice; this discipline and that discipline are not artificially divided anymore. Only through the enduring wisdom of restoring the sense of wholeness and establishing an integrative worldview and carrying out a holistic education could we meet the challenges of a changing world. (Fan, 2004)

References

Boyer, E. L. (1990). *Scholarship reconsidered: Priorities of the professoriate*. Jossey-Bass.

Braskamp, L. A., & Ory, J. C. (1994). *Assessing faculty work: Enhancing individual and institutional performance*. Jossey-Bass.

Chen, M., & Fan, Y. (2013). A review of the research articles from the genre of teacher training to faculty development in China. In Y. Fan (Ed.), *Comparative studies of faculty development between China and European countries: Based on multiple scholarship* (pp. 113–133). Southwest Jiaotong University Press.

Fan, Y. (2004). *From integrative worldview to holistic education: Theory and practice*. Southwest Jiaotong University Press.

Fan, Y. (2011). Comparative study on staff development in European and Chinese universities: Based on the perspective of multiple-scholarship. *Revista de Docencia Universitaria, 9*(1), 111–133. http://redaberta.usc.es/redu/index.php/REDU/article/view/196

Fan, Y. (2013). *Comparative studies of faculty development between China and European countries: Based on multiple scholarship*. Southwest Jiaotong University Press.

Fan, Y., Hoel, T., Tjedvoll, A., & Engvik, G. (2006). *Assuring university learning quality: Cross-boundary collaboration*. Tapir Academic Press.

Fan, Y., & Tan, M. (2009). Multiple-scholarship and staff development: Theory and practice. *Educational Research and Experiment, 131*(6), 27–32.

Fan, Y., Wang, J., Duan, Z., & Huang, T. (2017). Transforming teaching toward student-centered learning through participatory approach and action research: A faculty development case in Yunnan University, China. In S. Smith & K. E. Hudson (Eds.), *Faculty development in developing countries: Improving learning quality in higher education*. Routledge.

Feilberg, J., & Fan, Y. (2006). NTNU as a learning organization and an aligned institution. In Y. Fan, T. L. Hoel, A. Tjedcoll, & G. Engvik (Eds.), *Assuring university learning quality: Cross-boundary collaboration*. Tapir Academic Press.

Lin, Y. (2013). *A survey result demonstrated that half of the university teachers entered the profession after the year of 2000*. Phoenix New Media. http://news.ifeng.com/gundong/detail_2013_05/19/25470262_0.shtml

Ministry of Education (MOE). (2012). *Opinions on comprehensively improve the quality of education*. MOE.

National Education Association (NEA). (1992). *Faculty development in higher education: Enhancing a national resource*. Office of Higher Education.

O'Banion, T. (1997). *A learning college for the 21st century*. ORYX Press.

Pan, M., Fan, Y., & Zhu, Y. (2007). *Key to university quality assurance: Faculty development in global perspective*. Fujan Education Press.

Senge, P. (1990). *The fifth discipline: The art and practice of learning organization*. Century.

Trow, M. (1973). *Problems in the transition from elite to mass higher education*. Carnegie Commission on Higher Education.

Zhang, J. D., & Wang, J. (2013). *Exploring and sharing in the pursuit of teaching excellence*. Yunnan University Press.

4

Africa: The Evolution of Faculty Development in East Africa—A Tale of Three Transformation Stories

Charles Kingsbury, Mike Calvert, and Mary Omingo

Introduction

This chapter consists of three stories, each written by one of the authors, to share our personal accounts of gradually intersecting experiences with the transformation of faculty development in Kenya. Unlike universities in the UK which have benefited from government funding, faculty development in most African universities has been entirely driven by the faculty themselves.

A simple question about Bible school in our first story led Kingsbury to pursue a doctorate in faculty development and set up a Centre for Excellence in Teaching and Learning at a Kenyan university. Calvert's second story explains how an international partnership and funding led to vast institutional changes in teaching throughout Kenya. Finally, our last story details Omingo's first meeting with Calvert, a fortuitous event which would result in

---

C. Kingsbury (✉)
Daystar University, Aithi River, Kenya
e-mail: chip@kingsburyfamily.org

M. Calvert
York St. John University, York, UK
e-mail: trevlac1@googlemail.com

M. Omingo
Strathmore University, Nairobi, Kenya
e-mail: omingomary@gmail.com

© The Author(s), under exclusive license to Springer Nature Switzerland AG 2023
O. J. Neisler (ed.), *The Palgrave Handbook of Academic Professional Development Centers*,
Palgrave Studies on Leadership and Learning in Teacher Education,
https://doi.org/10.1007/978-3-030-80967-6_4

60   C. Kingsbury et al.

the creation of a network for professional faculty developers throughout East Africa. Despite some challenges, the outcome of each of these stories has been great, and we believe more will be achieved in future.

Story 1: An Individual Quest for Teaching Excellence

You don't learn things in Bible college that you can actually use. (Naphtali Gitonga)

For a short time in the late 1980s, I was an acting overseer for the Pentecostal Evangelistic Fellowship of Africa (PEFA) in the Nyeri district of Kenya. Each month we held a *baraza* (council meeting) for the pastors and leaders from the approximately 50 PEFA churches in the district. In one such *baraza*, I was chairing the meeting as we discussed some issue for which we were having trouble reaching consensus. African decision-making norms call for consensus building rather than a simple vote. We talked, debated, and danced around the issue for a long time. I was getting frustrated. In this exasperated state, I asked these pastors, many of whom had been to Bible college or seminary: "What did you learn in Bible school about this [issue]?" There was a long pause in the discussion. Finally, the district secretary, Naphtali Gitonga, who was seated next to me, looked at me and said, "Brother Chip, you don't learn things in Bible college that you can actually use." It took a moment or two for the enormity of that statement to grab my attention. When it did, I was stunned. Pastor Naphtali wasn't speaking tongue-in-cheek. He was entirely serious.

A couple of days later, I visited Naphtali as I wanted to pursue this further. This was a long time ago, and I don't have any notes from that visit. Neither do I have any verbatim recollections of our conversation on that day. Nevertheless, it had a life-changing impact on me. When I asked him about his statement—that one doesn't learn things in Bible college that can actually be used—he told me about learning that seemed disconnected from the life of ministry. He talked of education that was focused on memorizing information and then being able to reproduce that information in exams. He indicated that he could not think of anything he learned in Bible college that had helped him in his pastoral ministry.

Naphtali was a very good pastor, so I asked him, "Where *did* you learn how to be a pastor?" He explained that, while in Bible college, he had been assigned kitchen duty as part of his work study program. The older man who ran the kitchen was a part-time pastor at a local church. He had not been to

4 Africa: The Evolution of Faculty Development in East Africa... 61

theological training himself but had been pastoring for many years. Naphtali shared how during his three years working in the kitchen, this man's mentoring had helped him to become a pastor. All of this continued to astonish me. Obviously, something was terribly wrong. I had no idea what it was.

At the same time all this was happening, I was teaching at the very same institution Naphtali had attended, as well as in other programs of ministry formation in Central Kenya. I was discouraged with my work, in that while I taught many courses in theological institutions and conducted many workshops for those already in ministry, I could see very little fruit in the lives of those I was supposedly teaching. Almost as a lark, but more as a distraction, I enrolled in a master's-level, distance education course in intercultural studies from Wheaton College Graduate School in Illinois. I had no intention of doing a complete degree—I just wanted an academic challenge that would stir my thinking and possibly get me out of the doldrums. Then, at Wheaton, I experienced a world of learning that was absolutely transformative in my life. I was stretched and pulled, challenged and changed. I experienced a surfacing of my unexamined worldview in many areas of cross-cultural work. I had to think and examine myself. I had to recreate myself and become someone new—someone with a wider and deeper understanding of the world and my place in it.

I returned to Kenya in 1989 and went back to teaching. However, I was now different. I was no longer teaching *about* certain subjects and topics; I was a facilitator of transformation. The men and women in my classes began to recreate themselves, their futures, and their ministries. It was exciting. Soon, other institutions of higher learning began asking me to conduct training for their faculty. I started doing what I simply called 'teacher training workshops' grounded in the problem-posing pedagogy of Freire (1970) and the philosophies of transformative learning champions such as Mezirow (1990), Hope et al. (1995), Brookfield (2017), and Vella (2002). I quickly realized that I was both energized and terrified by the increasing opportunities I had to work with faculty members in East Africa: energized by the results I was seeing in the faculty I was training and terrified by the growing awareness that I had very little idea of what I was doing or needed to do.

I began looking for doctoral programs in faculty development with a strong emphasis on international development education. I ended up at Florida State University doing a program that was a perfect fit for me. My dissertation concerned establishing lists of the things that help and those that hurt the implementation of teaching for critical reflection and transformation by faculty who had experienced and received training in such facilitation (Kingsbury,

62 C. Kingsbury et al.

2002). I joined the faculty of Daystar University in Kenya in 1997, and I was asked to establish a full-time faculty development program.

The Centre for Excellence in Teaching and Learning was established in 2001. Even before it was established, we began offering a two-week intensive course called "Helping Learners to Think: Facilitating Critical Reflective Thought in Students." This course attracted participants from all over Africa. To date, over 800 faculty members representing more than 100 institutions from more than 20 nations have successfully completed this course. It is now part of Daystar University's Professional Certificate in Higher Education Teaching program. The course has also been conducted in nine nations in Africa.

During that time, the Deputy Vice Chancellor for Academic Affairs, Professor James Kombo, walked into the center one day in 2009 and introduced the person who was accompanying him, Dr. Mike Calvert of York St. John University in the UK.

Story 2: An England-Africa Partnership Collaboration

Transformation is a process, not an event. (Kotter, 1995)

My first involvement with faculty development in Kenya was the result of a bid by my university, York St. John University, to the British Council under the England-Africa Partnerships scheme. The proposal was for capacity building in the higher education sector with specific reference to pedagogy and a shift from teacher-centered, transmission-mode teaching to student-centered facilitation of learning. The one-year grant, scheduled from Easter 2007 until June 2008, and subsequently extended due to the post-election violence in December 2007, allowed for five visits to Kenya including a reconnaissance visit, a dissemination event, and three blocks of one week's training with 20 participants at the host university by a team of three. It also included a two-week fact-finding training program visit for 10 'leading members' of the team to York. The participants were to receive a postgraduate certificate, namely the Postgraduate Certificate of Academic Practice (PCAP), from York St. John University and Fellowship of the UK Higher Education Academy (now called Advance Higher Education). This program was already being offered at home and in Bahrain. The aim was to identify *multipliers* within the institution who might take forward the changes.

The program was a success in terms of the individual changes of views, attitudes, and behaviors of the staff attending. Almost all the participants completed the program and were awarded their certificates at a special graduation, generously funded and attended by the vice chancellor (VC) of York St. John University along with the former President of Kenya, Daniel arap Moi.

It would be fair to say that the level of pedagogy at the four universities (two public, two private) involved in the training was extremely limited, with few exceptions. Content dominated the overpacked curricula and learning outcomes were unclear or not defined. Some lecturers were underqualified and almost all were unprepared for the role. At the same time, the students were ill-prepared, having been served a diet of information which they had been required to recall for examinations. They expected lecturers to lecture and pass on information and were passive in their learning, assuming no responsibility and expecting to pass.

Two Anecdotes from my First Block of Teaching

The first involves a lecturer who had been a primary school teacher and still ran a primary school. She described to me how, once she had been given a post of lecturer, she had tried to find out what lecturers actually do. Being small of stature, she stood on tiptoes to look through the windows of the lecture rooms to see what lecturers were doing. She recalled that many of them were seated and appeared to be reading from a book or using their 'yellow notes' (yellow through age!) to impart information. She remembers thinking that there must be more to being a university lecturer than that.

The second involves a senior member of staff who, during the first week of teaching, was always the first to answer and was invariably wrong. He was quite a challenge as he enjoyed some status within the institution. When I arrived on the second week, he called me into his office. He stated to me that, prior to my first visit, he felt that as a pastor he had mastered his craft and had refined his marriage counseling training. During these sessions for married couples, he had divided up the couples depending on length of marriage and had proceeded to share his wisdom with each group in turn. After having spent a week on student-centered learning in PCAP, he went back to the training, and this time, after dividing them up, he let them talk amongst themselves. The session was due to finish at 2 pm but the participants asked to be allowed to continue after lunch. They left at 4 pm and asked for more of the same. He said to me: "Why didn't you come 15 years ago?"

Two years later, in 2009, after a challenging tour of duty in Rwanda with a similar program, a further call went out from the British Council. The grants were from the UK Department of Innovation, Universities, and Skills and were for partnership project grants with a clear emphasis on entrepreneurship and employability. Keen to develop the work we had done with the four universities, we applied and were successful. This time, we engaged five universities in Nairobi (four private, one public). We were able to advertise the program at the dissemination event referred to below and several universities were keen to host and others to take part.

With the second program, we asked the universities to identify one key multiplier and insisted, as far as possible, on the selection of appropriate staff who would have the ability and motivation to take forward development in their institution. The program also enlisted the involvement of former participants who we felt would be good ambassadors for the program and whose own skills and status would be enhanced by involvement as mentors and/or visiting lecturers.

The second programme involved a trip to the UK for the key multiplier in each university and three one-week workshops over nine months followed by a graduation ceremony. The funding was directed mainly to the host country and so meant that there were funds for only one UK lecturer as opposed to three. As usual, factors within the institution either promoted or mitigated the success of the program.

Two Anecdotes from the Second Program

One day, a psychology lecturer was invited to give feedback on the program so far. He got to his feet and, turning to me, he said: "Mike, you have ruined my life. I cannot go back to teaching how I did before, knowing what I know now."

An education lecturer had been so impressed with the treatment of assessment on the program that she had scrapped a written report by teacher training students on their practicum in favor of a presentation of a portfolio before a panel of educationalists involving teaching material, artifacts, photos, and any evidence that the student teacher wanted to present. We invited a student to the next block of training to present her portfolio. She was extremely impressive and proud of her achievements. It may well have been one of the first times that the lecturers actually listened to their students and heard their experiences first-hand.

The second program had a lasting impact on two of the universities in particular, and, along with one of the original universities, this led to further invitations to deliver training paid for by the universities. This enabled some key lecturers to develop their own skills and knowledge and for constructivist

4 Africa: The Evolution of Faculty Development in East Africa... 65

pedagogy to be more widely shared among institutions. Having worked with one institution for about five years, I was told one day by the academic registrar, who had been a key mentor in one of the universities, that they did not need me anymore. I took this to be a compliment.

In all, I worked with about a dozen Kenyan universities over a period of 10 years, and, throughout that time, it was obvious to me that the level of expertise within the country was such that local staff could deliver the programs as well as, or better than, I could. The staff had all studied with me and shared the same philosophies and had access to all the training materials. They had been encouraged to get together at alumni events and other occasions. While such a sharing approach was not favored by a number of universities who were often very competitive, it was popular among the lecturers.

In time, this led to the establishment of the Association for Faculty Enrichment in Learning and Teaching (AFELT), which has enabled more lecturers to become involved and for the organization to be recognized by an international program of faculty development, Transforming Employability for Social Change in East Africa (TESCEA). These efforts were funded under the Department for International Development, a UK government department responsible for administering overseas aid.

Reflecting on the programs and training that I have led and been involved with over the last 10–12 years, I would draw the following conclusions:

- As Kotter (1995) reminds us, "transformation is a process, not an event" (1). This means that faculty development, which includes changing the hearts and minds of the students as well as the personnel, will take time, strategic planning, political will, and does not come cheap.
- Having spoken to over 20 Kenyan VCs, I would say that many of them do not understand learning, education, or faculty development. Many are CEOs of large organizations faced with serious financial demands and can all too easily be caught up with neoliberal approaches to managing their institutions.
- Not all VCs, professors, deans, and lecturers are willing to surrender some of the power that knowledge gives them. Notions of co-constructing knowledge and sharing the learning and teaching experience are far removed from their thinking—although interestingly some have benefitted from education in other countries, such as the UK and the USA where student-centered learning is more firmly established.
- The challenge to government of funding, regulating policy, and managing higher education is enormous at a time of increasing demand by the growing middle classes in Kenya, fiscal constraints, huge public universities,

66   C. Kingsbury et al.

insufficient faculty to teach, pressures for those faculty to carry out research on top of teaching, and, in many cases, community engagement.

* Many lecturers want to change, and want better for their children who attend schools and universities, but need a supportive environment and the tools to do so. Just knowing what might be better is not enough for them to change.
* The lecturers who embrace student-centered constructivist approaches to learning appear to derive more satisfaction and enjoyment from their work and the metacognitive skills that they acquire often spill over into other aspects of their lives. They particularly value reflective practice.
* The best become 'dual professionals' who take an equal pride in their facilitation of knowledge and their own knowledge of their subject. Interactive teaching and learning are possible in large classes and adverse circumstances, but it takes skill and imagination and confidence to carry it out.

Story 3: Strathmore University Certificate Program

They were excited about shifting from a teacher-centred to a student-centred approach. (Mary Omingo)

In 2005, the management at Strathmore University in Kenya decided to introduce a Certificate in Lectureship after realizing that there was a need for lecturers to grow professionally. Most lecturers were expert in their specific discipline areas, such as accounting, financing, and entrepreneurship, but had very little knowledge on *how* to teach. Most of them tended to teach the way they were taught as students. The certificate course was offered in modules and was initially offered to all lecturers teaching degree courses; however, over time lecturers were not as enthusiastic to enroll in the course. In 2007, five members of the Academic Development Unit (ADU), under the academic registrar's office, conducted three focus groups of 13, eight, and 11 lecturers across the university to determine the lecturers' teaching needs.

I was one of the members of the ADU, and in 2007, I also became the academic registrar—which meant that I had now to chair the ADU. Based on the findings of the focus group discussions, I extracted the following themes/topics: Strathmore University Teaching Philosophy; Self-Management; Class Management; Innovative Teaching, Learning and Research; and Assessment and Feedback. However, I did not have a facilitator for sessions on these topics.

4 Africa: The Evolution of Faculty Development in East Africa... 67

In 2009, I was asked to attend a dissemination workshop at the Kenya School of Monetary Studies. The workshop was facilitated by Dr. Mike Calvert from York St. John University in the UK. During the workshop, Dr. Calvert took us through what he had accomplished, in the first round, on a one-year PCAP program. He wanted new partner universities for the second round of the project. After the workshop, I approached him and expressed my interest in Strathmore's lecturers participating in the program. The PCAP program ran for one year from 2009 to 2010. It was hosted at Strathmore University, and I was the coordinator. In addition, in 2009 I contracted Dr. Calvert to facilitate sessions on academic practice for Strathmore lecturers and my journey in this field began. Lecturers were excited about the program and embraced the paradigm shift from a teacher-centered to a student-centered approach.

In subsequent years, after the sessions that I organized on academic practice, some lecturers asked the question: *what next?* And others shared with me several changes that they were implementing in their classes. In most cases, I did not really know how to help them move to the next step, so when I decided to do my doctorate, I knew it had to be in academic practice. I wanted to respond appropriately to most of the questions that the lecturers asked, and I was also interested in learning more about what was going on in other universities. Although, I was mainly interested in following up with the PCAP members (as mentioned in Dr. Calvert's story), I also interviewed other non-PCAP members. During the interviews for my study, I realized that a number of lecturers had changed their teaching practice to support student learning and, at that moment, I thought of how these lecturers could share what they were doing. I contacted a few colleagues who were PCAP coordinators in their respective universities and broached the idea of forming a network.

The first meeting was held in Strathmore with four of us in attendance. By the end of the meeting, it was clear the way forward was to include more PCAP members. We later met as a group of PCAP members and deliberated on the constitution of the network. First, we decided to have a network covering the whole of East Africa, initially the *East African Association of Higher Learning Development*, but through consultation with other PCAP members, we settled for the *Faculty Enrichment in Learning and Teaching Network*. However, upon application for registration, the word "network" was rejected by the registrar of societies. We finally decided to register it as the *Association for Faculty Enrichment in Learning and Teaching*. The AFELT was officially registered on September 5, 2014. It currently has over 50 paid-up registered members.

Outcomes

Two major studies have since been carried out; the first on lecturers' learning to teach in private universities in Kenya (Omingo, 2016) and the second on pedagogies for critical thinking in Kenya (Omingo, 2018). They show that lecturers who participated in the above-mentioned programs are mainly facilitating students' learning rather than transmitting knowledge and the students' critical thinking skills are enhanced as they progress into their senior years.

Research: Applying a Learner-Centered Approach and Critical Reflective Thought

In Omingo (2016), a PCAP participant stressed the importance of planning, more so for students' activities. He explained how planning for students' activities was now ingrained in his teaching:

> Since [the] Postgraduate Certificate in Academic Practice, whenever I teach, every other course I teach, I plan an activity. I have to do it, there is no way I can go to class and do things off the cuff without knowing what I am doing. I give a bit of input for not more than 20 minutes or so and then an activity. A short input again, then an activity. It is sort of inbuilt. That I find I do it every time. (Participant 1, PCAP)

Similarly, a comment from another PCAP participant referred to planning but in a more structured way:

> Another thing I did after PCAP was I actually did a course outline where I included learning activities and even alignment of learning outcomes and activities. That is something I had not thought about before. I may have done alignment accidentally, like with the business planning, but it was not something intentional. (Participant 2, PCAP)

In planning learning activities, the above lecturers now focused on identifying the learning tasks that students needed to do in order to learn the material, rather than on the tasks that the lecturers needed to do in order to present or transmit knowledge. Such learning activities tend to enable students to engage in a dialogue which has the potential to challenge beliefs and produce conceptual changes (Wright, 2011). Biggs and Tang (2011) assert that students who engage in meaningful and purposeful learning tasks tend to adopt a deep learning approach.

4 Africa: The Evolution of Faculty Development in East Africa... 69

Incorporating the needs of an individual student in this planning seemed important to another participant who attended the Academic Staff Development Program (ASDP). His comment indicated that he considered the uniqueness of each student or group of students in relation to his subject, and not vice versa:

> The difference that has been there since the training is that I have learned to appreciate that each student is unique. The syllabus can be the same, but the students are unique. ... The main thing I learned from the training is that you need to appreciate the diversity of these students at different times, not necessarily making the syllabus longer or shorter, but being able to appreciate that each student or group of students is unique. (Participant, ASDP)

To get most students to use the level of cognitive processes needed to achieve the intended outcomes that more academic students use spontaneously, lecturers are facilitating students' participation. They facilitate participation in such a way that they let students take control of some of their learning. A comment from a PCAP participant demonstrated how categorical he was about students' participation:

> I move away from the podium, of the one who knows, of the lecturer; and I sit with the students at the same level and discuss with them issues and sometimes the classes can become quite involving. The idea of students' learning being participatory is not negotiable. When I am teaching, I have to think of how I will involve my students in the lesson, all of them! We have jelled, almost as sort of opposed to before PCAP where I could just read from my scripts. I would be dictating my notes. (Participant 1, PCAP)

The role of education, among other things, is to prepare students for the unknown future. This means that lecturers should endeavor to create a questioning and analytical mind in their students (Iversen et al., 2015). This, as mentioned in the above comment, can happen where lecturers appreciate students' contributions (Tom, 2015).

Lecturers are also assessing students by providing them with adequate time and space to reflect outside class and over time during the semester. A comment from a PCAP participant, and mentioned in one of the above stories, indicated that she preferred work-based students to write teaching portfolios rather than to do examinations:

> During PCAP we learnt about using portfolios to assess students. So, I implemented it here on how you can use a teaching portfolio to assess student teachers on teaching practice at a distance. (Participant 3, PCAP)

70   C. Kingsbury et al.

She further demonstrated how she used portfolios as an assessment tool:

> When you move students from [an] examination environment to preparing portfolios, they become very enthusiastic. They know they have three months to prepare the portfolio, because portfolio assignment cannot be done in a day or week. You give it at the beginning of the trimester and discuss the learning outcomes. At the end of the four months, they give you a portfolio, no examination. I would say that they put in more effort as they are not stressed. In addition, they collaborate and consult such that when another student's portfolio is good, the others want theirs to be better. (Participant 3, PCAP)

According to Moon (2007), learners require time and space in order to reflect and to learn to do so. For a lecturer who attended Critical Reflective Thought (CRT), effective students' reflection implied allowing the students to reflect on their values and write them down, what she referred to as "critical reflective thinking." She stated, "It is only when we work on the minds of thinkers; the students that society can change for the better" (Participant, CRT). Below is her account of what one of her students reflected on and documented:

> She says she doesn't know how life would be. She can't imagine how it would be, had she not come to my class, because she has always thought life made sense when you have a title, property, and you are a celebrity. Then, somehow, she has lost two friends who had all those and life came to a standstill. Generally, in every class, I push for some values that I think are important. She says, she is going to show how these values are going to or have made sense to her. So, that reflection, to give somebody that opportunity to bring it out, I think that is very important. (Participant, CRT)

According to Moon (2007), an environment where lecturers encourage reflection can lead to personal issues being unearthed in the learner that may seem unrelated to the task, as with the student mentioned in the above comment, but are important for the student's personal growth.

Research: Perceived Effect on Students' Learning

In Omingo (2018), the students who participated in focus group discussions (FGDs) in the universities where some faculty development had taken place felt that they were meaningfully engaged in learning by their lecturers. A comment from two students showed that the classes are interactive:

It is not one class where there is just one certain of answer and no one challenges ... there are a lot of challenges, there is kind of debate, classes that were not meant to turn into debate are turned into debate and there is a fun of it. (Student Participant, FGD)

I will say it is very interactive. It is not just students sitting and listening to the teachers that it just goes on and on. It is back and front; the teacher talks for some time and then we ask questions, we want to know more. It is not like he is just giving us information but we also give him information as well. We are also contributing to the lectures. (Student Participant, FGD)

Another student found learning at university different from that in high school. He explained learning at the university as being more practical:

I found it different from that in high school. Let me just add on to what he has said, you see, in high school, most of us were being taught the theoretical aspect, how to pass high school exams and nothing else, but my experience since I came to the university, even if it is a theory class like development studies, the lecturers try to emphasis on how we can change the society in our own way as opposed to high school where everything was 'get an A' and that was all. (Student Participant, FGD)

Studies on academic staff development mainly relate lecturers' learning to deep learning approaches where students are able to understand content qualitatively instead of quantitatively through knowledge construction (Biggs & Tang, 2011). However, students' learning, as illustrated in the above cases, needs to go beyond the passing of examinations; learning that actually has an impact on how students live their lives after the course is over and even after university (Fink, 2013).

AFELT Status

From its initial launch in 2014 to today, AFELT, and its influence on faculty development in East Africa, has grown. Since 2017, AFELT has been a partner in the 3½-year TESCEA project in Uganda and Tanzania:

[TESCEA] is helping young people in two other East Africa countries, Tanzania and Uganda, to use their skills and ideas to tackle social and economic problems. With partners in Tanzania, Uganda and Kenya, TESCEA supports universities, industries, communities and government to work together to create an

72 C. Kingsbury et al.

improved learning experience for students – both women and men. This improved learning experience fosters the development of critical thinking and problem-solving skills and allows for practical learning beyond the classroom that improves a graduate's employability. (TESCEA, 2018)

AFELT will hold its second international conference on the scholarship of teaching and learning in Nairobi. As a body of professional faculty developers and those interested in the same, AFELT will continue to have impact on higher education in the region and the rest of Africa. We see ourselves as champions for progressive higher education. AFELT's tagline, *Transformation, Innovation, Knowledge Creation*, is our guiding focus.

Currently, there is no Africa-wide body for the professional development of university faculty—only regional bodies exist. The need is great, and the energy is high for such an organization. We trust this story will continue.

Conclusion

In this chapter, we have narrated our stories around our involvement in faculty development. Faculty development as described by Clegg (2009a, 2009b) is becoming a career choice and a field of practice. In most countries, government policies, funding agencies, and quality assurance entities have supported faculty development. In Kenya, faculty development has mainly been supported by funding from the UK. Universities, quality audit entities, and government agencies in Africa may want to consider their support by funding faculty development, particularly by training faculty developers.

References

Biggs, J. B., & Tang, C. (2011). *Teaching for quality learning at university: What the student does* (4th ed.). McGraw-Hill, Society for Research into Higher Education and Open University Press.

Brookfield, S. (2017). *Becoming a critically reflective teacher* (2nd ed.). Jossey-Bass.

Clegg, S. (2009a). Histories and institutional change: Understanding academic development practices in the global "north" and "south". *International Studies in Sociology of Education, 19*(1), 53–65.

Clegg, S. (2009b). Forms of knowing and academic development practice. *Studies in Higher Education, 34*(1), 403–416.

Fink, L. D. (2013). *Creating significant learning experiences: An integrated approach to designing college courses* (2nd ed.). Jossey-Bass.

Freire, P. (1970). *Pedagogy of the oppressed*. Herder and Herder.

Hope, A., Timmel, S., & Hodzi, C. (1995). *Training for transformation: A handbook for community workers*. Mambo Press.

Iversen, A. M., Pedersen, A. S., Krogh, L., & Jensen, A. A. (2015). Learning, leading, and letting go of control: Learner-led approaches in education. *SAGE Open, 5*(4), 1–11.

Kingsbury, C. E. (2002). *Barriers and facilitators to teaching for critical reflective thought in Christian higher education in anglophone Africa* [Unpublished doctoral dissertation]. Florida State University.

Kotter, J. P. (1995, March–April). Leading change: Why transformation efforts fail. *Harvard Business Review* (pp. 59–67).

Mezirow, J. (1990). *Fostering critical reflection in adulthood: A guide to transformative and emancipatory learning* (1st ed.). Jossey-Bass.

Moon, J. (2007). *Reflection in learning and professional development: Theory and practice*. Routledge Falmer.

Omingo, M. (2016). *Towards sustainable lecturers' learning to teach in Kenyan private universities* [Unpublished doctoral dissertation]. Stellenbosch University.

Omingo, M. (2018). *Pedagogies for critical thinking in Kenya* [Unpublished].

Tom, M. (2015). Five C framework: A student-centered approach for teaching programing courses with diverse disciplinary background. *Journal of Learning Design, 8*(1), 21–27.

Transforming Employability for Social Change in East Africa (TESCEA). (2018). *Transforming employability for social change in East Africa*. TESCEA. https://www.inasp.info/project/transforming-employability-social-change-east-africa-tescea

Vella, J. K. (2002). *Learning to listen, learning to teach: The power of dialogue in educating adults* (revised ed.). Jossey-Bass.

Wright, G. B. (2011). Student-centered learning in higher education. *International Journal of Teaching and Learning, 23*(3), 92–97.

Part II

One Conceptual Model for the Field

Part II contains only Chap. 5: *Imagining the Ideal Academic Professional Development Center: An Attainable, Fact-Based Vision* by Linda B. Nilson, Clemson University, SC, USA. It is Nilson's response to a request for a summary of her ideas for the design of a model academic professional development center (ADC) and its initial evaluation parameters. The model can be used as a template for either the design or evaluation of a center. The following list of ADC functional tasks can be compared to the tasks listed in Fig. 3.1 (see Chap. 3).

Training

Improve the teacher development system, offer professional development, and improve teachers' ideological understandings and pedagogical competences.

Consulting

Meet the needs of teachers' growth while alleviating teachers' development confusion and stimulating teachers' development potential.

Exchange

Follow the development strategy of the university and build a platform for teachers to exchange, interact, and create a robust academic environment.

Resource Coordination

Build an allocation and sharing mechanism for teacher development resources and promote joint efforts between various institutions on campus for faculty development.

Quality Evaluation

Conduct teaching and learning quality evaluations, provide feedback to teachers and departments, and offer suggestions for improvement.

Regional Leadership

Take up the mantle of leadership to promote faculty development work beyond the campus and extend it to the region.

5

Imagining the Ideal Academic Professional Development Center: An Attainable, Fact-Based Vision

Linda B. Nilson

Introduction

This volume includes the stories and characteristics of academic professional development centers (ADCs) across the globe—an ambitious project that has never been undertaken before. Each center has a unique history, and some of the aspects of each reflect specific institutional and national contexts. But despite their differences, effective centers share some features, which suggest that we can step back and characterize an ideal center. This is the goal of this chapter, and it encompasses features and components such as mission, leadership, location within the institutional structure, relationship to the faculty and graduate students, size and staffing, organization, functions and services, activities and events, collaborations, marketing channels, connections to instructional technology, data sources, program planning, and internal evaluation and assessment strategies. In addition, it identifies components that are optional, depending upon the nature of the institution and the functions and services of other units.

To begin, this chapter considers the names of centers and how they have changed over time. For convenience, it uses the term "center" or "ADC"—for *academic professional development center*—to refer in general to the units of interest here.

L. B. Nilson (✉)
Clemson University, Clemson, SC, USA
e-mail: nilson@clemson.edu

© The Author(s), under exclusive license to Springer Nature Switzerland AG 2023
O. J. Neisler (ed.), *The Palgrave Handbook of Academic Professional Development Centers*,
Palgrave Studies on Leadership and Learning in Teacher Education,
https://doi.org/10.1007/978-3-030-80967-6_5

Names of Centers

Centers go by a variety of names, and no one name merits the status of "ideal." In fact, the titles largely reflect the history of the centers. Those established in the 1970s, 1980s, and 1990s typically feature the words "instructional development," "faculty development," or "teaching" but not "learning" in the name, unless the name has recently been changed. For instance, the Office of Instructional Development at University of California, Los Angeles, was established in 1975, New Mexico State University's Center for Educational Development in 1980, Vanderbilt University's Center for Teaching in 1986, the University of Kansas's Center for Teaching Excellence in 1987, Clemson University's Office of Teaching Effectiveness and Innovation in 1998, and the University of Georgia's Teaching Academy in 1999. Frostburg State University's Center for Teaching Excellence published its first electronic newsletter in late 2006, but its founding date does not appear on its website. New Mexico State closed its center in 2002 and immediately opened The Teaching Academy in January 2003 as an expanded, redesigned unit. The University of Michigan's Center for Research on Learning and Teaching was founded in 1962, but it originally focused on research, as the name implies, and broadened its mission over time.

In the early 2000s, the names of the newly established centers started to lengthen and incorporate "learning." The more common names were (and still are) "center for teaching and learning," "center for excellence in teaching and learning," "center for the enhancement of teaching and learning," "center for the advancement of teaching and learning," "center for the development of teaching and learning," and various combinations of those words. This change reflected a philosophical shift in the educational development community, emphasizing improved student learning as the measure of improved teaching as opposed to student evaluations or some determination of "performance." At the same time, the concept "student-centeredness" took on high value as a foundation of high-quality teaching, courses, and institutions. Other commonly used names outside the USA are "academic professional development center" and "academic development center."

Michigan State University changed its center's name twice. The unit started as the Office of Faculty Development in the 1970s, then became the Office of Faculty and Organizational Development, and, in 2016, the Academic Advancement Network, making a clear break from the title trend. The University of North Dakota presents another exception. What used to be the Office of Instructional Development (founding date unavailable) became the

Teaching Transformation and Development Academy in 2016—a name that, while longer, does not include "learning." The University of Kansas maintains a list of the names and website URLs of hundreds of centers around the world (University of Kansas, n.d.). However, the list is not exhaustive and misses most centers outside of the USA and Canada.

Mission

A model ADC has a mission statement that is prominently displayed on its website, often its home page, and just about all centers have this. This statement explains the purpose and often the goals of the unit, and a longer statement may lay out the means (strategic plan) for achieving those goals, such as the activities and services provided and the assessment strategies used. To encourage people to read it, a model ADC does not make its statement too long, and it links the mission web page to its activities and services.

The ideal center does not compose its mission in a vacuum. The statement reflects the mission of the larger institution. Some colleges and universities offer a wide range of disciplinary concentrations while others specialize in one or more areas: the liberal arts, music, art, business, technical areas, science, engineering, or workforce development. There are also schools of medicine, pharmacy, osteopathy, public health, and other medical and health specialties that house their own centers. In addition, some institutions offer strictly classroom courses, others only online courses, and most both. An increasing number of colleges and universities promote hybrid versions of classroom-based courses. A strong center's mission echoes these variations.

In their mission statements, virtually all ADCs declare their dedication to advancing high-quality teaching and learning (classroom, distance, and/or hybrid) through fostering many or all of the following: research-based best practices, an institutional culture that values teaching excellence, the scholarship of teaching and learning (SoTL), meaningful student assessment, supportive and inclusive learning environments for diverse students, and fair faculty teaching evaluations from multiple perspectives, including those of students. Some statements include goals such as developing academic leaders, cultivating lifelong learners, or building a collaborative community of learning of faculty, staff, and students. Other variations incorporate the unique mission of the institution, including its platform. Online institutions stress serving adults in the workplace, students in rural areas, or students around the globe.

80   L. B. Nilson

Therefore, no particular mission statement can appropriately cover all centers or be considered ideal. The model ADC honors a mission that incorporates the aims of its host college or university.

Leadership

Ideally, the center director is a full-time, experienced specialist who knows and contributes to the teaching and learning and/or educational development literature. The incumbent regularly makes presentations at relevant conferences and publishes research-based articles in respected journals and/or books with well-regarded presses. Such a strong academic record implies that the director has a multi-year background in running an ADC, along with at least five years of teaching experience in higher education, preferably at an institution with a similar mission. An additional expectation is familiarity with, if not mastery of, a few areas that neighbor or fall within educational development and teaching and learning—for example, cognitive psychology, instructional design, curriculum development, diversity and inclusion, graduate teaching assistant (GTA) development, leadership development, or organizational development in higher education. Having an outstanding teaching record is also critical, and having won teaching awards a plus.

To demand such a strong professional background means that the position is not a revolving door of interested faculty in other disciplines. Rather, it affirms the fact that educational development, especially in the area of teaching and learning, has matured into a scholarly, evidence-based discipline of its own. It does not rely on anecdotes, personal experience, and commonsense tips, as it did 50 years ago.

Another important aspect of center leadership is the level of the director's position in the broader organization's hierarchy. The higher the level, the better it is for the center. Designation as a vice or associate provost or an associate vice president of academic affairs (VPAA) is ideal. Such a high status implies that the director will hold membership in the provost/VPAA's central advising committee with influence on strategic plans and programs for academic improvement and student success. In other words, the director will have "a seat at the table" when centralized, high-level academic policies, procedures, plans, and visions are being discussed and decided. If institutions of higher education are mainly in the business of promoting student learning, the director of a model ADC belongs near the top.

Along with this elevated administrative status, the director holds faculty status in an appropriate discipline with the opportunity to teach at least one course a year. This status enhances the director's credibility with faculty (Mullinix, 2008). Keeping one's teaching experience current allows the incumbent to anticipate instructor concerns by experimenting with teaching and assessment methods and staying on top of teaching and technology challenges and changes in students' values and backgrounds. Given the vulnerability of an ADC within the larger institutional structure (see below), this status also offers the director some measure of job protection in the event of a center closure.

Especially in larger centers, a director assumes a wide range of roles, in particular in more complex institutions like comprehensive and doctorate-granting research universities (Sorcinelli et al., 2006). Therefore, in a model center, this person brings varied competencies to the job. Dawson et al. (2010) identified these competencies by using the World Café, a collaborative discussion-based method, at four Canadian and international conferences of educational developers. Of primary importance, they found, are the abilities to execute and balance the multiple roles of leader, scholar, and manager, to use time efficiently, and to plan and prioritize strategically. Additionally, the director is an expert facilitator of various activities, an advocate and leader for change, an effective interpersonal manager, a superior instructor, a policy developer, and a community builder.

Perhaps most critically, the director inspires the respect and trust of the faculty, which are a center's primary target clientele and main stakeholders. The incumbent's personality, competencies, academic background, faculty status, and publication record play key roles here, but so does the support that the top-level administration gives to the center.

Institutional Location

The most advantageous direct report line for the center director is to the provost/VPAA or an appropriate associate provost/VPAA holding campus-wide responsibility. This high, centralized status facilitates collaborations with the leadership of other academic and support units on campus. Typical collaboration partners for model ADCs include these units: instructional technology, instructional design, online learning, the library, the academic success center, student disability services, psychological/counseling services, the service-learning/community engagement unit, cultural and diversity centers, the first-year experience unit, academic advising, undergraduate studies, the career center, the research/external grant administration office, the assessment office, and institutional effectiveness/research—plus ADC directors at other institutions. These collaborative relationships may result in live or online training programs for faculty or graduate students, new instructor orientations, assessment initiatives, new classroom or online courses, undergraduate student success programs, diversity training, grants, reports, or publications, among other products.

Institutional Protection

ADCs occupy a vulnerable position in higher education. No matter how effective they have proven themselves to be, they and their directors come and go with budgetary ebbs and flows and high-level administrative changes (Flaherty, 2014; Nilson et al. 2011). After all, these centers do not bring in funding as do research grants and contracts, and teaching may play a secondary role in a research or research-aspiring university. An ideal ADC's budget is covered by a full endowment and is independent of the central administration for its funding. Unfortunately, few centers can claim this fiscally-independent status.

Staffing

The larger the institution in terms of the number of teaching faculty and GTAs served by the ADC, the larger the staff should be. In the model center, the ratio of personnel to institutional full-time-equivalent (FTE) positions is large enough to promptly serve all those who request services, including adjunct faculty and GTAs. No one individual "carries" the center. At a minimum, a campus-wide center has, in addition to a director, an associate or assistant director, educational developers and consultants with different specialties, administrative assistance staff, and student employees to help with clerical and simple technological tasks.

How the members of the staff specialize depends on the existence of other units that address those needs (e.g., online learning, service-learning, and disciplinary research). The personnel may include instructional designers and technologists, as long as the ADC is not housed within the instructional technology or online learning unit. Rather, it either houses such units itself or collaborates with them to offer embedded or integrated services. In addition, a model center influences the selection of instructional technologies and the learning management system, even if it does not control these functions (American Council on Education, 2017).

Data Collection and Analysis

The ideal ADC frequently surveys faculty and GTAs to assess their perceived needs and keeps track of the challenges that clients raise in workshops, online programs, social media posts, group meetings, and individual consultations. Chairs, academic deans, and GTA supervisors receive special survey forms asking about the needs of their departmental and college faculty and GTAs. The center's advisory board (called the "executive committee" in some places, such as the University of Georgia, Athens), which may consist of faculty, GTAs, and staff from collaborating units, also has input. The concerns heard shape much of the new programming, helping to ensure strong attendance and usage. According to the American Council on Education (2017), strong attendance means at least 30% of the teaching community across disciplines and position types in a given year. The training events and offerings demonstrate, preferably with attendee participation, as well as explain new teaching skills and methods. They also echo the priorities of the institutional and center's missions and cultivate professional growth and improvement. Some may target specific instructors (e.g., those teaching first-year seminars or lower-division science, technology, engineering, and math courses) while others address the challenges of all who teach.

In addition to needs assessment surveys, a model center collects and analyzes data to evaluate the effectiveness and impact of its programs, such as its workshops, webinars, online training programs, faculty learning communities, and individual services and consultations (see Table 5.1 for program specifics). These digitally stored data document attendance/usage, user satisfaction, evidence of changes in teaching practice, evidence of diffusion of best practices, and changes in students' achievement of learning outcomes. However, measuring the effect of a center's programming on student learning poses tremendous methodological challenges that few centers can surmount (Haras et al., 2017). The ADC uses these data not only for program evaluation but also for periodic self-assessment and annual assessment of the unit as a whole. It makes these anonymous digital records and reports available on its website, creating a repository for its institutional memory. Its annual assessment report may also have to appear in an institutional assessment database.

Table 5.1 Model ADC functions and services by the means to achieve/deliver them

ADC functions	Means to achieve/deliver them					
	Orientations for new faculty[a]	Professional development, training	Individual services and consultations	Consulting services to groups or units	Funding of faculty[a] growth efforts	Campus-wide special events and initiatives
Enhance[c] Faculty-to-faculty (classroom, studio, clinical) teaching[b]	Live and online presentations, workshops; information on ADC services	Workshops, webinars, and online training programs oriented toward individual faculty[a] or academic units	Confidential meetings with faculty,[a] preferably in a series, on challenges	Teaching[b] component of grants; teaching-relevant committees, task forces; curriculum development or revision	Travel to workshops, conferences	Campus conferences; well-known guest speakers and facilitators; participation in general education revisions
Develop, enhance online courses, teaching[b] (following Quality Matters standards)	Information on ADC services	Workshops, webinars oriented toward individual faculty[a] or academic units	Confidential meetings with faculty,[a] preferably in a series, on challenges	Teaching[b] component of grants; teaching-relevant committees, task forces; curriculum development or revision	Travel to workshops, conferences	Campus conferences; well-known guest speakers and facilitators; participation in general education revisions
Provide faculty[a] with during-course feedback on teaching[b]	Information on ADC services	Faculty[a] peers to provide during-course feedback or evaluation to colleagues	Classroom observations, class interviews, video recording reviews, online course reviews—all followed by confidential meetings with faculty[a]			

Provide faculty[a] with expertise on assessing student learning	Information on ADC services	Test and assignment design, posttest item analysis, course-level measurements of student learning	Confidential meetings with faculty[a]	Consultations on curriculum mapping, program-level measures of student learning		Measures of student learning in general education
Help faculty[a] ensure student equity, inclusion	Information on ADC services	Workshops, webinars, and online training programs oriented toward individuals or academic units	Confidential meetings (preferably a series) with faculty[a] on challenges		Travel to workshops, conferences	Campus conferences; well-known guest speakers and facilitators
Improve faculty[a] review and help faculty prepare for it	Information on ADC services	Workshops, webinars, and online training programs on interpreting student evaluations of teaching (SETs), writing a teaching statement/philosophy, assembling a teaching portfolio/dossier, explaining problematic student evaluations	Interpretation of SETs; help with writing a teaching statement/philosophy, assembling a teaching portfolio/dossier, explaining problematic SETs	Consultation to committees and task forces on SETs and the faculty[a] evaluation process		Evidence-based proposals to administrators on improving their use of SETs and the faculty[a] evaluation process

(continued)

Table 5.1 (continued)

ADC functions	Means to achieve/deliver them					
	Orientations for new faculty[a]	Professional development, training	Individual services and consultations	Consulting services to groups or units	Funding of faculty[a] growth efforts	Campus-wide special events and initiatives
Help faculty[a] learn from each other in peer communities	Information on ADC services		Workshops and webinars by faculty,[a] brown bags	Faculty[a] learning communities (FLCs) on teaching-related books, methods, or challenges	Books for FLCs	
Provide faculty[a] with print, video, and online teaching[b] resources	Information on ADC resources	Use or dissemination of resources	Use or dissemination of resources	Use or dissemination of resources	Mini-grants to faculty[a] to buy their own resources	Use or dissemination of resources
Help faculty[a] conduct research on teaching[b] (SoTL)	Information on ADC services	Workshops, webinars, and online training programs on conducting and publishing SoTL	Consultations on faculty[a] projects	Consultations on SoTL grants	SoTL mini-grants; information on and help applying for external grant opportunities	Dissemination of SoTL results

Reward, recognize faculty[a] for teaching[b] excellence and SoTL	Information on ADC services	Campus conferences, workshops, and webinars by faculty[a], online forums for students to recognize faculty,[a] brown bags, award and recognition ceremonies	Teaching-related and SoTL mini-grants (as rewards)	Dissemination of faculty's[a] creative and effective teaching methods and SoTL results

[a]The term "faculty" encompasses GTAs and adjunct faculty as well as tenure-track faculty

[b]Teaching includes course design and development, student-centered teaching, active learning methods, teaching higher-order thinking (critical, analytical, problem-solving), motivating students, student-learning assessment, test and assignment design, pedagogically sound uses of technology, and the evaluation of faculty teaching. Resources include a library of print books, journals, newsletters, and articles and DVDs for browsing and borrowing, as well as annotated online resources (text, video, audio, animation) on the ADC website

[c]Faculty-to-faculty

Communication, Marketing, and Physical Resources

A model ADC has robust communication channels with faculty and GTAs; a timely, proactive marketing plan based on responsiveness to instructor needs; a physical space with private offices; adequate facilities and equipment; a central campus location; and an easy-to-find, easy-to-navigate website with important teaching resources.

To elaborate, the main communication and marketing channels depend on the center having unrestricted access to comprehensive and up-to-date faculty and GTA mailing lists. These lists allow the staff to e-mail announcements of upcoming events and time-sensitive services and distribute an electronic newsletter. In addition, the model ADC maintains one or more social media sites, teaching handbooks, brochures, flyers, white papers, and a highly visible website with mutual links to the homepages of the institution and collaborating units. The materials that the center produces consistently promote its brand with a logo and memorable phrases.

Functions and Services and the Means to Achieve/Deliver Them

These are displayed in Table 5.1. Among the 10 functions and services of the ideal center are enhancing face-to-face, hybrid, and online teaching; providing instructors with during-the-term feedback; offering assessment expertise; supporting research on teaching; and helping faculty learn from each other, where the faculty beneficiaries encompass both tenure-track and adjunct faculty and GTAs. The means to achieve/deliver these functions and services range from orientations, training programs, and varied individual services to funding faculty research and travel, consulting for groups and units, and spearheading special events and initiatives.

Depending upon the nature of the institution and the offerings of other units, a model ADC may do the following as well:

* Organize and deliver live and online training programs in:

    - Research methods, scholarly productivity, scholarly writing (for publication), grant proposal writing, book proposal writing, and the like, especially in research-oriented universities

5 Imagining the Ideal Academic Professional Development Center...

- Academic leadership for new or future chairs and deans
- Using the campus learning management system
- Developing and managing an academic career and conducting an academic or nonacademic job search (e.g., vita, resume, and cover letter writing, interviewing, and teaching demo preparation)
- Integrating service-learning and community engagement experiences into a course
- Integrating undergraduate research experiences into a course or curriculum
- Teaching and grading for GTAs and undergraduate teaching assistants

* Organize faculty mentoring programs, or help departments do so
* Organize and lead writing support groups and/or writing retreats, especially in research-oriented universities
* Disseminate external grant opportunities in the disciplines, especially in research-oriented universities without a research office that does so
* Administer wellness services (e.g., self-care, stress relief, mindfulness, resilience, needs-based communication, work-life balance, work-values consonance)
* Run preparing-future-faculty programs for graduate students and postdoctoral fellows
* Develop and lead graduate courses on teaching, or help departments do so.

Conclusion: The Model as the Goal and Barriers to Attainment

The model center represents an exemplar to aspire to. Perhaps it can help unfunded ADCs convince their administrators to increase their funding. But not all centers will have the opportunity to grow into a model one because too many factors beyond a director's control shape an ADC's potential. For instance, the budgetary exigencies of the institution will restrict the center's operational budget, staff number, and staff salaries. Clearly, a strong center needs a fairly large, decently paid staff with a range of specialized skills—from online learning, social media, and website development to face-to-face teaching, assessment, and SoTL research. In addition, as campuses grow in size, many are cramped for space, leaving less available for any given unit.

Administrative priorities constitute another major influence. As mentioned above, ADCs are vulnerable units because they rarely add to the bottom line

90   L. B. Nilson

and are not as essential as admissions, financial aid, the registrar, and, on some campuses, athletic teams. A certain president or provost may shower a center with funding while, just a few years down the road, the next one may slash its staff and starve it, or even shut it down. Sometimes the faculty or deans concerned about ensuring the required teaching component in external grants can save an ADC, but sometimes not.

Even if centers fail to help an institution's fiscal bottom line, they do help "the other bottom line," which is student learning. While they may lack the resources to trace their impact on student outcomes, the literature provides evidence of this effect—on student success and retention at the community college level (Allen et al., 2019; Elliott & Oliver, 2016) and on student learning in a small liberal arts college and a large research university (Allen et al., 2019; Condon et al., 2016). Given this recent research, administrators should be less inclined to dismiss a robust, full-service ADC as an optional luxury.

References

Allen, D., McPherson, M., Nilson, L. B., & Sorcinelli, M. D. (2019). *ACUE student, faculty, and institutional impact research: Independent review process and findings.* Association of College and University Educators. https://acue.org/wp-content/uploads/2019/06/ACUE-Research-Review-Findings-2019.pdf

American Council on Education. (2017). *The faculty development center matrix.* American Council on Education. http://www.acenet.edu/news-room/Documents/The-Faculty-Development-Center-Matrix.pdf

Condon, W., Iverson, E. R., Manduca, C. A., Rutz, C., & Willett, G. (2016). *Faculty development and student learning: Assessing the connections.* Indiana University Press.

Dawson, D., Britnell, J., & Hitchcock, A. (2010). Developing competency models of faculty developers: Using the World Café to foster dialog. *To Improve the Academy, 28*(1), 3–24.

Elliott, R. W., & Oliver, D. E. (2016). Linking faculty development to community college student achievement: A mixed methods approach. *Community College Journal of Research and Practice, 40*(2), 85–99.

Flaherty, C. (2014, May 30). *A 'growth' field.* Inside Higher Ed. https://www.insidehighered.com/news/2014/05/30/some-teaching-and-learning-centers-have-closed-after-recession-field-growing-over

Haras, C., Taylor, S. C., Zakrajsek, T., Ginsberg, M., & Glover, J. (2017). Intended teaching effectiveness outcomes for instructors and faculty development. In C. Haras, S. C. Taylor, M. D. Sorcinelli, & L. von Hoene (Eds.), *Institutional commitment to teaching excellence: Assessing the impacts and outcomes of faculty development* (pp. 29–54). American Council on Education. https://www.acenet.edu/Documents/Institutional-Commitment-to-Teaching-Excellence.pdf

Mullinix, B. (2008). Credibility and effectiveness in context: An exploration of the importance of faculty status for faculty developers. *To Improve the Academy, 26*(1), 173–195.

Nilson, L. B., Nuhfer, E. B., & Mullinix, B. (2011). Faculty development as a hazardous occupation. *To Improve the Academy, 30*(1), 290–305.

Sorcinelli, M. D., Austin, A., Eddy, P. L., & Beach, A. L. (2006). *Creating the future of faculty development: Learning from the past, understanding the present.* Anker.

University of Kansas. (n.d.). *Other teaching centers.* University of Kansas. https://cte.ku.edu/other-teaching-centers

Part III

Mission Differences Lead to Structural Differences

Every case study in this book discusses the mission of its academic professional development center (ADC). However, the chapters included in this section and those referenced below have defined either an unusual mission or provided a clear depiction of how their mission influenced the ADC structure and/or how the mission led to programming choices for the ADC.

Chapters in Part III

Chapter 6: *Assessment Work in an Academic Professional Development Center.* Ingrid Novodvorsky, Elaine Marchello, and Lisa Elfring, University of Arizona, Tucson, AZ, USA.

This chapter details how the university's ADC program design changed as the mission for assessing student learning was clarified. There is a detailed description of the campus-wide learning outcomes assessment plan.

Chapter 7: *Implementing Academic Professional Development Strategies to Support Spiritual and Values-Based Engagement.* Sandra Sgoutas-Emch, University of San Diego, San Diego, CA, USA.

This chapter describes how the ADC supports the mission and values of the institution, specifically by supporting its Catholic identity and goals while promoting values-based education. Further, the ADC supports faculty members' spirituality in their search for meaning and purpose.

94   Mission Differences Lead to Structural Differences

Chapter 8: *Needs Analysis Leads to Sustainability: Development of a Medical Education and Informatics Department in the College of Medicine and Health Sciences, Sultan Qaboos University.* Nadia Mohammed Al Wardy and Rashid Al Abri, Sultan Qaboos University, Muscat, Oman.

Although an existing medical education and informatics unit predated the ADC at the university, the subsequent center now works independently toward a specific mission of excellence in clinical teaching and learning.

Chapter 9: *Tectonic Plates of American Higher Education: Yale University's Poorvu Center and a Multiplicity of Missions.* Kyle Sebastian Vitale, Temple University, Philadelphia, PA, (previously of Yale University), and Nancy S. Niemi, University of Maryland Eastern Shore, Princess Anne, MD, USA (previously of Yale University).

This case study provides insight into the navigation of change processes after a centuries-old research university embraced its mission to provide holistic integrated support for faculty and students. To implement the mission, the university merged related departments and services such as faculty development, program assessment, a student writing center, educational technology, a broadcast studio, digital education, student mentoring, and counseling into one organization located in a single centralized building.

Chapter 10: *Structural Changes Over Three Years: Evolution of Three Models to Support Learning and Teaching in a Large Research-Intensive University.* Tammy R. Smith, Kirsten Schliephake, and Barb Macfarlan, Monash University, Melbourne, VIC, Australia.

The ADC described in this chapter has changed both its mission and structure three times since it began in 2014 as a project management team reporting to the vice provost. Changes were based on analysis of program impact and on continuous needs assessment. The impact of university-level leadership and the results of building a community of practice are additional themes.

Other Relevant Chapters

Chapter 21: *Quality, Teaching, and Learning: A Networked Approach Across Pakistan and East Africa.* Tashmin Khamis, Aga Khan University, Karachi, Pakistan, and Zeenar Salim, Syracuse University, Syracuse, NY, USA (previously of Aga Khan University).

This chapter describes the establishment of integrated networks of quality, teaching, and learning which, while centrally led, are geographically dispersed across Asia and Africa in alignment with the institution's global mission.

Chapter 23: *Collaborative Faculty Development.* Jordan Cofer, Denise Domizi, Marina Smitherman, Jesse Bishop, and Rod McRae, University System of Georgia, Atlanta, GA, USA.

This chapter reveals a unique model in which an ADC-related consortium was established to facilitate institutional goals of planning, resource-sharing, and expertise across the 26 colleges and universities that comprise this higher education organization.

Chapter 24: *The Making of the Learning, Teaching, and Innovative Technologies Center: Building Upon an Internal Partnership.* Barbara Draude, Thomas Brinthaupt, and Sheila Otto, Middle Tennessee State University, Murfreesboro, TN, USA.

This faculty-led and supported ADC developed from a virtual center to a face-to-face 2,500-square foot facility. The mission of the ADC was designed entirely by a group of faculty delegates and informed the planning, activities, and environment of the center.

Chapter 28: *Building Community and Supporting Mentors in a Dispersed College for Adults: A Case Study.* Shantih E. Clemans, Center for Mentoring, Learning, and Academic Innovation, State University of New York Empire State College, Saratoga Springs, NY, USA.

This chapter recounts the experience of an ADC which provides a diverse array of educational programming for non-traditional adult learners across 36 campuses. Faculty are seen as mentors and this non-traditional teaching role has resulted in non-traditional professional development, with much of it aimed at building community via online programming. Mission and ADC structure are relevant as recent global issues are forcing higher education institutions to re-envision their missions and operations.

Chapter 29: *Virtual Faculty Learning Communities.* Angela Atwell and Cristina Cottom, Embry-Riddle Aeronautical University-Worldwide, Daytona Beach, FL, USA.

This chapter explains how an ADC uses technology-based programming to build communities of practice across 130 campuses in order to serve the institution's far-flung 1,800 faculty members.

6

Assessment Work in an Academic Professional Development Center

Ingrid Novodvorsky, Elaine Marchello, and Lisa Elfring

Introduction

The University of Arizona (UArizona) is a public university in the southwestern USA, with high research activity. Its total enrollment is 49,000 students, distributed across 390 degree programs; it employs some 3,200 faculty members. The Office of Instruction and Assessment (OIA) was created in 2010 for the consolidation of teaching support services that had previously been distributed across campus units. The decision to include learning outcomes assessment as a key mission for the new OIA was made in recognition that assessment is an organic complement to teaching and learning, and as a formal commitment to strengthening the campus's focus on learning outcomes assessment. The new unit merged personnel from three pre-existing support units: the Learning Technologies Center, which provided training and support in technology-enabled teaching; the University Teaching Center, which provided professional development to support teaching and learning; and one individual from the Office of Institutional Research and Planning Support, who was at that time the person assigned to supporting learning outcomes assessment across campus. In the intervening years, staffing has fluctuated, with 1.5 full-time-equivalent positions currently devoted to the support of

---

I. Novodvorsky (✉) • E. Marchello • L. Elfring
University of Arizona, Tucson, AZ, USA
e-mail: novod@arizona.edu; evm@arizona.edu; elfring@arizona.edu

© The Author(s), under exclusive license to Springer Nature Switzerland AG 2023
O. J. Neisler (ed.), *The Palgrave Handbook of Academic Professional Development Centers*,
Palgrave Studies on Leadership and Learning in Teacher Education,
https://doi.org/10.1007/978-3-030-80967-6_6

program-level learning outcomes assessment across campus. In this chapter, we describe the development of a campus-wide plan to support assessment of student learning in all degree programs, the evaluation of assessment reporting, changes in the campus-wide assessment landscape over the past 11 years, and the intersection of faculty development and assessment work.

Over time, the OIA's mission has crystallized into the following: *We build capacity for excellent teaching.* This mission statement recognizes that our goal is to empower instructors and other campus personnel so that they can make informed decisions about teaching, learning, and learning outcomes assessment. As much as possible, we avoid a prescriptive approach to teaching or assessment methods, with the belief that faculty members are best positioned to make decisions about the programs and student learning in their own disciplines (Suskie, 2018; Walvoord, 2010).

Funding and Organization of the OIA

The OIA currently has a permanent staff of 30 employees and an annual budget of just over US$2.8 million. Funding for the center comes largely from state funds (95%), internal funds (4.5%), and a small income (0.5%) from test scoring and media production. Fig. 6.1 provides an overview of the current organizational chart. The highest position at the OIA, the senior vice provost of Academic Affairs, Teaching and Learning, is a senior-level administrator who reports to the provost, the university's chief academic administrator, and oversees accreditation and assessment efforts and support of teaching and learning.

In addition to OIA's work in academic professional development and assessment, staff members also provide support for our campus learning management system, administer student course surveys, produce videos for classes and other projects, and develop websites and computer applications for the UArizona community.

Developing a Campus-Wide Learning Outcomes Assessment Plan

Initially, OIA's first assessment specialist, along with the new OIA director, convened an assessment committee composed of at least one representative from each college. The members were associate or assistant deans of academic programs or their designees. This Assessment Coordinating Council (ACC)

6 Assessment Work in an Academic Professional Development Center

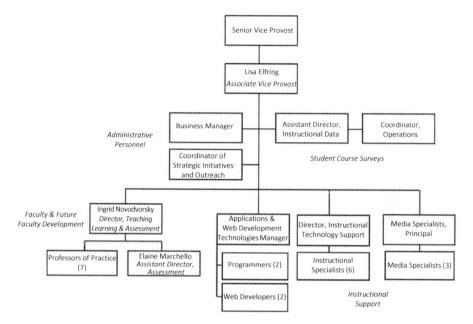

Fig. 6.1 OIA organizational chart

was tasked with formalizing the process of student learning assessment within programs, along with the reporting of assessment findings. With the guidance of the OIA director, the ACC adopted the guidelines presented by Walvoord (2010, 71) for department-level assessment of student learning:

- Construct assessment that you can use to improve student learning and that is sustainable in terms of time and resources
- A basic no-frills plan can work well, provided that you act on your assessment data
- Start now with an annual department meeting to examine whatever data you have
- Prepare data carefully for departmental discussion
- Choose your action item based on what is most important, most problematic, and feasible.

Initially, a website was created with a page for each degree program on campus. The OIA director asked each program to report on its assessment work on these web pages; the website was public to emphasize accountability across campus and to allow programs to learn from one another. Each unit assigned an assessment coordinator to add their programs' assessment information to the web pages. The required information included program learning outcomes, assessment activities, assessment findings, and changes in response to findings. To further emphasize the importance of assessment reporting, the ACC created a rubric with which to evaluate these web pages and give formative feedback to the programs regarding their assessment process. It was a good process, but with no incentives or penalties for participation, it was difficult to get all programs to report.

In 2010, UArizona was tasked by its accrediting agency with developing a more comprehensive learning outcomes assessment program; the existing assessment program did not include enough systematic oversight of learning outcomes assessment across campus. After attending an assessment institute in 2011, the OIA director, the senior vice provost for academic affairs and three faculty members developed an initiative to improve learning outcomes assessment. This early initiative of the OIA was one that embedded learning outcomes assessment reporting in the state-mandated Academic Program Review (APR) process. The APR is completed by each academic unit on a seven-year cycle and includes both a self-study and a site visit by a team composed of internal and external members who give formative feedback on all aspects of a unit's operations. Beginning with the 2011–2012 academic year, units were required to include learning outcomes assessment reporting in the APR Self-Study Reports. This structure has proven to be productive, helping departments to focus on the learning outcomes assessment in their programs at the same time that they are reviewing other important graduation outcomes (e.g., job placement, graduate/professional school admission, and time to graduation).

The Learning Outcomes Review Process

Using an updated version of the rubric that the ACC developed, the assessment team in OIA now evaluates the assessment plans in the APR Self-Study Report for each of a unit's degree programs and rates the plans. This rubric includes the following criteria: Program Learning Outcomes, Curriculum Map, Process of Assessment, Assessment Plan, Assessment Findings, and Changes in Response to Findings. The rubric focuses on the quality of the various sections of assessment reporting; in other words, whether the learning outcomes are clear and measurable, and the assessment activities are aligned to the outcomes. A written report is sent to the senior vice provost for academic affairs and the head of the unit in advance of the APR site visit.

6 Assessment Work in an Academic Professional Development Center 101

Following the APR review team's visit to campus, OIA assessment personnel meet with each unit, if necessary, to draft a post-APR action plan. These plans are tailored to each unit's needs, but typically focus on establishing a manageable and sustainable assessment plan. All units were also expected to make annual updates to their web pages on the university's assessment website. Programs are subsequently evaluated one, three, and five years post-APR, using the same rubric as for the APR. In order to emphasize the importance of the annual web page update, a letter from the provost (the university's chief academic administrator) with the evaluation history is sent to the unit heads. This letter is either congratulatory on a job well done or a warning that their assessment of student learning needs attention.

By year six of the seven-year APR cycle, the assessment team realized that the home-grown web pages were not sufficient for preserving historical assessment data, and assessment reporting was shifted into Taskstream by Watermark. After a pilot year, a series of workshops enabled the OIA assessment team to roll out Taskstream to the entire campus in 2018. This transition to a new system also allowed us to provide an important assessment refresher to units; this was helpful because there is a great deal of turnover among units' assessment representatives.

Evaluation of Assessment Reporting

Throughout the entire review process, OIA assessment personnel are available to provide feedback on assessment work, attend departmental meetings to explain assessment reporting requirements, and help units navigate Taskstream. As of the 2017–2018 academic year, we have completed one seven-year APR cycle, and so have worked with nearly every academic program on our campus; some units have delayed their APR due to leadership changes, and so will have their first formal relationship with the OIA assessment team during the second cycle.

For each of the seven years of the first APR cycle that required assessment reporting, we calculated the average rubric scores for the four major criteria. Each criterion is evaluated on a four-point scale, with a score of four being excellent and a score of one being inadequate. The number of programs evaluated each year ranged from 12 to 44. The average score for the Program Learning Outcomes increased from 2.5 to 3.8 over the course of seven years. The average scores for the other three criteria remained relatively unchanged across the seven years: Assessment Activities, average score of 2.3; Assessment Findings, average score of 1.8; and Changes in Response to Findings, average

102   I. Novodvorsky et al.

score of 1.8. It should be noted that the rubric referenced earlier includes two additional criteria: Curriculum Map and Process of Assessment. These were added to the rubric starting with the 2018–2019 cohort, to reflect reporting in Taskstream.

As indicated by the average rubric scores, most of the degree programs now have clear and measurable learning outcomes, and many have manageable and sustainable assessment plans. In the first few years of this process, many units initially developed overly complicated assessment plans that were not sustainable. The OIA assessment team has focused in recent years on encouraging simple plans to start with, so that units can collect some findings and make program changes in response to those findings, thus experiencing the benefits of using evidence of student learning to drive changes (Walvoord, 2010). This work on revising assessment plans presented in the APR year has slowed the collection of findings and changes in curriculum, thus explaining the stagnant average scores for these criteria in the first seven-year cycle. Additionally, many units report changes that are not linked to assessment findings or learning outcomes (e.g., new courses created because of new faculty hires or new advisors hired in response to increased student enrollment), further explaining the low average scores for that criterion. However, it appears that moving assessment reporting into Taskstream has improved the quality of that reporting. The average rubric scores for the 2018–2019 and 2019-20 academic years, for 45 programs, were: Program Learning Outcomes, 4.1; Assessment Plan, 2.9; Assessment Findings, 2.8; and Changes in Response to Findings, 2.7. The Assessment Activities criterion has been renamed Assessment Plan to reflect the structure of Taskstream.

Changes in the Campus-Wide Assessment Landscape

As the APR review process matured, the need for the ACC diminished, and the group was disbanded. However, the focus on outcomes assessment in many contexts remained important, and in 2015, the OIA assessment team leader invited faculty members and personnel from many units on campus to come together to discuss assessment on campus. This new group, the Assessment Leadership Team, includes representation from associate deans, various colleges, the UArizona Libraries, co-curricular programs, and the OIA. The team meets monthly throughout the academic year to share ideas and results of various assessments conducted in their respective units. This has helped provide a more comprehensive view of assessment efforts on our campus.

In 2017, the assessment team realized that UArizona did not formally recognize any institutional-level learning outcomes; that is, outcomes that all students are expected to demonstrate. Therefore, a proposal was put forward to adopt the General Education Learning Outcomes as the institutional learning outcomes (ILOs). After some revisions, these final institutional outcomes were approved by the UArizona Faculty Senate (the institution's governing body):

* Think critically
* Communicate effectively
* Understand and value differences
* Use information effectively and ethically.

The goal is to assess students both in general education and in degree programs to determine students' attainment of these ILOs during their academic careers. With the implementation of Taskstream, aligning program outcomes with the ILOs is off to a good start. For those undergraduate programs that have added outcomes to their Taskstream workspaces so far, all of them have mapped at least one program-level outcome to the ILO, "think critically". Percentages of program-level learning outcomes mapped to the other ILOs are 70% or above, indicating that most UArizona students are being asked to demonstrate the ILOs in their degree programs. Because of the vast number of general education courses distributed across all colleges, it is difficult to implement and track assessment of ILOs in those courses. However, this issue is being addressed as a new task force reviews and updates the general education program.

Intersection of Faculty Development and Assessment of Learning

Because the OIA includes both faculty developers and assessment professionals, we are positioned to integrate improvement in teaching practice with assessment of student learning, at both the course and program levels. When instructors consult with us about making changes to their teaching, modifying a course, or creating a new course, we quite naturally focus the conversation on what they want their students to learn. This is consistent with ideas concerning constructive alignment (Biggs, 1996; Biggs & Tang, 2011).

One example of this intersection has occurred over the past six years in our close relationship with the Computer Science Department. In fall 2015, we responded to a request from the department head to observe all of the department's instructors, video-record a class session, and meet with instructors after they had watched the recordings to provide feedback on their teaching. This mandatory coaching, which drew a skeptical response at first from many instructors, has allowed us to establish productive relationships and has resulted in a move toward evidence-based teaching practices (Ambrose et al., 2010; Bransford et al., 2000; Brown et al., 2014; Dunlosky et al., 2013; National Academies of Sciences, Engineering, and Medicine, 2018b) in both undergraduate and graduate courses. For example, many instructors are now using Think/Pair/Share cycles (Lyman, 1981) instead of just asking a question and waiting for volunteers to raise their hands. Think/Pair/Share involves posing a question to students, asking them to take a few minutes of thinking time, and then turning to a nearby student to share their thoughts. After a few minutes of pair discussion, some students are asked to share their ideas with the entire class. Several other instructors have restructured their class sessions so that students are working in small groups on coding activities, instead of listening to lectures. In an e-mail, the department head noted: "The biggest change that I'm seeing is discussion/adoption of active learning practices. While some are taking baby steps, I think the tide has turned in considering them to be valuable" (T. Proebsting, personal communication, 2018).

These ongoing classroom observations also led to the department paying 40% of the salary of one of our faculty developers for two years to work closely with the instructors of the introductory course sequence to revise the curriculum, establish clear and measurable course-level learning outcomes, and infuse even more evidence-based teaching strategies into those important early classes. Not too surprisingly, it is in these introductory courses that many female and underrepresented minority students decide that computer science is not for them (Margolis & Fisher, 2002; National Academies of Sciences, Engineering, and Medicine, 2018a).

After three years of intensive professional development and coaching of the instructors in the Computer Science Department, we also observed a positive impact on the department's work in assessing student learning in their degree programs. The previous assessment plans were developed in 2015 and were too complex to be sustainable, as they included too many outcomes and assessment points. Additionally, they were authored by a handful of instructors who did not consult the rest of the department. In 2018, the committees charged with developing assessment plans at the undergraduate and graduate levels worked to get faculty agreement with all parts of the plans and created streamlined plans anchored by fewer outcomes that are at a high cognitive level (e.g., evaluation and synthesis). The Undergraduate Curriculum Committee took time during the 2018–2019 academic year to refine the assessment measures and began collecting findings in the 2019–2020 academic year. We rated the 2018–2019 assessment reporting for the master's and doctorate programs as "Excellent" (a rubric score of 4) in all but one criterion. This is evidence that our work with Computer Science instructors on curricular reform and teaching improvements helped them to transfer some of those same principles to developing plans to assess student learning at the program level.

Lessons Learned

We have identified several lessons learned in our journey toward fully integrating assessment of student learning into all UArizona degree programs as part of OIA's mission to build capacity for excellent teaching.

Establish a Coaching Relationship

Just as with academic professional development work, a coaching relationship around assessment is critical. We work hard to meet faculty and staff members where they are in their understanding of assessment of student learning. Some are already well versed in assessment, and primarily need help with assessment reporting, while others know little about assessment. To support all levels of expertise, we have created a Program-Level Learning Outcomes Assessment resource website (OIA, n.d.).

Expect an Ever-Changing Cast of Characters

In the first few years of the first seven-year APR cycle, we kept being surprised by personnel changes, with new personnel never informed about their assessment-related responsibilities. We now update our list of department heads, program coordinators, and associate deans at the beginning of each fall semester. We also reach out via e-mail to new assessment personnel to invite their questions, share our resource website, and offer our support.

Establish a Standardized Reporting Structure

For programs to benefit from the collection of evidence of student learning over the years, it is crucial that the reporting structure is standardized and allows programs to see trends in findings over time. We made the switch from our own web pages to Taskstream because far too many programs would update their web pages by either deleting the previous year's findings or adding the year's findings to an aggregated set of findings. The standardized reporting in Taskstream, which is based on templates, makes it much clearer what and where information needs to be reported. As an added bonus, our evaluation of assessment reporting has become much more efficient, as we do not have to hunt all over a web page for the information we need to evaluate assessment reporting. We now have the capacity to provide formative feedback to every program each year, in addition to the formal evaluation one, three, and five years post-APR.

Evaluate Assessment Reporting

Associating assessment reporting with our APR process caused units on our campus to take it more seriously, and our regular rubric evaluation of assessment reporting further emphasizes that reporting is an expected part of a unit's work. This evaluation allows us to provide comments to improve assessment reporting in each annual cycle.

Enlist Administrative Support

Compliance with annual assessment reporting improved once we enlisted the provost's help in sending letters of commendation or warning after we complete our evaluation each year. We also reached out to the provost when we faced resistance from a program, who claimed that, since their program was externally accredited, they should be exempt from UArizona's assessment reporting. The provost issued a clear statement that all degree programs were expected to report on their assessment of student learning in their Taskstream workspaces. At this point, we still have a few programs which are not reporting on their assessment efforts: 6% have not yet entered any information into their workspaces, and 37% did not report on their assessment work for the 2018–2019 and 2019–20 assessment cycles. We are exploring what budgetary consequences might support full compliance across campus.

Conclusion

Although it is unusual to have assessment work housed in a faculty development center in the USA, we find that our assessment expertise is a great complement to our faculty development work. We are able to build on the coaching relationship we have with the instructors who seek us out for their teaching-related concerns and extend conversations to include assessment, both at the course and the program level. Additionally, unlike many assessment professionals who work in institutional research offices, we have experience as faculty members and so can draw on our work teaching courses and doing learning outcomes assessment in degree programs. Our work has helped UArizona units to develop robust and sustainable assessment plans that have allowed them to investigate student learning in their programs and, where necessary, make changes to improve student learning.

References

Ambrose, S. A., Bridges, M. W., DiPietro, M., Lovett, M. C., & Norman, M. K. (2010). *How learning works: Seven research-based principles for smart teaching.* Jossey-Bass.

Biggs, J. (1996). Enhancing teaching through constructive alignment. *Higher Education, 32*(3), 347–364.

Biggs, J., & Tang, C. (2011). *Teaching for quality learning at university* (4th ed.). McGraw Hill.

Bransford, J. D., Brown, A. L., & Cocking, R. R. (Eds.). (2000). *How people learn: Bridging research and practice.* National Academy Press.

Brown, P. C., Roediger, H. L., III, & McDaniel, M. A. (2014). *Make it stick: The science of successful learning.* Belknap Press.

Dunlosky, J., Rawson, K. A., Marsh, E. J., Nathan, M. J., & Willingham, D. T. (2013). Improving students' learning with effective learning techniques: Promising directions from cognitive and educational psychology. *Psychological Science in the Public Interest, 14*(1), 4–58.

Lyman, F. T. (1981). The responsive classroom discussion: The inclusion of all students. In A. Anderson (Ed.), *Mainstreaming digest* (pp. 109–113). University of Maryland Press.

Margolis, J., & Fisher, A. (2002). *Unlocking the clubhouse: Women in computing.* MIT Press.

National Academies of Sciences, Engineering, and Medicine. (2018a). *Assessing and responding to the growth of computer science undergraduate enrollments.* National Academies Press.

National Academies of Sciences, Engineering, and Medicine. (2018b). *How people learn II: Learners, contexts, and cultures.* National Academies Press.

OIA. (n.d.). *Program-level learning outcomes assessment.* OIA, University of Arizona. https://oia.arizona.edu/content/573

Suskie, L. (2018). *Assessing student learning: A common sense guide* (3rd ed.). Jossey-Bass.

Walvoord, B. (2010). *Assessment clear and simple: A practical guide for institutions, departments, and general education* (2nd ed.). Jossey-Bass.

7

Implementing Academic Professional Development Strategies to Support Spiritual and Values-Based Engagement

Sandra Sgoutas-Emch

Introduction

The purpose of higher education in the USA has come into question by both the public and politicians alike (Giroux, 2010; Harvey, 2000; Ladd Jr. & Lipset, 1975). Debates on what institutions of higher education should spend their resources on has led to some disruption of the current system (Bérubé & Nelson, 1995; Caplan, 2018; Slaughter & Leslie, 1997). Obtaining a degree from a college or university once meant the search for meaning, knowledge, and purpose (DeWitz et al., 2009; Nash & Murray, 2009; Parks, 2000). However, a shift occurred in the 20th century that pushed universities to become more secular and abandon the distinctly religious character that most colleges and universities previously espoused (Gross & Simmons, 2009; Kimball, 1990; Hartley, 2004). The emphasis on moral philosophy and religious studies was replaced with a greater focus on disciplines that are seen as more lucrative in our society.

These changes were instigated in some part by the many pressures placed on universities and colleges to prove their value in terms of graduation rates and the employment of and starting salaries for their graduates (Kelderman, 2017). Therefore, there is less emphasis on what are often called the "soft

---

S. Sgoutas-Emch (✉)
University of San Diego, San Diego, CA, USA
e-mail: emch@sandiego.edu

© The Author(s), under exclusive license to Springer Nature Switzerland AG 2023
O. J. Neisler (ed.), *The Palgrave Handbook of Academic Professional Development Centers*,
Palgrave Studies on Leadership and Learning in Teacher Education,
https://doi.org/10.1007/978-3-030-80967-6_7

skills" in the classroom, exploration of deeper questions and a search for purpose (Gewirtz & Cribb, 2009; Star & Hammer, 2008). Yet, many believe that ignoring the exploration of one's spirituality overlooks a key path to helping individuals find meaning and purpose—elements that should be part of the mission of higher education (Lindholm, 2007).

The term "spirituality" can mean different things to different people. In a holistic sense, spirituality encompasses the search for meaning and purpose, including that which gives us a sense of something beyond or greater than the self (Gardner, 2017; McSherry & Cash, 2004; Senreich, 2013). A survey of faculty showed that the majority consider themselves "spiritual being[s]" (Lindholm, 2007; Lindholm & Astin, 2008, 2011). Additionally, developing a meaningful philosophy of life was rated as essential by two-thirds of the surveyed faculty; yet, opportunities for self-reflection and spiritual growth are not always available (Lindholm & Astin, 2011). More than two-thirds of the surveyed faculty stated they seek out opportunities to self-reflect and grow spiritually. However, faculty who are in tenure-track positions, for example, have greater pressures on them to focus on their scholarship, writing grants, publishing in top-tier journals, and developing content for their teaching, and may not have time for more spiritual endeavors (Rawat & Meena, 2014; Van Dalen & Henkens, 2012).

Supporting faculty spirituality and values has many benefits for both individuals and institutions at large. Academic excellence is most likely the primary core value of any institution of higher education. Brown (2003) suggests that helping support faculty in their own search for meaning may in turn help institutions because these faculty are more likely to employ "student-centered" teaching approaches. Academic professional development centers (ADCs) have long evolved from a teaching-centered ideology to a student-centered emphasis because of the overwhelming evidence that this type of approach better supports student learning (Connell et al., 2016; Dole et al., 2016). Findings from a study completed as part of Project Muse showed that faculty who stated that spirituality was integrated into their lives were more likely to utilize "student-centered" pedagogies (Lindholm & Astin, 2008). Furthermore, Lindholm and Astin (2008) discussed the important link between faculty values and beliefs and the values and beliefs of the institution in which they work. Because faculty generally play a large role in shaping the culture of their institution, the faculty also play a role in helping to change it. Therefore, it is imperative that institutions consider the various ways in which faculty spirituality can be supported in a meaningful and non-judgmental way.

Finally, and most importantly, research shows that more and more students are seeking the answer to life's bigger questions and that faculty need to be better prepared to address these issues in their classrooms (Bryant et al., 2003). Case in point: although religious affiliation may drop while students are in college, levels of spirituality increase (Astin et al., 2007). Providing training for faculty on how to teach meaning and purpose-building is key to supporting the spiritual journey of both faculty and students. Developing purpose, exploring values, and creating clear goals has been shown to have positive outcomes for students. For example, a study published on the relationship between "grit" (passion and perseverance for one's goals) and finding purpose and direction in one's life found that having purpose in life was seen as a catalyst to achieving one's goals (Hill et al., 2016).

This chapter will outline a variety of ways in which our ADC addresses the following questions: *What role does an ADC play in supporting the mission and values of our institution? How can we help support other entities on campus with the primary role to support the Catholic identity of the university and the values-based education we hope to provide? What is our role in supporting faculty's own spirituality and search for meaning and purpose?*

Structure and Context of the Center for Educational Excellence at the University of San Diego

The role of designers and facilitators of ADCs around the globe can vary from institution to institution based on a number of factors, including the size of the faculty, the classification of the college/university, and the mission of the institution. Although all institutions of higher education have mission statements and values around academic excellence, faith-based schools have specific statements that support the religious foundations of their institutions. These types of institutions view education as a holistic endeavor to support mind, body, and spirit. Moreover, another important factor that is unique to faith-based institutions is how ADCs support the mission and values of the college/university that align with a particular religious affiliation. These statements are important to the identity of faith-based colleges and universities and are oftentimes lost alongside the many messages faculty and students are exposed to while at their institutions. Most faith-based schools have strong university ministries and mission offices; however, the role of those offices may be limited and outside the influence of the academic side of the institution. Thus, ADCs can play an important role in advancing not only the religious identity of an institution but also the spiritual growth and support of the faculty, staff, and students by working in partnership with other mission-driven centers and offices (Astin & Astin, 2010; Braskamp, 2007; Lindholm, 2007).

The Center for Educational Excellence (CEE) is located at the University of San Diego (USD), a medium-sized, contemporary, independent Catholic liberal arts institution. The mission of our center is "to support the USD community by providing integrated programs, events, and resources to promote the institution's core values of academic excellence, knowledge, creating a diverse and inclusive community, ethical conduct, and compassionate service" (USD CEE, n.d.-a). We offer a variety of programs, trainings, and group and individual development opportunities primarily focused on teaching and learning, but in other areas of educational development. Organizationally, we are housed in the Office of the Provost and report to the associate provost for faculty research and development. We currently have a part-time director, two full-time staff, four work-study students, and four faculty liaisons who help bridge the outreach to the different schools and part-time faculty. Our mission, organization chart, and programs are available on our website (USD CEE, n.d.-a).

Reshaping the Mission

Although many centers on faith-based campuses support the religious mission of the university, one of the roles of the CEE has been to examine the faculty development needs that align with the activities and goals of these other centers. For example, our Mission and Ministry Office often focuses on the students and community outreach of the institution and is less likely to hone in on faculty training needs to help support religious or spiritual identity work. Other centers exist to supplement the work of mission and ministry, including the Center for Catholic Culture and Thought (CCTC). This unit has a mission that is "concerned with helping USD and its neighbors to explore, understand and celebrate everything it means to participate in a university community that calls itself Catholic in the 21st century" (USD CCTC, n.d.). The Center for Christian Spirituality (CCS) is another example of a center that supports the mission by emphasizing "both faith and reason and wishes to support all who seek to shape their lives in a manner consonant with their deepest values and meaning" (USD CCS, n.d.).

A gap identified in the programming of these centers was how to assist faculty to engage in conversations about what it means to be located at a Catholic institution and how faith plays a role in the faculty's own search for meaning and purpose from an academic perspective. Furthermore, a question we explore is what might we offer to help support faculty in their ability to incorporate discussions about spirituality and Catholic social teaching (CST) in their teaching? CST is based on seven principles that include: (1) dignity of the human person; (2) call to family, community, and participation; (3) rights and responsibilities; (4) option for the poor and vulnerable; (5) the dignity of work and the right of workers; (6) solidarity; and (7) care for God's creation (Byron, 1999). It is hoped that faculty on our campus will infuse CST into their curriculum to support our Catholic identity, but not all faculty are equipped to do so in their courses.

Although explorations of faith, meaning, and spirituality are valued outside the academic space, it is important to note that the initiatives described below did not come easily. Interestingly, although USD is a faith-based institution, the director of the CCS and I met with some resistance from upper administration to our initial engagement into this subject matter of spirituality in the academy. As we were developing the initial programs, there was concern that the scholarship in the field of spirituality studies was not at the level of rigor and acceptability for some scholars, particularly in the Theology and Religious Studies Departments. It was feared that these discussions might water down theological and religious studies' disciplinary modes of inquiry. Apprehension also emerged as many faculty members felt ill-equipped to discuss spiritual matters in class or did not believe that it was the faculty's role to support this component of student development.

To strategically address the apprehension and build support, the CEE worked with the CCS and CCTC units on campus to design a series of discussions with world-renown scholars in the field of spirituality and the academy. Faculty, students, and staff were invited to a variety of discussions including dinners, breakfasts, and debates on the role of spirituality in the academy, as described in the next section of this chapter.

Methods and Implementation of the New Mission

Using a variety of methods to support faculty's spiritual growth, our development center has played a key role in supporting a number of diverse initiatives. Descriptions of some of the initiatives are provided in this section of the chapter.

Panels and Workshops

One of the first development opportunities the CEE offered on the topic of spirituality in the academy focused on the exploration of faculty spirituality in collaboration with the CCS. We wanted to ease into the topic by first gauging the extent of interest of the faculty. Over a two-year period, we organized panels, guest speakers, and discussions about the role of spirituality in the academy. We held a dinner discussion with a panel of faculty from different disciplinary backgrounds with the purpose of discussing the role that spirituality played in their lives and their teaching. The dinner was well attended, and there was so much interest in the topic that we followed up with a full-day workshop that included pedagogical and scholarship discussions. Renowned scholars in Christian spirituality such as Mary Frolich of the Catholic Theological Union, Douglas Burton-Christie of Loyola Marymount University, and Anita Houck of Saint Mary's College were invited to facilitate the workshop.

The workshop addressed methodology, the interdisciplinary nature of spirituality, teaching spirituality, and assessment of student learning around spirituality. Faculty delved into their own practice and how they could implement discussions to support student exploration of their own spirituality and either create new courses or modify current courses. The workshop was well received and led to the creation of more faculty development opportunities. At other events, scholars presented their research, talked about assessment of student learning outcomes, or facilitated discussions of various books such as Delio's *Christ in Evolution* (2008).

Similarly, the CEE worked closely with the CCTC to host panel discussions on important issues related to Catholic social justice (CSJ). Full-day workshops were offered yearly to help support faculty implementation of CSJ in their classrooms. Faculty were offered stipends of $250 to modify their syllabi and $750 if they modified their courses and completed assessment of student learning. These funds came from both the budget of the CCTC and the CEE. Additionally, the workshops helped support the implementation of the newly revised core curriculum in which CSJ was a central feature. Because USD is a Catholic university, a core curriculum that emphasizes theology, religious studies, ethics, and the liberal arts is paramount. All of these development opportunities for faculty laid the groundwork for the addition of a flagged competency of diversity, inclusion, and social justice in which the tenets of CSJ are highlighted. Because diversity, inclusion and equity are central to the mission of the university, these types of trainings are routine elements of faculty development.

7 Implementing Academic Professional Development Strategies...   115

Furthermore, our panel discussions in collaboration with the CCTC have provided venues for deep contemplation while addressing key, and sometimes controversial, issues that may impact one's faith. Topics such as the sexual abuse crisis in the Church, why women are not priests, the presidential election, the Black Lives Matter movement, nonviolence and peace, and the Pope's views on the environment have been explored by faculty, staff, and students. Because the topics can be upsetting to some, either because they are victims (such as the sexual assault talks) or because they are firm believers in the Church (because of the sometimes-critical nature of the discussions), the discussions are led by scholars in the field and include individuals with a diversity of thought on the matters discussed. It is amazing to see the depth of reflection that comes out of these thoughtful explorations.

An example of one of these panels that eventually helped stimulate curricular development was when we held a discussion on the Catholic Church and the LGBTQ+ community. Issues around homosexuality continued to be challenging conversations at a Catholic institution and addressing sexuality as a diversity and social justice issue can be complicated. In our case, the LBGTQ+ student population felt that they were being marginalized and held to a different standard; they specifically cited the lack of courses that represented their community's issues as problematic. Through these panel discussions, we were able to educate the attendees about CSJ and debate the interpretations of the Church on this topic. This inspired a group of faculty to request a learning community (the definition of which will be described later in this chapter) that would help facilitate the creation of a LGBTQ+ curriculum.

Common Book Read

In order to support the CSJ mission of the university, a common read program aptly entitled "USD Just Read!" was created and has been facilitated by the CEE for the past 10 years. A yearly CSJ theme is chosen, and a book is selected to match the theme. Events, course development trainings, and book discussions are scheduled throughout the year. Speakers present the Catholic Church's perspective and highlight the social justice themes in the text during the Just Read program. A key goal of Just Read is to help support the higher calling of education and engages the entire university and surrounding community in discussions of the challenges facing our society today. This inclusive program invites everyone to participate and have meaningful and thoughtful discussions that align with CSJ. Some of the previous books include *The Immortal Life of Henrietta Lacks* (Skloot, 2010) where ethical questions related

116 S. Sgoutas-Emch

to the ownership of one's body and patients' rights were examined. Another text entitled *Silent Spring* (Carson, 1962) prompted conversations on the Pope's writings on the environment and questions regarding how we are being good shepherds of this earth. This year's selection, *$2.00 a Day: Living on Almost Nothing in America* (Edin & Shaefer, 2015), focuses on poverty and the ethical and moral obligations of society to the poor around the world. Participating in these larger-question conversations has helped to support the campus community in their own path to meaning and purpose.

Faculty and Professional Learning Communities

A key tool which we use to support faculty spirituality and meaning-making is faculty and professional learning communities. The purpose of these communities is to give time and space to faculty and staff who apply to explore various topics over the course of an academic year. The communities meet once a month for two hours during an entire academic year and can range from six to 12 members. Members can come from any discipline or area on campus. The schedule gives faculty more time to engage in contemplation and deep thought about the topic at hand. Studies have shown that faculty learning communities (FLCs) are useful in engaging faculty and supporting faculty success (Cox, 2001, 2003; Furco & Moely, 2012). Over the years, the CEE has sponsored a number of learning communities that address themes of spirituality and values-based education. In fact, the very first learning community our center supported was cosponsored by the CCS and was entitled "Spirituality in the Academy." The call for the community stated:

> On the USD campus, a rich and diverse range of spiritualties and spiritual traditions are present among our students and employees. USD's newly instituted Living-Learning Community model includes a "Divine Living-Learning Community" which is designed for students to "investigate questions of ultimate meaning while growing in their own faith." In teaching and mentoring undergraduate students, the work of professors and staff may beckon for a way to intersect spirituality in an academic way. (USD CEE, n.d.-b)

This community of faculty and staff met for two years (the community requested an extension from the normal one year) and developed courses, workshops, and research projects. The community ultimately decided to change the name to "Contemplative Practices in Higher Education" to embrace the diversity of thought and religious/spiritual backgrounds. In fact, many of the faculty who participated continued their work by consulting with national organizations such as the Center for Contemplative Mind in Society to design programs and trainings at a national level.

Currently, in collaboration with University Ministry, the CEE is facilitating an FLC entitled "The Search for What Matters: Exploring Vocation in Our Contemporary World." The description of the community is as follows:

> As a Catholic university committed to educating students in the liberal arts, we have both a unique opportunity and a deep responsibility to create a robust mentoring environment where our students may productively engage questions of meaning and purpose, justice and solidarity. The troubling trend of higher education being viewed as a commodity or in instrumental, utilitarian terms, should increase our urgency to create a more personally engaging and transformative learning experience. This faculty learning community will consider the potential of vocational exploration (i.e., discerning and following authentic callings in life) as a particularly promising practice of creating a more effective mentoring environment for our students in their search for benevolent purpose in a complex, interdependent world characterized by both inequality and polarization. As a point of departure, we will refer to the description of vocation offered by Frederick Buechner: "The place God calls you to is the place where your deep gladness and the world's deep hunger meet" (Buechner, 1973, 119). (USD CEE, n.d.-b)

The goals of the FLC range from reading and discussing relevant literature on the purpose of higher education, the current and emerging pressures on liberal arts and Catholic institutions, vocational discernment and global solidarity, to exploring the range of courses and campus programs that currently address these issues, developing training to assist faculty in the implementation of vocation in their courses, and encouraging individual and collaborative research projects for both faculty and students.

Conclusions and Recommendations

Increased skepticism of the role of higher education in today's society contrasts with the desire of faculty and students to search for meaning and purpose in their lives. Furthermore, studies show that faculty who identify as spiritual and having a sense of purpose are more likely to implement pedagogies that engage students and address purpose meaning in their courses. Thus, universities need to identify ways to support faculty development that builds faculty's own sense of purpose and meaning as well as spiritual exploration.

118   S. Sgoutas-Emch

This chapter has provided some examples of types of programming that can help faculty in their own search for connection and meaning. ADCs are often focused on very traditional topics, especially around teaching and learning. However, with students wanting more guidance and thoughtful reflection, and faculty seeking ways explore their own spiritual paths, ADCs need to add more opportunities for faculty to seek meaning and purpose to help push our institutions back to the foundations on which higher education was built. In the end, faculty who feel connected with their purpose and their institutions are more likely to help their students find those same connections.

Centers that are looking to expand or change their mission to include values-based education and spiritual exploration should reach out to other units on campus that hold similar missions. An examination of potential collaborations that can help bridge the gaps in development opportunities for faculty that are more academically framed can help to support the institution overall and should be investigated. I would also recommend starting small and testing the waters to see what interest exists and where this interest is located. One may assume that faculty in Theology and Religious Studies Departments would be a natural fit, but this may not be the case. We had faculty from Physics, Nursing, Education, Leadership Studies, and Ethnic Studies, among others, who are still the change agents on our campus for promoting inquiry into meaning, ethics, and value-based and spiritual discovery. It is wise to gather change agents whom other faculty respect to lead the charge, so the push for more exploration is not seen as top-down, but more grassroots. Finally, try different modalities in delivering content that may appeal to a wider variety of faculty. We implemented small cohort exploration via learning communities but also supported larger, institution-wide discussions. For a more successful approach, meet resistance with a strategic plan and vocal advocates to support the change of direction.

References

Astin, A. W., & Astin, H. S. (2010). Exploring and nurturing the spiritual life of college students. *Journal of College and Character, 11*(3).

Astin, A. W., Astin, H. S., & Lindholm, J. A. (2007). *A national study of spirituality in higher education: Students search for meaning and purpose.* Higher Education Research Institute, University of California–Los Angeles.

Bérubé, M., & Nelson, C. (Eds.). (1995). *Higher education under fire: Politics, economics, and the crisis of the humanities.* Psychology Press.

Braskamp, L. A. (2007). *Fostering religious and spiritual development of students during college.* Social Science Research Council. http://religion.ssrc.org/reforum/Braskamp.pdf

Brown, K. L. (2003). From teacher-centered to learner-centered curriculum: Improving learning in diverse classrooms. *Education, 124*(1), 49–54.

Bryant, A. N., Choi, J. Y., & Yasuno, M. (2003). Understanding the religious and spiritual dimensions of students' lives in the first year of college. *Journal of College Student Development, 44*(6), 723–745.

Buechner, F. (1973). *Wishful thinking: A theological ABC.* Harper.

Byron, W. J. (1999). Framing the principles of Catholic social thought. *Catholic Education: A Journal of Inquiry and Practice, 3*(1), 7–14.

Caplan, B. D. (2018). *The case against education: Why the education system is a waste of time and money.* Princeton University Press.

Carson, R. (1962). *Silent Spring.* Houghton Mifflin.

Connell, G. L., Donovan, D. A., & Chambers, T. G. (2016). Increasing the use of student-centered pedagogies from moderate to high improves student learning and attitudes about biology. *CBE—Life Sciences Education, 15*(1), ar3.

Cox, M. D. (2001). Faculty learning communities: Change agents for transforming institutions into learning organizations. *To Improve the Academy, 19*(1), 69–93.

Cox, M. D. (2003). Fostering the scholarship of teaching and learning through faculty learning communities. *Journal on Excellence in College Teaching, 14*(2/3), 161–198.

Delio, I. (2008). *Christ in evolution.* Orbis Books.

DeWitz, S. J., Woolsey, M. L., & Walsh, W. B. (2009). College student retention: An exploration of the relationship between self-efficacy beliefs and purpose in life among college students. *Journal of College Student Development, 50*(1), 19–34.

Dole, S., Bloom, L., & Kowalske, K. (2016). Transforming pedagogy: Changing perspectives from teacher-centered to learner-centered. *Interdisciplinary Journal of Problem-Based Learning, 10*(1).

Edin, K., & Shaefer, H. L. (2015). *$2.00 a day: Living on almost nothing in America.* Houghton Mifflin Harcourt.

Furco, A., & Moely, B. E. (2012). Using learning communities to build faculty support for pedagogical innovation: A multi-campus study. *Journal of Higher Education, 83*(1), 128–153.

Gardner, F. (2017). *Critical spirituality: A holistic approach to contemporary practice.* Routledge.

Gewirtz, S., & Cribb, A. (2009). Understanding education: A sociological perspective. *Polity.*

Giroux, H. A. (2010). Bare pedagogy and the scourge of neoliberalism: Rethinking public education as a democratic sphere. *The Educational Form, 74*(3), 184–196.

Gross, N., & Simmons, S. (2009). The religiosity of American college and university professors. *Sociology of Religion, 70*(2), 101–129.

Hartley, H. V., III. (2004). How college affects students' religious faith and practice: A review of research. *College Student Affairs Journal, 23*(2), 111–129.

Harvey, L. (2000). New realities: The relationship between higher education and employment. *Tertiary Education & Management, 6*(1), 3–17.

Hill, P. L., Burrow, A. L., & Bronk, K. C. (2016). Persevering with positivity and purpose: An examination of purpose commitment and positive affect as predictors of grit. *Journal of Happiness Studies, 17*(1), 257–269.

Kelderman, E. (2017, June 22). Colleges face more pressure on student outcomes, but success isn't always easy to measure. *The Chronicle of Higher Education.* https://www.chronicle.com/article/Colleges-Face-More-Pressure-on/240422

Kimball, R. (1990). *Tenured radicals: How politics has corrupted our higher education.* Harper and Row.

Ladd, E. C., Jr., & Lipset, S. M. (1975). *The divided academy: Professors and politics.* McGraw-Hill.

Lindholm, J. A. (2007). Spirituality in the academy: Reintegrating our lives and the lives of our students. *About Campus, 12*(4), 10–17.

Lindholm, J. A., & Astin, H. S. (2008). Spirituality and pedagogy: Faculty's spirituality and use of student-centered approaches to undergraduate teaching. *Review of Higher Education, 31*(2), 185–207.

Lindholm, J. A., & Astin, H. S. (2011). Understanding the "interior" life of faculty: How important is spirituality? In M. D. Waggoner (Ed.), *Sacred and secular tensions in higher education: Connecting parallel universities* (pp. 63–85). Routledge.

McSherry, W., & Cash, K. (2004). The language of spirituality: An emerging taxonomy. *International Journal of Nursing Studies, 41*(2), 151–161.

Nash, R. J., & Murray, M. C. (2009). *Helping college students find purpose: The campus guide to meaning-making.* John Wiley and Sons.

Parks, S. D. (2000). *Big questions, worthy dreams: Mentoring young adults in their search for meaning, purpose, and faith.* Jossey-Bass.

Rawat, S., & Meena, S. (2014). Publish or perish: Where are we heading? *Journal of Research in Medical Sciences, 19*(2), 87–89.

Senreich, E. (2013). An inclusive definition of spirituality for social work education and practice. *Journal of Social Work Education, 49*(4), 548–563.

Skloot, R. (2010). *The immortal life of Henrietta lacks.* Crown Publishers.

Slaughter, S., & Leslie, L. L. (1997). *Academic capitalism: Politics, policies, and the entrepreneurial university.* Johns Hopkins University Press.

Star, C., & Hammer, S. (2008). Teaching generic skills: Eroding the purpose of higher education or an opportunity for renewal? *Oxford Review of Education, 34*(2), 237–251.

University of San Diego (USD) Center for Catholic Thought and Culture (CCTC). (n.d.). *Home page.* USD. https://www.sandiego.edu/cctc/

University of San Diego (USD) Center for Christian Spirituality (CCS). (n.d.). *Home page.* University of San Diego. https://www.sandiego.edu/ccs/

University of San Diego (USD) Center for Educational Excellence (CEE). (n.d.-a). *Home page.* University of San Diego. https://www.sandiego.edu/cee/

University of San Diego (USD) Center for Educational Excellence (CEE). (n.d.-b). *Learning communities*. USD. https://www.sandiego.edu/cee/programs/learning-communities.php

Van Dalen, H. P., & Henkens, K. (2012). Intended and unintended consequences of a publish-or- perish culture: A worldwide survey. *Journal of the American Society for Information Science and Technology, 63*(7), 1282–1293.

8

Needs Analysis Leads to Sustainability: Development of a Medical Education and Informatics Department in the College of Medicine and Health Sciences, Sultan Qaboos University

Nadia Mohammed Al Wardy and Rashid Al Abri

Introduction

Most medical schools around the world have well-established academic professional development centers (ADCs), referred to by different names. The development of such centers usually arises in response to certain needs, ranging from curriculum reform and the need for faculty training to accreditation requirements. The functions of these centers include teaching, research, and other educational support services, and they cater to a variety of audiences. Many of these centers first started as administrative units under their respective dean's offices, but then slowly evolved into independent academic units or departments. They tend to be operated by staff who come from different professional backgrounds, including the medical and educational fields, and have other part or full-time commitments (Davis et al., 2005). Overall, the establishment of these ADCs have had positive effects on their respective medical schools and support the continued development of medical education as a discipline (Al Wardy, 2008).

N. M. Al Wardy (✉) • R. Al Abri
Sultan Qaboos University, Muscat, Oman
e-mail: naiwardi@squ.edu.om; rabri@squ.edu.om

© The Author(s), under exclusive license to Springer Nature Switzerland AG 2023
O. J. Neisler (ed.), *The Palgrave Handbook of Academic Professional Development Centers*,
Palgrave Studies on Leadership and Learning in Teacher Education,
https://doi.org/10.1007/978-3-030-80967-6_8

This chapter will describe the steps taken to develop a Medical Education and Informatics Department (MEID) in the College of Medicine and Health Sciences (CMHS), Sultan Qaboos University (SQU) in Muscat, Oman. We will share our learning and development process, how we gathered information and resources to develop a model, our mission and objectives, and how we pulled together existing resources under the umbrella of a single unit which subsequently evolved into a department. We will also share the challenges and limitations of this model and end with recommendations.

History

The College of Medicine was first established in 1986 as one of the seven colleges of SQU (Hamdy et al., 2010). Subsequently, the scope of the college was expanded to include allied health science programs such as Biomedical Science (BMS) and Nursing; hence, the college was renamed in 2002 to 'College of Medicine and Health Sciences'. The SQU Hospital (SQUH) was established as the main teaching hospital to complement the college in its educational program. However, there are four other hospitals which share in the teaching with their affiliated clinical faculty. The number of staff and students has grown since the establishment of the CMHS. Currently, there are 83 academics (of whom 33 are clinician academics) and 329 affiliated clinical teachers. The annual intake of students is 170 in both the medical degree (MD) and BMS programs. The college also participates in clinical postgraduate training. The administrative structure of the CMHS consists of 19 departments which are discipline-based, a medical library, four assistant deans, and a director of administration.

The MEID was established initially as a *Medical Education Unit* (MEU) in 2006 under the Dean's Office of the CMHS. Its mission was to raise the standards of medical education in the college through various activities, including research, teaching, and providing educational support in the areas of curriculum development, assessment, mentoring, student counseling, methods of teaching and learning, and information technology (IT). In 2013, the unit was renamed the *Medical Education and Informatics Unit* (MEIU) to give recognition to medical informatics, which was a major section in the unit in terms of its technical staff and contribution to teaching in the new curriculum.

The MEIU had one full-time academic faculty and a few technical staff, but its activities depended mainly on the voluntary contribution of interested faculty and professionals from different departments of the CMHS, SQUH, and the Ministry of Health in Oman. The MEIU was headed on a part-time basis by the head of the unit who had a formal qualification in medical education in addition to a higher qualification in her own discipline. In 2009, the MEIU took on the responsibility of restructuring the existing Clinical Skills Laboratory, which then came under its administration, and, in 2013, a student counseling section was added to the unit. The MEIU functioned much like an academic department, but was facing several challenges and limitations due to its administrative status as a unit. Hence, in 2018, its status was changed to that of an official department.

Factors Leading to the Development of an MEU

Several factors led to the development of the MEU, including the need for faculty development, curriculum reform, the need to recognize core faculty, providing a home for dispersed college activities, and the global trend toward the development of MEUs.

Need for Faculty Development

Since its establishment, the CMHS has aspired to meet international standards of medical education. In 2000, the college recognized the need for curriculum reform and initiated several steps toward achieving this goal, one of which was holding its first international conference in medical education in 2002. Following the success of this conference, faculty development in medical education formally began. Around this time, developments in regional medical schools toward medical education were also taking place.

The Deans' Platform for Colleges of Medicine in the Gulf Cooperation Council (GCC)—of which the CMHS was a founding member—recognized the need for faculty development and established a short course in health professions education that covered key concepts in medical education and which was to be conducted in each GCC country on a regular basis. This course ran alongside the medical education conference as a three-day 'Train the Trainer' course and subsequently continued to be offered at the CMHS on a regular basis. The course was conducted mainly by inviting external experts in medical education. Both CMHS and SQUH faculty and other faculty anticipating affiliation were required to attend this course and be certified in health professions education.

Curriculum Reform and Increased Local Demand

The newly designed medical curriculum, with its emphasis on outcome-based education, integration of basic and clinical sciences, and early clinical exposure, required intensive and continuous faculty development. A needs assessment survey conducted just before the implementation of the new curriculum demonstrated the requirement for specialized workshops that enhanced the skills of faculty in areas of assessment, course and curriculum design, teaching and learning, e-learning, and research in medical education. With the implementation of the new curriculum, the need for faculty development became even more apparent.

Need to Recognize Core Faculty

Responsibility for the organization of the regular Train the Trainer course, and the delivery of faculty development courses, was given to a group of faculty members who had either obtained a formal qualification or had a strong interest in medical education. They were all affiliated with different departments. Through participation in the facilitation of this course, the group developed expertise and became the core group for faculty development initiatives in the college. They continued to teach and develop new courses, although this occurred on a voluntary basis with 'borrowed' time. Due recognition was needed for this faculty.

Finding a 'Home' for the Homeless

Several dispersed activities existed in the CMHS which did not come under the administration of any department. Such activities naturally fell under the MEIU, such as IT support, the Clinical Skills Laboratory, and the International Databases for Enhanced Assessments and Learning (IDEAL) Consortium databank (IDEAL Consortium, n.d.). An MEU was envisioned to provide a home for these activities. There was also an administrative need to provide a 'home' for staff returning to the CMHS with a medical education qualification.

Global Trend Toward MEUs as Standard Practice

At the time, many medical schools around the world were already responding to the need for curriculum reform by setting up their own MEUs and conducting faculty development programs for their teachers through in-house, regional, and international programs (Christopher et al., 2002). MEUs were also being established to provide support for teaching audits and appraisal activities demanded by accreditation and quality assurance bodies. In fact, certain accrediting bodies listed the existence of an MEU as a criterion for accrediting new medical schools (Davis et al., 2005).

Benchmarking Survey

In order to study the feasibility of establishing an MEU and learn from regional experience, a needs assessment survey was sent to other GCC universities (including Saudi Arabia, Kuwait, Bahrain, and the United Arab Emirates) to collect information regarding the establishment, structure, and role of medical education departments, units, or centers in their medical schools. The results of this survey showed that 10 out of 13 medical schools had such units (unpublished data). Of these, only two units operated independently, with the rest falling under the offices of their respective deans, or under another department in the college, although they aspired to become independent entities. The scope of their activities ranged from serving medical faculty only to all other health professions such as Dentistry, Pharmacy, Medical Technology, and Nursing. The duties of these MEUs included some or all of the following: faculty development; curriculum development; curriculum auditing, assessment and examinations; supervising preclinical and clinical training; continuing medical education; postgraduate residency training; teaching masters students; student selection; student advising; research in medical education; and IT services. This information informed our proposed structure, staffing model, and mission for establishing an MEU at the CMHS, SQU.

Organizational Reporting and Structure

Fig. 8.1 shows the current organizational structure of the MEID. This structure has gone through several developmental phases to become what it is now, as detailed below.

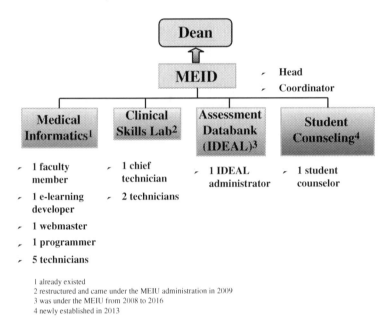

Fig. 8.1 Administrative structure and staffing of the MEID

Initial Structure

Due to the lack of full-time faculty in medical education, our ADC was 'kick-started' by being established as an MEU under the Dean's Office in 2006. This was in anticipation that it would become an independent department as it acquired full-time academic staff. A faculty member—one with a formal qualification in medical education in addition to a higher qualification in her own discipline—who had played a pivotal role in the establishment of the MEU was appointed as the head of the unit on part-time basis, reporting directly to the dean.

A core group of individuals assisted the MEU in its activities on a voluntary, but very committed, basis. This faculty had either a formal qualification or a strong interest in the field of medical education and served on critical college committees such as the Curriculum and Examination Committees. The MEU also drew on the voluntary participation of interested staff from the Ministry of Health. Only the IT staff were full-time.

Medical Informatics

An already-existing medical informatics group which had no administrative 'home' came under the administration of the MEU. It had two divisions:

technical and academic. The technical division was operated by several IT technical staff who dealt with IT troubleshooting, systems, and programming, and assisted in the technical aspects of teaching. The academic division had one faculty member who was responsible for teaching core courses in medical informatics to MD and BMS students.

The medical informatics group also provided consultations to staff regarding the application of medical informatics and the implementation of e-learning and e-assessment modalities, with the aim of strengthening the integration of medical informatics technologies in teaching, research, and service. In order to assist in the many activities of the group, a full-time assistant professor in medical informatics was recruited to the unit in 2009. Seeing as this group formed a major section in the unit, the MEU was subsequently renamed to the MEIU in 2013 to give recognition to the role played by the medical informatics group and their contribution to teaching in the new curriculum.

IDEAL Consortium

The CMHS had recently become a member of the IDEAL Consortium, an international collaboration of medical faculties which share a high-quality, voluminous assessment bank for medical education. Since one of the MEIU's objectives was to work toward implementing best practice and evidence-based assessment methods in the college, it was thought appropriate that the administration of the IDEAL databank should fall under the MEIU. An IDEAL Office was established in the college and an administrator recruited in 2008. The IDEAL Office housed the question bank and was responsible for dealings with the consortium, conducting relevant workshops, and providing item analysis services for all examinations in the CMHS. In 2016, however, these responsibilities were moved to the college's Examinations Office, an independent office that dealt with all aspects related to examination coordination in the CMHS. While both the Examinations and IDEAL Offices dealt with examinations and had to work very closely together, having different lines of administration was not conducive to their shared activities and the IDEAL Office was therefore moved under the Examinations Office.

Clinical Skills Laboratory

In 2009, the MEU took on the responsibility of restructuring the Clinical Skills Laboratory, an educational facility that existed under the Dean's Office and had one technical staff member. The laboratory then came under the administration of the unit, and a full-time chief technician and another technician were recruited in 2010. Since then, the laboratory has evolved into a learning environment that supports a wide range of skills across the curriculum and has hosted several national and international workshops. It provides medical students with the opportunity to develop and maintain competence in clinical skills, and allows them to practice physical assessment and procedural skills safely, and to demonstrate these skills under simulated conditions prior to attempting them on a patient. It has been equipped with a variety of instruments, simulators, and manikins to facilitate the training and assessment of students on clinical skills at different levels. In the last two years, the laboratory has been equipped with different high-fidelity simulators (such as the Victoria high-fidelity simulator) in order to enhance the training of medical students on sophisticated medical procedures.

Student Counseling

Although student academic advising services existed under the assistant deans, there was no student counselor role in the college. Assisting students in their adjustment to the university environment was carried out by the university student counseling center. The CMHS, however, thought it was necessary to have such a role 'in-house' for ease of access by the students and for their follow-up. Internationally, this role was being carried out by MEUs; therefore, having this service under the MEIU was thought appropriate. In 2013, the MD program was accredited by the Association for Medical Education in the Eastern Mediterranean Region (AMEEMR), in association and accordance with the standards of the World Federation for Medical Education (WFME) (SQU Quality Assurance Office, n.d.).

The report of the accreditation panel strengthened the position of the MEIU to appoint a student counselor in the same year, and a new section of student counseling was added to the unit. Now, this section assists the college administration in advising students on various issues—academic, personal, and social—and in adapting to university life. It is involved in teaching life skills to students and in conducting workshops on academic advising to faculty members.

Mission and Objectives of the MEIU

The MEIU was established with a mission to raise the standards of medical education in the college by providing educational services to support, evaluate, and enhance the educational role of the college. Its activities were to include teaching, research, and providing educational support in the areas of curriculum development, assessment, mentoring, student counseling, methods of teaching and learning, and IT. While adequate resources were not immediately available to support all of the listed objectives, it was thought important to develop an ideal plan to work toward this goal in stages. Areas in which expertise was available commenced first, while others were postponed and filed as long-term objectives until expertise became available. Some of these areas already existed and now fell under the MEIU.

Stage I

Stage I was effective immediately and included the following:

* Identifying the needs of faculty in the areas of teaching and learning and responding to those needs by conducting short courses, seminars, and workshops
* Alerting faculty about important issues in medical education, and facilitating access to external expertise in medical education
* Informing faculty about the MEIU's role and activities and promoting the availability of its services through the circulation of a medical education newsletter
* Working with the college's Examination Committee to standardize the assessment process
* Acting as a link with the IDEAL Consortium for sharing assessment banks
* Advising the college on updating educational facilities
* Collaborating with the university's Center of Educational Technology in studying the need for appropriate computing and communication equipment within CMHS and SQUH teaching sites
* Introducing staff to and educating them regarding the latest trends in educational technology
* Supporting the development of a web-based teaching and learning environment within the college, and providing the necessary support to faculty in running online examinations
* Teaching introductory courses in medical informatics to students
* Providing specialist advice and consultations on assessment, application of medical informatics, and the implementations of e-learning.

Stage II

It was anticipated that, as the unit grew and full-time expertise in each area became available, our objectives would expand to include the following:

- Providing award-bearing programs at the master's and doctoral levels
- Conducting and supporting research in medical education
- Participating in curriculum management and evaluation
- Developing and maintaining a databank of exam questions that had undergone validity and reliability tests
- Providing advice and short courses on study skills to students
- Enhancing the development of a sound student advising and counseling system in the college
- Taking responsibility for the running and maintenance of the Clinical Skills Laboratory
- Providing resource facility for training a cadre of simulated patients
- Designing telemedicine conferences and workshops
- Evaluating the effectiveness of different medical e-learning media
- Studying the feasibility of using virtual reality technologies in clinical training.

Activities and Programs of the MEIU

The MEIU has been very active in providing faculty development workshops to the CMHS, SQUH, affiliated staff, and other health professionals, particularly in the areas of teaching and learning, assessment, and e-learning. Mandatory courses such as the Certificate Course in Health Professions Education (CHPE) and Student Assessment Workshop (SAW) have been offered on a yearly basis. The CHPE covers several competency areas such as planning an educational activity, implementing the planned activity, and evaluating whether learning has taken place from the planned activity; in turn, the SAW focuses on areas specific to designing and conducting student assessment and examinations. More than 800 staff members (including faculty, clinicians, and other health professionals) have been certified through the CHPE and around 350 through the SAW. Several other workshops have been offered by the unit—by either invited experts in medical education or local faculty—in topics such as principles of curriculum and assessment design, evaluation, teaching, and assessment methodologies, instructional design for online courses, using the IDEAL databank, and data analysis using statistical programs.

The MEIU also initiated a lecture series to alert staff faculty to contemporary issues in medical education, as well as to act as refreshers for certain aspects that needed consolidation by the faculty. The unit's expertise has been sought both within and outside SQU, and several lectures and workshops have been delivered in this regard.

Impact of the MEIU

Self-reported and follow-up data from participants of the faculty development activities have shown their satisfaction and indicated that these activities helped them in their responsibilities as teachers. A substantial number reported changes in their teaching behavior. Participants reported they reviewed and changed their teaching objectives, wrote new teaching objectives, introduced changes to their teaching methodologies, reviewed and constructed new questions, and took steps to evaluate their teaching.

The faculty development courses built the expertise of the core group of faculty who were assigned to organize and coordinate these courses and assist the MEIU in its activities. Most of the faculty development courses were conducted by invited international faculty in medical education. The core group attended all these courses and helped in their teaching by, for example, facilitating small group activities. Eventually, this group of 'local experts' expanded and became trained to the level where they were able to replace the international faculty in the regular courses.

Although difficult to assess directly, several CMHS outcomes can be attributed, in part, to the faulty development program conducted by the MEIU. In 2013, the MD program was fully accredited by the AMEEMR in cooperation with the WFME for a period of 10 years; moreover, in 2014, the BMS program was accredited by the Institute of Biomedical Science, London, UK (SQU Quality Assurance Office, n.d.). The CMHS also received the Sheikh Hamdan Bin Rashid Al Maktoum Award for Medical Sciences in 2014 (Sheikh Hamdan Bin Rashid Al Maktoum Award for Medical Sciences, n.d.). Furthermore, CMHS faculty output in terms of medical education publications has increased.

Strategic Change: From a Unit to a Department

As a unit, the MEIU was able to provide diversified activities in the areas of teaching and learning, research, community, and administrative services, and functioned much like an academic department in its own right. However, it was facing several important challenges and limitations due to its administrative status as a unit. These included, for example, difficulties in registering the undergraduate courses offered by the unit, the inability to offer postgraduate courses, and logistic administrative issues in processing appointments and promotions for its academic staff. Despite its academic functions, the MEIU was not represented on the College Board, the supreme governing body of the college which consists mainly of heads of departments.

Hence, in 2018, the unit was upgraded to a department, the main objective of which was to overcome these aforementioned challenges. It is anticipated that the department will act to improve the standing of CMHS and SQU, both regionally as well as internationally, and will be able to attract academic staff from other academic departments in the college and senior clinicians from SQUH to contribute to its function. The department would continue to support collaboration among teaching faculty and support continuous professional development activities. In addition to other ongoing faculty development activities, it would foster concentrated faculty development for CMHS, SQUH, and affiliated faculty, with the expectation that they will then share their expertise through modeling.

Discussion

Since its inception, the MEIU, now the MEID, has been effective in fulfilling its stated mission. Many of the listed objectives have been implemented, while others are in progress. The department has brought together several dispersed educational activities in the CMHS and provided them with a 'home' and a proper line of administration. It has also gathered a group of committed faculty that have benefited both themselves and others though the faculty development program conducted by the department. In addition, the faculty development program has contributed profoundly to curriculum and assessment development in the college. Examples include the development of course and curriculum objectives, the introduction of team-based learning as a new strategy of teaching and learning in some courses, new assessment methodologies, and quality assurance of the assessment process in the college which, in part, resulted in the full accreditation of the MD and BMS programs.

Nevertheless, despite all these achievements, it was becoming increasingly obvious that sustainability could not be expected from the unit with its current level of, almost entirely absent, full-time academic staffing. The previous head of the unit, current head of department, and academic faculty were all (but one) affiliated and had full-time positions in their 'mother' departments.

It was therefore important to examine other strategies if the unit was to achieve its stated goals. Among the first steps needed was to change the administrative structure from a unit to a department, which would enable a critical mass of full-time academic staff. This change was also intended to facilitate the creation of adjunct or part-time faculty roles and make joint appointments to the department more attractive.

Although the change of status to a department has been successful, the recruitment of full-time academic staff has not occurred due to financial constraints. Augmenting the current staff by joint appointments or recruiting adjunct/part-time faculty from other departments might be more promising since there is already a number of faculty from other departments who are either qualified or have a strong interest in medical education. Such an appointment would facilitate their contribution to the MEID as well as allow them to act as a link with their 'mother' departments and get the necessary 'buy-in' from their colleagues in MEID activities. Furthermore, it will allow such adjunct/part-time faculty to become change agents in their own departments and advocates for the MEID.

The pool of faculty that have qualifications in medical education in the college can be increased by enabling existing staff to pursue a higher qualification in medical education and awarding scholarships to young faculty interested in pursuing specializations in medical education. Another important outcome of joint appointments to the MEID would be the long-awaited recognition and formalization of the role of the core group of faculty who undertook the responsibility of training teachers and conducting faculty development workshops in their 'borrowed' time. Once a critical mass of faculty is established, future plans for the department would include initiating a simulated patient program, establishing research links with international groups, and offering sustainable and award-bearing faculty development programs such as certificates, diplomas, master's degrees, and eventually doctorates.

Recommendations

The following points should be considered when establishing an ADC.

Have a Clear Vision

Starting an ADC in an organization where no provision for such a structure exists is challenging. A higher administration with a clear vision for such an endeavor is important to facilitate its establishment and for future administrative and financial support.

Learn About Regional and International Experience

Learning about other regional and international experiences in developing an ADC, and what is required to meet high standards and accreditation requirements, can help to secure the necessary administrative support for the establishment of an ADC locally.

Conduct Needs Assessment

Conducting a needs analysis survey will prioritize and focus the activities offered by the center and can be conducted at different stages of the ADC's development.

Capitalize on Faculty with Strong Interest in ADC Activities

Faculty with strong interest in educational development who have an impact on education in their departments or in the college can be recruited to the ADC. This will build a critical mass of educators that can help the ADC in its function and activities. Proper reward structures and incentives need to be in place to entice this faculty and get their 'buy-in'.

Gain Equal Administrative Status to Other Departments

It is important for an ADC to gain equal status to its 'sister' departments so that it can garner necessary respect, have a voice in decision-making, and secure proper financial and administrative support.

References

Al Wardy, N. (2008). Medical education units: History, functions, and organisation. *Sultan Qaboos University Medical Journal, 8*(2), 149–156.

Christopher, D. F., Harte, K., & George, C. F. (2002). The implementation of tomorrow's doctors. *Medical Education, 36*(3), 282–288.

Davis, M. H., Karunathilake, I., & Harden, R. M. (2005). AMEE education guide no. 28: The development and role of departments of medical education. *Medical Teacher, 27*(8), 665–675.

Hamdy, H., Telmisani, A., Al Wardy, N., Abdel-Khalek, N., Carruthers, G., Hassan, G., Kassab, S., Abu-Hijleh, M., Al-Roomi, K., O'Malley, K., El Din Ahmed, M. G., Raj, G. A., Rao, G. M., & Sheikh, K. (2010). Undergraduate medical education in the Gulf Cooperation Council: A multi-countries study (part 1). *Medical Teacher, 32*(3), 219–224.

International Databases for Enhanced Assessments and Learning (IDEAL) Consortium. (n.d.). *IDEAL Consortium*. IDEAL Coordination Centre. https://www.idealmed.org/2019/index.html

Sheikh Hamdan Bin Rashid Al Maktoum Award for Medical Sciences. (n.d.). *College of Medicine & Health Sciences, Sultan Qaboos University: Arab world awards— Hamdan award for the best medical college/institute or centre in the Arab World 2013–2014*. Sheikh Hamdan Bin Rashid Al Maktoum Award for Medical Sciences. http://www.hmaward.org.ae/profile.php?id=1516

Sultan Qaboos University (SQU) Quality Assurance Office. (n.d.). *Accreditation road map of the College of Medicine and Health Sciences*. SQU. https://www.squ.edu.om/qao/Accreditation-Road-map/College-of-Medicine-and-Health-Science-CoMHS

9

Tectonic Plates of American Higher Education: Yale University's Poorvu Center and a Multiplicity of Missions

Kyle Sebastian Vitale and Nancy S. Niemi

Introduction

If higher education can be described as having shifting tectonic plates, then those plates meet in academic professional development centers (ADCs). Because ADCs often form by the merger of pre-existing units on campus, they can incorporate institutional fault lines as they develop from many parts into a cohesive organism. In ADCs, we often see these fault lines around organizational mission, global trends in digital technologies, policies on disability, inclusive teaching practices, and the stratification of faculty and staff cultures, status, and purpose. These potential frictions provide the impetus for creating strategic bridges within ADCs in order to work across fault lines, if not close them wherever possible. Large ADCs, such as Yale University's Poorvu Center for Teaching and Learning (CTL), are no exception. As ADCs continue to work out their identities in a higher education landscape that also struggles to know its own mission (Stevens et al., 2008), we hope our story can provide insight for growing ADCs.

K. S. Vitale (✉)
Temple University, Philadelphia, PA, USA
e-mail: kyle.vitale@temple.edu

N. S. Niemi
University of Maryland Eastern Shore, Princess Anne, MD, USA
e-mail: nsniemi@umes.edu

© The Author(s), under exclusive license to Springer Nature Switzerland AG 2023
O. J. Neisler (ed.), *The Palgrave Handbook of Academic Professional Development Centers*,
Palgrave Studies on Leadership and Learning in Teacher Education,
https://doi.org/10.1007/978-3-030-80967-6_9

This chapter provides a brief history of the formation and large-scale goals of the Poorvu Center, before reflecting on team collaborations that developed the center's parts into far more than their sum. We conclude with a few recommendations gleaned from our own challenges and victories. The authors, both of whom are recent members of the Poorvu Center's Faculty Teaching Initiatives (FTI) team, have significant teaching backgrounds and have worked as the center's central classroom curricular support for over 5,000 faculty members. Our team navigated, and continues to navigate, an uneven terrain that involves various issues, such as a centuries-old institutional research culture; the center's significant digital education mission, with multiple teams subscribing to various extents to the belief that digital innovation can rapidly fix and improve student learning; and inconsistent personnel over the years. These tensions reflect many fault lines that mirror those present in American higher education today, such as the struggles to establish robust teaching cultures, the unsettled question of digital learning advantages, and tensions between those trained like faculty (mostly PhD holders) and those with uneven understandings of faculty life.

In one sense, we offer the following description as an illustration that, amidst inescapable debates and clashing cultures, the Poorvu Center still stands and does effective work. It is possible—if not necessary—to live with many of the tensions of higher education, rather than expect to solve them any time soon. In another sense, we have found strategies to turn those tensions into advantages. We recognize that the Poorvu Center's teams function best when allowed to focus on their own missions, collaborating where strategic on individual, department, program, and campus initiatives. The next section of this chapter will provide a brief history of the center's formation, followed by examples of collaboration. We conclude with some advice for new and growing ADCs.

History and Mission of Yale University's Poorvu Center

The Poorvu Center, originally the Poorvu CTL, was founded in 2014 with major backing by the president, provost, and board of Yale University to support students and faculty across campus. It was an unusual time in Yale's history, with a new president, provost, and decanal structure creating space in the Office of the Provost. That space was filled with a new position, the deputy provost for teaching and learning, whose first task was to build an ADC in

9 Tectonic Plates of American Higher Education: Yale University's... 141

alignment with President Peter Salovey's goal of making Yale "the research university most committed to teaching and learning" (Yale University Office of the President, n.d.).

The CTL embodied President Salovey's vision of 'One Yale' by integrating under one roof—literally and figuratively—various teaching, tutoring, writing, and technology-enabled learning programs previously distributed across the university. These original offices included the Yale College Writing Center, McDougal Graduate Writing Center, McDougal Graduate Teaching Center, Center for Scientific Teaching, Office of Online Education, Broadcast Center, and Instructional Technology Group for Instructional Technology Services. This idea of an umbrella structure sought to reduce audience confusion, allowing us to serve most university constituents or get them the help they needed swiftly. Crucially, the Poorvu Center's central location in the heart of the campus signals its centrality to Yale's educational mission.

As a central element of that vision, our founding executive director intentionally built the organization as a welcoming, nonevaluative resource, equipped to meet the needs of both new and senior faculty. The Poorvu Center happily assesses program strength and evaluates curriculums when invited to do so, but maintains a posture that combines support with leadership in the areas of effective teaching, diversity and inclusion, and educational research. This tone allowed us to build significant relationships with many departments and most professional schools, making us a 'household name' on campus as well as a valued strategic partner. That momentum led to our endowment in fall 2018 as the Poorvu CTL, solidifying our presence on campus.

At the time of the center's founding, Yale University was unusual in its absence of a faculty-serving teaching center. Various units, including the Center for Scientific Teaching and the still-separate School of Medicine Teaching and Learning Center and Center for Language Study, pre-existed the Poorvu CTL and were designed to serve targeted populations of faculty. Building a campus-wide resource for faculty was a new opportunity created by the formation of the Poorvu Center. Over time, our initial teams developed new identities and new teams were formed, establishing the following sections:

- FTI (the authors' team)
- Educational Program Assessment
- Science, Technology, Engineering, and Mathematics (STEM) Education
- Graduate and Postdoctoral Teaching Development
- The Graduate Writing Center

- Undergraduate Writing and Tutoring
- Digital Education
- Education Technology
- Education Technology and Media
- Broadcast Studio
- Communications
- Business Operations.

Whereas a number of distributed offices supporting various elements of teaching and learning had the potential to create uncertainty about where to go, our structure provided 'one door' for a variety of needs. There are now over 50 staff supporting effective course design and research-informed teaching methods for university instructors, including faculty and teaching fellows, across the university's undergraduate liberal arts college, the graduate school, and 12 professional schools.

The mission of the Poorvu Center is to promote equitable and engaged teaching throughout the university and support students across the curriculum as they take ownership of their learning (Yale Poorvu CTL, 2020). As part of a research institution, the center provides training, consultations, and resources designed to make teaching and learning more public and collaborative, so that every Yale instructor experiences the satisfaction that results from teaching well, and every student develops the critical reflection that marks deep and independent learning. The Poorvu Center's variety of teams are designed to focus in on certain populations and provide overlapping support across the institution.

Organizational Reporting and Structure

The Poorvu Center reports to the university provost's office, a structure aligned with its mission to work across all segments of the university. Because of the university's breadth of college and professional schools, our own location both constrains and frees us. On the one hand, the Poorvu Center is not embedded in any one community of learning and is therefore stretched to serve and explain our value to the entire university. On the other hand, the provostial line also makes the center free to work across the boundaries and siloes of a large research university.

The reporting structure of Poorvu Center is relatively flat: two executive directors lead the center both overall and in the digital education section, respectively, and senior directors from individual teams report directly to

9 Tectonic Plates of American Higher Education: Yale University's... 143

them. Various assistant and associate directors within teams report directly to their senior directors as well, creating a collaborative environment that ensures leaders are also colleagues. The center's funding structure is too vast for a legible diagram, comprised of multiple revenue sources and reflective of the various offices that merged in the formation of the center, including general funding from the university, grant funding, and donor funding.

To paint a picture of individual units, our former unit within the Poorvu Center, the FTI section, works as part of the faculty development profession more broadly and is "dedicated to helping colleges and universities function effectively as teaching and learning communities" (Felten et al., 2007). The team typically includes a senior director with various associate/assistant directors reporting to them. Work tasks are typically distributed evenly, with the senior director taking additional responsibility for departmental outreach, budgetary management, and senior strategizing. Team members are scholars in their own disciplines as well as leaders in faculty development, and host a huge variety of events for all Yale instructors including consultations, observations, workshops, institutes, and resources.

Our former team works at various points throughout the year with the Poorvu Center's other teams, overlapping most with the Graduate and Postdoctoral Teaching Development section and diverging most with the Digital Education section. When a faculty member wants to redesign a course, for example, the FTI team may co-consult with a member of the Educational Technology team so that questions about the learning management system (LMS) can be addressed in conjunction with curricular and pedagogical issues. The team has also been tapped occasionally to inform a particular learning design for one of the university's massive open online courses (MOOCs). These moments sometimes feel more like consultations for other teams than true collaborations, but over a given term our teams interact in a spectrum of ways. This chapter later explores true cross-team collaborations as well.

Because the team's work ranges across the entire university, participants in FTI programs frequently comment on the value offered by opportunities to speak to colleagues outside of their departments and disciplines. Moreover, such broad capacity offers Poorvu Center staff the chance to learn about the breadth of university resources, making it easier for us to connect different constituents and developments. In short, it functions as the hub for conversations and programming that the university hoped for when they created the Poorvu CTL.

The Poorvu Center's umbrella structure makes for different work environments for its staff. Perhaps most obviously, the FTI section is a relatively small team serving roughly 5,600 instructors. Because the FTI section tends to be staffed by PhD-holders with disciplinary expertise, it faces the additional challenge of its staff acting in full-time roles while still remaining legible as

K. S. Vitale and N. S. Niemi

teacher-scholars for Yale faculty. At Yale, this reality challenged us to be knowledgeable in our fields; experts in teaching and learning trends, tools, and research across all disciplinary domains; and seasoned teachers with authentic experience to draw on and share.

Campus Bridges and Fault Lines

It is perhaps ironic, especially for ADCs in our peer universities, that our research institutions still question and often reject the educational research upon which our work is based. All of our interactions took place in an institution that defines itself first and last as a place where new knowledge is created. Yale is classified as a doctoral university with very high research activity, in that it offers degrees from a bachelor's through to terminal degrees and focuses heavily on research activity. Yet Yale does not include a school of education among its programs of study or research. The Poorvu Center's emergence on campus—particularly that of the FTI section—suggests that at least some members of the Yale community see value in the cogent, committed exploration of effective teaching and learning. We found that focus on and acceptance of the disciplines of educational research and the science of learning vary across departments and schools. The FTI section's role in such a culture thus includes advocacy in addition to instruction and distilling and communicating the research that best engages Yale's teaching culture.

The major yield of this culture is, of course, various forms of the lecture model (Stains et al., 2018). It is evident from our experience, in ways much more trenchant than we realized, that higher education in general is built around the lecture—that is, it is clear that the one-way transmission of information from the professor's mouth (and, perhaps, their PowerPoint presentations) into students' heads (and their laptops) remains the primary mode of teaching. The actions of individual professors, the scheduling of auditorium-style classes, the instructional technologies that are in everyday use (LMS, lecture capture, MOOCs, etc.), the room-type designations (lecture rooms vs. seminar rooms), and even the teaching assistant positions (ours are called 'teaching fellows') often seem built to support the lecture-based modality of teaching.

Here lies a major fault line, for different areas of higher education and even different Poorvu Center teams see the lecture, and its alternatives, quite differently, and draw from different modes of research to defend their positions. 'Flipped' or recorded lectures are perceived as quick fixes for improving student engagement, whereas MOOCs purport to provide equitable access to

9 Tectonic Plates of American Higher Education: Yale University's...

learning, and traditional disciplines defend the 'sage-on-the-stage' lecture style as an adept lesson in notetaking and listening. Muddying the waters yet further, because assessment measures for digital education tend to be sparse (Esfijani, 2018), tension exists within the Poorvu Center—and similarly structured ADCs elsewhere—as to the role of digital strategies to meet various challenges and established beliefs.

In the midst of these challenges, we were often building bridges with fellow teams, traversing fault lines, and avoiding fault lines where they simply did not inform our work. What follows are several areas in which we found deep value and relational growth in collaborations that serve large swaths of the Yale University community.

Program Collaboration

Perhaps the single focus of the work of the FTI section is the conveyance of effective learning, with all of the research, internal and external contexts, and theoretical frames that shift and buffet its place in most aspects of academia. Two of the ways in which the Poorvu Center teams experience a number of these teaching and learning aspects are the center's Course (Re)Design Summer Institute and its midterm program, Course (Re)Calibrate. Close to 70 faculty have attended the Course (Re)Design Summer Institute in each of its three years running, and our newest initiative, the (Re)Calibrate program, saw 15 members attend its successful small-scale pilot, with plans to open the event to the entire faculty soon.

The Yale Summer Institute on Course (Re)Design is a three-day intensive workshop that helps instructors make changes to a new or existing course by: (1) examining principles of how people learn and applying them to teaching; (2) identifying assessment strategies to strengthen connections between student learning and course assignments; (3) identifying and refining components of classes that can be made more inclusive; and (4) identifying strategic actions to strengthen the culture of teaching and learning at Yale. After the success of the first year, it became apparent that this focal teaching and learning event represented more than just the FTI team; other units within Poorvu Center wanted to—and we felt needed to—participate in meaningful ways, showcasing the relationships of digital tools and technologies to teaching and learning development. This evolution in the program also kept pace with our internal evolution toward understanding how and where to collaborate productively.

However, we did not want to turn Course (Re)Design into an academic 'show-and-tell' of the Poorvu Center's offerings. As such, we integrated members of the Graduate and Postdoctoral Teaching Development and Educational Technologies teams in two ways: first, by assigning members of these teams to faculty cohorts that could work together throughout the program and, second, by describing, and making clearly available for individual consults, these teams' expertise. Embedding members of the teams into faculty discussions and whole-group instruction sessions allowed our nonfaculty-focused colleagues the ability to hear faculty conversations, participate in the development of coursework in real time, and listen to presentations of and discussions on pedagogical research. At the same time, we came to better understand the digital needs and expectations of Yale faculty and how our colleagues could meet those needs. Making sure that the faculty knew of our colleagues' expertise, and where to find them during individual work times, allowed our colleagues to meet faculty needs both immediately and individually.

The Course (Re)Calibrate program runs under a similar model: while we provide faculty with the resources and opportunities for energizing and recommitting during the midterm season, colleagues on our digital teams are available for individual consultations, providing that core 'umbrella' effect while ensuring our participants' needs are fully met. These strategies allow our nonfaculty-focused colleagues—particularly the technology-focused teams—to learn about education research, while helping us understand emerging trends in digital technology and education. We all end up learning alongside our faculty, and the various teams comprising our center subsequently use their knowledge in ways that are germane to informing the classes on which they are working.

Moreover, we built a variety of other programmatic bridges in the Poorvu Center. In addition to offering knowledge about teaching and learning to our technologically focused colleagues and vice versa, we have developed a series of small wins—events that are genuinely collaborative without creating forced connections. For example, we merged what were once separate teaching and technological tool-focused lunch time series into one ongoing event known as the Teaching and Learning Lunch Series. This allows the Poorvu Center to present a single face to the many Yale populations, erasing even in the titles the distinctions between a tech-focused talk and a learning-focused one.

Co-consultations

By contrast, the individual consultations that form one of the pillars of faculty development work can suffer when we force the issue of integrated teams, rather than paying attention to natural connections and divergences. Individual consultations are the heart of our work, and any successful

9 Tectonic Plates of American Higher Education: Yale University's... 147

consultation starts by building understanding and trust between both parties, a foundation built on a willingness to listen, recognition of shared expertise, and understanding of the other party's work environment. These factors can be easily disrupted by placing too many parties in the room, misaligning need with expertise, or signaling that the instructor's professional life is not understood. Forced integration has led to poor consultations and wasted time, while strategic co-consultations have been enriching when a complex ask can only be served by multiple teams and parties. Co-consultations, in short, are effective when the occasion calls for them.

There can be real friction across teams, at Yale University as at peer institutions, when co-consultations become sites for competing knowledge claims. On the one hand, a technologically focused consultation or project could benefit from the fundamentals of learning design. On the other hand, faculty developer expertise is often not sought as swiftly as it perhaps should be. However, our increasing collaborative work and exposure to one another across programming improved our knowledge base of others' work. We are experiencing a universal reality that no research paper will ever be able to satisfactorily quantify: time spent working together with open hearts and minds creates new pathways for knowledge and understanding.

Co-consultations have developed in a variety of ways: sometimes instructors have separate, consecutive conversations with different team members in the room, other times an issue, like use of polling software or integrating LMS blogs into an assignment, requires concurrent expertise and enables a true conversation between all parties. Individual faculty requests for support and help come in through many organizational doors, including via the LMS, through the classroom, and with online learning: the Poorvu Center continues to work out an effective system wherein the appropriate team handles the request with or without consultation from others, as needed. It is also crucial to recognize that these co-consultations often move in seasons, with several in a month and then none for a semester. We have learned that these patterns are not meaningful, and instead continue to stay alert to opportunities for our teams to work together for individual support.

Poorvu Center Conversations

In recent years, our executive director perceived that the Poorvu Center had reached a degree of positive, significant reputation on campus, in tandem with its teams reaching a certain level of maturity and cohesiveness, that would allow for more complex conversations about our work. These conversations developed into two ongoing streams: Common Ground and Impact Retreats. Common Ground has become a cross-cutting set of intellectual ideas that manifest differently, but should be present, in all areas of work—from digital to pedagogical and everything in between. The sophistication of this approach is in its nimbleness: while sharing a set of principles about effective teaching and learning, the Poorvu Center's directors cultivate intra-team conversations about how these principles might unfold differently in our work. This act of sharing principles while honoring subcultures allows the center to offer a cohesive front to Yale University while maintaining its unique ongoing practices.

The Impact Retreats, by similar token, have brought different teams together to discuss how we might measure our impact on Yale's teaching and learning culture and, by default, improve our practices and our data. Meeting every few months, these retreats have focused on particular kinds of data, sharing materials across teams, and establishing goals before the next meeting. The retreats have helped our leader develop theories of impact and change that apply specifically to Yale's institutional culture, and explore a complex, dynamic relationship between awareness of our services and the cultural adoption of the tenets we advocate.

Recommendations

The bridges we continually build and maintain are numerous—bridges across to our digital colleagues, to university leadership, and to senior culture-making faculty. Yet, because Yale is at once a liberal arts college, complex university, and self-described 'elite' institution, we believe the philosophies we have deployed can be helpful elsewhere. Distilling our experience down into a few recommendations looks like the following.

Consider Comprehensive Services

Every day, we have enjoyed the benefits of being able to respond to the vast majority of requests: "Yes, we can help with that." This regular response conveys a sense on campus that the Poorvu Center is "the place to go" for help with teaching and learning. Respecting differences in campus politics and histories, an umbrella organization takes years to develop and integrate, but once formed can become an authoritative and supportive figure in the minds of its users.

Collaborate Strategically

Just because teams work alongside each other does not mean they must, of necessity, collaborate at all points. There are vital early years to spend growing comfortable and familiar with each other's work and adopting other perspectives on learning. Strategic collaborations that allow various teams to exercise their expertise while challenging them to work together can increase confidence and understanding over time. When not collaborating, teams should be allowed to build out their work, brick by brick, unit by unit.

Start Gathering Data Now

Data informed our work, helped our directors emphasize our value and the need for continued support, and showed unsure faculty the extent of their colleagues' interactions with us. We counted the number of consultations we made, the conversations we had, the projects and observations we undertook, and the collaborations in which we engaged. These numbers helped us comprehend our departmental relationships, referrals from satisfied instructors, and outreach across instructor rank. At Yale University and elsewhere, we are keenly aware of differentiating quantitative, qualitative, and unmeasurable forms of impact as we consider all these outcomes, even as we need to provide evidence of our worth to the university that supports us. Because different teams gather different forms of data, we continue to debate the advantage of a central collecting system—Salesforce, for instance—compared to allowing teams to gather their own data in ways that can "talk" across the center.

Communicate

The Poorvu Center has made leaps and bounds in moments where our leadership modeled listening and patience, where strategic collaborations proved fruitful to all parties, and where invitations to converse led to new initiatives and the normalizing of our perceived unique challenges. There is something about working daily with one another that, like family, grows our willingness to like one another and try to understand different perspectives. This process also requires that each team decide, based on its principles, when to choose compromise, détente, or cession of their expertise in cross-center work. In this field, we are finding that integration for integration's sake is a nonstarter. The starting point must be learning, and then the best way to support that learning: subsequently, whatever expertise is called for at that point will dictate the blend of personnel required.

Conclusion

There will never be a Pangea in higher education—by its very nature, higher education is about growth and development, which is always messy and full of human imperfection. But ADCs can be places that own the messiness of learning and help colleges and universities support their priorities for students, however vast and seemingly contradictory. We can turn fault lines into frontlines and create earthquakes in education, rather than reacting to them. We do so by measuring our time geologically, rock by rock, and not digitally, second by second. When forging relationships and seeking to impact cultures of teaching and learning, it is the long, patient developments that create the bedrock for solid futures.

References

Esfijani, A. (2018). Measuring quality in online education: A meta-synthesis. *American Journal of Distance Education, 31*(1), 57–73.

Felten, P., Kalish, A., Pingree, A., & Plank, K. (2007). Toward a scholarship of teaching and learning in educational development. *To Improve the Academy, 25*(1), 93–108.

Stains, M., Harshman, J., Barker, M. K., Chasteen, S. V., Cole, R., DeChenne-Peters, S. E., Eagan, M. K., Jr., Esson, J. M., Knight, J. K., Laski, F. A., Levis-Fitzgerald, M., Lee, C. J., Lo, S. M., McDonnell, L. M., McKay, T. A., Michelotti, N., Musgrove, A., Palmer, M. S., Plank, K. M., … Young, A. M. (2018). Anatomy of STEM teaching in American universities: A snapshot from a large-scale observation study. *Science, 359*(6383), 1468–1470.

Stevens, M., Armstrong, E., & Arum, R. (2008). Sieve, incubator, temple, hub: Empirical and theoretical advances in the sociology of higher education. *Annual Review of Sociology, 34*, 127–151.

Yale Poorvu Center for Teaching and Learning (CTL). (2020). *About*. Yale University. https://poorvucenter.yale.edu/about

Yale University Office of the President. (n.d.). *Goals*. Yale University. https://president.yale.edu/goals

10

Structural Changes Over Three Years: Evolution of Three Models to Support Learning and Teaching in a Large Research-Intensive University

Tammy R. Smith, Kirsten Schliephake, and Barb Macfarlan

Introduction

Unfortunately, all teachers are not great teachers. In higher education, teachers (lecturers) are often experts in their disciplinary field, but have no expectation of formal qualifications in the art and theory of teaching or the field of education. As with any craft or discipline, teaching is something learned, practiced, and refined over time. Great teachers make teaching seem effortless; yet, that apparent effortlessness is a product of dedication, practice, and solid *effort*. So, how do we offer students great teaching across all courses in all disciplines, regardless of whose class they choose to be in or whose class they are allocated to?

In 2014, Monash University sought to answer this question. Theoretically, it can be answered. However, it presents a number of challenges practically, not least of which is the gamut of trials associated with making any change in a large, multicampus, highly regarded research institution. When that change involves tampering with traditional and familiar practices, the challenge increases exponentially.

T. R. Smith (✉) • K. Schliephake • B. Macfarlan
Monash University, Melbourne, VIC, Australia
e-mail: tammy.smith@monash.edu; kirsten.schliephake@monash.edu;
barb.macfarlan@monash.edu

© The Author(s), under exclusive license to Springer Nature Switzerland AG 2023
O. J. Neisler (ed.), *The Palgrave Handbook of Academic Professional Development Centers*,
Palgrave Studies on Leadership and Learning in Teacher Education,
https://doi.org/10.1007/978-3-030-80967-6_10

Background to the Initiative

Monash University is a member of the Group of Eight as one of Australia's leading research-intensive universities. It spans multiple campuses and teaching centers in Australia and abroad, catering to approximately 70,000 students. The university has 10 faculties that teach and conduct research in a range of disciplines from law, medicine, science, and engineering through to architecture, music, and the fine arts. That being the case, teaching contexts and environments are diverse and teaching sessions range from studio, tutorial, clinical placements, workshops, and laboratory work to very large lectures.

In June 2014, a central educational design team of six was assembled to actively support all faculties in the enhancement of their curriculum and improvement of teaching delivery. This included, among other strategies:

- Introducing blended learning techniques and practices, particularly for large classes
- Constructively aligning units of study and whole courses to enable a more fluent course progression and structure through accurate mapping
- Teaching practices that promoted student engagement in class and the application of material in seminar and workshop-style sessions in preference to lectures
- Educating lecturers in how to facilitate this alternate teaching style (something understandably quite daunting for those who had only ever lectured).

The educational development team consisted of one manager and five educational designers (EDs). This chapter is written from the perspective of the three remaining EDs from that original team and maps the journey from their centralized position as expert external support to faculties, to being embedded within and reporting directly to those faculties.

EDs as Change Agents

The role of 'educational designer' within Monash University is that of an educationalist with teaching and learning experience in the higher education sector, postgraduate qualifications, and extensive relevant experience and knowledge of the educational theory underpinning teaching. EDs are seen as change agents equipped to lead educational development across the curriculum and in the design of meaningful learning experiences and resources

(Macfarlan et al., 2017). Many other position titles are in use to describe this educationalist role, including educational/academic developer and learning consultant. Regardless of the title used, the role of those working in this area has become accepted within, and integral to, teaching and learning in higher education. The classification of the role has been debated with regard to whether it should have academic or professional status within the higher education sector or whether a third hybrid category is warranted to encompass the role's complex nature (Whitchurch, 2010).

Centers for Teaching and Learning

Many tertiary institutions have centralized offices of teaching and learning or centers of excellence dedicated to the improvement and support of teaching practice and creation of exemplary learning opportunities. At Monash University, the Office of the Vice Provost, Teaching and Learning (OVPLT) was the center fulfilling that function, and it was in that center in June 2014 that EDs were first employed. Since that time, the center has gone through restructures that changed the way EDs were able to interact with faculties and led to them being moved out of centralized OVPLT positions and embedded within each of the 10 faculties. Once in faculties, EDs continued implementation of the institutional agenda through targeted enhancement of units and courses. The aim was to improve the quality of teaching and learning to mirror the already-high standard attained by the university in research.

In this chapter, we share our journey through the educational design revolution and innovation evolution that has taken place across Monash University since mid-2014. The focus is on challenges faced and insights gained, with a view to inspiring and emboldening others who may embark upon or negotiate similar paths.

Transformation Models

Model one (June 2014–March 2015): A Project Management-Led Approach

In June 2014, we began working together in the OVPLT situated on the Caulfield campus, approximately 20 minutes' drive from the main campus at Clayton. We reported to the manager of educational design and began our

154   T. R. Smith et al.

tenure by planning how the envisaged program of innovation and improvement would be shaped and enacted. There were five of us, with each person being assigned two faculties with which to work. The first nine months while we were located in the OVPLT were formative and involved discovering how we could best contribute to teaching and learning outcomes and the education agenda. Upon reflection, this period took on three distinct stages through which we were:

1. Inducted into the role and worked together on background resourcing aspects
2. Introduced to the project managers (i.e., the change and engagement [C&E] team) and worked within a model led and negotiated by them
3. Refocused to undertake direct communication with the faculties and lecturers whose units of study needed development and/or improvement in some way.

During the first two stages, we had very little, if any, contact with the faculties or their lecturers. The approach set in motion an educational design journey through three different models of engagement with faculties, resulting in the EDs becoming an embedded and integral part of each of the university's 10 faculties.

Starting the Journey: Stage 1

Our initial task was to create and curate learning and teaching resources and strategies for use by lecturers. These were to enable implementation of the university's educational transformation agenda through a move away *from* reliance on lecture-based learning *to* approaches built upon more interactive teaching and learning techniques. The learning resources created included a variety of teaching templates, lesson planning tools, activities to assist lecturers in creating an online presence in their units, blended and flipped learning opportunities, and structures, ideas, and tips to encourage, support, and simplify the use of appropriate technologies.

Good practice examples were sourced from and supported with video interviews from teachers and innovators across the university. Existing teaching and learning support documents were reviewed for currency and content and, if found suitable, sorted into a purpose-built database. The introduction of a new web content management system was timely for the development of an OVPLT website, where 'Just in Time' teaching and learning tips were incorporated into a site known as the Better Learning and Teaching Bytes (Orchard et al., 2014).

The OVPLT then changed focus from resource provision and introduced a highly targeted and outcomes-based approach to promoting *teaching excellence* across the university. The aim was to improve teaching quality and to diversify offerings so that a range of knowledge and skills could be incorporated and measured. Given the heavy research focus of the university, such an emphasis on teaching was recognized as a challenging undertaking (James, 2013; Richman, 2015).

'Enhancement' was the term chosen to indicate the change. This was to occur through innovation in course and unit design, building teacher capacity, and encouraging teaching in preference to lecturing, so as to increase interaction *with*, and application *of*, content material. Each of the five EDs was responsible for two randomly assigned faculties.

Structural Fault Lines Disrupt Communication: Stage Two

At this time, the OVPLT also engaged the services of a C&E team consisting of two project managers. The transformation strategy and supporting business plan required this team to be the instigators of any interaction with faculties and to provide the catalyst and direction of educational change. We, as EDs, were to communicate with faculties via the C&E team and have no direct contact with faculties ourselves.

The project managers were each assigned five faculties. They met with the associate deans of education (ADEs) from those assigned faculties to identify units of study that would most benefit from the enhancement process, as outlined in the initial model of engagement. At this point, the aim was to reach the largest number of students possible with a new emphasis on interactive teaching and learning. To this end, large first-year units, some with more than 1,000 students enrolled, were considered ideal for identification and inclusion in the initiative, as they would show an impact on the greatest number of students. Once identified, these units had an enhancement plan developed by the project managers in consultation with the faculty lecturer (chief examiner) responsible for the unit. The EDs were not involved. See Fig. 10.1 for a diagram of the 2014–2015 procedures for interaction between the OVPLT and the 10 university faculties.

Project managers from the OVPLT engaged with the ADEs to identify units and negotiate enhancement terms and plans. Plans were then communicated to the EDs, who had to implement these without having prior

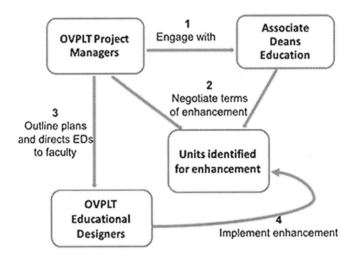

Fig. 10.1 Model one—initial method of engagement with faculties (2014–2015)

engagement with, or having formed any relationship with, the ADEs and lecturers. The project managers were not educators and approached their task from a business process perspective. This worked well for meeting attendance and the production of administrative charting and documents, but the approach fell short when decisions and planning on matters of educational significance were required. Given the context of the project, these matters arose with predictable regularity and created challenges to progress. Consequently, information transfer from the EDs to faculty lecturers was, when it occurred, quite inefficient. Miscommunication was not intentional, but more a product of the C&E team working outside of their project management expertise and attempting to provide guidance and rationale to education-based questions and problems posed to them.

This model of engagement dictated that the EDs *not* engage directly with lecturers in assigned faculties, and that they play no part in the innovation process until after the units were identified, the plan outlined, and the project contract for enhancement agreed upon and signed. Finalizing the process to that degree without any input from educationalists was fraught. It meant that changes to the units identified had to be done within the boundaries and expectations predetermined by non-educationalist project managers; although these predeterminations were made with the best of intentions, they were not always informed or realistic in terms of what was possible, practical, purposeful, or pedagogical.

10 Structural Changes Over Three Years: Evolution of Three Models… 157

We discussed this with the project managers, one of whom saw the problem and agreed that more cooperation and fuller communication was needed, and one of whom did not. Given this development, levels of communication and cooperation varied markedly depending upon which project manager was involved with liaisons.

In most cases, as the EDs each had responsibility for two faculties, they dealt at various times with both project managers. The variance in approach highlighted the importance of contextualizing project outcomes, because while the initiative itself had merit, its success was dependent upon which project manager was charged with enacting it and their particular perspective on how plans and interactions should look or be controlled.

This model proved problematic for decisions and understanding regarding:

* Education
* Identification of target units
* Capabilities, role and expertise of EDs, as interpreted by project managers
* What was required to enhance a unit, what was available, and what was possible
* Realistic timelines for designated tasks and other decisions (these were reliant on education design input, but were estimated by project managers rather than communicated to, and/or discussed with, EDs), and so on.

While well intentioned, this model hobbled communication and effective planning which made implementation of meaningful change extremely difficult. There was no opportunity for the cultivation of relationships or development of trust between the faculties and the EDs that would eventually be working with them. Cultivation of this type of relationship is a component vital to meaningful engagement (Cozolino, 2013; Moore, 2017). Over time, the obstacles to communication created by insisting on the project managers' role as conduit became more apparent and obstructive.

Addressing the Fault Lines: Stage Three

The EDs recognized the communication obstacles and sought leave, from management, to engage directly with faculty lecturers and form working relationships with them. After some valuable discussion, this was approved, direct communication commenced, and information flow immediately improved, as did planning for unit enhancement (UE).

158   T. R. Smith et al.

This new direct form of engagement between the EDs and faculty lecturers also quickly enabled planning for the implementation of several successful and ongoing enhancements. Two of these were:

1. A blended learning model making innovative use of the tools provided within the learning management system to guide student learning (Gleadow et al., 2015)
2. Integrating Science and Practice (iSAP), an online learning platform developed to use interactive case studies based on realistic clinical scenarios in a manner reflecting workplace practice (Williams et al., 2017).

These enhancements would not have been possible without direct communication and close collaboration between the EDs and faculty lecturers and the application of educational theory to the frameworks underpinning them. Making a significant change to teaching practice in a large research-focused university is complex and difficult (James, 2016; Lawson & Price, 2003), and requires a nuanced approach that is best left to educators with the ability to make education seem as simple as possible for highly qualified, highly regarded, highly intelligent, and extremely busy lecturers, many of whom have a first love of research and a requirement to teach.

In less than nine months, Model One evolved from a project management exercise led by a C&E team to an approach grounded in education theory about to be led by EDs. However, at the end of that short period, circumstances changed. The approach became the center of a redeployed education design workforce as part of a significant staff and role restructure within the OVPLT. The restructured OVPLT acknowledged the importance of educational leadership in the change process, with the removal of the project managers as intermediaries in what was, essentially, an educational domain. The remaining three EDs, if they wished to stay, would apply for positions embedded within faculties where they could liaise directly with lecturers. After this restructure, the OVPLT became known as the Monash University Office of Learning and Teaching (MU-OLT).

Staying True to the Vision

The move from a centrally located and controlled point was an important step forward for faculty engagement and for the enhancement of units and practice. This was important not simply from a proximity point of view, but from an ownership standpoint. We became *part of* the faculties, rather than *visitors to* them. Along with this, our reporting responsibilities moved from the central OVPLT to the faculty ADEs.

The move was more than physical. The 'us and them' divide that can exist between central offices and operational areas in large organizations also shifted during the move. It facilitated our transformation from outsiders to insiders, as we took up residence in our new faculty homes. There were, however, only three of us and 10 faculties, all with positions to fill. Positions within faculties had different position descriptions and were advertised widely. In a few months, faculties had filled their positions and the new model began. Recruiting continued and EDs came onboard to fill faculty positions throughout the remainder of the year.

With 10 faculties across several campuses, newly employed EDs, and no remaining instruction by, or location within, the MU-OLT, the danger of losing vision and focus loomed large. The three original EDs saw an urgent need to ensure communication and collaboration between the newly enlarged group of EDs. Although energy and expectations were high, these concerns were ever present. If the new EDs began work without any link to enhancement or to each other, particularly those already working toward the enhancement of units, then maintenance of the momentum that had been established and collaboration on a common purpose and shared goals would be impossible.

Up until this point, the criteria required for UE had not been clearly articulated beyond the initial ED group. If that was allowed to remain the case, then the enhancement concept could be interpreted inconsistently or not at all. We met with the vice provost of teaching and learning who shared our concerns. After discussions, he confirmed the direction and characteristics for UE. The consistent characteristics included:

- Alignment of:
    - Learning outcomes
    - In-class learning activities
    - Assessments
- Inclusion of:
    - Pre-class activities
    - Active learning and application of concepts in class
    - Post-class follow-up activities, where needed
    - Formative assessment
    - Timely feedback to students.

Establishment of this definition was crucial to the future consistency of outcomes. In order to measure, guide, and evaluate innovation and change, this clear basis was sufficient to invoke a consistent purpose across faculties while allowing sufficient flexibility to maintain the culture and flavor unique to each faculty. In practice and implementation, UE was an extended form of constructive alignment with the application of interactive learning principles and incorporation of formative activities and feedback/feedforward principles.

Commencement of a Community of Practice

As new EDs were recruited by faculties, the existing group welcomed them and provided support, explained what UE was and how it worked, shared resources, and established clear lines of communication among EDs across all faculties and campuses. This led to the impromptu formation of a community of practice (CoP) that met regularly, shared ideas, tips, and tricks, and built strong and valuable relationships across faculties.

The MU-OLT suggested that, as the EDs were funded by them, they should devote 10% of their time to MU-OLT-related activities. How these activities were to be decided upon or when this would happen was not made explicit. So, the CoP became the source of numerous, multifaculty collaborations and the development and implementation of a series of highly successful teaching symposia (the "Making a Difference" series).

CoPs are defined as "groups of people who share a passion for something that they know how to do and who interact regularly to learn how to do it better" (Wenger et al., 2002). These communities focus on building shared knowledge within learning dimension systems. These encompass engagement in social contexts that are dynamic and reflective of shared experiences and aspirations (Wenger, 2010). According to Lave and Wenger (1991), CoPs include three essential elements:

1. A *domain* of knowledge that creates a common ground and sense of common identity (i.e., what the community is about)
2. A *community* of people who care about the domain and create the social fabric of learning (i.e., how the community is formed and who should be part of it)
3. A *practice* developed to become effective in the domain (i.e., what is the shared practice that the community wants to get better at) (McDonald, 2014, 69).

The ED CoP at Monash University decided on terms of reference that included regular meetings rotationally facilitated by members of the core group. In addition, weekly informal meetings over coffee were instigated across the campuses and a very active chat forum was begun to answer any and every type of question or educational crisis. A sense of identity and belonging became very evident. The *community* developed over time based on mutual respect, honesty, reciprocity, and trust. The *practice* we shared was involvement in UE and the development of pathways and solutions to challenge lecturers to reimagine their delivery methods, thereby pioneering new teaching initiatives and guiding lecturers through any difficulties in transition. The shared knowledge *domain* was more than just working toward the same goal or working on similar projects; the members complemented each other with their abilities and skills, and they collaborated effortlessly toward the development of their social and knowledge capital.

Model Two (June 2015–June 2017): UE

The new model enacted between 2015 and 2017 was characterized by the following: expansion of the number of EDs (the three largest faculties were assigned one ED and one senior ED); continued funding of EDs by the OVPLT; and the location of EDs in the faculties. The ED roles remained centrally funded and supported. They also came with a defined budget for use by each faculty for support of the UE program. However, that was where linkages with the central office ended: the EDs now reported directly to faculty ADEs, with only a soft reporting line back to the central MU-OLT director. Most importantly, continuous communication through direct feedback channels and close proximity enabled the trust and relationships necessary for successful ED work and educational change (see Fig. 10.2).

Within each faculty or discipline, UE was enacted using a diversity of styles, approaches, and tools dependent on the idiosyncrasies of the discipline area. Sciences, for example, took a very different approach from that of arts or pharmacy, but each had a shared goal. In the Faculty of Medicine, Nursing, and Health Sciences (MNHS), the approach was to look at whole courses with a view to embed consistency across all year levels. Individual units were considered for inclusion based on the size of the cohort and student evaluations, but once a particular unit or units were identified, the whole course was taken into consideration. The change that the central ED team brought about was regarded positively in student feedback and helped to add momentum to

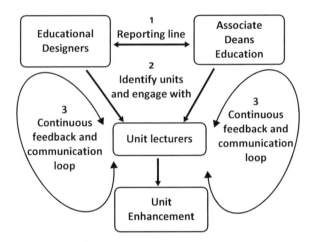

Fig. 10.2 Model two—revision of the initial engagement method (June 2015–December 2017)

the faculty-based approach. Schools within the MNHS have since employed more EDs to support lecturers within their particular disciplines (Schliephake et al., 2018).

As we neared the middle of 2017, three developments had a significant impact on UE initiatives. First, a new building was needed. After 12 months of this model, faculties had begun the UE process on more than 200 units of study and to support the process, a new purpose-built, state-of-the-art learning and teaching building (LTB) was constructed. The LTB provided a venue in which to teach enhanced units. Second, while the building was under construction, the deans and faculty members themselves advocated strongly for the retention of their existing EDs and an increase in their numbers. Response to this model of engagement was extremely positive. The EDs were accepted as part of the faculty education team, and their ideas and initiatives were, in the main, met with enthusiasm, respect, and approval. Third, with the recruitment of additional EDs, the CoP grew from 13, at the commencement of the model, to more than 30 by the middle of 2018.

Model Three (July 2017–Present): A Centrally Located Learning and ED Team in Addition to Faculty-Embedded EDs

Under new senior leadership, in June 2017, the MU-OLT changed its name to the Portfolio of the Deputy Vice Chancellor (Education), and a third model emerged combining aspects of the first two. A central, center-based, and directed

10 Structural Changes Over Three Years: Evolution of Three Models…

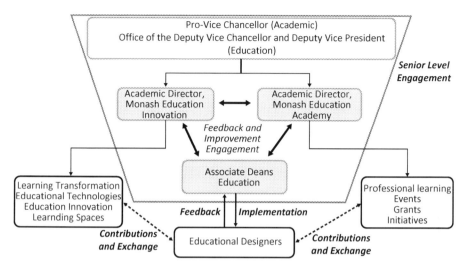

Fig. 10.3 Model three—addition of centrally located EDs (July 2017–present)

team of learning designers and EDs were specifically recruited to focus on reducing reliance on large lecture theater spaces. The use of technology and blended learning methods was strongly encouraged. Collectively, the new teams are known as the learning transformation (LT) team. They now work for a defined period of time on large cohort units (500+ students) to develop learning resources for online and face-to-face delivery. They collaborate on established faculty education goals to achieve their aims. EDs in the faculties continue working within their education teams to implement the newly defined Focus Education Strategy (Monash University, 2018), as shown in Fig. 10.3.

Conclusion

Monash University's aim of sustained growth at approximately 5% per annum put stress on physical learning spaces and has necessitated a greater reliance on the online learning environment. New learning spaces that focus on interactive learning sessions have been developed, and the LT team plays a pivotal role in supporting the work of faculty-based EDs and developing resources that can be shared easily across the university. This model is still in its infancy and has yet to be evaluated, but signs are promising. Four years after the first model was instituted to effect institutional change, the vision is clearer, the passion remains strong, innovation and change in units is ongoing, and the journey continues.

References

Cozolino, L. (2013). *The social neuroscience of education: Optimizing attachment and learning in the classroom*. W.W. Norton.

Gleadow, R., Macfarlan, B., & Honeydew, M. (2015). Design for learning – A case study of blended learning in a science unit. *F1000Research, 4*, 898.

James, N. (2013). 'How dare you tell me how to teach!': Resistance to educationalism within Australian law schools. *University of New South Wales Law Journal, 36*(3), 779–808.

James, N. (2016). Dealing with resistance to change by legal academics. In R. Field, J. Duffy, & C. James (Eds.), *Promoting law student and lawyer well-being in Australia and beyond* (pp. 204–217). Ashgate.

Lave, J., & Wenger, E. (1991). *Situated learning: Legitimate peripheral participation*. Cambridge University Press.

Lawson, E., & Price, C. (2003). *The psychology of change management*. McKinsey & Company. https://www.mckinsey.com/business-functions/organization/our-insights/the-psychology-of-change-management

Macfarlan, B., Hook, J., & Smith, T. R. (2017, October 1–14). *Agents for change: How a community of educational designers is changing educational practice in a large university* (Conference presentation), International Society for the Scholarship of Teaching & Learning (ISSoTL) 2017.

McDonald, J. (2014). *Community, domain, practice: Facilitator catch cry for revitalising learning and teaching through communities of practice*. University of Southern Queensland. https://altf.org/wp-content/uploads/2016/08/McDonald-J_NT_Final-report_-2014.pdf

Monash University. (2018). *Focus education: Agenda 2018–2020*. Monash University. https://www.monash.edu/__data/assets/pdf_file/0008/1386737/18P-0385-Focus-Education-digital.pdf

Moore, T. G. (2017, June 7). *Authentic engagement: The nature and role of the relationship at the heart of effective practice* (Keynote address), ARACY Parent Engagement Conference.

Orchard, A., Stewart, C., Gonzalez, A., Macfarlan, B., Schliephake, K., & Smith, T. (2014). BLT bytes: Timely takeaways for teachers [Conference presentation]. In B. Hegarty, J. McDonald, & S. K. Loke (Eds.), *Rhetoric and reality: Critical perspectives on educational technology* (pp. 722–725). Proceedings ASCILITE.

Richman, J. (2015). A student perspective on the causes of the commercialization of higher education and the movement of professors away from undergraduate teaching towards research and the effect those two movements have on undergraduate learning and education. *Visions for the Liberal Arts, 1*(1).

Schliephake, K., Baird, M., & Bui, D. (2018, July 21–23). *Transforming education at a faculty level* (Conference presentation). 25th International Conference on Learning.

Wenger, E. (2010). Communities of practice and social learning systems: The career of a concept. In C. Blackmore (Ed.), *Social learning systems and communities of practice*. Springer.

Wenger, E., McDermott, R., & Snyder, W. (2002). *Cultivating communities of practice*. Harvard Business School Press.

Whitchurch, C. (2010). Optimising the potential of third space professionals in higher education. *Zeitschrift fuer Hochschulentwicklung, 5*(4), 9–22.

Williams, I., Schliephake, K., Heinrich, L. M., & Baird, M. A. (2017). Integrating science and practice (iSAP): An interactive case-based clinical decision-making radiography training program. *MedEdPublish*, 1–10.

Part IV

Differences in Theoretical Foundations

While every chapter mentions some aspect of theories and principles that undergird the work of the academic professional development center (ADC) or its specific programs, the chapters in this section explain how the selection of theories or theoretical materials serves as a direct foundation for the design of ADC programs, activities, and often its evaluation.

Chapters in Part IV

Chapter 11: *Student Learning: A Framework for Designing Study Programs to Stimulate Deep Learning.* Hester Glasbeek, LEARN! Academy, Vrije Universiteit, Amsterdam, Netherlands.

The programs and activities of this ADC are founded on various theories and models, including the constructivist learning theory, constructive alignment, taxonomy of significant learning, and self-determination theory.

Chapter 12: *Theoretical Foundations for Online and Hybrid Faculty Development Initiatives.* Bridgette Atkins, Caroline Ferguson, Jeanette Oliveira, Sarah Stokes, and Susan L. Forbes, University of Ontario Institute of Technology, Oshawa, ON, Canada.

This chapter details how one university's mission to provide technology-enriched education for students is reflected in its ADC's mission which focuses on the use of technology when working with faculty. The first half of the

168   Differences in Theoretical Foundations

chapter explains the theories and frameworks that are foundational to the ADC programs: social constructivism, constructive alignment, backward design, and universal design for learning. The second half discusses the design of various hybrid and online programs, including a Certificate in University Teaching.

Chapter 13: *Mission-Aligned Teaching Center Initiative. Annie Soisson, Center for the Enhancement of Learning and Teaching,* Tufts University, Somerville, MA, USA.

The overarching framework for the design of programs at this ADC is the campus-wide shift to inclusive excellence. One strategy used includes partnerships with various campus identity organizations such as Asian, Latino, Africana, LGBTQ+, and the Women's Center, as well as garnering support from diversity officers and staff.

Other Relevant Chapters

Chapter 25: *Building Community: From Faculty Development to Pedagogical Innovation and Beyond.* Linda C. Hodges and Patrice McDermott, University of Maryland Baltimore County, Baltimore, MD, USA.

This chapter reveals how one ADC references theories related to inclusive excellence and the scholarship of teaching and learning in the design of its programs.

Chapter 31: *Achieving Certification and Innovation Simultaneously: Educational Leadership for Senior Faculty at a Research University in the Netherlands.* Joyce Brouwer and Rachna in't Veld, Vrije Universiteit, Amsterdam, Netherlands.

This ADC developed a specific model—the Systemic Innovation in Education model—that integrates several theories into a foundation for the design of its professional development programs.

Chapter 33: *Preparing Future Faculty: Developing Inclusive, Future-Focused Educators and an Adaptive Program.* Shamini Dias, Claremont Graduate University, Claremont, CA, USA.

Theories related to adaptive, inclusive pedagogy are combined with co-creative design and reflexive thinking to form the foundation for a higher education teaching certificate for graduate students.

Chapter 34: *Diversity and Coherence: The Continuum of Staff Development Actions Around a Common Core.* Dominique Verpoorten, Françoise Jérôme, Laurent Leduc, Catherine Delfosse, and Pascal Detroz, Institut de Formation et de Recherche en Enseignement Supérieur / Institute for Training and Research in Higher Education, University of Liège, Liège, Belgium.

This chapter details a set of five competencies and eight principles which undergird personalized certificate programs, providing faculty with the opportunity to earn a 10-credit certificate and a 60-credit master's degree in higher education teaching and learning.

Chapter 36: *Critical Reflection on Organizational Practice at a UK University Through Scholarship of Teaching and Learning.* Aysha Divan, Paul Taylor, and Andrea Jackson, University of Leeds, Leeds, UK, and Rafe Hallett, Keele University, Keele, UK (previously of University of Leeds).

Even though faculty at this university are already required to have higher education teaching certification as a condition of employment, this ADC supports faculty scholarship of teaching and learning projects focused on critical reflection theory to support academic outcomes.

Chapter 38: *Change in Practice: Achieving a Cultural Shift in Teaching and Learning Through a Theory of Change.* Grahame T. Bilbow, Centre for the Enhancement of Teaching and Learning, University of Hong Kong, Pok Fu Lam, Hong Kong.

This chapter describes how the theory of change was applied to manage the migration to new responsibilities and roles in an ADC.

11

Student Learning: A Framework for Designing Study Programs to Stimulate Deep Learning

Hester Glasbeek

Introduction

The mission of Learn! Academy is to strengthen the teaching and learning culture in higher education by empowering faculty and supporting them in order to integrate research-informed principles about learning and teaching into practice. For more information about how we empower and support faculty as well as information about our funding sources and reporting structure, please see Chap. 31. The focus in this chapter concerns the theoretical foundation of our mission, principles for course and program design, and the theories and principles we advocate with our faculties.

Designing Meaningful and Effective Study Programs

Learn! Academy aims to stimulate and support faculty to design meaningful and effective study programs; by that, we mean programs that contribute optimally to students' talent development and reduce unnecessary dropouts or study delays. Meaningful and effective programs help students to become

---

H. Glasbeek (✉)
LEARN! Academy, Vrije Universiteit, Amsterdam, Netherlands
e-mail: hesterglasbeek@reflectacademy.nl

© The Author(s), under exclusive license to Springer Nature Switzerland AG 2023
O. J. Neisler (ed.), *The Palgrave Handbook of Academic Professional Development Centers*,
Palgrave Studies on Leadership and Learning in Teacher Education,
https://doi.org/10.1007/978-3-030-80967-6_11

experts in their field by stimulating their interest and motivation and encouraging them to construct rich, adequate knowledge representations and acquire relevant academic and metacognitive skills (Glasbeek, 2015).

Theoretical Foundation

Constructivism

Our design approach is based on a constructivist view of learning. Thinking about this view and its implications is an eye-opener for many of our participants, since it contrasts with most novices' conception of teaching as 'teaching means telling what you know'. Common misunderstandings we meet about constructivism are that it is synonymous with the use of interactive teaching methods or with complete freedom for students to set their own goals. To solve these misunderstandings, it helps to clarify our position within the debate about constructivism and to contrast constructivism with more objectivist views of learning.

Constructivism is a popular and broad movement. Researchers and educational designers with a variety of ideas consider themselves to be constructivists. What they share is the assumption that learning is not a passive, knowledge-absorbing, and externally driven process, but an active, constructive, and self-directed process in which learners build up internal knowledge representations that form a personal interpretation of their learning experiences (Bednar et al., 1992). In our programs, we contrast constructivism against more objectivist views, such as the system approach (Merrill, 1983; Reigeluth & Stein, 1983), by pointing out the following differences:

* In a constructive approach, the student's perspective is central, whereas the objectivist tradition focuses more on the content and structure of instruction and the actions of the instructor.
* Constructivism attaches more importance to metacognitive skills and the ways in which knowledge is developed, whereas objectivist approaches put more emphasis on the body of knowledge that students must acquire. The aim of a constructivist education is not so much that the student knows things, but that they are capable of exploring ideas themselves and developing plausible interpretations from different perspectives (Cunningham, 1992).
* Constructivist approaches put more emphasis on interactive teaching methods. Some of our participants consider lecturing or having students

11 Student Learning: A Framework for Designing Study Programs... 173

read texts as 'passive' teaching methods. However, this does not follow from the constructivist view of learning. We tell our participants that every method can support the active construction of knowledge. While reading or listening, students can be actively connecting new information with existing knowledge with more intensity and a greater learning effect than while answering questions or following assignments all the time. What matters is that teachers keep wondering where students are in the process, and what experiences and activities they need in order to learn, instead of determining what students need to know and what information or instruction should be presented in which order.

Differences *within* constructivism relate to the question as to what extent meaningful knowledge construction is determined by the individual. Roughly two schools can be distinguished; namely, a radical school as well as one which is more moderate (Karagiorgi & Symeou, 2005). Radical constructivists believe that knowledge is unique for every individual and that every interpretation may be a good learning result, so long as that interpretation is meaningful and viable for the individual. The term 'viable' is used as an alternative to (the objectivist concept of) 'true' or 'correct'. Moderate constructivists believe that interpretations must also be socially viable and that construction of meaning takes place within the groups to which we belong (von Glasersfeld, 2001; Willis, 1998).

An interpretation that is only meaningful to the individual is inadequate; reality and the social context impose limitations on meaningful interpretations and claims. In addition, radical constructivism assumes that learners develop optimally if they are completely free to follow their own interests and set their own goals. The role of the teacher in this view is that of a coach or a process supervisor. Our design approach fits within a more moderate form of constructivism. It assigns a greater role to didactically skilled experts who can familiarize students with the codes and culture of the discipline and who can bring students in touch with goals, issues, and solutions they would not necessarily discover spontaneously.

Constructive Alignment

With his concept of constructive alignment, Biggs connects the constructivist view on learning to the concept of *alignment* derived from instruction theory (Biggs, 1996; Biggs & Tang, 2011). Alignment means that the various parts of a design are interrelated. In an aligned course (or curriculum), the goals,

174   H. Glasbeek

assessment forms, and teaching methods are all in agreement. In turn, *constructive* alignment implies that a course or curriculum is designed around the students' learning goals and activities, rather than around content and knowledge. This does not mean that content and knowledge are unimportant, as defining learning goals includes describing knowledge domains.

The implications of this concept can best be explained by describing an example of an 'unaligned' course. Suppose a teacher wanted their students to be able to draw connections between various theories, think critically, and analyze phenomena from different perspectives (i.e., the learning goals). This teacher offers seminars and assignments that serve these goals. Students are invited to unravel texts, come up with counterexamples for claims, apply concepts to real-life cases, and advocate various positions (i.e., the learning and teaching activities). However, for practical reasons (such as limited time and resources), the assessment is a multiple-choice exam in which facts, definitions, and unambiguous cases are questioned.

It is not difficult to predict which problems will arise in this course. If the students know beforehand that the assessment is a multiple-choice exam and that rote learning is the best strategy to pass, most will opt for this. They will not be motivated to take part in the class assignments and debates the teacher has in store for them. Moreover, although they will pass the exam, many of them will still not be able to see connections or think critically about the course subjects. The few students who are enthusiastic about the lessons and actively participate in class debates will be disappointed with the exam because it will not give them the opportunity to show what they have learned. Some from this group may fail, even though they have achieved the learning goals, because the examination asks for specific details whereas they have focused on larger concepts and connections.

Constructive alignment appears to be a simple but powerful concept in designing and evaluating courses and curricula. Although some of our participants think it is an open door at first glance, they gradually discover that their problems, like a lack of student motivation or low rates of achievement, can often be explained as a result of 'unalignment' at some level of their design.

Taxonomy of Significant Learning

A crucial step in educational design is constructing well-defined learning goals. The educational literature offers various taxonomies to support this step. Although there may be criticism as to their theoretical basis (Paul, 1985), these taxonomies appear to be helpful for teachers and designers. They meet

11 Student Learning: A Framework for Designing Study Programs... 175

the shared intuition that there are different kinds of knowledge and that to be able to reproduce a fact, term, or formula is different from being able to explain a fact, recognize a phenomenon in a new situation, and apply a formula properly at the right time. When novice teachers think about what students need to learn, they tend to think about specific areas and subjects (e.g., they must know about cell structure, cell processes, and photosynthesis). Working with a taxonomy helps them to define *how* students should be able to use their knowledge about these subjects (e.g., to describe and apply different cell processes at different organizational levels and to explain in their own words which factors influence these processes).

Commonly used taxonomies include those formulated by Bloom (Anderson & Krathwohl, 2001; Bloom & Krathwohl, 1956), Biggs (Biggs & Collis, 1982), and Miller (1990). In our programs, we use Fink's taxonomy of significant learning (Fink, 2013). Fink's taxonomy distinguishes six categories of learning goals: *foundational knowledge, application, integration, human dimension, caring,* and *learning to learn.*

We have several reasons for this choice. First, Fink encourages a broader view on academic learning, by distinguishing categories like 'caring', in addition to more traditional learning goals like 'applying' and 'analysing'. This fits with the importance our university attaches to societal impact and with its ambition to educate students to become responsible, critical, and committed academics who want to keep developing themselves. Second, Fink does not consider the acquisition of different types of knowledge as separate or successive processes, but as dynamic and interactive. Third, Fink's taxonomy is compatible with the Dublin descriptors, which describe the requirements all programs in European higher education must meet. This makes Fink an attractive model for determining and describing learning objectives at various levels.

However, one disadvantage of Fink's work, according to our participants, is that his categories are not clearly distinguished and defined, which makes the taxonomy hard to apply. Two remedies have proven useful to overcome this problem. Fink defines 'backward design' as a core principle in educational design; in other words, starting with the end in mind. One of the first steps attached to this principle is to finish this sentence: *"A year (or more) after this course is over, I want and hope that students will…".* This thought exercise stimulates teachers to look beyond learning goals like knowing and understanding. Also helpful to our participants are Fink's precise and meaningful examples of learning goals. For example, a year after this course is over, students will:

176 H. Glasbeek

- Remember the terms associated with microbial anatomy, biochemistry, and disease (*foundational knowledge*)
- Be able to perform a formal analysis of pictures when they visit an exhibition in an art museum in terms of the main elements of design (*application*)
- Integrate ideas about energy from chemistry and microbiology (*integration*)
- Become more confident regarding their ability to learn this material and be less intimidated by it (*human dimension*)
- Value the importance of precise language in this field of work, as part of professionalism (*caring*)
- Be able to identify important resources for their own subsequent learning (*learning how to learn*) (Fink, 2013, 76–78).

Student Motivation: Self-Determination Theory

Student motivation is a key issue for participants in our programs. Often participants express their disappointment with regards to the little interest students show in their subject and their high interest in passing exams. Many teachers believe that university students should demonstrate intrinsic motivation for their study. Our design approach does not consider interest and motivation as entry requirements, but as learning goals. Both intrinsic and extrinsic motivation are important for academic achievement and extrinsic motivation can develop into more intrinsic forms of motivation. A good degree program encourages and supports this development.

We find support for this position as well as starting points for design principles in the self-determination theory (SDT) proposed by Deci and Ryan (1985). The SDT acknowledges the power of intrinsic motivation as a natural wellspring of learning and achievement, resulting in high-quality learning and creativity. Besides this, the theory also states that intrinsic motivation can be systematically catalyzed or undermined by one's environment (Ryan & Stiller, 1991).

Deci and Ryan (1985) go on to describe two psychological needs that must be fulfilled for intrinsic motivation: the need for *competence* and the need for *autonomy*. People want to feel that they are capable of fulfilling the tasks they are assigned, that they are good at something. If the tasks are always too difficult, their need to feel *competent* is unfulfilled and there will be no room for intrinsic motivation. If the tasks are too easy, they get no chance to experience or show their competence and the intrinsic motivation they might have had will be extinguished. In addition, a sense of *autonomy* is required for intrinsic motivation. Students must feel they themselves are the cause of their sense of competence. Deci and Ryan (1985) refer to this as the need for an "internal perceived locus of causality". A tight structure with many small sub-tasks and little freedom to make one's own choices may contribute to the feeling of being competent, but still impedes intrinsic motivation because the need for a feeling of autonomy is not fulfilled.

Competence and autonomy are necessary conditions but not entirely self-sufficient for intrinsic motivation. People do not find every task interesting, even if they feel perfectly capable of carrying out the task and are allowed to make their own choices while doing so. For most students, their degree program includes subjects they do not find spontaneously interesting. For those subjects, they need a form of extrinsic motivation to persevere with and accomplish their goals. According to Ryan and Deci (2000), the distinction between intrinsic versus extrinsic motivation is generally presented too dichotomously. They suggest a continuum in which different degrees of motivation are distinguished, with intrinsic motivation as the highest form (Ryan & Deci, 2000, 61).

In the most autonomous form of external motivation, *integration*, students integrate the value of an allocated (not chosen) task into their own values and norms. Just as with intrinsic motivation, these students experience their actions as their own choice. The main difference is that student do not just act for the pleasure of reading and studying, but because of a value outside of that activity (e.g., doing well in your profession and being able to contribute to society). The quality of the learning outcomes of studying regulated by *integration* can be assumed to be comparable to intrinsically-motivated studying, whereas more externally regulated studying is related to more superficial learning and lower study effort (Kusurkar et al., 2013).

Study programs and teachers can support students to reach higher forms of external motivation. However, once again the human needs for autonomy and competence must be adequately met. In relation to extrinsic motivation, Ryan and Deci (2000) mention a third basic human need: the need for a sense of *relatedness*. In order for them to integrate the values the study program stands for, it helps for students to feel that they are seen and appreciated by their teachers and fellow students and that they belong to the study community.

The SDT appears to be inspiring for our participants. Teachers appreciate the positive view on education as it relates to the SDT, because it aims to help individuals develop into competent and independent professionals and members of society. In addition, the work by Ryan and Deci expresses a sense of reality (Deci & Ryan, 1985; Ryan & Deci, 2000). The power of intrinsic motivation is recognized, but they do not claim that students will do great as long as they can follow their own desires. By identifying autonomy, competence, and relatedness as basic needs that must be fulfilled to enable 'higher' forms of motivation, resulting in better learning, the SDT also offers starting points for design principles. These will be described later in this chapter in the recommendations section.

Empirical Foundation

In our programs on educational design, teachers think about the three components of Biggs' constructive alignment model—*learning goals and intended outcomes, assessment forms and feedback*, and *learning and teaching activities*—both separately and in conjunction, after an analysis of *relevant contextual factors* (Biggs, 1996; Biggs & Tang, 2011). Participants are encouraged to adopt a research-informed approach in doing so and consider empirical evidence, such as Schneider and Preckel (2017), Hattie (2013), Hattie and Timperley (2007), Kuh et al. (2011), Bain (2011), Nilson (2016), and Panadero and Jonnson (2013). The following section briefly summarizes relevant evidence for each component of the design process.

Analysis of the Context

The most important variables to consider in this step of the design process are student and teacher variables. These are more decisive than, for instance, characteristics of the institution or technology (Schneider & Preckel, 2017). In general, the students' starting level is the most important predictor for academic achievement. Other relevant student variables include motivation (Feltzer & Rickli, 2009; Kusurkar et al., 2013), metacognitive skills (Wang et al., 1990), and study strategies (Cotton, 2000; Vermunt, 2005). Study programs can take measures to improve the starting position of upcoming students, for instance, by:

* Helping students choose an appropriate degree program by giving good, realistic study information and organizing an informative introduction that promotes curiosity and involvement
* Knowing the students' qualities, interests, and knowledge gaps, for instance by using a formative entrance assessment
* Promoting academic and social integration from the first day
* Explaining and illustrating from the first day what is expected of students in terms of study behavior and effort, giving them feedback on these, and letting them reflect on differences with their previous education

- Offering targeted remedial education, on a voluntary basis, for students who are underprepared, for instance in math and academic reading or writing
- Being sensitive to diversity and ensuring that every student can feel at home.

According to Hattie (2009), the quality of the teachers is the most important influence on student performance over which schools have some control. This finding is in line with the findings of a meta-analysis by Schneider and Preckel (2017) on achievement in higher education. Good teachers invest time and effort in designing well-structured courses, establishing clear learning goals, and employing effective feedback practices. They stimulate meaningful learning with interaction, clear explanations, and demanding learning tasks (Schneider & Preckel, 2017). These findings emphasize the importance of well-thought-out strategies for teacher professionalization. As described in more detail in Chap. 31, Learn! Academy targets programs for university teachers at various levels, in which formal and informal forms of learning are blended and the development of teaching qualities is connected to leadership development.

Learning Goals and Intended Outcomes

Clear, meaningful, and challenging learning goals are associated with students' achievement (Schneider & Preckel, 2017). According to Fink's work and the SDT, it can be deduced that various types of learning goals should be combined in each module (Deci & Ryan, 1985; Fink, 2013). The traditional idea that first-year students need to acquire basic concepts and must not be confronted with more complex problems can be discouraging and demotivating.

More empirical evidence for this recommendation can be found in Billing (2007) and Renkl et al. (1996). Based on his research into the acquisition of academic skills, Billing (2007) concludes that there is little transfer of these skills when they are offered separately from domain-specific knowledge. Conversely, the isolated provision of domain-specific content leads to inert knowledge which is not activated in situations where this knowledge is needed (Renkl et al., 1996).

Assessment and Feedback

Students' study behavior is strongly influenced by their expectations about assessment (Sambell & McDowell, 1998). This result fits within the concept of constructive alignment: if deep processing is intended, deep processing must be assessed. Regular and good feedback has also been found to contribute considerably to more effective studying and better achievement (Gibbs & Simpson, 2004; Hattie, 2009; Hattie & Timperley, 2007). According to Hattie and Timperley (2007), good feedback enables students to answer three questions: *Where am I going to, How am I going,* and *What is my next step?*

Rubrics can be a useful feedback tool. Well-constructed rubrics can help students to understand the meaning of criteria, reflect on their own work, and stimulate the development of metacognitive skills (Jonsson & Svingby, 2007; Panadero & Jonsson, 2013). A prerequisite for success is that the use of a rubric is integrated into the learning process; simply handing out the rubric to the students at the beginning or the end of the course does not work.

Teaching and Learning Activities

There is much evidence that students learn more from teaching methods that explicitly invite them to think and talk about study material than from lectures where they mainly or exclusively listen (Schneider & Preckel, 2017). However, how 'activating' teaching methods must be is related to the students' level of self-regulation. For students who are highly self-regulating, too much activation can actually be unproductive (Vermunt & Verloop, 1999). And since most degree programs aim to educate autonomous, lifelong learners, it is recommended to reduce external regulation and activation over the course of the curriculum and to make clear to students that more initiative and independence is gradually expected from them (Glasbeek & Visser, 2018).

A point of attention is the relationship between contact hours and self-study. Van der Drift and Vos (1987) found that the optimal amount of contact hours is between 300 and 400 hours per year. Gijselaers and Schmidt (1995) mention an optimal number of 12 contact hours per week. With less contact time, students become less involved and give priority to other activities; with more contact time, students do not get enough room for self-study. An optimal relationship is determined not only by quantity, but also by quality. Students must experience alignment between self-study assignments and contact hours. They must notice that the outcome of self-study assignments returns in their lectures and that contact time must be used to structure self-study time as well as possible (Schmidt et al., 2010). Fink's idea of a 'Castle Top sheet' (Fink, 2013) is useful for achieving this alignment.

Conclusion and Recommendations

One of the conclusions teachers may draw from our teaching qualification programs is that course and program design is complex. Educational designers have to take into account a large number of factors and interests, some of which reinforce each other while others are in conflict. Programs must provide both sufficient space for student autonomy and sufficient structure and support to reinforce student competence. The optimal balance differs per individual. Students (like other people) want to learn and develop and most students want to get the best out of their studies, but also from the rest of their lives, given that studying competes with many other goals and activities. That is why students, although they may genuinely want to get the best out of their studies, regularly decide to take their exams with minimal effort.

Most teachers want to offer their students the best possible programs. But teachers are also human beings with their own goals and worries. Apart from teaching, they often have administrative and research tasks, the latter of which are often valued more highly. Three recommendations are therefore crucial for these kinds of dilemmas. They do not offer a guarantee of success, but do form the necessary conditions for success:

1. Keep balancing. Designing meaningful and effective study programs is a complex task and requires the art of balancing. Many factors and interests, interacting in many ways, must be considered.
2. Keep in touch. Teachers, students, alumni, education managers, and managers must keep searching for dialogue; keep asking and telling each other what you do and why you do it.
3. Keep searching for feedback (Hattie, 2009). Assume that a student's progress or lack of progress is feedback on the quality of the curriculum, rather than an evaluation of the student's talents.

References

Anderson, L. W., & Krathwohl, D. R. (2001). *A taxonomy for learning, teaching, and assessing: A revision of Bloom's taxonomy of educational objectives.* Longman.

Bain, K. (2011). *What the best college teachers do.* Harvard University Press.

Bednar, A. K., Cunningham, D., Duffy, T. M., & Perry, J. D. (1992). Theory into practice: How do we link. In T. M. Duffy & D. H. Jonassen (Eds.), *Constructivism and the technology of instruction: A conversation* (pp. 17–34). Routledge.

182 H. Glasbeek

Biggs, J. (1996). Enhancing teaching through constructive alignment. *Higher Education, 32*(3), 347–364.

Biggs, J. B., & Collis, K. F. (1982). *Evaluation the quality of learning: The SOLO taxonomy (structure of the observed learning outcome)*. Academic Press.

Biggs, J., & Tang, C. (2011). *Teaching for quality learning at university*. McGraw-Hill Education.

Billing, D. (2007). Teaching for transfer of core/key skills in higher education: Cognitive skills. *Higher Education, 53*(4), 483–516.

Bloom, B. S., & Krathwohl, D. R. (1956). *Taxonomy of educational objectives: The classification of educational goals. Handbook I: Cognitive domain*. Addison-Wesley Longman Ltd.

Cotton, K. (2000). *The schooling practices that matter most*. Office of Educational Research and Improvement, U.S. Department of Education. https://files.eric.ed.gov/fulltext/ED469234.pdf

Cunningham, D. J. (1992). Beyond educational psychology: Steps toward an educational semiotic. *Educational Psychology Review, 4*(2), 165–194.

Deci, E. L., & Ryan, R. M. (1985). *Intrinsic motivation and self-determination in human behavior*. Springer Science & Business Media.

Feltzer, M., & Rickli, S. (2009). *The influence of personality traits and other factors on dropout in higher education*. Tilburg University.

Fink, L. D. (2013). *Creating significant learning experiences: An integrated approach to designing college courses*. John Wiley & Sons.

Gibbs, G., & Simpson, C. (2004). Conditions under which assessment supports students' learning. *Learning and Teaching in Higher Education, 1*(1), 3–31.

Gijselaers, W. H., & Schmidt, H. G. (1995). Effects of quantity of instruction on time spent on learning and achievement. *Educational Research and Evaluation, 1*(2), 183–201.

Glasbeek, H. A. (2015). *What works in higher education? Recommendations for developing an educational and studyable curriculum*. Vrije Universiteit.

Glasbeek, H. A., & Visser, K. (2018). Motiveer mij intrinsiek!: Leidt verschoolsing tot motivatieverlies bij studenten? *Tijdschrift voor Hoger Onderwijs, 36*(3), 5–22.

Hattie, J. (2013). *Visible learning: A synthesis of over 800 meta-analyses relating to achievement*. Routledge.

Hattie, J., & Timperley, H. (2007). The power of feedback. *Review of Educational Research, 77*(1), 81–112.

Jonsson, A., & Svingby, G. (2007). The use of scoring rubrics: Reliability, validity and educational consequences. *Educational Research Review, 2*(2), 130–144.

Karagiorgi, Y., & Symeou, L. (2005). Translating constructivism into instructional design: Potential and limitations. *Educational Technology & Society, 8*(1), 17–27.

Kuh, G. D., Kinzie, J., Schuh, J. H., & Whitt, E. J. (2011). *Student success in college: Creating conditions that matter*. John Wiley & Sons.

Kusurkar, R. A., Ten Cate, T. J., Vos, C. M. P., Westers, P., & Croiset, G. (2013). How motivation affects academic performance: A structural equation modelling analysis. *Advances in Health Sciences Education, 18*(1), 57–69.

Merrill, D. (1983). Component display theory. In C. M. Reigeluth (Ed.), *Instructional design theories and models: An overview of their current states*. Lawrence Erlbaum Associates.

Miller, G. E. (1990). The assessment of clinical skills/competence/performance. *Academic Medicine, 65*(9), S63–S67.

Nilson, L. B. (2016). *Teaching at its best: A research-based resource for college instructors*. John Wiley & Sons.

Panadero, E., & Jonsson, A. (2013). The use of scoring rubrics for formative assessment purposes revisited: A review. *Educational Research Review, 9*, 129–144.

Paul, R. W. (1985). Bloom's taxonomy and critical thinking instruction. *Educational Leadership, 42*(8), 36–39.

Reigeluth, C. M., & Stein, R. (1983). Elaboration theory. In C. M. Reigeluth (Ed.), *Instructional-design theories and models: An overview of their current status*. Routledge.

Renkl, A., Mandl, H., & Gruber, H. (1996). Inert knowledge: Analyses and remedies. *Educational Psychologist, 31*(2), 115–121.

Ryan, R. M., & Deci, E. L. (2000). Intrinsic and extrinsic motivations: Classic definitions and new directions. *Contemporary Educational Psychology, 25*(1), 54–67.

Ryan, R. M., & Stiller, J. (1991). The social contexts of internalization: Parent and teacher influences on autonomy, motivation and learning. *Advances in Motivation and Achievement, 7*, 115–149.

Sambell, K., & McDowell, L. (1998). The construction of the hidden curriculum: Messages and meanings in the assessment of student learning. *Assessment and Evaluation in Higher Education, 23*(4), 391–402.

Schmidt, H. G., Cohen-Schotanus, J., van der Molen, H. T., Splinter, T. A., Bulte, J., Holdrinet, R., & van Rossum, H. J. (2010). Learning more by being taught less: A "time-for-self-study" theory explaining curricular effects on graduation rate and study duration. *Higher Education, 60*(3), 287–300.

Schneider, M., & Preckel, F. (2017). Variables associated with achievement in higher education: A systematic review of meta-analyses. *Psychological Bulletin, 143*(6), 565–600.

van der Drift, K. D., & Vos, P. (1987). *Anatomy of a learning environment: An educational economics analysis of university education*. Swets & Zeitlinger.

Vermunt, J. D. (2005). Relations between student learning patterns and personal and contextual factors and academic performance. *Higher Education,49*(3), 205.

Vermunt, J., & Verloop, N. (1999). Learning and instruction. *Congruence and Friction Between Leaving and Teaching, 9*(3), 257–280.

von Glasersfeld, E. (2001). The radical constructivist view of science. *Foundations of Science, 6*(1–3), 31–43.

Wang, M. C., Haertel, G. D., & Walberg, H. J. (1990). What influences learning? A content analysis of review literature. *Journal of Educational Research, 84*(1), 30–43.

Willis, J. (1998). Alternative instructional design paradigms: What's worth discussing and what isn't. *Educational Technology & Society, 38*(3), 5–16.

12

Theoretical Foundations for Online and Hybrid Faculty Development Initiatives

Bridgette Atkins, Caroline Ferguson, Jeanette Oliveira, Sarah Stokes, and Susan L. Forbes

Introduction

This chapter briefly explores the background and history of the Teaching and Learning Centre (TLC) at the University of Ontario Institute of Technology (Ontario Tech), its mission and institutional values, along with some of the theoretical foundations that inform the growth of its faculty development offerings. The chapter focuses on TLC programs and services that are delivered in online and hybrid (a combination of online and face-to-face) modalities.

Ontario Tech, one of Ontario's youngest universities, was founded in 2002 with the mission of providing technology-enriched education that prepares students for an evolving employment landscape and lifelong learning (Ontario Tech, 2019a). The emphasis on these goals was apparent by faculty members' integration of technology in the classroom, the use of a learning management system (LMS), and a mandatory laptop program for students. The university offers a variety of online courses and programs wherein students and faculty can connect remotely, either synchronously in real-time using video-conferencing tools or asynchronously using the LMS and other learning technologies. This

---

B. Atkins (✉) • C. Ferguson • J. Oliveira • S. Stokes • S. L. Forbes
University of Ontario Institute of Technology, Oshawa, ON, Canada
e-mail: bridgette.atkins@ontariotechu.net; caroline.ferguson@ontariotechu.ca; jeanette.oliveira@ontariotechu.ca; sarah.stokes@ontariotechu.ca; susan.forbes@ontariotechu.ca

© The Author(s), under exclusive license to Springer Nature Switzerland AG 2023
O. J. Neisler (ed.), *The Palgrave Handbook of Academic Professional Development Centers*, Palgrave Studies on Leadership and Learning in Teacher Education, https://doi.org/10.1007/978-3-030-80967-6_12

186   B. Atkins et al.

allows greater access to the university for students and/or instructors who are limited by their geographical location and are unable to attend the campus in person. Additionally, the flexibility of online courses provides greater opportunity for students who are engaged in part-time or even full-time employment to participate in courses offered by the university.

The key priorities of the TLC, which are described further in this chapter, closely reflect the mission, vision, and values of the university. An essential component of these priorities involves the integration of a variety of technologies (e.g., video editing software, online assignment systems, and polling software), which underscores the need for the TLC to support a wide range of educational tools and course delivery modalities. As such, the TLC has focused a considerable amount of attention on developing faculty training programs that are offered in online and hybrid modalities. Some of these programs include the New to Ontario Tech University Orientation, the Certificate in University Teaching (CUT) program, as well as a variety of online workshops and training sessions. Through these online and hybrid offerings, the center can model best practices in online and hybrid course development and facilitation, as well as provide faculty with opportunities to engage in professional development through these modalities.

Many of the faculty development programs and services offered by the TLC are grounded in a variety of theoretical principles and frameworks, such as social constructivism, constructive alignment, and backward design, as well as universal design for learning (UDL). An introduction of these theoretical foundations and principles will be followed by an exploration of key TLC offerings that are guided by these foundations. This chapter will conclude with lessons learned and future program directions.

Early Days of Teaching and Learning at Ontario Tech

Teaching and learning support at Ontario Tech started in 2002 under the leadership of Dr. William Muirhead, Director of Learning Technologies, and was primarily meant to support new faculty hires and the implementation of the mandatory laptop program (W. Muirhead, personal communication, October 3, 2019). Evolving over time to meet changing needs, the TLC went on to offer professional development, pedagogy/andragogy support, learning technology training, and multimedia development to those engaged in teaching at Ontario Tech. As the university and its faculty complement grew, additional demand was placed on the TLC. Educational multimedia requests drove much of the TLC support and workshop offerings. These requests grew out of the desire to use various multimedia within the LMS, such as videos, learning objects, and simulations (Brar & Drea, 2017), and reflect elements of the current organizational structure and services offered.

TLC Organizational Structure and Services Offered

The TLC consists of a specialized team that provides instructional support, multimedia development, and educational technology training for members of the Ontario Tech teaching community. The following section outlines the current organizational structure of the TLC, expands on current offerings, and concludes with the vision, mission, and priorities that guide the work of the center.

Organizational Structure

The current organizational structure of the TLC is shown in Fig. 12.1. The manager of the TLC oversees the team, which consists of a faculty development coordinator, five faculty development officers, four multimedia developers, an educational technology analyst, and an open educational resources laboratory supervisor.

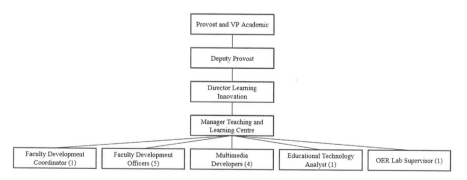

Fig. 12.1 Organizational structure of the TLC, Ontario Tech

Current Services

To support the variety of teaching modalities used in Ontario Tech courses, and the development needs of faculty who have varying schedules and places of residence, the TLC offers support in face-to-face, hybrid, and online formats, or via telephone where appropriate. Table 12.1 summarizes the current offerings of the TLC, as well as the modality used for each. Information regarding current offerings in this chapter pertains to services, programs, and workshops offered in 2019.

New Vision and Priorities

In August 2017, the TLC team explored the center's updated vision and mission statements and three key priorities, in order to better align its activities with those of the institution:

> The mission of the Teaching and Learning Centre at [Ontario Tech] is to empower faculty to reach their potential as educators and to create a culture where effective teaching is valued. We will champion the scholarship of teaching and implementation of pedagogy. We will create valuable teaching and learning professional development experiences. We will move [Ontario Tech] towards being a leader in teaching excellence, ultimately leading to greater student success. Key priorities:
>
> 1. Aiding and empowering faculty (and other university instructors) to enhance the learning experience for students.
> 2. Advancing the role and work of the Teaching and Learning Centre to create a culture that "inspires" faculty to reach their potential as educators.
> 3. Supporting the effectiveness and growth of online, hybrid, and experiential offerings. (Brar & Drea, 2017, 6)

Informed by these principles, a key focus of the TLC is to empower members of the teaching community to explore new and innovative tools and best practices with the intent of enhancing student learning.

Theoretical Foundations

The TLC strives to ground their educational development initiatives in relevant theoretical principles to promote best practices in teaching and learning. Recognizing the value that instructors bring to the teaching community, the

Table 12.1 Offerings of the TLC and their modalities

Service	Description	Modality
Teaching Support	Classroom observations and feedback, one-on-one or group consultations, and workshops on effective teaching methods, evaluation, assessment and feedback, and instructional design	Face-to-face, telephone, or online
Learning Technology	Support on a range of educational technology tools (e.g., classroom response systems, LMS, examination lock downs, online tests and assignments, screen capturing/video software)	Face-to-face, telephone, or online
Multimedia Design	Support in the development of video lectures, podcasts, learning objects, etc. Faculty can also receive training on creating their own multimedia or book the center's recording studio	Face-to-face
Professional Development	Two teaching development programs are offered, including a CUT program for faculty, PhD candidates, and teaching-related staff (e.g., clinical instructors and non-academic staff) and a CUT program for teaching assistants and master's students	Hybrid
Onboarding	The New to Ontario Tech University Orientation program is offered for individuals new to teaching roles at the university. New teaching assistants receive a similar program which is tailored to their specific needs. Tailored onboarding is also provided to programs and reflects their specific needs (e.g., clinical instructors in nursing, site supervisors/preceptors for medical laboratory sciences)	Hybrid or face-to-face
Resources	The TLC website provides various resources that support teaching practices and related areas (e.g., UDL, effective feedback, teaching online and hybrid courses, teaching dossier). The website also houses a Learning Library, which features tutorial videos, downloadable tip sheets, and other resources to support the implementation of a variety of teaching technologies	Online
Awards	The TLC honors teaching excellence and innovation through its annual awards. The Teaching Innovation Fund provides support for faculty to explore inventive teaching practices. The TLC also provides support related to external teaching awards	N/A

Data sources: Brar and Drea (2017) and Ontario Tech (2019b)

foundation for much of the programming offered by the TLC is underpinned by the theory of social constructivism. Additionally, the TLC has aimed to utilize a variety of relevant principles and frameworks for designing effective teaching and learning initiatives, including constructive alignment and backward design, as well as UDL. Many of these principles and frameworks, including constructive alignment and UDL, are commonly reinforced when TLC staff engage with faculty who are designing their own courses (Atkins et al., 2016). However, this chapter focuses on how these theoretical foundations, frameworks, and principles are applied in various TLC programs and workshops.

Social Constructivism

The theory of constructivism states that the process of learning occurs when the learner can connect new concepts with pre-existing knowledge (Naylor & Keogh, 1999). To build on this theory, social constructivism extends beyond an individual's learning and argues that the act of constructing knowledge is a shared experience (Prawatt & Floden, 1994). Viewing learning through the lens of social constructivism, individuals develop their own reality through interactions with their peers, instructors, coworkers, family members, or members of the community. Thus, deep learning can be facilitated through collaboration between individuals.

In an educational setting, social constructivism is leveraged when individuals come together to share their collective knowledge. In a traditional classroom, the instructor lectures while learners listen and absorb information. Alternatively, in a learning environment that is grounded in social constructivism theory, individuals are encouraged to interact with one another and share their thoughts and experiences to build upon their collective knowledge.

The theory of social constructivism can be applied to the design and delivery of educational experiences to encourage collaboration, value the experiences of participants, and remove the sense of isolation in learning. Applying social constructivist principles can help promote a sense of community among learners and enhance student engagement. This theory forms the foundation of many of the center's faculty development programs and currently plays a key role in curriculum planning, use of technology for delivery of programs, and interactions between facilitators and participants. Incorporating theories of social constructivism into the TLC's programs allows for rich and well-grounded educational opportunities for instructors across campus.

Additional Frameworks and Principles for Application

Several additional frameworks and guiding principles relevant to the social constructivist approach are applied in the design of the TLC's faculty development programming, including constructive alignment, elements of backward design, and UDL. This section discusses each of these guiding principles and frameworks and illustrates some of the ways they are applied by the TLC.

Constructive Alignment and Backward Design

In constructive alignment, teaching and learning activities and assessment methods aid in the achievement of learning outcomes (Biggs, 2003). In other words, learning outcomes, teaching and learning activities, and assessment methods should all be directly connected and relevant to one another. Similarly, backward design emphasizes awareness of the end or desired outcomes of a learning experience (Wiggens & McTighe, 2005). Learning outcomes are identified early in the program planning, before selecting relevant assessment methods, activities, and learning materials. This approach differs from models where specific learning resources and/or activities serve as the starting point for development (Wiggens & McTighe, 2005).

Additionally, and in keeping with the underlying theory of social constructivism, constructive alignment also acknowledges that learners "construct meaning through relevant learning activities" (Biggs, 2003, 3). To this end, faculty development programming offered by the TLC often places a focus on meaningful learning activities and engagement with peers rather than a primarily didactic or lecture-based approach. As such, participants' success depends on their willingness to engage in discussions and share their perspectives, questions and experiences.

UDL

UDL outlines ways to proactively consider and address potential barriers to learning. Three overarching UDL principles, explored below, emphasize the importance of providing multiple means of: (1) student engagement; (2) representation; and (3) action and expression (Meyer et al., 2014). Multiple means of engagement explores "the 'why' of learning" (Meyer et al., 2014, 52); a key aspect of this principle is the importance of flexibility, as what motivates one person may not motivate another. In contrast, multiple means of representation focus on "the 'what' of learning" (Meyer et al., 2014, 54); this principle involves varying ways in which content is provided to learners. Finally, multiple means of action and expression refer to "the 'how' of learning" (Meyer et al., 2014, 55), which involves supporting learners in their own goal-setting and planning. TLC facilitators endeavor to create and curate learning resources in a variety of modalities, vary the types of learning activities that are included in programming, and offer participants flexibility and choice wherever possible. Despite an awareness of UDL principles, better integration of these frameworks across all TLC offerings is something the center continually strives to improve.

The three principles discussed above enable teaching and learning professionals to plan programming that is engaging and accessible to members of the learning community, while also emulating good practices commonly explored in TLC programming. Examples of how these principles are applied in TLC programming are explained further in this chapter. Furthermore, while efforts to include elements of constructive alignment, backward design, and principles of UDL were applied in designing online and hybrid faculty development initiatives offered by the TLC, application of these principles to other areas of our offerings requires further development.

Design of Hybrid and Online Faculty Development Programs

This section outlines a few of the TLC's current offerings (in fall 2019) that are delivered in hybrid and online formats, including the New to Ontario Tech University Orientation workshop, the CUT program, as well as various TLC workshops that are offered online.

Onboarding

While the TLC offers tailored teaching and learning orientation programming for incoming groups such as teaching assistants, clinical instructors, faculty advisors, and other roles within the university, this section will focus on the new faculty orientation workshop, currently referred to as the New to Ontario Tech University Orientation. This hybrid offering provides new members of the teaching community with key information needed to get started in a teaching role at the university, meet other new colleagues, and

12 Theoretical Foundations for Online and Hybrid Faculty... 193

learn about future professional development opportunities to engage in teaching and learning initiatives.

There are two parts to the workshop programming, with part one being facilitated online through a web-conferencing platform, while part two is facilitated in a face-to-face modality. Providing the online component of this orientation allows TLC staff, as well as other members of the university, such as those working in the library, to connect with new hires who may not be located in close proximity to the campus or those who teach fully online, and allows participants to experience the use of online tools they may use in their own practice. Inclusion of the face-to-face component allows newly hired faculty to continue forming connections with new colleagues, while also becoming familiar with various campus locations and support staff that were not a part of the online sessions. The New to Ontario Tech University Orientation workshops feature discussions on UDL, classroom management strategies, inclusive teaching strategies, active learning strategies, academic integrity, library resources, student mental health services, a showcase of educational technology tools, and LMS training.

Following a social constructivist approach, the TLC has been mindful of incorporating opportunities for social learning in this orientation. As such, the TLC staff have placed an increased focus on designing session activities that allow attendees to explore key topics with peers. For example, a case-based approach was utilized in several of the workshop sessions in the summer/fall 2019 offering of the orientation to allow participants to exchange their own ideas, experiences, and questions related to topics explored and gain insight from the presenters. During these sessions, participants were given several case studies, which encouraged them to discuss classroom management strategies, consider approaches to support inclusive learning, and become familiar with procedures related to student accessibility.

In keeping with a UDL approach to program design and delivery, information exchange, the presentation of resources, and the means by which participants are able to contribute to this orientation session are varied. For example, the online and face-to-face components of the workshop provide participants with varied opportunities to engage in the sessions. In addition, information is presented in a variety of formats, such as through video, case studies, additional readings, training resources, and presentations.

The CUT Program

The CUT program is one of the TLC's main faculty development program offerings and is delivered in a hybrid format. The program encourages members of the Ontario Tech teaching community to develop their teaching practice by sharing their experiences and forming new connections with their colleagues. Although the TLC offers two CUT programs (please refer to Table 12.1 for more details), this section will focus on the main CUT program, which is offered for teaching staff, academic associates, sessional (part-time) instructors, and staff, as well as tenured and tenure-track faculty members.

A report on practice by Koroluk et al. (2016) outlines the foundational design decisions and components of this CUT program, including specific program requirements, the inclusion of guest facilitators for some of the module topics, and the program's constructivist roots. As explained in the report, TLC staff involved in designing early iterations of the program were cognizant of constructive alignment and applied a backward design approach (Koroluk et al., 2016). Overall program outcomes were determined first, before drilling down to determine relevant module topics, individual module outcomes, relevant learning activities, and completion requirements (Koroluk et al., 2016).

The CUT program consists of 14 modules, each focusing on a teaching-related topic. Current module topics include instructional design and learning outcomes, UDL, accessible instructional materials, assessment and effective feedback, active learning strategies, and technology and teaching. Three of the modules—mental health and wellness in education, finding and using open educational resources, and learning theories—are currently facilitated and/or co-planned by members of the university external to the TLC with relevant subject matter expertise.

A future direction noted by earlier facilitators of the CUT program was to increase the proportion of modules that were delivered in an online format, thus making the program more accessible for participants with scheduling conflicts (Koroluk et al., 2016). This suggestion has been implemented as the program evolved. Currently, of the 14 modules, five are delivered in a face-to-face format, three are delivered synchronously via a web-conferencing platform, and the remaining six are delivered asynchronously using an LMS platform to deliver content, facilitate group discussions, and retrieve assignment submissions. Additionally, participants must only complete 10 out of 14 modules, thus providing additional flexibility and the opportunity for

12 Theoretical Foundations for Online and Hybrid Faculty... 195

participants to choose which modules are of the greatest interest to them. As new iterations of the CUT program have been developed, with more and more online components replacing some of the face-to-face sessions, integrating elements of social constructivism to modules that were purely online—whether synchronous or asynchronous—became a major focus.

Whether face-to-face or online, facilitators provide resources for each module and drive discussions based on the topic of interest, while participants are encouraged to share their teaching experiences, ideas, and perspectives with the group. Whereas thoughtful integration of community-building activities in a classroom environment requires some planning and preparation, building community in an online environment can be a difficult task. In online modules of the CUT program, participants are asked to engage in personal reflections about their own teaching practice and respond to colleagues' posts in online discussion forums using the LMS. While given the option of sharing their discussion responses via text submissions, participants are also encouraged to respond in video format, thereby enhancing the feeling of community among participants in the program and allowing participants the option to choose their preferred mode(s) of communication. Additionally, CUT program facilitators create and share videos of themselves.

In addition to using discussion forums via an LMS, participants are asked to work collectively with their colleagues using various web-based applications that enable collaboration such as Google Docs, wikis, or Padlets. Furthermore, in online synchronous sessions via a web-conferencing platform, participants are often placed in breakout groups where they are asked to work collectively on a particular task and then report back to the larger group. In some modules, participants have been asked to supply case scenarios in advance to share for exploration during synchronous sessions.

Since programming offered through the TLC, including the CUT program, is not mandated, and formal recognition (via a transcript notation, for example) is not provided to participants upon completion, defining relevant assessment methods has been a key consideration (Koroluk et al., 2016). One area requiring further development identified by recent TLC facilitators of the CUT program is to include more effective assessment methods that would enable participants to also receive enriched feedback throughout the program. Current informal assessment methods within the program include the following:

* Completion of short, online 'exit tickets' at the end of each module (primarily for tracking completion and to provide facilitators with formative feedback)

- Classroom observation by TLC staff
- Reflection on a peer observation of teaching
- Submission of a teaching philosophy statement (for feedback)
- A brief presentation summarizing the key elements of one's own teaching philosophy (online or face-to-face) at the end of the program.

Currently, feedback provided to participants within the program is, for the most part, informal and unstructured. For example, rubrics are not currently used for required program elements. Inclusion of more formalized methods for assessment and feedback could aid in further demonstrating good practices in communicating assessment expectations and providing effective feedback to learners.

Faculty Development Workshops

This section explores two TLC workshop offerings provided in an online format using a web-conferencing tool that fall in line with a social constructivist approach: the Introduction to Adobe Connect workshop, which focuses on educating instructors on how to effectively teach online using a specific web-conferencing platform, and the Introduction to Universal Design workshop, which exposes faculty to flexible teaching approaches using the UDL framework outlined by the Center for Applied Special Technologies (2018).

When planning workshop offerings, TLC facilitators commonly identify a set of learning outcomes and then choose learning activities that are relevant to each of the outcomes and anticipated to be feasible to facilitate within the short time-frames typically given (i.e., one to two hours). Assessment methods employed in the workshops are largely informal and formative in nature. To set the tone for the workshop and promote engagement and interactivity, the facilitators turn on their webcams and encourage participants to do the same.

In the Introduction to Adobe Connect workshop, facilitators emphasize the benefits of encouraging all participants to use their webcams and microphones, focusing on the positive effects this can have on community-building in an online class. To encourage discussion among participants, each online session begins with introductions by the facilitators, along with introductions by each of the participants, where they are commonly asked to share their interests and goals for the session. This helps build a safe learning community and also provides participants with an opportunity to set up their audio and webcam and begin exploring and navigating the virtual room.

To create an interactive learning experience that fosters engagement and collaboration among participants, smaller group activities are structured and delivered using breakout rooms within the web-conferencing platform. This allows participants to build on their previous knowledge through interactions with their peers. For example, in a previous offering of the Introduction to Universal Design workshop, participants were organized into three breakout groups. Each group was placed in their own virtual breakout room and given the task of summarizing their assigned UDL principle and brainstorming three different examples of how they could incorporate this principle into their course. Once this was complete, all participants were sent back to the main meeting room, and each breakout group was given the opportunity to share their thoughts with the larger group.

Despite being facilitated completely online and over a shorter period of time than the other two professional development offerings explored in this chapter, these faculty development workshops serve to exemplify how the TLC seeks to facilitate professional development workshops that embody elements of the theoretical approach and good practices in teaching and learning that guide much of the center's other offerings.

Conclusions and Lessons Learned

This chapter explored some of the background and history of the TLC at Ontario Tech, along with theoretical foundations that inform the development and facilitation of its current online and blended/hybrid faculty development offerings. The use of technology is a significant part of the TLC's history for several reasons, given that Ontario Tech was an early adopter of a technology-enriched learning environment program through its mandatory laptop program for students.

Although Ontario Tech is currently transitioning from providing university-issued laptops to a bring-your-own-device model, the use of technology for teaching and learning is still highly relevant. This is also reflected in a key priority identified by the TLC: the need for supporting the effectiveness and growth of online, hybrid, and experiential offerings. As such, the continuous improvement of the center's online and hybrid faculty development initiatives is critical in modeling what is possible, in addition to providing faculty with opportunities to share their own ideas and experiences with these modalities.

Much of the faculty development programming offered to the teaching community at Ontario Tech by the TLC is rooted in a social constructivist approach to teaching and learning. Associated with this approach is the application of principles of backward design, constructive alignment, and UDL. However, despite efforts to model best practices, there is still room for growth with regard to how the faculty development programming at the TLC engages members of the teaching community in sharing their collective experiences. Lessons learned from this exploration into the work of the Ontario Tech TLC are summarized in Table 12.2.

These three lessons learned are areas the Ontario Tech TLC is currently exploring in order to improve the quality of faculty development at the university and may be of interest to other institutions who are in the process of establishing a teaching and learning unit. Reflecting on past and current initiatives, as well as their alignment with the theoretical constructs that informed their development, enables Ontario Tech TLC staff to focus on the next steps required to support the center's key priorities. In doing so, the TLC can work toward fostering a culture that enables members of the teaching community to "reach their potential as educators" (Brar & Drea, 2017, 6), as identified in the center's updated vision and mission statements and key priorities, thus further improving the learning experience for students (Brar & Drea, 2017).

Table 12.2 Lessons learned in faculty development programming and next steps to address them

Lesson	Next steps
Expand integration of core frameworks and strategies to all faculty development initiatives	Actively employ a theoretical foundation in designing and facilitating all teaching and learning activities. Apply best practices of UDL, constructive alignment, and backward design in faculty development offerings
Explore additional TLC offerings using various modalities with community stakeholders and subject matter experts	Identify additional TLC program offerings in various modalities (online, hybrid, or face-to-face) that could be co-planned or co-facilitated by additional members of the campus community who may be interested in lending their expertise to teaching and learning initiatives
Place assessment and evaluation at the core of all faculty development programming starting at the early phases of the design process	Improve assessment and evaluation methods in order to provide programs that are constructively aligned and in keeping with the best practices that faculty are encouraged to embody in their own teaching practices. Implement more rigorous assessment and evaluation methods to help ensure that the center is effectively meeting its goals

References

Atkins, B., Ryan-Harshman, M., Vogel, E., Jones Taggart, H., McLean, J., & Myco, C. (2016, November 2–4). *Designing a fully online social marketing course for 21st century learners* (Conference presentation). Higher Education in Transformation Symposium.

Biggs, J. (2003). Aligning teaching for constructing learning. *Higher Education Academy*, 1–4.

Brar, R., & Drea, C. (2017). *Teaching and learning centre proposed three-year plan* (Unpublished). University of Ontario Institute of Technology.

Center for Applied Special Technologies. (2018). *The UDL guidelines*. Center for Applied Special Technologies Professional Publishing. http://udlguidelines.cast.org/

Koroluk, J., Atkins, B., & Stranach, M. (2016). Designing for change: Engaging faculty through a blended Certificate in University Teaching program. Report of practice. *Journal of Professional, Continuing, and Online Education, 2*(1), 1–15.

Meyer, A., Rose, D., & Gordon, D. (2014). *Universal design for learning: Theory and practice*. Center for Applied Special Technologies Professional Publishing. https://www.cast.org/products-services/resources/2014/universal-design-learning-theory-practice-udl-meyer

Naylor, S., & Keogh, B. (1999). Constructivism in classroom: Theory into practice. *Journal of Science Teacher Education, 10*(2), 93–106.

Prawatt, R., & Floden, R. (1994). Philosophical perspective on constructivist views of learning. *Educational Psychology, 29*(1), 37–48.

University of Ontario Institute of Technology (Ontario Tech). (2019a). *University vision, mission and values*. Ontario Tech. https://ontariotechu.ca/about/uoit-info/university-vision,-mission-and-values.php

University of Ontario Institute of Technology (Ontario Tech). (2019b). *Teaching and learning centre*. Ontario Tech. https://tlc.ontariotechu.ca/index.php

Wiggens, G., & McTighe, J. (2005). *Understanding by design* (2nd ed.). Association for Supervision and Curriculum Development.

13

Mission-Aligned Teaching Center Initiative

Annie Soisson

Introduction

Effecting organizational change in higher education is a daunting task. Teaching centers often face the challenge of ensuring they are "at the table" to represent faculty needs and challenges, and to keep best practices for teaching and learning at the forefront of the university's mission and strategic planning. In its 12 years of operation, the Center for the Enhancement of Learning and Teaching (CELT) at Tufts University, USA, has significantly expanded and developed, embedding itself in the fabric of the university. As a Research One institution, Tufts University faces the challenge of balancing the dual mission of research and teaching. In this chapter, I will provide a history of the center and describe strategic steps that have made the CELT an integral part of the campus' teaching and learning conversation as well as a leader in introducing innovation into the classroom. Through the lens of one initiative, I will describe a three-year process that illustrates the center's approach to engaging in wide-scale organizational change.

A. Soisson (✉)
Center for the Enhancement of Learning and Teaching, Tufts University, Somerville, MA, USA
e-mail: annie.soisson@tufts.edu

© The Author(s), under exclusive license to Springer Nature Switzerland AG 2023
O. J. Neisler (ed.), *The Palgrave Handbook of Academic Professional Development Centers*, Palgrave Studies on Leadership and Learning in Teacher Education,
https://doi.org/10.1007/978-3-030-80967-6_13

201

History and Description of the Center

When the CELT was founded in 2006, a half-time director and an administrative assistant were appointed, joined in the second year by a teaching and learning specialist. In 2008, the director was made a full-time position. In 2012, a new full-time director joined the center, and, by 2018, the staff included three associate directors with specializations and a senior associate director in addition to the director. In the early years, the staff was small and developed primarily broad-based programming, but as the center grew, we have been able to identify and meet specialized needs in science, technology, engineering, and mathematics (STEM) disciplines and our professional schools and, more importantly, to increase inclusive teaching practices across the university.

Three initial strategic choices created the conditions for our center to flourish at Tufts University. First, we clarified our focus: we decided to provide support exclusively to Tufts faculty of all ranks rather than including teaching assistants or postdoctoral researchers. This emphasis differentiated our center from many other teaching centers, and made the CELT a welcoming place where faculty could engage in honest conversation with colleagues. Second, we made it clear that participation in the center's programs was completely voluntary—not simply for those with teaching challenges, but also to support faculty in advancing their understanding of the latest research on learning and best practices in teaching. For our inaugural program, Faculty Fellows, we carefully selected faculty leaders for the first cohort. This program was designed as a semester-long learning community supported by an external grant that engaged influential faculty who were already viewed as effective teachers. This was important to establish the CELT as proactive and to gain the support of persuasive and well-respected faculty leaders who would then promote the center to others. Third, while the CELT was originally founded by the dean of Arts and Sciences, in its third year we made the decision to move the center organizationally to report to the Office of the Provost, making it clear to faculty on all campuses that this was a university-wide service unit.

While these strategic decisions positioned the CELT to create organization-wide changes in teaching, working across three separate campuses and 10 schools demanded careful planning and creativity. Having our office located on one campus while serving two additional campuses posed challenges to the scope of our work. In order to make this work with a small staff, we have carefully focused and designed the programming and support we provide for our 1,500 faculty members to get the most impact.

As stated earlier, in its fifth year, a new director for the center was hired and the CELT established a faculty board of advisors from across all of Tufts University's schools and across all ranks. We also included the director of academic technology and the director of one of the libraries as ad hoc members. This group has guided CELT's work by informing us of their campus and school needs, promoting the center with their faculty, and advocating for the center to their deans and the administration.

The CELT's Model of Faculty Development

It is clear from the literature that successful faculty development is an ongoing process, requiring more time and engagement from faculty than short workshops can provide. Therefore, the CELT's primary focus is on longitudinal and high-impact programming. The core programs support course design, effective assessment, student-centered pedagogy, and inclusive teaching. Each of these institutes lasts between three and four full days, and requires faculty to focus on a course that they are teaching in the following semester. We have also given more prominence and resources to members of our Teaching Squares program and faculty learning communities, which meet over the course of a semester or year.

Early in the life of the center, we decided to expand our mission from focusing only on teaching to also include faculty development. For our first program, we collaborated with the Human Resources Department to develop an academic leadership development program for department chairs and faculty in lower-level leadership positions, such as program or laboratory directors. Several years later, we initiated a Mutual Mentoring program for recent assistant-level professors, a gap we had identified for faculty support. In the past two years, we shifted the Mutual Mentoring Program to one for faculty of color and have begun facilitating a roundtable for department chairs. While these professional development programs make up a relatively small part of the center's mission, the Academic Leadership Development Program, the Mutual Mentoring Program, and the department chairs roundtable connect us to a wide range of academic leaders who, in turn, advocate for the center to their faculty and the administration. While the CELT continues to offer programs for individual faculty, these programs give us access to whole departments and schools, where change can be more significant than at the individual level.

Now in its 13th year of operation, the CELT has a wide base of support and its staff members are trusted across the university and beyond. The next

"Coming In from the Margins"

As detailed in Schroeder et al.'s (2011) book, *Coming in from the Margins*, one of the challenges many learning and teaching centers face is how to weave the center's work into the fabric of the institution, and to be at the table for important decisions that can support the core mission of higher education—learning. At Tufts University, a Research One institution, finding the balance between research and teaching can be a challenge, and we needed to think strategically about how to ensure that teaching remained highly valued.

As all centers do, we follow emerging national higher education conversations and trends, making decisions about what might be important to integrate or adopt in our particular context. The national conversation on diversity, equity, and inclusion in higher education had taken center stage, and the term "inclusive excellence" was adopted by the American Association of Colleges and Universities (AAC&U). The AAC&U has defined inclusive excellence as:

> The collective responsibility to equitably engage all students in high quality, evidence-based educational experiences. An institution that commits to inclusive excellence intentionally designs experiences to accommodate differences in students' aspirations, life circumstances, ways of engaging in learning and participating in college, and identities as learners and students. (Witham et al., 2015)

By 2010, our center had already begun to integrate inclusive practices into our work, but ideas around inclusivity in the classroom had little visibility on campus. Tufts University had no chief diversity officer in place at the time, and there was a void in promoting and integrating efforts toward inclusion on campus. We saw a need not only to *get* to the table, but also to *create* the table. By 2011, when a new president who understood the importance of attending to issues of diversity and inclusion was inaugurated, we were already in motion to secure a grant and had begun to integrate inclusion into our work. He immediately assembled and led a Council on Diversity that met for a year to formulate recommendations on how to strengthen the institutional commitment to diversity, inclusion, and cultural competence. A year later, a new provost was hired, and he promptly began to formulate a 10-year strategic plan that included diversity and inclusion as one of its four major themes. We viewed this as a prime opportunity to prominently align the center with the mission and strategic direction of the university to gain visibility and an opportunity to support this organizational change. The center submitted an application for and was awarded a three-year grant from the Davis Educational Foundation to focus on teaching for inclusive excellence.

A Framework for Organizational Change Through the Lens of Inclusive Excellence

The organizational change process we followed for the grant-supported initiative on teaching for inclusive excellence was adapted from *Coming in from the Margins* (Schroeder et al., 2011); this model frames the steps we took to initiate, develop, and embed an inclusive teaching focus at Tufts University. The five stages of change we followed were: (1) exploring the context within and outside of the organization; (2) building relationships; (3) building capacity, both financially and with staffing; (4) evaluation of the initiative; and (5) capturing the outcomes.

Context, Goals, and Alignment

As we wrote the grant to support our teaching for the inclusive excellence initiative, we clearly articulated the national focus in higher education on equity and inclusion. We noted that, in our view, a critical part of our role at CELT was to anticipate future challenges and opportunities in teaching and learning. It was our responsibility to help the university understand these issues and to prepare Tuft University's faculty and the administration to address them, thus ensuring that the university would remain at the forefront of important national conversations in this area. Changing demographics in the USA toward a much more diverse student population and the lack of diversity in STEM disciplines have been an ongoing concern (Kezar et al., 2015), given that fully paying international students make up a large part of admitted students and women now maintain a majority presence in colleges and universities. Moreover, in spite of significant research on effective teaching for learning, teaching remains largely the same as it was 100 years ago.

While we understood that challenging old models would be difficult, we believed that this initiative was essential to the university's success. The goal of this grant was to develop learning communities to focus on how to teach

206   A. Soisson

inclusively and equitably. It was important to our center to secure the grant because grants are important currency on Research One campuses, drawing attention. More importantly, securing the grant allowed us to assist Tufts University in showing a long-term commitment to issues of equity and inclusion in the classroom, one of its articulated goals.

In order to engage support and demonstrate our value, we used language directly from the Tufts University's Strategic Plan and the report from the Council on Diversity, designing the grant to address the issues and goals outlined in those reports. We also carefully aligned our three-year plan to the social justice and global focus of the Tufts University mission, and our mission as a center. Aligning with the university's goals and highlighting Tufts as a progressive university at the forefront of an important national issue was deliberate to appeal to the university administration and the grantor. The provost and president both enthusiastically signed off on the grant, which brought the work of the CELT to their attention and garnered their public commendation of our work.

Building Relationships

As we wrote the grant, and later as we began the work, we deliberately chose key partnerships with others at the university who were doing similar work or who we considered to be strong allies (Cook & Kaplan, 2010). First, we met with the dean of Arts and Sciences, who was a co-chair for the Council on Diversity. We asked her to identify faculty from multiple departments and personally invite each to participate in one of the first two learning communities in the first year. She intentionally identified both early adopters and cynics and agreed to send personal invitations, which significantly increased the likelihood of participation. Second, we met with, and garnered the support of, the six identity centers on campus (the Asian American, Latino, Africana, LGBTQ+, Women's Center, and FIRST Resource Center) that work closely with students and understand the challenges they face in the classroom. Third, we met regularly with the new chief diversity officer to keep him informed about our progress and to make use of his expertise as an advisor. Lastly, we involved faculty we knew were committed to the work of inclusive teaching. These strong allies with a vested interest in and shared passion for supporting faculty and students helped sustain the initiative and further embedded the center as an important unit of support.

Because of these strategic partnerships, more people became aware of our work and we were invited to sit on a number of committees. The center was already a member of the university-wide Council on Teaching and Faculty Development, which gave us a platform for sharing our work. We were soon at the table of the Learning Outcomes Assessment Committee, the Diversity Council, and the Student Evaluation of Teaching Committee. Sitting on each of these committees ensured that the topic of inclusive teaching and assessment was always considered.

Building Capacity and Maintaining Visibility

Once we had partnered with other committed individuals and groups across campus and the grant was awarded, we reallocated the center's staff time and programming to work on the initiative. Each member of the center's three staff was involved in at least one learning community to help us build our own collective understanding of what it meant to teach inclusively and equitably. The design involved a multipronged approach to change (Takayama et al., 2017).

Two faculty learning communities with up to 12 participants would be formed each year, with a focus on topics selected by the center following conversations with our strategic partners. These topics would be inclusive teaching, 'difficult dialogues', inclusive teaching in STEM, inclusive online teaching, evaluation and student success, learning spaces and inclusion, and inclusive teaching in large enrollment courses. These topics allowed us to build a broad understanding of inclusive teaching, which would later inform our development of programming and a resource website for faculty (Soisson & Qualters, 2015). It also helped us frame a workshop we would go on to deliver at national conferences and use for our new faculty orientation.

In order to expand the work beyond the learning communities, we offered workshops led by external experts to all university faculty. This helped broaden the visibility of the initiative and generate enthusiasm for next year's learning communities. These half- or full-day workshops focused on topics such as the hidden curriculum, cultural competence, and implicit bias. We had identified in our previous work that faculty often lacked the courage to raise and facilitate classroom discussion on challenging topics, an important skill for success in work on inclusion. Drawing on our partnership with the chief diversity officer, who had strong expertise in facilitating difficult dialogues, we offered workshops centered on effective dialogue as an essential skill.

In the second year, in addition to beginning two more learning communities, we systematically began to integrate inclusive practices into all of our core programs. This integration was important for long-term success, making

208   A. Soisson

inclusive practices just part of good teaching, not separating them out as a "good thing" to do, or something done only by those in certain departments. It also increased the number of faculty who began to think more deeply about learning and inclusion and the use of effective teaching and assessment practices. At the end of the second year, with the work of four learning communities to share, we held an internal symposium. All faculty involved in the initiative thus far shared the changes they had made either in their thinking or in their teaching practice, and emphasized the importance of this work to their colleagues. Shifts in both thinking and practice were key to long-term change. We frequently see faculty adopt particular practices, but the change in approach and change in thinking increases sustainable practice (Soisson & Qualters, 2019). A sign of true commitment, the learning communities from both the first and second years continued to meet for an additional six months beyond our request.

In the third and final year, three more learning communities were formed. At the end of the third year, the CELT partnered with the New England Faculty Development Consortium to host a regional conference on Teaching for Inclusive Excellence. Each of the faculty learning communities from Tufts University, as well as faculty from across New England, facilitated workshops or created posters to share their learning and changes with their peers. Over 200 faculty members were in attendance on the day. This regional conference was an important part of sharing our learning and drawing on the work being done in other colleges and universities that might deepen our own initiative. It also positioned Tufts University as a leader on the topic of inclusive teaching.

Evaluation

In the semester following the program, we analyzed the data we had collected over the previous three years. The impact data analysis included a pre-post instrument to assess participants' understanding of inclusive teaching, interviews with participants, a reflective essay on their learning, and a review of responses to the student course evaluation question about inclusive teaching. We examined scores from the end-of-course student evaluations for all courses to the single question: *How would you rate the instructor's success in creating and maintaining an inclusive class, respectful of all students?* Our hypothesis was that those faculty who engaged the most frequently in CELT inclusive excellence programming would experience a higher average score on this question in the course evaluation survey compared to those who were non-participants in CELT programming. Based on the results, as shown in Fig. 13.1, we suggest

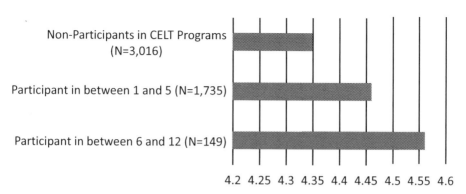

Fig. 13.1 Correlation between course evaluation scores* and participation in CELT programming
*Based on responses to the question: How would you rate the instructor's success in creating and maintaining an inclusive class, respectful of all students?

that scores for this course evaluation question were correlated to participation in CELT inclusive excellence programming. The more inclusive education programs that instructors attended, the higher students scored them on this question.

Quotes from Participants on Individual Change

The following excerpts from the reflective summaries of faculty participants illustrate how their approaches shifted toward greater intrapersonal awareness, interpersonal awareness, building communities of practice, and curricular changes—the four goals of the program.

Developing Intrapersonal Awareness

> In the classroom, I think I am just more aware of the fact that there are students in populations that may not have had mainstream experiences, or opportunities that I or many of the other students in the classroom have had. Some students may not have that vernacular or capital to draw on. So that can put students at a disadvantage in the classroom if people are not cognizant of that. (Faculty Participant 1, Tufts University)

> I think that what we have learned as a group ranges from the mundane to the profound: to learn our student's names and the correct pronunciation of those names; to be more flexible in terms of the assignments we design and the expectations that we have about the ways students can respond to those assignments;

to look for opportunities that broaden content and are more inclusive in terms of who is represented, explored, cited, imaged; to look closely at the language that we use; to query our own perceptions about the "neutrality" of that language; to not take lack of response as assent. Personally, I have been reminded to treat students with the respect and generosity with which I want to be treated. (Faculty Participant 2, Tufts University)

Probably the most important skill that I have deeply strengthened because of my participation in this group is the simple act of listening. Like most academics, I love to give my own opinion, and I have mountains of evidence for every argument I might make. (Faculty Participant 3, Tufts University)

Interpersonal Awareness

It has been very useful for me to view all discussion, even if doesn't deal overtly with charged issues like race, class, or gender, as something that can benefit from targeted techniques that enable the professor to strike a balance between faculty authority and student ownership, passionate expression and respectful listening, and objectivity and emotional engagement. (Faculty Participant 4, Tufts University)

Specific changes I have made are that I have diversified ways in which students can participate. Some feel comfortable talking in class, others feel comfortable in recitation. We incorporated learning catalytics to measure both content and opinions to generate discussion. (Faculty Participant 5, Tufts University)

Building Communities of Practice

... in a department retreat that focused on issues of diversity, I found that I was able to play a central and leadership role because of the work I'd done as part of this learning community, and that this was something that positioned me very well professionally, as I helped to disseminate some of the important learning we'd done." (Faculty Participant 6, Tufts University)

And the reason these good practices were reinforced during our 'difficult dialogues' discussions was because I finally saw other experienced, gifted teachers struggling with the same issues, sharing their failures and successes and frustrations and breakthroughs, and it brought it home to me that this is what good teaching is all about, and that it is ok to try and sometimes fail but to also learn and experiment. (Faculty Participant 7, Tufts University)

Facilitating Curricular Change

My goal was to help my students gain insights into and skills of facilitating difficult topics in museums. I decided to model an approach and chose terror lynching as the difficult topic to explore. For nearly three hours we confronted what to many of my students was a new facet of American history, and used our own (lack of) knowledge and emotional responses to the images of tortured individuals and gloating crowds to think about how (and why) we could help museum visitors engage with this awful past that continues to reverberate today. (Faculty Participant 8, Tufts University)

I wanted to tell you that I woke up this morning still thinking about last night's class. The class was like visiting a "difficult subject" exhibit—I felt totally immersed by the various ways you drew us in and prompted us to think more about such a painful subject. It was a great way to really understand how such an exhibit might be developed. So, strange as this may sound, thank you for a very powerful, disturbing evening. (Student response to Faculty Participant 8, Tufts University)

The objective was to change the assessment model that I use in organic chemistry courses to emphasize the use of exams as learning tools for students. The goal was to reduce test anxiety of students, which is known to reduce performance on exams. This is especially the case for underrepresented students in STEM. My approach was to allow students to re-answer questions on midterms exams for which they lost points. One week after receiving a graded exam back, students were permitted to submit revised answers to any questions, and required to explain why their original answers were incorrect. Students received 1/3 of the original point value back if they answered correctly on this second attempt. (Faculty Participant 9, Tufts University)

I thought it was really important that we were able to correct our exams, because it was clear [the] professor wanted us to learn, as opposed to just perform well on a test and then move on. (Student response to Faculty Participant 9, Tufts University)

These few examples give a taste of the kinds of changes documented by faculty in the learning communities during the time of the grant. While these are mostly at the individual level, the members were from many different departments, which each representing a voice in those departments as to the importance of paying attention to inclusive teaching. However, amid these testaments for individual change were some challenges to the broader goals of organization change.

Challenges

The path to a changed organization is not linear, and there are often stumbling blocks along the way. As a research institution, the time challenge has multiple facets. The balance between time committed to research and teaching can be a challenge to recruiting participants. The time required to participate in a year-long learning community was daunting to Tufts faculty, and resulted in smaller groups than we had anticipated. While it was difficult to get as many participants as we anticipated in the learning communities, those who joined were very consistent. Because of heavy faculty commitments, scheduling was also a challenge, and in several cases we lost participants because we were unable to find a common meeting time. The CELT staff carried a large part of the work of keeping the meetings organized, providing reading, and following up. This required a greater time commitment than we predicted, but was essential to provide the support that would lead to success. Each staff member worked with at least one learning community over the three years.

Three key allies left the university during the grant period. In the first year, the dean of Arts and Sciences had endorsed the participation of faculty by identifying both early adopters and resistors and personally inviting their participation. Her departure in the second year represented the loss of an important ally, and, as a result, we had to do much more outreach in the following two years. In the third year of the grant, the chief diversity officer, who had been hired in the first year, left the university. The individual who replaced him left within six months of being hired. The lack of stability in that role has been a challenge. Our third ally, the provost, left the university soon after the grant ended, and we were faced with gaining the support of a new provost. After losing these allies, our board and network building still provided stability for our programs, reinforcing our approach to network broadly. In the following section, I have outlined the broader indicators of organizational change that indicate impacts on the university.

Outcomes and Indicators of Organizational Change

In addition to the individual assessment of change, there are a number of other indicators of the continuing impact of this initiative. We have been able to use these outcomes to build on our initial work, and as a springboard for new grants and initiatives. The work of the following new learning communities, CELT programs, and other university-wide programs and initiatives can be traced back to the work from the three-year grant.

Learning Communities

Members of the STEM-focused learning community applied for and received a grant from the Howard Hughes Medical Institute to broaden participation and cultivate the talents of undergraduate students of diverse backgrounds in the natural sciences. This three-year, million-dollar award has allowed their work to continue. This grant was initiated and implemented by members of the STEM inclusive excellence learning community. Over the next three years, it is projected that 30 faculty from the sciences will be exposed to inclusive practices. A member of the 'difficult dialogues' learning community was awarded external funds to develop faculty learning communities to focus on social emotional learning, diversity and inclusion, and civic engagement. This project is in its second year, with more than 30 faculty involved.

CELT Impact

The approval to hire an associate director for teaching, learning, and inclusion was a significant outcome. This was an important symbolic and strategic decision. This signaled the Office of the Provost's and CELT's long-term commitment to diversity and inclusion in teaching, and has elevated the conversation across Tufts University. For example, invitations for CELT staff to attend department and school-wide faculty meetings to talk about inclusive teaching are frequent, and indicate that the center is seen as an important resource. The new associate director sits on several schools' diversity committees as an advisor. In addition, CELT has added a new core four-day Inclusive Learning Institute to its offerings.

The CELT principal investigator for the grant received the Faculty and Staff Multicultural Award at the end of the grant. The award recognizes the contributions of faculty and staff who have made significant efforts to define Tufts University as a multicultural environment. It is awarded by the president each year to one faculty member and one staff person whose efforts at Tufts best exemplify these ideals.

Since 2008, CELT continues to lead the new faculty orientation for arts, sciences, and engineering with inclusive and equitable teaching as the content, setting the tone for new faculty. This opportunity has been one of the key ways we continue to build capacity in the university. All new arts, sciences, and engineering faculty for the past 10 years have been introduced to teaching at Tufts through an inclusive lens.

University-Wide Impact

Extending the work begun in the learning community focused on 'difficult dialogues', the Bridging Differences Initiative was formed by the provost and is led by the chief diversity officers with representatives from across all campuses, including students. The Bridging Differences Initiative was launched in the fall of 2017 with the goal of developing a strategy that would position Tufts to lead nationally and internationally in supporting and developing structures, processes, and skills to engage constructively across differences. The CELT is recognized as a key representative in this initiative as the only member with direct responsibility for working with faculty to improve classroom teaching.

Departments and schools have significantly increased requests for CELT staff to facilitate faculty retreats, workshops, and meetings on topics related to diversity, equity, and inclusion. Most schools have now formed diversity committees, several of which were launched by those involved with the CELT initiative. CELT's associate director for learning, teaching, and inclusion is a strong resource for those groups. Furthermore, the Learning Outcomes Assessment Committee for the School of Arts and Sciences, a committee that maintains a focus on proactively meeting accreditation goals, now asks each department to select a course where they set goals for more inclusive practices and assess those goals.

The assistant dean of research for arts and sciences created the Visiting and Early Research Scholar Experience (VERSE) program. The VERSE program invites undergraduate students to participate in a 10-week summer research immnersion experience designed to (1) connect students to faculty mentors with active research laboratories and (2) provide students with valuable, mentored, hands-on research training that will build their confidence to conduct research and to design their own research projects in the future. The CELT supports the program by facilitating workshops for faculty to learn how to mentor underrepresented students in the laboratories.

Conclusion

As noted at the beginning of this chapter, advancing organization change in higher education is a daunting task as teaching centers have to ensure they are "at the table" to understand and represent faculty needs and to keep best practices for teaching and learning at the forefront of the university's mission. No

13 Mission-Aligned Teaching Center Initiative 215

department or center can make the change alone; however, in our experience, a network of committed individuals, departments, and committees working synergistically can affect organizational change (Soisson et al., 2018). As part of the larger efforts at our university to become more equitable and inclusive, the CELT has been an integral part of that change. Reflecting on the most important elements of our center's involvement, the following decisions and multipronged approach to change were instrumental to our progress:

* Initiating alignment with the mission of the center, the university, and national concerns in higher education made the case for acquiring internal and external resources
* Securing external funds and allocating internal resources allowed us to maintain a dedicated focus on fostering inclusive teaching, rather than offering a single program
* Creating partnerships and connections across the university with key leaders and parallel and synergistic efforts helped to create a broad network to foster real change
* Maintaining visibility of the work being done and the work yet to be done has made the conversation one that is ongoing and widespread
* Integrating our learning about inclusive teaching into all of our programs ensured the sustainability of our efforts beyond the grant and promoted inclusive teaching as simply good teaching
* Hiring a full-time staff member to support equity and inclusion in the classroom demonstrated our continued commitment to creating more inclusive classrooms.

Overall, there are a number of indicators that the CELT initiative significantly contributed to embedding inclusive teaching in the fabric of the institution. The model for change outlined in the chapter will hopefully prove a useful guide for teaching and learning centers at various institutions to adapt to their individual contexts, missions, and priorities.

References

Cook, C. E., & Kaplan, M. (2010). *Advancing the culture of teaching on campus: How a teaching center can make a difference*. Stylus Press.

Kezar, A., Gehrke, S., & Elrod, S. (2015). Implicit theories of change as a barrier to change on college campuses: An examination of STEM reform. *Review of Higher Education, 38*(4), 479–506.

Schroeder, C. M., et al. (2011). *Coming in From the Margins: Faculty development's emerging organizational development role in institutional change* (pp. 47–59). Stylus Press.

Soisson, A., Grooters, S., & Mirshekari, C. (2018, January 24–27). *How centers for teaching and learning can influence campus culture on emerging educational trends* (Conference presentation). Association of American Colleges & Universities (AAC&U) 2018 Annual Meeting.

Soisson, A., & Qualters, D. (2015, May 29–31). *Teaching for inclusive excellence* (Pre-conference workshop). Teaching Professor Conference 2015.

Soisson, A., & Qualters, D. (2019, October 3–5). *Mobilizing institutional structures and resources to influence educational change* (Pre-conference workshop). Leadership in Higher Education Conference.

Takayama, K., Kaplan, M., & Cook-Sather, A. (2017). Advancing diversity and inclusion through strategic multilevel leadership. *Liberal Education, 103*(3/4), 22–29.

Witham, K., Malcom-Piqueux, L. E., Dowd, A. C., & Bensimon, E. M. (2015). *America's unmet promise: The imperative for equity in higher education.* Association of American Colleges and Universities (AAC&U).

Part V

Differences in ADC Governance and Funding

Governance and funding are discussed in almost all of the chapters in this volume. However, this section highlights the exceptions to the usual university-level funding model of most academic professional development centers (ADCs), which generally involve a mix of faculty and staff reporting hierarchically through an academic affairs officer. All three of the chapters explain how faculty members led the development of their centers and how their voices have become central in campus policy conversations. They each share aspects of grassroots, bottom-up development activities discussed in Chap. 4, the overview of African academic professional development. The other five related chapters from other sections include explanations of other revenue streams that might incite new ideas for aspiring or existing ADC directors.

Chapters in Part V

Chapter 14: *At the Heart of the Campus: A Faculty-Led Teaching and Learning Center.* Gwendolyn Mettetal and Carolyn A. Schult, Indiana University South Bend, South Bend, IN, USA.

This chapter reports the experience at an ADC designed and led by faculty with a focus on enhancing student learning. The case study explains how the 18-member advisory board collected international data about ADC design and then cross-referenced that information with data from internal faculty needs assessment. This combination of faculty leadership, faculty research,

218   Differences in ADC Governance and Funding

and research-based program design could be a model for new center design. Grant funding is a key aspect of this chapter.

Chapter 15: *A Member-Driven, Donor-Supported Academic Professional Development Center: The New Mexico State University Teaching Academy.* Tara Gray, Teaching Academy, New Mexico State University, Las Cruces, NM, Laura Madson, Department of Psychology, New Mexico State University, Las Cruces, NM, and Morgan Iommi, Center for Teaching and Learning Excellence, Nevada State College, Henderson, NV, USA (formerly of New Mexico State University).

This chapter details how one ADC has been able to remain financially viable within its specific university context of deep budget and staff cuts. This model of a teaching academy, which incorporates anyone who either leads or attends a workshop, serves to build a community of practice whose members determine programming and donate funding to the center through payroll deductions. Other funding sources include allocations from college budgets, philanthropy, and planned gifts.

Chapter 16: *Faculty Leadership in Academic Professional Development Centers: Building a Case for a Three-Director, Faculty-Led Model.* Emily R. Smith and Carol Ann Davis, Fairfield University, Fairfield, CT, USA.

This case study describes how faculty have led the development of an ADC to its current model of leadership involving three directors. While this might be chaotic or competitive, the authors explain how this model has led to a collegial and collaborative environment for decision-making. The model bears more examination because it removes hierarchy and allows each director to focus on his/her area of expertise and responsibility within a structure that supports both autonomy and collaboration. Originally funded by grants, the ADC now operates from its endowment as well from yearly funding from the Office of the Provost.

Other Relevant Chapters

Chapter 6: *Assessment Work in an Academic Professional Development Center.* Ingrid Novodvorsky, Elaine Marchello, and Lisa Elfring, University of Arizona, Tucson, AZ, USA.

In this chapter, an ADC receives funding from the state budget, student technology fees, and the university budget.

Chapter 8: *Needs Analysis Leads to Sustainability: Development of a Medical Education and Informatics Department in the College of Medicine and Health Sciences, Sultan Qaboos University*. Nadia Mohammed Al Wardy and Rashid Al Abri, Sultan Qaboos University, Muscat, Oman.

This chapter reports how a change in administrative status from unit to department allowed one ADC to secure, among other things, proper financial support.

Chapter 13: *Mission-Aligned Teaching Center Initiative*. Annie Soisson, Center for the Enhancement of Learning and Teaching, Tufts University, Somerville, MA, USA.

This ADC has experienced changes in its reporting structure from being placed under the College of Arts and Sciences to the Office of the Provost. Grant funding is also an important component of its operations.

Chapter 25: *Building Community: From Faculty Development to Pedagogical Innovation and Beyond*. Linda C. Hodges and Patrice McDermott, University of Maryland Baltimore County, Baltimore, MD, USA.

This ADC oversees a $100,000 dollar-grant program designed to enable pedagogical innovation.

Chapter 27: *Promoting a Culture of Teaching Excellence in a Chinese Research University*. Yihong Qiu, Center for Teaching and Learning Development, Shanghai Jiao Tong University, Shanghai, China.

Teaching development grants are one part of the strategy employed by this ADC to promote teaching excellence at its respective university.

14

At the Heart of the Campus: A Faculty-Led Teaching and Learning Center

Gwendolyn Mettetal and Carolyn A. Schult

Introduction

Our teaching and learning center at Indiana University (IU) South Bend, USA, the University Center for Excellence in Teaching (UCET), has been in operation for 20 years and is highly respected and supported by faculty and administrators alike. A recent review using the American Council on Education (ACE) Faculty Development Matrix concluded that the center was highly effective, reaching a broad audience with varied programs. One major factor in its success is that it was initiated and designed by a large group of faculty and continues to be led by faculty directors supported by a large faculty advisory board. In this chapter, we recount the formation and governance of UCET and describe signature programs such as Back-to-School Week, the Scholarship of Teaching and Learning (SoTL) Institute and annual conference, promotion dossier preparation groups, and peer review of teaching. The Learn and Earn program that provides financial incentives to adjunct faculty for engaging in faculty development has nearly quadrupled participation, and we offer several other faculty grants programs to encourage innovation.

G. Mettetal (✉) • C. A. Schult
Indiana University South Bend, South Bend, IN, USA
e-mail: gmetteta@iusb.edu; cschult@iusb.edu

© The Author(s), under exclusive license to Springer Nature Switzerland AG 2023
O. J. Neisler (ed.), *The Palgrave Handbook of Academic Professional Development Centers*,
Palgrave Studies on Leadership and Learning in Teacher Education,
https://doi.org/10.1007/978-3-030-80967-6_14

Mission

UCET supports teaching and learning on the IU South Bend campus. Our mission is to enhance student learning by providing opportunity for faculty discovery, feedback, reflection, support, and collegiality by providing the following:
- A broad spectrum of ideas and strategies, including innovative and alternative methods of instruction
- Strategies and support for assessment of teaching effectiveness and student learning
- Services such as confidential consultations, workshops, mentoring programs, and conference funding
- Access to teaching technology and training
- Opportunities for university-wide dialogue on teaching and learning
- Overall support for the strengthening of teaching and learning on the IU South Bend campus (UCET, n.d.).

Developed by the Faculty

IU South Bend, part of the IU system, is a regional public university located in the northern part of the State of Indiana enrolling over 5,000 students taught by 300 full-time and 220 part-time faculty. Classes were first offered in 1933 at a local high school and the IU Center in South Bend opened on its current site in 1961 (Furlong & Vander Ven, 2010). By 1996, the campus had grown to over 4,000 full-time-equivalent students (about two-thirds of which attended part-time) and 248 full-time and 354 part-time faculty (IU Office of Institutional Research, 1996). Faculty development for teaching was provided by the Academic Senate Teaching Committee and a faculty development officer who was given one course release per semester to provide workshops and consultations about teaching and to implement a peer review of teaching program (J. Russo, personal communication, December 9, 2018).

In the mid-1990s, IU announced an internal Strategic Directions grants program to fund projects that would further the university's strategic goals (IU, 2001). In a review of faculty development, Ouellett (2010) notes that the 1990s were a time of institutionalizing and expanding faculty development on campuses, particularly larger research campuses. Two senior IU South Bend faculty members, Eileen Bender and Vince Peterson, saw this as an opportunity to develop a teaching center for our regional campus. Professor Bender had recently developed an IU-wide program, the Faculty Colloquium for Excellence in Teaching (FACET), that recognized outstanding teachers and provided support through retreats and various other programs (FACET, n.d.). She was aware of the rise of academic professional development centers (ADCs) at IU Bloomington and other large campuses and saw the potential for a similar model on a regional campus. Professor Peterson, a professor of counseling, collaborated on this opportunity to create a lasting structure to enhance teaching. In total, they received three grants totaling over $457,000 from that program, as well as similar contributions from the IU South Bend campus (E. Zynda, personal communication, October 23, 2018).

To plan the center, Professors Bender and Peterson formed a representative advisory board of 18 faculty and administrators and gathered information from ADCs across the USA and UK. They also surveyed IU South Bend faculty and students to learn what they wanted and needed. Based on the input from the needs assessment survey, they developed a plan for UCET. The mission of UCET was to enhance student learning through collegiality, discovery, feedback, reflection, and support. Their plan called for a half-time faculty director, a full-time instructional technology specialist, a part-time secretary, and student employees. The center would take over new faculty orientation (then provided by the Office of Academic Affairs), and provide workshops, consultations, and general support for teaching. A space was identified for the center—a classroom and several offices in a classroom building that had previously been used as the Psychology Laboratory and vacated when the department relocated to a new classroom building.

Professors Bender and Peterson secured further Strategic Directions grants in 1997 and 1998 to renovate and furnish that unused space as a teaching center. The administration committed funding for staffing and ongoing expenses, leading to the selection of the founding director (the first author of this chapter) and the hiring of a technology consultant. UCET began formal operations in August 1998 with faculty orientation, although the renovations were just beginning. The traditional one-day orientation was expanded into a 'Back-to-School Week' that included sessions on teaching, campus resources, and campus culture, with many sessions open to all faculty.

Current Staffing and Reporting Structure

UCET staffing has grown considerably over the years, as the administration became confident in its impact and its careful spending of available funding. In the early years, UCET staff included a half-time faculty director, a full-time instructional strategy consultant, and a half-time secretary. This staffing grew slowly to the current configuration seen in Fig. 14.1.

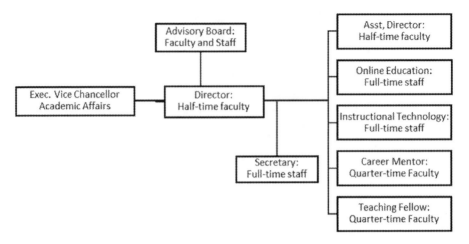

Fig. 14.1 Organizational reporting and structure of UCET

Directors

The center's director and assistant director are half-time positions filled by tenured faculty known for outstanding and innovative teaching. Although many ADC directors nationally are staff, the UCET planning committee felt that a tenured faculty member had several advantages. First, tenured faculty had quite a bit of experience teaching students at our campus and understood both the students and the context (the learning management system, curriculum, classrooms, etc.). Second, given our mid-sized campus with 520 full-time and part-time teaching faculty, an outstanding teacher was likely already known by many, and thus had credibility with the faculty. And third, tenured faculty had less concern over job security and could thus 'push back' against various pressures if appropriate. This last factor became particularly important when online learning needs completely engulfed many ADCs in the IU system. UCET was able to provide some support for online learning without giving up support for face-to-face teaching. Although our full-time instructional staff are extremely effective, even they have recognized the unique role that faculty leadership can play, and were supportive when a full-time staff person left and the position was changed to a half-time faculty assistant director who plays a lead role in our institutes, mentoring, and peer feedback programs.

Technology Consulting

Two full-time staff members support the use of teaching technology and online education. The instructional technology position is funded by the Office of University Information Technology (IT), but reports primarily to the UCET director. The online education and technology specialist receives funding via Academic Affairs. They both provide support through institutes, workshops, and consultations.

Career Mentor

The position of career mentor is a position not found in most ADCs. Funded by an endowment, the career mentor is a part-time faculty position held by a senior professor who organizes and leads a variety of career workshops and mentoring for all faculty ranks. The most intensive offerings are the dossier promotion preparation groups which meet frequently as faculty prepare their materials for promotion. This is described more thoroughly in a later section of this chapter.

Teaching Fellows

A teaching fellow is chosen each semester to develop and share expertise in some specific area such as mindset, classroom assessment, or best practice with peer mentors. Fellows can be tenured, pre-tenure, or lecturers. Some fellows work with a specific department or school to provide customized support. After the official period ends, fellows continue as 'campus experts' in their area and are often called upon to provide workshops or consultations.

Secretary

Our secretarial position has slowly evolved from a nine-month, part-time position to full-time, and this has made a huge difference in our operations. Our secretary keeps careful timelines for all events, plans the weekly newsletter, maintains the participation database, and handles travel and purchases. Her organization and efforts are particularly key to major events such as faculty orientation week and the annual Midwest SoTL Conference.

Faculty Volunteers

Faculty from across campus provide much of the programming, which also helps the center stay responsive to faculty needs. For example, most institutes are co-led by UCET staff and a faculty member, and faculty lead most book groups. Many of our institutes include faculty demonstrations of various teaching strategies, and we pull faculty from all ranks and units for these. During the 2017–2018 academic year, more than 50 faculty members helped UCET deliver services and programming. In these ways, faculty influence has always been critical to UCET success.

Advisory Board

The original intent had been to replace the large planning board with a smaller advisory board of seven to eight people, but the planning board members were very eager to continue their alliance with UCET. The director suggested a large Advisory Board with a smaller Executive Committee that met more frequently. This was the practice for many years, but eventually the Executive Committee was dropped and the larger Advisory Board continued. The Advisory Board has played a key role in keeping UCET faculty-centered. Over the years, the Advisory Board has ranged from 35 to 42 members including faculty, staff, and a few administrators, with most members staying for many years. A rotating limited term has recently been implemented to allow more faculty to serve. The board meets once a semester to brainstorm and advise, and members serve on committees, lead workshops, and otherwise help fulfill the UCET mission. Board members can serve as a liaison between UCET and their unit. At several points, board members were instrumental in pushing back against administrative initiatives that were deemed incompatible with the formative-development mission of UCET.

Funding Sources

The initial planning and renovations for UCET came through IU Strategic Directions grants as described above. Since that time, funding has come primarily through Academic Affairs. The annual budget includes replacement funds (adjunct rates) for the director, assistant director, and teaching fellows, and salaries and benefits for staff. The budget also covers stipends for faculty who are designing their first online course, basic office expenses, and some travel expenses for the staff. In addition, Academic Affairs supports several UCET small grants programs.

University IT Services funds the salary of the instructional technology consultant who reports primarily to the UCET director, but collaborates closely with other IU ADC consultants. FACET provides campus grants for programs available to all faculty (not just FACET members); our campus uses this money to support the annual Midwest SoTL Conference, small grants for faculty to attend teaching conferences, and the Bender Joy of Teaching event each semester.

The Midwest SoTL Conference is primarily funded through conference fees. As mentioned above, FACET provides a small amount. In recent years, the University of Notre Dame, Indiana, has also made a significant contribution and had our keynote speaker visit their campus as well. The IU Foundation accounts are funded entirely through contributions. The main account is used to purchase food for workshops, which cannot be funded through the regular account. A new endowed account provides some funding for a course release and modest expenses of a faculty career mentor.

Signature Programs

The Center has several 'signature programs' that have been especially useful and popular. More details can be accessed through the UCET website (UCET, n.d.).

Back-to-School Week

We provide new faculty orientation and embed it within a comprehensive Back-to-School Week that is open to all faculty. The sessions include backward course design, active learning pedagogy, campus technology basics, and some career planning. Even experienced faculty rave about the value of the week. This week also serves as a 'sampler' for our other offerings.

SoTL Conferences and Activities

SoTL has been a strong theme throughout UCET's history. In UCET's second year, we reached out to local universities to form a consortium to promote SoTL through an annual conference. In 2018, the 19th Annual Midwest

SoTL Conference drew 163 participants from 24 colleges across the nation. A SoTL Institute held during the fall semester supports faculty as they design and implement SoTL projects—their final product is a proposal for the conference. The *Journal of the SoTL*, a respected online peer-reviewed journal, was founded in 2001 by early directors of UCET and later moved downstate to the IU Mack Center for SoTL. SoTL work is greatly respected on our campus, and faculty may use it to document either their teaching or their scholarship for promotions and awards.

Promotion Dossier Preparation Groups

One of UCET's most popular programs has been the dossier preparation groups. As described in Mettetal and McGuire (2013), faculty are invited to meet every few weeks during the year as they construct their promotion dossier. Senior faculty serve as mentors and share policies, practices, and advice for a successful dossier. The cross-disciplinary nature of the group ensures that the vitae, teaching and scholarship statements, and materials provided will be understood by those at all levels of review. We started with groups for tenure candidates. When university policy required that lecturers seek promotion to senior lecturer, they were added to the tenure group and we found that this mix brought increased respect and collegiality across ranks. We recently added groups for professor-level dossier preparation, at the request of faculty. The mentors have become a powerful group on campus who work with the administration and Academic Senate to clarify and communicate career expectations.

Institutes

In recent years, we have moved much of our programming away from workshops to institutes—semester-long 'courses' that involve working on a project. We have a Course Design Institute, an Active Learning Institute (with a different emphasis each time, such as edu-gaming or technology), the Creative Grading Toolbox (non-traditional classroom grading/assessment of student learning), and the SoTL Institute mentioned previously. These institutes prompt more in-depth learning and allow faculty to implement what they have learned and friendships to develop across disciplines and ranks. Those who complete institutes earn a digital badge, and part-time faculty earn a small stipend through the Learn and Earn program.

Learn and Earn for Adjuncts

Our Learn and Earn program for part-time faculty has more than tripled our part-time participation rate. Faculty earn faculty development units (FDUs) per hour of participation (institutes and book groups have an overall rate that accounts for work done on their own). Then faculty receive a supplement to their final semester paycheck. In the past four years, we have seen total FDUs climb from 209 per year to 808 per year, with over one-third of our adjuncts participating. We offer an evening orientation program specifically for adjuncts, but many also attend our daytime offerings. Digital badges offer an 'independent study' option that works for faculty with tight schedules.

Peer Review of Teaching

The original IU South Bend academic professional development officers provided a formative peer review program, which was continued by UCET. Faculty volunteers were trained in multiple ways of providing confidential classroom observations and feedback to improve teaching. In the early 2000s, several FACET members (including the first author of this chapter) developed an all-university peer review course which became available online in 2015. Through UCET encouragement, our campus has the highest proportion of IU faculty who have completed FACET training (over half of all trained are from IU South Bend). UCET also worked with campus administrators to endorse completing peer review training, conducting reviews, and being reviewed as one type of documentation for teaching excellence.

Online Learning Stipends

Faculty who agree to develop online courses identified as high needs by the administration can receive stipends. They complete the Course Design Institute, a Quality Matters workshop, and design the first unit of their course. This is typically only available for the first course they develop.

Grants for Teaching

Two programs provide funding for faculty who would like to try new teaching strategies. Software and Equipment for Engagement and Discovery grants are available to faculty who want to try new teaching technologies, with the idea that they become beta-testers who can be role models to colleagues. Grants have funded everything from Surface Pros and iPads for innovative classroom uses to virtual reality systems and 3D printing materials. Materials for Active Learning Techniques is a similar program for nontechnology materials that has funded items such as learning games, poster-size post-its and markers, and 'scratch-off' scantron sheets.

Assessment

Overall

In 2018, UCET conducted a self-assessment based on a number of data sources, including extensive use of the ACE Faculty Development Matrix (Haras et al., 2017). This matrix provides rubrics to assess ADCs in the areas of organizational structure, center location, resource allocation and infrastructure, and programs and services. Each of these criteria has a number of subheadings. Each UCET staff member rated the center using the matrix and the Advisory Board members filled it out in small groups. Results were very similar across respondents and formed the basis for the assessment.

In particular, organizational structure and programs and services were rated as fully developed in all areas. These aspects are described more fully elsewhere in this chapter. The center location criteria had two areas rated as approaching fully developed. Web presence was rated lower because the site needs more asynchronous structured materials, such as webinars and online workshops. To remedy this, UCET staff contributed to an IU Teaching for Student Success online course for faculty. The center location subtopic was rated lower due to adjacent loud classrooms, and discussions about converting the classrooms to faculty space are ongoing. The resource allocation and infrastructure criterion included top ratings for budget, staffing, and IT support, but planning and data collection was rated as partially developed because the center collects participation data but does not collect direct evidence of changes in teaching practice as the result of participation. Plans were made for more formal tracking, at least using follow-up surveys in following semesters. Marketing was also noted as an area that could be improved and plans were made to use social media and announcements at departmental meetings in addition to current e-mail newsletters.

Participation

Our program has always been strong and has continued to grow in recent years. As at most universities, our assistant professors (pre-tenure) and lecturers (pre-promotion) are our most enthusiastic attendees. However, we also have relatively strong attendance across the ranks, including full professors, as seen in Fig. 14.2.

We are particularly proud of the effectiveness of our Learn and Earn program, which continues to impact the participation of our part-time faculty. From 2014 to 2017, participation nearly quadrupled from 209 to 809 hours. The Midwest SoTL Conference has continued to grow, allowing us to bring in nationally respected speakers. In four years, attendance increased from 111 to 200 registrants.

Satisfaction

We send out brief surveys after every event, with more comprehensive faculty satisfaction surveys for the Midwest SoTL Conference, institutes, and the dossier prep groups. With a very few exceptions, our participants are very satisfied with our offerings. They rate offerings very highly in terms of the usefulness of the content, but also in terms of collegiality/emotional support.

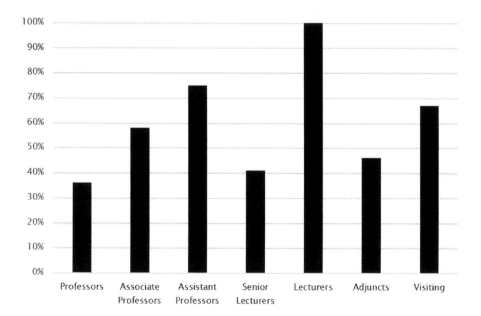

Fig. 14.2 UCET visits by faculty rank 2017–2018

Impact

Like many ADCs, our assessments have focused more on participation and satisfaction than on actual impact on teaching. Our participants are overwhelmingly enthusiastic about our offerings, saying that they are a good use of time. We are currently implementing a suggestion made by Fink (2013) and surveying past participants to ask what actual changes they have made to their teaching. At this point, we do not have enough data to analyze, but comments have been very positive. For example, past participants in the Course Design Institute wrote:

> "My teaching improved a great deal. I made my assignments more applicable and included language that made my expectations even clearer to students. For example, I now include rubrics in all my assignments" and "I continue to use some of the higher-order thinking skill sets shared during the Institute in my class. They have helped to elevate the questions, as well as the activities used in my class."

Past participants in the Grading Institute wrote: "I try to be more transparent with my students about why we are doing things the way we are" and "I have been reworking my rubrics to be clearer to the students." We plan to do more impact assessment in the future.

Summary and Recommendations

Having faculty take leadership in planning, implementing, and governing ensures a strong center that meets local needs and is a trusted resource for faculty. UCET has become an integral part of our campus, supporting faculty from orientation to retirement through institutes, consultations, mentoring, conferences, book discussion groups, and small grants programs. Although officially reporting to Academic Affairs, UCET is widely recognized to be faculty-led and responsive to faculty, much as the Academic Senate. UCET is often the first place that faculty turn to when they have questions or problems, knowing that UCET staff will either know the answer or know who to ask. Based on this experience, we believe that it is critical for ADCs to be faculty-led, but administratively supported. This collaboration ensures that the center meets the needs of a particular faculty and campus and becomes the 'heart of the campus.'

Acknowledgments The authors would like to extend special thanks to Cathy Dale, UCET secretary, who provided much of the data and archival material for this article.

References

Faculty Colloquium for Excellence in Teaching (FACET). (n.d.). *Faculty Academy on Excellence in Teaching*. Indiana University (IU). https://facet.iu.edu/

Fink, L. (2013). Innovative ways of assessing faculty development programs. *New Directions for Teaching & Learning, 133*, 47–59.

Furlong, P., & Vander Ven, T. (2010). *A campus becoming*. Wolfson Press.

Haras, C., Ginsberg, M., Magruder, E., & Zakrajsek, T. (2017). *The faculty development center matrix*. American Council on Education (ACE). https://www.acenet.edu/news-room/Documents/The-Faculty-Development-Center-Matrix.pdf

Indiana University (IU). (2001). *Indiana University strategic directions charter records, 1994–1998*. IU South Bend. http://webapp1.dlib.indiana.edu/findingaids/view?doc.view=entire_text&docId=InU-Ar-VAC1056

Indiana University (IU) Office of Institutional Research. (1996). *Number of faculty*. IU South Bend. https://www.iu.edu/~uirr/doc/reports/standard/fact%20book/fbook96/faclty96.html

Mettetal, G., & McGuire, G. (2013). Formal and informal support for pre-tenure faculty: Recommendations for administrators and institutions. *To Improve the Academy, 32*(1), 59–72.

Ouellett, M. (2010). Overview of faculty development: History and choices. In K. J. Gillespie & D. L. Robertson (Eds.), *A guide to faculty development* (2nd ed., pp. 3–20). Jossey-Bass.

University Center for Excellence in Teaching (UCET). (n.d.). *About us*. Indiana University (IU) South Bend. https://iu.instructure.com/courses/1683073/pages/about-us

15

A Member-Driven, Donor-Supported Academic Professional Development Center: The New Mexico State University Teaching Academy

Tara Gray, Laura Madson, and Morgan Iommi

Introduction

A member-driven, donor-supported model may be responsible for the success of our academic professional development center (ADC), the New Mexico State University (NMSU) Teaching Academy. About 200 members (regular participants) 'drive' our center by leading workshops and giving input. Over 100 donors a year have contributed a total of $1 million in cash and in planned (future estate) gifts. Member and donor generosity have allowed our ADC to prosper despite deep across-the-board budget cuts and poorly timed hiring freezes. Regardless of these setbacks, our center has flourished and has received

---

T. Gray (✉)
Teaching Academy, New Mexico State University,
Las Cruces, NM, USA
e-mail: tgray@nmsu.edu

L. Madson
Department of Psychology, New Mexico State University,
Las Cruces, NM, USA
e-mail: lmadson@nmsu.edu

M. Iommi
Center for Teaching and Learning Excellence, Nevada State College,
Henderson, NV, USA
e-mail: morgan.iommi@nsc.edu

© The Author(s), under exclusive license to Springer Nature Switzerland AG 2023
O. J. Neisler (ed.), *The Palgrave Handbook of Academic Professional Development Centers*,
Palgrave Studies on Leadership and Learning in Teacher Education,
https://doi.org/10.1007/978-3-030-80967-6_15

much local, national, and international recognition. The NMSU Teaching Academy offers a unique member-driven, donor-supported model for other teaching centers.

As a Hispanic-serving university situated in one of the five poorest states in the USA, NMSU may seem an improbable home for a center that has received recognition at home and abroad (United States Census Bureau, 2017). We specialize in science, agriculture, and engineering, with much reliance on externally funded research. Faculty members in these subjects are often in doctorate-granting programs and have low course assignments, typically two courses per semester, but with frequent buyouts from grants. In other subjects in which research is not usually externally funded and master's programs are more common, the course assignment is typically three courses a semester. For non-tenure-track faculty, the course assignment is usually four courses per semester.

The NMSU campus refers to itself as a research institution with a major push to earn the highest classification as a research university. Partly because of this focus, many faculty members do not view classroom teaching as their primary interest or duty. Since the recession of 2008, the campus has faced deep budget cuts and regular hiring freezes, which have reduced our center's budget by 55% and staff by 35%. Despite these challenges, we have thrived as a member-driven, donor-supported teaching center.

History and Mission

The story of the NMSU Teaching Academy began in late 2001 when our then-university president expressed a desire to enhance classroom teaching. At that time, he directed an administrator to begin conducting dozens of interviews with interested faculty, asking them for input on what would improve teaching at the university. By spring of 2002, a task force of faculty and administrators had been formed. By fall of 2002, a search for a center director was underway, and by January 2003 the director was in place. This all took place in about one year from the president's first expression of interest. This speed was the result of the decision to reshape the existing center, which had been established in 1980 and had fallen on hard times, rather than to start a new center. Our Teaching Academy is actually an ADC with paid staff, rather than a more traditional teaching academy, which in the USA often means a collaboration of faculty who are excellent teachers.

Since our center's establishment in 2003, our vision, mission, values, and motto have evolved to what they are today. Our vision is to help NMSU educators develop extraordinary teaching lives embedded in exceptional careers. Our mission is to provide robust professional development in teaching, scholarly writing, diversity, leadership, and mentoring, as well as promotion and tenure. Our values include lifelong learning, service, and leadership. Our motto was coined by John Cotton Dana, an American librarian: "Who dares to teach must never cease to learn."

The organizing principle of our center is to put educators first and address the full range of their needs (Boyer, 1990; Boyer et al., 2015; Glassick et al., 1997; Gray & Conway, 2007, 182). To that end, we devote almost half of our resources to issues other than classroom teaching, including the list of topics named above (a separate center provides professional development for online teaching). The decision to focus on the whole educator—on faculty or personal development—was made in response to feedback from faculty and within the context of the Boyer model (Boyer, 1990; Boyer et al., 2015; Glassick et al., 1997). Boyer and his colleagues shaped the thinking at that time with their emphasis on addressing a broad range of issues, including teaching. Instructors flourish when all their needs are addressed (Boyer, 1990; Boyer et al., 2015; Glassick et al., 1997; Sorcinelli et al., 2006). Instructors who come to our center to explore issues other than teaching often come back to explore teaching.

Our center is firmly grounded in the conceptual framework that successful centers should address faculty (personal), instructional, and organizational needs (Bergquist & Phillips, 1975). In addition to the faculty or personal development already discussed, we also address instructional and organizational development. We provide instructional development by offering dozens of one-time and multi-session workshops on teaching per year and provide organizational development by offering events for department heads and those aspiring to become department heads or deans. For department heads, we provide ongoing professional development, including one-time workshops and a book discussion group that reads one book per semester. For aspiring leaders, we provide a yearlong leadership program. Therefore, we work to change the organization by enhancing its faculty leadership, especially department heads.

Structure

The structure of the Teaching Academy includes everyone who leads workshops or who participates in them. All participants attend at least one event, while participants who lead a workshop or who participate in at least 10 hours

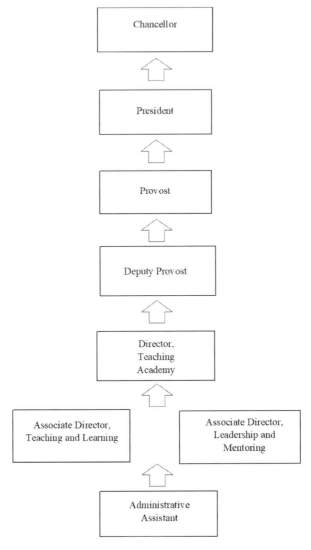

Fig. 15.1 Organizational chart* for NMSU Teaching Academy. *Accurate as of Spring 2020

of programming in a year earn a membership for the following year. Categories of membership are explained below.

We have three staff members who report to the director, who in turn reports to the deputy provost, who then reports to the provost (see Fig. 15.1). The staff includes the director, an associate director for teaching and learning, an associate director for leadership and mentoring, and an administrative assistant. Participants lead two-thirds of our center's programming, including a dozen fellows who are so named because they each lead a multi-session workshop approximately every other year. The majority (65%) of our participants are faculty, 15% are graduate students, and the remaining 20% are professional staff (many of whom also teach). Participants come from a total population of about 800 full-time and 250 part-time faculty members (NMSU Office of Institutional Analysis, n.d.-a), 600 graduate teaching assistants (College Factual, n.d.), and 2,500 staff (NMSU Office of Institutional Analysis, n.d.-b).

Our staff plans programming with input from participants. Participants are vocal about what programming they want: they provide input on workshop evaluations, through our advisory board, and by offering to lead workshops. To plan each semester's programming, staff relies heavily on our learning objectives and curriculum map, which ties every learning objective to the university's strategic plan (NMSU Teaching Academy, n.d.). The staff arranges about 60 different events each academic year, including a dozen multi-session workshops, taught about evenly by staff and fellows. We host many multi-session workshops because they have a profound impact on teaching, providing time for participants to reflect, practice, obtain feedback, and build community (Chism et al., 2012; Condon et al., 2016; Knight et al., 2005; Stes et al., 2010). Our director has formally evaluated several of these multi-session workshops (Gray, 2015; Gray & Birch, 2008; Gray et al., 2013, 2018; Gray & Meyer, 1997; Meyer & Gray, 1996; Sorcinelli et al., 2011).

A Member-Driven Center

What Is a Membership System?

In our membership system, faculty, staff, and graduate students who lead a workshop or who participate in at least 10 hours of events earn a membership for the following academic year. Three different levels of memberships are awarded: 10 hours (member), 20 hours (sustaining member), and 40 hours (distinguished member). We track and document these hours using an institution-wide training management database (Birch & Gray, 2009).

All three levels of members are honored at our gala, "Champagne & Chocolate," a grand affair that wraps up our membership year the way a ribbon wraps up a gift. The gala is held at the end of the academic year in the poshest room on campus, a room often reserved for donors. The gala has two parts: a reception followed by an awards ceremony. The university president and provost preside at the ceremony, which features awards for teaching, mentoring, outstanding members, and an outstanding workshop. The gala is a time for community and camaraderie. Our center pays for the gala because it is the best imaginable community-building event, not to mention the best publicity. At a recent gala, one graduate student member announced:

> When I read my first set of [student] evaluations, I cried out of sadness. When I read my second set, I cried out of happiness. I attribute the change to learning from experience and also from the Teaching Academy. (T. Busch, personal communication, April 29, 2019)

How Did a Membership System Develop?

The idea for membership came first from the faculty who served on the task force—and then from center staff who further developed the idea. The faculty on the task force said they did not mind doing faculty development, but wanted to be recognized for doing so. The center staff, in turn, wanted to give educators something concrete to put in their annual evaluations and their applications for promotion and tenure—by creating prestige around the idea of belonging to the center.

How Did the Membership System Lead to a Member-Driven Center?

The membership system was designed partly to give a greater sense of belonging to the center and thus have members drive the center with their commitment. Members drive our work in three key ways: by giving input to the staff, by leading workshops, and by donating money. First, members consistently give input to staff orally and in writing about which workshops they want. Overall, 30% of our members complete an impact survey every few years. The impact survey gives staff ideas for how to improve our center and gives us the data we need to demonstrate our center is working and should be sustained (for more information, please see the impact section of this chapter).

Second, members drive our work by leading more than half of our events. Each year, about 30 of our members lead one-time workshops or multi-session workshops, including book groups. Staff ask faculty to lead workshops whenever staff members learn that faculty are doing something especially effective in their classes. Members who give many successful workshops are invited to become fellows. The duty of fellows is to lead a multi-session workshop every other year. About a dozen fellows have graciously agreed to do this without course release or pay. The fellows are acknowledged at the gala and are featured prominently on our website.

Third, members drive our center by donating their own money. We believe that our membership and donor funding systems are intricately linked and that the membership system made the donor system possible.

A Donor-Supported Center

In addition to being member-driven, our center is also donor-supported. Donor support comes from participants, outside philanthropists, and other university units that supplement our base budget, which is provided by the university. Our fundraising approach has involved a lot of trial and error as we have adapted to the ever-changing conditions at the university and focused on approaches that were most successful given the current climate. Funding has also come from other university units who contribute from their university budgets, as well as from private individual donors giving from their personal monies through payroll deduction or through planned giving, as described below.

Funding from University Units

In 1998, five years before our center was launched, our director began her foray into fundraising. She began by raising money for the center that preceded the current center, where she was volunteering. The director raised this money from other university units, including seven deans, the provost, the vice president for research, the distance education department, and two former National Science Foundation (NSF) grants, including a grant from the NSF ADVANCE program. She initially raised money by soliciting it to pay participants who successfully completed multi-session workshops. She raised enough money to pay participants between $100 and $250, depending on the length of the workshop. By the time the current center was founded, our director had five years of experience soliciting money from university units.

There was nothing in the faculty development literature to explain how to raise money for a center, so our director used a one-on-one, data-driven approach. She met individually with each of eight college deans, giving them an annual update showing which faculty and graduate students participated from their colleges, their hours of participation, and the fraction of their participation as compared to the total from all colleges. Then she made a simple pitch—that faculty development was a shared responsibility and the center could not do it successfully alone. She approached the most generous deans first and then told the others that the deans she had approached earlier had donated. Our deans came to see the impact our center was having on their faculty and graduate students and most paid their fair share with a "minimum of grumbling" (Gray & Conway, 2007, 181). Using this method, the director was able to raise $100,000 per year.

Raising money from deans and other units was difficult in the beginning, but gradually became much easier. At first, such fundraising took around 40 hours of the director's time spaced over several months. It took so long because of the one-on-one meetings with each potential donor. Getting these appointments required some persistence initially. The last dean she approached had to be contacted by e-mail and phone six times before agreeing to the first meeting. When that dean asked our director why she had persisted despite being told "no" indirectly six times, she told him that she was persisting because she "knew he would do the right thing." He did eventually accept the meeting and contributed his fair share based on his college's participation rates. In subsequent years, fundraising became easier. After a few years, the director was spending about 15 hours a year on fundraising from campus units—an amazing return on investment!

In 2009, the money from the deans became permanent when our then-provost asked the deans to transfer the money they were donating to our permanent budget line (the NSF grants that were donating could not make this transfer). The transfer was not solicited by our director—our provost decided our director should not have to "beg" for money any longer. At that time, we received $75,000 of annual, recurring operating monies with the condition that we raise no more money from the deans.

In addition to this permanent line of funding we have secured from the deans, we still occasionally solicit funds from other campus units in the form of co-sponsorships for special events that are of mutual interest. For example, if we want to bring in a relevant diversity speaker, we might split the cost with a campus ethnic program office who co-sponsors the event. This allows us to bring in a greater variety of events.

Funding from Participants Through Payroll Deductions

In 2004, one year after our center was founded, we decided to start raising private money via payroll deduction from participants, including faculty members, staff, administrators, and graduate assistants. Payroll deduction is a mechanism for giving in which donors authorize a set amount to be automatically deducted pretax from their paychecks every pay period. Payroll deduction made raising money from employees practical. Virtually all small, recurring donations come to us in the form of payroll deductions. Small *one-time* gifts are sporadic at best, and do not account for any significant portion of our fundraising. Our university has a foundation (fundraising) office which collects and accounts for each donation, sending us a list of donors twice a month. Funds are available to us through a separate account. A payroll deduction system might be the one prerequisite for raising money from faculty and staff: in order to save a center a serious commitment in terms of accounting, the university might need to have a payroll deduction system.

To help with raising money from private individuals, we hired a part-time fundraising professional with experience raising money in a university setting. He started out working 10 hours per week on fundraising, but within a couple of years he shifted to five hours. He focused on helping the director establish a donor system, build relationships with stakeholders, and develop a fundraising campaign. Throughout his 10 years at our center, he raised at least five times what he was paid, much of it in planned gifts as described below.

During our first year, participation in events grew so rapidly that we had to knock out a wall to seat 50 individuals rather than 30 in our workshop room. We hosted a celebration that we used to kick off our payroll deduction campaign by 'passing the hat,' an age-old method for raising money in the USA in which one person takes off their hat and puts money in it before passing it around to everyone. Our director took off the construction hat that she was wearing for the occasion of the remodel, put her own payroll deduction form in it, and passed it from person to person throughout the room. One person filled out the payroll deduction form at that time, and others did so over a period of weeks and months, after we began to send members requests for funds.

We request payroll deduction gifts in categories of giving per two-week pay period. Our categories are $5 (Backers), $10 (Builders), $25 (Founders), and $50 (Benefactors). These set categories encourage donors to make larger gifts than they otherwise would (Sargeant & Jay, 2011). Giving through payroll deduction makes it easy and routine for donors to give. We raised

$8,000 that first year, which increased to $30,000 per year for 10 years (until 2014), before falling to $20,000 after our fundraiser took another job and was not replaced.

We conduct our ongoing fundraising campaigns requesting payroll deductions by working with our foundation's annual giving director. In the fall, we send a newsletter that contains a 'soft' or gentle ask, which precedes the formal fall direct request for funds by one day. In the spring, two requests for funds are also sent a day apart, with the pitch being an invitation to join our Wall of Honor. The Wall of Honor is a large banner, which extends across an entire wall in our workshop room, and lists the names of every donor by category. The e-mail depicts the Wall of Honor and says: "Your name could be here." We initially sent these requests for funds just to recent members, but then we began sending them to all participants, including graduate students and staff. Contacting participants as well as members has allowed us to extend our reach and garner new donors and support.

Our most successful fundraising efforts are accomplished in person and by phone. At special workshops with outside speakers and at the end of each multi-session workshop, we thank donors for "providing programming like this," point out the Wall of Honor, and invite others to join their colleagues by giving. Periodically, we call members and invite them to become donors; we also call donors and ask them to give at the next highest donor level, which usually means doubling their pledge. In both cases, we leave personalized voicemail messages on their office phones (few are reached in person). Calling 100 donors and/or participants takes about one day if you include the time it takes to send follow-up e-mails to each group of people you call.

Funding from Participants and Other Philanthropists Through Planned Gifts

A center must establish a culture of giving before large gifts will be forthcoming (Grant, 2013). Since we started this fundraising program, a half-dozen large gifts have been given (the first came from our former provost mentioned earlier). Other large gifts are planned gifts, also called estate gifts that are given upon the death of the donor. These gifts came after our effort to involve, inform, and acquaint donors with our vision. Our fundraising professional hosted 'Friends' Luncheons' in which faculty donors talked about what our center meant to them. These events were non-transactional lunches; that is, no direct solicitation of funds was made. Among the guests at one luncheon were a couple who were among the most generous university donors. We were able to invite them because it was a non-transactional lunch. At the end of the luncheon, they said to the director: "We are most impressed that faculty are giving. We need to see what we can do." Shortly thereafter, this couple gave a planned gift worth several hundred thousand dollars. Their gift was in addition to their other university gifts and was welcomed by our university's foundation office. Additionally, two $25,000 planned gifts were given by faculty as they neared retirement. These gifts were only subtly cultivated by us, but we had established a culture of giving and they gave. Finally, three other planned gifts were cultivated by our fundraiser: they came from our fundraiser himself, our director, and a long-time associate director. It was the small gifts that laid the groundwork for these larger gifts—without the small ones, no one, including the director, would have thought to put our center in their wills. The planned gifts will be worth about $600,000.

Donor Recognition

We recognize donors in a variety of ways. When donors first contribute, they receive a thank-you note from us and one from the university's foundation office. Every donor also receives a holiday card of thanks each year. On an annual fundraising day known nationally as "Giving Tuesday," our director calls donors and leaves personalized messages of thanks on their voicemail. Calling half our donors (about 50) in alternate years requires two hours to complete. At our annual gala, donors are given special nametag ribbons to wear that display their donor level, and they are asked to stand as a group and be recognized. Any donor who gives at the top level of payroll deductions also receives individual recognition as a new benefactor, which is our name for top-level donors. For more information about our fundraising methods, see Hohnstreiter (2011).

In sum, donors have contributed a combined total of $400,000 in payroll deductions and $600,000 in planned gifts, for a grand total of $1 million. More than a hundred donors have contributed to us each year over 15 years. We know that our donors are more committed to our success as a center because they give money to it. University administrators have told us that this unprecedented gesture of support is our biggest source of strength.

Impact Data

The Teaching Academy has been successful based on both internal and external metrics. Internally, we conduct impact surveys to demonstrate that our center positively impacts teaching, learning, and other elements of faculty careers. We administer the impact survey every three to five years so that a new survey can coincide with each change in upper administration, which occurs regularly. The impact survey is short (only nine questions), and we survey only recent members (i.e., those from within the last three years). Given that our programming changes over time, we feel that only recent members will know enough to comment meaningfully. Because we send the survey only to recent members and we announce upfront that there are fewer than 10 questions, we get a high response rate. In 2018, we surveyed about 600 members, of which 200 responded. The following percentages of members reported that, based on their experiences with our center, 92% made positive changes in their teaching, 80% observed improvements in their students' learning, and 82% enhanced their careers. Participants wrote:

> Thanks, Teaching Academy, for keeping me employed, fresh, and current, with tools to meet each individual's learning needs. (Participant 1, Teaching Academy)

> The only cost is time, and if someone wants to 'up their game', improve their CV, or move up in the ranks, they need to go no farther than the Teaching Academy. (Participant 2, Teaching Academy)

Based on this quantitative and qualitative data, we know we are making a difference internally.

Externally, we have received national or international recognition a dozen times, mostly regarding our unique status as a member-driven, donor-supported center. For example, both our membership and our donor programs have been finalists for the Innovation Award by the Professional and Organizational Development Network, the USA-based organization for faculty development. Our fundraising program was featured in a national online newspaper, *Inside Higher Ed*, with a circulation of almost two million (Basu, 2012). Our director has also been invited to keynote on our model both in the USA and abroad. In the USA, she has addressed three universities and faculty developers from 64 universities in the State University of New York system. Internationally, she keynoted at a conference in the United Arab Emirates and also addressed several hundred educators from across Thailand at an event sponsored by the Thai Secretary of Education.

Discussion and Recommendations

As we look back, we have several suggestions for those establishing new centers or directing mature ones. What has sustained us has been our members and donors. Whether or not you establish a donor system, consider establishing a membership system to create community and prestige about belonging to your center. If you fundraise, be patient and persistent. Don't be shy about asking for money. The first few dollars will be far harder to raise than subsequent dollars. Consider hiring a fundraising professional, even part-time, to get you started—and work closely with your foundation/fundraising office. Put your emphasis on raising money by making announcements at workshops and by phoning individual donors. And plan what you will do if you face budget cuts or hiring freezes.

Perhaps the biggest lesson is that the requirements for a successful center are not what one might presume. Our university does not have a multi-million-dollar endowment, a faculty uniformly devoted to excellent teaching, or a student body attracted by our rigor or reputation. We have benefitted from a handful of administrators who were open to the idea of creating an exceptional teaching center, a dedicated staff, and devoted members who give of their time, talent, and treasure.

Acknowledgments The authors of this chapter wish to thank the following three groups of readers for their sage advice: Jo Clemmons and Gayle Solfrank, both of Point Loma Nazarene University, San Diego, CA, and Linda Nilson, formerly of Clemson University, Clemson, SC, USA; NSMU faculty members, including Esther Devall, Department of Family and Consumer Sciences, Niki Mott, Department of English, Teaching Academy fellow, and Advisory Board chair, and Elise Sautter, Department of Marketing; and former and current Teaching Academy staff, including Mark Hohnstreiter, fundraiser, Sandy Katanayagi, administrative assistant, Alice Martinic, educational specialist, and Shawn Werner, associate director for leadership and mentoring.

References

Basu, K. (2012, April 30). Collective donating. *Inside Higher Ed*. http://www.insidehighered.com/news/2012/04/30/faculty-members-donate-money-teaching-academy

Bergquist, W. H., & Phillips, S. R. (1975). *A handbook for faculty development*. Council for the Advancement of Small Colleges.

Birch, A. J., & Gray, T. (2009). Ten ways to use a relational database at a faculty development center. *To Improve the Academy, 27*(1), 62–72.

Boyer, E. (1990). *Scholarship reconsidered: Priorities of the professoriate.* Jossey-Bass.

Boyer, E., Moser, D., Ream, T. C., & Braxton, J. M. (2015). *Scholarship reconsidered: Priorities of the professoriate* (expanded edition). Princeton University Press.

Chism, N. V. N., Holley, M., & Harris, C. J. (2012). Researching the impact of educational development: Basis for informed practice. *To Improve the Academy, 31*(1), 129–145.

College Factual. (n.d.). *The New Mexico State University- Main campus student to faculty ratio & faculty composition.* College Factual. https://www.collegefactual.com/colleges/new-mexico-state-university-main-campus/academic-life/faculty-composition/#secFullTime

Condon, W., Iverson, E. R., Manduca, C. A., Rutz, C., & Willett, G. (2016). *Faculty development and student learning: Assessing the connections.* Indiana University Press.

Glassick, C. E., Huber, M. T., & Maeroff, G. I. (1997). *Scholarship assessed: Evaluation of the professorate.* Jossey-Bass.

Grant, A. M. (2013). *Give and take: A revolutionary approach to success.* Penguin.

Gray, T. (2015). *Publish & flourish: Become a prolific scholar* (2nd ed.). NMSU.

Gray, T., Birch, A. J., & Madson, L. (2013). How teaching centers can support faculty as writers. In A. E. Geller & M. Eodice (Eds.), *Working with faculty writers* (pp. 95–110). Utah State University Press.

Gray, T., & Birch, J. (2008). Team mentoring: An alternative way to mentor new faculty. *To Improve the Academy, 26*(1), 230–241.

Gray, T., & Conway, J. (2007). Build it [right] and they will come: Boost attendance at your teaching center by building community. *Journal of Faculty Development, 21*(3), 179–184.

Gray, T., Madson, L., & Jackson, M. (2018). Publish & flourish: Helping scholars become better, more prolific writers. *To Improve the Academy, 37*(2), 243–256.

Gray, T., & Meyer, J. (1997). Peer coaching: Teachers helping teachers. *Journal of Criminal Justice Education, 8*(2), 273–284.

Hohnstreiter, M. A. (2011). Go for the gold: Fundraising for teaching centers. *To Improve the Academy, 30*(1), 262–276.

Knight, A. M., Cole, K. A., Kern, D. E., Barker, L. R., Kolodner, K., & Wright, S. M. (2005). Long-term follow-up of a longitudinal faculty development program in teaching skills. *Journal of General Internal Medicine, 20*(8), 721–725.

Meyer, J., & Gray, T. (1996). Peer coaching: An innovation in teaching. *Teaching in the Community Colleges (Electronic) Journal, 1*(3).

New Mexico State University (NMSU) Office of Institutional Analysis. (n.d.-a). *Factbooks: Faculty statistics for New Mexico State University- Las Cruces Campus [fall 2017].* NMSU. https://oia.nmsu.edu/factbooks-faculty/

New Mexico State University (NMSU) Office of Institutional Analysis. (n.d.-b). *Factbooks: Staff statistics for New Mexico State University- Las Cruces Campus [fall 2017].* NMSU. https://oia.nmsu.edu/factbooks-staff/

New Mexico State University (NMSU) Teaching Academy. (n.d.). *Teaching Academy learning objectives*. NMSU. https://teaching.nmsu.edu/teaching-academy-learning-objectives/

Sargeant, A., & Jay, E. (2011). *Building donor loyalty: The fund-raiser's guide to increasing lifetime value*. John Wiley & Sons.

Sorcinelli, M. D., Austin, A. E., Eddy, P. L., & Beach, A. L. (2006). *Creating the future of faculty development: Learning from the past, understanding the present*. Jossey-Bass.

Sorcinelli, M. D., Gray, T., & Birch, A. J. (2011). Faculty development beyond instructional development: Ideas centers can use. *To Improve the Academy, 30*(1), 247–261.

Stes, A., Min-Leliveld, M., Gijbels, D., & Van Pategem, P. (2010). The impact of instructional development in higher education: The state-of-the-art of the research. *Educational Research Review, 5*(1), 25–49.

United States Census Bureau. (2017). *Selected economic characteristics, 2013–2017 American Community Survey 5-year estimates*. U.S. Department of Commerce. https://www.census.gov/programs-surveys/acs/technical-documentation/table-and-geography-changes/2017/5-year.html

16

Faculty Leadership in Academic Professional Development Centers: Building a Case for a Three-Director, Faculty-Led Model

Emily R. Smith and Carol Ann Davis

Introduction

Effective academic professional development centers (ADCs) require leaders who can meet the diverse teaching and learning needs of educators on their campuses. Supporting faculty and staff to develop and sustain innovative teaching practices requires knowledge of and experience in pedagogy, learning theory, faculty development, management, and learning technologies, among other things. At the same time, ADC leaders must maintain credibility among the educators they serve, which typically grows from their direct experience as faculty scholars and teachers. Finding ADC leaders who possess both sets of expertise can be challenging.

This chapter draws on the literature on faculty development leadership models to illustrate the ways in which Fairfield University's Center for Academic Excellence's three-director, faculty-led leadership model provides the crucial knowledge and credibility needed for successful leadership. Drawing on examples from our work, we demonstrate how our integrated roles as faculty members and faculty developers enable and enrich our broadly shared work and offer other ADCs options for how they might think about organizing their respective centers. Although academic development is the

---

E. R. Smith (✉) • C. A. Davis
Fairfield University, Fairfield, CT, USA
e-mail: esmith@fairfield.edu; cdavis13@fairfield.edu

© The Author(s), under exclusive license to Springer Nature Switzerland AG 2023
O. J. Neisler (ed.), *The Palgrave Handbook of Academic Professional Development Centers*,
Palgrave Studies on Leadership and Learning in Teacher Education,
https://doi.org/10.1007/978-3-030-80967-6_16

larger field in which faculty development rests, in this chapter we use the term 'faculty development' because our center's mission, described below, explicitly focuses on faculty development, and our area of focus in this chapter is on the faculty buy-in that can accrue when faculty leaders are placed in positions of leadership at ADCs.

History of the Center for Academic Excellence at Fairfield University

The Center for Academic Excellence was formed in 2003 by faculty committed to providing Fairfield University, USA, with professional and organizational development support aligned with its institutional mission and priorities, including the Ignatian pedagogical tradition and best practices in teaching and learning. Since 2003, the center has supported innovation and scholarship in teaching and learning for faculty (full-time, part-time, visiting, and 'of the practice'), staff, and administrators. Originally funded by grants from the Davis Educational Foundation and others, the Center for Academic Excellence now operates from its endowment as well from yearly funding from the Office of the Provost, to which the center now reports. For the past 15 years, the center has been led primarily by faculty members, with assistance from nonfaculty assistant and associate directors hired from outside the university. In 2016, the center piloted a three-director, faculty-led model; this pilot model has stayed in place up to the present.

Organizational Reporting and Structure of the ADC

The Center for Academic Excellence's reporting structure has evolved with the changing leadership configurations in the center. With the move to a three-director model, our reporting pyramid has flattened somewhat, providing a collegial and collaborative structure of decision-making. Currently, the center's three directors report to the associate vice provost for Pedagogical Innovation and Effectiveness, who is also one of the three directors. This vice provost then reports to the provost (see Fig. 16.1).

The center also collaborates with several partners on campus, including the library, academic computing, the Center for Social Impact, and the Faculty Development and Evaluation Committee.

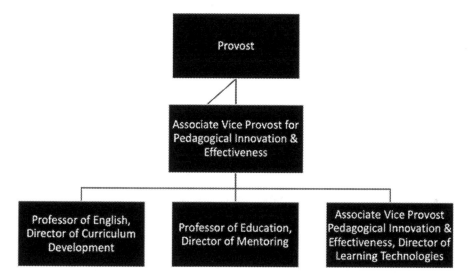

Fig. 16.1 Reporting structure of the Center for Academic Excellence

Leadership of ADCs

With the field of faculty development growing at an exponential rate (Gillespie & Robertson, 2010), we are learning more about leadership models in faculty development and the various ways in which institutions of higher education staff their ADCs. From the literature, we know that larger ADCs (and institutions) tend to have full-time directors with support staff, while smaller ADCs (and institutions) often support full-time faculty to direct with release time and/or stipends (Sorcinelli, 2002). ADC directors are often assisted by faculty fellows/liaisons, instructional designers and assistant/associate directors with specialized expertise (e.g., instructional technology, writing pedagogy, and assessment) (Gillespie & Robertson, 2010). Some ADCs hire internally from the faculty ranks, while others seek external administrators who bring expertise in the area of faculty development. A survey of ADC directors in Australian universities found that higher education institutions often hire staff from the secondary sector, as their faculty typically come from a research background rather than one in faculty development (Gosling, 2008). Another study of faculty development in North America found that faculty developers typically hold more than one position at their institution, with 45% of directors holding faculty status (Beach et al., 2016). With respect to capacity, a survey of

ADCs in the USA found a mean of 4.4 full-time-equivalent (FTE) staff, with a range of 0–25 FTE staff members (Herman, 2013).

Amid the diversity of these models, the literature is clear about the importance of knowledge and credibility among faculty development leaders. Although the knowledge base for faculty developers is not formally defined (Gray & Radloff, 2006; Sievers, 2016), there is a growing movement in the field to identify 'optimal skill sets' for faculty developers (Beach et al., 2016). Practitioners and scholars in the field agree that knowledge of theory and best practices in faculty development, as well as expertise in a scholarly discipline, are critical (Kolmos et al., 2001). Ideally, faculty developers should have experience with educational development, clinical and facilitation skills, and managerial and leadership skills (Gillespie & Robertson, 2010).

Equally important is the need for faculty developers to hold credibility among the faculty they support. Gillespie and Robertson (2010), among others, maintain that credibility is best achieved by colleagues who have been successful scholars and teachers, with insider knowledge of faculty experiences and needs. Faculty development programs, studies have found, "are most effective when they have strong faculty ownership and involvement" (Sorcinelli, 2002, 12) and when leadership is provided by respected teachers and scholars (Elbe & McKeachie, 1985). Effective centers, Gordon (2002) contends, align leadership with ownership.

The need for both faculty development expertise and credibility as faculty members poses a challenge for those charged with staffing faculty development centers: it is difficult to find people who possess both. Most faculty are experts in a discipline outside of faculty development, and people with faculty development expertise may not have experience as faculty members. As Gillespie and Robertson (2010) note:

> While faculty directors typically have a strong interest in teaching and success in the classroom, they may have no formal background in faculty development and limited familiarity with the literature and research base that supports it. (Gillespie & Robertson, 2010, 23)

The challenge is complicated by the finding that there is no clear or common path to becoming a faculty developer or developing the knowledge and skills required to succeed in the role (Gosling, 2008). In addition, standards related to qualifications or experience required to engage in faculty development are relatively scarce (Gray & Radloff, 2006).

Leadership in the Center for Academic Excellence: A Case of One Center

What follows is a description and discussion of our leadership model in which we share our efforts at managing these challenges while staffing an ADC at our midsize, liberal arts institution. Having a three-director leadership model with significant faculty involvement has enabled us to negotiate some of the tensions related to leadership credibility and knowledge. Our engagement as faculty directors has provided some of the necessary insights into faculty life and needs, as well as the credibility required to lead faculty development efforts on campus.

Since its inception in 2003, the Center for Academic Excellence has engaged with a variety of leadership configurations as it worked to meet the development needs of the roughly 300 faculty members at our Jesuit, liberal arts institution, Fairfield University. The center began with a single-faculty director on a reduced teaching load. As the work expanded, professional staff were added to its leadership: first an external associate director and then an assistant director and an administrative assistant were hired to support the faculty development work. Each of these professional staff did not have faculty status. Gradually, the center added stipended faculty liaisons to augment the activities and act as advisors for the director. Two full-time faculty members succeeded the inaugural director, accompanied by the professional staff mentioned above.

The first administrative director drawn from professional staff rather than faculty was appointed in 2014, when the third faculty director returned to her full-time teaching responsibilities. In 2016, the directorship returned to a faculty-directed model, with an associate professor of education (the director of mentoring) appointed to direct the center. At this point, a desire for collaborative leadership led to the hiring of two additional directors, an associate professor from the English Department (the director of curriculum development) and an administrator with faculty status from academic computing (the director of learning technologies).

As this short summary of our history indicates, leadership at the Center for Academic Excellence has evolved in response to an increased interest in faculty development around teaching and learning. As this increased interest has emerged, our faculty status has become even more significant to our leadership roles because the center is seen as part of faculty life and work. In what follows, we draw on examples from major center initiatives in recent years to illustrate the ways in which this three-director, faculty-led leadership model

256 E. R. Smith and C. A. Davis

has enabled us to round out the knowledge needs in faculty development leadership and demonstrate the credibility needed to sustain faculty buy-in to our work.

Covering the Knowledge Base in Faculty Development: A Synergy of Expertise

As the literature suggests, the ideal faculty developer possesses expertise in a scholarly discipline as well as knowledge of faculty development, leadership, and managerial skills. Because of the rarity of such as faculty member—or faculty developer—trained in all of these areas, our three-director model offers an alternative approach that combines the expertise of several individuals in a way that increases our ability to respond to faculty's individual needs and to collaborate across our areas of strength. In our case, one of our center's directors provides expertise in curriculum and instruction, another in pedagogies grounded in the development of low-stakes, writing-to-learn theoretical frameworks, and a third in the innovative use of educational technology. In addition, our collective engagement with both undergraduate and graduate students brings preparation with both young adult and adult learners. Finally, our collective academic experiences as managers, chairs, and directors provide a background in the leadership and managerial skills necessary to lead a center and to develop our faculty's capacity as leaders. In the case of the Center for Academic Excellence, we are able to extend our offerings to faculty—and to pivot to address institutional initiatives—because of this collaborative, faculty-led model.

Our Course Design Institutes are a good example of the ways in which our combined expertise provides the necessary knowledge and experience to support our colleagues' curricular revision process. The director of mentoring drew on her knowledge of curriculum development to structure a developmental sequence of course revision exercises, including identifying learning outcomes, designing authentic assessments, and outlining a sequence of learning activities. Using her own teaching as an example, the director of curriculum development drew on her extensive background in writing to illustrate how faculty can integrate low-stakes writing tasks into their teaching to facilitate formative learning experiences throughout a course. Finally, the director of learning technology's deep knowledge of and experience with diverse learning technologies helped to model the ways in which technology can be used as a tool to support active and authentic learning experiences.

Throughout these three-day institutes, we also invite faculty colleagues from across the university to share pedagogical examples of the design

16 Faculty Leadership in Academic Professional Development Centers... 257

principles we are modeling. As teachers, we can all draw on our work with Fairfield University students to illustrate the course design principles we promote. Our ability to share our campus teaching experiences brings us into communion with our faculty participants who share similar students and teaching challenges at our institution. Our faculty teaching also gives us insider knowledge of the pedagogical issues and innovations underway on campus. We are both *promoters* and *users* of the pedagogical and technological initiatives and innovations on campus, which gives us insight into the challenges and needs our faculty face, which in turn informs our planning.

Knowledge, Participation, and Credibility

Being teachers is important not only for our knowledge base, but also for our credibility. As noted, faculty development programs are most effective when there is faculty ownership and involvement (Sorcinelli, 2002) and when leadership is aligned with this ownership (Gordon, 2002). Thus, it is important that our directors are teachers who are visibly engaged in the 'bread and butter' of our university mission: teaching. Being an engaged teacher on campus is central to faculty buy-in as we lead teaching effectiveness efforts at the center. The same is true, we believe, for our engagement in faculty service. Because our faculty directors retain all of their faculty duties (with a reduced teaching load), they are fully engaged in faculty life, including faculty governance, committee work, and engagement with university initiatives. This involvement has proven to be both a key vehicle for remaining aware of faculty needs and concerns and a vehicle for maintaining credibility as faculty leaders.

Committee Work

One way in which we have earned credibility as faculty development leaders on our campus is through our faculty directors' continued involvement with various areas of faculty governance. Because faculty directors retain their faculty status (and are tenured associate and/or full professors) who at various moments hold chairships on committees, their work at the Center for Academic Excellence is integrated fully into the ways in which faculty engage in shaping the teaching, labor, and learning environments through governance. Here, we see the link between faculty/director involvement and ownership. In addition to consistently running for committee appointments through

258   E. R. Smith and C. A. Davis

their faculty status (for instance, one director served four years on the faculty's most important committee, the Academic Council, and another is the outgoing chair of Educational Technology as well as a member of the Undergraduate Curriculum Committee), the directors sit as nonvoting members on the Faculty Development and Evaluation Committee (FDEC), a committee each has chaired in the past from their faculty seat. In this role, we assist with the committee's twice-annual FDEC Day, an event that invites all faculty to convene on a topic of relevance to their teaching. FDEC Days in the recent past have helped to explore multicultural competency, introduced elements of a core revision, and tackled difficult topics such as how to encourage deeper and more critical reading. Through the center's involvement with FDEC Day, we are able to collaborate with faculty on a big stage and follow up with faculty back at the center, as these events open up areas of interest and growth for them. Faculty who seek out our assistance or attend our workshops see how our work as faculty members and faculty developers overlaps, informs, and enriches each other, thereby increasing faculty buy-in to what we do.

Faculty Evaluation

The "big days" are only part of the story, however; through involvement on committees at the level of ordinary committee business, our directors become aware of issues of importance to faculty and bring that work back to center programming. One example from the past would be that, after the FDEC Day on Multicultural Competence (itself a reaction to a sensitive racial incident on campus), the directors worked with the faculty chair on diversity to co-facilitate a series of brown-bag discussions titled 'Difficult Conversations in the Classroom'. More recently, the university was notified that our student course evaluation instrument, the Individual Development and Educational Assessment (IDEA) evaluation, was moving to another platform. The new interface meant that several questions on the instrument were revised, and the way in which faculty were asked to administer the form would also need to change. These issues were taken to the FDEC by the administration, but since the university was not given a choice about the changes, the committee was more of a sounding board for how to allay faculty fears than a request for permission.

In this context, the directors of the center, who had a decade's worth of knowledge of and direct experience with administration of the IDEA form as both teachers and committee members (and who had helped to facilitate

16 Faculty Leadership in Academic Professional Development Centers...

its original online implementation), were able to work with the administration to develop online materials that would educate faculty about these changes and to provide additional workshops and consultations for faculty. To prepare these materials, the directors met with the registrar and IDEA personnel so that all questions could be sufficiently and honestly answered. Once that work was complete, the directors attended the FDEC meeting in which the changes were discussed and were able to act as the contact for any faculty questions once the announcement was sent out by the provost. This allowed the chair of the FDEC the support he needed to continue his role as chair, rather than become the focus of this change, which was administrative in nature.

Center involvement in the work of committees, therefore, brings faculty development into the realm of service, which is an area where faculty collaborate across disciplines. The presence of the center (through faculty directors) is especially valuable there. In short, faculty status not only allows directors to be present at crucial junctures, but to assist faculty leaders from other areas when their expertise is most needed. This example of involvement in faculty governance demonstrates the ways in which the center becomes visible to faculty from within their work on committees and through their involvement with university initiatives (which flow through committees). In increasing our visibility, and the ways in which we can assist in deepening faculty development work through committee involvement, the directors raise the center's profile and knit the center's work directly to faculty work.

University Initiative

Because faculty directors are visible to colleagues on the level of governance and experience, collaborations with center directors as part of their service obligations, faculty in other areas of leadership begin to see the ways in which their own work and the work of the center interact. A long-term, vital role was played by center directors, for instance, as faculty leaders sought to bring forward a revision of the undergraduate core curriculum. After a task force identified that a core revision was needed and the provost appointed a director to explore its shape and feasibility, the center was asked to collaborate with the core director to facilitate the convening of working groups in the summer of 2016 to draft learning outcomes for three signature elements. More than 30 faculty met at the center to discuss and draft these learning outcomes, which became the basis on which the core revision proposal was built.

Those documents, forged with the facilitation of center leadership in collaboration with the core director, survived a two-year-long governance process and became the blueprint for the implementation of the new Magis Core Curriculum. As a result, core leadership (now a team consisting of the director and the coordinators of the three signature elements) collaborates routinely with the Center for Academic Excellence to develop the faculty resources to train faculty to teach in the Magis Core Curriculum (including Course Design Institutes and syllabus clinics), and the center cosponsored a faculty retreat to kick off the Magis Core Curriculum, which over 70 faculty attended. This type of collaboration would not be possible if faculty leaders from other areas did not see the center leadership as assistive with and intrinsic to their own work. Because of the directors' faculty status and ongoing engagement with issues central to faculty work, the center's work allies itself and tracks to the needs of faculty as they are situated in this university moment.

Managing the Dilemmas of Faculty Directorship

The faculty-directed center model is not without its difficulties, however; managing the tension between faculty-emergent initiatives (which the center encourages based on its high level of granular work and its overall position within the body politic) and university-driven ones (which come the center's way through its reporting structure within the Office of the Provost) is something directors continually negotiate and one that would not be as apparent if we were not faculty. Though faculty see the Center for Academic Excellence as a place where faculty lead, the administration still justifiably asks the center for assistance (and even leadership) on large projects that have faculty development as part of their initiative. As we move between our roles as faculty and as center directors, we need to be very transparent about what we do and how we do it—and we are accountable to faculty at all times about those choices. Maintaining a healthy balance between these roles allows us to maintain the transparency and credibility needed to ensure faculty buy-in and live out our roles as faculty and leaders.

Balancing Faculty and Administrator Statuses

One tension in our work arises when faculty are engaged in responding to university initiatives that may be administratively driven, either by necessary change (such as the IDEA form revisions) or because a timeline has been specified (such as with implementation of the Magis Core Curriculum). In those moments, we may not be seen as faculty but rather as administrators as we seek to facilitate faculty preparation for these (sometimes controversial) initiatives, or as growing pains are experienced in these transitions. At those moments, it is especially important for us to think through implications for faculty of these initiatives and voice these to the administration, along with other faculty leaders engaged in the initiative, to help articulate what faculty need to complete this university work. It is our role as faculty members that helps us to negotiate faculty concerns around particular initiatives, even when we are charged to carry out these initiatives out as administrators.

Maintaining Credibility in our Departments

A related drawback to the one described above becomes apparent on the departmental level. Although our roles as directors require a broad university lens and engage us in work that crosses many units of the university, we remain members of a single department, and departmental needs and obligations remain. Though we may be gaining credibility as faculty leaders precisely because we remain teachers, in our departments we can be seen as not pulling our weight because our teaching duties are reduced. It is important in this situation to be transparent both about the ways in which the position benefits the department (e.g., an increased voice in university initiatives, specific supports for faculty development, departmental program assessment, and review) and about the ways in which it presents challenges (i.e., a reduced teaching load).

Questions of Longevity

In addition to these obstacles, although we believe faculty gain institutional knowledge the longer they stay in faculty development leadership positions, longevity is not guaranteed because faculty typically serve in these positions on an at-will basis. Faculty leaders may find themselves negotiating the necessary tensions mentioned above without the assurance that their positions will remain supported. In some ways, as faculty leaders, we are only as secure as our last decision; still, because we are faculty first, we can always return to our departments.

Recommendations for Leadership in ADCs

We are aware that our perceptions of ADC leadership and effectiveness are highly situated within our specific context as a medium-size Jesuit university, but our conclusions are reflective of the literature in the field. This literature recommends that directors possess buy-in and two types of knowledge—disciplinary expertise as well as experience in faculty development. In our context, we have achieved these three crucial aspects by crafting a model that depends on faculty-led directors.

Do the Work of Faculty with Faculty

While, in our case, elements of buy-in and credibility are built through our faculty status, we are not convinced that these cannot be achieved by an administratively-derived director model. However, we recommend such a director engage in certain steps that would enhance their credibility and result in higher faculty engagement and buy-in inside the ADC. Whether or not a director is an administrative or professional staff person or a faculty member, we recommend working with faculty at the granular level, in the teaching and service work in which faculty are already engaged. This might include invitation to committees, outreach to committees, and clear communication to faculty units (departments, programs, and schools) about what the center is capable of offering to faculty. In our work, this means working on already-in-progress individual program reviews and self-studies, as well as core curriculum revision, and faculty evaluation.

Keep Teaching

We believe that faculty-driven center directors model themselves as reflective practitioners by continuing to teach, and reminding the university community that they are faculty. A nonfaculty director who teaches will develop more credibility with faculty than a nonteaching one.

Conclusion

Despite various drawbacks and tensions, we can conclude that faculty leadership at ADCs enriches the atmosphere of teaching and learning in a variety of ways, chiefly by providing the university with a way to support faculty development as well as further university initiatives. Our three-director model further serves to broaden the center's footprint and to draw different communities of faculty and professional staff into its orbit. It is our belief that greater faculty buy-in and the broader reach of a multidirector, faculty-led model together allow the center to become a locus of broad faculty activity because its leaders remain credible by continuing to teach and maintain active roles in faculty service and governance. Because we, as directors, remain not only *in*, but *of* the faculty, so too does the work of the center.

References

Beach, A. L., Sorcinelli, M. D., Austin, A. E., & Rivard, J. K. (2016). *Faculty development in the age of evidence: Current practices, future imperatives*. Stylus Press.

Elbe, K., & McKeachie, W. (1985). *Improving undergraduate education through faculty development*. Jossey-Bass.

Gillespie, K. J., & Robertson, D. L. (Eds.). (2010). *A guide to faculty development: Practical advice, examples, and resources*. Jossey-Bass.

Gordon, G. (2002). The roles of leadership and ownership in building an effective quality culture. *Quality in Higher Education, 8*(1), 97–106.

Gosling, D. (2008). *Survey of directors of academic development in Australian universities: Final report*. ResearchGate. https://www.researchgate.net/publication/255570433_Survey_of_Directors_of_Academic_Development_in_Australian_Universities_Final_Report/link/545b64820cf249070a7955ed/download

Gray, K., & Radloff, A. (2006). Quality management of academic development work: Implementation issues and challenges. *International Journal for Academic Development, 11*(2), 79–90.

Herman, J. H. (2013). Staffing of teaching and learning centers in the United States: Indicators of institutional support for faculty development. *Journal of Faculty Development, 27*(2), 33–37.

Kolmos, A., Rump, C., Ingemarsson, I., Laloux, A., & Vinther, O. (2001). Organization of staff development—Strategies and experiences. *European Journal of Engineering Education, 26*(4), 329–342.

Sievers, J. (2016). Educational developer 2.0: How educational development leaders will need to develop themselves in the era of innovation. *The Journal of Faculty Development, 30*(2), 107–115.

Sorcinelli, M. D. (2002). 10 principles for good practice in creating and sustaining teaching and learning centers. In K. H. Gillespie (Ed.), *A guide to faculty development* (pp. 9–23). Anker Publishers.

Part VI

Student Focus and/or Student Involvement Is a Major Focus

This section presents cases of academic professional development centers (ADCs) where the focus on students as partners, co-learners, and co-teachers drives the structure, programing, and assessment of either the ADC as a whole or one of its components.

Chapters in Part VI

Chapter 17: *The Centre for Student Engagement: A Research and Development Center for Students, Faculty, and Staff at the University of Winchester.* Tom Lowe, Centre for Student Engagement, University of Winchester, Winchester, UK.

This chapter explains how the design of a center for student engagement and a Postgraduate Certificate in Student Engagement revolves around the concept of student-faculty partnership. The chapter also describes other student-staff initiatives, such as the Winchester Student Fellows Scheme, which engages up to 60 student-staff partnerships a year on enhancement projects.

Chapter 18: *Partnerships Between Undergraduate Students and Faculty in the Assessment of Teaching and Learning: A Program Design Model.* Adriana Signorini, Cathy A. Pohan, and James Zimmerman, University of California Merced, Merced, CA, USA.

266   Student Focus and/or Student Involvement Is a Major Focus

In this chapter, an ADC involves students in a faculty-student partnership via a Students Assessing Teaching and Learning program. Students are co-developers, co-learners, and co-inquirers in both instructional development and the assessment of instruction.

Chapter 19: *A Holistic Approach to Student and Faculty Success: Integrating Careers, Advising, and Teaching.* Heather Keith, Radford University, Radford, VA (previously of Green Mountain College), Christina Fabrey, Virginia Tech, Blacksburg, VA (previously of Green Mountain College), and Serena Eddy, Mansfield Hall, Burlington, VT, USA (previously of Green Mountain College).

This chapter details how three centers have been incorporated into a one-location-based partnership to support student academic success with high-impact instruction, advisement, and career planning services. Although the college, and its related ADC, has closed recently, the collaborative model of academic professional development and student-focused engagement described in this chapter remains instructive.

Other Relevant Chapters

Chapter 8: *Needs Analysis Leads to Sustainability: Development of a Medical Education and Informatics Department in the College of Medicine and Health Sciences, Sultan Qaboos University.* Nadia Mohammed Al Wardy and Rashid Al Abri, Sultan Qaboos University, Muscat, Oman.

The ADC depicted in this chapter provides counseling to medical students as part of its mission to improve medical education outcomes.

Chapter 13: *Mission-Aligned Teaching Center Initiative.* Annie Soisson, Center for the Enhancement of Learning and Teaching, Tufts University, Somerville, MA, USA.

This chapter reveals how partnerships with campus identity organizations have been instrumental in ensuring the comfort, safety, and academic excellence of its diverse population of students and identifying the challenges they face in the classroom.

Student Focus and/or Student Involvement Is a Major Focus   267

Chapter 22: *Using Student Research Data to Shape the Teaching and Learning Activities of a New Academic Development Center in Turkey.* Elif Bengü, Abdullah Gül University, Kayseri, and Fatma Nevra Seggie, Boğaziçi University, Istanbul, Turkey.

The ADC at this university holds the responsibility for assessing student teaching and learning needs as well as conducting student evaluations of teaching.

Chapter 40: *From Workshops to Impact Evaluation: The Case of a Chilean Center for Teaching Development and Innovation.* Ricardo García, Héctor Turra, and Beatriz Moya, Universidad Católica de Temuco, Temuco, Chile.

This chapter discusses a Student Learning Assistant program that trains outstanding undergraduate students to support teaching and learning at its university.

17

The Centre for Student Engagement: A Research and Development Center for Students, Faculty, and Staff at the University of Winchester

Tom Lowe

Introduction

As higher education (HE) policymakers increasingly encourage student engagement, learning, and success at universities and colleges in the UK, the University of Winchester recently established an innovative Centre for Student Engagement to research and enhance staff and student engagement and development at the university.

The buzzwords "student engagement" have come to mean many things to different HE stakeholders (Bryson, 2014; Dunne, 2016). Student engagement is associated with student engagement in curriculum and learning (Finn & Zimmer, 2012), student involvement in quality assurance through student representation (Owen, 2013; Stalmeijer et al., 2016), and student-staff partnership projects related to teaching and learning (Marie et al., 2016; Matthews, 2016). This has also inspired much research into the student experience in wider HE on topics such as belonging, employability, and accessibility to education (Nghia Tran, 2017; Thomas, 2012; Department for Education Office for Students, 2018).

Western HE has placed significant emphasis on the catch-all term of "student engagement" as a means of activity, discourse, and enhancement to ensure students thrive, succeed, and can access an ever modernized and

T. Lowe (✉)
Centre for Student Engagement, University of Winchester, Winchester, UK
e-mail: tom.lowe@winchester.ac.uk

© The Author(s), under exclusive license to Springer Nature Switzerland AG 2023
O. J. Neisler (ed.), *The Palgrave Handbook of Academic Professional Development Centers*, Palgrave Studies on Leadership and Learning in Teacher Education, https://doi.org/10.1007/978-3-030-80967-6_17

marketized education sector which is increasingly accountable to their funders, including those who pay their tuition fees and the taxpayers (Frankham, 2017; Tran, 2015). The USA have also emphasized student engagement for decades in relation to their engagement in the curriculum and co-curriculum, inspired by Astin's *Student Involvement Developmental Theory* (Astin, 1984) and the research performed by Professor George Kuh encouraging multiple student engagement surveys worldwide, such as the National Survey of Student Engagement (University of Indiana, 2018), the UK Survey of Student Engagement (Advance HE, 2018), the Irish Survey of Student Engagement (Higher Education Authority, 2018), and the Australian Survey of Student Engagement (Australian Council for Educational Research, 2018).

Student engagement in the context of the UK has gone beyond the curriculum and a measurable survey, with universities being asked by sector bodies to engage students as partners, both collectively and individually, in the enhancement of learning and teaching (Department of Business, Innovation and Skills, 2011; Quality Assurance Agency for Higher Education, 2012, 2018). This had led to a plethora of activities, research areas, networks, and roles at HE institutions (HEIs), with three active journals under the banner of 'student engagement' (the *Student Engagement in Higher Education Journal, Journal of Educational Innovations, Partnership and Change*, and the *International Journal of Students as Partners*) and nationwide projects and networks such as the Researching Advancing and Inspiring Student Engagement network (Bryson, 2015) and the Student Engagement Partnership and Student Partnerships in Quality Scotland agencies, creating a significant amount of activity and scholarship.

With this vast array of activity and demand in the sector for student engagement, the University of Winchester, with its ambition to be a sector leader in student engagement practices, was keen to establish a research center to benefit the sector and students and staff at the institution (University of Winchester, 2015). This chapter will cover the core activities of the resulting center, the Centre for Student Engagement, following its establishment in August 2017.

Background

Since 2012, the University of Winchester, in partnership with the Winchester Student Union, has prioritized student engagement research and practice (Lowe et al., 2017; Sims et al., 2016), commended for training by the UK

Higher Education Academy (2014) and the Quality Assurance Agency for Higher Education (2016) and a recipient of the Guardian University Awards (*The Guardian*, 2015). The university's student engagement practices include creating innovative opportunities for students to participate in student voice roles on new committees, such as the strategic Student Academic Council, management and decision-making committees, and enhanced student-staff liaison committees at the program level.

The University of Winchester has also championed supporting students and staff to work in partnership by conducting research projects through the Winchester Student Fellows Scheme, which engages up to 60 student-staff partnerships a year on enhancement projects (Lowe et al., 2017; Sims et al., 2014). The university has also previously led national practice in developing accessibility to student engagement activities in the years 2015–2017, by conducting the sector-leading Realising Engagement through Active Culture Transformation (REACT) project, which facilitated critical development days and delivered content surrounding student engagement practice at over 20 HEIs across the UK (Lowe & Dunne, 2017). The REACT project also brought a significant amount of additional prestige and reputation to the University of Winchester as a seat of knowledge exchange in student engagement.

When funding for the REACT project came to an end in 2017, the university was keen to maintain its sector-leading reputation, so the management founded the nation's first Centre for Student Engagement. The REACT project, which aimed to enhance inclusivity and accessibility to student engagement practices, identified several aspects for further research, projects, and staff development at University of Winchester and across the sector in areas relating to student engagement, which the Centre for Student Engagement saw as a critical priority from its outset in 2017. These areas for development were to:

1. Create a staff development program for HE roles and responsibility for student engagement, such as engaging students in enhancement activities and researching students' experiences in the sector (Dunne & Lowe, 2017)
2. Conduct further research in the area of student engagement, especially for non-traditional HE students such as distance learning or alienated students (Shaw et al., 2017)
3. Holistically map student engagement/opportunities at the University of Winchester in an accessible format so students may become engaged in extra/co-curricular activities (Shaw & Lowe, 2017)

4. Assist departments (both academic and professional) in engaging students with regards to their delivery of a service or as academic programmers of study (Jones-Devitt et al., 2017).

The Centre for Student Engagement was not built into any pre-existing and established academic or professional service department, and instead reported directly to the deputy vice chancellor (deputy principal) of the university, allowing the center's manager to have free movement across the institution and the sector and, most importantly, quick access to decision-makers and key committees to have an impact quickly. In the first year of the center, the small team focused on three areas, including ensuring accessibility to student extracurricular opportunities (which included many of the student engagement practices outlined above), researching students' sense of belonging at the university, and validating a Postgraduate Certificate in Student Engagement in HE.

The team consisted of a manager (a full-time academic), a graduate intern who was then promoted to administrator from August 2018, and a selection of casual student/graduate interns and visiting fellows throughout the lifespan of the new office on campus thus far. See Figs. 17.1 and 17.2 for diagrams of the reporting structure for the center.

The significant emphasis on student engagement in UK HE has had complementary aims with the center's aims at the University of Winchester. Local missions include the University of Winchester's aspiration to be "sector leading in student engagement practices", which follows one of the university's three core values, "Individuals Matter". By valuing students' views and participation through student engagement activities, such as learning and teaching enhancement, quality assurance processes, and participation in student voice, the center aims to lead the university in fostering these practices through reflection, research, endorsement, and advocation of good practice.

Measures (often colloquially referred to as pressures) set by the UK HE sector also provide external aims for student engagement, such as the targets set out by the UK Quality Assurance Agency for Higher Education (2018), the emphasis on student voice and feedback loops in questions 23–25 of the UK National Student Survey (Department for Education Office for Students, 2017), and governmental policy that asks HEIs to place students at the heart of the system as learners (Department of Business, Innovation and Skills, 2011); in addition, more recently, pressures have been applied by customers who want to receive value for money in their education via high-quality teaching (Department for Education Office for Students, 2018; Department of

17 The Centre for Student Engagement: A Research... 273

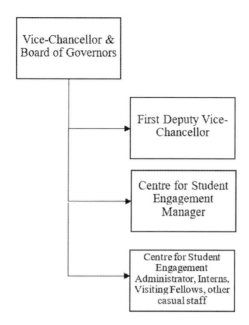

Fig. 17.1 Reporting structure for the Centre for Student Engagement

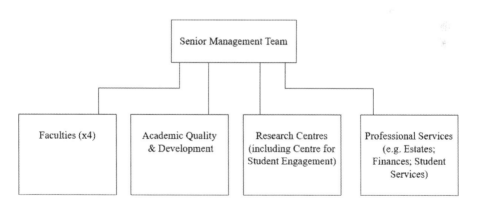

Fig. 17.2 Placement in the organization of the Centre for Student Engagement

Business, Innovation and Skills, 2011). These push factors have led student engagement, in its variety of forms (i.e., educational, developmental, feedback), to become a priority for all universities. The activities outlined below will further explore University of Winchester's practice in the area.

Creating a Staff Development Program for HE Roles and Responsibility for Engaging Students in Enhancement Activities/Researching Students' Experiences in the Sector

Following two years working on the externally funded REACT project mentioned previously, the center manager identified a desire and need in the sector for a new staff development postgraduate program for HE professionals who engage students on a weekly basis. Several new roles, strategies, working groups, and projects were appearing across HEIs, both small and large, including an increased number of publications in an emerging subdiscipline in its own right within HE studies, referred to as student engagement. Universities were investing hundreds of thousands of pounds into this area of activity, and the only learning opportunities for colleagues tasked with these targets were the emerging conferences and networking events throughout the year.

This was a new developmental area of activity and discourse for HE, and there were few experienced colleagues or scholars to provide advice in this area or who could draw together the vast amount of practice, research, and scholarship for a broad audience. There was also a gap in staff development for many in HEIs, who previously would have to study more general topics like education and philosophy or enroll in scholarship/practice of teaching and learning programs or business-related programs at the postgraduate level to advance their knowledge and careers. The University of Winchester chose to create a new program for those who engaged students in the area of student experience and develop and draw in a new audience to collaboratively learn across a year about student engagement outside of the curriculum in an accessible format for full-time professionals in the field.

The Postgraduate Certificate in Student Engagement in HE was validated in March 2018, offering a staff development part-time qualification for stakeholders who work in, or are researching, students' engagement in the HE community beyond the curriculum. A total of 10 students were recruited in 2018, followed by 17 in 2019, and 25 in 2020, from a diverse range of staff members who were a mixture of professional services, faculty, or employed in students' unions/associations. There is significant demand for the learning of best practices, creating spaces to assess practice critically, and gaining accreditation for colleagues working in this area.

The course was delivered in a 'blended' approach (part distance, part in-person); each of the two modules began with an in-person two-day retreat at the University of Winchester to create a cohort identity, which was then followed by distance learning across the semester via weekly evening lectures. The course had to fit around the participants' full-time HE roles, so the program assessment was made to be authentic, flexible (i.e., fit in with their work), and programmatic (thus one assessment fed into the next). The student cohort identity was one aspect that made the course a success, as the students were collaborative learners from small to large institutions who brought new perspectives and were open to learning from one another. Rather than only attending conferences a maximum of three times a year, with four- to six-month gaps in between, students were learning and collaborating weekly, which saw a staggering development in their student engagement practices and knowledge. This visible outcome was truly rewarding for the program team involved. In 2019–2020, due to its popularity, we validated the program to become a full degree program, a master's in Student Engagement in Higher Education. The first two years of the program (2018–2020) saw great success and satisfaction, with all students reporting themselves to be either satisfied or highly satisfied with the program. Here are some quotes from the students involved below:

> I was worried about feeling a part of a community and staying engaged from a distance, but it's been really good. (Participant 1, Postgraduate Certificate in Student Engagement in HE)

> Excellent knowledge of the staff. Very engaging even in the strange environment of an online lecture! (Participant 2, Postgraduate Certificate in Student Engagement in HE)

> [The] Retreat was great, and teaching at a distance was much better than anticipated. Lots of group work, which was useful and interesting. (Participant 3, Postgraduate Certificate in Student Engagement in HE)

> This is fantastic. The retreat kick-started this, allowing us to all get to know each other quickly and form this community of students. (Participant 4, Postgraduate Certificate in Student Engagement in HE)

> This course is great for networking opportunities! (Participant 5, Postgraduate Certificate in Student Engagement in HE)

> Loved getting to know everyone, I didn't expect this course to have such a great community feel. (Participant 6, Postgraduate Certificate in Student Engagement in HE)

The best award-bearing learning experience ever, and I have had a few. (Participant 7, Postgraduate Certificate in Student Engagement in HE)

Holistically Mapping Student Engagement Opportunities at the University of Winchester in an Accessible Format

As identified earlier, previous student-staff partnership projects at the University of Winchester had outlined the need for a single available space for students to access student opportunities at the university (Shaw, 2016). "Student engagement" as a term had created some momentum at the university; however, there were still differences in how the term was used, and there was a lack of consensus regarding which student engagement, extracurricular, and employment, and so on opportunities were perceived to be included under this term. A mapping of all student engagement opportunities beyond the curriculum was conducted in 2014, which paved the way for an online platform for student opportunities.

Once the senior management team had agreed it was to be part of the Centre for Student Engagement, the project began. However, it did not start without some initial turbulence. Politics from some of the over 160 opportunities coordinators initially critiqued the project, cautious of losing their individual opportunity's identity on campus. A Task and Finish Group of key stakeholders was set up to alleviate some of these concerns, and, further to this, the center manager prioritized close connections with key parties across the university, from the student union to careers, volunteering, and sports facilities, to ensure all parties felt represented and engaged along the way. The center recruited a graduate intern who had the time-intensive role of auditing all 150+ opportunities, interviewing each coordinator, and writing them up as case studies in a familiar tone of voice to be accessed by students in an internal database. This project has been disseminated across the sector and is recognized as being no easy undertaking across an HEI. The politics alone were slow and complicated, and the auditing of opportunities took over five months.

After six months, the 'Get Involved Project', originally named the 'Signposting Service for Student Opportunities', was completed by the launch of an accessible online platform for all student opportunities beyond the curriculum at the University of Winchester. This 'one-stop-shop' aimed to raise awareness of opportunities and overall student involvement by providing information and signposting to appropriate contacts. The project was desired by the university, as it was perceived to be in alignment with sector policy and research that brought together student involvement/engagement activities to enhance students' experiences, sense of belonging, integration into HE, and employability (Astin, 1984; Humphrey & Lowe, 2017; Thomas, 2012; Tinto, 1993). The 'Get Involved Button', the chosen name for the online platform, has now been in operation for over a year, bringing together activities from across the university.

As a platform to communicate with students directly, intentions for the Get Involved Button were to increase awareness and participation at the University of Winchester, which was understood to be mutually beneficial for both staff and students. It is placed on the top right-hand side of the university's internal virtual learning environment and allows students to "browse at their leisure" to gain access to opportunities at any time, showcasing employability benefits by listing skills gained and, most importantly, showing equal value between all occasions. The Get Involved Button project was a key output of the Centre for Student Engagement, which has led to the university requesting additional projects related to student employability and experience at the University of Winchester.

Assisting Departments (Academic and Professional) with Engaging Students in Regard to their Delivery of a Service or Academic Programmers of Study

Academic professional development centers have emerged across Western HE to provide staff development, leadership, research, and peer support in the development of course delivery, following an increased global emphasis on learning through excellent teaching (Lea, 2015). The University of Winchester has an active Learning and Teaching Development Unit, which had been established for over a decade by the time the Centre for Student Engagement began in 2017. Questions could have arisen as to why another supportive center, with a focus on student engagement, was initiated alongside an established learning and teaching center. However, the Centre for Student Engagement has proven to operate in new spaces, predominantly focusing on the aspects covered in this chapter, but also providing advice and guidance to any departments (professional or academic) who wished to review their engagement with students for enhancement reasons. The broad title of 'student engagement' allowed flexibility to focus on diverse projects and variety. The work of the Centre for Student Engagement at the University of Winchester is comparable with other centers for student engagement and

278   T. Lowe

development already established at the University of Calgary, which focuses on student leadership development (University of Calgary, n.d.), and California State University, which focuses on departmental development and student body research (California State University, n.d.).

In the first two years of its operation, the Centre for Student Engagement has been a point of consultation for many departments, and the team has met with 12 different directors and managers to assist them in making strategies for how they may gain student feedback or engage students as partners to review their activities. It was important that the center did not appropriate or replace the students' voices; instead, it aimed to enable and empower colleagues at the university to engage current students in order to gain their feedback. Many of the departments the center worked closely with were professional service teams who had a significant impact on students, but who were also struggling to gather student feedback on their experiences of these services. Such departments included the timetabling, library, campus chaplaincy, and student services departments. The manager of the center was also asked to sit on several university committees such as the Student Experience Committee and Employability Committee so these and any relevant research projects could be shared in strategic decisions. The team would also be called upon frequently to deliver sector talks on changes or developments in the HE sector to inform colleagues on policy developments. The center found its place through close communications between the center manager and other key stakeholders across the university, which ensured strategies aligned and portfolios did not cross. Although a new presence on campus is exciting, it is essential to take the time to embed the center within the institution, moving gently with projects to prevent political disruption.

Conclusion

In the years since the Centre for Student Engagement was established, the center manager and team members have conducted various projects at the University of Winchester with tangible outcomes. Alongside these projects, the center manager and team have also ensured that the university has remained engaged with the sector via publishing and presenting at international conferences on new research and reflections relating to student engagement in HE. Looking ahead to 2020 and beyond, the center now finds itself providing a catalyst service for institutional projects alongside running a new postgraduate program, which enrolled 10 students in its first year. Balancing portfolios with staff capacities is a continuous challenge, as while the team wishes to help and be involved in enhancement, it must also recognize the limitations of a small group.

Already from the 2018–2019 academic year, the center has been asked to assist with employability initiatives, assessment and feedback projects, and enhancing the student voice at the University of Winchester. Where 2020 and beyond will take the center remains unclear, but exciting. What is clear is that student engagement in HE—as an area of activity, discussion, debate, and even critique—is evolving, and in response, so must the center. A center for enhancement at any HEI must remain cutting-edge in its practices, scholarly in its work, and have impact which is measurable. All of these factors ensure it highlights the need for the center and provides demonstrable outputs in return for the time and money invested by management. The Centre for Student Engagement hopes to continue to show value and to help others (either individuals or departments) as it develops as part of the community of the University of Winchester.

References

Advance HE. (2018). *United Kingdom Engagement Survey (UKES)*. Advance HE. https://www.heacademy.ac.uk/institutions/surveys/uk-engagement-survey

Astin, A. W. (1984). Student involvement: A developmental theory for higher education. *Journal of College Student Personnel, 25*(4), 297–308.

Australian Council for Educational Research. (2018). *Australasian Survey of Student Engagement (AUSSE)*. Australian Council for Educational Research. https://www.acer.org/gb/ausse

Bryson, C. (2014). *Understanding and developing student engagement (SEDA Series)*. Routledge.

Bryson, C. (2015). Researching, Advancing, and Inspiring Student Engagement (RAISE). In J. Lea (Ed.), *Enhancing learning and teaching in higher education: Engaging with the dimensions of practice* (pp. 163–165). Open University Press.

California State University. (n.d.). *Division of student life: Center for Student Involvement*. California State University. http://www.calstatela.edu/studentservices/center-student-involvement

Department of Business, Innovation and Skills. (2011). *Students at the heart of the system*. Department for Business, Innovation and Skills. https://www.gov.uk/government/uploads/system/uploads/attachment_data/file/31384/11-944-higher-education-students-at-heart-of-system.pdf

Department for Education Office for Students. (2017). *About the NSS*. Office for Students. https://www.thestudentsurvey.com/about-the-nss/

Department for Education Office for Students. (2018). *Securing student success: Regulatory framework for higher education in England*. Office for Students. https://www.officeforstudents.org.uk/publications/securing-student-success-regulatory-framework-for-higher-education-in-england/v

Dunne, E. (2016). Preface – Design thinking: A framework for student engagement? A personal view. *Journal of Educational Innovation, Partnership, and Change, 2*(1).

Dunne, E., & Lowe, T. (2017). The REACT Collaborative Development Programme: Bringing universities together to enhance student-engagement activities for the 'hard to reach'. *Journal of Educational Innovation, Partnership, and Change, 3*(1), 40–45.

Finn, J. D., & Zimmer, K. S. (2012). Student engagement: What is it? Why does it matter? In S. L. Christenson, A. L. Reschly, & C. Wylie (Eds.), *Handbook of research on student engagement*. Springer.

Frankham, J. (2017). Employability and higher education: The follies of the 'productivity challenge' in the teaching excellence framework. *Journal of Education Policy, 32*(5), 628–641.

Higher Education Academy. (2014). *HEA & NUS students' union and institution partnership awards*. Higher Education Academy. https://www.heacademy.ac.uk/knowledge-hub/hea-nus-students-union-and-institution-partnership-awards

Higher Education Authority. (2018). *The Irish Survey of Student Engagement (ISSE): Results from 2018*. Higher Education Academy. https://studentsurvey.ie/sites/default/files/2019-10/ISSE-Report-2018-final.pdf

Humphrey, O., & Lowe, T. (2017). Exploring how a 'sense of belonging' is facilitated at different stages of the student journey in higher education. *Journal of Educational Innovation, Partnership and Change, 3*(1).

Jones-Devitt, S., Austen, L., Chitwood, E., Donnelly, A., Fearn, C., Heaton, C., Latham, G., LeBihan, J., Middleton, A., Morgan, M., & Parkin, H. (2017). Creation and confidence: BME students as academic partners… But where were the staff? *Journal of Educational Innovation Partnership and Change, 3*(1), 278–285.

Lea, J. (Ed.). (2015). *Enhancing learning and teaching in higher education: Engaging with the dimensions of practice*. Open University Press.

Lowe, T., & Dunne, E. (2017). Setting the scene for the REACT Programme: Aims, challenges, and the way ahead. *Journal of Educational Innovation, Partnership, and Change, 3*(1).

Lowe, T., Shaw, C., Sims, S., King, S., & Paddison, A. (2017). The development of contemporary student engagement practices at the University of Winchester. *International Journal of Students as Partners, 1*(1), 1–13.

Marie, J., Arif, M., & Joshi, T. (2016). UCL ChangeMakers projects: Supporting staff/student partnership on educational enhancement projects. *Student Engagement in Higher Education Journal, 1*(1), 393–351.

Matthews, K. (2016). Students as partners as the future of student engagement. *Student Engagement in Higher Education Journal, 1*(1), 1–5.

17 The Centre for Student Engagement: A Research...   281

Nghia Tran, L. H. (2017). Developing employability skills via extra-curricular activities in Vietnamese universities: Student engagement and inhibitors of their engagement. *Journal of Education and Work, 30*(8), 854–867.

Owen, D. (2013). Students engaged in academic subject review. In E. Dunne & D. Owen (Eds.), *Student engagement handbook: Practice in higher education.* Emerald Group Publishing.

Quality Assurance Agency for Higher Education. (2012). *UK quality code for higher education – Chapter B5: Student engagement.* Quality Assurance Agency for Higher Education.

Quality Assurance Agency for Higher Education. (2016). *Higher education review: University of Winchester.* Quality Assurance Agency. http://www.qaa.ac.uk/reviews-and-reports/provider?UKPRN=10003614#.WFLDB9Lc4dU

Quality Assurance Agency for Higher Education. (2018). *UK quality code advice and guidance: Student engagement.* Quality Assurance Agency for Higher Education. http://www.qaa.ac.uk//en/quality-code/advice-and-guidance/student-engagement

Shaw, C. (2016, May 18). *Student perceptions of "student engagement" at the University of Winchester* (Conference presentation). The Winchester Student Fellows Conference 2016.

Shaw, C., Humphrey, O., Atvars, T., & Sims, S. (2017). Who they are and how to engage them: A summary of the REACT systematic literature review of the 'hard to reach' in higher education. *Journal of Educational Innovation, Partnership, and Change, 3*(1), 51–64.

Shaw, C., & Lowe, T. (2017). The student participation map: A tool to map student participation, engagements, opportunities, and extra-curricular activities across a higher education institution. *Dialogue: Journal of Learning and Teaching, 1*, 45–50.

Sims, S., King, S., Lowe, T., & El Hakim, Y. (2016). Evaluating partnership and impact in the first year of the Student Fellows Scheme. *Journal of Educational Innovation, Partnership, and Change, 2*(1).

Sims, S., Lowe, T., Barnes, G., & Hutber, L. (2014). The student fellows scheme: A partnership between the University of Winchester and Winchester Student Union. *Educational Developments, 15*(3), 7–10.

Stalmeijer, R., Whittingham, J., de Grave, W., & Dolmans, D. (2016). Strengthening internal quality assurance processes: Facilitating student evaluation committees to contribute. *Assessment & Evaluation in Higher Education, 41*(1), 53–66.

The Guardian (2015, March 18). *Guardian university awards 2015: Winners and runners up.* Guardian Media Group. https://www.theguardian.com/higher-education-network/2015/mar/18/guardian-university-awards-2015-winners-and-runners-up

Thomas, L. (2012). *Building student engagement and belonging in higher education at a time of change: A summary of findings and recommendations from the What Works? Student Retention and Success programme.* Paul Hamlyn Foundation.

Tinto, V. (1993). *Leaving college: Rethinking the causes and cures of student attrition* (2nd ed.). University of Chicago Press.

Tran, T. (2015). Is graduate employability the 'whole-of-higher-education-issue'? *Journal of Education and Work, 28*(3), 207–227.

University of Calgary. (n.d.). *Leadership and student engagement.* University of Calgary. https://www.ucalgary.ca/student-services/leadership

University of Indiana. (2018). *National survey of student engagement.* University of Indiana. http://nsse.indiana.edu/

University of Winchester. (2015). *University of Winchester strategic plan 2015–2020.* University of Winchester. https://www.winchester.ac.uk/about-us/our-future/our-strategy/

18

Partnerships Between Undergraduate Students and Faculty in the Assessment of Teaching and Learning: A Program Design Model

Adriana Signorini, Cathy A. Pohan, and James Zimmerman

Introduction

> A great deal of communication is lost between students and faculty due to the hierarchical relationship between the two parties … students find it intimidating to communicate to their teachers … to voice personal viewpoints. … SATAL interns are a means to bridge the gap. … Students learn from the SATAL process that it is okay to communicate with faculty, and vice versa, in order to properly implement change (Intern 1, SATAL Program, UCM).

The University of California Merced (UCM) opened in the fall of 2005 as the newest campus in the University of California system and the first new American research university of the 21st century. The institution sits within California's Central Valley and is designated as a Hispanic-serving institution. Consistent with its relative youth, the campus currently serves 9,000 students, 75% of whom are first-generation college students from historically under-represented populations. UCM is home to three schools: the School of Engineering, School of Natural Sciences, and School of Social Sciences,

---

A. Signorini (✉) • C. A. Pohan • J. Zimmerman
University of California Merced, Merced, CA, USA
e-mail: asignorini@ucmerced.edu; cpohan@ucmerced.edu;
jzimmerman6@ucmerced.edu

© The Author(s), under exclusive license to Springer Nature Switzerland AG 2023
O. J. Neisler (ed.), *The Palgrave Handbook of Academic Professional Development Centers*,
Palgrave Studies on Leadership and Learning in Teacher Education,
https://doi.org/10.1007/978-3-030-80967-6_18

283

Humanities, and Arts. As a research university, UCM welcomes opportunities for undergraduate students to learn about research, be involved in research that attends to real-world problems, and develop the skills and dispositions of effective researchers.

Supported by the Division of Undergraduate Education, UCM's Center for Engaged Teaching and Learning (CETL) consists of three primary units: the Pedagogical and Curricular Design, Development, and Support Unit; the English Language Institute; and the Students Assessing Teaching and Learning (SATAL) program (UCM CETL, n.d.-b), the focus of this chapter (see Fig. 18.1).

When the institution underwent its first accreditation review in 2009, the CETL was instrumental in building cross-institutional assessment capacity. As a result, the SATAL program was designed to support faculty and program leads with the collection of actionable data related to teaching and learning (UCM CETL, n.d.-c). Since 2009, the SATAL program has evolved from a program designed to support accreditation efforts to a faculty-student partnership program in which faculty and students collaborate to rethink learning as a learner-centered process.

Since course evaluations occur at the end of the semester, student feedback comes too late for faculty to make modifications that might improve the learning experiences of those students providing said feedback. To rectify this situation, many educators advocate for mid-term course feedback. However, neither of these feedback practices addresses the real issue noted in the

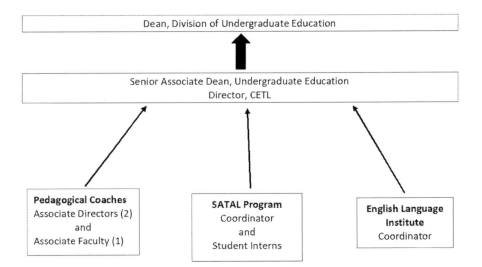

Fig. 18.1 CETL reporting and organizational chart

opening quotation. As the intern so aptly articulates, university students often feel intimidated in their new environment; therefore, it is not uncommon for them to fear voicing their opinions and/or perspectives regarding the effectiveness of the pedagogical approaches used by their instructors. For first-generation students and/or students from under-represented populations, this fear may be amplified. Even when they are willing, many students do not know how to provide actionable feedback to their instructors. This reality presents a dilemma for educators because the student voice is critical to any serious assessment of instructional approaches, planned learning experiences, and assessment of learning (Cook-Sather et al., 2014; Felten, 2014; Mercer-Mapstone et al., 2017). At UCM, the SATAL program provides a means to bridge the communication gap between faculty and undergraduate students and ultimately improve teaching and student success at this young institution.

This chapter is divided into three parts. The first section provides a review of the literature that informs faculty-student partnerships and sets the tone for SATAL program activities. The second section addresses the design of the SATAL program and offers a narrative about how undergraduate interns are prepared to collaborate with faculty partners in the assessment of teaching and learning experiences. Finally, the chapter takes a look at the ongoing development of the SATAL program and closes with concluding statements on ways in which academic institutions could further utilize the SATAL model and examples of methods to encourage institutions to allocate more resources to successful 'Students as Partners' (SaP) programs.

An Overview of Faculty-Student Partnership

Improving teaching and learning in higher education requires willingness on the part of faculty to assess their instructional practices and make the curricular and pedagogical changes needed to positively impact student learning. These assessment efforts require student participation as collaborators in their educational development. Scholars from a variety of disciplines across the country have been exploring possibilities for creating partnerships with students and engaging their voices in the scholarship of teaching and learning (SoTL) (Felton & Chick, 2018; Felton et al., 2007; McKinney, 2004). According to Mercer-Mapstone et al. (2017), the SaP movement implies that students collaborate with faculty and/or academic staff as they investigate the impact of planned teaching and learning activities on student learning. At UCM, we believe that assessment is an essential component to this partnership work, especially if we hope to make quality and impactful improvements to instruction, curriculum, and programs and ultimately improve student achievement and success.

The SATAL program was intentionally designed to engage a diverse group of instructional faculty, academic and nonacademic units' leads, and cross-program undergraduates in the selection and/or development of instruments and protocols to assess the student learning experience across the UCM campus. Our collaborative work program adopted the concept of faculty-student partnership (Cook-Sather et al., 2014) to characterize these student-faculty interactions. Based on Healey's Conceptual Model (Healey et al., 2014), the program positions students and faculty as codevelopers, co-learners, and co-inquirers, depending on the type of assessment assistance requested.

The SATAL program utilizes ongoing professional development (PD) of the undergraduate student interns who assist faculty with a variety of activities related to analyzing the classroom learning experience. Interns gather data related to the pedagogical approaches utilized and their impact on levels of student engagement. Following assessment activities, the assigned SATAL interns, program coordinator, and instructor meet to discuss findings, so the faculty can affirm what is working and adjust practices based on the feedback received (UCM CETL, n.d.-a). To that end, the SATAL program helps faculty and staff move from evidence to meaning and, ultimately, to action, working with faculty to identify best practices that are integral to the discipline and therefore more likely to improve student engagement and learning (Kinzie et al., 2019).

Design Elements

Data-informed decision-making is central to program improvement. To that end, the SATAL program employs a logic model that makes explicit the relationship between program activities and desired program outcomes. The logic model provides a comprehensive plan for the evolution of the program by identifying its vision, goals, outcomes, outputs, and inputs. Signorini and Pohan (2019) discuss the logic model elements of the SATAL program in detail; however, we have summarized the approach below.

Vision and Goals

Aligned with the UCM's mission of a student-centered research institution, the *vision* of the SATAL program is to provide exceptional student-assisted assessment practices, and to prepare UCM students to partner with faculty in ways that transcend a specific course. Ultimately, faculty seek this partnership to identify which aspects of a course, pedagogy, and/or program's organizational structure are working well, and which areas might need more focused attention. Thus, the *goals* for the faculty are as follows:

1. Faculty will make pedagogical and/or curricular modifications based on the assessment data gathered from student partners in their course(s) and programs
2. Faculty will (a) value the services provided, (b) report being satisfied with SATAL services, and (c) request SATAL assistance again as part of their continuous improvement efforts.

In turn, the *goals* of the SATAL program are to have undergraduate student interns report gains in skill sets related to:

1. UCM's general education hallmarks (academic and intellectual preparation, cultural awareness, community engagement and citizenship, self-awareness and intrapersonal skills, and interpersonal skills)
2. Research, including methodological design, data collection, analysis, and reporting.

Under the guidance of the program coordinator, SATAL undergraduate interns participate in research activities. Students and faculty collaborate throughout the entire research process—from study design, instrument identification and/or development, and data collection to the analysis of various forms of evidence and dissemination reports—in order to advance and improve faculty and program effectiveness.

Program Structure

The SATAL program aims to engage diverse, interdisciplinary undergraduates in learning experiences within a professional work environment. Undergraduates respond to an intern position announcement to join SATAL and collaborate with faculty in a SaP relationship founded upon the principles of shared respect, reciprocity, and responsibility (Cook-Sather et al., 2014). All enrolled undergraduates are eligible to apply to work six hours each week for this paid position. Interested students attend informational sessions and apply for the position, submitting the following: (a) a statement about their motivation to apply for this role, (b) a resume, and (c) letters of recommendation from faculty or staff members. Applicants are interviewed by the SATAL program coordinator and current undergraduate interns. The interview incorporates various questions, including their: (a) experiences providing constructive feedback, (b) perceptions of effective teaching, and (c) motivation for working in this program. The main asset that candidates bring to the program is their expertise as college students. No other knowledge or skills are needed to apply for the position.

Once selected, the new interns attend an orientation, participate in eight two-hour PD sessions, and complete the Institutional Review Board protocol. After this initial onboarding, interns participate in weekly meetings with seasoned interns and the program coordinator to discuss how best to partner with faculty and respond to their assessment requests productively. For the undergraduate interns, this program provides multiple opportunities to participate in research and other development activities that serve to propel their personal and professional growth (e.g., research and analytical skills, critical thinking, collaboration, and oral and written communication skills).

Apprenticeship Model

The SATAL program employs a comprehensive and systematic plan that articulates the intended results relevant to program services and intern development. Under an apprenticeship model, SATAL interns progress through three levels over multiple years, each with increasing responsibilities and a commensurate salary. *Year 1 interns* focus on learning about the different assessment tools utilized by the program, and shadowing and assisting a more experienced intern with faculty assessment requests. *Year 2 interns* conduct peer-led feedback workshops, utilize assessment tools, and analyze and summarize assessment results into reports. Finally, *year 3 interns* lead the PD and mentoring of the year 1 interns, develop and lead peer-led feedback workshops and projects, and—because of their expertise in data collection, analysis, and reporting—collaborate on special projects requested by campus programs and/or units. Additionally, interns at this level engage in the recruitment and hiring of new interns.

The SATAL program provides its interns with experience in a real-world work environment that may or may not be related to their career interests. There is a high degree of intentionality in the design of this internship, especially given the nature of the research institution and the need for graduates to possess a set of broad, flexible skills that enable them to be effective employees in an increasingly diverse global economy. Regardless of the paths the students eventually take, this internship helps students understand in a profound way that college is a time to explore their interests, clarify their values, and test their knowledge and skills in new settings.

PD Activities

The SATAL program is overseen by a coordinator who ensures that the program initiatives meet the needs of faculty partners and that support does not end simply because a group of interns has graduated. PD activities offered to interns utilize both active learning and flipped learning methodologies. Sample PD activities include:

* Weekly staff update meetings
* PD modules dedicated to the most requested assessment tools and services, such as Small Group Instructional Diagnosis (SGID) (Clark & Redmond, 1982), Classroom Observation Protocol for Undergraduate STEM (COPUS) (Smith et al., 2013; University of British Columbia, n.d.), video recording, focus groups, and mixed methods research
* Collaborative work sessions, including workshop development and rehearsal, tailoring assessment tools to specific faculty needs, and data analysis and report writing.

Once interns have completed the initial PD activities, they respond to assessment requests in groups of two or more, learn to work and solve problems in the company of others, and develop intellectual and practical competencies, such as oral and written communication and analytic skills. A key element in this program is the opportunity for interns to both reflect on their own learning experiences and apply what they are learning in new settings.

Any faculty member may request assessment support from SATAL interns. Since the inception of the program in 2009, SATAL interns have responded to over 1,000 assessment requests from 120 faculty members, 74% of whom are recurring program partners. Since many participating faculty members view SATAL assessment data as being critical to their ongoing improvement plans, we continue to serve many of the same faculty. Faculty partners vary in terms of teaching experience, role, and discipline, with the majority (65%) of requests representing the community of instructors teaching science, technology, engineering, and math (STEM) courses. Often, faculty conducting SoTL are supported by National Science Foundation grants, and thus driven by focused efforts to improve student retention, persistence, and completion rates across STEM-related disciplines.

In addition to quantitative data collection, SATAL interns collect qualitative data to provide a more holistic picture of students' learning experiences. SATAL interns facilitate focus groups and SGID with undergraduates to collect actionable feedback and identify student needs and perspective on their learning, information unavailable through simple paper or online survey formats. This process also motivates faculty at a research institution to approach assessment as inquiry and document the implementation and assessment of new practices.

Ongoing Development

The partnership model espoused by the SATAL program evolves according to the needs of the local context and adapts to the multiple facets of teaching expertise that can only be explained by triangulating data collected through different combinations. The SATAL program responds to faculty partners' feedback collected via a survey at the end of the semester (UCM CETL, n.d.-c). This section describes the evolution of the SATAL program data collection tools, with comments from faculty and students partnering to improve teaching and learning in the classroom.

The assessment approaches utilized vary depending on the expressed needs of the faculty member, with three-quarters of the faculty requesting a few tools in different combinations at various points in the academic year. As a result, faculty have access to multiple lines of evidence in support of their pedagogy and student learning experiences. Partnering with SATAL is entirely voluntary and all data remain confidential; only the requesting faculty member receives the summary report. Although individual faculty may choose to include SATAL assessment results in their professional dossier, these reports are not intended to be official evaluations of faculty performance. Among some of the faculty's motivations to partner with SATAL for assessment support and PD are those summarized in the following five contexts:

1. An extensive literature review suggests that active learning activities increase student performance in STEM disciplines; therefore, faculty implementing active learning in their courses plan on assessing the impact of these new practices
2. Faculty team-teaching in large introductory courses plan and collaborate on the delivery of their courses; therefore, student feedback helps these teams monitor students' engagement and learning experiences in the courses
3. Faculty's desire to document ongoing improvement, student engagement, and learning as part of their teaching effectiveness career path

18 Partnerships Between Undergraduate Students and Faculty... 291

4. Academic programs gather evidence of the learning outcomes achievement and activities that led students to that achievement, an aspect of the continuous improvement process
5. Federally funded projects with strong educational curriculum report baseline data and ongoing assessment activities for evaluation purposes.

To support faculty wishing to tell their stories about the undergraduate learning experience from multiple perspectives, different combinations of assessment tools are used to facilitate instructors' self-reflection and future-oriented conversations. These combinations are elaborated upon and illustrated below in more detail, with faculty comments from ethics-board-approved studies as well as informal feedback from staff and undergraduate interns.

Addressing a Specific Pedagogical Issue

The SATAL program partners with faculty for various reasons: (a) to identify and communicate their strengths; (b) to investigate how planned learning experiences impact student engagement and learning; and (c) to analyze aspects of their teaching in need of further development. The program aims its assessment efforts at the faculty member's specific pedagogical questions and/or concerns, thereby contributing to the faculty member's own PD by finding meaning in the everyday activities that make up the growth of their teaching expertise. For example, faculty may wonder how students are experiencing newly implemented active learning practices. Paired with focus group sessions, tools such as the SGID can assist in gathering data related to student engagement and perceptions of learning. One faculty member requesting this particular tool pairing noted:

> I requested a class assessment, and I received feedback that improved lectures. I also requested a post-observation at the end of the semester and compared results to the initial observation. Useful feedback included the incorporation of mid-lecture questions and minute papers in my classes. These mid-lecture questions provide students with a break from the lecture format and give them the opportunity to work in small groups to provide answers. They also allow me to encourage the participation of quieter students, thus evaluating their understanding of the material. By using minute papers at the end of the class, I am not only able to take attendance, but also to sample responses to assess what the students take away from the class. By incorporating these two tools into my lectures, students' grades increased because they were more engaged with the material. (Teaching Professor, School of Natural Sciences, UCM)

Documenting How Instructional Time Is Distributed in the Classroom

While there is no single best pedagogical approach, we know that effective instructors are flexible and apply research-based, high-impact practices in diverse situations (Kuh, 2008). In addition to using the SGID to gather data for faculty implementing new pedagogies (e.g., flipped learning, hybrid format), SATAL interns utilize COPUS to collect data on how instructional time is distributed across a typical instructional session. For example, because of initiatives aimed at improving retention and persistence rates among first-generation and female college students in STEM disciplines, the COPUS paired with the SGID and/or a class video recording is a particularly important protocol to assess the impact of new pedagogical practices implemented in STEM courses. Based on students' feedback received through a SGID-COPUS pairing, faculty implement changes in the course and then follow through to assess the impact of those changes, closing the assessment loop. One faculty member utilizing this tool pairing reported:

> Based on the course assessment findings, we implemented team-based learning in our introductory biology courses. Because of the administration of both the individual and team readiness assurance tests, our classrooms are now more raucous places where peer instruction is paramount. (Lecturer, School of Natural Sciences, UCM)

Collecting Mid-Semester Course Feedback

Students may provide some useful information on end-of-course evaluations, but the timing of this feedback makes it only useful for improving the next iteration of the course. To that end, the SATAL program implements the SGID to collect confidential information on students' learning needs and concerns midway through the term, which then allows faculty to adjust their pedagogy while the term is still in session. One faculty member using this COPUS-SGID pairing mentioned:

> My expectations were met because mid-term assessment feedback … gave me a clear picture of what my students think about my teaching as a whole … things they like or dislike in particular. Engagement has increased tremendously since I've learned the style in which students learn. I keep each of my lessons to less than 45 minutes, then I change my lesson focus for the other half of the session … [because] students had written that I tended to discuss a lesson too long. (Lecturer, Merritt Writing Program, UCM)

Supporting Program Assessment

The SATAL program partners with program leads and/or department chairs to conduct student focus groups, surveys, and/or SGID when assessing program outcomes achievement and the learners' perceptions of the curriculum. Some individual faculty members choose to include these reports as indirect evidence when submitting program-level assessment requirements connected with institutional improvement or accreditation. We find that surveys paired with focus groups is an effective tool for collecting actionable data regarding student perceptions of how a program is developing and their learning experiences in the classroom. For instance, a survey on the achievement of the program learning outcomes, instructional materials, or teaching practices could be immediately followed by a focus group to obtain specific information to better understand responses to the student survey. When questioned about the feedback collected through this pairing, program leads commented:

> My expectations were definitely met and even exceeded ... The assessment process was well-executed, logistically (scheduling, etc.), and surveys were well-devised. The analysis of survey results was thorough and meaningful. (Program Coordinator, School of Natural Sciences, UCM)

> We actually decided to: 1) make Math 150 a required course; 2) continue to include writing assignments in Math 141 and begin to include them in more of the upper division courses; 3) initiated a discussion on how to better coordinate the proof components in our core courses; and 4) incorporate more development and building of mathematical models into the core graduate curriculum. (Applied Mathematics Program Chair, School of Natural Sciences, UCM)

Supporting SoTL

At UCM, a research institution, the SATAL program presents its services as opportunities for faculty who treat the classroom as sites for inquiry and improvement to: (a) conduct SoTL in their classroom, online, or in our technology-enhanced active learning laboratories; and (b) utilize data collected through SATAL's assessment tools to document "teaching effectiveness" in the retention, tenure, and promotion process. For instance, to support a faculty member's action research and preparation of a manuscript, SATAL interns interviewed students attending the first 100%-online course offered by UCM's School of Engineering. The interns collected and analyzed student feedback regarding their learning experiences utilizing NVivo software.

Contributing with Peer-Led Workshops

SATAL interns have witnessed firsthand their peers' limitations at providing useful and meaningful feedback. To train undergraduates on how to provide actionable feedback in their courses, the SATAL program developed a peer-led presentation for situations where feedback is requested, such as peer review sessions, as well as for how to produce detailed and useful feedback. During the interactive workshop, SATAL interns guide small groups of students through problem-based activities designed to be solved cooperatively with the aid of a feedback rubric (UCM CETL, n.d.-a). SATAL interns ensure that students are actively and productively engaged with the materials and their peers throughout the activities. With the assistance of the rubric, examples of 'actionable' feedback, and practice feedback exercises, interns and faculty began to observe improvements in the quality of feedback undergraduates were providing. The study results affirmed the positive impact of the workshop on the students' abilities to provide meaningful and actionable feedback (Signorini, 2014). Since collecting actionable feedback from the students is of the utmost importance to the student-faculty partnership, a more formal investigation of the impact of these peer-led workshops became a priority, in particular when responding to the course evaluations or student evaluations of teaching (SETs).

Student-Assisted Assessment as Research

In 2016, the SATAL program received a grant from the Professional Organizational and Development (POD) Network to investigate the impact of a peer-led workshop on the quality of responses undergraduates were able to provide to a series of open-ended questions in end-of-course evaluations or SETs. A group of instructors in UCM's Merritt Writing Program agreed to participate in the study, inviting SATAL interns to deliver the workshop in their classes. The peer-led workshop was delivered in 11 classes to 205 students, midway and at the end of the semester, immediately before students completed their end-of-semester SETs. Data were analyzed to investigate whether the quality of student responses in the SETs improved after a peer-led presentation on the benefits of completing SETs and how to provide useful feedback using a rubric. Qualitative and quantitative data were collected to assess the quality of feedback undergraduates were able to provide to their peers after receiving the workshop (Signorini et al., 2020). This project entitled, "Students Helping Students Provide Valuable Feedback on Course Evaluation" (UCM CETL, n.d.-c) received the 2018 POD Innovation Award.

Based on these positive findings, as well as our limited capacity to deliver the workshop to a large number of classes, this peer-led presentation was captured in a brief video and shown to 362 students in 15 courses. In class, students completed both their mid and final SETs immediately after watching the video presentation. Based on an analysis of aggregated data, the findings indicated that feedback on the SETs improved across all questions. Interestingly, class standing was a highly significant predictor of feedback quality, with upper division (UD) students providing more useful feedback than lower division (LD) students. A total of 276 (70%) participating students rated the video as either highly effective or effective. Both UD and LD students rated their skill development equally. However, only students in UD courses performed better in their SET responses. Most of the students (88%) found the rubric helpful in guiding feedback, and the majority (81%) recommended that the video be delivered in other courses. Also, participating faculty recommended the video to other instructors, and upon analyzing students' feedback, the faculty identified concrete ways to improve the content and/or instruction in their courses.

The research study resulting from the video project received the POD Network's 2019 R. Menges Outstanding Research for Educational Development Award, along with a new line of funding to expand the project to other large and small courses on campus. SATAL program activities and publications have attracted campus visits from faculties from other institutions and individuals from media outlets wanting a firsthand look at program operations and to hold conversations with faculty and SATAL interns (Supiano, 2017).

Together with SATAL interns, the program coordinator and other faculty have collaborated on various conference presentations (including those organized by the POD Network and the International Society for SoTL) and publications (Signorini & Abuan, 2019; Signorini & Pohan, 2019; Signorini et al., 2020), offering undergraduate students important research opportunities that can help a research-focused institution fulfill its mission. In addition to research skills, interns report that the SATAL program has facilitated their development of a wide range of communication skills, such as providing constructive feedback, public speaking/oral communication skills, and academic report writing.

Clearly, when it comes to the interns, a major benefit of their involvement with the SATAL program is the professional growth and development they receive while being an undergraduate student. All of the participants surveyed noted their acquisition of a wide variety of skills that would positively impact their future profession. The following comments exemplify the benefits to our SATAL interns, some of which appear to be positively life-changing:

As a student, these skills have been crucial to my ability to progress in graduate school and even inspired multiple presentations which I had used to present at both national and international conferences in my field … deep understanding of survey methodologies have helped me drastically in my role as a … engineer (Intern 2, SATAL Program, UCM).

Before joining SATAL, I was pretty pessimistic about my career prospects. I didn't know what I wanted to do after college. I wasn't even sure what I wanted to do during college. But when I started getting into SATAL work, it encouraged me to really apply myself. Standing in front of an audience terrified me in my junior year of college. It was unthinkable. But it eventually became second nature to me after signing on to enough classroom assessments and peer-led workshops. Now I'm out here teaching [university] classes. In short, my involvement with SATAL guided me into a career path that I absolutely love. (Intern 3, SATAL Program, UCM)

Partnership Opportunities

Additional opportunities for faculty-student partnerships documented in the literature could be implemented. For instance, we could feature a panel of diverse students to discuss their experiences with learning, as well as topics such as blended learning, assessment, and inclusive teaching (Peseta et al., 2016). Interns could lead a conversation focused on using the university's assessment principles to plan their learning and introduce SaP programs such as SATAL in new faculty orientations and academic development sessions. This would create the opportunity for incoming faculty to engage in a dialogue not only with their colleagues, but also with students outside of the standard teacher-student relationship (Cook-Sather, 2016). Finally, there is an opportunity to fund and reward focused, cross disciplinary SoTL projects as part of the undergraduate research experience. The SATAL program will continue to conduct research on collaborative approaches to teaching and learning and, in particular, student feedback to support the regular ongoing work of faculty in their courses to bring students to higher levels of achievement.

Conclusion

Since its inception in 2009, assessment via UCM's SATAL program has become interwoven into the campus history and culture. Its evolving structure, attuned to the improvement of teaching and learning at UCM, has gained respect among the undergraduates and faculty partnering with SATAL. The program is not only meeting its identified goals, but serves as an exemplar for faculty-student partners displaying respect, reciprocity, and shared responsibility for teaching and learning (Cook-Sather et al., 2014). Indeed, both the faculty and student interns working with the SATAL program highly value their partnership and are driven by a desire to improve teaching and learning on the campus. Based in a research-focused institution, SATAL's research opportunities enhance each intern's education by offering new perspectives on teaching and learning and provide scholarly experiences that contribute to their resumes and future career paths. Moreover, this faculty-student partnership model steps forward and brings faculty development and assessment of student learning outcomes into greater alignment as they overlap and inform each other.

References

Clark, D. J., & Redmond, M. V. (1982). *Small group instruction diagnosis: Final report.* Washington University. https://eric.ed.gov/?id=ED217954

Cook-Sather, A. (2016). Undergraduate students as partners in new faculty orientation and academic development. *International Journal of Academic Development, 21*(2), 151–162.

Cook-Sather, A., Bovill, C., & Felton, P. (2014). *Engaging students as partners in learning and teaching: A guide for faculty.* Jossey-Bass.

Felten, P. (2014). Principles of good practice in SoTL. *Teaching & Learning Inquiry, 1*(1), 121–125.

Felton, P., & Chick, N. (2018). Is SoTL a signature pedagogy of educational development? *To Improve the Academy, 37*(1), 4–16.

Felton, P., Kalish, A., Pingree, A., & Plank, K. M. (2007). Toward a scholarship of teaching and learning in educational development. *To Improve the Academy, 25*(1), 93–108.

Healey, M., Flint, A., & Harrington, K. (2014). *Engagement through partnership: Students as partners in learning and teaching in higher education.* New York: Higher Education Academy. https://www.heacademy.ac.uk/engagement-through partnership-students-partners-learning-and-teaching-higher-education

Kinzie, J., Landy, K., Sorcinelli, M. D., & Hutchings, P. (2019). Better together: How faculty development and assessment can join forces to improve student learning. *Change: The Magazine of Higher Learning, 51*(5), 46–54.

Kuh, G. D. (2008). *High-impact educational practices: What they are, who has access to them, and why they matter.* Association of American Colleges & Universities.

McKinney, W. (2004). The scholarship of teaching and learning: Past lessons, current challenges, and future visions. *To Improve the Academy, 22*(1), 3–19.

Mercer-Mapstone, L., Dvorakova, L. S., Matthews, K. E., Abbot, S., Cheng, B., Felten, P., Knorr, K., Marquis, E., Shammas, R., & Swaim, K. (2017). A systematic literature review of students as partners in higher education. *International Journal for Students as Partners, 1*(1), 1–23.

Peseta, T., Bell, A., Clifford, A., English, A., Janarthana, J., Jones, C., Teal, M., & Zhang, J. (2016). Students as ambassadors and researchers of assessment renewal: Puzzling over the practices of university and academic life. *International Journal for Academic Development, 21*(1), 54–61.

Signorini, A. (2014). Involving undergraduates in assessment: Assisting peers to provide constructive feedback. *Assessment Update, 26*(6), 3–13.

Signorini, A., & Abuan, M., (2019, February 21). *Students helping students provide valuable feedback on course evaluations. Tomorrow's Professor.* Stanford University. https://tomprof.stanford.edu/posting/1700

Signorini, A., Abuan, M., Panakkal, G., & Dorantes, S. (2020). Students helping students provide valuable feedback on course evaluations. *To Improve the Academy, 39*(2), 75–105.

Signorini, A., & Pohan, C. A. (2019). Exploring the impact of the students assessing teaching and learning program. *International Journal for Students as Partners, 3*(2), 139–148.

Smith, M. K., Jones, F. H. M., Gilbert, S. L., & Wieman, C. E. (2013). The classroom observation protocol for undergraduate STEM (COPUS): A new instrument to characterize university STEM classroom practices. *CBE-Life Sciences Education, 12*(4), 618–627.

Supiano, B. (2017, November 19). What professors can learn about teaching from their students. *The Chronicle of Higher Education.* The Chronicle of Higher Education. https://www.chronicle.com/article/what-professors-can-learn-about-teaching-from-their-students/

University of British Columbia. (n.d.). *Classroom observation protocol for undergraduate STEM (COPUS).* Carl Wieman Science Education Initiative. www.cwsei.ubc.ca/resources/COPUS.htm

University of California Merced (UCM) Center for Engaged Teaching and Learning (CETL). (n.d.-a). *Providing constructive feedback rubric.* UCM. https://teach.ucmerced.edu/sites/crte.ucmerced.edu/files/page/documents/providing_constructive_feedback_rubric_2.pdf

University of California Merced (UCM) Center for Engaged Teaching and Learning (CETL). (n.d.-b). *Students Assessing Teaching and Learning (SATAL).* UCM. https://teach.ucmerced.edu/satal

University of California Merced (UCM) Center for Engaged Teaching and Learning (CETL). (n.d.-c). *Students helping students provide valuable feedback on course evaluations.* UCM. https://teach.ucmerced.edu/SATAL_Video

19

A Holistic Approach to Student and Faculty Success: Integrating Careers, Advising, and Teaching

Heather Keith, Christina Fabrey, and Serena Eddy

Introduction

At the small campus of Green Mountain College (GMC), USA, three separate centers—the Center for Excellence in Teaching and Learning (CETL), the Center for Advising and Achievement (CAA), and the Office of Career and Personal Development (OCPD)—were housed together under one Careers, Advising, and Teaching (CAT) Center in a central campus location. The result was that CAT Center staff worked together to support student learning, achievement, and career planning, from first-year experience to graduation and beyond. This integration resulted in a center focused on supporting student academic success with high-impact practices in a three-center collaborative approach that replaced traditional silos.

H. Keith (✉)
Radford University, Radford, VA, USA
e-mail: hkeith1@radford.edu

C. Fabrey
Virginia Tech, Blacksburg, VA, USA
e-mail: cfabrey@vt.edu

S. Eddy
Mansfield Hall, Burlington, VT, USA
e-mail: serena.eddy.7@gmail.com

© The Author(s), under exclusive license to Springer Nature Switzerland AG 2023
O. J. Neisler (ed.), *The Palgrave Handbook of Academic Professional Development Centers*,
Palgrave Studies on Leadership and Learning in Teacher Education,
https://doi.org/10.1007/978-3-030-80967-6_19

Each office contributed to this holistic integration, and their centralized physical location encouraged collaboration on a variety of student success initiatives. Having staff in these seemingly disparate centers working closely together led to more holistic approaches to student development. For example, while the students' first-year academic experience was guided by the CETL, it was also influenced by retention initiatives from the CAA, while postgraduation success activities were offered by the OCPD, such as Living and Learning Communities and career planning. Students also benefitted from academic coaching (under the CAA), faculty who were trained in teaching first-year writing (under the CETL), and persistence activities, such as working as a team on our college's outdoor adventure challenge course (under both the CAA and CETL). Faculty benefitted from workshops on high-impact teaching practices (under the CETL), holistic advising (under the CAA), and professional development opportunities offered by the OCPD, such as how to develop a LinkedIn profile.

In a typical week at the CAT Center, faculty and staff attended workshops on inclusive pedagogy, reading groups on effective academic or career-mentoring techniques, and workshops on professionalizing their social media presence, while students entered the space for academic advising and career preparation. The three centers worked together on many initiatives, such as student leadership programming, an online parent 'orientation course', and a holistic first-year seminar that integrated academic skills and content, professional goal-setting, and an exploration of student success resources. Bringing these three centers together created a vibrant space for facilitating faculty and staff development for holistic student success.

In 2013, GMC was the beneficiary of a five-year Title III Strategies for Student Success grant from the US Department of Education. With enhancing student retention and persistence via strengthening teaching and advising as the means of success, GMC founded the CETL and CAA. While it made sense to house both grant-funded centers together, the provost made the innovative decision to include the OCPD in the same space. The three centers—which comprised the CAT Center—were more successful together than separate centers would likely have been, and the shared space became a vibrant gathering place for students, faculty, and staff, and a center for holistic education from orientation to beyond graduation. The CAT Center was located in the heart of the campus in the student center, which was the primary gathering space for all students as it housed the only dining hall, a computer center, a student lounge, the mail center, the outdoor adventure program, and the student life offices.

This chapter details a unique experiment in student success involving the integration of teaching, advising, and careers as part of a holistic approach to student and faculty development. The following sections describe the unique nature of GMC's approach to holistic student success, detail the activities of the three centers, give an overview of the shared physical space, and explore the benefits (both expected and unexpected) of housing centers of teaching, advising, and career services together. Each center had a separate director, mission, and dedicated staff members, but the shared space encouraged teamwork toward a common goal of student success. During the five years of the Title III grant, we experienced an almost 10-point increase in first-year student retention, a major benchmark for the college. Here, we share the CAT Center's systems and initiatives during its five years of grant-funded activity to achieve this as well as other goals. Finally, we explore some challenges of shared space, although we believe that these are minor relative to the clear benefits of integrating centers of teaching, advising, and careers. Though GMC closed its doors for financial reasons in June 2019, our holistic model, both in terms of programming and shared physical space, enhanced retention and persistence of our students and provided opportunities for our faculty which were both meaningful and much in-demand.

GMC: Educating Holistically for a Just and Sustainable World

Between its founding in 1834 and our period of focus from 2013 onward, GMC held multiple identities, such as a high school, a junior college, a four-year liberal arts college, a women's college, a co-educational college, and, most recently, an institution that granted both undergraduate and graduate degrees. In 1995, GMC became one of the first American institutions to center its curriculum around the theme of 'environmental liberal arts', starting with an undergraduate core curriculum and several majors focused specifically on sustainability. In the early 2000s, the college added four master's degrees in Environmental Studies, Sustainable Food Systems, Resilient and Sustainable Communities, and Sustainable Business Management.

In recent years, the undergraduate and graduate education at GMC expressed a mission of fostering "the ideals of environmental and personal responsibility, civic engagement, entrepreneurial spirit, and global understanding" in engaging with students around issues of social justice and sustainability. For many years, the college ranked in the top 10 of *Sierra Magazine's* "Cool Schools" (for sustainability) and achieved the top rating for its curriculum under the American Association for the Advancement of Sustainability in Higher Education's sustainability tracking, assessment, and rating system.

Our centers of teaching, advising, and careers all aimed to support and promote this mission as we worked with both undergraduate and graduate students.

As previously mentioned, GMC received a US Department of Education Title III Strategies for Student Success grant in 2013. The aim of the grant was to aid the college in enabling better student retention and persistence through the development of the CETL and CAA. At the same time, the campus bookstore in our student center became vacant and the college decided to renovate this centrally-located space to house both the Title III-funded centers and the OCPD. There were many benefits to this integration of student-centered services in career development, advising, and pedagogy, as well as a few challenges.

Overview and History of the Three Centers

Although our three centers had separate directors and staff members and served varying audiences, from students and faculty to parents and administrators, we inhabited and maintained a shared space and collaborated daily on integrated initiatives, such as the first-year experience and senior capstone courses.

The CETL

One of the two major initiatives of the Title III grant, the CETL at GMC was established with three staff members: a director, an instructional designer, and an instructional technologist. In founding the center, the director connected with other teaching center directors around the country, exploring models of high-impact faculty development activities and spaces, and interviewing internal faculty to assess development needs on campus. The goals of the CETL were to enhance student retention and persistence toward graduation by training faculty in differentiated education techniques, making available to students open online educational resources, and working with the CAA on first-year initiatives and programming. The work of the grant was largely successful, as exemplified by a more than nine-point gain in first-year retention during the years of the grant.

The CETL specialized in a holistic view of faculty teaching development encapsulated in the college's sustainability mission, especially in our core curriculum. GMC's mission included preparing students to be engaged members of just and sustainable communities, and our core curriculum, from our first-year seminar to our senior capstone, aimed to give them the skills necessary to make sustainable personal choices and to contribute to a sustainable and just economy in their careers. Faculty who taught in our core curriculum regularly attended workshops in our teaching center and worked with the director on content and practices that engaged the college's mission in an active learning environment.

Faculty also consulted with CETL staff on approaches to differentiated instruction (Santangelo & Tomlinson, 2009), which involved balancing mastery learning for highly prepared students while simultaneously providing extra resources for students who were less prepared and required more opportunities to build skills. Mastery techniques included providing extra challenges in the classroom, as well as a robust undergraduate teaching assistant program in which students provided leadership in first-year and other lower-level courses. Students who needed to build more skills for college success were offered further resources (such as open educational resources, on-campus tutoring, and other local support) in both developmental and typical courses. Workshops on skills and motivation were at the same time offered to students in our Learning Center, under the umbrella of the CAA. Faculty were made aware of these opportunities and often incorporated them into students' coursework via both the CAA and CETL.

CETL staff also worked with faculty on applied and active learning techniques and designed new classroom spaces to fit practices that decentralized the faculty role and promoted peer teaching and learning (Baepler et al., 2014). We encouraged reflective pedagogical approaches and assessments, including students' engagement with their own learning, and faculty reflection on their growth as instructors. Finally, CETL staff supported faculty in the appropriate use of instructional technology in both residential and hybrid classrooms.

Our primary interaction with faculty was in course design, including the development and assessment of learning outcomes, and in course effectiveness, especially through the use of observations and midcourse reviews during which CETL staff interviewed students about their learning and the impact of instructional practices. We also offered frequent workshops on everything from efficient and effective evaluation of student work to maintaining civil classroom discourse when dealing with controversial issues. Faculty utilized our services via multiple modalities, including digital archives of high-impact practices, full-course design and assessment services throughout the term, workshops, and walk-in consultations. In partnership with the dean of faculty and the CAA, the CETL hosted a new faculty orientation in the wider CAT Center. We also communicated with faculty and the public on social media,

304 H. Keith et al.

at presentations, via a newsletter, and with a suite of digital 'tool kits for teaching'. In an internal study conducted during the third year of our grant, we found that student persistence from one year to the next was more likely if students were in multiple courses that had been redesigned with the CETL.

The CETL collaborated daily with advising and career development partners in the CAT Center. As we will explore later, teaching at GMC was inseparable from advising and mentoring students, both during and beyond their college years.

The CAA

In order to augment the college's holistic approach to teaching, and inspired by the research suggesting that academic and social engagement are important contributors to student retention, GMC established the CAA, also funded by the Title III grant. Prior to the establishment of this center, GMC's faculty advising model was decentralized and focused on prescriptive advising techniques. In creating the center, our main goal was to take a more holistic approach by focusing on intentional developmental advising, implementing targeted interventions for students at risk of academic failure, and identifying and developing institutional structures that promoted substantial academic and social integration. Knowing that engagement is, as suggested by Tinto (2000), the single most significant predictor of persistence, we shifted our academic advising to encompass discussions around educationally purposeful endeavors that connected students to the campus and provided them with leadership opportunities.

Starting with a focus group of faculty advisors, the CAA developed its mission and vision. After defining its greater goal—guiding students in exploring their academic, career, and personal ambitions in order to co-create a four-year experience that developed their individual potential as students, citizens, and professionals—this core group began to assess the strengths and weaknesses of the current advising model to better define gaps and opportunities moving forward. With our intention of creating a holistic advising system with the three centers at the core, the focus group looked at ways to involve the entire campus community in supporting students' personal, academic, and career development throughout their four years, including a number of key initiatives:

- Providing opportunities for learning best practices in faculty advising
- Defining and developing guidelines for advising at GMC
- Supporting developmental advising and first-year persistence by implementing an academic coaching program and electronic learning plan
- Employing new technology in proactive advising that employed predictive modeling, followed by comprehensive tracking and intervention for students exhibiting behaviors that placed them at risk of failure.

With an attractive and accessible advising center, we collaborated with the CETL and OCPD to offer holistic advising workshops and development opportunities to new and veteran faculty advisors in a number of different forms. An orientation for new faculty advisors assisted in providing them with essential advising knowledge and skills, while also helping them learn to synthesize conceptual issues and apply relational skills in their regular advising interactions with students. For seasoned advisors, the CAA offered advising 'mini-grants', which provided them with opportunities to have a positive impact on student success through programmatic and curricular advising innovations that served as models for others. Participants redesigned an element of their previous advising goals and systems with an added focus on student retention and advising best practices, and participated with their colleagues in three advising research discussions per semester. The culmination of the mini-grant process was an impact assessment and reflective statement, followed by opportunities to share their inspiring work in teaching and advising with other campus colleagues.

In addition to these unique opportunities, the CAA offered ongoing advising workshops. Featuring topics such as group advising, privacy and confidentiality with parents, and understanding financial aid, these workshops were open to all advisors, and in most cases, the entire campus community. Many of these workshops were facilitated internally, tapping into campus partners in academic advising. These workshops brought to life the content supplied in a newly developed advisor guidebook available on our advising platform that outlined both developmental and prescriptive techniques in advising specific to our unique sustainability curriculum.

Complementing our advisor development, the CAA initiated an academic coaching program to provide more intensive support and interventions for first-year students as they transitioned into the college environment. Initial research on coaching recognizes that the process helps to facilitate a successful transition from high school to college, increases students' intrinsic motivation and self-direction, and helps to improve student retention (Ashgar, 2010; Bettinger & Baker, 2011; Parker & Boutelle, 2009). As a collaborative, solutions-based, result-oriented process that facilitates the attainment of goals to improve a person's life experience, coaching provides students with a structure for personal and academic success. Our Learning Center, under the supervision of the CAA, brought professional staff into the CAT Center, offering students skills development and metacognitive strategy workshops to complement the work that our academic coaches provided.

From the time students confirmed their enrollment to their arrival on campus, the academic coaches were their initial contact via phone and e-mail outreach in helping to prepare them for their campus experience. A major component of their summer outreach included assisting students with choosing their first-year Living and Learning Community. In these interest-based, first-year seminars, our students lived together as a cohort guided by their first-year faculty advisor/instructor. With an academic coach connected to every Living and Learning Community, they worked closely with each student once they arrived on campus, and, via the CAT Center, were able to communicate regularly with faculty members on student progress. The faculty advisor guided students in defining their first-year academic goals in a formal writing piece known as an 'Academic Path'. In their weekly meetings with their academic coach, students tackled small actions identified in their Academic Path, moving them toward their ideal college experience. These small actions ranged from identifying ways to engage in the campus community to addressing academic or roommate challenges and working with the OCPD on job placement.

Finally, the CAA implemented an early alert platform. In addition to modeling student risk factors for proactive outreach, the early alert platform provided a strategic method of alerting CAA staff to academic and/or wellness concerns. The CAA was essential to defining student connections so that alerts could be assigned to campus professionals with the most natural relationships to the student on campus. Academic coaches and faculty advisors, as well as other support professionals, brought alert notifications into their meetings with students so that the student was supported in a plan to correct these concerns. Use of this technology encouraged more meaningful and frequent contact between a student and their campus support team.

Collectively, these strategies have an important role to play in student retention and persistence toward graduation. The CAA ensured the interconnectedness of student advising with learning support networks, early warning systems, and safety nets. Knowing that academic advising is essential to promoting student development and success, the CAA served as a visible and centralized location for faculty development and student academic planning and support. Within the five years of our grant work, our overall academic advising scores from the Noel-Levitz Senior Satisfaction survey reached their highest level within the previous decade. Seniors noted the strong improvement in advisor approachability, knowledge about academic requirements, individual care and concern about students, and facilitation of goal-setting. Partnering with the CETL on initiatives such as these allowed for the seamless connection of teaching and advising in faculty development.

The OCPD

With the integration of teaching, advising, and careers in the CAT Center, the former Career Services Office became the OCPD. For 25 years, the Career Services Office at GMC was nestled in a small space on the second floor of the library and generated limited foot traffic. When the college transformed the former bookstore in the student center into the CAT Center in 2014, the impact was immediate. In its new central building location, which allowed for partnership with advising and teaching services, student contact with the OCPD increased by 59% within two years.

Even more remarkable was the increase in collaboration between the OCPD and faculty members. Faculty requests for in-class, career-related workshops increased by 147% in the first three years and impacted 60% more students in 2016–2017 than it did in 2013–2014. The holistic reframing of student career services went beyond typical resources for writing resumes and finding jobs after graduation to the personal and professional development of each student from their first-year seminar to after graduation, both in the curriculum and in co-curricular opportunities. The OCPD was staffed by two professionals, the director and an employment relations manager, in addition to two work-study students. The mission of the OCPD was to support all GMC undergraduate students, master's students, and alumni as they explored their interests, developed a professional portfolio, pursued fulfilling careers, and achieved their personal goals.

Staff of the OCPD specialized in providing thoughtful, individualized guidance to students as they prepared tailored resumes and compelling cover letters, learned how to correspond with employers, and created a professional online presence. Students received constructive feedback on how to successfully interview, diplomatically network, research internship and employment options, and explore postgraduate educational opportunities, grants, and fellowships.

Partnering with the CAA, academic coaches incorporated career counseling into their advising sessions from the very first meeting and referred students to the OCPD as early as during the new student orientation. This partnership reinforced the idea that the college's career and personal development services were as much of an ongoing benefit to first-year students as they were to seniors. Indeed, GMC alumni of both undergraduate and graduate degree programs continued to take advantage of the career advising services throughout their professional lives.

In collaboration with the CAA and the CETL, OCPD career advisors presented career preparation workshops to all first-year students and administered and interpreted online skills and interest inventory assessments, including the CliftonStrengths Finder, the "What Can I Do With This Major" website, mind-mapping, and the Knowdell Motivated Skills Card Sort. In addition, GMC's Alumni Career Network connected students with alumni who provided valuable advice and helped them uncover job and internship opportunities. Via newly created Facebook groups and LinkedIn connections, thousands of GMC affiliates eagerly shared contacts and job leads with students and gave them tips on how to prepare for graduate studies. The CETL and CAA supported the OCPD in encouraging faculty members to actively participate in social media groups aimed at providing support to alumni throughout their careers. These online groups, with faculty engagement, have persisted beyond the closure of the college. Every spring, the OCPD collaborated with the CAA, CETL, and the Office of Alumni Engagement to host the 'Making a Difference & Making a Living Conference', during which GMC alumni, requested and invited by faculty, returned to campus to conduct mock interviews and share information (via panels and TEDx-style talks) about their career path and personal journey to finding fulfilling work.

Overall, 85% of GMC students completed at least one internship, externship, or practicum before they graduated. The OCPD maintained an internship database, several job boards, a JobLink platform (through Symplicity software), a resource library, and a video conferencing room. Staff also published monthly undergraduate, graduate, and alumni newsletters and offered an in-house, individualized job-matching service. OCPD staff also partnered with faculty and the CAA to match students with on-campus employment opportunities that provided them with valuable work experience and the transferable skills necessary to land attractive full-time jobs.

Because GMC prioritized individualized teaching and mentoring, graduates left GMC with recommendations from faculty who knew and appreciated their strengths and cared about their success beyond graduation. In partnership with faculty development initiatives in teaching and advising, especially in first-year programming, the OCPD supported close relationships that have outlasted the existence of the college itself. The shared space and ethos of the CAT Center allowed for formal collaboration on shared goals, as well as informal daily discussion of student success via faculty development.

Discussion: The Challenges and Benefits of Integrating Careers, Advising, and Teaching

The challenges of sharing a space between three important centers were predictable, but relatively easy to navigate. The directors occasionally had to negotiate for space and resources, but we created systems to manage our needs collectively, such as regulating the use of conference and other shared spaces. The OCPD was funded out of the college's budget, while the CAA and CETL were primarily funded from the Title III grant. Additional funding from the dean's and provost's budgets allowed the three centers to share incidental expenses, such as hospitality resources, workshop supplies, and outside facilitator costs. While each had separate work-study positions, our student workers were able to staff the shared CAT Center reception desk, as well as do work for individual centers. All three directors of the centers reported directly to the provost, which contributed to the sense that the staff of the separate centers were an integrated team.

The main benefit of sharing space and resources across the three centers was the holistic approach we were able to achieve in serving both students and faculty, especially in collaborating on important student success initiatives. The CAT Center was developed as a strategy for campus collaboration and strong partnerships in the holistic center focused on best practices in teaching and advising. While many faculty members spent a tremendous amount of time focusing on their teaching and advising responsibilities, the development of the CAT Center provided an additional opportunity for collaborating with key administrators, other faculty members, and staff. Among several benefits, the resulting outcome included a hub for proactive consultation on teaching, advising, career mentoring, and student support. The CAT Center became a place for accurate and consistent information for academic procedures, development, and student success resources.

The partnership between the CETL and the CAA allowed for intentional collaboration on workshops on teaching and advising. With directors in a shared space, ongoing collaboration focused on faculty professional development and progression toward grant targets (including the student retention and persistence initiatives), oversight of the budget, and facilitating external evaluations. The CAT Center offered the communal space to host the new faculty orientation and new student sessions, both of which provided a comprehensive overview of student success initiatives including teaching, advising, and early alert information.

Our first-year academic coaches were able to offload some of the faculty advisors' prescriptive work by introducing students to the advising process early on and reinforcing the importance of students initiating and developing a close faculty-advisee relationship. Having first-year academic coaches in close proximity to CETL staff and the consistent flow of faculty members in and out of the CAT Center provided regular opportunities for consultation about students' progress in courses, as well as frequent communication about the details of academic offerings, allowing coaches to tap into the expertise of the faculty's disciplines.

By bringing faculty members into our shared space for new faculty orientation, we were able to integrate advising and career mentorship into the faculty experience at GMC from day one. We followed up with holistic faculty workshops involving both teaching and advising. Likewise, the proximity of the OCPD allowed staff to work with faculty on career mentoring as part of their development for teaching and advising. Faculty collaborated with the OCPD through the CETL by incorporating nearly 50 in-class career workshops per year into the curriculum. Professors participated fully and reinforced job search best practices and skills for students to succeed in their personal career aspirations. The OCPD also supported student leadership initiatives, such as the work done by undergraduate teaching assistants and research assistants, by helping students to showcase valuable and practical relevant job experience in their internship and career searches.

The close collaboration between the CETL, the CAA, and the OCPD allowed communication to flow seamlessly between departments and classrooms. Faculty became adept at integrating career and academic advising in their work with students, in the classroom, and in advising meetings. The integration of career and advising services also allowed advising staff to support ongoing programming opportunities for students, such as building a professional profile, finding a job or internship, writing a resume, developing interviewing skills, considering summer experiences, and attending career conferences and job and graduate school fairs. The integration of careers, advising, and teaching also made possible holistic collaboration on major campus events and initiatives, such as the new student orientation, the Living and Learning Communities, and intersession leadership opportunities for students. The shared space allowed for shared resources, such as our student interview laboratory that was also used by faculty and staff search committees and a faculty development library that included resources on high-impact practices in teaching, advising, mentoring, and scholarship. We hosted open-house and 'family and friends' events for the college in our shared conference space and together built a parent 'orientation course' on our learning management system that acclimated parents to multiple aspects of their students' curricular and cocurricular education.

Our shared space was appreciated by the campus community. It became a vibrant hub of activity that involved students, faculty, and staff all at once. Other constituents on campus reserved the space in our central location for their own activities, bringing even more faculty, staff, and student traffic into the CAT Center. First-year students, especially, came to view the center as a pivotal place where they could find information, jobs, and advice. Faculty knew the center as a space they could stop by to schedule a career session in classes, learn about appreciative advising, and consult on best practices in teaching. To all campus constituents, the CAT Center became known as a friendly place to learn and grow and feel a sense of belonging.

Finally, after the announcement of the college's closure, the CAT Center was able to provide services to students and faculty in identifying immediate educational and career paths. CAA staff advised faculty on how to mentor students during the difficult transition, CETL staff provided targeted professional development programming for navigating the academic job market, and OCPD staff provided faculty, staff, and student workshops for writing cover letters and resumes, updating professional social media profiles, and exploring career opportunities.

Conclusion

During the five years of Title III grant-funded activity at GMC, we were pleased to have the opportunity to explore the integration of teaching, advising, and careers, which are usually considered separate and distinct entities on college campuses. We found that this integration resulted in a holistic treatment of student and faculty success that would have been unlikely with separate centers. Between 2013 and 2019, the year in which GMC shut its doors, the CAT Center was instrumental in launching many students into careers or other professional experiences, gave faculty countless opportunities for growth as teachers and advisors (and eventually helped them to explore career options elsewhere), and supported our mission by helping students, faculty, and staff to live our values as we supported students in achieving their goals for sustainable and resilient individual and community growth.

Acknowledgments Most of the activities mentioned in this chapter were made possible by a US Department of Education Title III Strategies for Student Success grant. We also acknowledge the support of Provost Thomas Mauhs-Pugh, supervisor of the grant.

References

Ashgar, A. (2010). Reciprocal peer coaching and its use as a formative assessment strategy for first-year students. *Assessment and Evaluation in Higher Education, 35*(4), 403–417.

Baepler, P., Walker, J. D., & Driessen, M. (2014). It's not about seat time: Blending, flipping, and efficiency in active learning classrooms. *Computers & Education, 78,* 227–236.

Bettinger, E. P., & Baker, R. (2011). *The effects of student coaching in college: An evaluation of a randomized experiment in student mentoring* (Working paper No. 16881). National Bureau of Economic Research. http://nber.org/papers/w16881.pdf

Parker, D. R., & Boutelle, K. (2009). Executive function coaching for college students with learning disabilities and ADHD: A new approach for fostering self-determination. *Learning Disabilities Research and Practice, 24*(4), 204–215.

Santangelo, T., & Tomlinson, C. (2009). The application of differentiated instruction in postsecondary environments: Benefits, challenges, and future directions. *International Journal of Teaching and Learning in Higher Education, 20*(3), 307–323.

Tinto, V. (2000). Taking retention seriously: Rethinking the first year of college. *National Academic Advising Association Journal, 19*(2), 5–10.

Part VII

ADCs Based on Partnerships and Collaboration

These chapters describe different types of partnerships and collaborations involving academic professional development centers (ADCs). Some are between and among organizations on the same campus, one is of directors across dispersed campuses, and others are between two or more higher education institutions, often sharing knowledge, resources, and support across national boundaries. One chapter discusses issues over creating partnerships versus mergers, a challenge faced by many campuses and ADCs. Every year this very question is raised at my own institution.

Chapters in Part VII

Chapter 20: *Creating through International Partnership: A Faculty Development Center at a Pakistani University*. Asif Khan, Karakoram International University, Gilgit, Pakistan, Michele A. Parker, University of North Carolina, Wilmington, NC, and Patricia Pashby, University of Oregon, Eugene, OR, USA.

This chapter elucidates a collaboration between three universities, one based in Pakistan and the other two in the USA.

Chapter 21: *Quality, Teaching, and Learning: A Networked Approach Across Pakistan and East Africa*. Tashmin Khamis, Aga Khan University, Karachi, Pakistan, and Zeenar Salim, Syracuse University, Syracuse, NY, USA (previously of Aga Khan University).

314   ADCs Based on Partnerships and Collaboration

This chapter relates the experience of a multinational collaboration between different departments and staff across one geographically dispersed university. The authors report on the impact, satisfaction rate, and instructional change resulting from the programs of integrated networks of quality, teaching, and learning operating across three continents, six countries, and 13 teaching sites. In addition, the ADC engages in online collaboration among existing educational development, library, information technology, and student support units to promote improvement in the learning environment and student success.

Chapter 22: *Using Student Research Data to Shape the Teaching and Learning Activities of a New Academic Development Center in Turkey.* Elif Bengü, Abdullah Gül University, Kayseri, Turkey, and Fatma Nevra Seggie, Boğaziçi University, Istanbul, Turkey.

Collaboration between an advisory group, students, faculty, and the staff of one ADC in Turkey was necessary to produce the research disseminated in this chapter in its drive to fulfil one university's mission to support teaching and learning, assess student satisfaction, and assess student needs.

Chapter 23: *Collaborative Faculty Development.* Jordan Cofer, Denise Domizi, Marina Smitherman, Jesse Bishop, and Rod McRae, University System of Georgia, Atlanta, GA, USA.

This chapter portrays the collaboration between directors and administrators from 26 distinct colleges and universities that are part of a single, structured consortium in the USA designed to improve teaching and learning across four research universities, four comprehensive universities, nine state universities, and nine state colleges, each with distinct core missions. The collaboration further works to mitigate the challenges of disparate resources, diverse services, inclusion, and attrition.

Chapter 24: *The Making of the Learning, Teaching, and Innovative Technologies Center: Building Upon an Internal Partnership.* Barbara Draude, Thomas Brinthaupt, and Sheila Otto, Middle Tennessee State University, Murfreesboro, TN, USA.

This ADC was formed on the basis of a partnership between two existing administrative units: academic affairs and informational technology. The ADC is designed to improve and integrate the creative and effective use of appropriate instructional technologies to enhance student learning.

Other Relevant Chapters

Chapter 9: *Tectonic Plates of American Higher Education: Yale University's Poorvu Center and a Multiplicity of Missions.* Kyle Sebastian Vitale, Temple University, Philadelphia, PA, (previously of Yale University), and Nancy S. Niemi, University of Maryland Eastern Shore, Princess Anne, MD, USA (previously of Yale University).

This chapter describes the challenges and benefits of a merger versus a partnership as it describes a situation wherein various departments such as faculty development, program assessment, a student writing center, educational technology, a broadcast studio, digital education, and student mentoring and counseling were integrated into one organization located in a single building.

Chapter 19: *A Holistic Approach to Student and Faculty Success: Integrating Careers, Advising, and Teaching.* Heather Keith, Radford University, Radford, VA (previously of Green Mountain College), Christina Fabrey, Virginia Tech, Blacksburg, VA, (previously of Green Mountain College), and Serena Eddy, Mansfield Hall, Burlington, VT, USA (previously of Green Mountain College).

This ADC involves a partnership between three campus centers to achieve an institutional mission of holistic student and faculty development.

Chapter 37: *Systematic Changes: Impact of Double-Helix Collaboration Toward Innovation in Faculty Development and Student-Centered Teaching and Learning.* Yihong Fan, Southwest Jiaotong University, Chengdu, and Xiamen University, Xiamen, China.

A partnership between a faculty development center and an academic affairs office provides support for long-term and sustainable faculty development and innovation in teaching and learning at a research university in China.

Chapter 38: *Change in Practice: Achieving a Cultural Shift in Teaching and Learning Through a Theory of Change.* Grahame T. Bilbow, Centre for the Enhancement of Teaching and Learning, University of Hong Kong, Pok Fu Lam, Hong Kong.

An international partnership with a professional membership scheme in the UK shows early signs of enhancing career prospects for faculty and graduate teaching assistants at a university in Hong Kong.

316   ADCs Based on Partnerships and Collaboration

Chapter 41: *Extending International Collaboration to Certify High-Quality Online Teaching in Higher Education.* Yan Ding, Center for Faculty Development / Research Institute for Higher Education, Fudan University, Shanghai, China, and Yaping Gao, Quality Matters, Annapolis, MD, USA.

This chapter details the international collaboration between an ADC and an American education quality assurance organization, which has allowed the center to provide course review and systematic teacher training services for teachers from more than 50 other member institutions in a national alliance to promote online course construction and blended learning reform.

20

Creating Through International Partnership: A Faculty Development Center at a Pakistani University

Asif Khan, Michele A. Parker, and Patricia Pashby

Introduction

Teaching practices in developed countries have improved significantly, with universities, as engines of change, making a robust contribution toward the socioeconomic development of their respective societies (McLean et al., 2009; Meizlish et al., 2017; Rathbun et al., 2017). However, most developing nations have not yet achieved the magnitude of growth expected as a result of university-level education (Lee et al., 2011). Without establishing a viable higher educational system and without nurturing skilled human resources, less developed nations cannot achieve sustainable development (Kruss et al., 2015a, 2015b).

This realization led the Government of Pakistan to initiate processes of reforming higher education in 2002, with the objectives of promoting excellence in teaching and learning and developing the capacity of faculties across

A. Khan (✉)
Karakoram International University, Gilgit, Pakistan
e-mail: asif.khan@kiu.edu.pk

M. A. Parker
University of North Carolina, Wilmington, NC, USA
e-mail: parkerma@uncw.edu

P. Pashby
University of Oregon, Eugene, OR, USA
e-mail: pashby@uoregon.edu

© The Author(s), under exclusive license to Springer Nature Switzerland AG 2023
O. J. Neisler (ed.), *The Palgrave Handbook of Academic Professional Development Centers*,
Palgrave Studies on Leadership and Learning in Teacher Education,
https://doi.org/10.1007/978-3-030-80967-6_20

the nation (Ali et al., 2013). Although the government achieved some of these reform objectives, such as establishing new universities in less developed areas, public sector universities still struggle with quality-related issues in terms of teaching and learning (Raza & Naqvi, 2011). Faculty development at the university level is therefore an emerging field in the Pakistani context.

History and Context of Faculty Development at Karakorum International University

The leadership of Karakorum International University (KIU), a newly established public sector university in Pakistan, recognized faculty development to be an urgent need. In early 2015, the vice chancellor appointed a coordinator of faculty development, who was affiliated with the Faculty of Education at the rank of an assistant professor with a PhD in Education. The coordinator received a mandate to establish an academic professional development center (ADC) to initiate professional development activities for the university faculty in order to address teaching and learning concerns. Three objectives identified for the faculty development program were to: (1) promote the professional growth of faculty through effective and innovative programs; (2) develop and identify materials and resources to support the faculty in effective teaching practices; and (3) conduct both formal and informal needs analysis research to determine the professional development needs of the faculty.

Established in 2002, KIU is situated in a semi-urban area of Pakistan. The university offers 15 majors in social and natural sciences and enrolls approximately 3,500 students. There are 128 faculty members, of which approximately 60 hold a PhD. Almost 95% of the faculty are employed at the academic ranks of assistant professor and lecturer, whereas the number of associate professors and full professors are few. Due to the remoteness of its geographical location, harsh weather conditions, and higher cost of living, KIU does not attract experienced and senior faculty.

Research Methodology

This chapter examines the faculty development initiative at KIU over a three-year span, including support from an American institution, the University of Oregon (UO). The data collection and analysis was guided by Stufflebeam's (1971) Context, Input, Process, and Product (CIPP) model and covers the context, input, and processes involved in the establishment of the initiative, focusing on the goals of the program, available resources, and program activities. Interviews, observations, document reviews, and focus groups were the methods used during the data collection period that spanned from June 2014 to July 2017. There were two phases: (1) a needs assessment in 2015; and (2) faculty feedback on workshops in 2017.

Needs Assessment

In 2015, a three-member committee led by the coordinator of faculty development at KIU was constituted to perform a needs assessment in the spring and fall, covering three areas: teaching approaches, course outline/syllabi, and weekly reading material. Since the university offers 15 major programs, three faculty members from each department were selected using a convenience sampling strategy. Faculty with more extensive teaching experience (not less than five years) were preferred. There was an equal representation of faculty from the social and natural sciences. This resulted in a total sample of 45 faculty members who underwent teaching observations and interviews; in addition, 15 department heads were also interviewed. Two separate interview protocols, one for faculty and one for departmental heads, were developed.

Furthermore, 15 focus group discussions (FGDs) were held with students from seven social science and eight natural science departments. All student participants were in their final semester. To authenticate the data, FGDs were held with the students in courses whose instructors had been observed as part of the classroom observations phase. The FGDs were conducted after the classroom observations, with 10–12 students being invited to participate in each group. The duration of each FGD was approximately one hour. The principal investigator asked the questions and two colleagues served as note-takers. Several guiding questions were used; however, other questions arose during the researchers' interaction with the participants.

Document review was the third method used to generate data. Some of the documents that were reviewed and examined were course outlines, graded answer scripts, reading materials, PowerPoint slides, and graded assignments. Through content analysis, data-derived codes were grouped to summarize the content in substantive categories. Using these categories, the researchers subsequently identified themes.

Faculty Feedback

The second phase of data collection was conducted from February to July 2017, during which time three formal professional development activities were initiated. Of over 50 faculty who attended the training sessions, 15

320   A. Khan et al.

faculty were selected through convenience sampling while maintaining an equal representation of members from social and natural sciences departments. Each person was interviewed to determine their reactions to the faculty development initiative, as well as any changes in their knowledge and improvement to their teaching.

Results

Utilizing the CIPP model, five themes surfaced across the various data sources:

1. Significant and careful planning led to the intentionality of implementing the faculty development program in this specific context; this included mentorship received by the coordinator of faculty development, which enhanced support involving stakeholders at various stages
2. Visiting professors and the coordinator of faculty development were instrumental in delivering high-quality sessions on teaching and learning
3. There were articulated needs for faculty development
4. Based on the initial programming, faculty reported changes after participating in the faculty development sessions
5. There are benefits to international partnerships for faculty development initiatives instituted in developing nations.

Input in the Form of the Needs Assessment

Highlighting the formal gaps in the teaching culture of the university and assessing the needs of the faculty were the first steps of the faculty development initiative. Although there was general agreement among the university faculty and students that the teaching practices at KIU met the maximum standards and contributed to the learning of the students, the results of the needs assessment indicated that some of the fundamental components of teaching and learning did not support this claim.

Reading Materials

Some instructors did not provide weekly reading materials to their students, while a small number of the faculty only assigned texts before the midterm and final exams. Students reported that sometimes their instructors provided resources upon request. Instructors shared different reasons for not providing course readings; for example, some faculty equated the provision of reading material by instructors to "spoon feeding," and argued that university-level students should themselves be responsible for finding literature from the library and other sources. Students reported that they could not access the books recommended by their instructors because they were neither available in the library nor the local market. On the other hand, some instructors explained that they provided students with PowerPoint slides as an alternative and students would prepare for their final exams by reading the PowerPoint slides. Although the majority of the students were content with the situation, a small number expressed concerns.

Course Syllabi

Many instructors did not follow the rule regarding the provision of detailed course syllabi at the beginning of the semester. In most cases, instructors did not provide any syllabi to their students, with the students seemingly indifferent to this situation. A small number of faculty provided a course syllabus to their students containing limited information about the courses. For instance, such course syllabi did not contain a description of assignments; instead, the instructors would provide this information a week before the assignment deadline. While commenting on this situation, students stated they were given a limited amount of time to complete an assignment, resulting in their frequently producing plagiarized work. These limited syllabi tended to contain a list of topics without details, such as when they would be discussed. Therefore, students would discover a weekly topic only after arriving to the lecture. One of the implications of this situation, as indicated by the students and observed by the primary researcher, was that teaching practices were devoid of student discussion and interaction, due to the lack of ability for advance preparation on the part of the students.

Teaching Practices

Substantial gaps were noted in teaching approaches, which were primarily teacher-centered. Instructors admitted that the lack of proper training for university teaching made them less effective in regard to their teaching methods. However, some instructors blamed the poor preparation and weak academic backgrounds of the students for the lack of interaction and discussion in their classes.

322 A. Khan et al.

Through observations, it was discerned that some instructors taught for 40–50 minutes, although the official duration of each class was 90 minutes. While reflecting on this situation, one of the instructors stated that students did not have the patience to sit for 90 minutes in each class; therefore, they reduced the class duration. Students claimed that some of their teachers frequently skipped classes on various pretexts, such as being a member of a committee and having to attend meetings. Many instructors complained that they had to teach too many courses, which resulted in deterioration in the quality of their teaching. According to the university rules, lecturers must teach five courses, assistant professors four courses, and associate professors two courses each semester.

Processes: Launching the Faculty Development Initiative

At the end of 2015, upon the completion of the needs assessment, the KIU vice chancellor scheduled a meeting with the academic heads of 15 disciplines, the deans of the social and natural sciences colleges, quality enhancement officials, and others to share the findings. The vice chancellor asserted that this meeting was an opportunity for the academic heads to address the teaching and learning gaps highlighted in the needs assessment results. He asked the academic heads to share the findings with their respective faculty with the anticipation of reviewing their teaching practices.

Previously, the university had developed an international academic partnership with an American university, the UO, to build the curriculum of two specific departments. Later, it was agreed to expand the scope of this collaboration with the provision of support from UO toward the establishment of a faculty development center at KIU. As a result of the partnership, the UO faculty contributed the following: (1) they conducted seminars for university faculty on effective teaching methods, the publication of research papers, and academic writing; (2) they provided learning resources such as books on faculty development; and (3) they offered an internship of three months at UO for the KIU coordinator of faculty development. Funding for the above was provided by the US State Department.

The internship for the KIU coordinator of faculty development took place from September to December 2016. The objective of the internship was to provide the coordinator with opportunities to develop an in-depth understanding of the concept of faculty development in the context of American higher education and accordingly design a context-oriented program for

KIU. The director of the UO's Teaching Engagement Program (TEP) served as mentor to the coordinator. After developing an understanding of the needs of the Pakistani university, the mentor identified a series of activities for the coordinator to attend. These activities included observing and participating in faculty development workshops and seminars arranged for novice and experienced faculty at UO; reviewing the literature on faculty development; observing best teaching practices in real classroom settings; and discussing different approaches of faculty development with those affiliated with the TEP. The coordinator met weekly with the mentor to reflect on how the professional development activities he observed could be adapted to the KIU context.

Objectives

The three objectives identified for the KIU's faculty development program—now called the Center for Human Resource Development (CHRD)—were to: (1) promote the professional growth of faculty through effective and innovative programs; (2) develop and identify materials and resources to support the faculty in effective teaching practices; and (3) conduct both formal and informal research to determine the professional development needs of faculty. From March to July 2017, three faculty development sessions were offered for visiting, novice, and mid-career faculty. Approaches employed in these sessions included pair and group activities, role-play, and discussions. Over 50 faculty from 15 departments participated, with each session attracting between 15 and 25 attendees.

Faculty Feedback on the Initial Training Sessions

This section provides details of the perceptions and feedback of the participants with regard to the three initial faculty training sessions. The first session was conducted for 25 faculty affiliated with different disciplines. The duration was four days (two hours each day) and the session covered the following themes: (1) designing course outlines; (2) designing assignments and rubrics; (3) reading materials and reading strategies; and (4) teaching approaches. These sessions were conducted by the KIU coordinator of faculty development and a member of the Faculty of Education.

Participants professed that, after attending the session, they started altering their practices by providing reading material, moving from teacher- to student-centered teaching approaches, and providing course outlines at the beginning of the semester. One of the faculty stated that he would previously

324   A. Khan et al.

provide the course outline only for the midterm exam, but now provided the course outline at the beginning of the semester. Another faculty member commented:

> Before coming to university, I was affiliated with a college where giving course outlines and providing reading material to the students was not part of the teaching culture and I only came to know about the practices of giving course outlines when I attended the training. (Participant 1, Faculty Development Session, KIU)

One of the instructors pointed out that although faculty come to universities with good content knowledge, delivering that knowledge in an effective manner necessitates specific skills that require guidance and training:

> There must be a mechanism of faculty development in every university of Pakistan ... each day we notice innovations in teaching practices and ... it is essential for the faculty to upgrade their knowledge on a sustainable basis. (Participant 2, Faculty Development Session, KIU)

While commenting on a change concerning teaching approaches, another instructor explained that his initial efforts were restricted to course completion with limited interaction with students, but that "after attending the training, now I have integrated interactive teaching practices with my students since one of the things that I got from the training is interactive teaching." On the topic of providing resources to students, one of the participants reported:

> I used to provide the reading material normally after the lecture, now I am providing the reading material before classes. This provides students with enough time to read and be prepared for classroom discussions. (Participant 3, Faculty Development Session, KIU)

The second faculty development session was conducted by the coordinator of faculty development as well as a master trainer who had recently completed extensive training on teaching effectiveness. This session lasted four days (two hours each day) and focused on microteaching and leadership in education. A total of 15 mid-career faculty attended the training. Each participant delivered a mock lecture, which was recorded for later evaluation of their teaching style.

When reflecting on the microteaching, faculty were candid in pointing out weaknesses and making connections to their actual teaching performances. One instructor commented on the benefits of the process:

Microteaching is a helpful tool that informs the instructors about their strengths and weaknesses. It provided us the opportunity to make our self-assessment and self-evaluation since, after watching our videos, we realized how can we improve our practices and areas which need further improvement. (Participant 4, Faculty Development Session, KIU)

Another participant stated: "I had a habit of watching the left side of the class while delivering lectures… I only noticed this habit when I watched my recording and participant's feedback during microteaching sessions."

To expand their understanding of the concept of leadership in education, the participants also took part in a collaborative activity called "The Marshmallow Challenge," in which they worked together to build a small structure out of unusual elements. Later reflecting on this, some participants acknowledged that their teaching practices were devoid of group work and activities, since they had the perception that teaching was the exclusive domain of instructors without the involvement of students. One participant summed it up as follows:

The participatory approach of learning helps the individual students to demonstrate their innate skills of creativity and innovation. Now I believe that involving students in group activities helps the students to take the lead and it provides a forum for the students to socialize with each other, which I think is one of the objectives of education. (Participant 5, Faculty Development Session, KIU)

The third session was conducted by four senior professors visiting from the University of Utah, USA. This two-day training focused on the following: (1) effective teaching; (2) use of teaching technologies; (3) curriculum development and improvement; (4) research management; (5) writing boot camps; and (6) academic governance. The duration of each session was two to three hours and 12 instructors (mid-career level) participated.

All of the participants expressed their satisfaction regarding the expertise of the session facilitators and the content selected for the workshop, in which many new ideas in terms of teaching and research were presented. As one participant explained:

Our knowledge and information about the usage of internet and computer was severely limited, but the training session expanded our knowledge about concepts such as the blended classroom and online learning. (Participant 6, Faculty Development Session, KIU)

326   A. Khan et al.

Another attendee immediately applied a technique introduced in the session:

> When I came back, I did some research to further expand my understanding of the said concept of the flipped classroom ... now I have started practicing the flipped classroom method which is an interesting experience for me. ... I ask the students to watch a brief video lecture at home before the classes and in class we discuss, review, and critique whatever they have viewed. (Participant 7, Faculty Development Session, KIU)

Other participants commented that one of the advantages of engaging foreign experts for professional development activities was that it provided an opportunity to compare practices: "It is essential to study the best practices of other countries as we experienced in this session. ... [W]e came to know about the culture of the American classroom, their teaching approaches." Another opined that Pakistani teaching approaches, as compared to teaching in American classrooms, are primarily teacher-centered, with limited emphasis on developing critical thinking skills. He suggested multiple reasons why these elements might be missing; one reason, he elaborated, was their teaching load, which prevented them from being more productive and innovative in their teaching practices.

Discussion

Instructor quality is one factor affecting student learning that is under the control of an institution (Bensimon, 2007; Yeh, 2009). In spite of competing workload requirements, faculty must help students navigate academic challenges (Hande et al., 2016). Student achievement gaps may be attributed to "cognitive and non-cognitive experiences, which can be compounded by institutional cultures and conditions that do not promote these students' success, as well as by faculty members' lack of teaching [preparation]" (Gillian-Daniel & Kraemer, 2015, 32).

At KIU, the coordinator of faculty development carefully planned activities to address faculty and student challenges. Research was conducted to identify faculty and student needs and present strategies for determining and implementing faculty development and support (Hande et al., 2016). Substantial planning led to an intentionality with regard to the implementation of a faculty development program for this specific context. This included the mentorship received by the coordinator, enhanced support, and the decision to involve stakeholders at various stages. In this "Age of the Networker," faculty developers are often "called upon to preserve, clarify, and enhance the purposes of the faculty development, and to network with faculty and institutional leaders to respond to institutional problems and propose constructive solutions as we meet the challenges" (Sorcinelli et al., 2006, 28).

The visiting professors and the KIU coordinator of faculty development were instrumental in delivering high-quality sessions focused on the effect of faculty instructional development on students' learning to improve courses. The initial programming involved single events and then multi-day events offered by center staff, additional faculty, and external faculty to meet articulated needs for development across faculty types (i.e., lecturer), ranks (i.e., assistant, associate, full professor), and years of experience (i.e., novice, mid-career, senior). Although the process involved extensive faculty engagement (Hande et al., 2016), support from KIU leadership resulted in high-quality, and necessary, faculty development activities.

The Benefits of International Collaboration for Faculty Development

The 'twinning' arrangement (Altbach & Knight, 2007, 294) between the director of the TEP at UO and the coordinator of faculty development at KIU was notable. Among other details, the network developed through the partnership helped the coordinator of the newly established CHRD clarify the vision of the center, identify issues, and make decisions. Each of these was a critical component in building an effective program (Gillespie & Robertson, 2010). Throughout the process, understanding the institutional culture of the partnership institution was just as important as understanding the culture of the institution wherein the new center was to be established.

Lee et al. (2011) note that communication across cultures is one of the main characteristics of a meaningful exchange program as part of an international collaboration. Given the full professional "toolkit" of academic development (i.e., techniques, experiences, ideas, values, theories), a specific approach was tailored for the development and implementation of an ADC in Pakistan. In doing so, elastic practice characterized by Carew et al. (2008) was demonstrated by an understanding of the necessary stages and approaches (e.g., needs assessment, FGDs) used to collect data that informed the design and delivery of programs specifically to benefit faculty at the Pakistani institution. In essence, the mode of engagement of the collaboration was elastic in nature and adapted to the requirements and culture of an international context (Lee et al., 2011).

It must be emphasized that the American university also benefitted from the international partnership. The director of UO's TEP, who served as mentor to the visiting KIU coordinator of faculty development, reported the experience as having "a positive impact" on the UO center:

> It was fascinating to learn about a very different institutional context, with different kinds of levers to pull to elevate teaching and a blank slate on which to craft the founding documents of KIU's teaching development center. (Director, TEP, UO)

She found particularly interesting the process of drafting descriptions of the role of department heads for the new KIU center, "articulating the specific and crucial role they play in setting a culture where teaching is valued," as well as the discovery that top administrators at KIU strongly supported not only the new center, but in making parts of its curriculum mandatory for faculty. This presented to her "a rare and unusual opportunity" to reflect on the core objectives of an ADC and its status on campus. Cook-Sather (2018) explains that international and intercultural development projects allow academics to "re-interpret our identities, positions, and power and how all of those inform the ways we work together in educational contexts" (5). The director of the TEP described her counterpart from Pakistan as "a wise and refreshing colleague who helped me think outside the limits of my own institutional context and toward some first principles about what matters most in our shared work."

Especially powerful effects were experienced by UO faculty who were able to travel to Pakistan. The word "transformational" was used by several team members who visited the KIU campus. Cruz and Parker (2018), in their introduction to *Rethinking the Scholarship of Global Partnerships: The Next Chapter*, prepare readers to move beyond the usual "paradigm of personal growth" (and the theme of the traveling academic as a kind of hero) toward more complex notions emerging from struggling with problems that may not be solved and discovering new approaches to thinking, functioning, and interacting. Cruz et al. (2018) highlight the intense personal impact of educational development abroad: "[W]e each found a part of our experiences to be deeply moving, transcendent, and, at times, even ineffable" (8). One UO faculty member, who had previously had little knowledge of Pakistan prior to the collaboration, visited the KIU campus three times and later made repeated trips to Pakistan to work on faculty development at other universities. For her, working with KIU was "life-changing" and inspired not only new ways of approaching professional tasks but shifted her whole notion of how the world works and her place within it.

Implications for Faculty Development in Emerging Higher Education Contexts

Given the success of the international partnership described in this chapter, as well as the resulting ADC and programming, the authors encourage others to use a comparable approach to faculty development in similar contexts. For the best potential international collaboration, it is appropriate to consider the questions raised by Altbach and Knight (2007), as well as their concerns about quality assurance and recognition in international partnerships. This remains salient for future partnerships and network arrangements, which are rapidly growing more prevalent. In this case, "periodic and ongoing collegial discussion about the detail and bases [of faculty development practice]" was helpful in terms of promoting elasticity (Carew et al., 2008, 4). In particular, for the development of ADCs in other emerging higher education contexts, we encourage "prompted reflective [thinking] and writing on the theoretical, philosophical and value bases of our accustomed approach to designing and delivering workshops" to promote elastic practice.

Conclusion

Increasingly, "academic developers from institutions and countries with established educational development programs and networks [are] being called upon to share their expertise and offer guidance to colleagues in emerging higher education contexts" (Lee et al., 2011, 2). This chapter makes visible the careful planning and articulation of embedded philosophies, pedagogical knowledge, and belief systems of faculty served by initial programming efforts at one institution involved in an international partnership.

References

Ali, A., Tariq, R. H., & Topping, K. J. (2013). Perspectives of academic activities in universities in Pakistan. *Journal of Further and Higher Education, 37*(3), 321–348.

Altbach, P. G., & Knight, J. (2007). The internationalization of higher education: Motivations and realities. *Journal of Studies in International Education, 11*(3/4), 290–305.

Bensimon, E. M. (2007). The underestimated significance of practitioner knowledge in the scholarship on student success. *The Review of Higher Education, 30*(4), 441–469.

Carew, A. L., Lefoe, G., Bell, M., & Armour, L. (2008). Elastic practice in academic developers. *International Journal for Academic Development, 13*(1), 8, 51–66.

Cook-Sather, A. (2018). Perpetual translation: Conveying the languages and practices of student voice and pedagogical partnership across differences of identity, culture, position, and power. *Transformative Dialogues: Teaching & Learning Journal, 11*(3).

Cruz, L., Manginelli, A., Michele, A., & Strahlman, H. (2018). Historia reimagined: Storytelling and identity in cross-cultural educations development. *Transformative Dialogues: Teaching & Learning Journal, 11*(3).

Cruz, L., & Parker, M. (Eds.). (2018). Rethinking the scholarship of global partnerships: The next chapter. *Transformative Dialogues: Teaching & Learning Journal, 11*(3).

Gillespie, K. J., & Robertson, D. L. (2010). *A guide to faculty development* (2nd ed.). Jossey-Bass.

Gillian-Daniel, D. L., & Kraemer, S. B. (2015). Faculty development to address the achievement gap. *Change: The Magazine of Higher Learning, 47*(6), 32–41.

Hande, K., Beuscher, L., Allison, T., & Phillippi, J. (2016). Navigating DNP student needs: Faculty advising competencies and effective strategies for development and support. *Nurse Education, 42*(3), 147–150.

Kruss, G., McGrath, S., Petersen, I., & Gastrow, M. (2015a). Creating world-class universities: Implications for developing countries. *Prospects, 43*, 233–249.

Kruss, G., McGrath, S., Petersen, I., & Gastrow, M. (2015b). Higher education and economic development: The importance of building technological capabilities. *International Journal of Education Development, 43*, 22–31.

Lee, V. S., DeZure, D., Debowski, S., Ho, A., & Li, K. (2011). Enhancing international collaboration among academic developers in established and emerging contexts: Moving toward a post-colonial perspective. *International Journal for Academic Development, 18*(1), 89–103.

McLean, M., Cilliers, F., & Vanwyk, J. (2009). Faculty development: Yesterday, today and tomorrow. *Journal of Medical Teacher, 30*(6), 55–84.

Meizlish, D. S., Wright, M. C., Howard, J., & Kaplan, M. L. (2017). Measuring the impact of a new faculty program using institutional data. *International Journal for Academic Development, 23*(2), 72–85.

Rathbun, G. A., Leatherman, J., & Jensen, R. (2017). Evaluating the impact of an academic teacher development program: Practical realities of an evidence-based study. *Assessment & Evaluation in Higher Education, 42*(4), 548–563.

Raza, S. A., & Naqvi, S. A. (2011). Quality of Pakistani university graduates as perceived by employers: Implications for faculty development. *Journal of Quality and Technology Management, 7*(1), 57–67.

Sorcinelli, M. D., Austin, A. E., Eddy, P. L., & Beach, A. L. (2006). *Creating the future of faculty development: Learning from the past, understanding the present.* Anker Press.

Stufflebeam, D. L. (1971). The relevance of the CIPP evaluation model for educational accountability. *Journal of Research and Development in Education, 5*(1), 19–25.

Yeh, S. S. (2009). The cost-effectiveness of raising teacher quality. *Educational Research Review, 4*(3), 220–232.

21

Quality, Teaching, and Learning: A Networked Approach Across Pakistan and East Africa

Tashmin Khamis and Zeenar Salim

Introduction

Established in 1983, the Aga Khan University (AKU) positions itself as "a university of and for the developing world" (Office of the Provost, 2014). Operating across three continents, six countries, and 13 teaching sites, there is no university in the world that functions quite like AKU. Guided by its four core principles of quality, access, relevance, and impact, AKU functions as one single, global university with integrated campuses distributed across Pakistan, Kenya, Tanzania, Uganda, and the UK. Thus, while meeting the regulatory requirements of each national context, AKU is governed by one Chancellor (His Highness, the Aga Khan), one Board of Trustees, one president, and one provost.

As stated in its mission, AKU aims to enable the "development of human capacities through discovery and dissemination of knowledge, and application through service" primarily in developing countries, and does so by "offer[ing] programs of international quality; prioritizing teaching and

---

T. Khamis (✉)
Aga Khan University, Karachi, Pakistan
e-mail: tashmin.khamis@aku.edu

Z. Salim
Syracuse University, Syracuse, NY, USA
e-mail: zsalim@syr.edu

© The Author(s), under exclusive license to Springer Nature Switzerland AG 2023
O. J. Neisler (ed.), *The Palgrave Handbook of Academic Professional Development Centers*,
Palgrave Studies on Leadership and Learning in Teacher Education,
https://doi.org/10.1007/978-3-030-80967-6_21

331

332 T. Khamis and Z. Salim

research that underpin intellectual innovation and change; and developing leaders through its educational programs" (AKU, n.d.-a). Despite its wide geographical spread, AKU remains a small, private, not-for-profit autonomous university with a merit-based, needs-blind admission process. Its student body numbers approximately 3,000, with an alumni force of 15,000 and a teaching faculty of around 500. A large staff complement of 13,000 supports the seven university hospitals, with current core disciplines in nursing, medicine, teacher education, Muslim cultures, and media and communications offered at both the undergraduate and graduate level (AKU, n.d.-b).

The university is part of the Aga Khan Development Network (AKDN)—one of the world's foremost development organizations whose scope encompasses health, education, community development, revenue-generating economic enterprise, and culture (AKDN, n.d.)—and thus serves as one of the organization's key human resource engines, impacting some seven million beneficiaries in the areas of health and education alone. In line with AKU's strategic imperatives of promoting excellence in teaching to strengthen the student learning experience, AKU established the integrated Networks of Quality, Teaching, and Learning (QTL_net) in 2013, encompassing the Network for Quality Assurance and Improvement (QAI_net) and the Network of Teaching and Learning (TL_net).

Rather than 'centers' of teaching and learning, these centrally led but geographically distributed support 'networks' were created in order to respond to the large geographic spread of AKU and to 'network' with academic departments (referred to hereafter as entities). Moreover, the QTL_net collaborates with existing educational development, library, information technology, and student support units to promote improvement in the learning environment and strengthen the student experience. The integrated networks have a university-wide role across all geographic locations with the following broad aims:

* The TL_net aims to advocate for teaching and support faculty with ongoing continuous educational development in the areas of pedagogy and curriculum, through short courses, workshops, and mentorship. Within the TL_net, the Network of Blended and Digital Learning is tasked with improving instructional quality through the uptake and application of information and instructional technologies and associated pedagogies across AKU's academic programs.
* The QAI_net aims to harmonize and standardize AKU-wide quality assurance (QA) policy and procedures, initially for the periodic review of exist-

ing programs, but also for the establishment of new programs and later for academic unit reviews.

Thus, the QTL_net supports academic entities and faculty by promoting a high-quality learning experience for its students through excellence in teaching and program delivery, in line with AKU's goals to be a research-led and student-centered university. Despite being located largely in Asia and Africa, our belief is that "We can quite reasonably strive to create a teaching and learning environment that rivals that of any university in the world" (Office of the Provost, 2014).

Theoretical Underpinnings

Centers for excellence in teaching and learning are developed to improve the quality and status of teaching and learning in higher education. The goals and activities of such centers have evolved over decades from providing remediation for faculty who are struggling or receiving poor evaluations on their teaching, to developing a community of practice focusing on the enhancement of quality of teaching and learning (Forgie et al., 2018; Gibbs, 2013). Beach et al. (2016) conducted a survey of 385 faculty developers who identified themselves as directors or coordinators of such centers and who were invited to participate through the listservs of the Professional and Organizational Development Network, Historically Black Colleges and Universities Faculty Development Network, and Society for Teaching and Learning in Higher Education. The findings indicated an increasing importance attached to the following three goals in educational development: (a) to create and/or sustain a culture of teaching excellence (75%); (b) to advance new initiatives in teaching and learning (57%); and (c) to provide support to individual faculty for their professional development (29%) (Beach et al., 2016).

Realizing the importance of collaboration among various stakeholders (such as teaching centers, academic departments, libraries, technology support services, research offices, and student support services) for fostering a culture of quality, teaching, and learning, the authors named this age in educational development the 'Age of Network' (Beach et al., 2016). Networked approaches enable these centers to foster the culture of QA and teaching and learning (QTL) required for sustainable changes in practices, priorities, and policies in order to improve, reward, and recognize scholarly and evidence-based teaching and learning (Sutherland, 2018). In light of the huge geographic spread of AKU and its interdependence of departments, a networked approach to supporting QTL was deemed the most viable approach compared to setting up a single teaching support center.

Background of the QTL_net

In January 2013, the AKU provost announced the establishment of two integrated networks—one for QA (the QAI_net) and the other for teaching and learning (the TL_net)—under the Office of the Provost, and appointed a director responsible for both networks. Consultations were initially conducted with entity heads and program directors to introduce the concept of the networks and seek input from senior leadership. Academic heads and program directors also appointed resource persons for both networks.

Resource persons for the TL_net were volunteer faculty members who had shown excellence in teaching or the scholarship of teaching and learning (SoTL), while those for the QAI_net were faculty or staff who would champion the process of self- and peer assessment of programs in their faculties. Participatory workshops were conducted for these individuals to raise awareness of best practices and create a common language of QTL at AKU. These resource persons built ownership of QTL processes and policies by participating in professional educational development programs, sharing learning resources, conducting needs assessments, and championing QA practices and teaching excellence within respective entities (Khamis, 2013).

Complementarity Between QTL

Over the last three decades, the field of educational development worldwide has grown exponentially, although not so much in the African and Asian regions where AKU is based. Nevertheless, there has only been cursory mention of how this field can be inclusive of faculty development, leadership development, and support for QTL (Rae, 2005; Scott & Scott, 2013). In this regard, the integration of the QAI_net and TL_net into the combined QTL_net is innovative, not only within Pakistan and East Africa, but on a more global scale.

The integration of the QA and teaching networks has had two key benefits. First, the focus has remained on support and enhancement, with initial suspicions and apprehensions regarding the role of the QAI_net being about 'quality control' having dissipated and no resistance from academic entities called upon to conduct their QA reviews. Second, it allows for the TL_net to nimbly respond to the improvement areas highlighted by external peer reviewers, which overwhelmingly relate to teaching and learning. Thus, this integration of the two networks has ensured that the focus remains on *improvement* in QA and teaching by enabling the support structure to be viewed not as 'punitive,' but rather as a community to which to belong in order to demonstrate a commitment to enhancing teaching practices and strengthening the learning experience.

Organizational Positioning and Geographical Locations

As the tradition of educational development and QA in higher education is nascent in the geographical locations in which AKU exists, the hiring of educational developers, instructional designers, and e-learning developers was not an option. Rather, developing the capacity of the resource persons and other faculty champions was deemed to be a more cost-effective and sustainable strategy and helped in advocating the work across the wider academy.

Currently, the QTL_net is led by a vice provost who reports directly to the provost. The network team plays a global role, working through technology and traveling across geographical boundaries to offer programs across the AKU campuses. The network staff in Kenya (n = 4) has a physical space in the Office of the Provost in Nairobi; however, staff in Karachi, Pakistan, are distributed between the workstations at the Office of the Provost (n = 3) and the Institute for Educational Development (n = 2), our school of teacher education.

As a newly established unit, a flexible approach with a distributed team encouraged receptivity to the services of the educational development unit and strengthened perceptions that the QTL_net team had made an effort to go to the faculty and deans to provide support. However, as the networks have built momentum, there is a need for more centralized space in a main campus building near the majority of our faculty and other support services. The lack of such a space creates inefficiencies, hampering synergies and productivity as faculty now struggle to find unit members to consult with, and do not have a place from which to access educational development resources. Management have been supportive in ensuring that the QTL_net unit is now included in the planning of new campuses and have space in libraries so that they can be viewed as a resource for faculty and students in their learning.

Policies and Frameworks

The QAI_net and TL_net developed frameworks to guide and harmonize QTL practices across AKU campuses. The AKU Academic Quality Framework (policy no. 30) guides the processes of self- and peer assessment of programs as a lever to improve the quality of teaching, learning, and curriculum in order to improve the students' learning experience (Harvey, 2002; Knight, 2002). The QAI_net engages the administration, faculty, and students in assessment of the quality of the program, identifying areas of improvement with resulting action plans.

The QA processes were developed after considering the requirements of the regulatory bodies in countries where our campuses are located, including the Quality Assurance Manual for Higher Education in Pakistan; the Quality Assurance Agency's Recognition Scheme for Educational Oversight; and the Inter-University Council for East Africa's (IUCEA) Road Map to Quality, itself a combined initiative of three government commissions, namely the Kenyan Commission for University Education, Ugandan National Commission for Higher Education, and Tanzanian Commission on Universities (IUCEA, 2015). The principles of the framework are that quality rests with the program and ownership must belong to those implementing the program (Biggs & Tang, 2011; Harvey, 2002; QAA, 2012). This ensures that the focus is on quality enhancement and improvement, and not on control (AKU, 2015).

In turn, the AKU Teaching and Learning Framework (policy no. 31) defines excellent teaching by benchmarking against Chickering and Gamson's (1987) highly cited seven principles of teaching and learning and identifying the attributes of AKU graduates through extensive university-wide consultations (Gibbs, 2013). In addition, it explains the need for and effectiveness of faculty development services providing support and reward mechanisms to develop a culture of excellent teaching at various levels of the organization, ranging from individual faculty members and course teams to entire departments and the university at large (Gibbs, 2013).

These frameworks complimentarily advocate for the engagement of faculty and staff members in assuring and improving the quality of programs through reflective practice, scholarship, and professional educational development. Moreover, the networks follow the principles of being evidence-based and needs-driven to create ownership, accountability, and continuous improvement in a safe and non-judgmental space (Scott & Scott, 2013). A recent impact review upon completion of our first five-year strategic plan concluded that

> [The QTL_net has been] remarkably successful in raising the profile of the importance of teaching and learning within AKU in a very short amount of time. The number of faculty who have taken advantage of the programs offered through the TL_net and who have very positive outcomes based on their experience is exceptional. (Unpublished external peer review report, 2019)

Program and Services, Including Reward and Recognition

In order to meet the overarching goals of AKU—to be a research-led and student-centered university upholding its commitment to excellence in its academic programs and to providing the best possible learning experience for its students (Office of the Provost, 2014)—and guided by the principles of quality, relevance, access, and impact, the QTL_net offers complementary programs and services in the areas of QA and faculty professional development. Through implementation of the AKU Academic Quality Framework, reviews are performed to identify areas requiring strengthening across the program, including curriculum review, stakeholder input, support for innovative pedagogies, strengthening of feedback, graduate supervision, and mentorship for new faculty members.

Addressing these areas, the TL_net planned and conducted workshops on pedagogical and instructional skills. These include the Instructional Skills Workshop (ISW), since renamed as the Teaching Learning Enhancement Workshop (TLEW), the Rethinking Teaching Workshop (RTT) focusing on course redesign, and the Blended Learning Faculty Development Program, as well as other initiatives, such as the graduate supervision program, faculty induction program, support mechanisms for curriculum review, use of a virtual learning environment (Moodle), and engagement in teaching with technology. In addition, the TL_net provides opportunities for faculty to engage in SoTL by organizing conferences and institutionalizing a competitive grant for SoTL projects at the university, including publication opportunities (Rodrigues et al., 2019).

The TL_net has also created reward mechanisms for excellent teaching through Teaching Enhancement Accredited Certification of the Higher Education Academy (TEACH) fellowships, a continuous professional development (CPD) scheme formally accredited by Advance HE in the UK—with

AKU being the first university in the developing world to ever achieve this accreditation. Designed and led by the TL_net, the TEACH CPD scheme enables AKU to award highly coveted and internationally recognized Higher Education Academy (HEA) fellowships and associate fellowships to its faculty and staff involved in faculty development who benchmark their teaching and educational development practices against the UK Professional Standards Framework (UKPSF), the only national framework in the world dedicated to supporting the development of teaching and learning staff in higher education. Participation in the TEACH CPD scheme is voluntary but we hope irresistible to faculty as a result of their being awarded a recognized teaching qualification in higher education. As the pool of accredited HEA fellows grows at AKU, it is envisaged that these teaching mentors will engage further with the delivery of QTL_net programs, activities, and resources and provide a sustainable resource for enhancing teaching and educational development at the university.

Recently, the QTL_net also established a Teachers Academy at AKU that aims to develop a community of HEA teaching fellows who have been recognized for their teaching excellence and who mentor other faculty through the activities of the TL_net to enhance teaching quality, the status of teachers, and SoTL. Membership in this academy is pegged to the UKPSF and the resulting criteria for HEA fellowships to ensure an open peer-review process benchmarked against international standards of teaching excellence; thus, senior fellowship with the HEA and demonstrable commitment toward teaching excellence are included in the eligibility criteria for membership. Members of the Teachers Academy are expected to serve the university by mentoring their peers and serving as members of committees that provide faculty with grants, travel scholarships, and teaching awards. We envisage that this academy fosters a more networked and communal effort toward sustaining the quality of teaching and learning at AKU.

Impact

Faculty Reach

Faculty reach is defined as the number of faculty who have accessed QTL programs/services at least once. Based on our data, the integrated networks have reached 60% of AKU faculty across all campuses, with two-thirds of faculty returning for more, particularly to the TL_net which has the most flagship courses. These results can be used as an indicator of the perceived value-add of the networks. Overall, demand and reach have far surpassed our expectations, particularly when benchmarking to other educational development units in our partner universities in Canada, which report a reach of 15–20% of their faculty after 20–40 years of existence. It should be noted that our Academic Council requires compulsory participation from all faculty in the TLEW and Virtual Learning Environment introductory course, which of course enhances our reach. The difficulty, though, is coping with the demand in an effective and sustainable manner in view of the 'lean team' that make up the three networks; in this regard, the importance of the HEA fellowship program and Teachers Academy is highlighted.

Faculty Satisfaction

While end-of-workshop evaluations are often dismissed as 'happy sheets,' MacCormack (2018) shows that faculty satisfaction is actually the first step toward changes in practice, and when faculty find a professional development activity 'relevant' they are more likely to apply their learning in practice.

Post-workshop evaluations of the flagship programs revealed that the faculty was satisfied with the quality of programs when evaluated immediately after the program offering (see Fig. 21.1). In order to triangulate the data captured immediately after these workshops with satisfaction after a time lapse after participation, an online faculty satisfaction survey (FSS) for all AKU faculty was conducted between September and October 2018, within

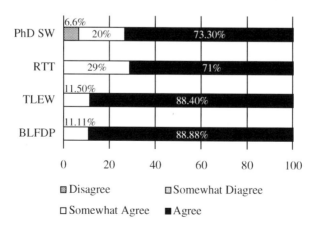

Fig. 21.1 Immediate satisfaction with QTL initiatives among participants

1–3 years of attendance at a flagship course (see Fig. 21.2). Despite the time lag, the programs were still rated as highly satisfactory by the faculty. Interestingly, in one case (the RTT course redesign workshop), the program was rated even more highly several months after the course. This implies that even after going back to their teaching practice, faculty found these programs relevant to their teaching and learning, and hence were more likely to implement innovation in their practice.

Five years after the establishment of the QTL_net, the faculty self-reported a higher use of active learning pedagogies (an increase of 14%) and a 7% reduction in lecturing. This was confirmed in the FSS, in which those who had attended QTL_net programs confirmed that they were more likely to plan their lessons and use technology in teaching (see Fig. 21.3). These findings may explain why almost all of the QTL_net workshops are regularly oversubscribed.

Factors Accelerating the Change Process

The networks were faced with a huge task of change management—to create centralized support services for academic units in the integrated areas of quality enhancement and educational development for faculty. In order to challenge the expected hesitation and, indeed, resistance from academic units out of a fear of centralized control, much consultation had to be done to ensure

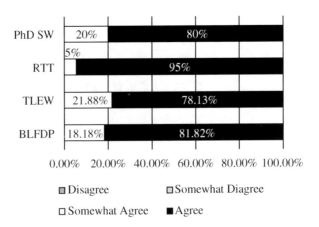

Fig. 21.2 Impact of QTL initiatives on knowledge and conceptions of teaching and learning after 1 to 3 years

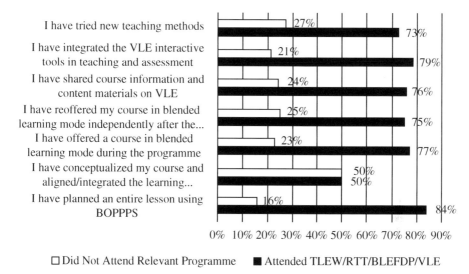

Fig. 21.3 Comparison of teaching practices according to QTL_net program attendance after 5 years

that the support was seen to add value by being needs-based, promoting improvement rather than being punitive in nature, and creating safe, non-judgmental, and inclusive spaces for faculty. As mentioned in the unit review, the large faculty reach attained over a short period of time (60% in five years) is unprecedented. Factors that have enabled this uptake are explained below.

Creating Buy-in Through Consultations

An initial discussion paper regarding the establishment of the QTL_net was distributed across all levels of the Teaching Academy (Khamis, 2013), followed by consultations with resource persons and teaching champions across all departments. These group discussions provided an opportunity for faculty, staff, and students to provide their input on the conceptualization of the networks; one example is that the title "QA officers" was changed to "QA resource persons" to avoid a 'policing' connotation. Special care was taken to establish a balance between accountability and improvement (Vroeijenstijn, 1995), with emphasis being placed on self-regulation, internal QA, and ownership of improvement plans. Those in support of the networks also endorsed engagement in the self- and peer-review mechanisms, establishment of local buy-ins, practices benchmarked against international best practices, and engagement of the university faculty and administration in QA and faculty development areas, so that the networks could result in "learning, dialogue and improvement" (Harvey, 2002; Knight, 2002; Lemaitre, 2014).

Evidence-Based Practice

At AKU, the QTL_net promotes evidence-based and contextually relevant practice with both the Teaching and Learning Framework and Academic Quality Framework carefully developed through consultations and benchmarking against good practices in higher education within relevant contextual realities (Biggs & Tang, 2011; Chickering & Gamson, 1987; Gibbs, 2013; Harvey, 2002; Quality Assurance Agency for Higher Education [QAA], 2012). Not only are the adopted policies and frameworks rooted in strong theoretical foundations, but also the practices implemented exemplify best practices. For example, the contextual adaptation of tried and tested programs was institutionalized, such as the Canadian Instructional Skills Workshop, renamed as the TLEW (Dawson et al., 2014; Macpherson, 2014), and the RTT course redesign workshop (Amundsen et al., 2008; Saroyan & Amundsen, 2004).

To ensure their contextual relevance, each of the programs and services was evaluated using measures such as post-workshop evaluation, small-scale research studies (Khamis & Chapman, 2017; Khamis & Dhamani, 2017; Khamis & Scully, 2020; Rodrigues et al., 2019), and testimonials to identify areas of improvement in the design and delivery of each program. Moreover, in order to "practice what we preached," the QTL_net engaged in a unit review after its first five-year strategic plan following the self- and peer-review process conducted in early 2019 to assess its outcomes.

Mentoring: Learning from the Experience of Others

While these areas of teaching and learning support may have been new to AKU, they certainly were not among our partner universities, and hence a conscious decision was made not to "reinvent the wheel," but to adapt and contextualize good practices from elsewhere. The TL_net collaborated with Academics Without Borders (AWB) and recruited experienced volunteer staff, including educational developers, to work with the team to support the development of QTL frameworks, strategic plans, QA processes, and faculty development programs focusing on technology-enhanced teaching and learning, course redesign, instructional skills, and so forth. The volunteers mentored and built the capacity of QTL_net staff to be evidence-based and adopt good

Needs-Driven Support and Development

A needs-analysis survey was sent to all AKU faculty members in 2013 via e-mail, with 25% of faculty members responding to the survey and faculty representation from all entities at the university. The survey was conducted just after the launch of the QTL_net. When faculty were asked about their current methods of teaching, a majority of the faculty shared that they predominantly used a lecture-based approach for teaching as this was the method they had themselves been taught. Faculty were also asked about their professional needs, with the results showing their top priorities to be student engagement, assessment, and SoTL. A repetition of these questions five years after establishment of the QTL_net revealed increasing realization among faculty of the need to engage students in teaching and learning (as evidenced by an increment of 22%).

Subsequent to the identification of needs through needs assessment surveys and program reviews, the findings were presented to deans and program heads and next steps were mutually decided upon. As with other academic development units (Knapper, 2016), the QTL_net initially faced resistance from academic units reluctant to create a central mechanism due to a fear of centralized control. Being needs-based and consultative enabled ownership and perception of the QTL_net to shift to a support service, providing a safe, nonjudgmental, and inclusive space for faculty, administration, and leadership to seek support and assure and improve the quality of teaching and learning (Aelterman, 2006; Biggs, 2003; Jordens & Zepke, 2009; Kanuka, 2010).

Faculty and Staff as Ambassadors of Academic Quality

The QTL_net engaged faculty, staff, and students in the process of program reviews as well as faculty development activities. The engagement of faculty and staff in co-planning and co-implementing QTL programs and services has been a lever for change as it creates buy-in and ownership and, as a result, encourages faculty champions who advocate for quality across the academy. These faculty champions have been trained through the completion of certified programs like the ISW Faculty Development Workshop and the HEA TEACH fellowship scheme. Faculty learn best through peer mentors, their fellow faculty champions, as they can exchange applicable, relevant, and practical examples of best practices from their classrooms (Geertsema & Bolander Laksov, 2019; van der Rijst et al., 2019). These faculty champions are housed in their respective entities which allows for the creation of a community of practice around 'signature pedagogies' where peer mentoring is offered as and when required.

Indeed, evaluations show that certain TL_net flagship courses that are *not* discipline-specific, such as the ISW and RTT course redesign workshops, are often the first time that faculty interact across disciplines and learn from each others' teaching approaches in a safe space where they are 'unknown' and hence more confident to try out new teaching methods. These workshops also help to dispel myths that "teaching is different in my discipline" and build a layer of trust, connections, as well as in-house support. Moreover, fellows in the Teachers Academy (as discussed previously) foster a community of practice where sustained peer-mentoring support is ensured. In addition, this community helps create awareness about QTL_net programs and services as teaching fellows advocate for other faculty to connect with the QTL_net to enhance academic quality.

Breaking the Silos of Discipline and Geography Through Building Partnerships: Quality Across the Academy

QTL_net programs and services invite faculty, staff, and students from all entities, disciplines, and geographical locations, hence creating an inclusive space for all to contribute to academic improvement. Other faculty support units are automatically resource units for the QTL_net, creating a community of practice and inclusion. By offering SoTL grants and conferences, encouraging faculty to design multidisciplinary SoTL projects, and conducting faculty development workshops and program review exercises for all disciplines and geographical locations, the integrated networks attempt to break the silos of disciplines and blur geographical boundaries to foster deep cross-geographical and cross-disciplinary connections, also emphasized by Gibbs (2013), as cited in Knapper (2016).

These inter-entity connections help AKU to function as 'one university,' providing a quality student experience across geographical locations. For example, to establish the generic graduate attributes, a consultation was held with all program directors to identify what each of the 23 programs at AKU, at that time, aimed to achieve for its students. A common set of graduate attributes was agreed upon. This enabled a discussion across our various campuses regarding how we were ascertaining that AKU graduates were actually meeting these learning outcomes, ensuring the standardization of an AKU degree from any of our geographic locations. The consequence of this was that faculty began questioning how they were actually ensuring their teaching was promoting these various competencies, such as leadership, critical thinking, problem-solving, effective communication, and lifelong learning (Bhutta et al., 2015).

A Safe and Non-Judgmental Space for Reflective and Scholarly Practice

Based on literature demonstrating that faculty learn best from their peers (Geertsema & Bolander Laksov, 2019; van der Rijst et al., 2019), the QTL_net engaged academic programs as well as their faculty and staff in the deliberate processes of peer learning, reflection, and self-assessment, as suggested by Billing (2004) and Knight (2002). For example, the QAI_net supports the program leadership, staff, and students in assessing their own programs and subsequently undergoing the process of peer review. On the other hand, the TL_net conducts workshops that do not provide 'one-shot' solutions for the problems of teaching, but engage faculty in active and collaborative learning experiences, exploring theoretical underpinnings, reflective practice, and self-assessment in interdisciplinary settings. Thus, principles of peer learning, reflection, and self-assessment help the QTL_net to create a safe, inclusive, and non-judgmental space, as stressed by Fyffe (2018). In his account, Fyffe (2018) enlightens educational developers to "help people develop their own judgement and make their own decisions about their teaching, research, and academic careers based on sound scholarly reasoning" (364).

A department chair, on completion of a cluster review, stated:

> Initially we felt threatened and defensive towards having to participate in the cyclical review process. However, as we went through the self-assessment process, the act of identifying our own issues means we are more likely to make the needed changes for improvement. It was a very useful process! (Participant, external peer review, Pakistan).

Another participant from a professional development workshop in East Africa reiterated how the 'safe space' engaged her in the experimentation of new teaching strategies, stating: "My confidence has increased as I moved along TLEW, not because I think I am perfect (definitely not), but I am more at

346   T. Khamis and Z. Salim

peace when trying out new things, even if these fail, since it becomes a learning opportunity." It is evident that the QTL_net acts much like a safe haven or 'the Switzerland of AKU,' by ensuring that the networks are the go-to place for support on QTL, rather than a punitive place.

Conclusion

Impact reviews have documented that, in a short span of five years, the QAI_net has supported more than half of all AKU programs with self- and peer assessments. Real changes for improvement have resulted, such as regular curriculum reviews, support for faculty in teaching, and the acknowledgment of students as partners in QA reviews. In addition, an overwhelming 60% of faculty have accessed TL_net services, with two-thirds even attending further TL_net faculty development activities. These numbers compare favorably with much older, more established teaching learning innovation centers elsewhere in the world, confirming the value-add of the programs and safe spaces created by the AKU QTL_net.

These impacts over a relatively short period were due to the timely and expert input of AWB mentors who have helped AKU to leapfrog development of support for quality enhancement and faculty teaching and align this support with best practices elsewhere. Indeed, it could be argued that, in setting up these new structures, AKU capitalized on opportunities that older universities have taken much longer to embrace; for example, accreditation for the professional recognition of teaching for AKU faculty through Advance HE fellowships is something that universities in North America are just beginning to think about.

The QTL_net's achievements have been enabled by various factors, including leadership support from the senior-most management cadres (i.e., the president, provost, and Board of Trustees); volunteer mentors (through the AWB) who have given of their time and expertise to leapfrog development by learning from others without reinventing the wheel; advisory bodies promoting lessons from good practice; a cohesive and committed team; faculty champions who serve and see the networks as their 'second home'; and consultation, consultation, consultation across all levels of the academy and with experts in the fields of quality, teaching, and technology in the higher education sector.

As pioneers of QTL units in the regions served by AKU, members of the QTL_net have had opportunities to influence policy and practice through further 'networking' and sharing lessons by being invited to serve on various regional and international boards related to quality and educational development, such as the Association for Faculty Enrichment in Learning and Teaching, the East African Higher Education Quality Assurance Network, and the International Network of Quality Assurance Agencies in Higher Education. Thus, the networked approach used by the QTL_net has positively influenced AKU as well as other institutions and networks outside of the university to promote quality teaching and learning in Asia and Africa.

References

Aelterman, G. (2006). Sets of standards for external quality assurance agencies: A comparison. *Quality in Higher Education, 12*(3), 227–233.

AKDN (n.d.). *Overview of the Aga Khan Development Network.* Aga Khan Development Network. https://d1zah1nkiby91r.cloudfront.net/s3fs-public/factsheets/AKDN-factsheet.pdf

Aga Khan University (AKU) (2015). *Academic Quality Framework: policies and procedures* (Policy No. 30). AKU. https://www.aku.edu/admissions/Documents/policy-quality-framework-030.pdf

Aga Khan University (AKU) (n.d.-a). *Our vision.* AKU. https://www.aku.edu/about/at-a-glance/Pages/our-vision.aspx

Aga Khan University (AKU) (n.d.-b). *AKU at a glance.* AKU. https://www.aku.edu/about/at-a-glance/Pages/home.aspx

Amundsen, C., Weston, C., & McAlpine, L. (2008). Concept mapping to support university academics' analysis of course content. *Studies in Higher Education, 33*(6), 633–652.

Beach, A. L., Sorcinelli, M. D., Austin, A. E., & Rivard, J. K. (2016). *Faculty development in the age of evidence: Current practices, future imperatives.* Stylus Press.

Bhutta, S. M., Khamis, T., & Notta, F. (2015). *Teaching and assessing critical thinking: the development of a learning outcomes project at the Aga Khan University* (Conference presentation), East African Higher Education Quality Assurance Network Conference AKU.

Billing, D. (2004). International comparisons and trends in external quality assurance of higher education: Commonality or diversity? *Higher Education, 47*(1), 113–137.

Biggs, J. (2003). *Teaching for quality learning at university.* Society for Research into Higher Education and Open University Press.

Biggs, J., & Tang, C. (2011). *Teaching for quality learning at university* (4th ed.). Society for Research into Higher Education and Open University Press.

Chickering, A., & Gamson, Z. (1987). Seven principles for good practice in undergraduate education. *American Association for Higher Education Journal, 39*, 2–7.

Dawson, D., Borin, P., Meadows, K. N., Britnell, J., Olsen, K., & McIntyre, G. (2014). *The impact of the instructional skills workshop on faculty approaches to teaching.* Higher Education Quality Council of Ontario.

Forgie, S. E., Yonge, O., & Luth, R. (2018). Centres for teaching and learning across Canada: what's going on? *The Canadian Journal for the Scholarship of Teaching and Learning, 9*(1).

Fyffe, J. M. (2018). Getting comfortable with being uncomfortable: A narrative account of becoming an academic developer. *International Journal for Academic Development, 23*(4), 355–366.

Geertsema, J., & Bolander Laksov, K. (2019). Turning challenges into opportunities: (re)vitalizing the role of academic development. *International Journal for Academic Development, 24*(1), 1–6.

Gibbs, G. (2013). Reflections on the changing nature of educational development. *International Journal for Academic Development, 18*(1), 4–14.

Harvey, L. (2002). The end of quality? *Quality in Higher Education, 8*(1), 5–22.

Inter-University Council for East Africa (IUCEA). (2015). *A road map to quality: Handbook for quality assurance in higher education: Combined volume 1 & 2: Guidelines for internal and external program assessment.* IUCEA. https://iucea. org/?mdocs-file=5698

Jordens, J. Z., & Zepke, N. (2009). A network approach to curriculum quality assessment. *Quality in Higher Education, 15*(3), 279–289.

Kanuka, H. (2010). Characteristics of effective and sustainable teaching development programs for quality teaching in higher education. *Higher Education Management and Policy, 22*(2), 1–14.

Khamis, T. (2013). *Office of the Provost discussion paper: AKU networks of teaching and learning and quality assurance and improvement.* Aga Khan University. https:// www.aku.edu/about/Provostoffice/Documents/2013%2011%2005%20 Networks%20of%20QA%20and%20Improvement%20and%20TLDP.pdf

Khamis, T., & Chapman, M. (2017). Reflections on an innovative mentoring partnership: Facilitators and inhibitors to success in faculty development. *Journal of Higher Education in Africa, 15*(1), 105–124.

Khamis, T., & Dhamani, K. (2017). Quality assurance self-assessment: A catalyst for the Aga Khan University. *Journal of Higher Education in Africa, 15*(1), 125–134.

Khamis, T., & Scully, S. (2020). Questioning the efficacy of quality assurance frameworks for teaching and learning: A case study from East Africa. *Quality in Higher Education, 26*(1), 3–13.

Knapper, C. (2016). Does educational development matter? *International Journal for Academic Development, 21*(2), 105–115.

Knight, P. T. (2002). The Achilles' heel of quality: The assessment of student learning. *Quality in Higher Education, 8*(1), 107–115.

Lemaitre, M. J. (2014). Quality assurance in Latin America. In *Quality assurance in higher education* (pp. 160–177). Palgrave Macmillan.

Macpherson, A. (2014). *The Instructional Skills Workshop as a transformative learning process* (Doctoral thesis). Simon Fraser University Faculty of Education. https:// wiki.ubc.ca/images/1/17/ISWasTransformativeThesis111117.pdf

Office of the Provost. (2014). *Setting strategic academic priorities: A university "of and for" the developing world*. Aga Khan University. https://www.aku.edu/about/Provostoffice/Documents/2014%2004%2003%20Strategic%20Priorites%20Document.pdf

Quality Assurance Agency for Higher Education (QAA). (2012). *The UK quality code for higher education, part B: Assuring and enhancing academic quality*. QAA.

Rae, B. (2005). *Ontario, a leader in learning: Report and recommendations*. Ontario Ministry of Colleges and Universities.

Rodrigues, S., Bhutta, S. M., Salim, Z., Chauhan, S., & Rizvi, N. (2019). Implementing a teaching and learning enhancement workshop at Aga Khan University: Reflections on the implementation and outcomes of an instructional skills workshop in the context of Pakistan. *SOTL in the South, 3*(1), 100–110.

Saroyan, A., & Amundsen, C. (2004). *Rethinking teaching in higher education: From a course design workshop to a faculty development framework* (1st ed.). Stylus Press.

Scott, D., & Scott, S. (2013). *Future trends in academic professional development*. University of Calgary. http://www.ucalgary.ca/provost/activities/iltp

Sutherland, K. (2018). Holistic academic development: Is it time to think more broadly about the academic development project? *International Journal for Academic Development, 23*(4), 261–273.

van der Rijst, R., Baggen, Y., & Sjoer, E. (2019). University teachers' learning paths during technological innovation in education. *International Journal for Academic Development, 24*(1), 7–20.

Vroeijenstijn, A. I. (1995). *Improvement and accountability: Navigating between Scylla and Charybdis. Guide for external quality assessment in higher education* (Higher Education Policy Series 30). Taylor and Francis.

22

Using Student Research Data to Shape the Teaching and Learning Activities of a New Academic Development Center in Turkey

Elif Bengu and Fatma Nevra Seggie

Introduction

According to the Higher Education Information Management System in Turkey, there were 207 higher education institutions in Turkey as of 2020, including 129 public institutions, 74 non-profit institutions run by foundations, and four foundation vocational schools (Higher Education Information Management System, 2021).[1] The Council of Higher Education (CoHE), established in 1981, is an institution that oversees all of these institutions and is responsible for "the strategic planning of higher education, coordination between universities, and, most importantly, establishing and maintaining quality assurance mechanisms" (CoHE, 2018, 1). Out of these 207 instititutions, around 12 have created mechanisms and built structures to further improve teaching and learning on their campuses. In other words, these institutions have established centers, units, or offices to provide support for teaching and learning in their institutions. For the purpose of this chapter, all units, offices, and centers will be referred to as *center*.

E. Bengu (✉)
Abdullah Gül University, Kayseri, Turkey
e-mail: elif.bengu@agu.edu.tr

F. N. Seggie
Boğaziçi University, Istanbul, Turkey
e-mail: nevra.seggie@boun.edu.tr

© The Author(s), under exclusive license to Springer Nature Switzerland AG 2023
O. J. Neisler (ed.), *The Palgrave Handbook of Academic Professional Development Centers*,
Palgrave Studies on Leadership and Learning in Teacher Education,
https://doi.org/10.1007/978-3-030-80967-6_22

351

352   E. Bengu and F. N. Seggie

Within this context, the aim of this chapter is to first describe the establishment, organizational structure, and activities of a new teaching and learning center at a public university in Turkey. The chapter then discusses its contributions to the university. Next, it displays the major findings of needs analysis research conducted with 80 students to explore students' needs for a better learning environment; these findings have been used as a support for the improvement of the center's actions. The chapter concludes with a critical discussion of the opportunities and challenges of the center within the context of the Turkish higher education system.

The Teaching and Learning Center

The academic professional development center (ADC) is located at a public university in the region of Anatolia, Turkey. According to the coordinator of the center (personal communication, October 15, 2018), the university was designed as a research university with the explicit vision and foundational purpose of contributing substantially to society and science. The coordinator of the center emphasizes that one cannot rely solely on research activities and that the institution needs to strengthen its education in order to achieve their goals (personal communication, October 15, 2018).

One of the missions of the university is to support faculty members on their way to better preparing their undergraduate students for the challenges of an ever-changing world (Sorcinelli, 2007). To achieve this aim, the center focuses on increasing the quality of teaching, thereby leading to an increase in student satisfaction (Bok, 2017). The center's other mission is to educate individuals who are eager to learn and share what they have learned to shape the future of the community (Ackoff & Greenberg, 2008; Kolb & Kolb, 2017). Thus, the ADC we describe in this chapter was established in 2016 to provide support for teaching and learning on campus (Hagner, 2001).

Mission of the Center

The establishment of the center can be viewed as one of the university's efforts to put its mission into practice in the 21st century. In addition to playing an active role in faculty development, the center aims to bring disciplines together and develop curricula according to the needs of the students and industry (Eskandari et al., 2007; Parsons & Taylor, 2011). It also aims to follow

Organization of the Center

The center consists of a coordinator, a statistician, and two graduate assistants (GAs). One of the GAs is a doctoral student in educational technology and provides support to faculty on the use of technology in their instruction. The other GA provides administrative and research support. Since the beginning of 2019, the center has reported to the advisor of the rector. In the fall semester of the 2018–2019 academic year, an education committee was established to serve as the university's advising body on educational matters. Since the spring of 2018, the coordinator of the center has shared with the committee important matters related to the functioning of the center, such as its evaluation process and planned activities.

Contributions of the Center

In accordance with its goals, the center aims to continue its contribution to the development, implementation, and evaluation of teaching and learning strategies relevant not only in the classroom but also out of the classroom. New attempts are made to highlight the value of teaching, learning, assessment, and research on campus. For example, at the end of the 2018–2019 academic year, a teaching award was given as a result of student surveys for the first time. The center has also undertaken other collaborations and initiatives to promote its activities, such as conference presentations and research projects, which are believed to contribute positively to the quality of education at the university.

The center also collaborates with the quality assurance committee of the university in the yearly reporting period, as well as with deans of the Student's Office in conducting orientation for the incoming students, and specific departments in designing rubrics for the assessment of the courses and internships. Additionally, it assists the library in conducting creative drama workshops for children.

Activities of the Center

The center, which is located on campus, organizes teaching and learning activities to support academic instruction in the departments and an orientation program for incoming full-time faculty members. The center also conducts impact research on the effectiveness of its own activities and faculty members' needs within the context of teaching and learning. In the center, foundational knowledge in the field of adult education and teaching and learning theories in various disciplines (e.g., engineering education) are used to help instructors facilitate teaching and learning. In addition, the center sees teaching as a scholarly practice. The coordinator of the center collaborates with the industrial and mechanical engineering departments to conduct research on instructional methods in those disciplines. With that notion, the center works with faculties to share their best teaching practices and publish their findings.

In addition, the coordinator of the center is an educator by training with a specialization in measurement and evaluation in education, and conducts student evaluations of teaching (SETs) at the end of each semester in the courses they have taken. Collecting SETs at the end of the semester is not mandated by the Turkish CoHE, although some universities in Turkey conduct SETs on their own initiative. However, while the objectives of these evaluations are consistent—for measuring teaching effectiveness and teaching quality as well as for decisions on hiring, promoting, and firing instructors (Boring et al. 2016)—their application methods may vary from one university to another. Students might be asked to fill out the SET to see their final grades or they might be asked to fill it out within the last week of the semester.

At our institution, the course evaluations are collected on paper in the last two weeks of the semester. Each course evaluation questionnaire includes 38 items that ask students to rate their perceptions of instructors and courses based on a 5-point Likert scale ranging from "strongly disagree" to "strongly agree" as well as four open-ended questions. The results of the SET are used to evaluate student satisfaction and explore ways to increase the quality of teaching. These evaluations have so far been collected for three consecutive semesters. On campus, the coordinator of the center receives active support from faculty secretaries to distribute the evaluations to the students. As of the 2018–2019 academic year, they also help the coordinator with data entry. Subsequently, the center coordinator shares the quantitative results of the 38 close-ended items in the evaluations with the instructors through their university account e-mail.

As for the qualitative data resulting from the students' answers to the four open-ended questions, instructors arrange a one-on-one meeting with the coordinator of the center on a voluntary basis the following semester. According to the center's records, 20% of instructors request a one-on-one meeting with the coordinator to discuss the written comments of the students and the SET results. The meeting usually takes between an hour and an hour and a half. Two weeks after the meeting, the coordinator checks with the instructor through e-mail and meets the instructor one-on-one again upon request. However, the coordinator of the center often faces challenges as a result of overseeing the administration of the evaluations and collection of the data. As an example, instructors and departments may take the results personally and some prejudices and biases toward the center occur. This leads to resistance from some faculty members when it comes to collaborating more closely with the center.

The questions used in the end-of-semester SET were prepared as a result of detailed work. The first author of this chapter conducted meetings with coordinators of teaching and learning centers at different universities, both in Turkey and abroad, and discussed potential problems and challenges of existing SETs in order to learn from their experiences and design questions that would highlight challenges commonly faced by other institutions. Students' evaluations of the same course taught by the same professor often vary based on individual student differences in knowledge, intelligence, motivation, and interest. These challenges were in line with a study conducted by Uttl et al. (2017). Other potential problems that may arise are student biases toward specific academic disciplines/fields of study, the instructor's gender or accent, grade expectations, classroom size, classmates, and class meeting time (Boring et al., 2016).

The evaluations were checked for validity and reliability several times by professionals in their field. The user-friendliness of the questions was also checked with students. Nevertheless, the center has received criticism regarding the results of the evaluations. The main criticism has been that the results were mainly based on the questions which heavily depended on quantitative items. In addition, the four open-ended questions were deemed to be insufficient to support the quantitative data because students did not always elaborate on the answers in detail. Theall and Franklin (2002) confirmed that many universities face this challenge.

So that the results could be explored further and in more detail, faculty members raised their wishes to also cross-check and triangulate the outcomes with qualitative data, and also to receive more detailed information in relation

356   E. Bengu and F. N. Seggie

to the data collected via evaluation forms. Accordingly, the center coordinator conducted a focus group study in September and October 2018.

Student Needs Analysis: A Qualitative Approach

Focus groups were conducted in Turkish and then translated into English for the purpose of this chapter. Each focus group meeting lasted 60 to 90 minutes. Eight focus groups were conducted with 80 undergraduate students (10 students from each of the eight departments of the university). Of these, 32 were female and 21 were fourth-year, 22 were third-year, and 37 were second-year students. To ensure anonymity, the students were given participant numbers ranging from 1 to 80 as reference numbers during the documentation of the data.

The interview protocol used in the focus group study is an adapted version of an interview protocol developed by one of the authors of this chapter with a research team for use in a previous study. In this interview protocol, in addition to the items assessing the students' demographics, questions were explored in three sections: (1) teaching practices and perspectives of their course instructors; (2) the students' needs for skills, materials, and management; and (3) the support/training they received from the university (see Table 22.1).

Table 22.1 Interview protocol

1. About teaching practices and perspectives:
a. Can you describe your typical class, 30 minutes into it?
b. What is your teacher doing?
c. What are you doing/thinking as a student?
d. Are there any constraints/boundaries in your courses that prevent you from doing what you want to do?
e. Are you happy or unhappy? What is working and not working?
2. About their needs for skills, materials, management, etc.:
a. What do you have and what do you need (materials, resources, incentive, etc.) to be able to learn?
b. What are three things that you wish your instructors would change in your class to facilitate learning and why?
c. What are three things that you wish to change about your learning style/ practice and why?
d. How have you tried to address those issues?
3. About their support/training experiences:
a. What type(s) of learning support have you received from your university?
b. What types of support do you wish the university provided?
c. What are the things that you are happy the university provides?

Reproduced with permission

22 Using Student Research Data to Shape the Teaching and Learning... 357

Data analysis included procedures of the constant comparative method (Merriam, 1998) and three main categories as the findings of the study appeared. These are the needs of the students from (a) the departments, (b) the instructors, and (c) the campus. The findings were first shared at a meeting at which all department heads were present. During this meeting, only general themes where shared. Following that meeting, the center coordinator had a series of one-on-one meetings with the department heads on a voluntary basis.

Findings

In this chapter, only findings related to the needs of students from their departments and their instructors are documented, since the needs of the students from their campus environment do not fall within the scope of the ADC of the institution in question. Findings incorporate the input received from both student evaluations and focus groups.

Needs of the Students from Departments

The results of the SET indicated a high rate of satisfaction with the school (score: 4.28 out of 5) and from all the departments that were included in the study. Likewise, the outcomes of the focus groups also highlighted that students generally felt satisfied with their departments. They were usually happy with the resources provided by departments and appreciated the open-door policy of the department heads and course instructors. One fourth-year female student highlighted the fact that "our department listens to us... they let us voice our opinions" (Participant 2). However, during the focus groups, students also expressed two specific needs from their departments to improve their academic learning: (1) a more systematic academic advising system; and (2) more effective methods of communication.

Recommendations for the improvement of the academic advising system included more frequent contact between students and their advisors. Their perceptions indicated desire for a system where they could remain in touch with their academic advisors throughout the semesters. A fourth-year female student explained: "I wish I had seen my advisor more often after the course selection session. I wish we had held meetings together during the semester" (Participant 49).

358 E. Bengu and F. N. Seggie

Students also expressed their needs for different methods of communication. One wish was for a departmental meeting. Specifically, students in general emphasized their desire to have more time together with their peers and academics in their departments to build better connections with one another and with their instructors.

Needs of the Students from Instructors

The results of the SET indicated a high-to-moderate level of satisfaction with instructors (score: 3.9 out of 5). Likewise, the results of the focus groups highlighted three main categories regarding students' perceived needs from the instructors: (1) better teaching assistant (TA) preparation; (2) more diverse use of teaching and learning methods; and (3) more effective use of the syllabi.

Most of the students in the focus groups indicated that TAs should be able to better collaborate with students and be better equipped with communication skills. They also thought that TAs did not seem to always be as fully prepared as they should when assisting learning. A second-year male student explained that sometimes TAs might indicate that they "did not have enough time to look at all of the questions" (Participant 42). Another, a second-year female student, explained:

> If I were a TA, I would make sure to come ready before standing in front of undergraduate students. I would not want to stand in front of the undergraduate students and not be able to, for example, solve the question. (Participant 48)

One other theme heavily emphasized by the students was a desire for various teaching and learning methods. Generally, while students were very pleased with the content competence of their instructors, they reported that they would like them to use fewer slides in the classroom. As explained by a fourth-year female student: "If an instructor uses 90 slides in one lecture in 45 minutes, the class becomes boring" (Participant 53). In addition, several students wished to be provided with opportunities where they could apply the knowledge they had learned. The aforementioned student indicated that: "If we are not provided with a platform to apply the knowledge, it will not stay permanently" (Participant 53). Similarly, a second-year male student explained that: "Based on the information that the instructor gives, I would like to see how I can apply that to a project, otherwise the information does not stay and will be forgotten" (Participant 58).

Most of the students emphasized that they learned better when their instructors used active teaching and learning methods in the classroom. They wanted their instructors to use the PowerPoint presentations as a tool, but not as the lecture itself. Rather than product-oriented, they wished their evaluation to be process-oriented where they could receive ongoing constructive feedback. Students also indicated that they would like to work on real-life projects that would make learning relevant to their life. A second-year female student explained: "If the instructor is doing his best to give us something with projects, that motivates me to come to his course" (Participant 20). Another second-year female student similarly stated that "courses should be conducted through active teaching and learning methods; slides should not be read [aloud]" (Participant 77).

One last point mentioned by some students was the more effective use of syllabi. Students mentioned that the syllabus distributed by course instructors at the beginning of the course should also include the kind of competencies expected by the end of the course and, in turn, instructors should follow the syllabus closely. A second-year female student supported this argument by reporting:

> Instructors think that we do not check the syllabus, on the contrary ... We do not want the syllabus to change frequently. Instead, we would like to know what kind of competencies we will have gotten by the end of the course. (Participant 10)

Discussion and Recommendations

The findings from both the student evaluations and focus groups indicate that the students' needs generally revolved around the professional development of both graduate students and faculty members as two emerging issues. The center has used the findings of this study as a support to further improve its operations and has identified three future actions.

First, it appears that there is a need for a GA support program. This is a program that is tailored to prepare GAs in their future roles as faculty members. This kind of program provides primarily doctoral students with opportunities to observe and experience faculty responsibilities in different types of institutions (Austin, 2002; Bok, 2017). As the first step toward such a program, based on the findings, the first action of the center was the decision to design a new graduate course titled *Principles of University Teaching and Learning*. This is a credit-based course required for all graduate students which aims to contribute to their preparation as future faculty. A second future action was to meet one-on-one with each department head and report the results of the course evaluations. Whereas these meetings had been conducted on a voluntary basis previously, the decision was made to make these meetings a requirement going forward. The third action was the decision to conduct departmental workshops on the fundamentals of teaching and learning. These workshops will be coordinated in such a way that the academic development center will work closely with each department and document their best teaching practices.

In addition to these three actions, one other aim of the center is to establish policy guidelines for the distribution and use of data collected through student evaluations or focus groups over the three consecutive years. The center would like to use formative data for classroom assessment and research and "allow formative evaluation to explore innovative techniques without the threat of failure" (Theall & Franklin, 2002, 53) for faculty members.

Concluding Remarks

The way this ADC operates and adapts itself in order to address the institutional weaknesses exposed in the findings of the needs analyses and assessments it conducts is a good example of how a new center can better develop itself and contribute to the improvement of teaching and learning on a campus. Future actions, when implemented, are believed to constitute a step forward toward creating a sustainable support mechanism for faculty members and GAs within the context of teaching and learning when needed.

In the long run, we expect that more and more higher education institutions in Turkey will establish teaching and learning centers. It is important to note that the role of these centers is not limited to conducting course evaluations at the end of the semesters. In the USA, for example, they can also provide support for existing faculty members by addressing the challenges of managing new and expanding faculty roles (Austin & Sorcinelli, 2013; Sorcinelli, 2007), support new faculty members in their orientation into the campus culture, and aid in the preparation of GAs for their future academic roles (Austin & Sorcinelli, 2013; Bergquist & Phillips, 2016).

According to related research in the field (Austin & Sorcinelli, 2013; Bergquist & Phillips, 2016; Sorcinelli, 2007), "student-centered teaching was identified as one of the top challenges" for higher education faculty (Austin & Sorcinelli, 2013, 92) that can be addressed by ADCs. Other challenges seem to be the integration of technology in teaching and learning processes as well as the assessment of learning outcomes (Austin & Sorcinelli, 2013). From this perspective, a well-built center in each higher education institution can be a great asset to overcome these challenges and contribute to the quality assurance mechanisms established by the CoHE within the context of teaching and learning.

Collecting data from two different sources (i.e., student evaluations and focus groups) was helpful to see and analyze the needs of the students and to cross-check the results, as some of the needs were visible in one of the sets of data but not the other. For example, the urgent need to provide support for TAs was not an issue raised in the student evaluations, but instead revealed itself in the focus group data.

We conclude by proposing that existing ADCs might consider opening channels for closer collaboration with one another. This would create significant opportunities to learn from one another due to the breadth and depth of expertise of each specific teaching and learning center. Furthermore, such a collaboration also has the potential to create a nationwide collaborative faculty development network in the future, which, in turn, would positively contribute to the improvement of university teaching and learning practice and research in Turkey.

Acknowledgments Permission to refer to and adapt the interview protocol used in this chapter's research was taken from the research team leader of the previous study in which the protocol was first developed.

Note

1. The reason we cannot give an exact number is that the Higher Education Information Management System only documents the statistics of active and passive research and application centers, and not individual units or offices. Looking at these statistics, we searched for "teaching and learning" separately and obtained a list of public and foundation institutions with the words "teaching", "learning", or "teaching and learning" only, and eliminated the ones that included the words "lifelong", "open", "distance", "micro-analysis", "social interaction", and "teacher". This left us with a total of seven active and passive research and application centers in seven higher education institutions. We also did a Google search with the terms "teaching and learning" and came across two more centers in Turkey which included "learning" in their title; however, these did not appear in our search in the Higher Education Information Management System. In addition, our Google search displayed three units or offices directly attached to the Rectorate in the organizational chart. Therefore, it is possible that some centers, units, or offices in Turkey were omitted which focus on supporting teaching and learning but operate under different names that do not include either of these words.

References

Ackoff, R. L., & Greenberg, D. (2008). *Turning learning right side up: Putting education back on track.* Prentice Hall.

Austin, A. E. (2002). Preparing the next generation of faculty: Graduate school as socialization to the academic career. *Journal of Higher Education, 73*(1), 94–122.

Austin, A. E., & Sorcinelli, M. D. (2013). The future of faculty development: Where are we going? *New Directions for Teaching and Learning, 2013*(133), 85–97.

Bergquist, W. H., & Phillips, S. R. (2016). Components of an effective faculty development program. *Journal of Higher Education, 46*(2), 177–211.

Bok, D. (2017). *The struggle to reform our colleges.* Princeton University Press.

Boring, A., Ottoboni, K., & Stark, P. B. (2016). Student evaluations of teaching (mostly) do not measure teaching effectiveness. *ScienceOpen Research.*

Council of Higher Education (CoHE). (2018). *History of the Council of Higher Education.* CoHE. http://www.yok.gov.tr/en/web/cohe/history

Eskandari, H., Sala-Diakanda, S., Furterer, S., Rabelo, L., Crumpton-Young, L., & Williams, K. (2007). Enhancing the undergraduate industrial engineering curriculum: Defining desired characteristics and emerging topics. *Education + Training, 49*(1), 45–55.

Hagner, P. R. (2001). *Interesting practices and best systems in faculty engagement and support.* National Learning Infrastructure Initiative. http://216.92.22.76/discus/messages/21/FD_Entrepenuers_vs__Second_Wave-1844.pdf

Higher Education Information Management System. (2021). *Current number of students by type.* Higher Education Information Management System. https://istatistik.yok.gov.tr

Kolb, A., & Kolb, D. A. (2017). Learning styles and learning spaces: Enhancing experiential learning in higher education. *Academy of Management Learning & Education, 4*(2), 193–212.

Merriam, S. (1998). *Qualitative research and case study applications in education.* Jossey-Bass.

Parsons, J., & Taylor, L. (2011). Improving student engagement. *Current Issues in Education, 14*(1).

Singer, S., & Smith, K. A. (2013). Discipline-based education research: Understanding and improving learning in undergraduate science and engineering. *Research Journal for Engineering Education, 201*(4), 468–471.

Sorcinelli, M. D. (2007). Faculty development: The challenge going forward. *Peer Review, 9*(4), 4–8.

Theall, M., & Franklin, J. (2002). Looking for bias in all the wrong places: A search for truth or a witch hunt in student ratings of instruction? *New Direction for Institutional Research, 2001*(109), 45–56.

Uttl, B., White, C. A., & Gonzalez, D. W. (2017). Meta-analysis of faculty's teaching effectiveness: Student evaluation of teaching ratings and student learning are not related. *Studies in Educational Evaluation, 54*(2017), 22–42.

23

Collaborative Faculty Development

Jordan Cofer, Denise Domizi, Marina Smitherman, Jesse Bishop, and Rod McRae

Introduction

The University System of Georgia (USG), USA, comprises 26 public colleges and universities in the State of Georgia, collectively governed by the Board of Regents. The USG's Consortium on Teaching and Learning (GA-CTL) was founded in 2007 and comprises directors or representatives from the centers for teaching and learning (CTLs) of USG institutions. The GA-CTL was established by the USG to "strengthen quality teaching and learning through the coordination of policies and programs that support faculty development across the University System of Georgia" (GA-CTL, 2008). In 2018, the GA-CTL was officially recognized as a USG Regents Advisory Committee.

Structure

Membership in the GA-CTL consists of one voting representative from each USG institution. Typically, this is the CTL director, their representative, or some other designee on campus who holds a leading role in faculty

---

J. Cofer (✉) • D. Domizi • M. Smitherman • J. Bishop • R. McRae
University System of Georgia, Atlanta, GA, USA
e-mail: jordan.cofer@gcsu.edu; denise.domizi@usg.edu;
msmitherman@daltonstate.edu; jebishop@highlands.edu; rmcrae@westga.edu

© The Author(s), under exclusive license to Springer Nature Switzerland AG 2023
O. J. Neisler (ed.), *The Palgrave Handbook of Academic Professional Development Centers*,
Palgrave Studies on Leadership and Learning in Teacher Education,
https://doi.org/10.1007/978-3-030-80967-6_23

development. A representative from the USG's Office of Academic Affairs serves as an ex-officio liaison between the system and the members. The liaison participates in all official GA-CTL activities, serves as a resource, and informs members of system initiatives with regard to faculty development. Recently, members elected to include a second non-voting representative from institutions where responsibility for faculty development is divided or shared.

An executive committee—comprising a chair, chair-elect, and advisory chair—organizes and leads biannual face-to-face meetings and monthly online meetings, conducts elections, and submits recommendations to the USG. Committee members hold three-year positions, with the newly elected committee member cycling through first as chair-elect, then as chair, and finally as advisory chair. Duties vary based on the role and include supporting the mission of the GA-CTL, organizing the agenda for all meetings, representing the GA-CTL on USG committees or at events, and mentoring representatives who are new to the field of faculty development.

Challenges

The USG comprises four research universities, four comprehensive universities, nine state universities, and nine state colleges. Many of these institutions have multiple instructional sites. Given this variety of institutional contexts, we have identified five key challenges that the CTLs often face and have leveraged the collective resources of the CTLs to help mitigate these challenges. In this section, we will introduce the challenges; in a later section, we will discuss the avenues taken to moderate the challenges.

Different Missions of Different Sectors

Each of the four sectors has a distinct core mission. Research universities, for example, are expected to have a "statewide scope of influence" (USG, 2018), with a commitment to teaching and learning, research, and public service, and include baccalaureate, master's, and doctoral-level degrees, as well as professional programs. State colleges, on the other hand, are primarily local, associate-level access institutions, remain committed to teaching a diverse population, and hold a responsibility to address local needs (USG, 2018). As such, the different missions of the institutions within the four sectors factor into collaborations between institutions of different sizes, in which different institutional priorities and cultures come into play.

Disparities in Resources

A dedicated physical space can be an indicator of an institution's commitment to faculty development (Brown et al., 2018). This space could include an office, an area in a library, or a dedicated classroom. Of the 26 USG institutions, nine have a faculty development space at each one of their instructional sites, whereas five of the institutions have no dedicated space on their campus. In addition to space, a disparity in resources can impact how much time is devoted to faculty development. One of the research universities has nine full-time faculty developers, whereas several of the state colleges have only a single person on a part-time contract; therefore, it is clear that the levels of resources available to support faculty development vary widely from institution to institution.

Diversity of Services

Centers within the USG offer a diverse range of programming. The majority of centers offer workshops (92%), new faculty orientation (81%), and peer observations of teaching and individual consultations with faculty (69%). Many support scholarship of teaching and learning (SoTL) (58%), facilitate book groups and teaching circles (54%), have faculty learning communities (FLCs) or communities of practice (CoPs) (50%), and offer support for online learning (50%) and for their institution's quality enhancement plan (50%).

Serving All Faculty

Travel between USG institutions in Georgia—the largest state in terms of landmass east of the Mississippi River—can prove challenging. With up to two hours' travel distance between some campuses at multisite institutions, and up to six hours between the furthest institutions, faculty developers have to think creatively in order to serve all of their faculty. This varies from a director who commutes significant distances to each of five sites on different days of the week, to one who provides synchronous and asynchronous web-based options for workshops, book groups, and other programming.

Attrition

Consistency of vision and quality programming between institutions relies on experienced faculty developers. Within the GA-CTL, there has been consistent turnover every few years—with less than 20% of institutions retaining

366   J. Cofer et al.

the same representative over a period of 5–10 years. This lack of consistency disrupts institutional continuity and can interrupt or impede collaboration within the consortium.

The GA-CTL as a CoP

According to the literature, CoPs are "groups of people who share a concern, a set of problems, or a passion about a topic, and who deepen their knowledge and expertise in this area by interacting on an ongoing basis" (Wenger et al., 2002). Members of these communities collectively find purpose and value in their interactions, actively share resources, support each other's endeavors, collaborate toward shared goals, and engage in collective problem-solving. Wenger-Trayner and Wenger-Trayner (2015) describe three key characteristics that define purposeful CoPs: domain, community, and practice. Each of these characteristics is present in the GA-CTL, thereby indicating that this group functions essentially as a CoP.

Key Characteristics

Domain

Members in a CoP have a shared understanding of what the community values and deems important. They each bring expertise to the community, and they value the contributions of all members. In the GA-CTL, each representative brings a unique understanding and experience from within the context of their institution, sector, students, and faculty. At the same time, despite varying degrees of expertise, there is a shared understanding of best practices in both faculty development and teaching and learning based on an established body of evidence from published research in the field.

Community

In a CoP, members meet and interact with each other, collaborate, and share ideas as they build relationships in their community. They learn from each other, ask and answer each other's questions, and share in the successes and failures of members of the group. The GA-CTL meets face-to-face twice a year to share ideas and to learn with and from each other; members also have monthly online meetings during which they update their community on their current work or ask questions of the group. Members of the community co-present at conferences, co-author articles or chapters, and meet both formally and informally at conferences. Some visit other institutions to conduct workshops or offer consultations.

Practice

The practice of a CoP is the developed set of resources, stories, and tools that combine to make a shared practice. Members are practitioners of the domain. Through many sustained interactions over the years, GA-CTL members learn with and from each other as they design and develop a shared understanding of their practice. Countless conversations have helped to shape new faculty orientations, fellowship programs, FLCs, classroom observations, and workshops. A shared Dropbox, a cloud-based file hosting service, serves as a repository for materials developed. As new faculty developers join the group, members reach out to welcome and mentor them as they learn how to participate within the group. Although community members share resources and ideas, they maintain autonomy in terms of determining how best to serve the needs of their own campuses.

Structural Elements

Operating within these three domains allows the GA-CTL to support faculty developers in a variety of ways, from the professional to the political to, at times, the personal. Framing the GA-CTL as a CoP yields richer meaning from the work of sharing evidence-based practices with faculty. Moreover, three structural elements emerge from negotiating meaning in practice: mutual engagement, joint enterprise, and shared repertoire (Pyrko et al., 2017; Wenger, 1998). What people do and how, the problems they address, and the concepts and artifacts they create are related not just to the community itself, but also to individual practitioners within the CoP.

Wenger's characteristics are helpful for understanding the structure and participation of CoPs (Wenger, 1998); however, a more practical understanding of what makes CoPs work is perhaps best summed up in the notion of "thinking together" (Pyrko et al., 2017, 390). Conceptually, thinking together relates to how groups share tacit knowledge to guide one another "through their understanding of a mutually recognized real-life problem" (Pyrko et al., 2017, 390). As a result, participants in a CoP who think together develop and sustain the domain and practices around these problems. The GA-CTL reflects this process of thinking together in many ways. Specifically, the monthly check-in sessions and the listserv allow for regular and sustained interaction, allowing the group to share knowledge around problems that each member is facing at their institution—problems that are often very real and require immediate attention.

Although there is a structure in place for membership in the GA-CTL, participation varies. This is consistent with Wenger's ideas of levels of participation, which indicate that there is often a small core of participants who take a leadership role in the development of the group (usually 10–15% of the community), another group that regularly participates in meetings and activities, and a third group that plays a more passive role, although these participants may still be learning from the group (Wenger et al., 2002). In the GA-CTL, the formal core group tends to include a revolving executive committee, but informally also includes past members of the executive committee and the USG liaison.

Methods of Collaborative Work

An extended benefit of membership of the GA-CTL is the sustained contact and networking opportunities. Each month, center directors are invited to take part in a monthly video conference check-in meeting. The agenda for each monthly check-in is developed by the GA-CTL chair. During these meetings, center directors share updates on their CTLs and get advice and perspectives from other representatives, and the USG liaison updates members on system happenings.

The GA-CTL also hosts a face-to-face business meeting once a semester at a different campus around the state, with the current GA-CTL chair typically hosting one of these meetings. Each spring, the GA-CTL holds officer elections during the business meeting. Although these were one-day meetings initially, they have been expanded to two days, with the first day typically dedicated to a business meeting and the second day to the professional development of the members. During the business meeting, members may share plans for how they are managing a new USG initiative or might discuss ideas for revising new faculty orientation, for example. This time has been used for everything from developing programming and refining workshops to writing faculty policy or composing white papers. These meetings may also bring in important guest speakers, such as top-level administrators from within the system. Adding the day of professional development was the result of feedback from the group saying that they wished to have more time to learn

23 Collaborative Faculty Development

together and to develop themselves professionally. Consequently, members offer their expertise to the group in the form of workshops and activities, or they can solicit outside experts to present on shared areas of interest. These meetings are practical and educational but also offer an important networking component for directors.

As both the GA-CTL and its meetings have evolved over time, the USG provided support for three retreats for its members—with the first taking place in 2016, the second in 2018, and the third in 2019. The goals of each retreat were different but were shaped around USG initiatives; in all cases, faculty developers were given the opportunity to work together for long periods of time without distraction. The end result of the first meeting was a white paper that outlined an expansion of the understanding of CTL responsibilities with regard to the USG's plan for Complete College Georgia. The second and third retreats—described in more detail later in this chapter—resulted in the development of four interactive workshops each year that support the Momentum Approach—a key USG initiative—and are available to all CTL directors in the USG.

In between the face-to-face and monthly check-in meetings, members of the GA-CTL have access to both synchronous and asynchronous digital resources at their fingertips. The GA-CTL has an active listserv that is made up of members and administrators, as well as those who work in the USG System Office. The members of the listserv regularly field questions ranging from the extremely general (e.g., book recommendations for new CTL directors building a lending library) to more specific (e.g., suggestions for how to choose institutional nominees for state-wide teaching awards), as well as sharing professional opportunities, such as calls for proposals for local teaching conferences and job position openings.

Each member also has access to a repository of resources where members may upload their own materials and download those shared by others. These workshop materials, handouts, schedules, assessments, and other resources are available for all members to use and customize for their own institution. As the GA-CTL is composed of 26 different institutions, this repository represents a wealth of knowledge developed by many skilled faculty developers. This resource also serves as a valuable tool for onboarding new faculty developers and directors. Often, especially at smaller institutions, new faculty developers who are charged with their institution's faculty development may have no formal experience in the field; this resource offers customizable programming at their fingertips.

Mentoring is frequently talked about as vital for the success of new faculty (Phillips & Dennison, 2015) and serves as a way for new faculty to become socialized to the norms of their professional lives (Cawyer et al., 2002). Faculty developers are often asked to run mentoring programs (Beane-Katner, 2014). However, mentoring for new faculty developers themselves has been less explored. Although it is not a prescriptive and formalized aspect of the GA-CTL, it is another benefit of the collective experience. As is often the case, there is some turnover among the members of the GA-CTL. Often, especially in small institutions, CTL directors find themselves in a role for which they feel unprepared—whether because of a lack of administrative experience or due to feeling overwhelmed by the broad scope and demands of the position. In these cases, the GA-CTL seeks to match up new directors with mentors. Leaders, especially those in the same Carnegie classification or institutional sector, are identified and reach out to the new directors. This interaction creates another level of information-sharing that keeps faculty development as the central focus. These mentors can open up networking contacts, programming ideas, scholarship recommendations, and other resources for new directors.

In the same vein, the GA-CTL allows a place for faculty directors—both seasoned and new—to confidentially discuss the difficulties of navigating this position. Often faculty developers are tapped by university administration to help strategize initiatives and gain faculty buy-in. However, the role of the faculty developer varies. Some directors are full-time administrators, whereas some directors may only receive a course-release, or even a small stipend, to serve as a single-person center for an entire institution. The GA-CTL offers a support network for developers to strategize, share success stories, and try to gain seats at powerful tables (Chism, 2011) in order to advocate for faculty and faculty development.

This network extends beyond the strategic. Since CTL directors find themselves attending many of the same meetings, both inside and outside the state, the GA-CTL offers a professional and social network for its members. There are official GA-CTL meet-ups and GA-CTL-sponsored presentations at major conferences within the faculty development field, such as the Professional Organization Development (POD) Network, the International Consortium for Educational Development, and the annual meeting of the Southern Regional Faculty and Instructional Development Consortium. This network is not limited to faculty development; members of the GA-CTL have made presentations and had meet-ups at many higher education conferences, ranging from the Gateway Course Experience Conference to the Southern Association of Colleges and Schools Commission on Colleges. As the GA-CTL continues to grow, so does its reach, helping faculty developers assist their respective institutions through a host of initiatives.

Seeing as many of its members are involved in parallel projects, the GA-CTL network has led to external collaborations beyond the GA-CTL itself. Often, members have been involved in other strategic initiatives within the State of Georgia, such as the Momentum Approach, a multi-pronged student success initiative; Georgia's Gateway to Completion initiative, which focuses on retention; Affordable Learning Georgia, which centers around low-cost and no-cost textbooks; and LEAP Georgia, which supports the Liberal Education and America's Promise (LEAP) initiative of the Association of American Colleges and Universities (AAC&U). Still others work together on national initiatives, working with organizations like the AAC&U and POD Network. Even when the scope of projects starts to move away from faculty development, the GA-CTL has provided a foundation that has given birth to many different collaborations.

Outcomes of Collaborative Faculty Development

Since the establishment of the GA-CTL in 2007, the level of collaboration between members of this CoP has evolved significantly. For the first eight years, the group maintained a basic level of collaborative work. Members of the group served as peer-mentors, and the group functioned as a brain trust, sharing faculty development resources and strategies for success between fellow center directors at face-to-face meetings. This has evolved to higher levels of collaboration from jointly created and shared workshops or collaborative conference presentations to consortium-wide research projects and group advocacy efforts for improved support for teaching and learning across the state. The quality of the outcomes and the advocacy of this collaborative work have diversified and improved over time because of this evolution.

This development has occurred as a result of three different, unique features of the community. Relationships strengthened as trust was built between members over time, particularly as a result of the open sharing of resources. Expectations of the collaborative nature of the group normalized this kind of sharing within the community. In addition, an appreciation for the shared benefit of high levels of collaboration between members has developed to the point that research can be embedded into programming through cooperation. Accordingly, the whole achieves more than the sum of its parts. This is one area of the USG where the long-held notion of institutions as competitors for students and resources fades, paling in comparison to the communal passion for exceptional teaching and learning for all students within the university system.

372   J. Cofer et al.

The following section describes how the outcomes have evolved at each level of collaborative work as a CoP, along with the benefits for teaching and learning in Georgia.

Level 1: Resource-Sharing Outcomes

From the outset, the GA-CTL aimed to serve as a vehicle for sharing pointers for success in leading CTLs across the state. At face-to-face meetings, those newer to the role interacted with more experienced directors and the subsequent sharing of best practices enabled the group to avoid recreating the metaphorical wheel. Thus, the function of meetings as input-seeking led to basic supportive functions for each center director and individual institution. This focus on resource-sharing ranged from tips for the successful leadership of CTLs to workshop materials to supplemental documents between/among institutions—even including assisting each other in conflict management. For instance, when one director had been asked to create a year-long program for new faculty, another director who had created one previously shared faculty learning outcomes, along with a plan to serve as the basis for the development at the other institution.

In another example, a director created a One-Button Studio, which enables faculty to record, at the push of a button, lectures for flipped classrooms and also allows students to record themselves doing presentations for class to reflect and refine their performances. Upon presenting this setup to the GA-CTL at a face-to-face meeting, the GA-CTL members discussed the outcomes of the technology and asked pertinent questions, probing the idea for viability at their respective institutions. This presentation then led to further discussions with three other USG institutions, each of which benefited from the initial presentation and later implemented its own version of the One-Button Studio. Additionally, the GA-CTL listserv has provided instant access to members of the community during the intervals between face-to-face meetings so that new questions can be answered at any time.

Level 2: Sharing the Workload Outcomes

Although openly sharing resources and strategies for success helps to create a sense of a supportive community for directors who are often isolated in individual institutions, institutional contexts vary widely, and directors can face disparity in resources across the USG. To mitigate these disparities, members have pooled resources for the mutual benefit of several institutions at one time. For example, when several of the institutions were interested in having a nationally recognized speaker work with their faculty, they pooled resources and shared travel expenses to bring the speaker to Georgia. As a result of this mutually beneficial planning, the speaker visited and presented at both institutions during one visit. Furthermore, because of the level of collaboration between institutions through the GA-CTL, directors of those two centers invited faculty from surrounding institutions to participate, thus expanding the impact of this single event.

In addition to this, members began to collaborate in designing workshops that could be delivered to faculty at any of the institutions in the system. For example, after several GA-CTL members saw a presentation on transparency in learning and teaching (TILT) at the 2016 POD Network Conference, they came back to Georgia and shared the framework with the group. After one face-to-face meeting and several online video conferencing meetings, a group of six GA-CTL members collaboratively designed a one-hour interactive workshop that they piloted at one of the biannual GA-CTL meetings. After receiving feedback from this group of experts, they revised the workshop and started facilitating it—individually or together—to faculty across the USG, usually at the invitation of GA-CTL members who had participated in the first workshop. They later went on to design and deliver three-hour TILT workshops. At the time of writing, they have presented TILT to over 950 faculty in Georgia.

The success of this collaborative model of workshop design and delivery has provided a model for subsequent workshops that were developed in support of the USG's "Momentum Year" initiative (USG Academic Affairs and Policy, n.d.). In 2018, 22 members of the GA-CTL—representing 20 of the 26 institutions in the USG—met for a three-day USG-sponsored retreat to work collaboratively to design workshops that they delivered later that fall to FLC facilitators from every institution in the USG. These four workshops—small teaching and active learning, inclusive pedagogies, course design, and academic mindset—were also used by GA-CTL members on their own campuses to help recruit participants to these FLCs.

In 2019, a second iteration of the sponsored retreat gathered GA-CTL members to design another set of four workshops collaboratively. The topics for the workshops—high-impact practices, brain-based learning methods, SoTL, and TILT—were chosen as complementary to the previous set of workshops. As with the 2018 workshops, these workshop materials and supplemental documents were made available to all members of the GA-CTL to use and modify. Further variations of these workshops have since been presented to faculty at large during the annual USG Teaching and Learning Conference.

Level 3: Large-Scale Advocacy and Creative Scholarly Outcomes

The most commonly utilized models of leadership within higher education tend to focus power and control on the leaders within individual institutions, often resulting in isolated leadership. What works in teaching and learning has been well-established in the literature for decades, yet many college classrooms remain unchanged. Higher education needs models of leadership that are less hierarchical and more collaborative. In so doing, institutions successfully adopt effective teaching and learning practices, continue to evolve, and remain competitive globally. A study of four universities in Australia (Jones et al., 2012) showed that focusing on collective collaboration through distributed leadership was effective in building capacity in and for innovative teaching and learning. This is the model of leadership that forms the framework of the GA-CTL.

Along these lines, another development within the GA-CTL is the creation of shared scholarship across institutions, facilitated by strong relationships and trust through the open sharing of materials built at face-to-face meetings and other local conferences. The third evolutionary phase in the activities of the GA-CTL has been joint creative and scholarly activities tied with group-wide advocacy for improved teaching and learning across the state. The goal and net result of this is 26 institutions working collaboratively together to enrich faculty development.

The first example of these activities was a retreat for the GA-CTL members to focus on where instructional innovation needed to fit in support of USG's Complete College Georgia plan to improve graduation rates. This retreat led to the creation of a group-authored white paper to the USG and the inclusion of this document in the goals of the initiative. Another example of GA-CTL shared scholarship activities can be found in an ongoing research project based on the revised American Council on Education and POD Network's CTL matrix, a tool developed to evaluate levels of service provision offered by CTLs. Although at an early phase at the time of writing, this project will enable the GA-CTL to engage in an external review of the CTLs within the USG to help collectively advocate for improved resources that support excellence in teaching and learning across Georgia. This represents a future evolutionary leap in our collaborative efforts and mirrors what is occurring nationally with external reviews of centers by CTLs as a mechanism to ensure that faculty receive the best support. In addition to the use of the CTL matrix for external reviews, the GA-CTL is also using it as the framework for a

Concluding Remarks: Stability and Sustainability

Though more often applied to ecological and corporate domains, sustainability serves a vital role in GA-CTL's success as a CoP. Because of the complex nature of the GA-CTL, the differing missions of its institutions, and their diverse contexts, sustaining the CoP plays an integral role in the continuation, efficacy, and impact of the group. Although delegated membership exists in the GA-CTL, participation is not required. As noted previously, institutions can choose their level of participation, from leadership to active participation to passive membership. The flexibility and organic nature of variation that makes the GA-CTL a strong CoP also results in challenges to its sustainability.

One of the key elements of the success and stability of the GA-CTL is the involvement of the USG liaison, Dr Denise Domizi, who provides continuity for CTLs within the consortium. As of 2018, most of the members of the GA-CTL have been in their roles for less than five years. Although they may have worked for more than five years in faculty development in some capacity, only a few have surpassed five years of serving in this group in their current role. Whether through job changes, retirements, promotions, and so on, the turnover rate of CTL directors within the consortium creates a potential knowledge vacuum for the group. The resulting potential for unsteadiness is stabilized by the role of the liaison.

When a new CTL director is identified at an institution, the USG liaison sends a welcome e-mail to that person with information about the consortium's monthly check-ins, face-to-face meetings, listserv, and the names and e-mail addresses of the executive committee. The new member is introduced and welcomed at their first meeting; at the same time, they are informally introduced to the norms of the group through the modeling behaviors of existing members. As such, new members are usually quick to learn how the overall group interacts and also how members support each other.

These new members often find themselves mentored by more experienced members. One of the unique aspects of this mentorship relationship is how quickly participants engage one another regarding a problem or concern. Some of the mentoring is by design, whereas some is wholly organic. The monthly virtual meetings and biannual face-to-face meetings allow for individuals to get to know one another, gaining levels of comfort that are essential to sharing their knowledge and their ways of knowing. In addition to these regular interactions, the GA-CTL highlights numerous opportunities for individuals to interact and collaborate through various system-level events and through the routine course of professional experiences, such as the USG Teaching and Learning Conference, the POD Network Conference, and other ad hoc events.

Faculty developers come from a variety of academic, professional, and intellectual backgrounds (Ouellett, 2010). This is certainly true of the GA-CTL. This diversity of backgrounds provides rich spaces for ideas to flourish, but it can also present significant challenges to sustaining itself over time because individuals may not initially see themselves as similar to their counterparts. However, by *thinking together*, faculty developers in the GA-CTL engage one another in ways that can promote sustainability for the group and, arguably, the field of faculty development. When members share their knowledge, they share more than just "technical, practical, or theoretical knowledge"; moreover, they ultimately share an "understanding of the historical relationships and communities" relevant to the group (Pyrko et al., 2017, 394). Engagement around specific, non-routine problems leads to the creation of artifacts and norms that can guide the next generation of GA-CTL representatives through their own development.

From a sustainability perspective, focusing on the development of individuals within the GA-CTL creates a situation in which some of the most active participants end up leaving the group because of job changes, such as promotions or changes in location. Although these changes would presumably decrease stability in the group and hinder sustainability, our experience is the opposite. Because of the frequent additions of new personnel, there is little time for individuals to become apathetic or disaffected, which is common in many other areas of professional academic life. The frequent, structured changes in leadership of the group ensure that no one person (or institution) can dominate the direction or will of the group. Likewise, this variability provides all sectors of institutions with opportunities to engage with system-level leaders and gives voice to smaller USG institutions. At the same time, those members who move on or upwards continue to serve as resources, mentors, or collaborators—albeit in a more informal role—indicating that these strong relationships often endure even after the position changes.

References

Beane-Katner, L. (2014). Anchoring a mentoring network in a new faculty development program. *Mentoring & Tutoring: Partnership in Learning, 22*(2), 91–103.

Brown, E. C., Haras, C., Hurney, C. A., Iuzzini, J., Magruder, E., Sorcinelli, M. D., Taylor, S. C., & Wright, M. (2018). *A center for teaching and learning matrix.* American Council on Education.

Cawyer, C. S., Simonds, C., & Davis, S. (2002). Mentoring to facilitate socialization: The case of the new faculty member. *International Journal of Qualitative Studies in Education, 15*(2), 225–242.

Chism, N. V. N. (2011). Getting to the table: Planning and developing institutional initiatives. In C. M. Shroeder et al. (Eds.), *Coming in from the margins: Faculty development's emerging organizational developmental role in institutional change* (pp. 47–59). Stylus Press.

Jones, S., Lefoe, G. E., Harvey, M., & Ryland, K. (2012). Distributed leadership: A collaborative framework for academics, executives and professionals in higher education. *Journal of Higher Education Policy and Management, 34*(1), 67–78.

Ouellett, M. L. (2010). Overview of faculty development: History and choices. In K. J. Gillespie & D. L. Robertson (Eds.), *A guide to faculty development* (pp. 3–20). Jossey-Bass.

Phillips, S. L., & Dennison, S. T. (2015). *Faculty mentoring: A practical manual for mentors, mentees, administrators, and faculty developers.* Stylus Press.

Pyrko, I., Dörfler, V., & Eden, C. (2017). Thinking together: What makes communities of practice work? *Human Relations, 70*(4), 389–409.

University System of Georgia (USG). (2018). *Core mission statement.* USG. https://www.usg.edu/institutions/

University System of Georgia (USG) Academic Affairs and Policy. (n.d.). *What is a momentum year?* USG. https://www.usg.edu/academic_affairs_and_policy/complete_college_georgia/momentum_year

University System of Georgia (USG) Consortium on Teaching and Learning (GA-CTL). (2008). *Bylaws for Georgia Consortium for Teaching and Learning (GA-CTL).* USG.

Wenger, É. (1998). *Communities of practice: Learning, meaning, and identity.* Cambridge University Press.

Wenger, É., McDermott, R., & Snyder, W. M. (2002). *Cultivating communities of practice: A guide to managing knowledge.* Harvard Business School Press.

Wenger-Trayner, É., & Wenger-Trayner, B. (2015). *Introduction to communities of practice: A brief overview of the concept and its uses.* http://wenger-trayner.com/introduction-to-communities-of-practice/

24

The Making of the Learning, Teaching, and Innovative Technologies Center: Building Upon an Internal Partnership

Barbara Draude, Thomas Brinthaupt, and Sheila Otto

Introduction

Middle Tennessee State University (MTSU) is a public research doctoral university located in the southeastern USA. It serves approximately 22,000 national and international students and employs over 900 faculty members on a main campus of more than 500 acres. MTSU's faculty center, the Learning, Teaching, and Innovative Technologies Center (LT&ITC), was founded in 2004. Professionals in the field of faculty development emphasize that successful faculty centers establish collaborations and partnerships across campus (Austin & Sorcinelli, 2013; Chism, 2004; Ellis & Ortquist-Ahrens, 2010). However, in practice, these collaborations and partnerships are usually limited in scope.

Most faculty development in the USA is provided through a centralized center with a dedicated staff, and the majority of these centers report exclusively to the institution's chief academic officer, often through an associate or assistant provost (Beach et al., 2016). The faculty center at MTSU, however, began as a unique partnership, a collaborative effort between two existing administrative offices: the Academic Affairs and Information Technology (IT)

B. Draude (✉) • T. Brinthaupt • S. Otto
Middle Tennessee State University, Murfreesboro, TN, USA
e-mail: barbara.draude@mtsu.edu; tom.brinthaupt@mtsu.edu; sheila.otto@mtsu.edu

© The Author(s), under exclusive license to Springer Nature Switzerland AG 2023 **379**
O. J. Neisler (ed.), *The Palgrave Handbook of Academic Professional Development Centers*,
Palgrave Studies on Leadership and Learning in Teacher Education,
https://doi.org/10.1007/978-3-030-80967-6_24

380   B. Draude et al.

divisions. Although it started with extremely limited resources, the LT&ITC has established itself as a valuable instructional and professional development asset to the university. We were unable to find any existing models that describe best practices for developing partnerships specifically between Academic Affairs and IT divisions. However, we have published a paper that presents a framework for strategically leveraging on- and off-campus resources to enhance center success (Brinthaupt et al., 2019). That framework guided many of the programs that we describe in this case study.

Historical Overview

During the 1980s and 1990s, faculty development opportunities at MTSU were limited to activities such as local workshops and seminars, invited guest speakers, and university-sponsored travel to professional conferences. For a number of years, the university sponsored small groups of faculty to attend conferences on teaching and learning and asked those faculty members to present workshops on their return to campus. In the early 1990s, the faculty senate president (who was part of these early faculty development efforts) presented a proposal to the provost to establish a center for faculty teaching excellence. In the late 1990s, when teaching with technology was in its beginning stages, MTSU's IT administration began preparing for the expansion of technology integration by asking one of the authors of this chapter, Barbara Draude, to move from a full-time faculty position to an administrative position in the Office of IT, thus providing a teaching and learning perspective to the work of that office. In 2001, a new university president initiated the development of an Academic Master Plan. Committees working on various components of the plan identified the establishment of a faculty teaching and learning center as a priority for the university.

These converging developments provided the impetus for and led to the conception of a unique cross-divisional partnership between the Academic Affairs and IT divisions. Draude and the vice president for IT, who also served as the chief information officer, approached the university provost and proposed developing a collaborative teaching and learning center to support the teaching excellence and student-centered learning goals included in the new Academic Master Plan. The process of establishing a center was begun by Draude, representing the IT division, and the assistant to the provost for special projects, who oversaw faculty development efforts, representing the Academic Affairs division. With no additional staff and a limited budget, these co-directors, along with a delegation of 22 faculty volunteers, researched learning centers at other universities and developed a plan for creating a center at MTSU.

From its humble beginnings as a "virtual" center, with no dedicated space on campus, the current LT&ITC occupies a large area (approximately 2,500 square feet) in the campus's main library, with workshop facilities, informal meeting areas, and staff offices. In addition to the co-directors from the two divisions, the LT&ITC staff now includes two half-time faculty appointments, a full-time instructional designer, and a graduate assistant who is employed on a 12-month contract for 20 hours per week. Associated instructional technology staff include two instructional technologists, a multimedia developer, an instructional accessibility specialist, two systems analysts, a statistical software consultant, and a second graduate assistant on a 20-hour-per-week, 12-month contract.

A defining feature driving the success of the LT&ITC is faculty support and involvement. This orientation is reflected in the participation of the original faculty delegates, many of whom continue to support the center as advisors and as members of its Executive Board. Additional support is provided by faculty who have completed the LT&ITC Faculty Fellows program, and partners from the university library, distance learning administration, general education, the campus-wide quality enhancement program, and the Office of Student Success. Through multiple university and divisional administrations, the LT&ITC has maintained a "by the faculty, for the faculty" philosophy.

In this case study, we discuss how our center started small and has matured; how the initial faculty delegation established our mission; how we were able to provide services during the early years primarily using faculty volunteers; and how we established the business case for growing the LT&ITC. Throughout the chapter, we describe the value of our unique partnership along with the challenges that it has presented.

Reporting Structure and Funding Sources

The Academic Affairs and IT partnership supporting the LT&ITC necessitates a unique reporting and funding structure (see Fig. 24.1). Currently one administrator from each administrative division—the assistant vice president for academic and instructional technologies from the IT division and the vice provost for faculty affairs from the Academic Affairs division—function as the center's co-directors. Their role is to request and approve funding, oversee

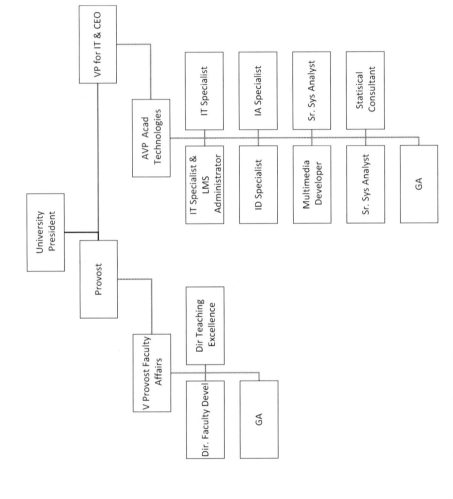

Fig. 24.1 Organizational chart of the LT&ITC

operations, and advocate to their respective vice presidents on the center's behalf. With no separate budget or staffing lines for the LT&ITC, both administrative division partners contribute to its operation.

Initially, funding for the LT&ITC was provided fairly equally by the two divisions, with IT funding an administrative assistant position and operational costs and Academic Affairs funding faculty stipends and outside speakers. The co-directors did not receive any additional salary and incorporated their new responsibilities into their job descriptions. However, as a result of the increase in technology staff working with the center, the current funding model has changed but is still collaborative. The IT division funds the professional staff and covers operational costs, and Academic Affairs provides funding for faculty appointments and program stipends for faculty participants. Professional staff report to the assistant vice president for academic and instructional technologies, and the two faculty with half-time appointments report to the vice provost for faculty affairs.

The Establishment, Growth, and Development of the LT&ITC

In 2004, following approval of the divisional partnership, the co-directors convened a group of 22 faculty delegates, nominated by their respective deans, to discuss the process of establishing a center. Delegates included several faculty members who had earlier advocated for a center for teaching excellence. Teams of delegates visited five established and respected teaching and learning centers in the USA. During those visits, the teams reviewed mission statements, interviewed staff, and collected information on best practices. The delegates then met for a two-day strategic planning retreat and established the new center's name, mission statement, and goals, as well as a plan for its first year of operation. The mission statement was to "create a community of faculty who develop, improve, and integrate creative and effective use of pedagogies and technologies to enhance student learning" (Brinthaupt et al., 2019). Among the major goals identified by the delegates were to (1) establish the LT&ITC as a primary campus resource for teaching excellence; (2) develop, provide, and promote learning, teaching, and technology opportunities for faculty; and (3) foster a culture to promote collaboration, collegiality, and mentoring to enhance the scholarship and practice of effective teaching.

Services in the first two years included a workshop series provided by the co-directors and faculty volunteers, faculty consultations with the co-directors, guest speakers on teaching and learning topics, a monthly newsletter, the initiation of an annual Faculty Showcase, and support for two one-quarter-time faculty fellow appointments. From 2006 until 2010, the center employed an administrative assistant, but that position was lost in 2010 due to budget cuts. Office and presentation space in an academic building acquired in 2007 was lost in 2009 due to other institutional priorities. During these years, the LT&ITC continued to expand services offered with limited or no space and only the co-directors and faculty fellows as staff.

A tipping point occurred in 2010, when space in the university's main library became available, and the two faculty fellow appointments, which had been unfunded the previous year, were combined into a half-time appointment of a director of faculty development. In addition, in a partnership with the distance learning administration, a position was transferred to the IT division for the hiring of an instructional design specialist, who would be housed in the LT&ITC. A second tipping point occurred in 2014 with the addition of a second half-time faculty appointment, a director of teaching excellence, and further integration of the LT&ITC and instructional technology staff into a more cohesive instructional and professional development team.

The LT&ITC has evolved to provide a wide variety of services across three major domains. With respect to faculty and professional development programming, the center now offers a Faculty Fellows initiative, an intensive year-long professional development program; faculty and professional learning communities, which provide groups of faculty the opportunity to study and discuss issues of interest; mentoring programs; a faculty wellness workshop series; a badging program; weekly faculty writing groups and two-day writing retreats; scholarship of teaching and learning (SoTL) consultations; and statistical and research design consulting.

In the domain of teaching excellence, the LT&ITC offers frequent workshops during each academic term; mid-term teaching check-ups for instructors; numerous teaching consultations; retreats and institutes, including an annual Course Design Institute; a 10-week Graduate Teaching Assistant Teaching Preparation certificate program; faculty reading groups; and an Open Classrooms initiative, where award-winning faculty open their classrooms to visitors. A full description of our programs and services is located on the center's website (LT&ITC, n.d.).

Finally, the closer relationship between the LT&ITC and instructional technology staff has allowed for significant progress in offering course design/development programming, including administrative support for our learning management system, instructional systems and tools (e.g., student response systems, lecture capture, media servers), and the use of electronic portfolios. The new relationship has also created opportunities for formal instructional design and redesign programs, consultations, auditing, and remediation services for course accessibility, multimedia resource development, and multi-member course design teams.

Strengths, Accomplishments, Challenges, and Barriers

Despite its modest beginnings and ongoing limitations in budget and staffing, we continue to build the case that the LT&ITC provides a valuable service to our university. The primary strengths of our center are its foundational partnership and its "by the faculty, for the faculty" approach. The foundational partnership provides a strong relationship between the administration of the two divisions with respect to teaching and learning topics. Having a common ground for discussion has encouraged each division to consider the other's perspectives when setting priorities and allocating resources, thus helping to bridge the traditional gap between faculty and IT staff. From an institutional perspective, we have profited by promoting teaching excellence and faculty success using a single voice. The partnership also sends a strong message that pedagogy and technology are inseparable and must work together to promote teaching excellence and faculty success. This linking of pedagogy and technology is a crucial feature given the dramatic increase in instructional technologies across all delivery modes.

With respect to faculty involvement, we have, from the beginning, depended on faculty to share their knowledge and passion for teaching with their colleagues. The co-directors, having long tenures as faculty on campus, provided the first faculty foundation for the center. The original delegates were carefully recruited to provide representation from all ranks, departments, and colleges. Delegates were chosen for their reputations as excellent instructors and their willingness to explore new teaching methodologies, including technology integration. The first faculty fellows were chosen from the delegates to support the center's "by the faculty, for the faculty" philosophy.

The faculty-driven philosophy has been instrumental to the center's growth. In 2010, when the half-time director of faculty development position was approved, the opportunity was offered to a faculty member with sterling credentials. He had a long history of working with the center, had served as a faculty intern in the IT division, had expressed commitment to faculty development, and was a respected scholar. In 2014, when services had expanded

386   B. Draude et al.

and additional funding was approved, the half-time position of director of teaching excellence was offered to a well-respected faculty member with a long history of supporting teaching excellence as director of the university's general education program and as a member of the center's Executive Board. By adding these two appointments to the LT&ITC staff, we were able to further support the center's mission by providing faculty expertise despite our limited budget.

We continue this faculty-driven commitment by encouraging faculty to involve themselves as both facilitators and participants in LT&ITC programs and services, and we also continue our commitment to establishing partnerships across campus. Increases in participation and collaboration have been steady. For example, workshop attendance increased from 395 in 2015–2016 to 606 in 2017–2018; moreover, in the 2017–2018 academic year, LT&ITC workshops were facilitated by a wide range of faculty who represented almost half of the university's 39 departments and all of the university's 10 colleges. The development of partnerships across campus continued in 2017–2018 as numerous divisions and offices were represented among the workshop presenters, including Student Affairs, University Advancement, International Affairs, Counseling Services, and the Office of Student Success. Participation in the Faculty Fellows program continues to increase, with a total of 69 faculty having completed the year-long program. Involvement in faculty learning communities (FLCs), which are proposed and facilitated by faculty members, doubled between the academic years 2015–2016 and 2017–2018 from 24 to 48, with groups studying topics ranging from sustainable study abroad to problem-based learning and students as knowledge creators.

In addition, the LT&ITC hosts multiple reading groups each year, with approximately 40 faculty participating annually. The center also continues to expand its programs and services, as evidenced by the Open Classrooms initiative, which was first implemented in the 2018 spring semester, with five faculty opening their classrooms to visitors for a week in February. Another new initiative in 2018—two-day faculty writing retreats that attracted 108 faculty—emerged out of a partnership between the university library and the Office of Research Services. In addition, in 2018, three faculty were sponsored as LT&ITC Academic Year Teaching Fellows to implement a teaching/learning project proposed from work they had started during their participation in the Faculty Fellows program. This kind of expansion of our center's programs and services has been possible because of our commitment to seeking and nurturing collaborations across campus.

However, as is often the case with collaborations, the lack of a separate institutional divisional identity has also provided challenges, including lingering confusion about the services and support provided by the LT&ITC. For example, because the LT&ITC and instructional technology staff are housed in separate locations on campus, faculty members are sometimes perplexed about where to go or whom to contact for questions and services. Some faculty mistakenly think that the LT&ITC is primarily technology-focused and are unaware of its teaching and professional development resources. The lack of a dedicated administrative staff or funding lines has also made the expansion of services difficult.

Nevertheless, we have been able to weather those challenges and the LT&ITC is now, after 15 years, a mature teaching and learning center. Since our founding, we have seen an increase in requests to collaborate with various departments and colleges. Our joint sponsorship of FLCs and experiential learning and discipline-specific events has earned us much positive press. Evidence of our success can be seen in a steady increase in attendance at events and in the use of our resources. Total faculty participation in LT&ITC programs and services more than doubled between the academic years 2015–2016 and 2017–2018 from 636 to 1,296 participants.

Over time, we have established the center as a mission-critical university service, essential to our strategic planning. For example, the latest quality enhancement plan (QEP), a requirement for our university's regional accreditation, centered on "integrative thinking." Activities and assessments within the QEP (e.g., faculty retreats, ePortfolio training, FLCs, and other workshops) were built specifically using the faculty development, teaching excellence, and course design services offered by the LT&ITC.

Impact Data

We are able to demonstrate the impact of the center's services through data such as our calendar of offerings, attendance records, post-event surveys, and anecdotal accounts. See Table 24.1 for a sampling of services offered by the LT&ITC from our annual report for 2017–2018. In general, the number of workshops per semester averages 20–25, with attendance ranging from 15 to 20 attendees per event.

Event evaluations have also shown consistently high satisfaction levels. We have received anecdotal feedback, such as the following:

> My first year at MTSU has been both challenging and rewarding. I am grateful for the opportunity to work at this institution and to participate in the Teaching and Professional Development program. This program gave me the opportunity

388   B. Draude et al.

to share with and learn from experienced professors, as well as with others during their first year (MTSU Faculty Fellow).

I especially appreciate hearing the various perspectives and experiences from the different faculty members as we discuss ways to foster and build a true "learning community" at MTSU. We are all at different points and places in our careers, and this has greatly enriched our conversations. As our mission states, we should foster an environment conducive to learning and personal development, and I witness this in our meetings (FLC Participant).

I had a lot of creative ideas about how I wanted to redesign the class, but I could have never executed my ideas without the design team (Subject Matter Faculty Member for the Instructional Design Team).

In addition, needs assessments conducted every five years show high evaluations of the services we provide, and provide us with ideas for future planning. Additional evidence of the center's impact includes the continuing and new partnerships we have established (e.g., the library and QEP) as well as invitations for the co-directors to serve on university planning committees (e.g., the new Academic Master Plan, Quest for Student Success, QEP) in order to include faculty development and teaching excellence perspectives in

Table 24.1 Sampling of services provided by the LT&ITC in 2017–2018

Services	Number of offerings/events	Estimated number of participants
Faculty visits	1,300	–
Instructional consultations	102	–
Teaching excellence workshops	42	606
Special events (i.e., collaborations with other campus departments/programs)	24	518
Accessibility/universal design for learning workshops	5	24
Reading groups	5	40
Writing groups	5	40
Faculty writing retreats	2	67
Graduate Teaching Assistant (GTA) Certificate program	2 cohorts	11
FLCs	6	73
Faculty Fellows program	1 cohort	11
LT&ITC academic year teaching fellows	–	3
Open Classrooms initiative	5	39
Mid-semester course check-up	3	–

the initial planning stages. Analysis of student success data also shows impact in the domain of the center's course design/development programming. For example, a comparison of final grades before and after course redesigns for three cohorts has shown an improvement in student success rates.

For many years, our center has fostered a focus on SoTL, which permeates much of what we do. We believe it is essential to inform both the field and other teaching and learning centers of the innovative, interesting things we do. Reflecting that focus, we have published several papers that highlight IT and online teaching and learning issues (Brinthaupt et al., 2009; Raffo et al., 2015), outcomes of our FLCs (Brinthaupt et al., 2011; Otter et al., 2013), and activities and conceptual frameworks that have emerged from our work (Brinthaupt et al., 2014, 2016, 2019).

Conclusion and Recommendations

This case study has detailed the success story of the LT&ITC, built on a cross-divisional collaboration between the IT and Academic Affairs divisions, which started small and has steadily matured in its ability to provide essential services to our campus. Working within the advantages and challenges created by a partnership with limited resources and with the assistance of many highly motivated and generous faculty, we have provided quality support for the instructional design, instructional technology, and professional development needs of our campus.

Acknowledgments We want to thank all past and current faculty and staff who have contributed to the growth and operation of our center. We also want to acknowledge several of our past and present administrators who were instrumental in starting our center and supporting its growth: Lucinda Lea, former vice president for information technology/chief information officer (retired); Dr Diane Miller (retired); Dr Kaylene Gebert (retired); Dr Bard Bartel, former provost; and Faye Johnson, associate provost (formerly assistant to the provost for special projects) and original co-director of the center (retired).

We would also like to extend our gratitude to our current vice presidents, Dr Mark Byrnes (provost) and Bruce Petryshak, vice president for information technology/chief information officer, who support the continuing partnership. An additional thank you is due to Faye Johnson, associate provost, and Cheryl Torsney, vice provost for faculty affairs, for their review, comments, and suggestions for this chapter.

References

Austin, A. E., & Sorcinelli, M. D. (2013). The future of faculty development: Where are we going? *New Directions for Teaching and Learning, 2013*(133), 85–97.

Beach, A. L., Sorcinelli, M. D., Austin, A. E., & Rivard, J. K. (2016). *Faculty development in the age of evidence: Current practices, future imperatives.* Stylus Press.

Brinthaupt, T. M., Clayton, M. A., & Draude, B. J. (2009). Barriers to and strategies for faculty integration of IT. In P. Rogers, G. Berg, J. Boettcher, C. Howard, L. Justice, & K. Schenk (Eds.), *Encyclopedia of distance learning* (Vol. 1, 2nd ed., pp. 138–145). IGI Global.

Brinthaupt, T. M., Clayton, M. A., Draude, B. J., & Calahan, P. T. (2014). How should I offer this course? The course delivery decision model (CDDM). *Journal of Online Learning and Teaching, 10*(2), 326–336.

Brinthaupt, T. M., Cruz, L., Otto, S., & Pinter, M. (2019). A framework for the strategic leveraging of outside resources to enhance CTL effectiveness. *To Improve the Academy, 38*(1), 82–94.

Brinthaupt, T. M., Fisher, L. S., Gardner, J. G., Raffo, D. M., & Woodard, J. B. (2011). What the best online teachers should do. *Journal of Online Learning and Teaching, 7*(4), 515–524.

Brinthaupt, T. M., Neal, A., & Otto, S. (2016). A faculty wellness workshop series: Leveraging on-campus expertise. *To Improve the Academy, 35*(2), 377–394.

Chism, N. V. N. (2004). Playing well with others: Academic development as a team sport. *To Improve the Academy, 22*(1), 226–236.

Ellis, D. E., & Ortquist-Ahrens, L. (2010). Practical suggestions for programs and activities. In K. J. Gillespie & D. L. Robertson (Eds.), *A guide to faculty development* (2nd ed., pp. 117–132). Jossey-Bass.

Learning, Teaching, and Innovative Technologies Center (LT&ITC). (n.d.). *Welcome to the Lucinda Taylor Lea Learning, Teaching, and Innovative Technologies Center!* Middle Tennessee State University (MTSU). https://www.mtsu.edu/ltanditc

Otter, R. R., Seipel, S., Graeff, T., Alexander, B., Boraiko, C., Gray, J., Petersen, K., & Sadler, K. (2013). Comparing student and faculty perceptions of online and traditional courses. *The Internet and Higher Education, 19*(2013), 27–35.

Raffo, D. M., Brinthaupt, T. M., Gardner, J. G., & Fisher, L. S. (2015). Balancing online teaching activities: Strategies for optimizing efficiency and effectiveness. *Online Journal of Distance Learning Administration, 18*(1).

Part VIII

Strategies for Building Community

Several academic professional development centers (ADCs) implement programs specifically aimed at creating one or more communities of practice. The goal is to change or enhance conversations about teaching and learning at the program, college, and university levels as motivation and support for instructional change. Some ADC programs begin with a small group activity such as a monthly book discussion group. At the other end of the spectrum is a large worldwide institution needing to facilitate faculty collaboration.

Chapters in Part VIII

Chapter 25: *Building Community: From Faculty Development to Pedagogical Innovation and Beyond*. Linda C. Hodges and Patrice McDermott, University of Maryland, Baltimore, MD, USA.

This chapter relates how a center can align all facets of ADC programming to build community among the faculty. That community also expands to include students in a joint focus on inclusive academic excellence.

Chapter 26: *A Holistic Vision of Faculty Excellence: Creating Sustainable Programming that Expands Community, Infrastructure, and Capacity*. Jennifer Keys and Abiódún "G-P" Gòkè-Pariolá, North Central College, Naperville, IL, USA.

One ADC has created a holistic program to deepen faculty teaching, mentoring, research, and citizenship roles.

392   **Strategies for Building Community**

Chapter 27: *Promoting a Culture of Teaching Excellence in a Chinese Research University*. Yihong Qiu, Center for Teaching and Learning Development, Shanghai Jiao Tong University, Shanghai, China.

This chapter discusses how new faculty orientation, scholarship of teaching and learning, and midterm student feedback influence a culture of teaching excellence at a research university.

Chapter 28: *Building Community and Supporting Mentors in a Dispersed College for Adults: A Case Study*. Shantih E. Clemans, Center for Mentoring, Learning, and Academic Innovation, State University of New York Empire State College, Saratoga Springs, NY, USA.

In this chapter, one ADC serves a geographically dispersed, experimental institution catering to adult students. The role of faculty—who act as mentors rather than traditional teachers—leads to non-traditional professional development, with much of it aimed at building community via online programming.

Chapter 29: *Virtual Faculty Learning Communities*. Angela Atwell and Cristina Cottom, Embry-Riddle Aeronautical University-Worldwide, Daytona Beach, FL, USA.

This chapter explains how one ADC uses technology-based programming to build virtual communities of practice for its large, remote faculty base.

Chapter 30: *Planting Seeds for a Campus-Wide Conversation on Teaching and Learning in Oman: The Faculty Fellows Program at the Center for Excellence in Teaching and Learning, Sultan Qaboos University*. Thuwayba Al Barwani and Otherine Neisler, Sultan Qaboos University, Muscat, Oman.

A Faculty Fellows program developed by one ADC is a catalyst for the development of communities of practice in 11 teaching units.

Other Relevant Chapter

Chapter 23: *Collaborative Faculty Development*. Jordan Cofer, Denise Domizi, Marina Smitherman, Jesse Bishop, and Rod McRae, University System of Georgia, Atlanta, GA, USA.

This chapter details the community of practice established by a state-wide consortium of directors and administrators from 26 colleges and universities.

25

Building Community: From Faculty Development to Pedagogical Innovation and Beyond

Linda C. Hodges and Patrice McDermott

Introduction

The Faculty Development Center (FDC) at the University of Maryland Baltimore County (UMBC), USA, a medium-sized, public research university, has an enviable history. The center was created in 1999 in response to an identified need from the faculty, voted in by the faculty governance system, and subsequently endorsed by the provost. The center leveraged this bottom-up, top-down initiative to connect to institutional values and build community around teaching and learning, establishing itself as an integral part of the fabric of the institution. In this chapter, the current director and vice provost for faculty affairs share how the FDC has acted synergistically in institutional change, serving both as a sensor and a stimulus for the evolving needs and priorities of the institution.

Almost from its inception, the FDC played a role in organizational, as well as instructional, development at the university, a situation that deviates somewhat from the norm (Schroeder et al., 2011). Critical to the achievement of this integration was our continuing focus on building a sense of community around teaching and learning. In retrospect, we can see how, over the years, the center directors, knowingly or unknowingly, capitalized on social

---

L. C. Hodges (✉) • P. McDermott
University of Maryland Baltimore County, Baltimore, MD, USA
e-mail: lhodges@umbc.edu; mcdermot@umbc.edu

© The Author(s), under exclusive license to Springer Nature Switzerland AG 2023
O. J. Neisler (ed.), *The Palgrave Handbook of Academic Professional Development Centers*,
Palgrave Studies on Leadership and Learning in Teacher Education,
https://doi.org/10.1007/978-3-030-80967-6_25

393

cognition and cultural theories of organizational development (Kezar, 2001) and worked within Senge's (1990) framework of learning organizations to foster change. For example, cultivating a shared vision and fostering team learning via community building are integral elements in systems thinking (Senge, 1990).

Guided by the institutional mission and responding to evolving institutional priorities and national pressures, the focus of our community-building process changed over time. In this chapter we tell our story, from the establishment of the center with its focus on professional development through its evolution to become a hub for both effective teaching and pedagogical innovation and research. We hope that lessons we learned from our experience—especially about the importance of forming institutional relationships and connecting to institutional priorities and values to build a community around teaching and learning—may inform the field going forward.

History of the Center

In 1966, UMBC was established in recognition of the Baltimore area's large student demographic base and the potential for growth in scientific research and development. From its beginning, UMBC was open to people of all races and backgrounds. Through the years, the university has grown to encompass almost 14,000 students and over 500 full-time faculty, and its mission has continued to reflect its emphasis on inclusive excellence. Beginning with the presidency of Dr Freeman Hrabowski in 1992, UMBC sought to brand itself as a research university that provided a distinctive undergraduate experience for all students. The university committed to providing programming appropriate for an honors university and supportive of students of diverse backgrounds.

As a new university, UMBC faced the demands of handling growth in enrollment, developing new programs, expanding research capacity, and adding faculty. Faculty were faced with the tensions of balancing research and creative agendas while offering courses and programs that effectively supported all students as learners. More and more, as the university sought to distinguish itself for the quality of its undergraduate experience, faculty development became an obvious need.

In 1998, the university appointed an ad hoc committee, the Faculty Senate Committee on Faculty Development, to undertake a needs assessment to determine the status of faculty development at the university. This committee reviewed existing documents that looked at faculty development on campus, such as reports from the Committee on Faculty Rewards, the Provost's Committee on University Priorities Subcommittee on Faculty/Staff Development, and the Faculty Development Section in the 1996 report to UMBC's accrediting body. They also compared existing faculty support processes at the university to practices of other higher education institutions, especially those institutions considered peers. The conclusion from the Committee on Faculty Development was that UMBC was notable in the absence of support for faculty development. Thus, establishing an academic professional development center was a logical next step in the advancement of the university.

The FDC was established in 1999 and soon became instrumental in helping the university achieve its vision, acting as an agent for institutional transformation. As we reflect on the FDC's history, we see how the center utilized elements of the approach of systems interdependence within Senge's (1990) model of learning organizations to build community and promote change, in this case specifically by (1) drawing on institutional interrelationships and (2) responding to larger institutional and national pressures. In addition, we can identify two different emphases historically in the FDC's efforts to build community around teaching: initially as a focus on teaching as part of one's professional practice and, later on, teaching as scholarly practice. We explore each of these phases below.

Organizational Reporting and Structure of the FDC

From its beginning, the FDC was positioned in direct administrative connection with the faculty through the vice provost for faculty affairs (see Fig. 25.1).

Building Community Around Teaching as a Professional Practice

Based on UMBC's institutional needs, the Committee on Faculty Development recommended that the center's mission should be *to assist all faculty with professional development in teaching, research, and service*, a motion approved by the Faculty Senate in December 1998. In the committee's report to the Faculty Senate, the decision to address all three responsibilities of the faculty

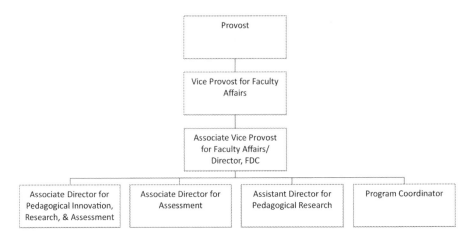

Fig. 25.1 FDC organizational chart

role was based on one of the priorities of the center to *emphasize inter-relationships of the traditional triad of teaching, research, and service, including research about teaching, teaching as research, and service learning*. The need for a physical center was based on the belief that *only by being given an institutional identity can faculty development become part of the university culture and have a lasting positive effect on the campus*.

Drawing on Institutional Interrelationships

Initially, the Committee on Faculty Development advocated for the center to be led by a faculty member, affirming the importance of faculty connection in this work. The appointment was a half-time assignment, and the faculty member worked closely with a steering committee composed of faculty and administrators, including the vice provost for faculty affairs and designees from the deans. Given that the first director had no formal training in faculty development, a consultant with experience at a teaching and learning center was brought in to advise and support early efforts. This first year was spent in exploring priorities with the steering committee and department chairs and in establishing a presence for the center via a website, newsletter, and high-profile events. The director faced the challenge of reconciling diverse needs while creating a coherent vision for the center. At the same time, he dealt with scarcity of human and fiscal resources and physical space. As a result, progress in establishing a credible presence for the center was slow.

This model, in which centers are led by less than full-time directors, was common in early eras of faculty development. For example, in Erickson's (1986) study, only 14% of the reporting institutions claimed a dedicated center for faculty development. Instead, faculty development was usually provided by an individual administrator charged with that responsibility, among others. However, by the time of a survey by Sorcinelli et al. (2006), only 19% of respondents reported a model in which faculty development was led by an individual faculty member or administrator. Furthermore, in a study by Beach et al. (2016), only 20 of 155 responding directors (about 13%) noted that they were less than full-time, and these were directors primarily at comprehensive universities or liberal arts colleges. Presumably, the transition to dedicated staff and centers reflects growing demands for faculty development and recognizes the professional training required for promoting personal and institutional change.

In recognition of the difficulties inherent in starting a new center with limited resources and staffed solely by a part-time director, the university conducted a national search for a new full-time director in spring 2000. The university hired an established, respected faculty developer with experience at a teaching and learning center at Stanford University. He and a half-time administrative assistant working with a modest budget from the university were tasked with supporting institutional aspirations to provide distinctive student experiences.

Although the senior administration was open to a developing vision of what the FDC should and could do, they were clear from the beginning that general faculty development was a priority. The FDC director formed key connections with departments and colleges, in collaboration with the nascent instructional technology unit, and planned programming that made extensive use of faculty peers—thus drawing on interrelationships to build community. In these early days, the work was both responsive to existing needs within institutional structures and proactive in advancing university aspirations. For example, working with other university offices, the director implemented much-needed faculty orientations. Similarly, the director worked with academic departments that expressed the need for guidance in training graduate teaching assistants. He also collaborated with the then-small instructional technology unit, expanding its reach and providing pedagogical framing for technology use. In responding to these identified needs, the center validated its usefulness to the community, established relationships with institutional units, and simultaneously promoted practices for effective teaching.

At the same time, however, acting in concert with faculty committees, the director helped establish the FDC as a proving ground for new initiatives.

During the 1990s, the institution branded itself as an honors university that supported the development of all students. An Honors Task Force had identified three initiatives to support these goals: first-year seminars, first-year success courses, and a Writing in the Discipline program. The FDC worked with faculty charged to undertake the establishment of these programs, providing them with a home, structured opportunities for collaboration, necessary background information, and administrative support to distribute resources and push the initiatives forward, thus creating a community around first-year success initiatives and the teaching of writing. Supporting and advancing these interrelated programs contributed to a systems change—by 2002, in recognition of the growth in size and importance of these programs, the university institutionalized them in an Office of Undergraduate Education. During this era, the center came to be seen as a trusted resource in the professional practice of faculty and a creative nexus for curricular innovation, promoting the university's growing reputation as a leader in undergraduate education.

Responding to Larger Institutional and National Pressures

As the university moved through the first decade of the 21st century, its commitment to inclusive excellence had resulted in a growing national reputation, especially for its innovative programs supporting under-represented minority students in science, technology, engineering, and mathematics (STEM) fields. Expanding on this work, the university received major external grant funding in 2010 for a study to compare evidence-based approaches for STEM student support. Similarly, the university participated in state-funded initiatives to innovatively redesign courses across the curriculum to increase student access, enhance student success, and reduce institutional costs. The growing emphasis in higher education on evidence-based teaching and data-driven decision-making, however, also posed challenges. Specifically, universities were being held to higher and higher standards for assessing student learning outcomes and acting on findings to improve student learning and success. The university had to respond to concerns raised in its 2005 accreditation review about the university's efforts in systematizing its processes for the assessment of student learning outcomes.

In the midst of these opportunities and challenges, the inaugural director left after eight years of leadership. At about the same time, a new provost was appointed who sought to continue and extend the university's focus on student success. In recognition of the changing imperatives at multiple levels, after a two-year trial with an interim director, the university launched a national search for a new director of the FDC. In preparing for this transition, the incoming vice provost for faculty affairs was authorized to narrow the emphasis of the center's mission and programming, focusing it on support for teaching effectiveness, pedagogical innovation, and research and assessment related to teaching and learning.

Building Community Around Teaching as a Scholarly Practice

In hiring the third full-time director of the FDC, the university again brought in a seasoned leader, one with a background in the scholarship of teaching and learning (SoTL). The new director had eight years' experience in faculty development, including directing a teaching and learning center at an elite research university. Acting on the institutional vision for advancing teaching at the university, the director built on the existing community base and actively sought to connect teaching and research at the university. She shaped conversations with faculty and departments to be less about standards of teaching excellence and more about the research on student learning and how to address student difficulties (Bransford et al., 1999). She framed teaching challenges as intellectual problems (Bass, 1999), connecting to the research mores of the faculty and the common ground of scholarly practice, and thus connected teaching more closely to the community of practice around research.

Building up Institutional Interrelationships

To develop an interrelationship between teaching and research, the new director recognized the need to act on Shulman's (1993) admonition to open the doors on our teaching. Shulman (1993) posited that teaching was usually treated as personal property, not as community practice. In his view, this isolation inhibited the advancement of teaching and learning as a field. The new director sought to make the center a hub for conversation, collaboration, and community around teaching and research in teaching and learning, thus both championing and advancing the evolving vision of the university as a national leader in pedagogical innovation and research.

In recognition of the constraints for tenure-stream, research-focused faculty to engage in pedagogical research, the director provided a platform for the work of the teaching-track faculty through the FDC. This group (representing about 20% of the full-time faculty at our institution), are often at the margins of the power structure in universities (Thedwall, 2008). However,

400   L. C. Hodges and P. McDermott

they were at the vanguard of pedagogical innovation at our institution. The teaching-track faculty frequently acted as early adopters, experimenting with new approaches, addressing difficulties, and adapting them to the institutional context. Within FDC programs and through the interrelationships of department cultures, these faculty were encouraged to share their work with the broader audience of the university and act as resources and thought leaders for all faculty.

Changes in the Assessment of Student Learning

A critical corollary to pedagogical innovation and research is the systematic assessment of student learning. The vice provost for faculty affairs was charged with this work, and she and the director sought ways to support the university's efforts to improve faculty and department perspectives and practices. They recognized that faculty and programs often still struggled with the concept and requirements of assessing student learning outcomes, finding it difficult to make the work meaningful and doable within their existing workload constraints. The center director reached out to administrators responsible for assessment work in colleges and departments, offering to join meetings and conduct workshops. She helped faculty and programs develop and refine their student learning outcomes and create reasonable and meaningful plans for assessing their effectiveness in achieving them. Key to this work was her involvement in organizational structures such as the General Education Committee. This group was charged not only with reviewing courses for general education status, but also with reviewing assessment efforts in general education as a whole. General education encompassed the institutional-level learning outcomes as they manifested in both general education courses and program-level outcomes. Again, she attempted to shift assessment processes from an emphasis on compliance to a focus on scholarly examination of practice, in keeping with the evolving ethos of the university.

The center's emphasis on pedagogical innovation and research also coincided with growing requirements of government grant funding agencies. Proposals for pedagogical research as well as new faculty career grants often called for rationales based on educational research and robust assessment plans documenting student learning. The center connected to several high-profile pedagogical research projects on campus, providing consulting or assessment support, integrating the center more fully into the research mission of the university, and adding to the center's reputation and its impact on institutional culture.

Center Impact

Centralized within the institution and utilizing a multifaceted approach for community-building, the FDC was able to act as an engine of change. Working within the communities and structures of the university, engaging faculty on their own terms and connecting with their interests, the FDC was a generative force in the advancement of the university as a leader in undergraduate education. On average, the FDC had annual contact with about 40% of the university faculty. Through its interrelationships with various groups on campus, the center garnered new resources. For example, a committee allocated additional monies for the FDC when the university received special state funding for student success initiatives, allowing the center to hire an associate director to support pedagogical innovation and research and to establish faculty learning communities. Likewise, when academic program reviews for several departments noted increased needs for assessment support, the university designated funding for an assessment specialist and recognized that the logical and most productive home for this person was the FDC.

The growing reputation of the center and its perceived value in advancing university initiatives were critical in expanding the work of the center and further enhancing its impact on institutional transformation. For example, in 2012, the university administration recognized the challenges to pedagogical innovation and the role of the FDC in supporting and catalyzing these efforts by creating a new institutional system: a high-profile internal grant program awarding up to $100,000 per year, named for President Hrabowski and designed to enable pedagogical innovation through funding for resources such as course release and support personnel. In 2014, the provost further promoted the status of this work and created a new disseminating structure by asking the FDC to organize a yearly symposium on teaching and learning, showcasing faculty and staff projects for student success.

The center now had three interrelated themes in its mission of faculty support for teaching: faculty development, pedagogical innovation and research, and assessment of student learning outcomes. Enhanced resources meant that the center was able to add to its programming and engage faculty in more sustained learning experiences, such as faculty learning communities and certificate programs. These experiences have the potential to create an even greater sense of community among participating faculty and promote more lasting transformation in practice (Beach & Cox, 2009; Borrego & Henderson, 2014; McAlpine & Weston, 2000), outcomes we are now beginning to document through faculty surveys, reflections, and observations of teaching.

402 L. C. Hodges and P. McDermott

Moreover, critical for the institution's effectiveness and reputation, assessment support from the FDC was instrumental in the university receiving positive recognition on its assessment processes in its 10-year review by its accrediting body. The growth of the center and the expanded initiatives on campus around pedagogical innovation, research, and assessment reflect the interrelationship between the center's work and the university's vision of itself as a leader in undergraduate education.

Re-envisioning for the Future

The first 20 years of our center illustrated the themes articulated earlier, namely that such centers can influence change by working within existing structures, recognizing and capitalizing on interrelationships in the organization, and being both responsive and proactive in evolving aspects of higher education. As we look ahead, we are guided by the university's strategic plan of 2015. In recognition of the importance of teaching and learning in the university's vision, one of the four focal areas of the plan was *innovative curriculum and pedagogy*. Discussions with student, faculty, and staff groups in a number of settings over several years resulted in the recommendation to *enhance the capacity of the FDC to provide support for research on and training in best pedagogical practices and transform it into the Center for Teaching Excellence*. Planning for this new center is currently under way.

Conclusion

We began the FDC with an emphasis on supporting the university's goal of providing a distinctive undergraduate experience for all students. To promote change, the directors recognized the need to create community among faculty and connect to institutional priorities. As the university evolved to frame its distinctiveness around pedagogical innovation and research, the FDC became a hub for information on evidence-based teaching and assessment of student learning outcomes, and provided community around SoTL, bringing the research and teaching missions more closely together. This alignment resonated with and re-envisioned the aims expressed in the original proposal for the FDC. The changing landscape of learners in higher education in the USA places new demands on faculty to connect with students—both intellectually and culturally—to create meaningful, transformative educational experiences. As we both look ahead and reflect on the past, this growing imperative of inclusive practice brings us full circle to the founding principles of the institution. The new center will continue to build interrelationships and respond to institutional needs and national pressures to advance the work of the university in achieving its vision of inclusive excellence in teaching.

Acknowledgements We gratefully acknowledge the help of Dr Jack Prostko in providing historical information necessary for this chapter. We also recognize and appreciate the many people at the university who, over the years, were instrumental to the establishment and success of the center.

References

Bass, R. (1999). The scholarship of teaching: what's the problem? *Inventio: Creative Thinking About Learning and Teaching, 1*(1).

Beach, A. L., & Cox, M. D. (2009). The impact of faculty learning communities on teaching and learning. *Learning Communities Journal, 1*(1), 7–27.

Beach, A. L., Sorcinelli, M. D., Austin, A. E., & Rivard, J. K. (2016). *Faculty development in the age of evidence: Current practices, future imperatives.* Stylus Press.

Borrego, M., & Henderson, C. (2014). Increasing the use of evidence-based teaching in STEM higher education: A comparison of eight change strategies. *Journal of Engineering Education, 103*(2), 220–252.

Bransford, J. D., Brown, A. L., & Cocking, R. R. (Eds.). (1999). *How people learn: Brain, mind, experience, and school.* National Academy Press.

Erickson, G. (1986). A survey of faculty development practices. *To Improve the Academy, 5*(1), 182–196.

Kezar, A. J. (2001). *Understanding and facilitating organizational change in the 21st century: Recent research and conceptualizations.* Jossey-Bass.

McAlpine, L., & Weston, C. (2000). Reflection: Issues related to improving professors' teaching and students' learning. *Instructional Science, 28*(5), 363–385.

Schroeder, C. M., et al. (2011). *Coming in from the margins: Faculty development's emerging organizational development role in institutional change.* Stylus Press.

Senge, P. M. (1990). *The fifth discipline: The art and practice of the learning organization.* Century.

Shulman, L. S. (1993). Teaching as community property: Putting an end to pedagogical solitude. *Change, 25*(6), 6–7.

Sorcinelli, M. D., Austin, A. E., Eddy, P. L., & Beach, A. L. (2006). *Creating the future of faculty development: Learning from the past, understanding the present.* Anker Publishers.

Thedwall, K. (2008). Non-tenure track faculty: Rising numbers, lost opportunities. *New Directions in Higher Education, 143*, 11–19.

26

A Holistic Vision of Faculty Excellence: Creating Sustainable Programming That Expands Community, Infrastructure, and Capacity

Jennifer Keys and Abiódún "G-P" Gòkè-Pariolá

Introduction

North Central College (NCC) is a comprehensive liberal arts institution located in a thriving suburb just west of Chicago, Illinois, USA. Enrollments of 2,770 undergraduates and 200 graduate students, average class sizes of 20, and a student-to-faculty ratio of 14:1 enables us to live by our cardinal rule, which is: *Everything that we do begins with our students.* We pride ourselves on inspired instruction by 151 full-time (108 tenure-track) faculty who love to teach, and who support students inside and outside of the classroom, helping them realize their direction.

History

The earliest academic professional development centers (ADCs) emerged at larger institutions with a heavy emphasis on research, such as the University of Michigan, where publications and grants were the principal determinant of tenure and continued success (Cook & Kaplan, 2011). As the focus on student learning grew, ADCs were designed to address the "problem" of deficient

---

J. Keys (✉) • A. "G-P". Gòkè-Pariolá
North Central College, Naperville, IL, USA
e-mail: jennifer.keys@northwestern.edu; agokepariola@noctrl.edu

© The Author(s), under exclusive license to Springer Nature Switzerland AG 2023
O. J. Neisler (ed.), *The Palgrave Handbook of Academic Professional Development Centers*,
Palgrave Studies on Leadership and Learning in Teacher Education,
https://doi.org/10.1007/978-3-030-80967-6_26

pedagogical preparation for newly minted doctorates. Smaller institutions that had always focused primarily on teaching also began to establish centers. To overcome the remediation stigma—the pervasive belief that their existence was to remedy the problem of ineffective teaching—ADCs sought to reframe their work by accentuating intentional teaching practices and critical reflection (Reder, 2010).

Consistent with our heavy institutional emphasis on inspired instruction, NCC faculty must first concentrate on the establishment of a record of success in their teaching. Faculty are then expected to broaden their impact by becoming effective mentors, engaged scholars, and active faculty citizens. At every rank, faculty must continue to engage in self-reflection and demonstrate growth in all four of these areas of evaluation. At NCC, the Center for the Advancement of Faculty Excellence (CAFÉ) was created to help ensure that faculty members are not only equipped to meet the multifaceted standards for promotion and tenure, but that faculty are fully supported in their continued efforts to flourish in all the interconnected areas of their professional life.

Our college's first ADC, which launched in 2009, was not an integrated model. The concept had been developed over several years by the now-retired vice president of academic affairs (VPAA) in collaboration with a small group of interested faculty. The charter document stated that the purpose was *to foster excellence in teaching and learning and to extend and heighten the impact of conversation and inquiry around student learning as a core dimension of institutional identity*. It followed a typical pattern for institutions of our size: the director was released from two of seven classes required annually, the center occupied a very small space in one of the least desirable spots on campus, and it had a small budget of $ 7,000. A separate faculty committee awarded summer research grants. This was essentially the extent of the investment made in faculty development.

In 2015, a new provost/VPAA was brought in with a wealth of experience from other institutions as a passionate advocate of faculty development. Rather than trying to tweak the status quo, he challenged the campus community to consider the following: *How would we build a center if we were starting from scratch?* The answer was to adopt a backward design approach, which shifted the focus from addressing a narrow, predetermined "problem" toward much bolder end-goals:

1. How can we leverage a new ADC to not only contribute to the core institutional mission of teaching and learning but also to help advance other strategic priorities?

2. How can the ADC stimulate broad faculty interest and develop sustainable programs that positively affect student success?
3. How can the ADC help create an environment in which faculty are engaged and thriving so that our students can be as well?

These questions did not assume that there were deficiencies in faculty work. What these questions did reflect was a dual focus on individual-level faculty support and broader organizational development, which—to paraphrase Gillespie (2010)—refers to efforts geared toward shaping institutional processes, facilitating and/or leading change initiatives, and enhancing overall organizational functioning by taking both human and structural interactions into account. The provost/VPAA moved quickly to seek input from key stakeholders, including the elected Faculty Steering Committee, and these ideas were embedded in the leadership charge. The provost/VPAA successfully pitched the importance of this institutional investment to the President's Cabinet.

Organizational Reporting and Structure of the ADC

In 2016, we launched a competitive national search for a director who would provide leadership for all faculty professional development programs. To establish the break from the past and to chart the new course for the future, the scope of the ADC was expanded, and the name was changed from the "Center for Teaching and Learning" to the "Center for the Advancement of Faculty Excellence." The director would be a full-time administrator, reporting directly to the provost/VPAA; Sorcinelli (2002) identifies this as a key principle of good practice, as it signals strong financial backing and a shared agenda with the Academic Affairs division of the college. The inaugural director would also sit with the deans and other key academic leaders on the Provost's Council (see Fig. 26.1) and attend the Board of Trustees Academic Affairs Committee where system-level changes and the future direction of the institution is ultimately determined—this acknowledges the vital role that educational developers can play in helping colleges navigate the continually shifting landscape of higher education (Chism, 1998).

The ideal candidate would have a terminal degree, an active scholarly agenda, and a demonstrated record of excellence as an educator. To serve as a model for pedagogical innovation, the director would be given the opportunity to teach

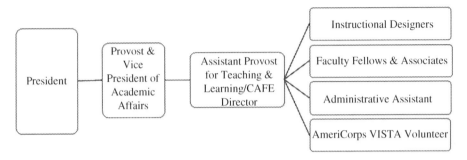

Fig. 26.1 Diagram of the reporting structure of the CAFÉ

one or two classes per year. This is consistent with the employment patterns of educational developers worldwide. According to an international survey conducted by Green and Little (2016), 59% of directors hold a doctorate and nearly all have teaching responsibilities (96%) and conduct research (84%), although only 29% are in primarily administrative roles. The search culminated with the hire of an internal candidate who had come up through the faculty ranks; her familiarity with the institutional culture has proven to be an asset. Reder (2010) advises: "Directors who are known and respected by the faculty and who have teaching experience bring to the position a strong base of knowledge and credibility" (302); however, it is a "somewhat ironic move" to pluck an excellent teacher-scholar for this new enterprise (299).

The total annual institutional budget commitment of the center, including personnel, is about $400,000. The CAFÉ director also serves as the provost/VPAA's designee on the elected Faculty Development and Recognition Committee (FDRC), which allocates additional funding for faculty research grants, sabbaticals, and awards. We regard this substantial investment as critical for helping us retain top-notch faculty who will ensure that our students receive the high-quality education that they deserve.

Mission, Vision, Goals

The director crafted an aspirational mission statement:

> CAFÉ provides a distinctive, holistic model of faculty development. The vibrant array of programming utilizes evidence-informed best practices to support faculty at all stages of their careers in their efforts to grow and thrive as teachers, mentors, scholars, and campus leaders, which is critically important for bolstering student

success. CAFÉ also contributes to college-wide strategic initiatives by helping to create the optimal conditions in which faculty can thrive.

In terms of space, the CAFÉ is more centrally located in the library with a suite that is large enough to accommodate the director, staff, a conference table, and a One Button video recording studio. Now in its fourth year, the CAFÉ has become known as an inviting, full-service office that offers robust support and the resources to achieve higher levels of impact. It has sparked campus-wide interest and participation in faculty development workshops, seminars, institutes, and learning communities. The biggest accelerator of faculty buy-in has been word of mouth about the value of CAFÉ's offerings and individualized faculty consultations. We devote the remainder of this chapter to sharing observations about our efforts to expand community, infrastructure, and capacity to achieve our holistic vision of faculty excellence.

Expanding Community

Our determined effort to expand community can be seen most clearly in our processes for acclimating new faculty, matching collaborative colleagues, showcasing knowledge, and orchestrating collegial events. As a new faculty administrator kindly remarked about our opening week schedule, there is "so much cheer."

We recognize that the socialization of new faculty is key for shifting culture, which is why we devote considerable attention to welcoming colleagues into our community. A unique feature of our ADC is that the director plays a role in recruitment by meeting with every faculty candidate to highlight the rich array of career-spanning faculty development opportunities. Three members of the current cohort specifically mentioned the CAFÉ as part of what attracted them to our campus. As our professional programs at the graduate level continue to grow, the CAFÉ sends a clear signal that we will help prepare skilled practitioners who are teaching for the first time. Our new faculty orientation has been completely reimagined from what it was five years ago. The former two-day talking head marathon has been replaced with Navigating North Central, a program that focuses on cohort bonding and interactive sharing of the essential institutional knowledge needed to get classes off to a great start. Over the course of the academic year, the CAFÉ sponsors informal gatherings hosted by the deans and new faculty are invited as the guests of honor.

Acclimating conversations continue with the New Faculty Academy, which promotes empowerment and the exploration of pathways to impactful teaching, dedicated mentoring, engaged scholarship, and vibrant campus leadership in a small college environment. The extended format makes it easier to absorb the information when it is most applicable, such as a discussion of student evaluations (i.e., how to avoid fixating on outliers, research on validity and bias, etc.) after the faculty member has received fall semester feedback. The New Faculty Academy is guided by a shared reading list that includes *Shaping your Career* (Haviland et al., 2017) and a clear set of learning outcomes. All aspects of this innovative learning community (Cox, 2004) are geared toward demystifying institutional expectations and propelling the members of the first-year cohort toward promotion/tenure. Attendance and completion of the assignments are required for early-career, tenure-track faculty members with reassigned CAFÉ time (equivalent to one four-credit course release)—this is an additional investment from the provost/VPAA's budget. Faculty who come in with prior experience may also join us for any sessions that are of interest.

We connect new faculty to passionate teacher-scholars who have a proven track record of effectiveness and a growth mindset, including our Distinguished Teaching Award and Scholarship prize winners and Ruge Fellows—programs that the CAFÉ now oversees. We also provide Let's Connect Coupons to encourage new faculty members to be proactive in inviting a colleague to coffee or lunch (Rockequemore, 2010). As Johnson (2016) observes in *On Being a Mentor,* high-quality mentoring of junior faculty not only facilitates a smoother transition, it leads to important proximal and distal outcomes, including more effective teaching and service, a stronger record of scholarly productivity, a greater sense of commitment to the institution, higher rates of retention, promotion, and tenure and enhanced career satisfaction (162). By placing a diverse collection of exemplary community members in their orbits, we are helping new faculty build their own mentoring constellation, one that will provide a range of professional and personal support throughout their careers (Johnson et al., 2013).

As Boice (2000) reminds us, "exemplary professors" regularly seek advice. It was in this spirit that we launched the Collaborative Colleagues Matching Program, which facilitates knowledge-sharing and reciprocal relationships at every career stage. The match can hone in on challenges in any area of faculty work, from creating inclusive classrooms to effectively mentoring undergraduate researchers, seeking external grants, adjusting to a department chair role, and maintaining work-life satisfaction. To date we have made over 20 matches. With just the small cost of a lunch for two, we are nurturing an ethos of mutual support within our community. Indeed, "breaking bread together" has long been intuitively understood as a way to enhance cooperation and feelings of closeness and has also been substantiated by research (Woolley & Fishbach, 2019). As Sorcinelli (2002) suggests, "even small rewards such as a luncheon or refreshments act as a positive motivation and add greatly to creating a congenial setting" (19) and she lists fostering collegiality and community as one of the 10 principles of good practice for faculty development.

Our Lunch and Learn series, which attracts between 30–40 attendees per semester, nourishes the body and mind. The director has partnered with faculty in Psychology, Chemistry, Mathematics, and Education to showcase the latest research, which has been a great way to bring more voices and perspectives into the conversation. The format features key takeaways from a recently published book in higher education and, in recognition of the constraints on faculty time, no advance reading is required. The CAFÉ's instructional designer and director drew from Eynon and Gambino's (2017) *High-impact ePortfolio Practice* to gauge and ignite interest in this integrative pedagogy. We also began a tradition of holding a Fall Faculty Colloquium with a featured speaker to invite inspiring ideas, foster dialogue on critical issues in higher education, and unite us in our shared purpose as intellectuals and educators. Most recently, Hanstedt (2018), author of *Creating Wicked Students*, gave a talk entitled "Constructing Engaged, Powerful, Transformative Students," which stoked the flames of curricular creativity that have been burning during our reimagining of general education.

The CAFÉ hosts other events that are intended to deepen social connectedness. Fête Friday is an open-house event that offers a momentary step away from the fast pace and a chance to unwind and converse with colleagues across the campus. For example, the director and provost cohosted a "Higher Ed Happy Hour" to combat proliferating laments and spark conversation about our industry's strengths (Brint, 2019). We were both struck by how the faculty we invited to serve as discussants were honored to have been identified as embodying a positive outlook. While events like these cannot repair fractures from tectonic shifts, they can remind us that there is greater strength in community.

Expanding Infrastructure

As a sociologist, the director is driven to create sustainable organizational structures. In this next section, we offer four illustrations of how the CAFÉ has worked to expand the college's infrastructure so that we can scale up high-impact practices (HIPs), enhance educational technology, bring greater

412   J. Keys and A. "G-P". Gòkè-Pariolá

transparency to our faculty recognition programs, and create a fair system for professional leave and sabbaticals.

NCC has recently transitioned from a three-credit, seven-course teaching load (2-2-3) to a semester calendar with a four-credit, five-course teaching load (2-3). Fewer start-ups and preps combined with greater flexibility in the "fourth hour" will enable us to embed more HIPs (Kuh, 2008). As part of the lead-up to this calendar conversion, the provost appointed the CAFÉ's director as co-chair of the HIP strategic planning team, which heightened CAFÉ's influence and visibility as a hub for disseminating research on these transformative pedagogies. To build the necessary infrastructure for HIPs, the director also collaborates closely with the dean of engaged learning and honors programs, who concentrates on the student side of the equation, to implement tactics and systematically track progress.

We have made the greatest progress to date with community-engaged learning (CEL); disparate threads have been woven together to make this HIP one of our signature programs. We brought together early adopters to form a CEL Faculty Council that agreed on shared terminology. NCC defines CEL as:

> …an educational experience in which students collaborate with community partners to apply academic knowledge and critical thinking skills to meet societal needs. Through critical reflection on their activities, students gain a deeper understanding of course content, a broader appreciation of the discipline, and an enhanced sense of civic efficacy and responsibility.

After our proposal to require every NCC student to take a CEL course was accepted, we worked with faculty to develop their applications for the General Education Committee. A "train the trainer" approach was utilized to cultivate a cadre of CEL workshop leaders, peer consultants, and role models, which enabled more rapid diffusion across the campus. In a stipend-supported CEL Summer Collaboratory for early adopters, participants crowdsourced a thought-provoking reading list, deepened their understanding of the multi-faceted benefits of CEL, developed exemplary CEL projects and courses, received and provided peer feedback, and engaged in a one-day reflective retreat. We put the final pieces of the CEL infrastructure into place by curating resources for a CEL faculty toolkit, securing funding for a CEL mini-grant, hiring four federally funded work-study students to serve as engaged learning facilitators, and training faculty and students to use the new portal to find CEL opportunities. We are also hosting our third AmeriCorps Volunteer in Service to America who serves as liaison between faculty members and community organizations.

We have also been rapidly expanding our infrastructure to support technology-enhanced teaching and learning. The director oversees the instructional design team and provides leadership for the smooth integration of technology to make educational experiences more dynamic. To achieve our strategic plan objective of scaling up high-quality blended and online courses, the CAFÉ developed an Online Pedagogy Institute, open to any faculty member ready to discover, experiment, and revolutionize their courses. This eight-week, stipend-supported online course equips instructors with the knowledge and skills necessary for effective teaching in a blended or online learning environment. Participants engage in dialogue, reflection, and collaboration, and they get hands-on practice integrating technology and utilizing online communication tools. By experiencing an online course from a student's perspective, participants also gain valuable insights into the many benefits and unique challenges of learning online. These kinds of communities of practice have been shown to enhance the application of knowledge as well as social relationships and can lead to performance improvement (Abigail, 2016).

To make the CAFÉ even more integral, the oversight and administration of a variety of faculty-centered initiatives have been added to the portfolio of the director, including all faculty recognition programs and the new sabbatical/professional leave program. We have made tremendous progress in building out both areas and have developed clear pathways and far more transparent decision-making processes. Previously, the selection committees and criteria for faculty awards had always been cloaked in mystery. The director and FDRC engaged in a multiyear systematic review of our awards process that has led to the creation of clearer guidelines; each committee is now assembled with broad faculty representation, there is a confidentiality agreement, and nominations can be made year-round. We have filled in the gaps by adding new awards for mentoring, online teaching, and for visiting faculty, elements that were overlooked in our previous structure.

As part of faculty governance, the FDRC can hold open meetings and hearings on big issues like the creation of our new banked professional leave/competitive sabbatical program, which recognizes the transformative potential in periodic opportunities to take a break from habitual routines. It supports the faculty member's pursuit of thoughtfully chosen and uniquely individual professional pathways. This was one of the enticements for faculty to move to a semester calendar. The director has been a lead architect of this complex new system—including eligibility, cycles, application forms, and review criteria—which involved building an entire infrastructure. Working

Expanding Capacity

The CAFÉ is also making inroads in three other areas of faculty evaluation—mentoring, citizenship, and scholarship—and the capacity of our ADC and its director has been significantly expanded. To support faculty as they are exploring new ways to make mentoring connections, the director partnered with student success and student affairs departments to create and catalogue opportunities in an e-book.

Faculty had expressed uncertainty regarding their new role as we transitioned to a team of professional advisors. This advising staff is trained to ensure that students are meeting their graduation requirements, but their large caseloads and perceived lack of disciplinary expertise garnered some skepticism. In our old model, every faculty member, regardless of their commitment to mentoring, was assigned an advising load of approximately 20 students. Meetings were required for registration and advisors were responsible for checking in with students about unsatisfactory progress reports. Many faculty advisors, of course, went beyond this by encouraging students to reflect on their broader aspirations and so the desire to safeguard our existing practices was not surprising. We know that, beyond college:

> If graduates recalled having a professor who cared about them as a person, made them excited about learning, and encouraged them to pursue their dreams, their odds of being engaged at work more than doubled, as did their odds of thriving in all aspects of their well-being. (Ray & Kafka, 2014)

To inspire a new vision for mentoring, the director helped draft new faculty evaluation guidelines and the CAFÉ began to offer workshops highlighting other impactful forms of faculty-student interaction, which research demonstrates have a positive impact on students' persistence and academic achievement (Crisp & Cruz, 2009).

All faculty are expected to be engaged as campus citizens and there are opportunities for them to move into leadership roles. Although there had been sporadic training opportunities in the past for deans and department chairs, the CAFÉ now offers a half-day workshop at the start of each academic year. These typically focus on the most critical areas—onboarding new faculty, budgeting, course scheduling, interpreting student ratings, and faculty evaluation. In an attempt to move beyond troubleshooting, we have discussed ways to foster strengths and cohesion in a holistic department (Weiner, 2015) and positive academic leadership, which Buller (2013) describes as a proactive approach that emphasizes what is working well over fixing what is flawed. This year, the CAFÉ director partnered with a professor of Psychology to explore emotional labor (Hochschild, 2012) in an interactive presentation playfully titled "Why Some People Suck the Life Out of You and What You Can Do About It." We hope to further expand department chairs' leadership capacity by positioning them as drivers of diversity and inclusion (Chun & Evans, 2015).

With so much institutional change, our faculty frequently lament the lack of time left to devote to their scholarly and creative work. Thus far, the CAFÉ has been unsuccessful in sustaining faculty writing groups, but we are gaining momentum in the scholarship of teaching and learning (SoTL). On behalf of the Associated Colleges of the Chicago Area, NCC hosted the 2019 Scholarship of Pedagogy Symposium, an initiative that brought faculty together across disciplines and institutions for a dynamic exchange of innovative pedagogical strategies. In the lead-up to the submission deadline, one of our CAFÉ associates, an experienced SoTL practitioner, offered a seminar series for faculty to consider ways to engage in this systematic and reflective process. By learning about our own teaching and from one another, we can make a deeper impact on student learning.

CAFÉ associates and fellows further extend the reach of the ADC. The annual request for proposals seeks associates who wish to devote energy to a targeted strategic initiative that has broad institutional value like internships or inclusive teaching. Fellows work closely with the director to: (1) identify needs and prioritize CAFÉ initiatives that have the greatest potential to foster both faculty and student success; (2) build capacity for scaling-up intensive pedagogies; (3) disseminate evidence-informed best pedagogical practices and stimulate innovation in teaching and mentoring; (4) bolster the infrastructure of support that faculty need for their scholarly and creative pursuits; (5) establish indicators of CAFÉ's success and assess measured outcomes; and (6) enhance the institutional impact and reputation of the center. The work of associates is recognized as a significant form of service in the faculty evaluation process and fellows receive two credits of reassigned time—this small investment has been an effective way to grow CAFÉ programs in a resource-constrained environment.

In 2018, the director was promoted to assistant provost for teaching and learning and this new title came with an enlarged scope of strategic tactics related to fostering a culture of creativity and risk-taking, rewarding innovation and excellence, increasing prestigious awards and fellowships, partnering with department chairs and deans on strategies for faculty recruitment, retention, and success, and shaping policies and practices that help sustain a diverse, inclusive, and equitable community.

Conclusion

Tenured faculty members report receiving insufficient recognition for their work and a lack of encouragement in their professional development; however, faculty at smaller private institutions tend to be most emotionally and intellectually connected to what they do (Jaschik & Lederman, 2015). This puts the CAFÉ in an enviable position. All too often, one observes low faculty patronage of ADCs, but the CAFÉ has been set up to be integral to our vision of faculty excellence. The more faculty that can be proactively supported as teachers, mentors, scholars, and campus citizens, the more dynamic, inclusive, and transformational the educational experience can be for students. We offer the CAFÉ as a model for expanding community, infrastructure, and capacity to unleash faculty members' full potential and achieve the highest aspirations for student learning.

References

Abigail, L. K. M. (2016). Do communities of practice enhance faculty development? *Health Professions Education, 2*(2), 61–74.

Boice, R. (2000). *Advice for new faculty members: Nihil nimus.* Allyn & Bacon.

Brint, S. (2019). *Two cheers for higher education: Why American universities are stronger than ever—And how to meet the challenges they face.* Princeton University Press.

Buller, J. L. (2013). *Positive academic leadership: How to stop putting out fires and start making a difference.* John Wiley & Sons.

Chism, N. V. N. (1998). The role of educational developers in institutional change: From the basement office to the front office. *To Improve the Academy, 17*(1), 141–153.

Chun, E., & Evans, A. (2015). *The department chair as transformative diversity leader: Building inclusive learning environments in higher education.* Stylus Press.

Cook, C., & Kaplan, M. (2011). *Advancing the culture of teaching on campus: How a teaching center can make a difference*. Stylus Press.

Cox, M. D. (2004). Introduction to faculty learning communities. *New Directions for Teaching and Learning, 2004*(97), 5–23.

Crisp, G., & Cruz, I. (2009). Mentoring college students: A critical review of the literature between 1990 and 2007. *Research in Higher Education, 50*(6), 525–545.

Eynon, B., & Gambino, L. M. (2017). *High-impact ePortfolio practice: A catalyst for student, faculty, and institutional learning*. Stylus Press.

Gillespie, K. (2010). Organizational development. In K. Gillespie & D. Robertson (Eds.), *A guide to faculty development* (2nd ed., pp. 379–396). Jossey-Bass.

Green, D. A., & Little, D. (2016). Family portrait: A profile of educational developers around the world. *International Journal for Academic Development, 21*(2), 135–150.

Hanstedt, P. (2018). *Creating wicked students: Designing courses for a complex world*. Stylus Press.

Haviland, D., Ortiz, A. M., & Henriques, L. (2017). *Shaping your career: A guide for early career faculty*. Stylus Press.

Hochschild, A. (2012). *The managed heart: Commercialization of human feeling* (3rd ed.). University of California Press.

Jaschik, S., & Lederman, D. (2015). The 2015 Inside Higher Ed survey of college and university faculty workplace engagement: A study by Gallup and Inside Higher Ed. *Inside Higher Ed*. https://www.insidehighered.com/booklet/2015-survey-college-and-university-faculty-workplace-engagement

Johnson, W. B. (2016). *On being a mentor: A guide for higher education faculty* (2nd ed.). Routledge.

Johnson, W. B., Barnett, J. E., Elman, N. S., Forrest, L., & Kaslow, N. J. (2013). The competence constellation model: a communitarian approach to support professional competence. *Professional Psychology: Research and Practice, 44*(5), 343.

Kuh, G. D. (2008). *High-impact educational practices: What they are, who has access to them, and why they matter*. Association of American Colleges and Universities.

Ray, J., & Kafka, S. (2014). *Life in college matters for life after college*. Gallup. https://news.gallup.com/poll/168848/life-college-matters-life-college.aspx

Reder, M. (2010). Effective practices in the context of small colleges. In K. Gillespie & D. Robertson (Eds.), *A guide to faculty development* (2nd ed., pp. 293–308). Jossey-Bass.

Rockequemore, K. (2010). Get out there and shake it! *Inside Higher Ed*. https://www.insidehighered.com/advice/2010/02/15/get-out-there-and-shake-it

Sorcinelli, M. D. (2002). Ten principles of good practice in creating and sustaining teaching and learning centers. In K. H. Gillespie (Ed.), *A guide to faculty development: Practical advice, examples, and resources* (pp. 9–23). Anker Publishers.

Weiner, T. (2015). Re-imagining the academic department: Conceptualizing a holistic department. In N. H. Hensel, L. Hunnicutt, & D. A. Salomon (Eds.), *Redefining the paradigm: Faculty models to support student learning* (pp. 21–39). New American Colleges and Universities.

Woolley, K., & Fishbach, A. (2019). Shared plates, shared minds: Consuming from a shared plate promotes cooperation. *Psychological Science, 30*(4), 541–552.

27

Promoting a Culture of Teaching Excellence in a Chinese Research University

Yihong Qiu

Introduction

While many Chinese universities and colleges have a tradition of new faculty orientation, educational development is a fairly recent idea in China, which has developed only in the past decade. One of the earliest academic professional development centers (ADCs) in China, the Center for Teaching and Learning Development (CTLD) of Shanghai Jiao Tong University (SJTU), runs various events and programs to promote teaching and learning capacities on campus. This chapter briefly introduces the history, mission, and structure of the CTLD, and describes various workshops, the new faculty orientation, and a special event for advancing teaching culture, before delving in more detail into the midterm student feedback (MSF) service and scholarship of teaching and learning (SoTL)-related activities. The influence of the CTLD on teaching culture is investigated and discussed. Evidence shows that the CTLD has successfully made itself visible and respectable in a short period of time and plays an important role in promoting a culture of teaching excellence on campus.

Y. Qiu (✉)
Center for Teaching and Learning Development, Shanghai Jiao Tong University, Shanghai, China
e-mail: yhqiu@sjtu.edu.cn

© The Author(s), under exclusive license to Springer Nature Switzerland AG 2023
O. J. Neisler (ed.), *The Palgrave Handbook of Academic Professional Development Centers*,
Palgrave Studies on Leadership and Learning in Teacher Education,
https://doi.org/10.1007/978-3-030-80967-6_27

419

History of the CTLD

Established in 1896, SJTU is one of the oldest Chinese higher education institutions, and is a comprehensive, research-intensive, and internationalized first-class university. The university provides bachelor's, master's, and doctoral degree programs in economics, law, humanities, science, engineering, agriculture, medicine, management, and the arts. More than 3,000 full-time faculty members educate about 16,000 undergraduates, 30,000 postgraduates, and 2,700 overseas students (SJTU, n.d.).

The CTLD of SJTU was established in 2011 to meet the need for improving teaching and learning capacity and quality. It is among the first ADCs in China, particularly since educational development is a fairly new concept in the country. In response to strong national concern over improving teaching and learning quality in the context of the rapid expansion of enrolment in higher education (Vithal, 2018), the Ministry of Education (MOE) and Ministry of Finance jointly launched the Project of Undergraduate Teaching Quality and Teaching Reform in 2011, in which the construction of ADCs was suggested. Since then, many universities and colleges have established their own ADCs. The CTLD is also one of 30 national model centers supported by the MOE with extra funding (¥ 1 million each year for five years), with responsibilities to conduct practical research on the construction of the ADC and to organize training for ADC staff in the region.

In 2013, the CTLD joined 13 other ADCs to form the Chinese Higher Education Development (CHED) Network with the mission to promote educational development in Chinese universities and colleges and jointly improve the quality of teaching and learning in higher education across the country. In 2014, the CTLD hosted the first annual conference of the CHED Network in Shanghai.

Mission, Organizational Reporting, and Structure of the CTLD

Bearing the responsibility for supporting teaching and learning development, the mission of the CTLD is to disseminate research-based and innovative teaching ideas and practices, advance a culture of teaching excellence, facilitate inquiry of teaching and learning, and provide a network for discussing teaching and learning.

Currently, the CTLD has a director, deputy director, two assistant directors, an advisor (the founding director), and 12 staff members. Eight professionals have different academic backgrounds in education, psychology, science, and engineering, and five of them have participated in the Center for Research on Learning and Teaching Fellowship Program offered by the University of Michigan, USA. The director reports to the executive vice president in charge of undergraduate education (see Fig. 27.1). The CTLD is fully financially supported by SJTU, including staff salaries, everyday operation fees, grants, and the costs of hosting conferences and staff training, etc. In addition, donations are received from the School of Continuing Education, especially for the CTLD Excellence in Teaching Award.

The CTLD collaborates with other teaching support units, such as the Network and Information Center (NIC) and Educational Technology Center (ETC). At the beginning of its establishment, the CTLD obtained the permission of SJTU to send its event notice through the university's e-mail system by the NIC. Because the CTLD is now widely recognized among faculty and staff, the ETC often collaborates with the CTLD to publicize and implement their educational technology training.

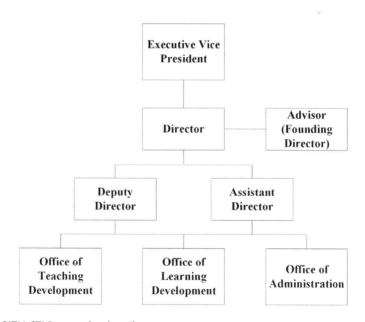

Fig. 27.1 SJTU CTLD organization chart

Activities and Programs of the CTLD

The CTLD runs various face-to-face activities, in addition to using website and WeChat (a popular Chinese social messaging application) resources to reach as many teachers and students as possible. CTLD activities and programs fall into four general categories: (1) one-time activities to increase awareness of educational development, such as workshops, teaching assistant training, and the new faculty orientation; (2) in-depth services to better support faculty (Cook, 2011), such as the MSF service and teaching development grants; (3) awards to faculty members who have devoted themselves to teaching and achieved excellent learning outcomes; and (4) services for schools and departments through customized programs and the establishment of a subcenter.

Workshops, Seminars, and Luncheons

The CTLD runs workshops, seminars, or luncheons one to two times each week during the spring and fall semesters, usually at lunch time with a light lunch served. On average, each event attracts about 50 participants. Topics range from pedagogy, instructional design, educational technology, mentoring of postgraduates, and personal career growth to the experience of an overseas visit. The workshops are usually facilitated by CTLD professionals, and sometimes external experts are invited. The CTLD invites faculty members with excellent histories of teaching or mentoring postgraduate students to give seminars and luncheons and share their good teaching practices and teaching innovations. From time to time, foreign faculty members or visitors are invited to give seminars, which are also very popular.

Assessment data are collected at the end of each event, as most similar programs do (Plank & Kalish, 2010; Wright, 2011). Participants are invited to fill out a feedback form in which they are asked about whether they are satisfied with the event, what they have learnt, and what changes they would henceforth make in their teaching. These data are used both to show the effectiveness of these activities and to improve subsequent events. By the end of 2018, more than 11,500 people had participated in these events, and the overall satisfaction rate exceeded 95%.

New Faculty Orientation

The new faculty orientation is mandatory, and it is a prerequisite for new faculty members to obtain a Qualification Certificate for Teachers in Colleges and Universities. The Office of Human Resources organized the new faculty orientation for many years before the establishment of the CTLD. Since 2013, CTLD has taken over the training module of pedagogy for the orientation. Anyone who already has teaching experience in other universities can be exempted from this module. The two-day training includes student-centered teaching philosophy, instructional design, learning about students, sharing teaching experience, and the practice of microteaching. Each year, about 100 new faculty members participate in the pedagogy training module, with an overall satisfaction of 97.2%.

The 'Thanks a Million, Dear Teacher' Event

As SJTU is a research university, research is often perceived to be more visible and valued than teaching during the annual review, reward, and promotion processes. In recent years, like other research universities (Cook, 2011), SJTU has made teaching a priority. In order to create an atmosphere of appreciation for teachers and thus advance a culture of teaching excellence, the CTLD has organized an event since 2015 during the SJTU anniversary celebration month known as "Thanks a Million, Dear Teacher." Specially designed cards are provided in multiple locations to current students and alumni so that they can write down their appreciation and blessings to their favorite instructors. Completed cards can be put into a collecting box at any of the predesignated collection places. After the event, the CTLD sorts out the cards and hands them over to the recipients. Some of the instructors who have not used CTLD services learn about the CTLD in this way. In the first event, about 600 cards were distributed to recipients.

Most recipients are pleasantly surprised when they receive such cards. They are gratified because their former students still remember them many years later, and they feel that their engagement in teaching is well rewarded. As one instructor said: "Seeing these words is really the warmest moment in my heart. I am very pleased!" Another said: "The students' sincere gratitude gives me a great sense of happiness and promotes me to improve myself."

The CTLD obtains the consent of instructors who have received a lot of cards to record a short video of them wherein they can express their joy and talk about their teaching philosophy. These videos are then published on the

424   Y. Qiu

CTLD webpage to reach more people. To be more efficient and environmentally friendly, a mobile app has been developed recently to avoid the use of paper cards. Students and alumni can choose different e-cards in which to write their gratitude and blessings, with these e-cards then e-mailed to the recipients.

Midterm Student Feedback

Student ratings of teaching have been collected at SJTU for many years. However, due to the fact that the rating is done near the end of courses and the lack of appropriate explanation of the results, many instructors believe that these ratings do not help them improve their teaching. However, formative student feedback can effectively enhance teaching practice, especially with the help of professional consultants (Clark & Bekey, 1979; Diamond, 2004; Finelli et al., 2008). Therefore, the MSF service was launched shortly after the establishment of the CTLD.

The MSF Process

The MSF service is adapted from the formative assessment technique known as Small Group Instructional Diagnosis (Clark & Redmond, 1982). The five-step process is briefly described as follows (Black, 1998; Finelli et al., 2011). Step one, the consultant and the instructor have a first meeting to get to know each other. The consultant introduces the process to the instructor and then learns about the learning outcomes, assessment methods, classroom activities, and the instructors' concerns, after which they schedule a classroom observation. Step two, the consultant arrives at the classroom before the scheduled class time and observes and records the teaching and learning activities until about 15 minutes of class time are left. The instructor then hands over the class to the consultant and leaves the classroom. The consultant explains the purpose and procedure of the data collection to the students before dividing them into groups of three to five. Each group receives a form with two questions: *What are the strengths of this course?* and *What changes could be made to help you learn better?* Students first discuss these questions in small groups before writing down their responses, and then the consultant facilitates a whole class discussion to determine their collective responses. Step three, the consultant writes a report based on the students' feedback. Step four, the consultant meets with the teacher, usually before the next class, to share the report, students' comments, and the observation data, and to discuss how to respond to the comments and how to improve the instructor's teaching. Step five, near the end of the semester, the CTLD invites the instructors and their students to take a follow-up survey to assess the effectiveness of the MSF service.

Publicizing the MSF Service

The MSF service is a one-on-one teaching consultation with which most faculty members are not familiar. Therefore, in order to make it more widely known, the CTLD uses a variety of ways to publicize the service, such as introducing it on its website, posting leaflets on the walls of elevators in classroom buildings, and putting leaflets in the teacher's lounge. In order to eliminate the worries that those who seek teaching consultations have poor teaching practices, the CTLD also holds informational luncheons from time to time. Instructors who have used the MSF service are invited to interact with participants face-to-face, sharing why they chose the MSF service and how they benefited from the consultation. This kind of communication conveys the message that anyone who wants to better their teaching should utilize the MSF service. It is so effective that some participants have even applied for the service on the spot.

Although the MSF service is promoted in various ways, the number of instructors using this service is about 40 each year. One possible reason for this is that publicity of the service has failed to attract the attention of teachers. Another possible reason is that many teachers think their teaching is good enough and so they lack the motivation to pursue teaching excellence. A campus survey showed that more than 98% of faculty members regarded their teaching to be either excellent or good, and that intense research pressure and busy academic activities affected their engagement in teaching.

Effectiveness of the MSF Service

In the 2017 academic year, 42 instructors used the MSF service. The CTLD invited all these instructors to take a follow-up survey and requested that they invite their students to take a student survey approximately 7–8 weeks after the MSF service. The instructor questionnaire included items related to their perception of the MSF service with multiple-choice responses or Likert scale ratings, as well as three open-ended questions concerning what changes they had made in their class, what aspect was most helpful from the MSF service, and what could be done to improve the MSF service (Finelli et al., 2008). The student questionnaire consisted of items regarding the service's effectiveness, perceptions of teaching changes, and the impact the service had had on their learning with either multiple-choice responses or Likert scale ratings, as well as an open-ended question to determine how their learning had changed as a result of the experience (Hurney et al., 2014). A total of 29 instructors took the instructor survey, and 15 asked their students to participate in the student survey, with 391 anonymous student responses collected.

From the perspective of the instructors, 100% were satisfied with the MSF service, 96.6% thought it was worth taking the time to undergo the service, 93.1% regarded the service as having a positive influence on the instructor-student relationship, and 93.1% reported what they had changed in their teaching practice. In response to the question *What was most helpful of the MSF?*, one participant wrote: "Compared with asking students' opinions directly, CTLD as a third party, can obtain students' real feelings and opinions about their learning, which is more helpful for me to improve my teaching quality." Another expressed that: "The MSF service is great! The consultant is very experienced and professional. Although her subject background is different from mine, she grasped the key points and gave me some effective suggestions."

From the perspective of the students, 93.1% regarded the MSF process as efficient, 91.6% perceived some changes in their class, 91.6% regarded the service as having a positive influence on the instructor-student relationship, and 88.2% expressed that their motivation was increased due to the MSF experience. One student wrote: "My teacher has known our opinions and improved his teaching methods. I'm more engaged in this course." Another stated that "My teacher writes [on] the blackboard clearly now, and I am more willing to take notes."

These results show that the MSF service does help teaching and learning, findings that are consistent with those reported in other studies (Diamond, 2004; Finelli et al., 2008; Hurney et al., 2014).

SoTL-Related Activities

About 10 years after Boyer's (1990) paper, *Scholarship Reconsidered: Priorities of the Professoriate*, articles discussing SoTL began to appear in Chinese journals (Yu & Yu, 2000; Geng, 2002). Although most Chinese university teachers are unfamiliar with the concept or definition of SoTL, inquiries on teaching and learning are carried out in various disciplines. As one of the pioneer advocates for SoTL in China, the CTLD launched teaching development grants in 2012 to support SoTL projects. These projects align with the center's mission to facilitate the inquiry of teaching and learning on campus. The CTLD believes that SoTL projects will be an efficient way to encourage instructors to commit themselves to improving their teaching (Mårtensson et al., 2011; McAlpine & Gandell, 2003) and thus advance a culture of teaching excellence institutionally.

Teaching Development Grants

Teaching development grants include both phased levels of funding and specific funding to support instructors to better understand and improve teaching and learning through evidence-based inquiries. These grants are eligible for multiple applications and awarded upon completion of the project. A-level grants are eligible to those who have completed an A- or B-level project and who are expected to make a significant contribution to the field with further funding. B-level projects are open to all applicants for evidence-based classroom practice that incorporates advanced teaching ideas and pedagogies. The Internationalization Project—initiated in 2017 in cooperation with the University of Hong Kong, Hong Kong University of Science and Technology, and Hong Kong Baptist University—supports the investigation of issues encountered in developing students' international vision and competency as well as cross-cultural understanding and tolerance.

These projects usually last for one year, and a final report is required at the end of the project. If the project undertaker cannot complete the project in time, they can apply for an extension of one year. To ensure the quality of these projects, the CTLD has standardized processes for application, proposal review, midterm inspection, and final report review (Cook & Marincovich, 2010).

Impact

From 2013 to 2018, 27 A-level and 324 B-level funding proposals were approved, of which 18 and 298 projects were successfully completed, respectively. In most cases, failure to complete the project was due to the inability to submit a final report, or lack of solid evidence of practice or inquiry in the report. The grants were awarded across schools, with the largest number of awards granted to the School of Foreign Language (12.6%), followed by the School of Life Science and Technology (7.3%). The grants have supported 203 applicants, of which 41.4% have obtained grants multiple times. The grant recipients have made eight keynote speeches and about 120 oral presentations at various teaching conferences and have published 65 peer-reviewed journal papers.

The Annual SoTL Conference and Creation of a Community of Practice

To publicly share the grantees' work and get peer critiques (Malfroy & Willis, 2018), thus inspiring other faculty members and promoting a teaching culture, SJTU's first annual SoTL conference was held in 2016. The university president delivered the welcome speech, one domestic and one overseas expert gave the keynote speeches, three domestic journal editors discussed the scope of their journals and the criteria for paper review, and 28 faculty members shared the results of their inquiry in parallel sessions. The conference successfully attracted more than 300 participants from about 60 universities. More journal editors were invited to the 2017 and 2018 annual conferences, and each attended one parallel session to give instant feedback to help speakers further improve their research. At the 2018 annual conference, six speakers from other universities were invited so that the academic exchanges were more diverse and extensive.

Faculty members at SJTU often face challenges related to the lack of certain basic skills for conducting SoTL work, such as having difficulties clarifying their inquiry questions and setting research baselines, as well as being unfamiliar with relevant literature (Richlin, 2001), so the CTLD provides "a full cycle of research support" (Vithal, 2018). In addition, a community of practice for SoTL was started in 2017. Currently, the community has about 140 members who meet regularly during semesters to discuss their studies and exchange ideas. Workshops and consultations are provided in proposal development, research design, data analysis, and paper writing.

The Role of the CTLD in Improving Teaching

In the first half of 2018, SJTU initiated a big discussion on educational philosophy. The CTLD actively participated in this by conducting an online survey to gain an in-depth understanding of the teaching practices and teaching development needs of the faculty, thus providing reference information for decision-making units. The questionnaire included 31 questions, with either multiple-choice responses or Likert scale ratings, and covered various data, including the instructor's characteristics, basic information about the courses being taught, teaching philosophy and practices, perceptions of teaching culture, knowledge of and access to teaching development activities, and expectations of support for teaching. In addition, one open-ended question, *What suggestions do you have for improving the undergraduate teaching evaluation system?*, was also included in the survey (Briseño-Garzón et al., 2016; Chalmers & Gardiner, 2015). The CTLD asked the NIC to send an e-mail to full-time faculty inviting them to participate in the online survey and received 671 valid responses with a response rate of approximately 22%.

Perceptions of Teaching Culture

Regarding perceptions of teaching culture, 75.8% of the participants agreed that "both SJTU and my school emphasize the importance of teaching," while 41.9% agreed that "effective teaching matters in the annual review, reward, and promotion in my school." These findings are similar to those reported by Briseño-Garzón et al. (2016). However, 81.4% of the participants agreed that "continuously improving teaching is one of my goals," while only 47.2% agreed that "continuously improving teaching is one of my colleagues' goals." These differences indicate that the current teaching culture is not sufficient to motivate all faculty members to make more of an effort in their teaching.

Support for Teaching

Overall, 85.3% of the participants knew about the CTLD and its educational development activities. While only 46.2% had previously used CTLD services, another 10.8% expressed a willingness to participate in such services in future. Unfortunately, 14.7% did not know about the CTLD. Individuals who reported participation in CTLD activities were distributed across disciplinary areas and career stages, and 57.1% of them reported that they applied what they learned in these activities to improve their teaching practice. In response to the question *What kind of support do you expect SJTU to provide to improve your teaching?*, the largest response was that SJTU should highlight the value of teaching, and the second most frequent answer was that SJTU should provide opportunities and resources to learn advanced teaching ideas, methods, and technologies. These results show that the CTLD has made a great contribution to helping instructors improve their teaching practice. At the same time, the needs of educational development are broad and diverse; the CTLD should therefore strike a balance between being responsive to instructors' needs and SJTU's initiatives.

Conclusions

After several years of effort, the CTLD at SJTU has gained visibility and credibility on campus. It plays an important role in promoting a culture of teaching excellence and won first prize for the Shanghai Higher Education Teaching Achievement Award in 2017. Currently, the CTLD is more actively involved in SJTU decision-making processes for education reform and strategically redesigns its activities or designs new programs to proactively serve the university's critical initiatives (Cook & Marincovich, 2010).

References

Black, B. (1998). Using the SGID method for a variety of purposes. *To Improve the Academy, 17*(1), 245–262.

Boyer, E. L. (1990). *Scholarship reconsidered: Priorities of the professoriate.* Jossey-Bass.

Briseño-Garzón, A., Han, A., Birol, G., Bates, S., & Whitehead, L. (2016). Faculty perceptions of challenges and enablers of effective teaching in a large research-intensive university: Preliminary findings. *CELT Collected Essays on Learning and Teaching, IX*, 133–143.

Chalmers, D., & Gardiner, D. (2015). An evaluation framework for identifying the effectiveness and impact of academic teacher development programs. *Studies in Educational Evaluation, 46*, 81–91.

Clark, D. J., & Bekey, J. (1979). Use of small groups in instructional evaluation. *POD Quarterly, 1*(2), 87–95.

Clark, D. J., & Redmond, M. V. (1982). *Small group instructional diagnosis: Final report.* Fund for the Improvement of Postsecondary Education. https://files.eric.ed.gov/fulltext/ED217954.pdf

Cook, C. E. (2011). Introduction: CRLT and its role at the University of Michigan. In C. E. Cook & M. Kaplan (Eds.), *Advancing the culture of teaching on campus: How a teaching center can make a difference* (pp. 1–12). Stylus Press.

Cook, C. E., & Marincovich, M. (2010). Effective practices at research universities: The productive pairing of research and teaching. In K. J. Gillespie & D. L. Robertson (Eds.), *A guide to faculty development* (2nd ed., pp. 277–292). Jossey-Bass.

Diamond, M. R. (2004). The usefulness of structured mid-term feedback as a catalyst for change in higher education classes. *Active Learning in Higher Education, 5*(3), 217–231.

Finelli, C. J., Ott, M., Gottfried, A. C., Hershock, C., O'Neal, C., & Kaplan, M. (2008). Utilizing instructional consultations to enhance the teaching performance of engineering faculty. *Journal of Engineering Education, 97*(4), 397–411.

Finelli, C. J., Pinder-Grover, T., & Wright, M. C. (2011). Consultations on teaching: Using student feedback for instructional improvement. In C. E. Cook & M. Kaplan (Eds.), *Advancing the culture of teaching on campus: How a teaching center can make a difference* (pp. 65–79). Stylus Press.

Geng, B. (2002). Preliminary study of scholarship of teaching and learning of university teachers. *Degree and Postgraduate Education*, (2–3), 60–63.

Hurney, C. A., Harris, N. L., Prins, S. C. B., & Kruck, S. E. (2014). The impact of a learner-centered, mid-semester course evaluation on students. *Journal of Faculty Development, 28*(3), 55–62.

Malfroy, J., & Willis, K. (2018). The role of institutional learning and teaching grants in developing academic capacity to engage successfully in the scholarship of teaching and learning. *International Journal for Academic Development, 23*(3), 244–255.

Mårtensson, K., Roxå, T., & Olsson, T. (2011). Developing a quality culture through the scholarship of teaching and learning. *Higher Education Research & Development, 30*(1), 51–62.

McAlpine, L., & Gandell, T. (2003). Teaching improvement grants: Their potential to promote a scholarly approach to teaching. *Journal of Further and Higher Education, 27*(2), 187–194.

Plank, K. M., & Kalish, A. (2010). Program assessment for faculty development. In K. J. Gillespie & D. L. Robertson (Eds.), *A guide to faculty development* (2nd ed., pp. 135–149). Jossey-Bass.

Richlin, L. (2001). Scholarly teaching and the scholarship of teaching. *New Directions for Teaching & Learning, 2001*(86), 57–68.

Shanghai Jiao Tong University (SJTU). (n.d.). *Overview of Shanghai Jiao Tong University*. STJU. https://www.sjtu.edu.cn/xxjj/index.html

Vithal, R. (2018). Growing a scholarship of teaching and learning institutionally. *Studies in Higher Education, 43*(3), 468–483.

Wright, M. C. (2011). Measuring a teaching center's effectiveness. In C. E. Cook & M. Kaplan (Eds.), *Advancing the culture of teaching on campus: How a teaching center can make a difference* (pp. 38–49). Stylus Press.

Yu, X., & Yu, Q. (2000). Focus on improving capacity of scholarship of teaching for university teachers. *Chinese Higher Education*, (13–14), 25–27.

28

Building Community and Supporting Mentors in a Dispersed College for Adults: A Case Study

Shantih E. Clemans

Introduction

Empire State College, part of the State University of New York (SUNY) in the USA, is a 50-year-old experimental institution dedicated to adult learners. The college offers flexible learning opportunities for students pursuing associate, bachelor's, and graduate degrees. More than 1,300 full- and part-time faculty mentors work with amazingly diverse, "nontraditional" students whose varied life experiences, goals, interests, and educational commitments inform their learning paths.

At Empire State College, the faculty are referred to as mentors, an important distinction in language and terminology. Mentoring is our core function and a source of institutional pride and distinctiveness. Beyond advising, the process of mentoring involves working closely with students in the process referred to as educational planning where, over time and through many conversations, students create what are known as individualized degree programs. Flexibility and accessibility are core values of Empire State College; students have the option to take studies in several different modalities, such as study

S. E. Clemans (✉)
Center for Mentoring, Learning, and Academic Innovation, State University of New York Empire State College, Saratoga Springs, NY, USA
e-mail: shantih.clemans@esc.edu

© The Author(s), under exclusive license to Springer Nature Switzerland AG 2023
O. J. Neisler (ed.), *The Palgrave Handbook of Academic Professional Development Centers*,
Palgrave Studies on Leadership and Learning in Teacher Education,
https://doi.org/10.1007/978-3-030-80967-6_28

433

434   S. E. Clemans

groups (small classes), independent studies, online studies, and residencies. Moreover, the mentors teach and advise in different ways for different students.

While the main campus of Empire State College is in Saratoga Springs—a small city in northeastern New York at the foot of the Adirondack Mountains—there are 35 other distinct and varied locations across New York State, including Albany, Binghamton, Brooklyn, Manhattan, Buffalo, Fort Drum, and Plattsburgh, among other places. Faculty mentors are therefore physically spread out and thus have limited opportunities to connect with their colleagues (or sometimes their students) in person. As with an increasingly number of traditional and nontraditional colleges, Empire State College has a robust online program in which students can choose to study totally or partially online. Also, with the increasing emphasis on online teaching and interacting at a distance with students and colleagues, faculty are more often required to teach and mentor in new (and, for some, less comfortable) ways. This tension between the needs of students and the skill and comfort of faculty provides a rich opening for the creation of responsive approaches to faculty development, which will be a theme of this chapter.

The Center for Mentoring, Learning, and Academic Innovation (CMLAI) at SUNY Empire State College offers thoughtful and responsive ways to build community and encourage faculty and staff to connect with each other, strengthen their practice, and experiment with new ways of teaching. Through a menu of annual programming, and a spirit of deliberate inclusiveness, the CMLAI prioritizes community-building and helps faculty feel listened to, supported, and valued.

Below is the mission of Empire State College, which informs the mission of the CMLAI:

> SUNY Empire State College provides motivated adult learners with access to innovative, flexible and quality academic programs that empower people and strengthen communities. We build on the diversity of our students, their work and life experiences and their individual, personal, and professional goals. (SUNY Empire State College, 2017)

Over the years, Empire State College has developed a series of institutional commitments that guide the priorities of the college community. These commitments include:

* Critical reflective inquiry that encourages active engagement in the local and global community
* Promoting social justice

- Ensuring a healthy democracy that recognizes and respects diversity in all its forms
- Supporting the individual goals of our students in a collaborative mentoring environment (SUNY Empire State College, 2017).

History of the CMLAI

The Center for Individualized Education

Efforts and programs to support and nurture faculty mentors at SUNY Empire State College have existed in one way or another since the founding of the college in 1971. The original academic professional development center, known as the Center for Individualized Education (CIE), was founded in 1974 with funding from a foundation. The CIE operated for only three and a half years. This early prototype offered professional development workshops across the college on various topics, including learning contracts, assessment process, and the role of the mentor (A. Mandell, personal communication).

The Mentoring Institute

The next iteration of the center in 1993 was the Mentoring Institute with its slogan "Mentors for Mentors", which sprang up from the ideas and content of the CIE. The Mentoring Institute included a cohort of mentors committed to traveling to various locations of the Empire State College system to offer workshops on topics relevant to mentoring practice and work with students. This 'traveling work' was rooted in generosity, a deep interest in helping each other, and the purpose and joy of celebrating a community of learning. In addition to workshops in local centers, the Mentoring Institute developed a plan for 'mentoring companions', a version of a faculty buddy system. One could volunteer to be a mentor companion or reach out if one wished for a companion of one's own.

An important and lasting component of the Mentoring Institute was the creation and distribution of a newsletter, *All About Mentoring*, dedicated to thoughts, practices, and reflections on mentoring. The first issue was published in September 1993 (A. Mandell, personal communication). A note from the editors in the first issue of *All About Mentoring* emphasized the value of and need for a thoughtful and inclusive faculty development plan:

The near ubiquity and brilliant flexibility of the College make our work nearly invisible, even to each other. For powerfully good reasons, we lack classrooms and libraries. It's to our honor that at this college one can't tell the teachers from the students. The intense, wondrous encounters between mentors and students, shining four, five, six times a day, every day in our offices, flicker and wink across dark distances. How shall we make a visible posterity? (Herman & Tatzel, 1993, 1)

During these years of experimenting with approaches to faculty development, all of the efforts to offer and participate in workshops were voluntary, a theme and tension still relevant today. The need to help each other and to receive support from a peer colleague continues to be a strong college commitment (Clemans et al., 2016).

In 1997, the Mentoring Institute became part of the Office of Academic Affairs and was recognized as an official part of Empire State College, with the first director being named. There were both positive aspects and drawbacks of this move to the Office of Academic Affairs. Overall, the institutional visibility of the Mentoring Institute was helpful and positive. However, on the negative side, the "voluntary-community-building side of things faded" according to Alan Mandell, the Mentoring Institute's first director (A. Mandell, personal communication). The new Mentoring Institute offered workshops, was responsible for the New Mentor Orientation program as well as other programs focused on mentoring and teaching, and provided other college-wide services, for example in organizing Empire State College's annual Fall Academic Conference.

The Center for Mentoring and Learning and CMLAI

More changes were underway for the center. Over time, the college decided that it wanted an even fuller integration of the Mentoring Institute into the Office of Academic Affairs. A new iteration of the Mentoring Institute was developed, the Center for Mentoring and Learning (CML), the origin of the title of college professor of adult learning and mentoring (CPALM). The first director of the CML, who was not a faculty member, held the position for six years and then retired. More efforts to 'reshape' faculty development at Empire State College followed with yet another manifestation of CML, the current CMLAI, in which the term "academic innovation" was added to the title, with a faculty member on a full-time, renewable, two-year release as its director. Fig. 28.1 illustrates the structure of the center within the larger college context.

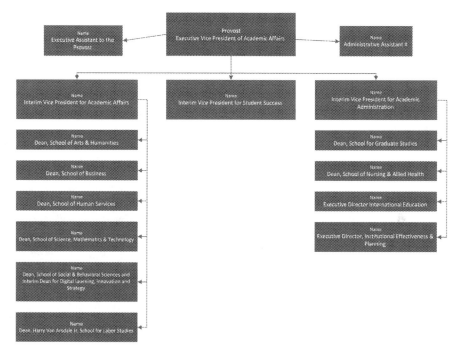

Fig. 28.1 Organizational reporting and structure of the CMLAI

Political Context Within the University

At the time of writing, Empire State College is amid a dramatic and, for some, disruptive, multiyear restructuring process. Prior to this restructuring, the college was organized around geographic locations. Now, similar to traditional institutions, it is academic divisions/areas that function as the college's organizing framework. The impetus for the restructuring was to improve academic quality and to safeguard quality of teaching and mentoring across locations and academic disciplines. As a consequence, faculty currently have less 'local culture' and arguably more experiences of isolation and disconnection. At the same time, financial pressures have restricted the hiring of new faculty.

In an effort to reach more students, Empire State College has intensified online options for students; this has added to the need for faculty to learn to connect with their students (who are often in geographically distant areas from their mentors) in new and effective ways, for example through the learning management system, Moodle, and/or through Skype videoconferencing or on the phone. It has been crucial for the CMLAI to be attuned to changes

438 S. E. Clemans

in the college and the need to remain responsive to supporting faculty in whatever way necessary.

Activities and Programs of the CMLAI

Mission

The CMLAI, which is now situated within the Office of Academic Affairs, offers a range of college-wide opportunities and programs to support mentors in their everyday work with students. The CMLAI is about building community through regular, predictable offerings where faculty and staff have opportunities to talk honestly about the sometimes challenging, often exhilarating work with adult students. We are faculty-directed and faculty-focused and have a 'come one, come all' spirit to our priorities and programs. The CMLAI offers nonjudgmental programs and opportunities for faculty mentors to develop, experiment, share, and be together. Because of the geographically dispersed nature of the Empire State College, most of the programs offered by the CMLAI are Skype videoconferencing sessions that present both challenges and opportunities.

What follows are examples of the priorities and activities of the center:

* We focus on the ongoing professional development and renewal of faculty mentors (both full-time, part-time, and adjuncts), as well as professionals and administrators engaged in the specific practice of teaching and mentoring
* We are a service center dedicated to helping faculty develop and strengthen their teaching and mentoring practice with adult students
* We prioritize community-building, support, and discussion of everyday teaching and mentoring work
* We offer workshops and events across the college
* We provide supportive forums for sharing questions, ideas, projects, and approaches related to the practice and scholarship of mentoring, teaching, and learning
* We emphasize inclusivity and care in all of our programs and events
* Each year, we offer faculty reassignments to support faculty and encourage scholarship and research connected to teaching and learning (CMLAI, 2017).

Team

Located in different areas of the college, the current CMLAI team includes a director, a faculty member who is the CPALM, two professionals (a senior staff associate for professional development and a coordinator for instructor development), a secretary, and three rotating faculty members on one-year reassignments. A small advisory group of select faculty and administrators interested in faculty development also participate in strategic planning initiatives.

Faculty Reassignments/Release Time

Each academic year, CMLAI sponsors three faculty on release time so that faculty can have sustained time to pursue projects connected to mentoring, teaching, and learning. It is also the expectation that faculty on these reassignments join the CMLAI team and participate in weekly thinking, planning, and leadership of center activities. After garnering support from their respective deans, faculty apply for either quarter- or half-time release from teaching and mentoring duties. The half-time position is referred to as a faculty associate; the faculty member in the position serves as a vital member of the CMLAI team—planning, strategizing, and delivering various workshops and programs connected to mentoring and teaching.

For these annual reassignments, faculty apply through a college-wide announcement and application process in which they are required to describe the goals of their teaching and learning project. Moreover, faculty are asked to articulate their interest in being part of the CMLAI team and actively participating in decisions and year-long planning and programming. A small committee reviews the applications and submits recommendations to the provost who makes the final decisions. CMLAI faculty reassignments have multiple purposes: (1) to support faculty in giving sustained time to work on a project connected to mentoring, teaching, and learning; (2) offering a sense of belonging and community by joining the CMLAI team and participating in planning, programs, and events; and (3) serving as a component of professional development for the faculty member through regular check-in conversations with the director to plan, for example, opportunities to share work via a webinar or other college-wide presentations.

Weekly Open Mic Discussion Group

The center's most iconic offering is a weekly videoconferencing meeting wherein faculty and staff come together on Skype to talk about a problem, situation, or question to do with their work with students. The Open Mic discussion group is a confidential, regularly scheduled hour offered three times a month in which faculty and other members of the college community talk openly about their teaching and mentoring and receive support, validation, and ideas from colleagues. Although the focus of Open Mic is on teaching and mentoring, the forum exercises a 'come one, come all' philosophy. Open Mic is facilitated by two members of the CMLAI team. We go around the virtual room and ask participants to state their name/role in the college and indicate if they have an issue, question, or 'case' to bring to the group.

Every Open Mic fosters discussion around a range of teaching-specific issues and concerns, such as plagiarism, workload, designing meaningful assignments for adult students, and fear and vulnerability in the teaching role. Each session begins with these words spoken by the director:

> Open Mic is a time and space for you to share issues, topics, questions related to your mentoring practice and your work with students. This is a non-judgmental forum where we invite you to listen, share and learn together. We don't always (or often) have clear answers. Many questions are ongoing and unfolding. Please respect the confidentiality of this meeting—whatever is said in here, stays in here. (S. Clemans, personal communication)

Once everyone has had a chance to introduce themselves, we begin with the first pressing issue or topic. On any given Open Mic session, the number of participants ranges from 8 to 20, including faculty, professionals, and staff. Although we have not systemized a formal evaluation of these Open Mic sessions, the feedback is overwhelmingly positive. Participants indicate that it is their 'favorite' time of the week. Open Mic enjoys a loyal core group who come every week. Our next challenge is to find ways to spread the word so as to involve more colleagues.

New Mentor Orientation Program and Mentor Workshops

Historically, the CMLAI was responsible for orienting new faculty mentors to their college responsibilities, specifically to help newcomers develop a practice of serving students in caring, responsive, and attentive ways. The New Mentor

28 Building Community and Supporting Mentors in a Dispersed...

Orientation program is also a way for colleagues to connect across the college and (hopefully) develop lasting and nurturing bonds. The New Mentor Orientation program begins as an in-person residency with various sessions on topics including writing learning contracts, meeting a new student, and working with struggling students. Interspersed throughout these content sessions are opportunities to 'meet and greet' and socialize with colleagues, both new and seasoned, from near and far. After the residency, the New Mentor Orientation program continues with regular Skype check-in conversations and other meetings and workshops.

As a result of recent financial pressures, there have been fewer new hires. In response, the center's traditional New Mentor Orientation program has been restructured. Most recently, the CMLAI offered an in-person workshop for new and seasoned faculty focused on the theme of "mentoring and teaching at a distance: strengthening our practices." The introductory words highlight the spirit and intention of this new workshop, especially our decision to bring new and seasoned faculty together:

> All voices, experiences, styles of learning, questions, expertise, and hesitancies are welcome. Some of us have lots of experience working at a distance; others among us have less experience. Everyone has something valuable to contribute. (S. Clemans, personal communication)

Institute on Mentoring, Teaching, and Learning Summer Residency

The Institute on Mentoring, Teaching, and Learning (IMTL) begins as a summer residency that provides time and support to those who mentor, teach, or are involved in research relevant to mentoring, teaching, and learning, allowing these individuals to pursue projects that further their development and enhance their mentoring and teaching practices. Faculty and professionals are invited to apply each year. The application process requires describing a project connected to teaching, mentoring, and students. The IMTL kicks off with an in-person residency in Saratoga Springs that includes voluntary sessions on conducting research and how to apply to the Institutional Review Board, among other topics. Interspersed between these sessions, participants are given time (and private office space) to dive into their writing, thinking, planning, and collaboration activities.

Members of the IMTL receive no money or release time; they participate out of a desire to be part of a peer group of interested colleagues all working

442   S. E. Clemans

on projects with teaching and mentoring at their heart. After the three-day residency, participants receive continuous opportunities throughout the year to share their progress and receive support and feedback from their peers.

Podcast Series on Mentoring Practices

In tune with the mission and history of Empire State College, the CMLAI has experimented with new approaches to entice and engage our college community in conversations connected to teaching, learning, and mentoring. Our newest initiative is a podcast series on mentoring practices. The purpose of the podcast series is to share two- to four-minute audio recordings of specific practices and approaches that help us learn from colleagues. We save the recordings in order to build a library of resources to guide and support our faculty in their work with students. Each podcast offers one mentor's take on assignments or grading or other topics. These become easily accessed 'pearls of wisdom' that create a community-based form of collaborative faculty development. We are currently considering a platform for sharing the podcasts with others outside our institution who are also working with adult students.

Discussion

Empire State College, like many other student-centered and adult-serving colleges and universities, is rapidly and dramatically changing, in part to meet the needs and interests of more diverse students. However, along with changes to stay current with technology and be partners in this digital age, Empire State College faces a dilemma: *How can the college maintain its distinctiveness of mentoring and building relationships with students that are based on respect, reciprocity, and a deep desire to learn and/or to develop skills and knowledge for the workforce?* At the CMLAI, we must navigate the tension everyday between supporting faculty in doing the work that they love—teaching and mentoring students—while, at the same time, helping faculty develop new research-based 21st century teaching and learning skills.

Additional tension is created as we grapple with navigating ways in which the CMLAI can remain responsive to the interests and needs of the faculty while also responding to the administration of the college. The center has enjoyed a certain kind of autonomy and freedom to create and facilitate programs and conversations that emphasize faculty learning together to strengthen teaching practices. We have so far resisted pressure to mandate that faculty take certain workshops or participate in specific trainings or orientations.

Conclusion

At its core, the CMLAI is about community, learning, and connection—connection across ideas about teaching and across ways to write, think, and present as members of a vibrant college community. We also seek to navigate changes in higher education, such as the challenges introduced by more colleges vying for a relatively small number of students, fewer faculty hired to teach and mentor, pressure, and the need to connect at a distance with student and colleagues across geographical miles, sister colleges, and differences in academic approach or discipline. Our mission is to welcome, nurture, and engage adult students who are trying again, or maybe for the first time, to finish a degree program; while they have doubts and worries, they also have experience, expertise, and a certain kind of perseverance to continue against difficult odds.

References

Clemans, S., Mandell, A., & Wright, A. (2016). Brown bag on mentoring practices. *All About Mentoring, 48*, 74–76.

Center for Mentoring, Learning, and Academic Innovation (CMLAI). (2017). *About the center for mentoring, learning and academic innovation.* State University of New York (SUNY) Empire State College. https://sunyesc.sharepoint.com/oaa/cmlai/AboutCMLAI/Home.aspx

Herman, L., & Tatzel, M. (1993). From the editors: The "real thing": A visible culture to honor our work. *All About Mentoring, 1*, 1–2.

State University of New York (SUNY) Empire State College (2017). *College mission and vision.* SUNY Empire State College. https://www.esc.edu/about/college-mission/

29

Virtual Faculty Learning Communities

Angela Atwell and Cristina Cottom

Introduction

Virtual opportunities are on the rise in the field of academic development. Online education and professional development from a distance are not new concepts. Geographic location no longer dictates which universities instructors choose to affiliate with or where an instructor teaches. However, distance from a physical campus location can impede sense of belonging, as well as lead to feelings of isolation and disconnectedness. Faculty learning communities (FLCs) have found success developing a sense of belonging in traditional face-to-face environments, but virtual applications of these experiences are underexplored. While referred to with various titles, such as communities of practice and/or professional learning communities, FLCs are groups of individuals who come together to focus on improving a practice.

This chapter describes the experience(s) created to address the needs of an international, globally-dispersed faculty population. In response to these needs, grant funding was received to create a series of virtual FLCs (V-FLCs). These experiences focused on various teaching and learning topics that would benefit the growing needs of diverse students in higher education. These types of asynchronous experiences are appropriate for an international audience as

A. Atwell (✉) • C. Cottom
Embry-Riddle Aeronautical University-Worldwide, Daytona Beach, FL, USA
e-mail: atwella2@erau.edu; cottomc@erau.edu

© The Author(s), under exclusive license to Springer Nature Switzerland AG 2023 **445**
O. J. Neisler (ed.), *The Palgrave Handbook of Academic Professional Development Centers*,
Palgrave Studies on Leadership and Learning in Teacher Education,
https://doi.org/10.1007/978-3-030-80967-6_29

446   A. Atwell and C. Cottom

they allow for connectedness, collaboration, and community at the user's convenience, regardless of time zone. The various interactions of these V-FLCs led to the development of a framework. While this framework was designed to support globally-dispersed faculty, it has many applications. It can assist others in various locations, departments, and disciplines in creating a virtual space for collaboration.

Embry-Riddle Aeronautical University-Worldwide (ERAU-W) is home to approximately 23,000 students. While most students choose to take courses in the online modality, students can also take face-to-face courses through web-conferencing technology or in person at one of the 130 satellite campus locations around the world. ERAU-W's academic programs are managed by three academic colleges, the College of Aeronautics, the College of Business, and the College of Arts and Sciences. Approximately, 1,800 faculty are active within the ERAU-W system. Full-time faculty teach only a fraction of the course sections, with the majority taught by globally-dispersed adjunct faculty. In 2017, more than 86% of courses were taught by adjuncts. Many of the adjunct faculty are subject-matter experts who are currently active in their field. Although some of these faculty members may have online teaching experience, others do not.

In order to be eligible to teach for ERAU-W, all faculty must complete online, facilitator-led faculty development courses through the Rothwell Center for Teaching and Learning Excellence-Worldwide (CTLE-W). Reporting to the vice chancellor of online education and chief digital learning officer, the CTLE-W team includes a director, a research specialist, and two faculty developers (see Fig. 29.1). The CTLE-W does not have a physical center for faculty to meet and collaborate since the faculty are located all over the world. However, faculty have 24/7 access to an internal resource site that serves as a virtual center, providing a variety of pedagogical resources, including asynchronous discussions and helpful teaching tools. In addition to the required faculty development courses, the CTLE-W offers a number of optional professional development opportunities, including monthly webinars, quarterly special sessions, and self-paced workshops.

The CTLE-W's mission statement is as follows:

> CTLE-W aims to foster and support all faculty in teaching excellence through a variety of educational experiences and resources such as workshops, consultations, and just-in-time support. CTLE will research and continuously improve/innovate to ensure we are a source and model of the most accurate and current strategies in teaching and learning. We offer friendly and informed opportunities for faculty to reflect on their practice and increase student engagement and learning. (Rothwell CTLE-W, n.d.)

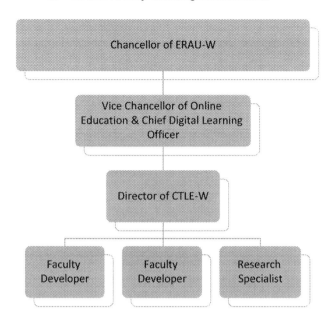

Fig. 29.1 Reporting structure for CTLE-W

Background

Most often, organizations evaluate programs to ascertain their value using a needs assessment model. Needs assessments are intended to identify gaps in services as well as the needs of patients, customers, employees, students, and faculty (Travis et al., 1996). In an educational setting, it is important to evaluate faculty development programs on a regular basis to ensure that formal and routine offerings meet the needs of the faculty. Course and program evaluation should occur on a schedule to ensure course content remains updated and reference materials align with course and program objectives. By conducting an established needs assessment study, faculty developers can identify what to offer and how to improve their current service catalog. A needs assessment study starts with a systematic plan that focuses on a reflective review of specific issues and concerns (Altschuld & Kumar, 2010).

A recent needs assessment conducted by the CTLE-W specifically focused on the end of course surveys from faculty development courses. This assessment included responses from newly hired full-time and adjunct faculty at ERAU-W from January 2016 to September 2017. Faculty completed an informed consent form at the beginning of the course and a survey at the end of the course. The survey was anonymous with no identifying information noted. Remarkably, although the survey was voluntary, there was a high faculty participation rate. The total participant sample during this period was 1,805. The total number of participants who completed the end of course survey yielded an 81% participation rate (n = 1,462). When analyzing the data from this needs assessment survey, it was noted that faculty requested differentiated and advanced training. In addition to the end of course survey data, the CTLE-W also collected and analyzed data from an annual survey. Each year, the CTLE-W sent a survey to all faculty in order to assess departmental effectiveness and obtain feedback on CTLE-W services. Although the CTLE-W facilitated a variety of offerings, data from the needs assessment survey, as well as feedback from annual surveys, validated the need for advanced, differentiated, collaborative experiences.

In the absence of a traditional campus location, faculty have limited access to each other and campus resources, often leaving them feeling seemingly disconnected (Benton & Li, 2015; Dailey-Hebert et al., 2014). Professional development, provided by institutions, can combat these feelings of seclusion by encouraging collegiality (Dailey-Hebert et al., 2014). Furthermore, teaching and learning in the online modality can intensify these challenges. Students and faculty alike can experience feelings of alienation and isolation (Dolan, 2011; Samuel, 2015). Engaging students who are not physically present requires a skill set that differs from pedagogical strategies traditionally used in face-to-face classroom settings (Samuel, 2015). Combating these feelings of isolation and alienation, in addition to providing an outlet for faculty to share best practices in online teaching, is critical as online teaching and learning continues to influence all areas of higher education (Dykman & Davis, 2008; Magda et al., 2015). Based on current literature, coupled with the nature of the ERAU-W campus, the CTLE-W applied for and received the 2016–2017 Early Researcher Grant, from the Professional Organizational Development Network, in the amount of $1,000 to explore faculty development in a virtual environment. These funds were utilized to purchase materials associated with this research project, including a book focused on online teaching provided for each participant.

V-FLC Experience

Face-to-face FLCs have demonstrated their effectiveness in promoting faculty engagement (McKenna et al., 2016). In addition, these collaborative experiences can encourage faculty to take advantage of instructional support (Nordin & Anthony, 2014). FLCs can be initiated by a center for teaching and learning, may engage eight to 12 participants, and can vary in structure (Cox & McDonald, 2017). Due to geographical distance, FLCs in the traditional, face-to-face format are not available to ERAU-W faculty. However, a virtual collaborative option can encourage and enhance community identification, knowledge sharing, and innovation (Sarma & Matheus, 2015).

In accordance with the needs assessment and annual survey results, as well as research supporting virtual options for collaboration, the CTLE-W created a V-FLC inspired by the principles of FLCs. This included consistent membership of eight to 12 participants over a period of eight weeks. The CTLE-W identified an opportunity with adjuncts teaching in the online modality, as they teach the majority of ERAU-W courses. In the fall of 2016 and spring of 2017, this V-FLC was marketed to all ERAU-W online adjunct/part-time/contingent faculty. These faculty are contracted on a term-to-term basis and teach less than 10 courses per year. This open-ended experience allowed adjunct faculty to share best practices in online teaching and learning through weekly discussions organized in Canvas, ERAU-W's learning management system (LMS). Faculty developers organized the experience within Canvas, but were not active participants. These weekly discussion prompts were developed and facilitated by participants. At the end of this eight-week experience, participants were asked to describe their greatest takeaway in the form of a teaching tip to be shared with their peers on the CTLE-W's internal, virtual resource site. Faculty reported that this V-FLC was beneficial and worthwhile. The asynchronous component allowed for flexibility, but the focused topics and regular engagement provided a feeling of belonging and connectedness. The virtual aspect allowed for collaboration regardless of time and location.

Impact

The V-FLC was well received by the faculty. As previously noted, the participants stated they enjoyed this experience as is evident from some of their comments. These comments include statements such as: "Thank you for this

450   A. Atwell and C. Cottom

opportunity, allowing us to come together as peers in a virtual community to learn and share our teaching experiences," "I found the book interesting, helpful, and the interaction with other faculty very beneficial," and "I want to [say] thank you [to] everyone for their time and words of wisdom. I have learned something from each of you. Well worth the time." Furthermore, the participants stated they wanted to continue interacting with their peers: "I'm excited to keep this going and learning more. This is a great group of diverse instructors and I'm glad I signed up for it," and "I would welcome opportunities to keep in touch with this great learning community."

To support further collaboration among these participants, the CTLE-W created a V-FLC group within the CTLE-W internal, virtual resource site. These comments, in combination with other qualitative data, were analyzed to establish the common themes that emerged from this experience. The themes that were identified were: building relationships; sharing; university community; best practices; and learning from others. There were also sub-themes of gratitude, isolation, and resource sharing. Upon successful completion of the V-FLC experience, the CTLE-W decided to continue offering V-FLCs for faculty to collaborate and engage in discussions around best teaching and learning practices. Interestingly, 10 adjunct faculty who had participated in the fall 2016/spring 2017 V-FLC returned for the 2017–2018 V-FLC iteration.

Although the V-FLC was an overall success, there were opportunities for improvement. After the fall 2016 offering, the CTLE-W reviewed trends from the experience and this reflection impacted the development of the spring 2017 iteration. In the fall, participants were asked to sign-up to choose weekly discussion topics, which were open to participants only during that week. The CTLE-W team found this difficult to manage because some of the faculty did not contribute for that week, some failed to facilitate their discussion topic, and some weeks contained multiple discussion topics. To combat this problem in the spring, the weekly topics were available throughout the experience, which led to deeper conversations that lasted longer than just one week. In addition, in the fall, it was noted that some faculty were not engaging by posting in the discussions, and several withdrew from the experience. To address this situation in the spring, faculty leaders were chosen by the participants and they reached out to their peers who were not engaging. Interestingly, all participants completed the spring V-FLC.

Lastly, the CTLE-W recognized that utilizing the university's LMS may have led to confusion for V-FLC participants. The LMS is used for other faculty development offerings, which may have impacted how faculty engaged in the experience. For instance, faculty are accustomed to the faculty developers engaging in discussions and being more hands-on throughout faculty development experiences. However, in accordance with FLC principles, during the V-FLC, the faculty developers were not involved. This may have led to some confusion, as some faculty likened the V-FLC to a CTLE-W faculty development course. The open-ended, faculty-led structure of the V-FLC was unfamiliar to participants. Also, the LMS required a certain level of technological skill, which varied depending on the faculty's experience with the tool. Despite these challenges, faculty enjoyed the V-FLC. Throughout the 2016–2017 V-FLC experience, these lessons learned were utilized to create a framework.

V-FLC Framework

At the conclusion of this experience, the *CTLE-W Framework for Virtual Faculty Learning Communities* was created (Atwell et al., 2017). This framework can be used by others to plan and facilitate their own V-FLCs. This framework outlines 12 steps to develop, implement, and evaluate a virtual collaborative experience for faculty (see Fig. 29.2).

This framework contains seven sections, which includes an introduction, a step-by-step guide with probing questions, answers to these questions based on the CTLE-W V-FLC, a discussion of lessons learned, references, and examples of documentation utilized in the CTLE-W experience. Below are the questions created to assist others who are interested in developing a V-FLC. While this framework was initially intended for those in faculty development, the CTLE-W realized that V-FLCs have other applications as

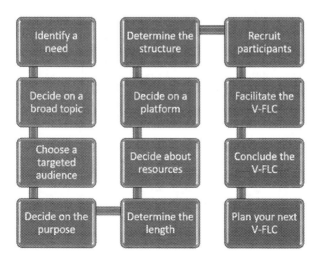

Fig. 29.2 V-FLC framework steps

452   A. Atwell and C. Cottom

well. This framework can be used within departments, between programs, or across disciplines. It can also be used to forge inter-university collaborations or make connections within a committee. The complete framework is available for download on the CTLE-W website (Atwell et al., 2017).

Implementation Framework Category Questions

1. **Identify a need**

    a. What need will this V-FLC address (professional development, community building, communication, etc.)?

2. **Decide on a broad topic**

    a. What topic will you focus on (online learning, feedback, mentorships, content-specific, etc.)?

3. **Choose a targeted audience**

    a. Who will participate (adjuncts, online instructors, full-time faculty, new instructors, etc.)?
    b. What is your ideal number of participants?
    c. What will you do if the response is more or less than expected?

4. **Decide on the purpose**

    a. What are your objectives?
    b. Will this be a research project?

5. **Determine the length**

    a. Who will decide this?
    b. If you are deciding, how long will it be?
    c. If the participants are deciding the length, will you provide parameters and what will they be?

6. **Decide about resources**

    a. Will you have a budget?
    b. Will you provide resources/materials? If so, will the resources be used once or multiple times?
    c. What kind of materials will you use (books, videos, articles, all of the above)?
    d. Will participants identify resource(s)?

29 Virtual Faculty Learning Communities

7. **Decide on a platform**

   a. How do you want the participants to interact?

      i. Will the experience be synchronous or asynchronous?
      ii. Will participants use videos, discussions, chat tools, small groups, etc.?

   b. Where do you want the participants to interact?

      i. Will you use your university's LMS?
      ii. Will you use an external tool (Yellowdig, Voicethread, etc.)?
      iii. Will you integrate an external tool within your LMS?
      iv. Will you use web conferencing (Blackboard Collaborate, Adobe Connect, Zoom, Skype, etc.)?

8. **Determine the structure**

   a. How will you define and/or explain a V-FLC to participants?
   b. How will you create a community?

      i. How will you build a community?

         1. Will you introduce yourself?

   c. How much structure will you provide?

      i. Will you state your expectations for participation?

         1. Will participants post discussions, share examples, create videos, etc.?
         2. How often will participants engage in the above activities (one topic per week or no due dates, etc.)?

      ii. Will participants develop their own guidelines?

         1. How often will participants contribute?
         2. Will participants select topics?
         3. Will participants select leaders for the V-FLC?

   d. Will you model engagement?

      i. How will you engage with the content, if at all? How so (videos, announcements, e-mails, feedback, contributions to discussions, etc.)?

   e. Will there be a deliverable?

      i. Will this deliverable be shared beyond the V-FLC?

9. **Recruit participants**

   a. How will you market the experience?
   b. Will there be incentives?

      i. If you have provided an incentive and a participant withdraws before the experience begins, how will you manage this?

   c. If it is a research project, how will you collect informed consent?

10. **Facilitate the V-FLC**

   a. Will you document your reflections during the V-FLC?

      i. If so, how?

   b. How will you handle withdrawals or lack of participation during the experience?
   c. How much time will you budget to manage the V-FLC?

11. **Conclude the V-FLC**

   a. How will you acknowledge completion and participation?

      i. What evidence of completion will you provide for their professional development portfolio?

   b. How will participants communicate with each other beyond the V-FLC experience?
   c. How will you reflect on your overall experience?
   d. What will you collect and analyze from the V-FLC (artifacts, discussions, organizer reflection, etc.)?
   e. Will this experience be repeated?

      i. What areas of opportunities were identified at the conclusion of the V-FLC?
      ii. How will you make the necessary changes?

   f. Will you disseminate your findings?

12. **Plan your next V-FLC**

   a. What will you do next?

Conclusion

As virtual teaching and learning becomes more prevalent in higher education, faculty may find themselves working at a distance and potentially feeling disconnected and isolated. A V-FLC is a great opportunity to share best practices, collaborate, and connect. Moving forward, the CTLE-W team continued offering V-FLCs focusing on various teaching practices. For example, the 2017–2018 V-FLC was open to all ERAU-W faculty, regardless of status (full-time and adjunct), and centered on effective feedback practices. The 2018–2019 V-FLC focused on instructor self-care. Regardless of the topic, offering a virtual opportunity to connect is a necessity.

References

Altschuld, J. W., & Kumar, D. D. (2010). *Needs assessment: An overview*. SAGE Publications.

Atwell, A., Cottom, C., Martino, L., & Ombres, S. (2017). *CTLE-W framework for virtual faculty learning communities*. Embry-Riddle Aeronautical University Scholarly Commons. https://commons.erau.edu/publication/1372/

Benton, S., & Li, D. (2015). Professional development for online adjunct faculty: The chair's role. *The Department Chair, 26*(1), 1–3.

Cox, M. D., & McDonald, J. (2017). Faculty learning communities and communities of practice dreamers, schemers, and seamers. In J. McDonald & A. Cater-Steel (Eds.), *Communities of practice* (pp. 47–72). Springer.

Dailey-Hebert, A., Norris, V. R., Mandernach, B. J., & Donnelli-Sallee, E. (2014). Expectations, motivations, and barriers to professional development: Perspectives from adjunct instructors teaching online. *The Journal of Faculty Development, 28*(1), 67–82.

Dolan, V. L. (2011). The isolation of online adjunct faculty and its impact on their performance. *The International Review of Research in Open and Distributed Learning, 12*(2), 62–77.

Dykman, C. A., & Davis, C. K. (2008). Part one: The shift toward online education. *Journal of Information Systems Education, 19*(1), 11.

Magda, A. J., Poulin, R., & Clinefelter, D. L. (2015). *Recruiting, orienting, & supporting online adjunct faculty: A survey of practices*. The Learning House.

McKenna, A., Johnson, A. M., Yoder, B., Guerra, C., Rocio, C., & Pimmel, R. (2016). Evaluating virtual communities of practice for faculty development. *The Journal of Faculty Development, 30*(1), 31–40.

Nordin, E., & Anthony, P. J. (2014). Supporting online faculty holistically: Developing a support website resource. *Higher Learning Research Communications, 4*(1), 30.

Rothwell Center for Teaching and Learning Excellence (CTLE-W). (n.d.). *Home page*. Rothwell CTLE-W. https://rctle.erau.edu/

Samuel, A. (2015, May 20–23). *Faculty perception of "presence" in the online environment* (Conference presentation). Adult Education Research Conference. https://newprairiepress.org/aerc/2015/papers/47/

Sarma, M., & Matheus, T. (2015). 'Hybrid' open source software virtual communities of practice–a conceptual framework. *Technology Analysis & Strategic Management, 27*(5), 569–585.

Travis, J. E., Hursh, D., Lankewicz, G., & Tang, L. (1996). Monitoring the pulse of the faculty: Needs assessment in faculty development programs. *To Improve the Academy, 15*(1), 95–113.

30

Planting Seeds for a Campus-Wide Conversation on Teaching and Learning in Oman: The Faculty Fellows Program at the Center for Excellence in Teaching and Learning, Sultan Qaboos University

Thuwayba Al Barwani and Otherine Neisler

Introduction

This chapter describes the process of establishing the Faculty Fellows Program, an initiative which has been pivotal in initiating changes to the teaching and learning culture of Sultan Qaboos University (SQU), a public university based in the Sultanate of Oman. As an institution, SQU takes great pride in its diverse array of faculty originating from over 45 countries worldwide. International faculty members comprise approximately 60% of the full-time teaching staff, representing 1,000 members from a wide variety of academic cultures, languages, and religions. While this is a rich and healthy environment in which to instill learning, it can become problematic when attempting to unify institutional processes and teaching standards. At the same time, Omani faculty members also have diverse academic backgrounds, given that they normally pursue their doctoral certifications outside of the country, such as in the UK, USA, Canada, and Australia, as well as in nearby Arab nations like Egypt, Jordan, and Morocco.

T. Al Barwani (✉) • O. Neisler
Center for Excellence in Teaching and Learning, Sultan Qaboos University, Muscat, Oman
e-mail: thuwayba@squ.edu.om; neisler@squ.edu.om

© The Author(s), under exclusive license to Springer Nature Switzerland AG 2023
O. J. Neisler (ed.), *The Palgrave Handbook of Academic Professional Development Centers*, Palgrave Studies on Leadership and Learning in Teacher Education, https://doi.org/10.1007/978-3-030-80967-6_30

Faculty members are not required to take any professional development training prior to being given teaching responsibilities at SQU, nor are they asked to provide any evidence of any previous teaching certification. Moreover, the university bylaws do not require that teaching faculty possess teaching certificates upon employment and, more importantly, teaching excellence is not considered during faculty promotions or contract renewal. This leaves a huge information gap and an uncertainty as to what is actually happening behind the closed doors of the classroom.

In recent years, a drive for quality, standards, rankings, and accreditation required that SQU break away from traditional modes of teaching and focus more on active learning and student-centered methodologies that are more relevant to the needs and realities of today's labor market. The university was cognizant of its burden of responsibility in preparing graduates who could lead the country into the future. These 21st-century students required a different set of skills in order to survive in an increasingly competitive employment environment. As such, it became apparent that the faculty too needed a new set of skills. To drive that change, a designated center for teaching and learning was necessary to ensure the sustainable and planned professional development of the faculty.

Accordingly, the SQU Center for Excellence in Teaching and Learning (CETL) was established in 2014 and, shortly after, began operating in 2015. To begin with, the center had a staff of three reporting directly to the deputy vice chancellor (DVC) for academic affairs, training, and community service, an office equivalent to that of the academic vice president. Despite having no designated headquarters or budget, and exceedingly little administrative and technical support, the CETL flourished. Within the span of the year, the center had assisted over 200 of the 992 faculty members, hosted various speakers and workshops, consulted with individual faculty members, and established the Faculty Fellows Program. By 2020, although still hindered by resource limitations and other hindrances, the CETL had a small suite of offices and, more importantly, was responsible for a revolutionary campus-wide transformation in perceptions about teaching and learning.

History of the Establishment of the Center

The center started as an idea in 2010 at the SQU College of Education (COE). As other colleges were rapidly applying for international accreditation, the need to define our teaching and to collect evidence of its impact on student learning became more pronounced. Specifically, the quest for accreditation from the National Council for Accreditation of Teacher Education for the COE, and from the Accreditation Board for Engineering and Technology for the College of Engineering, called for evidence that student learning goals were being met. This led to an evaluation of outcome-based learning objectives and the instructional methods best suited to achieving them; in other words, it was the process of documentation of student learning which led to an examination of teaching.

Another source of pressure for change came from students, graduates, and employers. Much like other countries around the world, modern-day Omani students required a different set of skills in order to compete in an increasingly challenging labor market. However, most of these skills were either not taught at all or were tackled only in piecemeal and random fashion by select faculty members as a result of their personal teaching backgrounds and exposures. The faculty therefore urgently needed to enhance their existing pedagogical knowledge and skills.

Planned Goals of the Center

The CETL was established to support faculty in developing new instruction designed to maximize student learning. It was intended to be a focal point for the dissemination of research, for scholarly discussion, and for modeling the best research-based practices. The center operates under the following vision—to position SQU at the forefront of research-based teaching and learning practices in higher education. Its mission was, and still is, to:

- Promote learning by supporting and enhancing effective higher education teaching and learning practices evidenced by current research on teaching and learning and in alignment with the requirements of major accrediting bodies
- Create a learning community that continually explores the relationship between teaching and learning
- Encourage research and scholarship in teaching and learning in higher education
- Provide consultancy services in the areas of teaching and learning in higher education.

As such, the planned goals of the center were as follows: (1) integration of technological tools to enhance learning; (2) course design/redesign; (3) assessment of student learning; (4) integration of problem-solving strategies and activities in the classroom; (5) implementation of active learning strategies; (6) inclusion of higher-order thinking skills instruction; and (7) management of research on teaching and learning.

Structure of the Center

Official approval of the organizational structure of the CETL was granted in 2014 (see Fig. 30.1). The intended structure of the center was presented to the University Council for approval as part of the original proposal document (CETL, 2014). However, it is important to note here that with dwindling resources, severe budgetary constraints, and competing priorities, the center

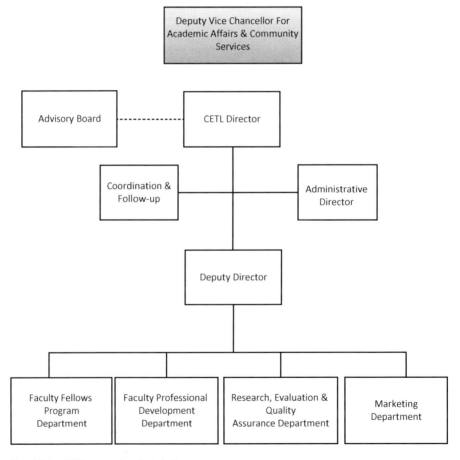

Fig. 30.1 CETL organizational chart

was left to survive with minimal human and financial resources. Thus, much of what was planned for the center could not be achieved.

In reality, the CETL has a director who is a full professor with a reduced teaching load; a full-time deputy director with higher education teaching experience and a doctorate in instructional design; one to two administrative support staff; and a couple of other staff members whose positions, duties, and responsibilities change according to availability and necessity (e.g., acting as instructional designer, training manager, or faculty consultant). Nevertheless, the success of the CETL can be attributed to its relationships with the other centers that also serve the university, together with the community that it has built as a result of its Faculty Fellows Program.

Utilizing the resources and expertise available at the SQU Center for Educational Technology and Center for Information Systems, the CETL has been able to implement its programs and achieve its goals by capitalizing on the technical know-how of these two centers. In addition, grants and donations have been used to fund international speakers and workshop facilitators. However, some of the biggest supporters have been the COE faculty who have been indispensable in providing the academic expertise needed to conduct workshops and engage in research. At the same time, support for the planning and implementation of CETL activities has been made possible as a result of the center's strong connections with its faculty fellows (FFs), as well as other faculty volunteers from across 11 teaching units, including the nine SQU colleges, the Center for Preparatory Studies (CPS), and the Sultan SQU Hospital.

Activities of the Center

The years between 2015 and 2020 have witnessed the implementation of a planned program whose activities have addressed four main faculty groups. These activities are mainly based on the priorities identified during a needs assessment survey conducted in the first year of the center's establishment. For the first group—consisting of all faculty members from all nine SQU colleges—workshops are organized and delivered by renowned scholars in the area of teaching and learning. The second group—comprising specific departments or programs—is similarly served with workshops tailored to their needs. The third group—consisting of FFs—is required to enroll in specific workshops culminating in the Certificate of Higher Education Teaching and Learning (CHETL), and the fourth of individual faculty members who come to the CETL for individual consultations regarding specific issues related to their classroom practice.

Other activities conducted by the CETL include research on teaching and learning, orientation programs at every college, an orientation workshop for all newly appointed faculty, and book discussions. From 2018, the CETL initiated a new activity in collaboration with the Risk Management Office (RMO) whereby faculty members are invited to present proposals detailing innovative instructional approaches that they have implemented in their classrooms based on data collected over a specified period. This activity provides faculty with a platform to showcase their work and, at the same time, gives visibility and value to teaching and learning. Submitted proposals undergo a rigorous selection procedure, after which chosen proposals are shared at a two-day event organized by the center. In general, our activities focus on the needs identified by faculty, department heads, and deans. All activities are designed to reimagine teaching to maximize student learning and to assist faculty in authentic assessment as well as the documentation of learning.

The Faculty Fellows Program

Following a visit to the academic professional development center (ADC) of the University of Kansas, USA, and a meeting with its director, Daniel Bernstein (Bernstein et al., 2006), the SQU administration decided to adapt the Kansas Faculty Fellows model to the Omani context. In 2015, the CETL requested all college deans as well as the director of the CPS to nominate two faculty members each to serve as FFs to the CETL (CETL, 2015). Subsequently, a total of 21 FFs were nominated to represent their colleges at the center, with the dean of the College of Science insisting on three members representative of the diversity of the college programs. To determine whether a faculty member was suitable as an FF, the following eligibility criteria were used:

1. Nominee must be a full-time faculty member teaching undergraduate and/ or postgraduate students
2. Nominee must have a minimum of two years of teaching experience at SQU
3. Nominee must have good oral and written English communication skills
4. Nominee must be nominated by his/her college dean based on leadership or interest in the following areas:

(a) Inspiring students to excel while promoting critical thinking, problem-solving, reading, writing, and student research
(b) Assessing student learning as a guide for selecting effective and innovative instructional strategies and technologies
(c) Working with students outside of the classroom, as evidenced by mentorship/supervision of undergraduate students, master's thesis/dissertation supervision, field supervision of students, and/or student club sponsorship
(d) Conducting research and training that promotes excellence in teaching and learning
(e) Improving the quality of teaching at SQU by working with other faculty members, developing the curriculum, or developing assessment tools.

The goals for the FFs required them to complete the requirements for the CHETL; facilitate conversations about teaching and learning in their college or center; lead campus committees related to teaching and learning (including assessment of learning and evaluation of instruction); conduct research on teaching and learning; and facilitate CETL workshops as appropriate. There was also a strong element of continuance in the role as demonstrated in the program motto: "Once a Faculty Fellow, always a Faculty Fellow". Upon completion of their two-year cohort term, each member becomes a senior FF, still expected to participate in workshops, meetings, committees, and research, but not obliged to attend the monthly meetings and workshops. These contributions are integral to the success of the CETL. The most important goal of the FF program was the creation of a community of practice (CoP).

Current research suggests that faculty CoPs provide an excellent platform for faculty professional development (Cox, 1999; Jakovljevic et al., 2013). In these groups, faculty members get together to discuss pedagogy, share resources, exchange best research-based practices, solve problems, and observe and comment on the implementation of innovative teaching approaches. According to Jakovljevic et al. (2013), CoPs are "groups of people who share a concern or a passion for something they do and learn how to do it better as they interact regularly" (1,107). The members of such communities collaborate to map projects designed to solve problems and bridge gaps in the organization, especially in learning; compile information and data; garner experience; work in coordinated and synergistic ways; discuss developments; and share new information.

Cox (1999), on the other hand, defines a CoP as a group of faculty members brought together to explore concepts and instructional approaches

464   T. Al Barwani and O. Neisler

through an extended and facilitated process. Wenger (1998) adds two elements to this definition: first, that the group works toward a common goal and, second, that members have a shared vocabulary and/or common resources to aid in the negotiations toward shared meanings as they solve problems or address issues. This process culminates in the construction and development of a base of faculty knowledge and skills surrounding specific issues or topics through cooperative faculty learning, as well as the development of an integrated network which supports its members and works as a catalyst for further growth and involvement.

Implementation of the Faculty Fellows Program

The first of the three FF cohorts at SQU were inducted into the program in January 2015. One of their initial tasks was to conduct a needs assessment survey within each of their respective colleges. The data from the survey was subsequently used to build a foundation for planning subsequent CETL activities from 2015 to 2020. During the period of their service as FFs, the nominees participated in over 150 hours of activities, including monthly meetings, workshops, research projects, book discussions, committee meetings, peer assessments, and critical thinking tasks. These activities were designed to expose them to topics geared toward the enhancement of teaching and learning at SQU. Workshop topics included outcome-based learning objectives, authentic assessment, course alignment, mentoring models, portfolio development, student engagement and motivation, course development, technology-enhanced instruction, and a variety of course design models and teaching tools.

While the original FF term of service was intended to cover a fixed period of two years, the first group requested that their duration be extended for an extra year. This was seen to be an encouraging reflection of the positive nature of the FF experience, given that their academic departments did not grant them reduced teaching loads or any exemptions from other academic duties during their term of service. Training for the first batch of FFs was based on the priority areas identified by the faculty during the needs assessment survey, with scholars from different universities in the USA invited to conduct workshops.

In 2015, the first FF orientation was conducted by Bernstein, director of the University of Kansas ADC, in which he addressed a variety of topics such as becoming an FF, faculty and student expectations for learning, teaching as inquiry, FF resources, working with CETL, and consultation models to promote inquiry into the scholarship of teaching and learning (SoTL). Other workshops conducted for this cohort over the following three years included outcome-based assessments and rubrics (Anderson & Krathwohl, 2001; Wiggins & McTighe, 2005); 21st century teaching; diverging trends in the form and value of teaching (Bain, 2004); developing inquiry in teaching and learning through peer collaboration; teaching portfolios; alignment of assessment and learning outcomes; creating significant learning experiences (Fink, 2003); research-based best teaching practices (Nilson, 1998); teaching critical thinking skills for 21st century citizens; the new SQU course design template; and using interactive technology to engage students in deeper learning. What distinguished this first batch of FFs in particular was their enthusiasm, motivation, and willingness to promote and collaborate in CETL activities.

In February 2018, a second batch of 18 FFs was inducted into the program. Their work with the center over the next two years exposed them to similar workshops and activities as the previous batch with the introduction of a new online critical thinking course and a more formalized version of the CHETL. Another significant change was the introduction of workshops conducted by experts from teaching centers in other parts of the world apart from the USA, such as Europe, Asia, and the Gulf region. The overall program followed the same format except that the week-long orientation was eliminated. Motivation, enthusiasm, and participation were not as high as for the first group. Also, while all FFs in the 2015 cohort earned the CHETL, only half of the 2018 cohort completed the more rigorous requirements for the revised CHETL program.

The CHETL is organized around 28 credit units which are offered in the form of workshops in addition to a peer review report and a teaching portfolio submission. Faculty members are encouraged to enroll and are given two years in which to complete the program. The content of the teaching certificate program includes the content or activities usually offered via workshops, consultations, discussion groups, or online modules (see Table 30.1).

Originally, the CHETL was intended to be piloted on the FFs first. Subsequently, in 2019, enrolment was expanded to include other faculty members from the SQU colleges. Ultimately, it is intended to be opened to faculty members from all other colleges and universities in Oman.

In February 2020, a third cohort of 21 FFs started to work with the center. It is important to note here that this cohort has shown exceptional enthusiasm and commitment from their very first meeting, which consisted of a four-day orientation led again by Bernstein. From the beginning, quite a number of them believed in the work that CETL was doing and had in fact participated

Table 30.1 CHETL content modules

Modules	Credit load
Introduction to CHETL	1
Educational philosophy and learning theory	2
Outcome-based learning	3
Course design	3
Assessment and rubric design/selection	5
Use of technology in teaching	2
Research-based teaching (SOTL)	4
Peer review	2
Teaching critical thinking	5
Capstone teaching portfolio	1
Total	**28**

in some of the CETL workshops prior to joining the program. After the orientation, FFs who had not previously known each other began to exchange ideas, resources, and experiences via a WhatsApp chat group as well as by tweets and e-mail.

Thus, as a result of the Faculty Fellows Program, a CoP was born at SQU. To this day, innovative ideas continue to be shared and silos shattered as we witness exchange and collaboration across various disciplines. As we prepare the final edits to this chapter, we can see in real time continuous use of the three cohort group chats as current and former FFs communicate and discuss a myriad of issues, from instructional strategies and online tools to student concerns and their own fears as they move to emergency remote teaching as a result of the global coronavirus pandemic which has disrupted teaching and learning activities worldwide throughout 2020–2022.

The Creation of Communities of Practice

Building upon the characteristics of CoPs described earlier, additional CETL workshops were conducted to expose the FFs to the principles of building a CoP both within and across disciplines. The CETL also decided to define the target issue of the CoP as "How to teach critical thinking across the disciplines". This problem had been originally identified during the 2009–2013 research conducted by CETL staff during the early approval stages of the center. All incoming student cohorts were required to complete the California Critical Thinking Skills Test (Facione, 2000); however, scale scores from the 34-question test indicated that SQU students entered the university with critical thinking skills well below the expectations of the faculty (Neisler et al.,

2016; CETL, 2017). The research was presented to the FFs in particular, as well as to the entire faculty and administration. Face-to-face workshops on this topic were followed by the development and implementation of an online Teaching Critical Thinking Course in 2018.

In order to facilitate a continuing dialogue, the CETL adopted various social networking and communication avenues like WhatsApp groups, e-mail, Instagram, and Twitter as platforms to encourage the faculty to support each other and share any information that they might find useful in their practice. In addition, the CETL and RMO provided venues to showcase innovative teaching that generated evidence of enhanced student learning. These strategies have sustained open communication between the CETL and FFs, as well as between the FFs themselves. Lastly, these activities, particularly the teaching and learning showcase events, have moved the Faculty Fellows Program into the center of the campus dialogue about teaching and learning.

Evaluating the Faculty Fellows Program

According to Rutz et al. (2012), "The tacit assumption underlying faculty development programs is that when faculty learn more about teaching, they teach better, which in turn improves student learning" (41). Indeed, the authors lament that this assumption is one of the most poorly tested in higher education despite its popularity in these institutions, of which SQU was by no means any different. Evaluations collected after every workshop indicated satisfaction with the quality of speakers, importance of the topics covered, and the appropriateness of the logistical arrangements. However, this was hardly enough to establish the impact of the Faculty Fellows Program on student learning. Lingering questions continued to trouble us.

Fearing that its work could not be justified without evidence of tangible outcomes, the CETL decided to embark on a study to investigate the impact of the Faculty Fellows Program on professional growth, as well as the impact of professional learning on course development and subsequent student learning. A questionnaire containing a total of 12 closed- and open-ended questions was administered to the first two FF cohorts (N = 39). A total of 33 members (85%) responded, of which 16 represented the 2015 cohort and 17 the 2018 cohort.

468   T. Al Barwani and O. Neisler

Impact of the Program

With regard to the impact that each FF had in initiating conversations about teaching and learning, 28 out of the 33 respondents (85%) indicated that they had either a big (n = 11) or an average (n = 17) impact. Only 15% perceived themselves to have a small or no impact. The respondents were also asked to select which out of 10 activities they were able to conduct in their colleges as a result of their training. Table 30.2 shows the frequencies and percentages of their responses.

Of the specified activities, the FFs most frequently indicated that they were able to engage in consultations with individual faculty (n = 24), initiate curriculum change at the department or unit level (n = 21), and present about teaching and learning at the department/college levels (n = 20). Some also indicated that they were able to offer consultations to the college administration and conduct workshops for their colleagues as a way of cascading their training. Five FFs also provided information about other activities not included in the list, including service on quality assurance committees and accreditation teams.

Overall, it appeared that FF leadership in these activities had resulted in three major outcomes: expanded the work of the small CETL staff; established the FFs as a valuable resource within the colleges; and affirmed the prestige and importance of being nominated and selected as an FF. In addition, the respondents were asked to identify the CETL activities that they found to be most useful. See Table 30.3 for the frequencies and percentages of their responses.

Table 30.2 Types of activities conducted by FFs at the college/center/university levels

Rank	Types of activities[a] conducted by FFs	Frequency
1	Consulted with individual faculty	24
2	Initiated curriculum change at the college or department level	21
3	Presented at the college or department level about teaching and learning	20
4	Conducted workshops	15
5	Consulted with college administration	15
6	Conducted peer review at the college or department level	9
7	Conducted SoTL research on teaching and learning	6
8	Published a paper on teaching and learning in their discipline	6
9	Other	5
10	Presented SoTL research at a conference/meeting	4
11	Conducted book discussions	4

[a]The 33 respondents marked as many of the 11 types of activities that they had conducted as FFs

30 Planting Seeds for a Campus-Wide Conversation on Teaching... 469

Table 30.3 CETL activities that the FFs found most useful

Rank	Most useful CETL activities[a]	Frequency	Percentage
1	Workshops conducted by invited speakers	27	20.1
2	Discussions with other FFs	21	15.7
3	CETL presentations	20	14.9
4	Critical thinking course	15	11.2
5	Consultations with CETL staff	13	9.7
6	CETL monthly meetings/activities	12	9.0
7	Book discussions	10	7.5
8	CETL resources	9	6.7
9	CHETL program	7	5.2
	Total	**134**	**100**

[a]The 33 respondents marked as many of the 9 types of activities that reflected their experience

Workshops conducted by invited speakers were by far the activity perceived as being of most use to the FFs (n = 27), followed by discussions with other FFs (n = 21) and CETL presentations (n = 20). Less frequently mentioned activities included the CHETL program (n = 7), CETL resources (n = 9), and book discussions (n = 10). However, it is important to note that both the CHETL program and the book discussions constituted the newest and least available activities. For example, at the time of the survey, only four book discussions had taken place with limited enrollment for each session, resulting in a maximum of 16 participants out of a total pool of 1,000 faculty members. These book discussions have since become the most in-demand activity of the center, and ongoing conversation about these books is the focus of a new CETL research project.

Hindrances to the Program

We were also interested to learn if the FFs had encountered any obstacles while accomplishing their mission. See Table 30.4 for the frequencies and percentages of their responses. A large proportion of the respondents mentioned difficulties with their heavy workload (n = 28), followed by a lack of enthusiasm from colleagues (n = 18) and difficulty in scheduling activities (n = 14). Interestingly, only five FFs identified lack of support from the administration as a barrier; we had expected this obstacle to be much more frequently reported.

In general, FFs receive no release time and no recompense; only the very first cohort received a small stipend at the end of their three-year tenure in the program. Nevertheless, there is growing evidence that either the prestige, the work, and/or the experience of being an FF compensates for the increased workload and additional responsibilities involved with taking on this role.

470   T. Al Barwani and O. Neisler

Table 30.4 Obstacles encountered by the FFs

Rank	Obstacles[a] encountered	Frequency	Percentage
1	Heavy workload	28	41.8
2	Lack of enthusiasm from colleagues	18	26.9
3	Difficulty in scheduling activities	14	20.9
4	Lack of support from administration at the college or department level	5	7.5
5	Insufficient knowledge to conduct required activities	1	1.5
6	Insufficient support from CETL staff	1	1.5
	Total	**67**	**100**

[a]The 33 respondents marked as many of the 6 obstacles that reflected their experience

Improvements in Student Learning

Maximization of student learning is the main focus of CETL's work, and CHETL participants are required to provide an analysis of student learning as part of their capstone portfolio. When asked if they had observed any improvements in their students' learning, the majority of FFs either agreed (n = 21) or strongly agreed (n = 8). Only three FFs strongly disagreed, and one person provided no response. In the open-ended section of this question, the FFs identified evidence of this change as follows: improvement in student motivation/enthusiasm; increase in student classroom participation; better grades and quality of assignments; improvement in student responsibility for their own learning; and increase in student-to-student interaction.

Changes in Perspective

When questioned as to whether they believed that their exposure to CETL activities had changed their perspective on teaching and learning, the responses of the FFs were overwhelmingly positive (n = 29). Examples provided in the open-ended section included becoming a reflective practitioner; using a wider variety of teaching methods; realizing that students can become autonomous learners; and understanding that students learn best from each other through group projects and assignments.

Similar findings were observed with regard to the FFs' perceptions regarding whether their job as faculty members had changed as a result of their exposure to CETL activities. The majority responded in the affirmative (n = 23), giving examples such as giving more importance to teaching; engaging in systematic planning of their course and caring about its quality; becoming more patient and flexible; and customizing teaching to respond to students' needs.

Changes to Teaching

A qualitative analysis of the responses to the open-ended questions also elicited further information regarding specific changes that the FFs had made to their teaching as a result of their exposure to CETL activities. The majority of the FFs had introduced a variety of new teaching strategies in their courses and focused primarily on flipped classroom and active learning methodologies. Other frequently mentioned changes were related to assessment and feedback techniques, as well as rapid response applications to check on student understanding and the development of rubrics for each assignment. Some mentioned the promotion of critical thinking in their teaching, the enhanced use of technology, and a greater degree of student involvement in the course. The development of outcome-based learning objectives completed the list, together with the use of learner-centered methodologies and enhanced attention to the course outline.

In summary, the evaluation confirmed that the Faculty Fellows Program provided activities of sufficient value and utility and that—despite compelling obstacles like the increased workload and lack of administrative support—the program had changed how the FFs viewed their jobs, helped them modify and enhance their teaching, led to improved student learning, and placed them at the very center of departmental and program-level discussions about teaching and learning.

The Way Forward

As demonstrated in an analysis of student, faculty, and institutional impact research at 10 institutions in the USA conducted by the Association of College and University Educators (2019), while a lot still needs to be done in evidence-based instruction, it is clear that "teaching and student learning have assumed a much more prominent place in the academic landscape" (8). Further, their findings revealed that "good teaching matters and that students learn more from faculty who invest in their development as teachers" (8).

Many campuses have gone on to adopt CoPs or faculty learning communities (FLCs) as a strategy to promote cross-disciplinary collaboration and to encourage faculty members of different disciplines to come together to learn, discuss, and share knowledge about teaching and learning. Existing evidence suggests that FLCs are effective for improving instructional practice, while also building knowledge and confidence around new topics (Glowacki-Dudka & Brown, 2007). According to Cox (1999), FLC participants are more likely to collaborate across disciplines, create more active learning student environments, and support a culture of teaching and learning. However, while anecdotal evidence is easily available, very few such programs have presented evidence demonstrating the success of these communities or their impact on student learning. This may well be one of the areas of research that the CETL should focus on in the future.

Among the few studies that have investigated the impact of CoPs on student learning is that of Eliott et al. (2016), a group of researchers who created an FLC wherein the instructors of a large biology course developed new pedagogies, adapted active learning strategies, discussed challenges and progress, critiqued and revised classroom interventions, and shared materials. Their findings revealed that this collaborative work led to the increased implementation of active learning strategies and an improvement in student learning. In particular, their study showed that student learning gains correlated with the amount of time spent on active learning modes of teaching.

Bosman and Voglewede (2019) investigated the effectiveness of a CoP on the classroom practices of 28 faculty members from an engineering college. Over four semesters, during which time they were assigned books to read, the members met to discuss and reflect on the innovative ideas therein and then sought to implement these in their own classrooms. Subsequently, they reflected on the experience of implementing these ideas and participated in peer observation sessions. Both qualitative and quantitative data was collected and analyzed. Among other things, the findings revealed that the CoP strengthened relationships, peer-to-peer sharing, and the implementation of newly learnt pedagogies. Similarly, a number of value propositions were identified in the faculty members' reflections, of which the most important was the power of peer observations. Overall, the findings indicated that the participants changed their teaching practices after they had observed their peers.

The CETL intends to be guided by this research and will continue to promote learning-centered methodologies, active learning pedagogies, and advocate for higher-order thinking skills. We will continue to encourage faculty to make their teaching visible by engaging in peer-to-peer observations, collecting evidence of the impact of instructional changes on student learning, and publishing and disseminating our findings in peer-reviewed SoTL journals. We will encourage FFs to reimagine teaching across all facets. Considering all that has been achieved so far, there is great hope that the CETL, particularly the Faculty Fellows Program, will continue to transform the teaching and learning conversation at SQU.

References

Anderson, L. W., & Krathwohl, D. R. (Eds.). (2001). *A taxonomy for learning, teaching, and assessing: A revision of Bloom's taxonomy of educational objectives*. Pearson.

Association of College and University Educators. (2019). *Student, faculty and institutional impact research – Independent review process and findings*. Association of College and University Educators. https://acue.org/wp-content/uploads/2019/06/ACUE-Research-Review-Findings-2019.pdf

Bain, K. (2004). *What the best college teachers do*. Harvard University Press.

Bernstein, D., Burnett, A. N., Goodburn, A., & Savory, P. (2006). *Making teaching and learning visible: Course portfolios and the peer review of teaching*. Jossey-Bass.

Bosman, L., & Voglewede, P. (2019). How can a faculty community of practice change classroom practices? *College Teaching, 67*(3), 177–187.

Center for Excellence in Teaching and Learning (CETL). (2014). *Proposal*. Sultan Qaboos University.

Center for Excellence in Teaching and Learning (CETL). (2015). *The CETL annual report*. Sultan Qaboos University.

Center for Excellence in Teaching and Learning (CETL). (2017). *The CETL annual report*. Sultan Qaboos University.

Cox, M. D. (1999). Peer consultation and faculty learning communities. *New Directions for Teaching and Learning, 1999*(79), 39–49.

Eliott, E., Reason, R., Coffman, C., Gangloff, E., Raker, J., Powell-Coffman, J., & Ogilvie, C. (2016). Improved student learning through a faculty learning community: How faculty collaboration transformed a large-enrollment course from lecture to student centered. *CBE Life Sciences Education, 15*(2), ar22.

Facione, P. (2000). *The California Critical Thinking Skills Test (CCTST)*. California Academic Press.

Fink, L. D. (2003). *Creating significant learning experiences*. Jossey-Bass.

Glowacki-Dudka, M., & Brown, M. P. (2007). Professional development through faculty learning communities. *New Horizons in Adult Education and Human Resource Development, 21*(1/2), 29–39.

Jakovljevic, M., Buckley, S., & Bushney, M. (2013). *Forming communities of practice in higher education: A theoretical perspective* (Conference presentation). Management, Knowledge and Learning International Conference 2013. http://www.toknowpress.net/ISBN/978-961-6914-02-4/papers/ML13-368.pdf

Neisler, O., Clayton, D., Al-Barwani, T., Al Karusi, H., & Al-Sulaimani, H. (2016). 21st century teacher education: Teaching, learning and assessment of critical thinking skills at Sultan Qaboos University. In M. Flores & T. Al Barwani (Eds.), *Redefining teacher education for the post-2015 era: Global challenge and best practices* (pp. 77–95). Nova Science Publishers.

Nilson, L. B. (1998). *Teaching at its best: A research-based resource for college instructors*. Anker Publishing.

Rutz, C., Condon, W., Iverson, E. R., Manduca, C. A., & Willett, G. (2012). Faculty professional development and student learning: What is the relationship? *Change: The Magazine of Higher Learning, 44*(3), 40–47.

Wenger, E. (1998). *Communities of practice: Learning, meaning, and identity.* Cambridge University Press.

Wiggins, G., & McTighe, J. (2005). *Understanding by design* (2nd ed.). Association for Supervision and Curriculum Development.

Part IX

Certification Program Examples

Both the UK and certain European countries require some form of higher education teaching certification for employment and/or tenure. This section provides examples of various teaching and learning certificate programs implemented by academic professional development centers (ADCs). Such ADC certification programs are implemented in various forms from a two-year master's degree to a short series of workshops. Some programs require face-to-face cohort attendance, while others are self-paced and delivered using online or hybrid modalities.

Chapters in Part IX

Chapter 31: *Achieving Certification and Innovation Simultaneously: Educational Leadership for Senior Faculty at a Research University in the Netherlands*. Joyce Brouwer and Rachna in't Veld, Vrije Universiteit Amsterdam, Amsterdam, Netherlands.

This chapter details how one ADC uses their Systemic Innovation in Education model as the foundation for a senior teaching qualification which is a pre-tenure requirement.

Chapter 32: *Higher Education Faculty Certificate Program: Foundations of Reflective Teaching*. Christopher E. Garrett and Christine A. Draper, Nevada State College, Henderson, NV, USA.

476 Certification Program Examples

At this university, the ADC offers two levels of certification for new and adjunct faculty. The Foundations of Teaching Certificate and the Advanced Certificate: Reflective Practitioner are self-paced programs offering flexible campus and online options for remote faculty.

Chapter 33: *Preparing Future Faculty: Developing Inclusive, Future-Focused Educators and an Adaptive Program.* Shamini Dias, Claremont Graduate University, Claremont, CA, USA.

Theories related to adaptive, inclusive pedagogy are combined with co-creative design and reflexive thinking to form the foundation for a higher education teaching certificate for graduate students.

Chapter 34: *Diversity and Coherence: The Continuum of Staff Development Actions Around a Common Core.* Dominique Verpoorten, Françoise Jérôme, Laurent Leduc, Catherine Delfosse, and Pascal Detroz, Institut de Formation et de Recherche en Enseignement Supérieur / Institute for Training and Research in Higher Education, University of Liège, Liège, Belgium.

A set of five competencies and eight principles undergird personalized certificate programs that enable faculty to earn either a 10-credit certificate or a 60-credit master's degree in higher education teaching and learning.

Other Relevant Chapters

Chapter 11: *Student Learning: A Framework for Designing Study Programs to Stimulate Deep Learning.* Hester Glasbeek, LEARN! Academy, Vrije Universiteit, Amsterdam, Netherlands.

While the structure of the certificate programs at this university is discussed in more detail in Chap. 31, this chapter presents additional information as to how the intersections of constructivist learning theory, constructive alignment, taxonomy of significant learning, and self-determination theory help faculty reimagine teaching with the certificate programs.

Chapter 12: *Theoretical Foundations for Online and Hybrid Faculty Development Initiatives*. Bridgette Atkins, Caroline Ferguson, Jeanette Oliveira, Sarah Stokes, and Susan L. Forbes, University of Ontario Institute of Technology, Oshawa, ON, Canada.

This ADC offers hybrid and online components for its Certificate in University Teaching.

Chapter 38: *Change in Practice: Achieving a Cultural Shift in Teaching and Learning Through a Theory of Change*. Grahame T. Bilbow, Centre for the Enhancement of Teaching and Learning, University of Hong Kong, Pok Fu Lam, Hong Kong.

This chapter explains how the university has partnered with a British professional membership scheme to provide certification opportunities for its faculty and graduate teaching assistants.

Chapter 40: *From Workshops to Impact Evaluation: The Case of a Chilean Center for Teaching Development and Innovation*. Ricardo García, Héctor Turra and Beatriz Moya, Universidad Católica de Temuco, Temuco, Chile.

This ADC offers an online Certificate of Teaching and Learning that is oriented towards the development of teacher competencies, ethical college teaching, and analysis of teaching practice.

31

Achieving Certification and Innovation Simultaneously: Educational Leadership for Senior Faculty at a Research University in the Netherlands

Joyce Brouwer and Rachna in't Veld

Introduction

Higher education (HE) is in a state of constant flux as diversity and overall student populations continue to grow (Nuffic, 2017). Alongside the massification and internationalization of HE, a third global trend is digitalization—a tool that acts as a catalyst for the former two elements (van der Zwaan, 2017). All of these developments mean that HE programs are continually being (re) developed and that the curriculum development work is never done.

The lion's share of such development work is done by teaching staff working in HE institutions. This work has not gone unnoticed by educational thinkers who want to stimulate innovative and research-based teaching in tertiary education. Since 2000, several teaching guides have been published containing new ideas about student-focused learning aimed at the classroom and course level (Ambrose et al., 2010; Fink, 2003; Nilson, 2010). Much has been written on how to organize change at the level of the institution and institutional policies (for instance Kezar, 2001). The connecting link, however, where policy meets the classroom is at the curriculum or program level, where head of programs are usually the ones responsible. The focus in this case study is precisely there (called the senior level at most universities),

---

J. Brouwer (✉) • R. in't Veld
Vrije Universiteit Amsterdam, Amsterdam, Netherlands
e-mail: joyce@reflectacademy.nl; rachna@reflectacademy.nl

© The Author(s), under exclusive license to Springer Nature Switzerland AG 2023
O. J. Neisler (ed.), *The Palgrave Handbook of Academic Professional Development Centers*,
Palgrave Studies on Leadership and Learning in Teacher Education,
https://doi.org/10.1007/978-3-030-80967-6_31

479

because we wholeheartedly agree with Scott et al. (2008) that the roles on this level crucial in achieving real change in teaching and learning:

> The role least recognised for its critical role as the final arbiter of whether a desired change is actually taken up and actioned locally is that of Head of Program. If these people do not engage then they will not focus and assist their staff to learn how to make the desired change work in practice. (Scott et al., 2008, xvii)

On this level, these seniors lead teams of teachers in designing the actual structure of the students' learning experiences. To make educational change sustainable, this level is where change should be consolidated and where ownership should be secured. In this chapter, we discuss a model to support senior faculty in bringing about meaningful change and how our academic professional development center (ADC) engenders that support from its specific position within the university structure.

Who Are We?

LEARN! Academy is the ADC of the Vrije Universiteit Amsterdam (VUA), Netherlands. Our mission is to strengthen the teaching and learning culture at VUA by empowering teachers and educational leaders at all levels and supporting them so that they can put research-based principles about learning into practice. This is embedded in our university's mission on education (VUA, 2019). For more details regarding our ADC's central ideas about teaching and learning, please see Chap. 11.

Our university currently has over 22,000 students enrolled in over 50 bachelor degree and over 100 master degree programs. The VUA employs 2,196 full-time-equivalent academic staff, of which 50% are doctoral students (who are considered part of the academic staff in Dutch research universities) and 25% are staff with teaching responsibilities. The VUA is a broad research university with 11 faculties. Learn! Academy is a subdivision of Learn!, an interdisciplinary research center under the Faculty of Behavioral and Movement Sciences (see Fig. 31.1).

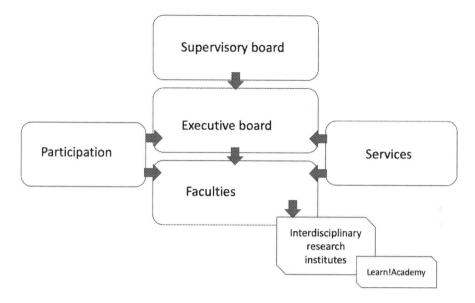

Fig. 31.1 Reporting structure of the VUA in connection to Learn! Academy

Influence by Proxy: Combining Teacher Qualification Programs with Innovation

As can be seen in our reporting structure, our ADC is not part of the central hierarchical structure of our university. Although this might not be the ideal position (see Chap. 5 for a discussion of the ideal position for a model ADC), we have found an approach that nonetheless stimulates educational innovation inside all faculties. We call this *influence by proxy*—not hierarchical or top-down influence at the policy level (although we are included in central initiatives and are 'at the table' in that respect), but influence garnered by supporting bottom-up innovation by teacher staff, thereby creating a bridge between the classroom and policymakers and ensuring ownership and empowerment of the teachers in all faculties. We achieve this by making concrete contribution to the learning environment a prerequisite for certification in our qualification programs at all teaching levels.

How Does Bottom-Up Innovation Connect to Qualification Programs?

In Dutch research universities, although faculty members are mainly selected for their research work—see, for instance, the case study of the University of Twente (Graham, 2018)—teaching (as part of the academic core tasks, next to research) is more and more recognized. Since 2006, getting a teaching qualification is a prerequisite for university staff to receive tenure according to the Dutch University Teaching Qualification criteria. This qualification is aimed at classroom practice and course development (Expertise Network Higher Education [EHON], 2016; Vereniging van Universiteiten, 2018). Since 2015, the VUA offers a follow-up qualification, the Senior Teaching Qualification (STQ), and, from 2017, all teaching levels have been covered with the development of the Educational Leadership Program (KnowVUA, 2017) (Table 31.1).

Table 31.1 Connection between teaching levels, qualification structure, and teaching and learning products for qualification at each level

Teaching level	Qualification needed to get a contract at that level	Role in the organization	Focus of the ADC qualification program	Concrete contribution to the VUA teaching and learning environment
Junior and middle-level teacher	University Teaching Qualification	Teacher and course coordinator	Classroom teaching skills and course design	Research-based improvement course design and lesson design
Senior-level teacher	STQ	Head of program or program coordinator	Improvement of the teaching and learning environment and the program level and development of leadership qualities	Innovation project at the program level
Expert-level teacher	Educational Leadership Program	Educational provost, head of department, or dean	Educational leadership at the policy level	Contribution to the teaching and learning environment at the policy level

Senior-Level Teachers as Linking Pins

As can be seen in the preceding table, contribution at the senior level takes the form of an innovation project. In Dutch research universities, senior-level teachers represent the link between the administration, who make policies, and academics, who conduct research and teach (Kallenberg, 2016). They lead bachelor and master program teams and ensure that the curricula meet the standards and conditions agreed on by decision-makers at the policy level. Scott et al. (2008) pinpoint an important characteristic of this group: they usually do not have mandate over resources like the money or time allocated to staff for teaching. What they *can* develop, however, is *educational leadership*, leading change that directly impacts the teaching and learning environment (Grunefeld et al., 2015). To make sure all participants are stimulated to use this special position, we have operationalized this influence in the following exit qualifications of the STQ:

* The candidate demonstrates that he or she is capable of initiating and leading innovation in education with a real impact at the curriculum level
* The candidate is sufficiently knowledgeable about educational theory and possesses the vision to carry out educational innovations in a substantiated manner
* The candidate displays a professional and development-oriented attitude and has made progress in their leadership development.

How to Best Support the Development of Senior Teachers?

We can conclude that the innovation projects that the senior teachers carry out are crucial. Accordingly, this gives us, as ADC staff, a special responsibility: we have to make sure we support these teachers to enable them to successfully implement relevant innovation. So far, at the program and course level, a lot is written about *what* should be done to improve the learning outcomes of students (Biggs & Tang, 2011; Glasbeek & Visser, 2018; Schneider & Preckel, 2017). However, having a set of prerequisites to enhance learning outcomes is not the same as knowing *how* to implement these improvements that stimulate successful learning. The literature on this topic is diverse. On the one hand, there is specialized literature on educational change, for instance, *The Meaning of Educational Change* by Fullan (2007) and the subsequent translation of his recommendations for HE (Elton, 2003). They offer broad guidelines for instigating change in HE institutions. On the other hand, while various project-based management guides exist (Bos & Harting, 2006; Kotter, 2018), the language in these innovation guides does not appear to appeal easily to academics (Kenny, 2012).

As program leaders of the STQ, we felt the need to develop a tool that would help us to support and empower our senior teachers in a language they can easily engage with. Our leading question was: *Can we devise a model that helps senior staff in HE to successfully lead an innovation project aimed at the development of both their programs and their educational leadership?*

What Do STQ Participants Experience in Their Innovation Projects?

Our design journey started from our own experience as program leaders in the STQ. Together, we coached approximately 150 STQ participants and, thus, have been close spectators of their experiences and had an in-depth view into their development and innovation projects. After about two years of searching for methods and debating the patterns we saw, we devised a questionnaire to get a more general view of our participants' experiences in the innovation process. The questionnaire consisted of four open-ended essay questions:

1. What is the most important lesson you learned in your innovation project?
2. Which intervention had the biggest positive impact on the outcome?
3. What was the biggest stumbling block in the project?
4. What would your advice be to your STQ successors who are starting their own innovation project?

In total, 48% of our STQ alumni filled in the questionnaire. Using qualitative data analysis methods, we explored the data to identify themes that encapsulated the various struggles and successes that our alumni had encountered. The most prominent theme that emerged was the need to act strategically. By far the most commonly shared question was how to get shared ownership with all the stakeholders involved in the project. For example, one participant advised that successors should "try to build an individual relationship with those people. Make an inventory of the different concerns." Another reported that "the biggest stumbling block was that the degree program committee was not interested."

This is closely connected to the second theme that emerged from the data, which was that the participants needed more skills like collaboration, listening, and asking relevant questions. These interpersonal skills, the participants felt, needed to be supported by personal leadership qualities like flexibility, 'guts,' persistence, and patience. One participant stated that the most important lesson they had learned from the project was that "you are a leader when you can act as a bridge between the people involved, departments and students." In turn, another admitted that the intervention that had the biggest positive impact on the outcome of their project was "a frank conversation with the provost."

A third prominent theme that emerged from the data was a practical need for hands-on knowledge regarding project design. For example, one STQ participant advised future applicants to "not only give clear direction in the success criteria, but also have a good think about the project team you want to form."

These outcomes directed our attention to the strong need to focus on the social side of innovation. How do you involve others in the process without losing the focus on your goals and intentions? We iteratively drew a model and started exploring it in different educational leadership programs and among our own team of STQ program leaders. Following trials with nine different course groups at three Dutch universities and a workshop with EHON, the Dutch association for teacher educators, our ideas crystallized and resulted in the Systemic Innovation in Education (SIE) model.

The SIE model has a twofold purpose: first, to give guidance to the change process by advocating for a specific sequence of getting a teacher team to commit and join the work on innovation, and, second, to address the issue of the process of change from the senior position (i.e., what kind of leadership skills do you need to steer the innovation process successfully?). In the model, we try to connect the concerns and experiences of our participants with relevant literature on leadership and project management. In the next section, we will discuss the model itself, before examining what we gain from using it in our programs.

The SIE Model: Two Dimensions and a Sequence

The word 'systemic' in the title of our model signifies that a system thinking perspective is key. To find critical thinking power in academia is easy, but as Fullan and Scott (2009) provocatively argue, critical analysis is both the strength and the Achilles' heel of university thinking. In critical analysis, problems are unraveled into smaller units until the core of the problem reveals itself. When this is done, you will know what problem to address. In contrast, the core idea of system thinking is that problems are complex, which means that the component parts of problems are not stand-alone elements to be identified, but elements that are interconnected and interact and influence each other (Senge, 1990). This is no different in HE; in his paper on successful change in HE, Elton (1999) states that change in this context is a systemic phenomenon and that any change strategy must take this fact into consideration. Without a systemic view, it is impossible to understand why innovations in education fail or succeed (Serdyukov, 2017). The SIE model stresses that it is important to move back and forth between the project leader's analysis and the different stakeholders' views and perspectives; together they can come to a systemic view of the situation and the needs that can be addressed. This leads to our first dimension.

Dimension: Taking/Sharing the Lead

This dimension is the leadership dimension of the model—to start with, every innovation project needs someone to instigate action and move the project forward, whether out of personal commitment or as a consequence of an assigned task or role. This individual represents the project leader (Kirschner et al., 2004). At the start of an innovation, the project leader needs to find a real need for the innovation—one that is recognizable and motivates others to be at least interested in the project.

To find this need, a systemic analysis is necessary, because a single person does not have the resources or the complete oversight to do so. As such, the project leader needs to involve all stakeholders in the process. In HE, this means teachers and students, first of all, as well as management, support staff, and representatives and experts from the specific professional field. Fullan (2007) shows that the most important reason that innovation fails is because the people who are actually implementing the change or who are in concrete contact with the learners are not involved. Even though there might be a discourse of change, the innovation never actually enters the classroom. Professionals need to know why things have to change, especially knowledge workers like academics. They need to be taken seriously with their analysis of the situation. If their knowledge is not considered, they will feel attacked at their core identity as professionals and they will revert to the practice they feel most comfortable with (Weggeman, 2007).

This systemic view and this kind of complexity require a specific kind of leadership. Uhl-Bien et al. (2007) call this *leadership for complexity*, or in

Peters' (2016) terminology, *contextual leadership*. The key leadership skill to lead in this complexity and for an understanding of complex systems, like universities, is listening (Fullan & Scott, 2009).

Dimension: Creation to Implementation

The second dimension is between creation and implementation; in other words, what to do when and how to ensure clear decision-making and focus:

> Innovation involves both the creation of a new idea, and the implementation, dissemination, and adoption of that idea by an organization. (Sawyer, 2012, 254)

In any innovation project, the process will consist of several phases. The need to make a distinction between creation and implementation is supported by West (2002). He states that creativity and implementation represent two very different stages in an innovation process. Creative analysis occurs when all involved expand and diverge their thinking individually and with others. On this end of the dimension, it is important to keep options open, look for underlying questions, invite new ideas, in order to keep an open mind. This is opposed to moments where the project gears toward implementation, where the project converges, action is instigated, and plans are implemented and evaluated. In those moments, one needs a goal-oriented mindset (Bos & Harting, 2006).

A Grid and a Route

When combined, these two dimensions form a grid with four quadrants (see Fig. 31.2). In the STQ, we use the different quadrants as positions that you can take in an innovation project. Quadrant 1 refers to *exploration*, where an initial analysis is explored. Quadrant 2 is *commitment*, where the analysis is shared, the stakeholders heard, and commitment for the innovation is developed. In quadrant 3, the *design* of the project, the systemic shared analysis is translated into a feasible plan that team members can join. And, lastly, quadrant 4 refers to the *realization* of the project where the innovation is implemented. These distinctions provide us with a language for opening up a dialogue about the innovation process.

The other central idea to the SIE model is that there is a helpful route through the different quadrants. This route holds the shape of an infinity symbol. This connects the model to the idea that development and change in

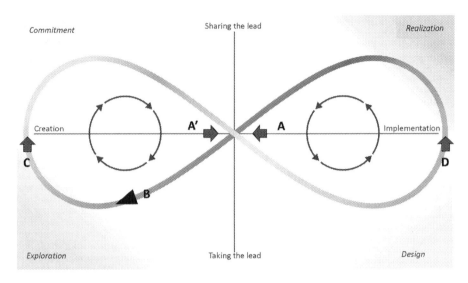

Fig. 31.2 Diagram of the SIE model depicting crucial moments in the innovation process

learning organizations are in constant flux and the goals of innovation are constantly adapted to new situations (Senge, 1990). In that sense, innovation is never done and you have to move back and forth in iterative cycles to get innovation moving and connected. This is in accordance with Fullan and Scott's (2009) advice to adopt a cyclical, action-oriented approach to innovation; they point out that linear planning is one of the reasons that universities are "change-averse." In linear planning, more energy is put into analyzing and writing a plan rather than doing the plan.

We thus decided to adopt a cyclical, action-oriented approach to innovation. However, the ability to use such an approach is not a given for all participants. Connecting the innovation process with leadership qualities helps us in our courses to address the leadership development that is needed to move innovation forward. We distilled a set of leadership qualities for each quadrant based on Peters' (2016) ideas about contextual leadership. For example, the commitment quadrant of the SIE model requires interpersonal leadership and people management.

This is the human component of system awareness—you have to be able to read and handle human processes and networks. For this, you need to develop certain qualities, such as being tuned toward cooperation and partnership, being trustworthy and loyal, and being able to foster collectivity in order to create movement and innovation. The infinity symbol also connects to underlying ideas of contextual leadership. In Peters' (2016) list of contextual leadership qualities, this is called *cheerful resilience*, the ability to simultaneously keep an eye on the course of the project and react flexibly to everything that pops up. In their guide for project-based creation, Bos and Harting (2006) describe this as "the art of playing with the Bermuda triangle"; in other words, being able to act strategically yet playfully to both foreseen and unforeseen circumstances.

Using the SIE Model for Support and Learning

Working with the SIE model in our courses, we discovered that the model diagram (see Fig. 31.2) helps our participants to get oversight of the innovation process and reflect on what is actually happening. The visualization of the model gives them a tool to look forward and backward and plan their next steps. During our coaching and the plenary, and small-group sessions of the STQ program, we learned that there are specific moments in the innovation process that are worthwhile to explore in depth with the use of key questions. Below you find some examples of these moments and questions connected to specific locations in the model diagram:

* What is going on? What do you see? Start with a thorough exploration and take time to reflect on your own (from **A** to **B**)
* Is there a real need for the project? Is it really worthwhile to get wider commitment on the plan, does it need to be now? (see **C**, crossing from phase 1 to 2)
* How can you involve your context? Is the focus and the analysis clear and shared? What are your strengths and weaknesses in this process? Take several iterative rounds of exploring as project leader and as a team (depicted by the **circle on the left side**)
* Do you have commitment, a focus and a team? (see **A**, before crossing through the middle from phase 2 to 3)
* Do you have a feasible project design? (see **D**, before crossing upward from phase 3 to 4)
* Is the design shared and adjusted together with the team? (as depicted by the **circle on the right side**)
* Is there a need for a structural renewal of the plans and/or the team? (see **A**, going to the middle again from 4 to 1).

We connect these key moments and questions to our participants' leadership development by offering them workshops, literature, and individual coaching to support their project work. At the end of the program, an assessment

490   J. Brouwer and R. in't Veld

interview based on written reflection on the innovation process determines if the participant will get the qualification or not.

Our Next Step as Educators

As we have described above, the SIE model is a tool that helps us support grassroots innovation in all departments of our university. With our support, we hope to empower the senior teachers in our courses and indirectly improve the teaching and learning in their departments. The model is based on referenced literature and, above all, on the reactions and evaluations we receive from both the people participating in the STQ and our colleagues giving the course. We are very much aware, though, that we need to take a next step.

In our alumni group, we now have approximately 100 teachers who did not work with the model and approximately 100 who did work with the model. Our next research step will be to compare the experiences of these groups and the outcomes of the innovation projects they lead. To establish the real worth of the model, we will do a systemized document analysis on the assessment dossiers of both groups to see if the model is used and in what way. Also, we want to repeat our questionnaire and see if the second group has different experiences during the innovation project, especially whether they feel more able to deal with the question of how to get shared ownership with the right people and if they feel better equipped with hands-on project design in comparison to their predecessors.

Our Next Step as an ADC: A Resolution and a Recommendation

In a way, one could say that all of the above is just a "cunning plan" to make the most of an unfortunate situation—the fact that our ADC is not part of the central decision-making on teaching and learning in our university. This is partly true; as an ADC, we are dependent on representation by our faculty board in central decision-making. On the other hand, you could say that this position is a blessing in disguise. By working with teachers, heads of departments, and students, we have a strong connection with actual teaching and learning and we are not considered to be suspicious or even "contaminated" by the power structure of the university. We are not part of top-down policy-making. In a sense, we form a third sphere together with the teaching staff, a sphere in between the academic and administrative spheres, as Kallenberg (2016) would call it. This makes us both credible and approachable.

So, what do we recommend? Work on the grassroots level and have strong alliances with policymakers. In recent years, we have invited policymakers to join our courses or designed special courses for them so that they get to know us and, more importantly, the reality of teaching and learning at VUA. This has proved fruitful for us.

Conclusion: A Wish

We hope that our model contributes to transforming passive knowledge about teaching and learning into meaningful innovations. By focusing on innovation processes and implementation in day-to-day practice, we foster the bottom-up process of educational development. We wish that our model, and our use of it in the STQ, inspires senior teachers and program leaders worldwide. Especially, we hope that by working with the SIE model, we give active meaning to Fullan and Scott's (2009) description of leadership as acting through a rising spiral of learning and doing. Finally, by doing this, we hope to contribute to our university as an innovative and inspiring place for our teachers and students, from the classroom to the boardroom.

References

Ambrose, S., Bridges, M., DiPietro, M., Lovett, M., & Norman, M. (2010). *How learning works: Seven research-based principles for smart teaching*. Jossey-Bass.

Biggs, J., & Tang, C. (2011). *Teaching for quality learning at university* (4th ed.). McGraw-Hill.

Bos, J., & Harting, E. (2006). *Project creation 2.0, completely revised edition*. Scriptum.

Elton, L. (1999). New ways of learning in higher education: Managing the change. *Tertiary Education and Management, 5*, 207–225.

Elton, L. (2003). Dissemination of innovations in higher education: A change theory approach. *Tertiary Education and Management, 9*, 199–214.

Expertise Network Higher Education (EHON). (2016). *The BKO in practice: Inventory and analysis of all BKO programs at Dutch universities*. EHON. https://www.ehon.nl/bko/

Fink, L. (2003). *Creating significant learning experiences: An integrated approach to designing college courses*. Jossey-Bass.

Fullan, M. (2007). *The new meaning of educational change* (4th ed.). Teachers College Press.

Fullan, M., & Scott, G. (2009). *Turnaround leadership for higher education.* Jossey-Bass.

Glasbeek, H., & Visser, K. (2018). Does schooling lead to a loss of motivation in students? *Tijdschrift voor Hoger Onderwijs, 36*(3), 5–22.

Graham, R. (2018). *The career framework for university teaching: Background and overview.* Royal Academy of Engineering. https://www.raeng.org.uk/publications/reports/career-framework-for-university-teaching-backgroun

Grunefeld, H., van Tartwijk, J., Jongen, H., & Wubbels, T. (2015). Design and effects of an academic development programme on leadership for educational change. *International Journal for Academic Development, 20*(4), 306–318.

Kallenberg, T. (2016, October 10). *Innovation in the 'patchwork' university. The balancing act of academic middle managers in and between the micro-cultures of the interacting spheres* (Conference presentation). EFMD Higher Education Research Conference.

Kenny, J. (2012). Managing innovation in educational institutions. *Australian Journal of Educational Technology, 18*(3), 359–376.

Kezar, A. (2001). *Understanding and facilitating organizational change in the 21st century: Recent research and conceptualizations.* Jossey-Bass.

Kirschner, P., Hendricks, M., Paas, F., Wopereis, I., & Cordewener, B. (2004). *Determinants for failure and success of innovation projects: The road to sustainable educational innovation* (Conference presentation). 27th Convention of the Association for Educational Communications and Technology.

KnowVUA. (2017). *Framework for teaching performances at Vrije Universiteit Amsterdam.* Vrije Universiteit Amsterdam (VUA). https://knowvu.nl/wp-content/uploads/2017/11/Framework-2017.pdf

Kotter, J. (2018). *Eight steps to accelerate change in your organization.* Kotter. https://www.kotterinc.com/wp-content/uploads/2019/04/8-Steps-eBook-Kotter-2018.pdf

Nilson, L. (2010). *Teaching at its best: A research-based resource for college instructors* (3rd ed.). Jossey-Bass.

Nuffic. (2017). *Internationalisation: Facts and figures.* Nuffic. https://www.nuffic.nl/en/subjects/research/internationalisation-facts-and-figures

Peters, F. (2016). "We don't need another hero". A leadership profile for a diverse future. *M&O, 5,* 69–78.

Sawyer, K. (2012). *Explaining creativity: The science of human innovation* (2nd ed.). Oxford University Press.

Schneider, M., & Preckel, F. (2017). Variables associated with achievement in higher education: A systematic review of meta-analyses. *Psychological Bulletin, 143*(6), 565–600.

Scott, G., Coates, H., & Anderson, M. (2008). *Learning leaders in times of change: Academic leadership capabilities for Australian higher education.* University of Western Sydney and Australian Council for Educational Research. https://research.acer.edu.au/cgi/viewcontent.cgi?article=1001&context=higher_education

Senge, P. (1990). *The fifth discipline: The art and practice of the learning organisization*. Century.

Serdyukov, P. (2017). Innovation in education: What works, what doesn't, and what to do about it? *Journal of Research in Innovative Teaching & Learning, 10*(1), 4–33.

Uhl-Bien, M., Marion, R., & McKelvey, B. (2007). Complexity leadership theory: Shifting leadership from the industrial age to the knowledge era. *Leadership Quarterly, 18*(4), 298–318.

van der Zwaan, B. (2017). *Higher education in 2040: A global approach*. Amsterdam University Press.

Vereniging van Universiteiten. (2018). *Professionalization of university lecturers: The BKO and afterwards*. The Hague: Vereniging van Universiteiten/Association of Universities in the Netherlands. http://www.vsnu.nl/files/documenten/ Professionalisering%20van%20docenten%20aan%20de%20universiteit.pdf

Vrije Universiteit Amsterdam (VUA). (2019). *Mission and profile*. VUA. https:// www.vu.nl/en/about-vu-amsterdam/mission-and-profile/index.aspx

Weggeman, M. (2007). *Leading professionals? Do not! About knowledge workers, craftsmanship and innovation*. Schiedam.

West, M. A. (2002). Sparkling fountains or stagnant ponds: An integrative model of creativity and innovation implementation in work groups. *Applied Psychology, 51*(3), 355–387.

32

Higher Education Faculty Certificate Program: Foundations of Reflective Teaching

Christopher E. Garrett and Christine A. Draper

Introduction

With the current microscope aimed at supporting the diverse student body in higher education, being knowledgeable in one's own content area is no longer enough. Instructors must improve their knowledge and understanding of different approaches to teaching, learning, and assessment, including the use of effective and appropriate technologies to support student learning. Faculty need support in developing skills relevant to teaching and facilitating learning and being reflective and self-critical of their progress. By utilizing a structured teaching certificate program, institutions can provide their instructors with significant, structured professional development opportunities to enhance their teaching effectiveness.

Concern for the quality of teaching and learning in colleges and universities in the USA intensified after the mid-1970s (Rice & Kreber, 2006), and this has become an issue of critical importance internationally as well in the 21st century (Eaton, 2004; Kotecha, 2012; Landinelli, 2008; Miles & Polovina-Cukovic, 2012; Miranda, 2008; Department for Education and Skills, 2003; United Nations Educational, Scientific and Cultural Organization, 2014).

C. E. Garrett (✉) • C. A. Draper
Nevada State College, Henderson, NV, USA
e-mail: chris.garrett@nsc.edu; christine.draper@nsc.edu

© The Author(s), under exclusive license to Springer Nature Switzerland AG 2023
O. J. Neisler (ed.), *The Palgrave Handbook of Academic Professional Development Centers*,
Palgrave Studies on Leadership and Learning in Teacher Education,
https://doi.org/10.1007/978-3-030-80967-6_32

With diverse demographic changes and students often coming to college less prepared than in previous generations, effective teaching practices have been more closely scrutinized and are being reassessed (Binder et al., 2012; Swail, 2002; Ward & Selvester, 2012). The issue often lies in the fact that we tend to teach as we were taught. Many new professors are graduate students who attend large research universities that have been historically slow in adopting active learning strategies, thus leaving lecture as the primary modeled instructional method.

The push for quality teaching has led to numerous responses, including private foundations launching major funding grant initiatives (e.g., the W.K. Kellogg Foundation and Eli Lilly Foundation), and the formation of major organizations such as the Professional and Organizational Development Network, the International Consortium for Educational Development, and the Staff and Educational Development Association. The scholarship of teaching and learning (SoTL) and its implications were first introduced by Boyer (1990). SoTL is an approach that integrates research, teaching, and student learning with a focus on improving learning outcomes and assessment in higher education.

Looking at the characteristics of institutions that strongly support teaching and learning, one feature often included is the existence of faculty or educational development efforts (Feldman & Paulsen, 1999; Patrick & Fletcher, 1998; Paulsen & Feldman, 1995; Smith, 1998; Woods, 1999; Wright, 1996). This in turn has led to the formation of academic professional development centers (ADCs), which are known by a variety of names (e.g., centers for teaching and learning and faculty development centers), on campuses worldwide. These initiatives were all created to support effective teaching in higher education (Ward & Selvester, 2012).

Support for Quality Teaching

The notion of quality teaching needs to be supported by the institution to be effective and meaningful. In today's diverse world, students often enter college less prepared than previous generations. In the USA, the 2016 National Center for Education Statistics study projected an increase in minority students from 2012 to 2023, including more women, more diverse age groups, and more nontraditional students enrolling in college (U.S. Department of Education, 2018). Colleges and universities must ensure that their faculty are prepared to meet the needs of this increasingly diverse student population. There is a substantial body of literature that defines effective research-based teaching practices and high-quality teaching as a key factor in college persistence and graduation (Gyuorko et al., 2016). Therefore, it is essential that higher education institutions invest in professional development as a part of their overall strategic plan for ensuring successful students and improving graduation rates. This is needed for all teaching faculty, including tenure-track faculty, full-time lecturers, and adjunct instructors.

Inclusive Professional Development for Adjunct and New Faculty

Lyons (2007) stated that adjunct instructors teach half of all course sections offered at many institutions; similarly, the Coalition on the Academic Workforce (2012) reported that 75.5% of faculty members at many institutions in the USA were in "contingent positions" and not on track for tenure. Adjunct instructors are often "the invisible faculty" (Lyons, 2007, 6), receiving little or no training or support from their hiring institutions. Numerous authors and educational leaders have suggested that college administrators need to be concerned with providing optimal working conditions to increase the retention and productivity of instructors (Ballantyne et al., 2010; Halcrow & Olson, 2008; American Federation of Teachers, 2010). Many adjunct instructors often feel isolated, unsupported, and like second-class citizens (Gaillard-Kenney, 2006). Sadly, very few college leadership teams direct their efforts toward supporting adjunct faculty because these instructors are viewed as transients who typically have short tenures; consequently, few resources are invested (Halcrow & Olson, 2008). Furthermore, few institutions consider that the needs of their adjunct faculty may differ.

By considering the needs and wants of these part-time faculty and supporting them, colleges and universities can help improve overall teaching performance to benefit a larger number of students (Leslie & Gappa, 2002). Magda et al. (2015) surveyed 202 deans, directors, and provosts at two- and four-year higher education institutions and found a large portion of course design and delivery functions were placed on adjunct faculty's list of responsibilities, and there were few professional development sessions or opportunities that were not offered face-to-face. In order to retain high-quality adjunct faculty and provide them with the tools and sense of community they need, but do not often see, training opportunities offered through a structured teaching certificate program can help increase satisfaction, remove isolation by engaging adjuncts with a supportive community of practice that can enhance retention (Magda et al., 2015).

498   C. E. Garrett and C. A. Draper

This is not just an issue with adjunct faculty. In the USA, very little pedagogical training is offered to most graduate students. Faculty typically are hired into tenure-track positions based on their disciplinary knowledge and not their teaching skills. Consequently, institutions often provide workshops on pedagogy, course design, or assessment via educational development programs. Research shows that lecturing is rarely effective for the vast majority of learners who receive a D grade, fail, or withdraw (DFW); indeed, DFW rates under traditional lecturing increased by over 55% compared to students engaged in active learning (Freeman et al., 2014). To be an effective teacher, one needs to consider student learning, motivation, engagement, and much more. Workshops and 'one-and-done' piecemeal training can promote new ideas and fresh thinking, but how do we know that faculty are being exposed to a set of foundational principles on teaching or that they are actually implementing any of the content from these workshops? Creating a structured teaching certificate program is one way to fulfill this need.

Overview of the ADC

Context and Mission

Nevada State College is located in Henderson, Nevada, which is part of the Las Vegas metropolitan area, located in the Southwest USA. Founded in 2002 with just 200 students, Nevada State College now enrolls 7,000 students and is currently the second fastest-growing public state college in the USA. As a four-year college, we employ about 110 full-time faculty and over 200 part-time instructors. Many of our adjunct faculty members teach remotely, and many do not reside within Southern Nevada. Offering professional development opportunities can help retain online adjunct faculty from term to term (Magda et al., 2015). Established in 2016, our Center for Teaching and Learning Excellence (CTLE) has sought to ensure that our instructors receive adequate support and are able to participate in a variety of training opportunities and experiences that are offered beyond our physical campus.

Our ADC's mission addresses the need to provide professional development opportunities for all full-time and part-time faculty in order to improve student learning outcomes and support the college's academic mission. One of the significant initiatives that we have created to support faculty and build a community of life-long enthusiastic learners of effective teaching is through the Teaching Academy Certification Program. Learning objectives include participants examining their own assumptions about teaching and learning;

engaging in the process of experimenting, assessing, and revising teaching strategies and practices in order to improve student learning; and practicing critical reflection to catalyze one's professional growth as a teacher. This self-paced certificate program addresses the foundational teaching topics of learning theory, course design, methodology, and assessment and can be completed within 1–2 years.

Organizational Reporting and Structure

The CTLE provides professional development programs for full-time faculty and part-time instructors employed in Nevada State College's School of Liberal Arts and Sciences, School of Education, and School of Nursing. The CTLE staff are led by a director who also holds a tenure-track position in the School of Education. In addition to his administrative duties overseeing the ADC program, the CTLE director also teaches one undergraduate course per semester. The director reports to the associate provost for academic initiatives. The team of CTLE staff includes two instructional designers, one instructional technologist, and a student worker who serves as a part-time office assistant (see Fig. 32.1).

Funding Sources

The CTLE receives funding for its operational expenses from the Office of the Provost, with funds allocated on an annual budgetary cycle. We submit our budget requests for professional development programming for the fiscal year

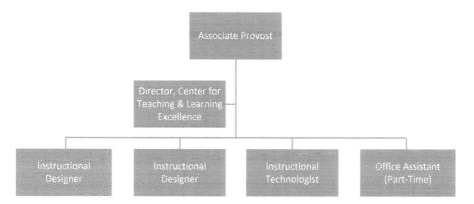

Fig. 32.1 Reporting structure of the CTLE, Nevada State College

Discussion on the Need for Teaching Certificates

(from July 1 to June 30) to the college's executive leadership team, who then review and prioritize needs before submitting proposals on to the college's Budget Committee for approving allocations. The CTLE receives approximately $50,000 dollars annually to fund professional development programming, excluding conference travel expenses and staff salaries.

Discussion on the Need for Teaching Certificates

Some countries require newly appointed faculty to undergo teacher training, such as Sri Lanka and Denmark. However, in the absence of national policies, universities in many countries design and implement their own teacher training programs. For example, most higher education institutions in Sweden require formal training of their faculty. Similarly, universities in Denmark mandate that all assistant professors must engage in teacher training courses. In Australia, most universities design and offer their own structured professional development programs generally labeled as Graduate Certificates in Higher Education for Teaching and Learning (O'Connor & Wisdom, 2014).

While ADCs in the USA offer a variety of activities, relatively few provide structured certificate programs. Those that do, typically have a primary requirement based on workshop attendance. For example, DePaul University's Teaching and Learning Certificate Program requires participants to attend six workshops and create a digital teaching portfolio (DePaul University, 2018). At Oklahoma City University, the Faculty Teaching Academy Fellow program established by Chris Garrett in 2008 continues to offer a certificate to those who attend seven workshops, participate in a faculty learning community (FLC) or teaching partnership, and complete a teaching portfolio (Oklahoma City University Center for Excellence in Teaching and Learning, 2018). In contrast, the University of Alabama at Birmingham offers four distinct certificates, each utilizing a gamification approach in which faculty earn points and badges toward certification by attending workshops, participating in classroom observations, and developing teaching materials and artifacts (University of Alabama at Birmingham Center for Teaching and Learning, 2018). Part-time instructors at Valencia College in Orlando, Florida, are encouraged to pursue a special certification program; after completing 60 hours of professional development activities, the adjunct instructor not only receives a certificate but also earns the designation of associate faculty member and receives a salary increase (Valencia College Office of Faculty Development, 2018).

Several organizations offer opportunities to complete a certificate program online with an enrollment fee to participate. The Association of College and

University Educators provides an online course in effective teaching practices that requires approximately 50 hours to complete and includes modules in course design, learning environment, active learning techniques, higher-order thinking, and assessment (Association of College and University Educators, 2018). However, institutions must make a significant investment for a large cohort of faculty to enroll in the course before they can participate. In contrast, individuals from any institution can pursue the Bok Teaching Certificate awarded by Harvard University (2018). Inspired by their own face-to-face seminar, this eight-week online course requires an investment of 8–10 hours per week as participants work through modules on topics such as how learning works and using feedback to improve teaching. The course is led by an instructor with a set calendar of activities and costs $2,400 to enroll.

Designing the Teaching Academy Certification Program at Nevada State College

Nevada State College's Teaching Academy Certification Program strives to engage faculty in teaching strategies, practices, and reflection. This encourages participation, provides a structured program to address particular faculty learning outcomes, and delivers tangible proof of participation and engagement that faculty can include in their teaching review portfolios for annual reviews and promotion and tenure evaluations. Participants can choose workshops and sessions based on foundational teaching topics, including learning theory and strategies, course design, teaching methods, and assessment. Because we have a large part-time instructor base, including many who teach remotely, we also offer the option of pursuing Teaching Academy certificates online, which accommodates instructors who are unable to physically come to campus for professional development activities. This ensures that participants have a well-rounded and robust experience understanding teaching, engaging with peers, and reflecting on their personal growth.

In order to assist participants in exploring ways to enhance their teaching practice and to connect with colleagues in our teaching community, we designed two levels of programming for our diverse participants: the Teaching Academy: Foundations of Teaching Certificate and the Teaching Academy Advanced Certificate: Reflective Practitioner. The learning experiences were designed to ensure participants could engage in a community of practice through discussion and reflection to critically evaluate their teaching strategies and philosophy. Participants are encouraged to complete all of the requirements for the Foundations of Teaching Certificate during a 1–2-year period.

502 C. E. Garrett and C. A. Draper

The structured learning experiences for the Foundations of Teaching Certificate involve approximately 13 hours of work to achieve certification, including:

* Attending at least five CTLE workshops that include at least two foundational teaching topics
* Actively engaging in an FLC on a teaching and learning topic for at least one semester (with active engagement considered attendance at a minimum of 75% of scheduled FLC meetings)
* Participating in a CTLE Teaching Circle (an interdisciplinary partnership focused on formative feedback), including receiving two teaching observations from colleagues and providing one of their own, as well as engaging afterward in reflective sessions
* Writing a 1–2-page reflective essay about their personal growth as a teacher during these learning experiences, sharing reflections on new activities and innovative ideas that they implemented into their teaching, and recording how they assessed the impact of those implementations. This reflective essay is then shared at the annual celebratory event for the Teaching Academy.

Learning experiences for the Advanced Certificate: Reflective Practitioner are very similar, but continue to build on the foundational certificate and encourage the participants to articulate a teaching portfolio based on their personal investigations and analyses of teaching and learning. At this level, participants engage in approximately 10 additional hours of professional development, including:

* Attending at least two CTLE workshops that address a third foundational teaching topic
* Actively engaging in another FLC on a teaching and learning topic
* Participating in an additional CTLE Teaching Circle, including receiving two teaching observations from colleagues and providing one of their own, as well as engaging afterward in reflective sessions
* Requesting mid-semester feedback from students (i.e., Small Group Instructional Diagnosis), a service conducted by the CTLE, and engaging in the consultation process to discuss student responses
* Submitting their teaching portfolio (e.g., narratives of their teaching philosophy statement, teaching strategies, assessment methods, response to course evaluations, and statement on professional development) to the CTLE to post in a digital repository to share with fellow faculty

* Writing a 1–2-page reflective essay about their personal growth as a teacher during these learning experiences, sharing reflections on new activities and innovative ideas that they implemented into their teaching, and recording how they assessed the impact of those implementations. This reflective essay is then shared at the annual celebratory event for the Teaching Academy.

Peer Review of Teaching: Opportunities for Formative Feedback

In higher education, peer review stands as a vital means of receiving expert assessment for ensuring high-quality scholarship. While peer review is well-established as a means of evaluating research across the disciplines, it is often less common when assessing teaching performance. Peers can go beyond the expertise of students, since they are experienced teachers themselves and can offer colleagues important perspectives to inform efforts to improve teaching. When done well, peer review leads to a number of benefits including more vigorous conversation about the criteria for excellent teaching, greater sharing of teaching successes and challenges among colleagues across disciplines, and often an increased perception of teaching excellence at the institution.

CTLE Teaching Circles support formative, peer review observations. The circles are organized as interdisciplinary partnerships, focused on feedback. During this experience, participants receive two teaching observations from their Teaching Circle colleagues and engage afterward in reflective sessions, as well as provide one teaching observation for a colleague, providing feedback afterward in a reflective session. It takes approximately 2–4 hours for a participant to observe their colleague's course, provide feedback through a reflective session, and receive feedback from their CTLE liaison. Including this type of peer feedback and reflection encourages the participant to learn about their strengths and to consider future teaching goals for their classroom.

Both of the Teaching Academy certification levels use and encourage evidence-based teaching practices that foster student engagement and assessment activities that provide facilitators and participants alike with evidence of learning and opportunities for formative feedback. This component is essential since these certificate programs are informal and ungraded. Both levels also have fully online options for completion for participants not located geographically close to campus or those unable to attend professional development sessions face-to-face due to time constraints. This ensures that we are providing completion options for instructors who want to improve their craft of teaching but who are unable to attend due to limited time or access to on-campus offerings.

Reflections and Informal Assessment

Our faculty certificate programs offer foundational principles for effective teaching. However, the design of similar programs at other institutions would really depend upon the needs of the faculty. Some certificate programs are focused on teaching with technology and others may have a special concentration on topics like assessment. As for the essential components of your certificate program, make sure to include stakeholders in the design (e.g., members of your center's faculty advisory board or professional development committee). In our case, faculty told us that peer review of teaching was important to them, so we created the Teaching Circles (as described above) and incorporated this experience into our criteria for the certificate.

When designing the Teaching Academy certificates, we tailored our requirements and offerings in direct correlation with our faculty learning outcomes. These include:

* Expanding evidence-based pedagogical awareness
* Incorporating evidence-based best practices in course design, instructional delivery, and assessment
* Collaborating within a community of teaching scholars
* Engaging in reflective practice.

These outcomes are what frame our offerings to identify expected competencies and encourage faculty to examine their own assumptions about teaching and learning and to engage them in the process of experimenting, assessing, and revising their teaching strategies and practices in order to improve student learning.

Certificate programs are valuable for several reasons. First, a certificate program provides structure for faculty development activities. In some departments, faculty may be asked in their annual reviews to create an individual development plan (IDP) and track their progress toward reaching those goals. Faculty appreciate certificate programs because they can function as a significant piece of their IDP and, when completed, represent tangible proof of reaching those professional development goals. Secondly, when a university offers a certificate program to its faculty, this inherently shows how much that institution values professional development. This also provides an opportunity to recognize the achievements of individual faculty members who invest time and effort toward improving their teaching knowledge and skills.

32 Higher Education Faculty Certificate Program... 505

Over the past four years since commencing the program, 36 instructors have completed the requirements of the Foundations of Teaching Certificate, with the pool of recipients comprising five tenured faculty, 17 tenure-track faculty, 12 lecturers, and two part-time instructors. In addition, eight faculty members have earned the Advanced Certificate: Reflective Practitioner. At the time of writing, there are currently 21 instructors enrolled in the Foundations of Teaching Certificate program, including four tenure-track faculty, five lecturers, and 12 part-time instructors.

We informally surveyed current participants and found that there were three main incentives for pursuing Teaching Academy certification. These included exposure to evidence-based practices that can improve the participant's teaching and the experiences of students in their courses; opportunities to collaborate and network with colleagues both within their own and from different disciplines; and, finally, formal documentation and evidence this certification can provide for annual reviews and goals for both full and part-time faculty and for their promotion and tenure packet for those faculty on the tenure track.

In addition, many of the participants spoke to the certification program providing opportunities to learn and relearn new methods and strategies for engaging students and in providing them with equitable and challenging learning experiences. Participants also referred to the importance of learning, seeking and providing feedback, sharing with each other what works and what does not, and how the scope and sequence of courses across campus works to support students at various levels. The participants also mentioned their personal motivations for enrolling in the program to make not only their individual classes, but the college experience as a whole, a better one for students enrolled at Nevada State College.

Several certificate recipients acknowledged the importance of having the CTLE on campus and the need to support the center's initiatives. These faculty participants felt that the certificate program demonstrated the institution's long-standing commitment to teaching excellence for its diverse population. These individuals stated that they had enjoyed attending events and found the information very beneficial and useful for their classrooms. Furthermore, participants also appreciated the opportunity to engage and collaborate with instructors with the same aspirations. Finally, several participants spoke to the importance of self-reflection on one's teaching and that improving one's teaching is a process, not a destination. They felt that the certificate program was an effective medium used to engage with a cohort of faculty who not only enjoyed teaching but were also willing to share and learn from each other.

When designing our Teaching Academy certificates in alignment with our faculty learning outcomes, the CTLE team decided to create the advanced level to encourage participants to take their teaching and learning even further. Respondents who had completed the advanced certification noted that this level provided them with a more focused approach to their classroom and engaged them with a variety of colleagues to gain additional feedback and perspectives on their teaching. They felt that the advanced certificate enabled them to focus on specific courses and reflect on their teaching practices in a more effective and detailed manner than they had the opportunity to engage in previously. This provided a unique format to showcase their commitment and dedication to the craft of teaching and effective learning.

Recommendations and Conclusion

As educational developers, we hope that every college teacher will fully engage in our ADC offerings and pursue completing a certificate program. However, relatively few tend to do so. Many who choose not to enroll state that the investment of time is the major obstacle. Therefore, one of the challenges to creating and sustaining a certificate program is developing an initial cohort of faculty who can champion the cause and encourage colleagues to follow their example. It is important to identify opinion leaders on your campus who you can personally reach out to and invite to participate. If funding is available, you may want to consider offering small stipends to those who complete your certification program. It is essential to use every opportunity to promote and advertise the program at workshops, faculty meetings, and convocations. Moreover, ADCs need to make sure they introduce this certification program to new faculty at orientation events. Tenure-track faculty and part-time instructors also tend to be responsive to invitations. Discussing the merits of the certificate with deans and department chairs to enlist their support is also vital to the success of the program.

A well-planned program for the development of faculty can yield rich rewards. Our institution's Teaching Academy Certification Program has helped to build a community of lifelong, enthusiastic faculty learners to improve the quality of students' learning experiences and enhance learning outcomes.

References

American Federation of Teachers. (2010). A national survey of part-time/adjunct faculty. *American Academic, 2*, 1–16.

Association of College and University Educators. (2018). *Certificates*. Association of College and University Educators. https://acue.org/courses/certificates

Ballantyne, S., Berret, B., & Harst, W. (2010). Full time faculty perceptions of leadership in adjunct faculty to maintain Franciscan identity. *Research in Higher Education Journal, 9*, 1–9.

Binder, M., Chermak, J., Krause, K., & Thacher, J. (2012). The teacher penalty in higher education: Evidence from a public research university. *Economics Letters, 117*(1), 39–34.

Boyer, E. L. (1990). *Scholarship reconsidered: Priorities of the professoriate*. Jossey-Bass.

Coalition on the Academic Workforce. (2012). *A portrait of part-time faculty members*. Coalition on the Academic Workforce. http://www.academicworkforce.org/survey.html

Department for Education and Skills. (2003). *The future of higher education*. Higher Education Council. http://www.educationengland.org.uk/documents/pdfs/2003-white-paper-higher-ed.pdf

DePaul University. (2018). *Teaching and learning certificate program*. DePaul University. http://tlcp.depaultla.org

Eaton, V. (2004, July 14). *Some initial feedback on the NFPTS consultation exercise* (Presentation). PG Cert Leaders Northern Network.

Feldman, K. A., & Paulsen, M. B. (1999). Faculty motivation: The role of a supportive teaching culture. *New Directions for Teaching and Learning, 1999*(78), 69–78.

Freeman, S., Eddy, S. L., McDonough, M., Smith, M. K., Okoroafor, N., Jordt, H., & Wenderoth, W. P. (2014). Active learning increases student performance in science, engineering, and mathematics. *Proceedings of the National Academy of Science, 111*(23), 8410–8415.

Gaillard-Kenney, S. (2006). Adjunct faculty in distance education: What program managers should know. *Distance Learning, 3*(1), 9–16.

Gyuorko, J., MacCormak, P., Bless, M. M., & Jodl, J. (2016). *Why colleges and universities need to invest in quality teaching more than ever: Faculty development, evidence-based teaching practices, and student success* (White paper). Association of College and University Educators. https://acue.org/wp-content/uploads/2018/07/ACUE-White-Paper1.pdf

Halcrow, C., & Olson, M. R. (2008). Adjunct faculty: Valued resource or cheap labor? *Focus on Colleges, Universities, and Schools, 2*(1), 1–8.

Harvard University. (2018). *Bok teaching certificate*. Harvard University. https://online-learning.harvard.edu/course/bok-teaching-certificate

Kotecha, P. (2012). *A profile of higher education in southern Africa – Volume 1: A regional perspective*. Southern African Regional Universities Association.

Landinelli, J. (2008). Scenarios of diversification, differentiation, and segmentation of higher education in Latin America and the Caribbean. In A. L. Gazzola & A. Didriksson (Eds.), *Trends in higher education in Latin America and the Caribbean* (pp. 149–172). International Institute for Higher Education in Latin America and the Caribbean, United Nations Educational, Scientific and Cultural Organization.

Leslie, D. W., & Gappa, J. M. (2002). Part-time faculty: Competent and committed. *New Directions for Community Colleges, 2002*(118), 59–68.

Lyons, R. E. (2007). Deepening our understanding of adjunct faculty. In *Best practices for supporting adjunct faculty* (pp. 1–12). Anker Publishers.

Magda, A. J., Poulin, R., & Clinefelter, D. L. (2015). *Recruiting, orienting, & supporting online adjunct faculty: A survey of practices*. Learning House.

Miles, C. A., & Polovina-Cukovic, D. (2012). *The role of new faculty orientation in improving the effectiveness of university teaching—Part I: University sector*. Higher Educational Quality Council of Ontario.

Miranda, X. Z. (2008). Regional integration and internationalization of higher education in Latin America and the Caribbean. In A. L. Gazzola & A. Didriksson (Eds.), *Trends in higher education in Latin America and the Caribbean* (pp. 173–232). International Institute for Higher Education in Latin America and the Caribbean, United Nations Educational, Scientific and Cultural Organization.

O'Connor, K. M., & Wisdom, J. (2014). *The preparation of university teachers internationally*. International Consortium for Educational Development. http://icedonline.net/iced-members-area/the-preparation-of-university-teachers-internationally/

Oklahoma City University Center for Excellence in Teaching and Learning. (2018). *Awards: Faculty teaching academy fellows*. Oklahoma City University. https://www.okcu.edu/campus/resources/cetl/cetl-awards

Patrick, S. K., & Fletcher, J. J. (1998). Faculty developers and change agents: Transforming colleges and universities into learning organizations. *To Improve the Academy, 17*(1), 155–170.

Paulsen, M. B., & Feldman, K. A. (1995). Taking teaching seriously: Meeting the challenge of instructional improvement. *Journal of General Education, 50*(1), 75–80.

Rice, R., & Kreber, C. (2006). Enhancing the quality of teaching and learning: The U.S. experience. *New Directions for Higher Education, 2006*(133), 13–22.

Smith, B. (1998). Adopting a strategic approach to managing change in learning and teaching. *To Improve the Academy, 17*(1), 225–242.

Swail, W. (2002). Higher education and the new demographics: Questions for policy. *Change: The Magazine of Higher Learning, 34*(4), 14–23.

U.S. Department of Education. (2018). *Digest of education statistics, 2016* (NCES #2017094). Institute of Education Sciences, National Center for Education Statistics. https://nces.ed.gov/pubsearch/pubsinfo.asp?pubid=2017094

United Nations Educational, Scientific and Cultural Organization. (2014). *Higher education in Asia: Expanding out, expanding up*. United Nations Educational, Scientific and Cultural Organization Institute for Statistics.

University of Alabama at Birmingham Center for Teaching and Learning. (2018). *CTL certification programs.* University of Alabama at Birmingham. https://www.uab.edu/faculty/ctl/programs

Valencia College Office of Faculty Development (2018). *Associate faculty certification.* Valencia College. https://valenciacollege.edu/faculty/development/programs/adjunct/certificateProgram.cfm

Ward, H. C., & Selvester, P. M. (2012). Faculty learning communities: Improving teaching in higher education. *Educational Studies, 38*(1), 111–121.

Woods, J. Q. (1999). Establishing a teaching development culture. In R. J. Menges (Ed.), *Faculty in new jobs: A guide to settling in, becoming established, and building institutional support* (pp. 268–290). Jossey-Bass.

Wright, D. L. (1996). Moving toward a university environment which rewards teaching: The faculty developer's role. *To Improve the Academy, 15*(1), 185–194.

33

Preparing Future Faculty: Developing Inclusive, Future-Focused Educators and an Adaptive Program

Shamini Dias

Introduction

This chapter presents the evolution of the Preparing Future Faculty (PFF) program, a national initiative in the USA that both teaches an adaptive, inclusive pedagogy and practices the same principles in its program design. The program responds to significant changes in higher education. In addition to increasingly diverse, nontraditional student populations (Center for Law and Social Policy, 2015), higher education is undergoing rapid change as a result of increased globalization and the emergence of a digitally interconnected knowledge economy (Adams & Carfagna, 2006; Appadurai, 1996; Davidson, 2016; Friedman, 2005; Robinson, 2011, 2018). Teaching must adapt to these new contexts and diversities to better prepare students for their futures. The PFF Teaching Certificate content is based on an integration of systems and ethical, cocreative design and reflexive thinking to prepare graduate students to become inclusive, future-focused educators who understand the importance of working adaptively. These same principles structurally helped us to develop a fluid, responsive, and inclusive program.

S. Dias (✉)
Claremont Graduate University, Claremont, CA, USA
e-mail: shamini.dias@cgu.edu

© The Author(s), under exclusive license to Springer Nature Switzerland AG 2023
O. J. Neisler (ed.), *The Palgrave Handbook of Academic Professional Development Centers*,
Palgrave Studies on Leadership and Learning in Teacher Education,
https://doi.org/10.1007/978-3-030-80967-6_33

511

512   S. Dias

History and Mission

The program's mission is tied to concern in American higher education regarding the changing role of teaching. The national PFF initiative began in 1993 led by the Association of American Colleges and Universities and the Council of Graduate Schools to explicitly address graduate student preparation for faculty careers and to promote teaching. Boyer's (1990) report, *Scholarship Reconsidered: Priorities of the Professoriate*, redefined traditional scholarship to include the scholarship of *teaching* in parallel importance to the scholarships of *discovery*, *integration*, and *application*. Other scholars have added to the conversation about teaching responsibility (Glassick et al., 1997; Huber & Hutchings, 2005; Hutchings & Shulman, 1999; Shulman, 1999; Shulman & Shulman, 2004). Barr and Tagg's (1995) analysis of shifting from an instructional to a learning paradigm also shaped the educational mission, criteria for success, the place of pedagogy, and the significance of the learning sciences.

Early career faculty face various institutional and disciplinary pressures and often struggle to engage with teaching innovations (Matthews et al., 2014), as much as with developing a professional identity in teaching (Alsup, 2005; Friesen & Besley, 2013). However, graduate students—in their formative transition from students to scholars—represent an optimal population for developing teaching identities and knowledge. Unfortunately, many graduate programs still work within the pre-Boyer model, where scholarly development is primarily disciplinary research. Claremont Graduate University (CGU), as a small, graduate-only institution with 2,038 students in 2019, identified a unique opportunity to implement a program that helps graduate students discover and craft their identities and knowledge as educators in parallel to becoming researchers. Teaching is a scholarly and leadership process, and hence, a significant responsibility. Locating teaching as a meaningful part of graduate studies helps foster future faculty who will in turn make learning meaningful for their students and advocate for teaching excellence, seeing themselves as active engaged scholars who participate in the scholarship of teaching and learning.

Organizational Reporting and Program Structure

Program development began in 2013 and officially launched in fall 2014 as part of CGU's student services. In 2018, the PFF program, together with the Center for Writing and Rhetoric (CWR), the Career Development Office

(CDO), and the Transdisciplinary Studies program, formed a collaborative department known as Academic Professional Development. This move signaled an explicit connection with students' academic pathways and positioned the program to evolve as a faculty resource. The PFF program collaborates with the CDO, CWR, and the Transdisciplinary Studies program on an annual Careers in Higher Education Conference as well as Re-Orientation, a one-day event designed to help post-coursework students in designing their futures. In addition, the PFF program and the Claremont Colleges Library work in collaboration on scholarly communication workshops. As of 2019, the program reports directly to the vice president for academic innovation, student success, and enrollment management in the President's Office.

Program Structure

The PFF Teaching Certificate program comprises two courses using a teaching portfolio for reflexive practice. The courses for the certificate program include Transdisciplinary Pedagogy for Ethical Education, and Teaching Practicum and Portfolio. The courses are offered in the fall, spring, and summer semesters; students take them in sequence, but can take time off between them as needed. Students begin by familiarizing themselves with the course's learning management system (LMS) through an orientation, online introductions, and setting up their teaching portfolio. A portfolio approach helps students curate, organize, and synthesize learning. They respond weekly to a reflexivity worksheet, select and organize resources, and manage their course projects in their portfolios. These portfolios also help students who may choose to pause the PFF program to focus on research and life issues to later resume the program more coherently. Furthermore, learning to work with portfolios prepares students to sustain this practice during their continuing professional development.

The first course, Transdisciplinary Pedagogy for Ethical Education, is an online synchronous course adapting a flipped classroom model. It introduces key frameworks and establishes complexity and systems and design thinking as foundations for understanding and working adaptively with changing educational contexts. This foundation supports developing a future-focused, ethical pedagogy and operationalizes aspects of inclusive teaching, including: identities and community; active learning; assessment and feedback; teaching modalities; and digital tools. As part of this development, students create an active learning teaching demonstration with peer review and feedback. They also engage in a transdisciplinary group project to practice systems thinking

514   S. Dias

in reimagining education, proposing a transformation of a selected aspect of education in a creative format of their choosing. The course supports development of their teaching philosophy and diversity statements.

In the asynchronous online Teaching Practicum and Portfolio course, students apply what they have learned by creating a set of items to add to their teaching portfolio. They work on observing and reflecting on undergraduate teaching and inclusive course and syllabus design—including constructive alignment of outcomes and assessments, syllabus schedule and assignments, syllabus policies, tone, and logistical details—as well as a sample LMS and a teacher-scholar website. These assignments are done through a formative draft-feedback-revise process. While there are no whole class meetings, students have weekly one-on-one meetings with PFF fellows, advanced graduate students who teach in the program to support their work development. This enables us to balance structure and flexibility with deadlines for drafts and final submissions. As students complete the program, they write a final integrative reflection to synthesize their learning. Students complete the program with a portfolio of useful items that prepare them for the job market, but more importantly with a robust start to ethical teaching practice.

Theoretical Foundations of the FPP Program

Five Mindsets for Inclusive Future-Focused Pedagogy

We define flexible, inclusive, future-focused pedagogy as ethically grounded teaching designed for all learners to meaningfully construct knowledge, while building capacities for flourishing in their future. Education is a complex endeavor or a "wicked problem" (Buchanan, 1992; Handstedt, 2018; Rittel & Webber, 1984), comprising multilayered webs of multiple players, disciplines, issues, and levels of power and action. *Ethical and systems mindsets* question legacy education bounded by racist, oppressive, transmission modes of teaching (Freire, 1970/2005; Giroux, 2020; Hooks, 1994; Love, 2019), especially illuminated by global complexities of rapid change and uncertainty, multiple perspectives, and interconnectedness. This helps students to design for inclusivity and justice, address systemic inequities, and to integrate plurality, multiple perspectives, hope, and growth in their teaching. *Design and cocreative mindsets* activate ethical systems thinking supporting intentional, student-centered, collaborative approaches. These mindsets are the basis for facilitating flexible, responsive, inclusive learning processes in which students

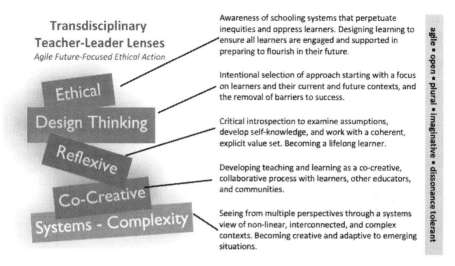

Fig. 33.1 The five mindsets for inclusive future-focused pedagogy

are partners on the learning journey. Finally, *reflexive mindsets* sustain educators in understanding the 'self' that teaches (Palmer, 2017), especially in emerging, complex contexts. Critical introspection of one's assumptions, values, and beliefs fosters openness to change and supports responsive, adaptive teaching (Argyris, 1999; Flavell, 1985; Schön, 1983, 1987). Figure 33.1 provides more details as to how each of these five mindsets contributes to a transdisciplinary teacher-leader lens.

A Complexity Lens for Inclusive, Adaptive Teaching

Understanding complexity is critical to inclusive pedagogy (Davis et al., 2015; Meadows, 2008; Patton, 2011; Snowden & Boone, 2007), because it helps us engage in situation recognition and responsiveness (Patton, 2011) and sense-making (Snowden & Boone, 2007) when responding to diverse contexts. This supports the complex, adaptive nature of inclusive teaching to honor and work with a diverse population of students, multiple perspectives, and emerging contexts in active knowledge construction. The PFF program uses Snowden and Boone's (2007) Cynefin framework to help educators make sense of different teaching-learning contexts.

The framework presents five ontological and epistemological spaces: clear, complicated, complex, chaotic, and aporetic/confused. These spaces differ in terms of the level of rigidity of the constraints on thinking and action. *Clear*

516   S. Dias

and *complicated* contexts have relatively tight and linear relationships between cause and effect, whereas *complex* and *chaotic* contexts have more degrees of freedom between cause and effect (i.e., more potentialities and choices). *Aporetic* contexts, located in the middle, involve situations where we find ourselves confronting paradoxical or multiple truths which, if we can embrace them, help us avoid falling into a crisis of thought. In clear contexts, everything is known and undisputed. Here, we sense the situation, fit it to preestablished categories and rules, and take predetermined actions. From a learning perspective, no growth happens. In complicated contexts, although not everything is known, there are governing constraints in the form of canonical knowledge and experts who can help us understand how to respond. We like these spaces; they feel safe and stable, and business as usual can proceed. In these efficient spaces, however, we can fall into "entrained thinking" or conditioned responses as a result of past experience, training, and success (Snowden & Boone, 2007). We become reluctant to change, persisting in legacy actions, blind to the need to adapt as situations shift.

Legacy education is rooted in these spaces, with long-established norms and practices based on racism and other oppressive social paradigms, as well as disciplinary and learning assumptions. Not recognizing the mismatch between legacy education and changing contexts, emerging futures, student diversity, and calls for justice, we are easily in danger of perpetuating multiple oppressions. The legacy model with the teacher at the center has a one-way, one-size-fits-all approach that excludes those who do not "fit," when in fact everyone can flourish if learning processes work flexibly in inviting a diversity of students' voices, histories, and identities to make learning meaningful. Understanding the dangers of entrained thinking in clear and complex domains by practicing reflexivity to pay attention and question legacy systems can help us work adaptively to include all learners and foster their capacities to help them flourish.

Complex domain thinking is critical in sensemaking and working adaptively. Here, things are unknown and emerging. Both learners and teachers experience this. Learners venturing into new topics and skills do not feel comfortable or safe; they might feel overwhelmed and easily perceive situations as chaotic when things emerge in ways they cannot understand. A typical instinct is to resist or withdraw, to disengage from learning. Teachers, too, face ever-shifting unknowns with diversity in learners' contexts, emotions, and life situations. However, in adopting complex domain thinking, we pay attention to and accept emergence and uncertainty, seeing multiple perspectives and possibilities as *enabling* constraints that facilitate adaptation and innovation. We are better able to use intentional, inclusive design to sustain engagement and

33 Preparing Future Faculty: Developing Inclusive, Future-Focused... 517

support students in persisting through the natural dissonance of learning. Transparent goals, flexible and safe-to-fail learning processes, and intentional scaffolding prevent learners from experiencing learning as *chaotic*. They are better able to take risks in mastering knowledge and skills. This facilitates meaningful, integrative active learning connecting new and old knowledge and experiences (Dewey, 1938; Hinton et al., 2012; Piaget & Cook 1952; Vygotsky, 1978).

In addition, by approaching teaching and learning as complex adaptive processes, teachers can build on opportunities (amplify) and reduce barriers (dampen) as they emerge. This is akin to improvisation, or what Snowden (2015) refers to as "the evolutionary potential of the present moment." Complex domain thinking reframes diversity, plurality, uncertainty, emergence, and error as natural in learning, locating inclusive teaching as a complex adaptive process of intentional, flexible design. This moves us well away from the transmission model based on unquestioned assumptions of academic mores and motivations. Teaching becomes an ethical, co-creative, emergent process with all students (Cavanagh, 2016; Handstedt, 2018).

Reflexive Practice

Reflexivity is critical in teaching (Brookfield, 1995; Cartwright, 2002; Dewey, 1933; Greenwood, 1998; Loughran, 2002; Schön, 1983, 1987; Van Manen, 1995; Zeichner & Liston, 1996). From the perspective of the Cynefin framework, reflexivity is the key to adaptive teaching that avoids entrainment. Building on Argryis's (1999) model of double-loop learning, reflexivity enables engagement in a critical self-introspection of assumptions, values, and beliefs and thus supports transformative learning. As Archer (2012) argues, reflexivity is an imperative in the face of diversity and fast-emerging change; we cannot afford habituated thinking.

In the PFF program, we foster reflexivity as a central process (Argyris, 1999; Bean & Stevens, 2002; Pintrich, 2002) through in-class reflexive writing and discussions, metaphor explorations, and parallel development of reflexive thinking after each class. These processes allow students to critically examine their past experiences as learners to surface and disrupt habituated or conditioned assumptions and beliefs about teaching and learning. Through an intentional selection of values, goals, and methods as educators, students develop teacher-leader identities, positionality, and fluid practice for the future. In locating teaching in the *complex* space, as a flexible, emergent process, reflexivity becomes critical for developing openness, self-awareness, and

518   S. Dias

to continuously challenge assumptions and change how we think. Reflexivity supports adaptive capacity and growth for justice.

Design Thinking

As a human-centered process explicitly based on empathy with users and contexts, design thinking operationalizes diversity, inclusivity, and responsiveness in practice to transform teaching and learning (Brown, 2009; Cross, 2011; Seelig, 2015; IDEO U, n.d.). Design thinking is a key program framework to help our students expand backward design (Wiggins & McTighe, 2005) for adaptive, inclusive pedagogy. The "Empathize" and "Define" stages of design thinking ground teaching in a student-, context-, and systems-based approach to shape the learning outcomes from which course development proceeds (the "Ideate" and "Prototype" phases). The "Test" phase underscores the fluidity of teaching. In remaining responsive to students' needs, voices, and interests, as well as emerging challenges, we adjust teaching as we go to adapt and support learning. Hence, reflexivity in a continuous formative evaluation of teaching is integral to design thinking and fosters Boyer's (1990) concept of the teacher-scholar where reflexivity and agility serve the quest for excellent, ethical engagement as much with teaching as with research.

Program Innovation Through Reflexive, Design Thinking

The PFF program's pedagogy has also guided its development. Starting as a one-person office and growing incrementally, systems and design thinking, reflexivity, and a co-creative, ethical approach have empowered the evolution of the program. Our emergent process has been a co-evolutionary, innovative response to emerging student and institutional needs and opportunities. Integrating teaching professional development into graduate education is a complex challenge. Participation in the PFF program is not a requirement; students elect to commit to it on top of their doctoral research, full- or part-time work, and family commitments. Therefore, flexibility is critical in order to evolve responsively to emerging needs, similar to a developmental evaluation process (Patton, 2011), ongoing formative assessment without a fixed logic model.

Figure 33.2 details the evolution of the PFF program from inception to its current form. Phase 1 of the program (spring 2013 to fall 2014) consisted of

33 Preparing Future Faculty: Developing Inclusive, Future-Focused...

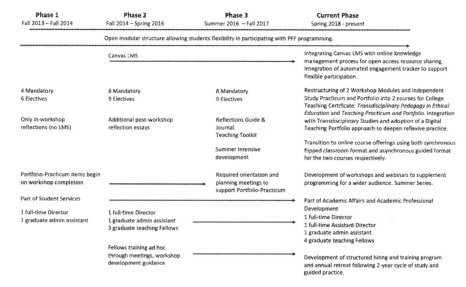

Fig. 33.2 Evolution of the PFF program over time

a fluid prototype of open workshops integrating reflection writing. This enabled us to test key ideas to extract foundational principles. Subsequently, in Phase 2 (fall 2014 to fall 2015), the second prototype was launched, which included a pioneering team of graduate student fellows as workshop facilitators and the use of an LMS. We explored tailoring the program to specific departments with teaching artist workshops, and providing some exemptions for psychology students who had completed their department's Teaching Seminar course. In turn, in Phase 3 (fall 2015 to summer 2017), in response to witnessing participants' struggle with submitting their reflections, we streamlined our workshops to consolidate reflections. The addition of orientation and planning sessions scaffolded engagement and persistence in building PFF Teaching Certificate items. We also assigned a PFF peer advisor who tracked and supported engagement. In this phase, we tested a Summer Intensive Module that proved popular.

As of the time of writing, we are currently in Phase 4 (spring 2018 to date). A faculty subcommittee reviewed the PFF program's potential and made a recommendation to the Board of Trustees to add an assistant director. We also developed an internal tracking system to automate and enable proactive outreach to help students engage and persist in the program to completion. This provides live data to study enrollment, engagement, and completion trends, and to monitor work submission and feedback rates. Continuing review of reflective practice as well as further exploration of graduate life contexts led to

520   S. Dias

structural changes; we adopted a portfolio-based approach, transitioning to a model of two connected courses that provide a more coherent process. We also moved to an open access model with most of our online materials and resources. As we move forward, we are developing a more structured process for PFF fellows in a two-year cycle that includes authoring webinars, blog-posts, and resources, and an annual team retreat. We are also developing a PFF "reader" of key scholarship that underpins the program. As of spring 2020, the PFF Teaching Certificate program is fully online.

Program Innovation Principles

In developing the PFF program using the same pedagogical model we teach, the following principles have emerged as critically important.

Accessibility

We want all graduate students to participate; therefore, no application restrictions or selection process are applied and the program is open to both current students and alumni. To encourage participation, there are no program fees (except when a department requires a unit-bearing course as a teaching tool). Alumni pay a minimal administrative charge. We continue to work with academic departments to seek integration so that they encourage, endorse, or make the PFF program part of their degree completion requirements.

Flexibility and Adaptiveness

A modular structure enables busy graduate students to engage, persist, and complete the PFF Teaching Certificate. Key strategies include: (1) spacing out the two program courses, and (2) offering multiple ways in which to engage with the program. While the two courses are linked, students can space them out when their work, lives, or doctoral studies need more attention. The teaching portfolio they develop in the first course ensures that they do not lose any work and allows them to easily review materials before they resume the second course. We also offer one-on-one meetings as needed to help students prepare for the second course.

In addition, students who find themselves not ready or unable to take the PFF Teaching Certificate courses can still engage in other teaching professional development activities by attending workshops on an ad hoc basis.

These workshops are designed to stand alone so students are not adrift with references to concepts from previous workshops. In addition, students can also work one-on-one with the PFF program team to discuss teaching ideas and issues, develop resources, get feedback on teaching documents, and practice teaching.

Reflexivity

Reflexivity is core to our evolving program development. As is typical of organizational growth, we require a balance between the need for structure and continuing emergence (Csikszentmihalyi, 1996; Sagiv et al., 2010). Brown and Duguid (2001) describe this as moving from being a self-organizing string quartet toward an orchestra needing a conductor. Our team-based, co-creative response to emerging student and institutional needs is essential for adaptive program innovation. Yet, as the program grows, we also need clear business processes and mission-critical design decisions that balance the program's structure with the fluidity of individualizing to serve diverse needs and circumstances. We are formalizing our reflexive process in a developmental assessment cycle and have instituted semesterly staff reflection meetings to ensure we remain responsive within our organizational structure.

Impact of the PFF Program

The impact of the PFF program can be seen in various ways. Our program reach grew significantly from 82 to 244 attendees in the first phase, and from 382 to 701 in four academic years. Our participants include alumni and are well distributed across different subject areas, including areas not typically associated with teaching such as business and information systems. With the move toward the two-course structure, we are also seeing higher completion rates in terms of earning the certificate. In 2020, 68 students earned their PFF Teaching Certificate, compared to an average of 6–8 per year previously.

In addition, faculty and institutional endorsement of the program was seen in the vote to add an assistant director. Individual faculty recommending the program to students has supported program outreach and we have stronger integration with academic departments. Three academic departments, the CGU Center for Information Systems and Technology, Division of Behavioral and Organizational Sciences, and the School of Community and Global Health, have added the PFF foundations course as a doctoral requirement.

522   **S. Dias**

With this disciplinary integration, we remain mindful of the importance of crossing boundaries and engaging in novel thinking in dismantling and transforming legacy education. Therefore, we more strongly articulate the development of transdisciplinary pedagogy as the basis for ethical education.

In addition, the program has seen a small but steady line of inquiry from non-CGU graduate students who have asked to join the program. As we build capacity, there are possibilities for including external fee-paying students in developing ethical pedagogies. In 2017, the PFF team were approached by the Office of Civic and Community Engagement at the University of La Verne, California, to partner with them in developing a mentoring program to help future faculty integrate community-based learning in teaching their own disciplines. The Partnership for Community Engagement and Democracy program immersed graduate students from both institutions under faculty mentorship in community service courses; they then went on to develop and teach their own courses the following semester.

Finally, even students not seeking faculty careers engage with the PFF program. Our framing of ethical pedagogy as responsive, learning leadership attracts students seeking careers in business, consulting, evaluation, entrepreneurship, public health, and the arts industries. The program's student-oriented flexible approach enables individualizing work so students can write a leadership philosophy, develop training programs, or public education outreach programs instead of a syllabus.

Conclusion

We firmly believe it is not sufficient today to merely teach pedagogical methods. The scholarship of teaching in a diverse, dynamically interconnected, and complex world also requires a disposition toward complexity and ethical systems thinking. This continues to inform our three increasingly complex foci: (1) fostering teaching identities and positionalities rooted in complex, adaptive thinking grounded in an awareness of legacy systems and ethical transformation; (2) equipping future teacher-leaders with future-focused pedagogical knowledge and skills for inclusive design; and (3) maintaining a complex, adaptive program that sustains responsive innovations to meet emerging opportunities in the university and academia at large.

References

Adams, J. M., & Carfagna, A. (2006). *Coming of age in a globalized world: The next generation*. Kumarian Press.

Alsup, J. (2005). *Teacher identity discourses: Negotiating personal and professional spaces*. Lawrence Erlbaum Associates.

Appadurai, A. (1996). *Modernity at large: Cultural dimensions of globalization*. University of Minnesota Press.

Archer, M. S. (2012). *The reflexive imperative in late modernity*. Cambridge University Press.

Argyris, C. (1999). *On organizational learning*. Blackwell.

Barr, R. B., & Tagg, J. (1995). From teaching to learning: A new paradigm for undergraduate education. *Change: The Magazine of Higher Learning, 27*(6), 12–25.

Bean, T. W., & Stevens, L. P. (2002). Scaffolding reflection for preservice and in-service teachers. *Reflective Practice, 3*(2), 205–218.

Boyer, E. L. (1990). *Scholarship reconsidered: Priorities of the professoriate*. Jossey-Bass.

Brookfield, S. D. (1995). *Becoming a critically reflective teacher*. Jossey-Bass.

Brown, J. S., & Duguid, P. (2001). Creativity vs. structure: A useful tension. *MIT Sloan Review, 42*(4), 93–94.

Brown, T. (2009). *Change by design: How design thinking transforms organizations and inspires innovation*. Harper Collins.

Buchanan, R. (1992). Wicked problems in design thinking. *Design Issues, 8*(2), 5–21.

Cartwright, S. (2002). Double-loop learning: A concept and process for leadership educators. *Journal of Leadership Education, 1*(1), 68–71.

Cavanagh, S. R. (2016). *The spark of learning: Energizing the college classroom with the science of emotion*. West Virginia University Press.

Center for Law and Social Policy. (2015). *Yesterday's non-traditional student is today's traditional student* (Table). Center for Postsecondary and Economic Success. http://www.clasp.org/resources-and-publications/publication-1/CPES-Nontraditional-students-pdf.pdf

Cross, N. (2011). *Design thinking*. Bloomsbury Academic.

Csikszentmihalyi, M. (1996). *Creativity: Flow and the psychology of discovery and invention*. Harper Collins.

Davidson, N. (2016). Debating the nature of capitalism: An engagement with Geoffrey Hodgson. *Competition and Change, 20*(3), 204–218.

Davis, B., Sumara, D., & Luce-Kapler, R. (2015). *Engaging minds: Cultures of education and practices of teaching* (3rd ed.). Routledge.

Dewey, J. (1933). *How we think: A restatement of the relation of reflective thinking to the educative process*. DC Heath and Company.

Dewey, J. (1938). *Experience and education*. Kappa Delta Pi.

Flavell, J. H. (1985). *Cognitive development*. Prentice Hall.

Freire, P. (1970/2005). *The pedagogy of the oppressed*. Continuum.

Friedman, T. L. (2005). *The world is flat: A brief history of the twenty-first century.* Farrer, Straus, and Giroux.

Friesen, M. D., & Besley, S. C. (2013). Teacher identity development in the first year of teacher education: A developmental and social psychological perspective. *Teaching and Teacher Education, 36*, 23–32.

Giroux, H. A. (2020). *On critical pedagogy.* Bloomsbury Academic.

Glassick, C. E., Huber, M. T., & Maeroff, G. I. (1997). *Scholarship assessed: Evaluation of the professoriate.* Jossey-Bass.

Greenwood, J. (1998). The role of reflection in single and double loop learning. *Journal of Advanced Nursing, 27*(5), 1048–1053.

Handstedt, P. (2018). *Creating wicked students: Designing courses for a complex world.* Stylus Press.

Hinton, C., Fischer, K. W., & Glennon, C. (2012). *Mind, brain, education* (The Students at the Center Series). Jobs for the Future Project, Nellie Mae Education Foundation. https://www.howyouthlearn.org/pdf/Mind%20Brain%20Education.pdf

Hooks, B. (1994). *Teaching to transgress: Education as the practice of freedom.* Routledge.

Huber, M., & Hutchings, P. (2005). *The advancement of learning: Building the teaching commons.* Jossey-Bass.

Hutchings, P., & Shulman, L. S. (1999). The scholarship of teaching: New elaborations, new developments. *Change: The Magazine of Higher Learning, 31*(5), 10–15.

IDEO U. (n.d.). Online learning experiences. IDEO. https://www.ideou.com

Loughran, J. (2002). Effective reflective practice: In search of meaning in learning about teaching. *Journal of Teacher Education, 53*(1), 33–43.

Love, B. L. (2019). *We want to do more than survive: Abolitionist teaching and the pursuit of educational freedom.* Beacon Press.

Matthews, K. E., Lodge, J. M., & Bosanquet, A. (2014). Early career academic perceptions, attitudes and professional development activities: Questioning the teaching and research gap to further academic development. *International Journal for Academic Development, 19*(2), 112–124.

Meadows, D. H. (2008). *Thinking in systems.* Chelsea Green Publishing.

Palmer, P. J. (2017). *The courage to teach: Exploring the inner landscape of a teacher's life.* Jossey-Bass.

Patton, M. Q. (2011). *Development evaluation: Applying complexity concepts to enhance innovation and use.* Guildford Press.

Piaget, J., & Cook, M. T. (1952). *The origins of intelligence in children.* International University Press.

Pintrich, P. R. (2002). The role of metacognitive knowledge in learning, teaching, and assessing. *Theory Into Practice, 41*(4), 219–225.

Rittel, H., & Webber, M. (1984). Dilemmas in a general theory of planning. In N. Cross (Ed.), *Developments in design methodology* (pp. 135–144). John Wiley & Sons.

Robinson, K. (2011). *Out of our minds. Learning to be creative.* Capstone.

Robinson, K. (2018). *You, your child, and school: Navigate your way to the best education*. Viking.

Sagiv, L., Arieli, S., Goldenberg, J., & Goldschmidt, A. (2010). Structure and freedom in creativity: The interplay between externally imposed structure and personal cognitive style. *Journal of Organizational Behavior, 31*(8), 1086–1110.

Schön, D. A. (1983). *The reflective practitioner: How professionals think in action*. Basic Books.

Schön, D. A. (1987). *Educating the reflective practitioner: Toward a new design for teaching and learning in the profession*. Jossey-Bass.

Seelig, T. (2015). *Insight out: Get ideas out of your head and into the world*. Harper Collins.

Shulman, L. S., & Shulman, J. H. (2004). How and what teachers learn: A shifting perspective. *Journal of Curriculum Studies, 36*(2), 257–271.

Shulman, P. (1999). Taking learning seriously. *Change: The Magazine of Higher Learning, 31*(4), 10–17.

Snowden, D. J. (2015, August 21). *Change through small actions in the present*. Cognitive Edge: http://cognitive-edge.com/blog/change-through-small-actions-in-the-present/

Snowden, D. J., & Boone, M. E. (2007). A leader's framework for decision making. *Harvard Business Review, 85*(11), 69–76.

Van Manen, M. (1995). On the epistemology of reflective practice. *Teachers and Teaching: Theory and Practice, 1*(1), 33–50.

Vygotsky, L. S. (1978). *Mind in society: The development of higher psychological processes*. Harvard University Press.

Wiggins, G., & McTighe, J. (2005). *Understanding by design*. Association of Supervision and Curriculum.

Zeichner, K. M., & Liston, D. P. (1996). *Reflective teaching: An introduction*. Lawrence Erlbaum Associates.

34

Diversity and Coherence: The Continuum of Staff Development Actions Around a Common Core

Dominique Verpoorten, Françoise Jérôme, Laurent Leduc, Catherine Delfosse, and Pascal Detroz

Introduction

Higher education is still confronted with a considerable challenge when it comes to direct attention, reflection, discussion, and action focused on excellence in teaching and learning. If faculty engagement in such matters remains relatively tepid, the needs for training in higher education pedagogy vary considerably according to individuals' personal and professional interests. In order to promote quality teaching, many universities support their teachers by offering opportunities for pedagogical development at the various stages of their career. However, in order to do so, a coherent approach to higher education pedagogy is needed.

This chapter focuses on a continuum of pedagogical development designed by the learning and teaching center of the University of Liège in Belgium. Based on a set of five competencies, the continuum combines eight principles aiming at pedagogical quality, with three levels of development and corresponding accreditation. The three levels—basic, intermediate, and advanced—are respectively composed of a few thematic '*à la carte*' sessions (the **FormaStart**

D. Verpoorten (✉) • F. Jérôme • L. Leduc • C. Delfosse • P. Detroz
Institut de Formation et de Recherche en Enseignement Supérieur / Institute for Training and Research in Higher Education, University of Liège, Liège, Belgium
e-mail: dverpoorten@uliege.be; fjerome@uliege.be; laurent.leduc@uliege.be; catherine.delfosse@uliege.be; p.detroz@ulg.ac.be

© The Author(s), under exclusive license to Springer Nature Switzerland AG 2023
O. J. Neisler (ed.), *The Palgrave Handbook of Academic Professional Development Centers*, Palgrave Studies on Leadership and Learning in Teacher Education, https://doi.org/10.1007/978-3-030-80967-6_34

527

program), a personalized certificate program (the **FormaPlus** program), and a full master's degree program (the **FormaSup** program).

The purpose of the continuum is twofold. It aims, on the one hand, at offering diversified training opportunities in response to faculty's individual interests, needs, constraints, and teaching experience. On the other hand, it makes it possible for teachers to individualize their progression by leaning on previous achievements and by undertaking projects attuned to their pedagogical ambitions. We believe that such integrated approaches to higher education pedagogy are particularly apt to promote teaching and learning at the university level. They also enable learning and teaching centers to account effectively for their implication in staff development and for their bearing on institutional orientations.

Overview of the Institute for Research and Training in Higher Education

History and Missions

The learning and teaching center of the University of Liège is known as the Institute for Research and Training in Higher Education (IFRES). It was created in January 2005 by the management board of the university. Its missions as decreed in 2005 are to:

* Promote teaching at the university
* Support faculty and departments in their teaching activities, both in face-to-face and distance settings
* Coordinate the offer of pedagogical training
* Support and conduct research projects in higher education pedagogy
* Facilitate the development of technology-enhanced learning and teaching, especially by resorting to the university's virtual campus.

Organizational Reporting, Structure, and Funding

The center is operated by a staff of about 30 members attached to four distinct domains of activities (see Fig. 34.1). The first domain consists of a secretary and teaching assistants under the responsibility of the IFRES president, while the second domain comprises staff related to a unit dedicated to freshmen pedagogy, under the responsibility of a lecturer. The third domain is a unit of

34 Diversity and Coherence: The Continuum of Staff Development... 529

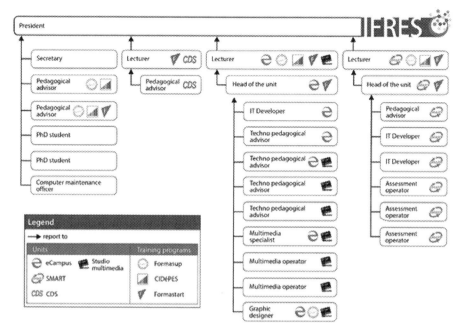

Fig. 34.1 Staff and hierarchy of the IFRES

technology-enhanced learning and teaching supervised by a lecturer and combining two lines of action: (1) the information technology-management of the institutional 'e-Campus' e-learning platform and the organization of training sessions meant for teachers wishing to use it and (2) the management of a multimedia studio in charge of the production of video material for learning and teaching purposes. Finally, the fourth domain is the SMART Methodological System to Support Testing Unit, a unit supervised by a lecturer and specialized in assessment techniques and optical reading systems for tests and exams.

The head of IFRES is a full professor from a faculty background who keeps the major part of his/her regular academic duties during their mandate. This choice is deliberate: it prevents the risk that the learning and teaching center becomes disconnected from field reality (Bråten, 2014; Raaheim & Karjalainen, 2012). The president dedicates about 20% of his/her workload to the IFRES and acts as a strategic advisor as well as an interface between the university's management board, the deans, and the IFRES staff. Practically, the day-to-day management of the center is left to the three lecturers.

With a few exceptions of external funding (i.e., projects supported by European, Belgian, and Walloon funds), the wages and operating costs of the IFRES are covered by the university. Overall, the total expenses of the

530   D. Verpoorten et al.

center equate to around €1.5 billion per year (equivalent to approximately $1.8 million) for a university of 23,700 students, 660 faculty members, and nearly 800 teaching assistants. As the IFRES is mainly concerned with staff training (since services for students have their own units and funding), the University of Liège displays a rounded ratio of one pedagogical advisor to every 100 staff members.

The IFRES Continuum of Pedagogical Development

The third mission of the center—to coordinate the offer of pedagogical training—has led to a reflection on the training needs of teachers and on how to meet them. The result was a training program that has been growing steadily since 2005. Progressively, the various initiatives took on the form of a training continuum based on five major pedagogical competencies (Palmer et al., 2011) (see Fig. 34.2).

This continuum of pedagogical development is sustained by eight 'quality principles' (Robson, 2017) serving as guidelines for the conceptualization, implementation, and adjustment of the training sessions and programs.

The Eight IFRES Quality Principles

Principle 1: Training in Higher Education Pedagogy Means Developing Five Key Competencies

To a lesser or larger extent, each IFRES training program seeks to promote the development of five competencies grouped in a referential framework named "CREER" for: (1) **C**onceive coherent courses; (2) **R**ealize the course design; (3) **E**nact teaching face-to-face and at a distance; (4) **E**valuate student learning and give feedback; and (5) **R**egulate one's teaching through reflection-on-action. The referential framework is both used to communicate training goals to teaching staff and to monitor training programs, courses, and sessions. The framework is IFRES's answer to the question: *What kind of teachers do we want to train in regard to the future of higher education?*

34 Diversity and Coherence: The Continuum of Staff Development...

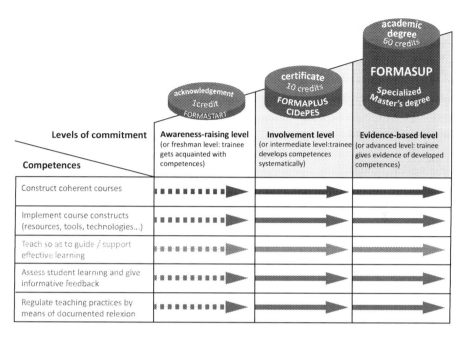

Fig. 34.2 Continuum of pedagogical development designed by the IFRES

Principle 2: Promotion of Career-Long Pedagogical Development

The IFRES seeks to foster the career-long pedagogical development of teaching staff (Clarke & Hollingsworth, 2002) in the following ways:

- By offering a coherent training structure so as to meet the needs of teachers at any phase of their teaching career (Huberman, 1989)
- By enabling teaching staff to capitalize on previous pedagogical experiences; the developmental approach to pedagogical training adopted by the IFRES makes it possible for trainees to move from one level to the next while benefiting from reduced registration fees and/or program adjustments on the basis of previous achievements
- By supporting growing autonomy; the various training programs provide occasions and instruments of reflection on personal teaching practice with the purpose of fostering autonomous pedagogical development.

532   D. Verpoorten et al.

Principle 3: Promotion of Differentiated Mentoring

Although it is not possible to know about the specificities of each teaching context and, accordingly, to propose fully customized training activities, the IFRES tries to a certain extent to:

* Take into account the needs and specific interests of trainees, either by collecting relevant information at the outset of the training session, course, or program, or by enabling trainees to organize their learning activities according to considerations that make sense for them
* Adapt the training instrument and the learning pace to perceived and expressed needs
* Adapt learning demands to perceived capabilities of trainees; in this respect, the IFRES has experimented with a few practices of ipsative assessment (Hughes, 2011).

Principle 4: Practical Significance of Pedagogical Training

Without denying the relevance of knowledgeability regarding educational sciences, the IFRES favors action-oriented training. It seeks to highlight the practical aspects of pedagogical training by:

* Enabling trainees to discuss and reflect on their teaching experiences
* Adjusting training to trainees' experiences so that it makes sense for them
* Offering learning experiences and training activities likely to be used and mobilized by trainees in their own teaching context
* Emphasizing the applicability of pedagogical concepts and approaches to authentic professional situations (Herrington & Herrington, 2006).

Principle 5: Isomorphism and Pedagogical Diversity

This can be achieved by adopting various strategies, including:

* Offering a variety of training programs and courses resorting to varied pedagogical methods such as lectures, workshops, simulations, and experiential learning
* Introducing trainees to innovative methods, such as serious games, hands-on activities, role-playing games, etc., according to the conviction that

isomorphism is a powerful means of teaching and learning (Jérôme & Verpoorten, 2014).

Principle 6: Debate and Exchange of Experiences Across Varied Disciplinary Backgrounds

Beyond individual gains in pedagogy, the IFRES training programs and courses (especially the FormaStart training sessions) energize a larger debate about the institution's teaching mission (Verpoorten et al., 2019). They do so by:

* Organizing programs and courses in a way that teaching staff from all faculties, departments, and disciplines can come together and talk about their teaching practice
* Soliciting testimonies from teachers with diverse disciplinary backgrounds
* Fostering debate and experience-sharing within each training session
* Granting hardly any exemption from participation in mandatory training courses as absenteeism impedes collective engagement in pedagogical issues.

Principle 7: Fostering Trainees' Interest in Higher Education Pedagogy

In practical terms, that implies:

* Enthusiasm and dynamism on the part of the IFRES staff members in charge of training courses and sessions
* Availability of trainers and their attention to every trainee
* Demystification of abstruse theories by adopting a more pragmatic discourse on pedagogical issues.

Principle 8: Monitoring the Effects of Training with the View of Improving Programs

This means collecting and analyzing—as regularly as possible—data likely to provide information regarding the impact of the programs, courses, and sessions on participants (Detroz et al., 2019; Leduc & Verpoorten, 2017; Van de Poël & Verpoorten, 2014).

534   D. Verpoorten et al.

The Three Levels of Pedagogical Development

FormaStart or the Awareness-Raising Level of Pedagogical Development

In 2007, the University of Liège decided to impose a pedagogical training program on new teaching assistants as well as on newly appointed academic staff (Trowler & Bamber, 2005). Accordingly, since then, newcomers among the assistants (Edmond, 2010) and faculty must enroll in training sessions within the first two to five years of their appointment, in order to attain a total of 10 units of pedagogical training (UPTs). Most training sessions last half a day, which amounts to five days of mandatory training.

Each year, the IFRES publishes a catalogue of approximately 60 training sessions distributed according to topic and format. Sessions known to attract a large number of participants are organized several times during the academic year. The catalogue is distributed by mail to all members of the university and made available on the IFRES website, which means that those who are under no obligation to register can, all the same, attend sessions if they wish to do so. Thus, besides serving as initial training in higher education pedagogy, the FormaStart sessions can also be part of in-service training. Over the past five years, FormaStart training sessions have welcomed 1,000 participants, of which 179 were under no obligation to participate.

The FormaStart training program offers sessions of three different types or formats. Half-day sessions worth one UPT each fill up half of the annual catalogue and constitute the first type of FormaStart training. They are led by one or two IFRES collaborators (usually senior lecturers and/or adjunct staff) according to their familiarity with the topics in question. The half-day sessions are dedicated to generic and rather pragmatic topics, such as "Starting in a teaching position at the University of Liège: my survival kit", syllabus design, constructive alignment, student motivation, active learning, introduction to learning assessment, avenues of professional development in higher education, introduction to e-learning, and so on. They can also be focused on more specific or technical issues such as the design of effective teaching materials, deontology, organization of practical or laboratory work, performance-based assessment, project-based learning, learning portfolio, dissertation tutoring, and guidelines on how to use the institutional e-Campus platform. The program also includes specific training sessions each year dedicated to the enhancement of first-year student learning. Thus, teachers and teaching

34 Diversity and Coherence: The Continuum of Staff Development... 535

assistants can choose the sessions they wish to attend according to their needs or special interests, before registering via the IFRES website.

The second type of FormaStart training corresponds to 'hands-on' seminars organized in a tutored hybrid learning modality. Each seminar is worth three UPTs and entails a workload of approximately 10 hours. Such seminars (i.e., flipped classrooms, gamification, peer reviewing, bottlenecks to learning, media literacy, online course development, etc.) give trainees the opportunity to design and implement a small-scale teaching project with the support of a pedagogical advisor. The third type of FormaStart training takes place once a year in the form of a one-day conference dedicated to teaching and learning at the University of Liège first implemented in 2007. For newly recruited teaching staff, attendance at the conference is credited with one UPT.

To obtain validation of their mandatory training in higher education pedagogy, trainees have to write an end-of-program reflection report in which they list attended sessions and give a brief account of the benefits they received in terms of pedagogical knowledge, know-how, and reflection.

FormaPlus or the Involvement Level of Pedagogical Development

The intermediate level of pedagogical training corresponds to a 10-credit program called the Interfaculty Certificate of Pedagogical Development in Higher Education (CIDePES). The CIDePES program was created by the IFRES five years ago in order to complete its range of training programs in relation to higher education pedagogy. Teachers at the University of Liège are under no obligation to enroll in the CIDePES program; those who choose to do so are personally convinced of the added value that pedagogy can bring to their teaching practice. Participants are mostly young fellow lecturers and their interest in the CIDePES program often stems from their previous participation in the mandatory training sessions and/or from the urgency with which they have to prepare for and give courses. Therefore, the CIDePES program aims at their pedagogical development by means of the conceptualization and implementation of a personal pedagogical project in direct relation with their teaching practice. In addition, a variety of training activities (i.e., course design assignments, microteaching sessions, experimentation with methods of classroom assessment, etc.), ad hoc resources, and individual tutoring sessions are also part of the training program.

The main characteristics of the CIDePES program are flexibility, proximity to the participants' individual teaching concerns, reasonable training requirements, and practice-related assignments. The underlying idea is to make

536 D. Verpoorten et al.

participants work on aspects of teaching that they would anyway have to tackle on their own as part of their professional activities. Thanks to the CIDePES program, they can benefit from encouragement, guidance, and feedback. The CIDePES also offers them the opportunity to evolve as teachers despite their endemic lack of time. Another boon is that teachers can put forward their participation in the program when trying for promotion. In order to do so, they can use the individual blogs (Poole et al., 2007) in which they have recorded their achievements and reflections during training to showcase their commitment to teaching and higher education pedagogy.

FormaSup or the Evidence-Based Level of Pedagogical Development

The upper part of the training continuum is the FormaSup program resulting in a specialized Master's in Higher Education Pedagogy. This program is organized at the University of Liège by IFRES staff (two senior lecturers and two pedagogical counselors shoulder most training activities). The FormaSup program aims to target the professional development of college and university teachers from all over the world. In this respect, it offers organizational flexibility; participants may choose to attend the program either in a hybrid combination of face-to-face sessions and online activities or entirely from a distance. Each year, approximately 10 teachers enroll in the program. The FormaSup program amounts to 60 UPTs and lasts for one year, although it can also be divided into two years. It comprises three high-stake assignments due for summative assessment. Each assignment is related to one of the three courses or modules that compose the core curriculum: (1) framing and analyzing teaching and evaluation practice, (2) regulation of teaching and evaluation practice, and (3) a professional portfolio.

The end-of-course assignment for the first of these courses involves writing a syllabus describing accurately the pedagogical organization of a course they are in charge of. In order to prove and improve its pedagogical value, the syllabus must also contain appropriate references to pedagogical theories and models. For the second course, the end-of-course assignment consists of writing a 'regulation article' in which the participant reports in a scientific manner the main characteristics and the effects on their students' learning of a pedagogical innovation implemented in one of their own courses (see the section below on scholarship of teaching and learning [SoTL] within the FormaSup program). Finally, the FormaSup master's degree is awarded partly on the basis of a portfolio in which the participant shows evidence of their progress regarding the five key pedagogical competencies and of their professional development as a whole. The portfolio has to be presented and defended orally in front of a jury of three experts in higher education pedagogy.

Optional courses complete the core curriculum. Some of these are organized face-to-face whereas others can be attended online. Topics such as problem-based learning, student assessment, quality assessment, teaching methods, educational technologies, and so on enable participants to deepen their understanding of the aspects of teaching and learning in which they are particularly interested.

SoTL within the FormaSup Program

The most innovative and ambitious part of the FormaSup program consists in giving participants the opportunity to conduct full-scale SoTL research. The importance of SoTL as a means of enhancing teaching quality and developing professionally is widely acknowledged: "[SoTL] stimulates you to think about your teaching and what you expect students to gain from it. It enriches both your conceptual thinking about education and your repertoire of skills" (Svinicki & McKeachie, 2011, 343). The SoTL research is embedded in the regulation of teaching and evaluation practice module. The module amounts to 18 credits (out of the 60 credits for the whole program) and takes place in the second half of the academic year. The timespan of the SoTL project is rather short, so participants have to shoulder a heavy workload.

In order to initiate their SoTL project, participants have to single out one innovative aspect of their teaching practice in relation to one of their courses. The innovative course regulation often involves trying out new activities (i.e., problem-based learning, case studies, group work, fieldwork, experiential learning, etc.) in an otherwise routine context, with a view to enhancing student learning and motivation to learn. Participants have been led to reflect on their course regulation before starting the SoTL module. The final output is a SoTL-related article wherein participants describe their context, their initial problem, the solution they brought, the literature they inspected, the type of data they collected—with the FormaSup program imposing a '3P' data sources matrix; that is, the gathering of **p**articipation, **p**erception, and **p**erformance data (Parlascino et al., 2017)—an analysis of it, the limitations of the study, and recommendations for further work. The SoTL research is made public through a poster session and, for some participants, is disseminated further in a conference presentation or publication of an article in a SoTL-themed research journal (Fenton & Szala-Meneok, 2011).

538   D. Verpoorten et al.

The approach to SoTL research, as it is organized within the FormaSup program, is delineated and quite prescriptive in regard to methodology and final assignment. In order to meet this tight agenda, participants can also rely on the individualized support of a pedagogical counselor, either face-to-face or at a distance via online sessions. This counseling (Jérôme et al., 2017) is geared toward empowering participants to carry out their classroom research and to account for it in the form of a research article. The concept of utilizing mentorship to facilitate SoTL research is by no means new:

> Situational support for SoTL research in complex academic (institutional, curricula and/or classroom) settings enhances the possibilities for such research in the already busy lives of academics and contextualizes theory in meaningful environments, thereby holding more relevance and immediate impact for both mentor and mentee. (Hubball et al., 2010)

Discussion

To date, nearly two-thirds of faculty and assistants of the University of Liège have had, at minimum, contact with the basic training program organized by the IFRES, resulting in a rather high level of satisfaction according to the feedback questionnaires that every training participant is required to complete. Regarding effects on the field, they are easy to assess for the FormaSup and CIDePES programs since training requirements include changes in the practice. As for the FormaStart program, small-scale actions are already claimed by participants to have taken place in their courses. Other participants only mention an increased awareness of the stakes of pedagogy and, sometimes, their intentions to do more (Leduc & Verpoorten, 2017; Van de Poël & Verpoorten, 2014). The IFRES is currently busy with a thorough analysis of the final reports which are soon to be incorporated alongside meetings with other staff members in order to initiate a longitudinal study of the short and long-term effects of the available training stages.

Another effort is also planned to populate the FormaPlus stage with more than the CIDePES. For instance, more and more teachers are involved in faculty initiatives regarding different aspects of teaching and learning; to acknowledge that this is part of the continuum makes sense. Although attendance has been growing since the program's inception, CIDePES participants remain scarce. As the CIDePES is strategically important insofar as it constitutes an intermediary stage of pedagogical development between the basic FormaStart and the elaborate FormaSup programs, further efforts will take place in future to better promote the program. Concerning the more mature FormaSup program, experience has taught us that, despite promotion and adaptation efforts, the average number of participants remains uniform. This gives credit to Ramsden's (1999) early prediction regarding SoTL: "Just as only a small proportion of university staff are outstandingly productive and respected researchers, so only a few academics will emerge as brilliant scholars of teaching" (4). For this minority, the FormaSup is an essential program matching their needs and desire to go further in pedagogy. Some of them will become, at the institutional level, role models for their colleagues and natural relays and supporters for further IFRES actions in faculties and departments.

Recommendations

Consider staff development programs as 'relationship boosters.' A larger effect of the continuum should be mentioned—from the feedback questionnaires collected from participants, especially in FormaStart, it appears that teachers and assistants especially value the mixed audience in the training sessions, beyond the theoretical and practical gains in pedagogy. In addition, staff development programs may represent occasions of permanent pedagogical brainstorming. The training curriculum is worth seeing as an instrument to initiate and maintain a collective reflection on pedagogy by making it, individually and collectively, an object of attention, conversation, transformation, and study.

References

Bråten, H. (2014, August 27–30). Searching for the holy grail-excellence in teaching and learning in Norway: A study of Centres of Excellence in Education (SFUs) (Conference presentation). European Higher Education Society 36th Annual Forum.

Clarke, D., & Hollingsworth, H. (2002). Elaborating a model of teacher development. *Teaching and Teacher Education, 18*(8), 947–967.

Detroz, P., Alonso Vilches, V., Delfosse, C., Hausman, M., Jérôme, F., Leduc, L., & Verpoorten, D. (2019, January 22–24). *Quality assessment of a training path for higher education instructors* (Conference presentation). 32nd Association pour le Développement des Méthodologies d'Évaluation en Éducation-Europe.

Edmond, N. (2010). The role of HE in professional development: Some reflections on a foundation degree for teaching assistants. *Teaching in Higher Education, 15*(3), 311–322.

Fenton, N., & Szala-Meneok, K. (2011). *The research on teaching and learning guidebook*. McMaster University Center for Leadership in Learning. https://research.mcmaster.ca/app/uploads/2018/08/redo_guidebook-1.pdf

Herrington, T., & Herrington, J. (2006). *Authentic learning environments in higher education*. Information Science Publishing.

Hubball, H. T., Clarke, A., & Poole, G. (2010). Ten-year reflections on mentoring SoTL research in a research-intensive university. *International Journal for Academic Development, 15*(2), 117–129.

Huberman, M. (1989). The professional life cycle of teachers. *Teachers College Record, 91*(1), 31–57.

Hughes, G. (2011). Towards a personal best: A case for introducing ipsative assessment in higher education. *Studies in Higher Education, 36*(3), 353–367.

Jérôme, F., & Verpoorten, D. (2014). A blog rather than Word? Feedback from the inclusion of an online course in a higher education teacher training program. *Education & Formation, e-302*, 94–107.

Jérôme, F., Verpoorten, D., & Detroz, P. (2017). Documenting the parameters of effective SoTL counselling. In R. Andersson, K. Martensson, & T. Roxa (Eds.), *Proceedings of the 2nd European Conference for the Scholarship of Teaching and Learning* (pp. 29–35). University of Lund.

Leduc, L., & Verpoorten, D. (2017, February 11–14). *Ten years of pedagogical training sessions for faculties teaching freshmen* (Conference presentation). 36th Annual Conference on the First-Year Experience.

Palmer, S., Holt, D., & Challis, D. (2011). Strategic leadership of teaching and learning centres: From reality to ideal. *Higher Education Research and Development, 30*(6), 807–821.

Parlascino, E., Jérôme, F., Verpoorten, D., Denis, B., Devyver, J., Borsu, O., Van de Poël, J. F., Navet, R., & Haubruge, E. (2017). *Innovative instructional and methodological support for the jobs@skills – SCES – Liège-Luxembourg incubator: Guidelines for developing blended learning*. Institute for Research and Training in Higher Education (IFRES), University of Liège.

Poole, G., Taylor, K. L., & Thompson, J. (2007). Using the scholarship of teaching and learning at disciplinary, national and institutional levels to strategically improve the quality of post-secondary education (Invited essay). *International Journal of the Scholarship of Teaching and Learning, 1*(2), 1–16.

Raaheim, A., & Karjalainen, A. (2012). *Centres of excellence in university education: Finland 1999–2012 – An evaluation*. Finnish Education Evaluation Centre.

Ramsden, P. (1999). Teaching and learning – An informal discussion. *Hersda News*, 3–4.

Robson, S. (2017). Developing and supporting excellent HE teaching: Opportunities and challenges. In A. French & M. O'Leary (Eds.), *Teaching excellence in higher education: Challenges, changes and the Teaching Excellence Framework* (pp. 109–137). Emerald Publishing.

34 Diversity and Coherence: The Continuum of Staff Development... **541**

Svinicki, M., & McKeachie, W. J. (2011). *McKeachie's teaching tips: Strategies, research, and theory for college and university teachers* (13th ed.). Wadsworth.

Trowler, P., & Bamber, R. (2005). Compulsory higher education teacher training: Joined-up policies, institutional architectures and enhancement cultures. *International Journal for Academic Development, 10*(2), 79–93.

Van de Poël, J., & Verpoorten, D. (2014). Two years of training and techno-pedagogical support at ULg: Audience, impact and perspectives. *Education & Formation, e-302*, 122–130.

Verpoorten, D., Leduc, L., Mohr, A., Marichal, E., Duchâteau, D., & Detroz, P. (2019). Feedback first year – A critical review of the strengths and shortcomings of a collective pedagogical project. In J. Friberg & K. McKinney (Eds.), *Applying the scholarship of teaching and learning beyond the individual classroom* (pp. 162–181). Indiana University Press.

Part X

ADC and Faculty Research About Teaching and Learning

The four academic professional development centers (ADCs) described in Part X share methodologies, designs, and findings from their research exploring various aspects of teaching and learning. These projects include needs assessment, faculty perceptions, classroom teaching and learning research, and oversight of student assessments of teaching and learning.

Chapters in Part X:

Chapter 35: *Needs Analysis Research Leads to Specialized Faculty Development Programs.* Pang Haishao and Zhang Yeye, Beijing Institute of Technology, Beijing, China.

This chapter describes how ADC staff conducted needs assessment research focused on faculty knowledge and interest in higher education pedagogy. The analysis of their data led to the development of programs to meet the needs of three specific groups: new faculty, mid-career faculty, and graduate teaching assistants.

Chapter 36: *Critical Reflection on Organizational Practice at a UK University Through Scholarship of Teaching and Learning.* Aysha Divan, Paul Taylor, and Andrea Jackson, University of Leeds, Leeds, UK, and Rafe Hallett, Keele University, Keele, UK (previously of University of Leeds).

544 ADC and Faculty Research About Teaching and Learning

This chapter describes how one ADC supports faculty scholarship of teaching and learning projects focused on critical reflection of their academic outcomes. A key aspect of these projects is collaborative faculty writing groups.

Chapter 37: *Systematic Changes: Impact of Double-Helix Collaboration Toward Innovation in Faculty Development and Student-Centered Teaching and Learning.* Yihong Fan, Southwest Jiaotong University, Chengdu, and Xiamen University, Xiamen, China.

Faculty at this research university engage in action research as part of the teaching reform projects. The reform and research help faculty develop new innovative courses.

Other Relevant Chapter

Chapter 22: *Using Student Research Data to Shape the Teaching and Learning Activities of a New Academic Development Center in Turkey.* Elif Bengü, Abdullah Gül University, Kayseri, Turkey, and Fatma Nevra Seggie, Boğaziçi University, Istanbul, Turkey.

The ADC at this university is responsible for assessing student needs related to teaching and learning. Furthermore, the center conducts student evaluation of teaching. This chapter presents major findings from a needs analysis of 80 students as well as the ways in which these needs have subsequently been incorporated into the operations of the ADC.

35

Needs Analysis Research Leads to Specialized Faculty Development Programs

Pang Haishao and Zhang Yeye

Introduction

With the rapid development of higher education in China, the Chinese Government fully recognizes the importance of supporting the development of college teachers. From 2000, a pre-post training program was launched to provide new teachers with a series of theoretical and practical training, which resulted in a teacher qualification certificate for those passing the examinations. Since 2010, several express provisions have been issued by the Chinese Government to encourage universities to set up teaching development centers (Ministry of Education, 2010).

Development Path and Overview of the Center for Enhanced Learning and Teaching at the Beijing Institute of Technology

At the Beijing Institute of Technology (BIT), pre-post training for new teachers has been provided since 1998. The main focus of the training is learning education theory and educational technology. An educational technology

---

P. Haishao (✉) • Z. Yeye
Beijing Institute of Technology, Beijing, China
e-mail: panghaishao@163.com; zhangyeye@bit.edu.cn

© The Author(s), under exclusive license to Springer Nature Switzerland AG 2023　**545**
O. J. Neisler (ed.), *The Palgrave Handbook of Academic Professional Development Centers*,
Palgrave Studies on Leadership and Learning in Teacher Education,
https://doi.org/10.1007/978-3-030-80967-6_35

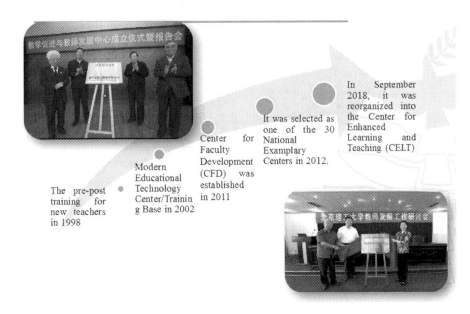

Fig. 35.1 CELT development path.

training center and a specialized training base were established by the Personnel Department and the Modern Educational Technology Center in 2002. Subsequently, the Center for Faculty Development (CFD) was established in 2011. At the time, most of the part-time experts in the CFD originated from the Institute of Education. The center was selected as one of 30 national exemplar faculty development centers in 2012 (see Chap. 3 for more information regarding the context and evolution of faculty development work in China). In September 2018, the center was reorganized and renamed as the Center for Enhanced Learning and Teaching (CELT), as shown in Fig. 35.1.

Faculty development in Chinese universities is often divided and scattered across different management departments. However, this dispersed, nonprofessional, traditional teacher training no longer meets the needs of higher education professional development. Setting up a specialized agency for faculty development at the university level is vital to create a system that is specialized, institutionalized, and normalized (Pang et al., 2017).

Since 2011, the CELT has provided teacher training, research support, and consulting services for entry-level and senior teachers across the university. The purpose of the center is to help teachers learn innovative teaching methods, improve teaching quality, and enhance career development (Du, 2014), as shown in Fig. 35.2.

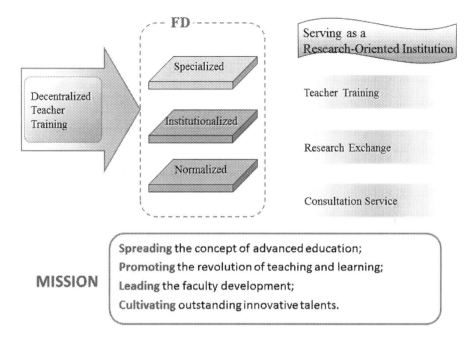

Fig. 35.2 Mission and attributes of the CELT.

Faculty Development Practice and Achievements

Between February 2011 and May 2019, the CELT held a total of 287 diversified faculty development activities. More than 13,000 teachers participated in these activities, and the rate of satisfaction was over 95%. Members of the center have participated in many domestic and international academic exchange activities, including those organized by the Professional and Organizational Development Network, International Consortium for Educational Development, International Society for the Scholarship of Teaching and Learning (SoTL), and other professional development training organizations. In addition, the center has cooperated with various other institutions, such as the University of Michigan's Center for Research on Learning & Teaching, Brown University, the University of California Los Angeles, the Chinese University of Hong Kong's Centre for Learning Enhancement and Research, Hong Kong Polytechnic University's Educational Development Centre, Macau University, and Taiwan University's Center for Teaching and Learning Development. Overall, the center has received nearly 300 visitors and the center's expert team has given hundreds of lectures and workshops for over 100 other colleges and seminars.

Planning for the achievements listed above began in 2011 when the director of the CELT, a professor of Education, integrated various professional development activities that had been previously scattered over different departments. She led the team to create a faculty development system that was specialized, institutionalized, and normalized (see Fig. 35.2). Specialization has been achieved by designing a series of faculty development training projects for teachers specific to their career development stages. Two examples are the Honghu School, a pre-post training program for entry teachers, and the Teaching Innovation Contest, designed to motivate mid-career teachers who have taught for several years to improve their teaching and update their methodologies. In addition, the center also provides specialized training for teachers with specific needs under an initiative known as the Jinggong Training Camp.

At BIT, faculty development is institutionalized by being embedded into the overall planning of the university, particularly through the development and implementation of university goals. Thus, university policy underpins the faculty development program, for instance with the document *Several Opinions on Improving the Quality of Undergraduate Talent Cultivation* (BIT, 2013). This document stipulates certain faculty development requirements, including the participation of entry-level teachers in the pre-post training program and the participation of all teachers under the age of 45 years in a minimum of 1–2 training programs per year. As a result, faculty development is normalized as a regular part of the academic teaching role, appearing in work plans and the like.

Needs Assessment Survey

In 2011, a survey of teaching performance and faculty development needs was conducted for all BIT faculty. This survey was designed to understand the teachers' challenges, needs, and their expectations of teaching and of the faculty development center. The survey also looked at what kind of activities the teachers would be willing to participate in.

Specialized Faculty Development Programs

Based on data from the needs assessment survey, the CELT developed specialized faculty development programs, including the Eagle Project (for experienced teachers), the Honghu School (for entry-level teachers), and the Chuyan Academy (for teaching assistants). These programs were designed to meet the specialized requirements of teachers at different stages in their careers. In addition, the center organized various forms of activities and created a series of signature programs, such as the Mingli Lectures (a series of lectures given by renowned professors), the Jinggong Training Camp (special seminars to meet specific teachers' needs), and the Qizhi Salon, as well as themed workshops and micro-class demonstrations.

The content of these activities combines features of educational reform and pedagogical trends to highlight characteristics of engineering education, *suzhi* education (a concept unique to Chinese education) (Pang et al., 2020), and general education. All of these activities contribute to a specialized, institutionalized, and normalized faculty development system (Du et al., 2017).

Honghu School: The Entry Teachers' Growth Training Camp

There are two types of courses in the Honghu School pre-post training program. It is a reasonable training system combining both online and face-to-face course modalities, some of which are compulsory and some elective. The theoretical content is offered by the Teacher Training Center of the Beijing Higher Education School. The online program contains four courses: Higher Education, Higher Education Psychology, Higher Education Regulations, and the College Teachers' Professional Ethics. The timing and format of the program is designed so as to be flexible and convenient for teachers. The face-to-face program component utilizes a menu-based selection of compulsory and elective courses designed to complement the flexible online program.

The course menu was formulated based on the results of the needs analysis survey carried out in 2011. According to this survey, the 10 issues that teachers were most concerned with included: (1) teaching methods; (2) teacher-student interactions; (3) career planning, (4) expression and communication skills; (5) research ability enhancement; (6) dealing with work-related stress; (7) the application of technology in teaching; (8) how to evaluate student learning; (9) organization and leadership; and (10) social etiquette. In order to address these concerns, seven modules were designed for incorporation into the face-to-face course (see Table 35.1).

After meeting the basic requirements of the program, teachers can take additional elective courses according to their own time limitations, demands, and interests. The program is constantly revised to reflect contemporary understandings of higher education. It embodies a people-oriented approach; moreover, the inclusion of compulsory peer observations allows teachers to

Table 35.1 Description of the component modules of the Honghu School pre-post training program

Module	Elements	Requirement
1. Opening ceremony and BIT overview	Introduction to the faculty development support policy and an overview of the history and spirit of BIT	Compulsory
2. Professional ethics and political quality	The mission and responsibility of college and university teachers, teacher morality, and the experiences of national exemplar teachers	Compulsory
3. Educational concept and curriculum design	Student-centered undergraduate education reform, the concept and practice of faculty development in the university, results-based teaching reform, the reform of the higher education cultivation model from specialist education to general education, how to carry out the teaching design of a course, and the concept and implementation of peer teaching methods	Elective
4. Teaching and academic research and publication	Statistical methods, software and technology in educational academic research, and the writing and publication of educational research papers	Elective
5. Teaching skills training workshop	Effective teaching design skills training using the bridge-in, objectives, pre-assessment, participatory learning, post-assessment, and summary (BOPPPPS) model	Elective
6. The growth and development of young teachers	Skill and life planning for new teachers, balancing teaching and research, etiquette and communication, and how to respond to stress for young teachers	Elective
7. Micro-curriculum display and teaching ability assessment	National exemplar teachers, pedagogical experts, professional teachers, and responsible professors, etc. are invited to form a team to analyze and review a teaching video submitted by the participant	Compulsory

observe each other and exchange information regarding best practices for teaching and learning (Du & Gao, 2018).

A total of 430 teachers participated in the Honghu School between 2013 and 2018. Subsequently, the CELT surveyed participating teachers using questionnaires and interviews from October to December 2018. The survey results showed that the teachers had high overall satisfaction with the training courses. The top three modules considered to be most beneficial to the teachers were modules 1–3. In particular, the new teachers particularly valued learning the latest national and school policies in module 1, the professional ethics models in module 2, and educational philosophy and teaching methods in module 3. Overall, they reported that the program modules were very helpful in improving their teaching ability.

Eagle Project: The Excellent Teachers' Training Camp

The Eagle Project is designed to help teachers with several years of teaching and research experience to be more creative in their teaching and discipline-based research. The overall goal is to develop a 'pipeline' of excellent teachers. As such, the center implemented the Teaching Innovation Contest. This competition encourages mid-career teachers to update their educational concepts, change traditional teaching methods and activities, implement a student-centered teaching approach, and explore contemporary instructional strategies such as flipped classroom, research-based, and outcome-based teaching approaches, thereby achieving deep learning for students.

In 2018, the top nine Chinese universities of science and technology (known as the "Excellence 9")[1] organized the Young Teachers' Teaching Innovation Contest. Preliminaries were held in June and, in September, the "Excellence 9" recommended a total of 69 teachers for the quarterfinals. Of these, 31 teachers moved on to the finals where 21 experts reviewed their micro-course videos and teaching innovation design report. The contestants competed against each other and showcased their pedagogical knowledge and achievements using various formats such as poster presentations, videos of lectures, and oral presentations. The experts made on-the-spot comments regarding the design of the teaching objectives, teaching challenges, the innovation of design, and the impact on student learning.

The Teaching Innovation Contest is a unique event that has been highly praised by experts and contestants alike as an interdisciplinary experience and platform for learning about teaching innovations (Sui, 2018). From 2019 to 2020, the center promoted the contest at additional universities through the Chinese Association for Suzhi Education; moreover, the scope of the contest will soon be expanded to cover teaching innovation activities in general education.

Jinggong Training Camp

In conjunction with education and teaching reforms at BIT, the CELT conducts specialized training under the Jinggong Training Camp, an initiative that focuses on providing personalized training programs for teachers. The following is a list of the training topics provided in recent years:

- Student-centered quality assurance system
- Integrating general education teaching and learning
- Improving the academic ability of young teachers in research and teaching
- Micro-class design and effective teaching structure of the BOPPPS model
- Engineering professional certification and outcome-based education practice
- SOTL and publication
- Cultivation of quality assurance system construction
- Improving the leadership and research ability of university teachers
- Emerging engineering technologies and engineering education
- Professional curriculum construction and innovative education.

Other Teaching Training and Professional Development Activities

As there is a strong need to strengthen the quality of general education provided at BIT, the director of the CELT led the center to carry out a series of training workshops and activities. To begin with, the center formed the General Education Teaching (GET) community of practice. The GET community of practice was formed so that teachers could communicate with each other regarding teaching and learning practices in general education courses. Everyone learns through themed activities provided in both online and offline modalities, such as the Breaking Teaching Solitude event and interdisciplinary teaching cooperation and exchanges. More than 110 teachers had joined the GET community by the end of 2018. The main activities have been carrying out online activities on the WeChat platform (a Chinese social messaging app), publishing information related to relevant themed activities and domestic and international conferences, and sharing *suzhi* education ideas, curriculum resources, and materials (Zhang, 2019).

Secondly, the center carried out a number of offline activities, including expert lectures, themed seminars, and teaching and research general education courses, and also provided consulting services for teachers. As of 2018, the center has helped 14 teachers to conduct mid-term student feedback evaluations of their courses. These 14 teachers all came from different disciplines, and the teaching problems they faced were both common and specialized. The center also arranges one-to-one consultations for teachers with suitable consultants according to their different needs. The center maintains files independently for teachers who request consulting services and keeps them anonymous (Sui, 2019).

Third, the center organized the General Symposium on Teaching and Learning of General Education, in which various experts and scholars from Peking University, Tsinghua University, Fudan University, Nankai University, Southwest Jiaotong University, Ocean University of China, and Ohio State University were invited to discuss concepts and practices related to general education courses. Hundreds of teachers have attended these activities so far.

Through organizing a series of activities, the CELT has worked to improve understanding of the concepts, purposes, and teaching methods of the BIT general education curriculum and its teachers. Moreover, the Department of Undergraduate Academic Affairs has issued a series of incentives to encourage the establishment of general education courses, resulting in much improvement in the number of general courses being offered. In the past, there were only 120 general courses for students to choose, making it difficult to meet their needs. Now, the number of general education courses has more than doubled.

Over the past eight years, the center has undertaken many faculty development projects, including the establishment of a specialized agency for faculty development at the university level to consolidate scattered teacher training. The formation of this new mechanism has helped teachers to improve the quality of their instruction. After years of hard work, the CELT's teaching program—Specialized, Institutionalized, and Normalized Faculty Development System Construction and Practice—won the BIT 14th Excellent Teaching Achievement Prize in 2018, as well as the second prize for the Excellent Teaching Achievement Award issued by the Beijing Municipal Government.

Future Prospects

Serving at a research-oriented organization, the CELT is dedicated to the research and practice of advanced pedagogy, curriculum design, instruction, and faculty development to enhance the quality of higher education teaching and learning at BIT. The center conducts research in the areas of engineering education reform, *suzhi* education, and general education. In addition, the center also actively conducts exchanges and collaboration initiatives both nationally and internationally to lead faculty development practice.

In terms of our future prospects, the center will focus on practice-based research and will develop faculty development special projects by drawing on the experience of faculty development in developed countries. In addition, there are plans to provide relevant training services for faculty development staff as well as the front-line teachers of national universities. It will train professional faculty development trainers, teaching consultants, and course designers, as well as masters and doctoral students in the field of faculty development so as to develop a professional pipeline for faculty development centers of Chinese universities in line with its important mission of spreading the concept of advanced education; promoting the revolution of teaching and learning; leading faculty development activities; and cultivating outstanding innovative talents.

Note

1. The "Excellence 9" consist of the BIT, Chongqing University, Dalian University of Technology, Southeast University, Harbin Institute of Technology, South China University of Technology, Tianjin University, Tongji University, and Northwestern Polytechnical University.

References

Beijing Institute of Technology (BIT). (2013). *Several opinions on improving the quality of undergraduate talent cultivation* (Document no. 22). BIT.

Du, J. (2014). General information of center for faculty development. In *Center for Faculty Development, CFD, 2013 annual report*. Center for Enhanced Learning and Teaching (CELT). http://celt.bit.edu.cn/docs/20140325095931945095.pdf

Du, J., & Gao, X. (2018). Honghu School, entry teachers' growth training camp. In *2017 annual report of Center for Faculty Development, BIT*. Center for Enhanced Learning and Teaching (CELT). http://celt.bit.edu.cn/docs/20180529021420992387.pdf

Du, J., Pang, H., & Gao, X. (2017). Practices of new faculty orientation in Chinese higher education institutions. *Higher Education Development and Evaluation, 33*(02), 74–80.

Ministry of Education. (2010). *Outline of national medium and long-term education reform and development plan (2010–2020)*. Ministry of Education.

Pang, H., Cheng, M., Yu, J., & Wu, J. (2020). Suzhi education and general education in China. *ECNU Review of Education, 3*(2), 380–395.

Pang, H., Zhang, Y., & Song, W. (2017). Construction and implementation of the faculty development system. *Higher Education Development and Evaluation, 33*(02), 50–58.

Sui, Y. (2018). The 2nd excellent University Alliance College young teachers' teaching innovation contest and the "student-centered" teaching innovation forum ended in perfection. Center for Enhanced Learning and Teaching (CELT). http://celt.bit.edu.cn/gzdt/136365.htm

Sui, Y. (2019). Mid-term student feedback. In *2018 annual report of Center for Enhanced Learning and Teaching, SHSS, BIT.* Center for Enhanced Learning and Teaching (CELT). http://celt.bit.edu.cn/docs/20191025030926784435.pdf

Zhang, Y. (2019). Teaching community and Qizhi Salon. In *2018 annual report of Center for Enhanced Learning and Teaching, SHSS, BIT.* Center for Enhanced Learning and Teaching (CELT). http://celt.bit.edu.cn/docs/20191025030926784435.pdf

36

Critical Reflection on Organizational Practice at a UK University Through Scholarship of Teaching and Learning

Aysha Divan, Paul Taylor, Andrea Jackson, and Rafe Hallett

Introduction

> The University of Leeds has a long-standing commitment to excellent, research-based student education, evidenced … through being named University of the Year 2017 by *The Times* and *The Sunday Times*. As such, we support the Teaching Excellence Framework's core aims: to raise teaching standards, provide greater focus on graduate employability, and widen participation in higher education. (Ward, 2017)

Deputy vice chancellor of education, Tom Ward's reflection on the University of Leeds gold-rated submission to the UK's Teaching Excellence Framework (TEF) raises important questions for leaders of higher education (HE), both at the University of Leeds and elsewhere (Department for Business, Industry, and Skills, 2016): *What does "excellence" mean? How can we "evidence" it? How can we "raise standards" and simultaneously "widen participation"?* The establishment of the Leeds Institute for Teaching Excellence (LITE) in 2016

A. Divan (✉) • P. Taylor • A. Jackson
University of Leeds, Leeds, UK
e-mail: a.divan@leeds.ac.uk; p.c.taylor@leeds.ac.uk; a.v.jackson@leeds.ac.uk

R. Hallett
Keele University, Keele, UK
e-mail: r.hallett@keele.ac

© The Author(s), under exclusive license to Springer Nature Switzerland AG 2023
O. J. Neisler (ed.), *The Palgrave Handbook of Academic Professional Development Centers*,
Palgrave Studies on Leadership and Learning in Teacher Education,
https://doi.org/10.1007/978-3-030-80967-6_36

provided an opportunity to consider how a large research-intensive university in the UK might respond to such challenges productively and scaffold meaningful dialogue with stakeholders across the university.

We were attracted to theoretical frameworks from the field of critical management education. In particular, an approach initially articulated by Vince (2002), and drawing on work performed by Reynolds (1999), titled *Organizing Reflection* advocates for the "collective questioning of assumptions that underpin organizing to make power relations visible [and] contribute towards democracy in the organization" (Vince & Reynolds, 2009). A central theme emerging from this research is the opportunity to move beyond individual, private practitioner reflection as a means of personal development toward collective, public reflection (Kemmis, 1985). This repositioning of reflection is accompanied by a shift in timeframe from evaluating something in the past to an active process within the present and a further shift of understanding about the nature of managerial authority, resulting in critical, reflective organization as a shared responsibility.

Perhaps surprisingly, Vince and Reynolds' (2009) invitation to HE institutions (HEIs) to organize reflection in this collective, critical way has not yet been accepted widely (Brunstein & King, 2018). On the other hand, the LITE works to create and link 'reflexive spaces' (Cotter, 2014) for critical reflection within the University of Leeds, adopting and simplifying the schema from Vince and Reynolds (2010) that shows how both 'public' and 'productive' reflection can contribute to the 'organizing reflection' of an institution (see Fig. 36.1).

Herein, we present case studies that exemplify modes of public reflection and productive reflection, discuss how an academic professional development center such as the LITE can organize reflection across a large university, and consider how staff can be supported in this new environment. In passing, we

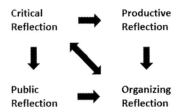

Fig. 36.1 The organization of reflection based on Vince and Reynolds (2010) framework

36 Critical Reflection on Organizational Practice at a UK University... 559

note that the terminology and methods utilized in the emerging field of the scholarship of teaching and learning (SoTL) may provide a useful language for communication in a critical, reflective HEI:

> [SoTL is] the systematic study of teaching and learning, using established or validated criteria of scholarship, to understand how teaching (beliefs, behaviours, attitudes, and values) can maximize learning, and/or develop a more accurate understanding of learning, resulting in products that are publicly shared for critique and use by an appropriate community. (Potter & Kustra, 2011, 2)

Organizing Reflection: The LITE

From its inception in 2016, the LITE has aimed to strike a balance between its role as a strategic university institute and its malleability as a reflexive and self-critical community. Working toward explicit teaching enhancement aims and its establishment in the early days of the UK's TEF meant that strategic and political considerations certainly influenced the institute's manifesto. The LITE aimed to "establish the University of Leeds as an international leader in the pedagogy and scholarship of research-led education and research-based learning, and as a centre for the development and dissemination of innovative teaching practice" (LITE, 2016).

This kind of strategic imperative for organizing SoTL activity is not uncommon. After a flurry of institutionally sponsored activity over the last five years, most HEIs in the UK now fund and host institutes or centers whose function, in part, is to articulate and advertise the particular 'teaching excellence' that characterizes each university. For example, several Russell Group universities, including the Universities of Durham, Liverpool, and Bristol, all set up or reformed institutes for teaching enhancement and scholarship between 2016 and 2018, often recruiting new 'leaders' to do so. Thus, UK universities are acutely aware that their scholarship communities need a heightened external profile and a clearer 'story of excellence' to tell.

Some of the rhetoric emanating from these centers is driven by changing sector-wide expectations and key performance indicators as to what constitutes 'excellent' educational design and scholarship. Messages and projects concerning research-led teaching, assessment diversity, and blended learning dominated the SoTL scene five years ago, to be eclipsed more recently by commitments to inclusive and personalized learning, students as partners, and student resilience and well-being. Employability, repeatedly pushed by UK Government policy, has retained prominence throughout. This institutional 'marketing' of educational investment and priority is common and thus makes such initiatives vulnerable to strategic clichés and parroting.

So, what did the LITE do internally to construct a more reflective and collaborative culture, which might fulfil a strategic function but also "open itself up as a space of scholarly exchange, debate and critique" (LITE, 2016)? The prime structural tactic was that of *affiliation*—a promise that the LITE would not just showcase internal teaching projects and communities but define itself as a network that fed off and into other scholarship communities in the university. The hub diagram depicted in Fig. 36.2 demonstrates some of the satellite scholarship communities involved. The 'gravitational pull' of each shifted the emphasis of the LITE as it developed, so that the institute's orbit was pulled into spheres of, for example, medical education pedagogy, science, technology, engineering, and mathematics (STEM) enhancement projects, and language learning scholarship during its first year of development.

This scholarship structure of 'hub and satellite' has developed an important etiquette through which the core institute has avoided a hierarchical status in relationship to the (often well-developed and internationally respected)

Fig. 36.2 Structure of affiliation of the LITE

36 Critical Reflection on Organizational Practice at a UK University... 561

satellite groups. The LITE co-funds or co-brands scholarship reports, events, and projects, but does not define themes, methods, or authorship. The LITE website acts as a catalyst for the project results and storytelling developed in the affiliate communities, and, whilst working with design templates, is porous to the particular narrative emphases these carry with them (LITE, n.d.).

This structure of affiliation is loyal to Vince's (2002) model of organizing communities of practice that promotes "engagement at the boundaries between organizational sub-systems and ... interactions with the power relations that characterise organizations" (Vince, 2002, 67). By affiliating scholarship subgroups, making visible their contrasting objectives and outputs, and obliging their interaction, an SoTL family is created. But like any blended family, relationships are not always easy, and 'storming and forming' took place as well-established groups with international reputations (e.g., the Leeds Institute for Medical Education) jostled with new arrivals (e.g., the Centre for Innovation and Research in Legal Education) and occupied common ground within the LITE. Power relations needed to be recontextualized—the kudos of international grant income held by an established group was juxtaposed with the new energy and momentum of a fresh scholarship community, with each needing recognition and voice.

Therefore, a *necessary* self-disruption and critical reflexivity comes with an affiliation model of SoTL. The LITE's Work in Progress seminars, in particular, host and broadcast the contrasting outputs and ambitions of the SoTL family of the University of Leeds. The quantitative and qualitative methods deployed by the different affiliate groups are tested in front of a critical audience. An atmosphere of critical confrontation as well as dialogue emerges, and far from 'adopting' any particular scholarship methods (as the 'filial' etymology might suggest), the LITE instead allows a space for challenging, but progressive, institutional debate. This model of interaction plays out some of the core principles of organizing reflection distilled in Vince and Reynolds's (2010) framework. It shifts priority from the individual to the social (in terms of groups as well as scholars), encourages an awareness and reassessment of power relations (especially between established and new groups), and, with a democratic etiquette, lays bare assumptions of scholarship practice within particular subjects and fields (Vince, 2002).

The next step in this affiliate structure of scholarship would most ambitiously be an external one, which would seek to draw together all UK institutes of SoTL in genuinely public and critical reflection about the nature and 'ends' of teaching scholarship. Although the LITE is gesturing toward this through its hosting of institute 'partners,' this step is fraught with counterforces and obstacles. Increased protectionism around teaching initiatives,

562   A. Divan et al.

spaces, and resources in the context of the UK's TEF rivalry may impact on the 'free trade' of teaching scholarship, and indeed on academics' willingness to admit to fault lines or failure in their practices. Polished institutional narratives of teaching excellence do not always rest easily with honest and self-critical reflection. A commitment to public and critical reflection, however profound its disruptions, will hopefully win out, so that institutional orbits of scholarship might ebb and flow in relation to each other, to the benefit of SoTL in both the UK and on an international scale.

Public Reflection: The Role of Writing Groups in Collaborative SoTL Activity

A number of activities have been set up under the auspices of the LITE to bring together individuals from across the institution to promote dialogue and foster collaboration. One of these is the establishment of collaborative writing groups (CWGs). These comprise individuals from different disciplines coming together to research and write about learning and teaching topics through structured writing retreats and pre- and post-supported activities. The CWGs act to bridge the space between current LITE scholars who typically work individually or in pairs, and the discipline-specific affiliations embedded within the various departments of the university. Thus, the key aims of the CWGs at the University of Leeds are to:

* Encourage cross-institutional collaboration in learning and teaching research and discourse
* Facilitate high-quality publication outputs such as books or book chapters, publications for peer-reviewed journals, or grant proposals
* Increase capacity and competence in learning and teaching scholarship through supported writing and mentorship.

The benefits of structured writing retreats and writing groups are well-documented in the literature, including in building communities of practice, providing opportunities for networking, and supporting academic writing competence. Such groups can also facilitate measurable increases in academic publication outputs (Kent et al., 2017; Kornhaber et al., 2016). Discipline-specific work, particularly in STEM subjects, is increasingly done in teams (Wuchty, et al., 2007), and hence such papers are usually written by several authors. In comparison, collaboratively writing a multiauthored paper in learning and teaching occurs with much less frequency (Kahn et al., 2013; MacKenzie & Myers, 2012), and writing groups typically consist of multiple writers meeting for mutual support and feedback whilst working on their own articles. However, literature on international CWGs (ICWGs) in the context of SoTL is now beginning to emerge (Marquis et al., 2014).

The CWGs established at the University of Leeds are informed by the experiences of these ICWGs (Motley et al., 2019), as well as the literature around academic writing retreats, in particular the work of Kornhaber et al. (2016) and Vince and Reynolds (2010). In a systematic review of the literature relating to academic writing retreats, Kornhaber et al. (2016) identify institutional support—in providing time and space for writing and providing mentorship opportunities—as key to the success of such groups. Vince and Reynolds (2010) highlight the transformational potential of public reflection within an organization, as encapsulated in the following quote:

> Public reflection provides an environment within which we can distinguish 'what is measured and critical from that which might be self-fulfilling and self-justificatory.' (Vince & Reynolds, 2010, 8)

Structure of the CWGs

The CWGs at the University of Leeds were set up in August 2018 and are designed to run every two years, with manuscripts arising from the work of the groups submitted to publishers within one year of the writing group first coming together. The CWG initiative is managed by a working group drawn from across the institution, including the LITE director, two other academic members of staff who have experience in collaborative writing and educational research, and a member of staff experienced in running writing retreats. Each CWG comprises four to five members, including a mix of professional and academic staff drawn from across the institution with different disciplinary backgrounds and levels of experience in researching and writing in learning and teaching. The topics for writing are selected from the themes prioritized by the LITE; examples include student resilience and well-being, work placement and employability, and learning spaces.

In parallel, the working group has been tracking the journey of the participants to evaluate the process and impact of the initiative. Some of the early feedback speaks to the motivations for engaging in the activity and the

564   A. Divan et al.

potential challenges they may face. Accordingly, key motivations for engaging in the collaborative writing initiative include:

* To gain confidence and experience in academic writing through a collaborative approach
* To gain more experience of writing for publication in pedagogic contexts and to learn from colleagues with greater experience in this area
* The opportunity to network with people with similar interests.

In turn, potential challenges that have been highlighted include:

* Balancing activities with demands of current employment
* Managing the expectations of self and others, with regards to collaborative writing practices
* Collaborating with colleagues that are not known before starting the project
* Finding ways of combining different perspectives and voices in a productive way.

Our aim is to evolve the current institution-wide CWGs into ICWGs. This would be in line with the next phase in the development of the LITE—to facilitate an outward-facing, critical, and public dialogue of learning and teaching informed by international perspectives and different cultural contexts.

Productive Reflection: The Impact of Undergraduate Research

> Productive reflection has a developmental character with an intention to build agency among participants; to promote confidence that they can act together in meaningful ways. (Vince & Reynolds, 2010, 10)

Interpreting the idea of productive reflection in the context of an HEI invites us to think inclusively about who should be engaged in our critical reflection. In the previous section on public reflection, we highlighted how different stakeholder groups such as academic staff (faculty members) and professional services staff can collaborate in critical reflection. In this section, we focus on the inclusion of students as reflective agents.

The 'student as producer' concept (Neary & Winn, 2009) sees participation in the research culture of a university as a way to transform students from consumers to co-producers of knowledge (Zepke, 2015). Programs that train, empower, and resource our students to develop as researchers are explicitly designed to build agency, either as critical agents in their own disciplines, or pedagogic scholars reflecting on the education their institution provides. Such initiatives are enhanced by opportunities for students to present their research findings through journals such as *Reinvention: an International Journal of Undergraduate Research* and at conferences such as the British Conference of Undergraduate Research (BCUR) and other regional and international undergraduate research (UR) conferences, such as the Australasian Council of Undergraduate Research, National Conference on Undergraduate Research, International Conference of Undergraduate Research, and World Congress on Undergraduate Research (Walkington, 2015).

The University of Leeds takes the idea of the 'student as producer' very seriously. But how can we be sure, referring back to the aforementioned ideas of Vince and Reynolds (2010) above, that this new 'agency' among student participants is meaningful? The LITE has realized that we must do more to engage former students in the university's critical reflection processes, so that we can evaluate the actual impact of our work in the real world. Despite UR being noted as a 'high-impact practice' (Kuh, 2008), there is limited evidence that UR has impacts beyond graduation other than improved performance in graduate school (Bauer & Bennett, 2003).

As a pilot study, we contacted 36 former students from one of the faculties of the University of Leeds who had been supported to attend the BCUR through the period of 2013–2016. Four volunteered to undergo semi-structured interviews about their UR experience, as described below (names changed to protect their privacy). Sarah was completing a master's course elsewhere in Europe, Matt was near the end of a doctoral program at a UK university, Veronica was undertaking a multicenter international master's program, and David was employed as an information technology researcher. All four had undertaken an assessed final year project at the University of Leeds, had engaged with either a voluntary project as part of a placement or a summer research internship, and had presented the results of the latter at the BCUR.

Strikingly, the non-assessed projects had *all* had a lasting impact. Sarah's research had initiated a new international collaboration between professors at her new institution and the University of Leeds. Matt had been invited to present his project at a significant public engagement event. Veronica's findings were, to date, the only ecological research data from the region she had visited and were guiding subsequent charitable projects. The impact on David was more about his development as a researcher, since he was still using the

566   A. Divan et al.

same methodologies in his commercial role. All four rated the BCUR as a key part of their UR experience: "A good first experience" (David), "A supportive environment. A steppingstone, but also a broad [multidisciplinary] experience" (Matt), "It was nice to see it all come together—to work out what's really important" (Sarah), and "The culmination of my research … I was really proud and excited" (Veronica).

When asked to reflect on their entire programs of study against the concept of a 'high-impact experience,' all four participants rated only their voluntary UR experiences and their field trip or industrial placement as having had a high impact. Strikingly, none selected their assessed final-year projects. From this limited pilot study, we can conclude that UR that is not assessed is a high-impact educational practice, that the BCUR is a 'stepping stone' to new research roles, and that UR can have real impact, leading to a new international research collaboration, new practice in commerce and the third sector, and public engagement work.

Most importantly, we find that the idea of productive critical reflection has led the LITE and the University of Leeds to ask some important and rewarding new questions regarding the inclusion of students as reflective agents, which can be explored with our students and alumni through scholarly research.

Supporting Individuals in a Reflective Organization

Launched in January 2017, the LITE mentoring scheme was conceived as a bespoke framework of support across the student education network at the University of Leeds in three key areas:

1. Mentoring for those who want to pursue more *formal teaching scholarship and pedagogy*. Advice for mentees includes support for developing scholarship project ideas; putting together funding applications; understanding and implementing research methodologies; research ethics, project management, project evaluation, and support for dissemination and publication.
2. Mentoring for those seeking *career development through student education* at the University of Leeds. Advice for mentees includes how to get involved in ongoing and new student education projects/developments across campus; contributing to the governance and committee structure; targeting student education roles and responsibilities; joining networks within the university; and advice on how to explore external, national, and international networks of innovation and scholarship.

36 Critical Reflection on Organizational Practice at a UK University...   567

3. Mentoring for those *progressing with curriculum design and student educa-tion project delivery*. Advice for mentees might include significant module, program, and assessment design; student support development; and digital developments. For this strand, mentees are asked to also seek advice from other structures of educational delivery, such as schools, faculties, units, and from other centers of teaching innovation, where relevant.

The first call for volunteers for the scheme successfully attracted 45 indi-viduals, resulting in 27 mentor-mentee pairings (as some staff volunteered to mentor more than one mentee). Staff representation encompassed all nine faculties (departments) of the university and across all grades (including teaching fellows, senior teaching fellows, lecturers, associate professors, and professors). All staff who applied as mentees were paired with a mentor. Subsequent calls for the scheme have resulted in 70 volunteers from across the institution.

Participants were contacted after 18 months to ascertain whether they wished to continue the mentor-mentee relationship, if they would like a new pairing, or if their support needs had been met and no further relationship was needed. Questionnaires were also sent at this time to gauge the impact of the LITE mentoring scheme; overall, the feedback suggested that the scheme has had a positive impact on participants. For example, mentees reported that their mentors had been a great source of encouragement in offering advice, guidance, and support, including providing ideas and suggestions for taking forward projects; suggesting relevant networks in which to get involved; pro-viding feedback on promotions; giving advice on applying for conferences; giving advice on how to approach a new field of scholarship; suggesting career development opportunities; balancing personal development versus team responsibilities; and suggesting new contacts. One mentee had been invited to participate in the research of their mentor, leading to the award of a LITE scholarship.

As well as practical support, mentees also reported positive personal bene-fits including their mentor helping them feel more confident in their practice, being better informed, and having raised their aspirations. Several mentees noted that they enjoyed having a mentor outside of their department to offer a different perspective:

> It's been really useful to get an additional perspective on my career development, from outside my faculty and subject discipline. My mentor has challenged me, and also put me in touch with others who can advise me, which has been extremely helpful. I'm looking forward to our future meetings. (Participant 1, LITE Mentorship Scheme)

I have found the scheme extremely helpful and supportive ... The scheme has provided me with renewed confidence ... It has opened up new opportunities that I wouldn't have considered. As my mentor is from a different department, he will hear of opportunities that I don't, especially as I belong to a service. Also, it provides me with a new network of contacts that I wouldn't naturally have had access to. (Participant 2, LITE Mentorship Scheme)

Want to feel more confident about your approach to scholarship and/or the outputs from your scholarly activity? Get a mentor! It has made a significant difference to how I feel about this part of my role and the actions I have taken as a result of being able to share ideas, discuss approaches, get constructive feedback and take next steps. It has raised my aspirations too. (Participant 3, LITE Mentorship Scheme)

The strands of the scheme where most staff requested support were in pursuing more formal teaching scholarship and pedagogy and seeking career development through student education; however, the majority of staff offered support for progressing with curriculum design and student education project delivery. This proved a difficulty when matching mentors and mentees. Although no one asked for a change of pairing, and feedback from the vast majority of mentees showed that their support needs had been met, an aim for the scheme has been to attract more experienced mentors. It is anticipated that this will be addressed through the development of the LITE in supporting staff in pursuing more formal teaching scholarship and pedagogy.

Although workshops have been held to support the role of a mentor, feedback suggests that more guidance would be welcome and, as such, resources are being put in place on a dedicated webpage for staff to refer to as needed. Other suggested areas for improvement to the scheme include wider advertising and network-building events where mentees and mentors meet both separately and as a group.

In summary, the LITE mentoring scheme has been successful so far in attracting 70 volunteers, and testimonials suggest that the scheme is having the intended positive impact on staff. It has also raised awareness of areas where staff need further support, for instance in designing robust pedagogic projects, developing methodologies, analyzing qualitative and quantitative data, and writing for journals. This is an area that is being addressed as the LITE develops its portfolio of activities, including the establishment of CWGs and other group-based training events.

Concluding Comments

By engaging with a theoretical framework for critical reflection, the LITE avoids creating new hierarchies, working instead to prioritize activities that catalyze dynamic public and productive reflection across and beyond the university. Using language and methods from the international movement around SoTL, the LITE can organize critique by facilitating collaboration among stakeholder groups and supporting individual agents through mentoring. It is far too early to judge the eventual success of such an approach as we respond to institutional needs and sectoral changes, but already valuable networks are emerging, including thematic-based groupings and mentoring for pedagogical research. All of this enables and supports us to ask important questions about what "teaching excellence" means in our specific context.

References

Bauer, K. W., & Bennett, J. S. (2003). Alumni perceptions used to assess undergraduate research experience. *The Journal of Higher Education, 74*(2), 210–230.

Brunstein, J., & King, J. (2018). Organizing reflection to address collective dilemmas: Engaging students and professors with sustainable development in higher education. *Journal of Cleaner Production, 203*, 153–163.

Cotter, R. J. (2014). Reflexive spaces of appearance: Rethinking critical reflection in the workplace. *Human Resource Development International, 17*(4), 459–474.

Department for Business, Industry, and Skills. (2016). *Success as a knowledge economy: Teaching excellence, social mobility and student choice.* Williams Lea Group. https://www.gov.uk/government/publications/higher-education-success-as-a-knowledge-economy-white-paper

Kahn, P., Goodhew, P., Murphy, M., & Walsh, L. (2013). The scholarship of teaching and learning as collaborative working: A case study in shared practice and collective purpose. *Higher Education Research & Development, 32*(6), 901–914.

Kemmis, S. (1985). Action research and the politics of reflection. In D. Boud, R. Keogh, & D. Walker (Eds.), *Reflection: Turning experience into learning.* Kogan Page.

Kent, A., Berry, D. M., Budds, K., Skipper, Y., & Williams, H. L. (2017). Promoting writing amongst peers: Establishing a community of writing practice for early career academics. *Higher Education Research & Development, 36*(6), 1–14.

Kornhaber, R., Cross, M., Betihavas, V., & Bridgman, H. (2016). The benefits and challenges of academic writing retreats: An integrative review. *Higher Education Research & Development, 35*(6), 1210–1227.

Kuh, G. D. (2008). *High-impact educational practices: What they are, who has access to them, and why they matter*. Association of American Colleges & Universities.

Leeds Institute for Teaching Excellence (LITE). (2016). *Vision statement*. Leeds University.

Leeds Institute for Teaching Excellence (LITE). (n.d.). *About the institute*. Leeds University. https://teachingexcellence.leeds.ac.uk/

MacKenzie, J., & Myers, R. A. (2012). International collaborations in SoTL: Current status and future directions. *International Journal for the Scholarship of Teaching and Learning, 6*(1), 1–8.

Marquis, E., Healey, M., & Vine, M. (2014). Building capacity for the scholarship of teaching and learning (SoTL) using international collaborative writing groups. *International Journal for the Scholarship of Teaching and Learning, 8*(1), art12.

Motley, P., Divan, A., Lopes, V., Ludwig, L., Matthews, K., & Tomljenovic-Berube, A. (2019). Collaborative writing: Partnerships & identity formation. In N. Simmons & A. Singh (Eds.), *Critical collaborative communities* (pp. 212–227). Brill.

Neary, M., & Winn, J. (2009). The student as producer: Reinventing the student experience in higher education. In L. Bell, M. Neary, & H. Stevenson (Eds.), *The future of higher education: Policy, pedagogy and the student experience* (pp. 192–210). Continuum.

Potter, M. K., & Kustra, E. D. H. (2011). The relationship between scholarly teaching and SoTL: Models, distinctions, and clarifications. *International Journal for the Scholarship of Teaching and Learning, 5*(1), 23.

Reynolds, M. (1999). Grasping the nettle: Possibilities and pitfalls of a critical management pedagogy. *British Journal of Management, 9*, 171–184.

Vince, R. (2002). Organizing reflection. *Management Learning, 33*(1), 63–78.

Vince, R., & Reynolds, M. (2009). Reflection, reflective practice and organizing reflection. In S. J. Armstrong & C. V. Fukami (Eds.), *The SAGE handbook of management learning, education and development* (pp. 89–103). SAGE.

Vince, R., & Reynolds, M. (2010, April). *Organizing reflective practice* (Conference presentation). 3rd Conference of Organisational Learning, Knowledge, and Capabilities. http://www2.warwick.ac.uk/fac/soc/wbs/conf/olkc/archive/olkc3/papers/contribution115.pdf

Walkington, H. (2015). *Students as researchers: Supporting undergraduate research in the disciplines in higher education*. The Higher Education Academy.

Ward, T. (2017). *Submission to the teaching excellence framework 2017*. University of Leeds. http://www.leeds.ac.uk/download/505/submission_to_the_teaching_excellence_framework_2017

Wuchty, S., Jones, B. F., & Uzzi, B. (2007). The increasing dominance of teams in production of knowledge. *Science, 316*, 1036–1039.

Zepke, N. (2015). Student engagement research: Thinking beyond the mainstream. *Higher Education Research & Development, 34*(6), 1311–1323.

37

Systematic Changes: Impact of Double-Helix Collaboration Toward Innovation in Faculty Development and Student-Centered Teaching and Learning

Yihong Fan

Introduction

Southwest Jiaotong University (SWJTU), located in Chengdu, Sichuan Province, Southwest China, is a comprehensive research university with a 125-year history. Founded in 1896, SQJTU currently has 20 schools, 2,610 teachers, and about 45,000 students, including undergraduate, master's, doctoral, and overseas students. Faculty development (FD) work is imperative for such a large university so as to support the development and growth of both the faculty and students to assure learning quality.

History and Evolution

The Center for Faculty Training was established in 2001 and began offering a one-year Training and Consultation Program for Novice Teachers (TCpNT) (for more details, please see the latter part of this chapter). Subsequently, in

---

Y. Fan (✉)
Southwest Jiaotong University, Chengdu, Sichuan Province, China

Xiamen University, Xiamen, Sichuan Province, China
e-mail: 1400201046@qq.com; fanyihong@aliyun.com

© The Author(s), under exclusive license to Springer Nature Switzerland AG 2023 **571**
O. J. Neisler (ed.), *The Palgrave Handbook of Academic Professional Development Centers*,
Palgrave Studies on Leadership and Learning in Teacher Education,
https://doi.org/10.1007/978-3-030-80967-6_37

2011, the name of the center was changed to the Faculty Development Center (FDC). In October 2012, it was one of 30 centers in China granted the honor of being named a national exemplary FD center and was granted an annual budget of ¥1 million from the Ministry of Education. Besides a vice director and a director, the FDC has four staff members who directly report to the vice president for academic affairs at SWJTU.

Overall Mission, Main Goal, and Shared Vision

The *overall mission* of the FDC is to contribute to the enhancement of quality education at SWJTU by promoting improvement and innovation in teaching and learning through FD work. The *main goal* is providing academic faculty with various teaching and learning theories, approaches, and pedagogy to facilitate students' deep learning, innovation, and creativity. The *shared vision* is to nurture faculty to be holistic educators and students to be holistic persons.

Support System for Innovation in FD and Teaching and Learning

The FDC has joined efforts with the Academic Affairs Office (AAO) at SWJTU to develop a systematic support system. It starts with system thinking and arrives at a shared vision for facilitating the faculty to develop into holistic educators and students into holistic persons. Figure 37.1 offers an illustration of the support system of SWJTU. Across the center vertically, collaboration between the FDC and AAO is represented as a double-helix driving force to facilitate systematic changes, including organizational learning, FD, and teaching innovation, thereby affecting students' deep learning and development.

The words in bold in Fig. 37.1 correspond with the explanations on either side of the double helix, while the abbreviation of each explanation is shown at each level of the helix. As can be seen, from the bottom to the top of the double helix, there are seven levels of development from *System Thinking* to *Shared Vision*. This starts with the *career-stage FD* designed by the FDC, supported by the *five measures* offered by the AAO, before moving to the FDC-facilitated *five phases of promoting teaching competencies for young teachers* (PTCYT), before the FDC and AAO join forces to offer a *continuous FD program* with the goal of achieving a *five paradigm shift* and developing *five innovative courses*.

37 Systematic Changes: Impact of Double-Helix Collaboration...

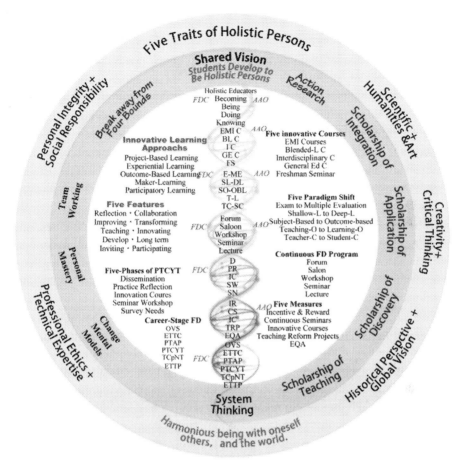

Fig. 37.1 Support system at SWJTU for FD and innovation in teaching and learning

Throughout the whole process, the faculty develop to integrate their learning and practice to become holistic educators (Fan, 2004). All programs that are offered incorporate the *innovative learning approaches* and *five features* (see the top left of the double helix). Once the faculty have become holistic educators, they are better able to help students become holistic persons who possess the five traits shown in the very outer circle: personal integrity and social responsibility; scientific capacity and humanistic and artistic tendencies; professional ethics and technical expertise; creative spirit and critical thinking; and historical perspective and global vision. The ultimate purpose of being a holistic person is shown at the very bottom of the far outer circle: to live harmoniously with oneself, the others, and the world.

574   Y. Fan

The second outer circle demonstrates the four conceptual underpinnings that lead to these systematic changes and development in the university concerning FD work, pedagogical innovation, and the development of innovative courses. These are organizational learning, multiple scholarship, action research, and breaking away from the four bounds.

Four Conceptual Underpinnings for the FD Support System

According to Senge (1990), the five elements that contribute to the organizational learning and changing process consist of shared vision, system thinking, changing mental models, personal mastery, and teamwork. In turn, the four domains of multiple scholarship (Boyer, 1990)—namely, scholarship of teaching, scholarship of discovery, scholarship of application, and scholarship of integration—contribute to redefining the faculty's academic roles and responsibilities, thus promoting innovative course design and implementation (Fan, 2011, 2013; Fan & Tan, 2009). Action research empowers teachers as practice-researchers who engage themselves in the whole process of "plan-act-observe-reflect" (Carr & Kemmis, 1986). Finally, when designing and implementing innovative courses, teaching teams need to break away from the four bounds of classroom learning; namely, time-bound, space-bound, role-bound, and efficiency-bound (O'Banion, 1997), and go beyond the classroom into the community. In this way, students not only learn knowledge in the classroom, but also serve the community's needs with their innovative project products, thus promoting qualities like civic responsibility, professional ethics, and broad social perspectives. These theories and models serve as a guide to FD program development at SWJTU. The following programs demonstrate how the support system works in practice.

Career-Stage FD Programs

The FDC of SWJTU has developed teacher development projects for faculty serving at different career stages, including the Entry Teacher Training Program, TCpNT, PTCYT program, Postgraduate Teaching Assistant Training, Promotion Evaluation, Young Teachers' Teaching Contest, and sending teachers abroad on a overseas visiting scholarship, etc. Two signature programs, the TCpNT and the PTCYT, are discussed in the following sections.

The TCpNT Program

The TCpNT has been offered since 2001 for novice university teachers. It is a one-year program that has a comprehensive program scheme embedded within an apprenticeship learning approach that is centered on the organization of mentor groups at both the school and university levels. The novice teachers need to attend their mentors' and peer teachers' classes to observe how they are planned and organized. The mentors also attend the novice teachers' classes, offering suggestions for improving their lesson plans and their class organization. Through classroom observations and video evaluation of their micro-course teaching, the mentors give thoughtful feedback at each step, guiding the novice teachers to develop their teaching competencies. The novice teachers need to go through two formal teaching demonstration sessions at the end of the year under the inspection of the mentor group, one at the school level and the other at the university level.

Besides mentor review, the novice teachers must also undergo faculty peer review, a student course evaluation survey, self-reflection on teaching, and provide a summary report of what they have learned through the whole program. The novice teachers receive the university teaching certificate after they have successfully passed all components of the TCpNT program.

The PTCYT Program

The PTCYT is a one-year program designed in the fall of 2015 as a joint effort of the FDC and AAO aiming to help teachers develop new concepts and approaches for teaching reform and learning innovation. The ultimate purpose of the program is to help teachers to achieve a *paradigm shift* from teacher-centered teaching to student-centered learning. As Zhao (2016) maintains, universities need to embark on a systematic change and paradigm shift to ensure that teaching reform reaches its full potential and is geared toward student-centered learning.

Each round of the PTCYT program admits about 50 teachers and offers a dozen seminars and workshops for them to learn new ideas, approaches, and strategies of innovative teaching. To date, after five years, the PTCYT completion cohort consists of about 250 teachers who have gone on to become teaching-reform pioneers on campus. The PTCYT has five features and four modules that contribute to the long-term effects of the program, as outlined below.

Five Features of the PTCYT Program

First, this program changed the organizing scheme from demanding to inviting teacher participation. Second, the program systematically supports teachers to steadily engage in a paradigm shift focused on student-centered, innovative teaching. Third, through the Mao Yisheng Honors College, faculty design and implement innovative courses. Fourth, collaboration between the FDC and the AAO supports faculty teaching projects. Fifth, action research facilitates teachers' reflection on both their teaching and their students' learning.

Four Modules of the PTCYT Program

In the past five years, scores of seminars and workshops have been offered over four modules. These are: (1) facilitating student active learning, including project-based learning to facilitate student-centered learning, outcome-based learning, how to help students become self-directed learners, and how to tap into a student's potential, creativity, and innovation; (2) information communication technology-supported teaching and learning, including mobile learning, how to design massive open online and small private online courses, and how to facilitate blended learning; (3) assessing and evaluating learning outcomes, including using rubrics to assess students' learning outcomes, using a development portfolio to evaluate a student's development and growth, and using multiple evaluation and quality assessment (EQA) for student-centered learning; and (4) research-oriented seminars, including action research in designing and implementing innovative courses, multiple scholarship for interdisciplinary course design, and design thinking for project-based learning, etc.

Collaboration Between the FDC and AAO to Develop a Learning Organization

To achieve profound organizational change, we must first embark on a journey to build a learning organization on campus; in other words, arriving at a shared vision, applying system thinking, changing mental models, gaining personal mastery of the new way of teaching, and facilitating teamwork (Senge, 1990), both for the teachers and students.

The *shared vision*, as mentioned earlier, is to help students develop the five traits of holistic persons in order to be harmonious with oneself, others, and the world (see Fig. 37.1). However, in order to accomplish this, teachers must first develop themselves into holistic educators.

At SWJTU, we developed a five-phase FD scheme to engage faculty in multiple scholarship development. The phases consisted of: (1) investigating their developmental needs; (2) offering seminars and workshops to serve their needs; (3) providing opportunities to engage themselves in teaching and learning reform projects by designing and implementing their courses in innovative ways; (4) reflecting on the development and growth of themselves and their students after implementing the innovative courses; and (5) disseminating or sharing their experiences with other teachers. All programs helped the faculty change mental models and achieve a paradigm shift from teacher-centered teaching to student-centered learning.

The AAO initiated teaching research and reform projects for faculty to apply new ideas and approaches in their teaching. When the teachers meet obstacles or problems in their teaching process, the FDC adviser gives guidance and offers further seminar and workshops for teachers to carry out the innovative courses successfully. In this way, we help teachers develop a personal mastery of new approaches of teaching as well as teamwork when designing new courses, thus demonstrating all five elements of a learning organization as advocated by Senge (1990).

Long-Term and Continuous FD Programs Supporting Innovative Teaching

Besides the programs offered by the FDC, the AAO also initiated a series of seminars, forums, workshops, and salons on theme-based exploration and discussions for promoting teaching reform and innovation, through which faculty have engaged in designing and implementing innovative courses. In 2015, the AAO invited Ken Bain, renowned higher education researcher and author of *What the Best College Teachers Do* (Bain, 2004), to give a series of lectures, seminars, and workshops on how to be excellent university teachers and what innovative approaches could be used in teaching and learning. Subsequently, from 2016 to 2018, the AAO together with the FDC created learning opportunities for faculty and helped teaching teams to design and implement innovative courses, such as freshmen seminars, general education courses, blended learning courses, and interdisciplinary courses.

Designing and Implementing Innovative Courses

From the fall of 2015 to the fall of 2019, SWJTU developed and offered 64 interdisciplinary courses, 55 blended learning courses, and 99 general education courses, through which both faculty and students were able to discover their own potential and creativity and gain a significant sense of success in teaching and learning.

Impact of the Innovative Courses

By 2017, the teaching and learning innovation at SWJTU had caught the attention of FD developers at other universities as well as the Higher Education Academy of China. Three forums for teaching innovation were organized, held at each of the SWJTU campuses, with each one attracting hundreds of participants from all over China. Our teaching team got the chance to communicate and exchange their experiences of designing and implementing their innovative courses with university teachers from various parts of China.

Five Measures Ensuring Teaching and Learning Innovation

The AAO at SWJTU developed five measures to support teaching and learning innovation. These include: (1) a student-centered EQA system; (2) teaching research and reform project as incentive; (3) a continuous seminar for improving teaching and learning approaches; (4) opportunities to design and implement innovative courses, and (5) a reward system to acknowledge excellence in teaching and learning innovation among teachers.

Multiple Scholarship and Action Research Boosting Innovative Courses

A multiple scholarship model was introduced to help teachers to enlarge their scope of academic roles and responsibilities and action research for teachers to develop themselves as practice-researchers. Most of the teaching research and reform projects initiated by the AAO were geared toward developing new and innovative courses (i.e. the freshmen seminar and general education, blended learning, and interdisciplinary courses).

Multiple Scholarship Boosts Interdisciplinary Courses

In the fall of 2015, the AAO of SWJTU decided to develop and offer interdisciplinary courses to students of Mao Yisheng Honor's College. We shared the notion that creative and innovative ideas most likely emerge when teachers or students from different fields of study communicate and engage with each other as result of the sharing of different perspectives and ways of thinking. Interdisciplinary teacher teams were formed during the Project-Based Learning Workshop of the FDC. Through the co-mingling of teachers from different fields and the generation of heated discussions about solving real-life problems, the interdisciplinary teams came up with ideas for interdisciplinary courses. Through this process, they gained awareness of the need to pay attention not only to teaching and learning, but also to connecting theory to practice (Chen, 2009) and integrating knowledge from different fields, thus incorporating the tenets of the multiple scholarship into their real-life teaching practice.

Action Research and Teaching Reform

Action research was also incorporated into the teaching team to empower them to be practice-researchers. The interdisciplinary teaching teams arrived at a general idea about "learning outcome" through a discussion of the goal of the course and how to modify the curriculum outline and implementation strategies to achieve the best result from all teachers' and students' collective intelligences and endeavors. Through the process of action research, the teachers learned to ask fundamental questions regarding the ultimate purpose of their courses, henceforth realizing that passing on knowledge is not as important as stimulating students' interests, tapping into their potential, and fostering their spirit of creativity.

The teaching teams learned to collect data over every major step of their teaching by using questionnaires at the beginning of the course to learn more about their students' interests and needs. They designed experiential learning tasks to stimulate the students' interests and engagement in project-based learning to accomplish what the students themselves would like to explore and create. The teaching team also incorporated a mid-term evaluation of the students' learning to determine whether they needed to modify their course plan. They also learned to use multiple evaluation for assessing students' learning outcomes. At the end of the course, both the students and teachers wrote reflection reports of the course.

Interdisciplinary Courses That Foster Creativity and Innovation

Between 2015 and 2020, 64 interdisciplinary courses were developed and offered at SWJTU, all aimed at fostering creativity and innovation in both the faculty and students. Examples of these courses include 'From Codes to Things: Make almost everything', 'Nanotechnology and Life', 'Sports, Science, Technology, and Wise Life', 'Thinking on Learning', and 'Thinking on Designing', to name a few. These interdisciplinary courses were designed to discuss, engage with, and solve real-life problems, thus triggering the students' intrinsic motivation and task-driven inspiration and promoting teamwork so as to stimulate self-directed learning.

Most of the courses were project-based and the groups were formed of students from different disciplines so that they could contribute to their projects through different fields and perspectives. All teams presented their products at the end of the course. These experiences of exploring real-life problems and designing new products to solve these problems gave the students the sense that they were engaging in meaningful study and contributing to their community and society. In this way, they demonstrated a much stronger motivation to learn, create, and contribute, and in turn, they also developed a stronger sense of social responsibility.

The interdisciplinary teams applied project-based teaching, inquiry-based learning, and research-oriented learning, which combines teaching, extracurricular activities, and hands-on practice in a laboratory. After having participated in the interdisciplinary courses, students realized concepts such as the integration of knowledge and gained a better sense of their own creativity, innovation, and development and growth.

Teachers Become Pioneers of Teaching and Learning Innovation

After having been involved in the FD process at SWJTU, quite a number of teachers have since become pioneers of education reform and teaching innovation. For example, more than half of the teachers engaged in interdisciplinary courses were from PTCYT cohorts. In 2016, 30% of the teachers who won the Tang Lixin Excellent Teachers Award at the university were members of PTCYT cohorts. As one of the teachers from the 'Sports, Science, Technology, and Wise Life' course teaching team put it:

37 Systematic Changes: Impact of Double-Helix Collaboration…

Life is interdisciplinary! If we need to solve real-life problems, we need to combine what we've learned from all disciplinary fields. We need to help the students to become T-type persons, who have enough breadth as well as depth in their knowledge base and competencies. (Teacher 1, SWJTU)

One teacher and former member of the PTCYT cohort reported: "Now I will pay attention to students' interests and understand the feelings of students and realize the enrichment of university teachers, and the significance of the valuable impact teachers could have on the students" (Teacher 2, SWJTU). Another said: "The workshop of PTCYT inspired my educational heart and touched my educational soul, and then opened a 'heart journey' to devote myself to educational research and innovative teaching practice" (Teacher 3, SWJTU).

One of the teachers of an interdisciplinary team claimed that:

The designing and implementing of the interdisciplinary course lent me a totally different perspective than what I used to have. Previously, I only cared about my specialty, nothing else. Now, I've sensed connections from all related disciplines and areas of studies, thus more robust ideas have come into being, helpful for both teaching and research. (Teacher 4, SWJTU)

Another teacher stated:

The program of faculty development and activities inspired my inner motivation. Now that the fire in my heart has been lit up for teaching in new approaches, I decided to make a great effort to light up the fire in students' hearts, giving them opportunities to discover their own potentials and creativity. (Teacher 5, SWJTU)

Students' Development and Growth

Innovative teaching opens up a brand-new learning horizon for students. The following section provides some insight into SWJTU students' gains, development, and growth as summarized by the students themselves.

Discovering Their Own Potential and Creativity

One student from the 'Sports, Science, Technology, and Wise Life' course wrote in his reflection report that:

The experience of this course gave me the opportunity to discover my own potentiality and creativity. When we saw what we designed and made finally work, how proud we were of ourselves, of our team and, in turn, our self-confidence has grown. (Student 1, SWJTU)

Another student said:

At the early stage of the course, we learned that we'll need to make sports-related devices as the final project outcome, but at the time we did not believe we could do it, since we were only freshmen or sophomores in our group. But as the course went on, we learned knowledge from different fields, design thinking, and creativity methodology. With the help of the teachers and several rounds of brainstorm, we finally were able to come up with [a] feasible design. When the design came out as real product, how happy and excited we were! We started to believe we have endless potential and creativity. (Student 2, SWJTU)

Opportunity to Sense Their Own Success

Moreover, the course gave the students the opportunity to gain self-confidence and a sense of their own success. As one student wrote in their reflection report:

The course gave me the opportunity to design, develop, and make our own products. In the end, when the product got to work, we were so excited that we made it, thus we experienced a strong sense of achieving success through our own efforts. (Student 3, SWJTU)

Another wrote:

Before attending this course, I was just an invisible person in the class. But during the process of making investigation, coming up with ideas for products, and finally making the product, I learned to contribute to the group and finally gained the sense of becoming an important member of the group and finally share the success with the group. I was so happy to be able to contribute to the group project, thus I started to have a stronger self-confidence. (Student 4, SWJTU)

Teamwork and Collaboration

The opportunity for collaboration also enhanced teamwork and spirit. One student reported that working in teams gave them much more enjoyment when studying and solving problems:

When group members from different disciplines work together, we were able to learn from different perspectives and ideas, using knowledge from different fields, thus it was much easier to come up with new ideas to solve problems and achieve results. And when we faced with difficulties we put our heads together to solve the problems. In the end, when we witnessed our own product work, we were so proud of our team! (Student 5, SWJTU)

Similarly, when the teachers saw the students' products, including such innovative devices as Smart Mountain Climbing Sticks, Neck Exercise Device, Basketball Practice Device, and Rock-Climbing Apps, they felt incredible joy that the students were able to devise and accomplish these products within such a short period of time. Based on the students' feedback, we learned that the students had really enjoyed the innovative courses, which had given them more space to use their heads, hands, feet, and minds, thereby facilitating their all-around development. The teachers were also able to continue to maintain communication with their students and further improve their teaching effectiveness.

Long-Term Continuous Student Innovation

If the students really cherish their experience in a course, the end of the course does not necessarily mean the end of their interaction with the teachers. One of the students in the 'Sports, Science, Technology, and Wise Life' course designed a logo for the course during his summer break, long after he had finished the spring course. When the teacher received the logo via e-mail, she was touched as she knew that the student had developed a sense of belonging and wanted to contribute to the long-term development of the course. The student-designed logo of the course is shown in Fig. 37.2.

Based on the aforementioned reflections and feedback, we see clearly that the teachers and students have developed and grown together at the same time during the process of implementing these innovative courses.

Gaining Worldwide Recognition

In April 2018, when Bain, came to SWJTU for the second time, he was very impressed by the interdisciplinary courses offered on campus. He chose to include the 'Sports, Science, Technology, and Wise Life' course in his new book *Super Courses: The Future of Teaching and Learning*, which describes innovative courses from around the world (Bain, 2021).

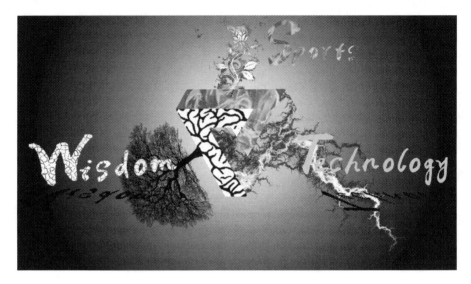

Fig. 37.2 A student-designed logo for the interdisciplinary course 'Sports, Science, Technology, and Wise Life' (Figure reproduced with permission)

Summary

This chapter elaborates on how the FDC and AAO at SWJTU collaborated to achieve systematic changes with a shared vision for developing holistic teachers and students who can live harmoniously with themselves, others, and the world. Armed by four conceptual underpinnings—organizational learning, multiple scholarship, action research, and breaking away from the four bounds of classroom learning—the FDC and AAO joined forces, coming up with long-term, systematic programs and measures to drive seven levels of FD, resulting in a paradigm shift from teacher-centered teaching to student-centered learning and the development of various innovative courses. Effective teaching and learning should lead the students into realistic situations and give them real-life experience. Thus, the goal of education is not to fill the brain with knowledge, but to ignite a spark in the student to unlock their inner potential and creativity.

References

Bain, K. (2004). *What the best college teachers do*. Harvard University Press.
Bain, K. (2021). *Super courses: The future of teaching and learning*. Princeton University Press.

37 Systematic Changes: Impact of Double-Helix Collaboration... 585

Boyer, E. (1990). *Scholarship reconsidered: Priority of the professoriate.* Jossey-Bass.

Carr, W., & Kemmis, S. (1986). *Becoming critical.* Falmer Press.

Chen, X. (2009). *Bridging praxis and theory: A study of teachers' practical knowledge.* Education Science Press.

Fan, Y. (2011). Comparative study on staff development in European and Chinese universities: Based on the perspective of multiple-scholarship. *Revista de Docencia Universitaria, 9*(1), 111–133.

Fan, Y. (2004). *From integrative worldview to holistic education: Theory and practice.* Southwest Jiaotong University Press.

Fan, Y. (2013). *Comparative studies of faculty development between China and European countries: Based on multiple scholarship.* Southwest Jiaotong University.

Fan, Y., & Tan, M. (2009). Multiple-scholarship and staff development: Theory and practice. *Educational Research and Experiment, 131*(6), 27–32.

O'Banion, T. (1997). *A learning college for the 21st century.* Oryx Press.

Senge, P. (1990). *The fifth discipline: The art and practice of learning organization.* Century.

Zhao, J. (2016). On the new three centers: Concept and history – One of the researches on SC undergraduate teaching reform in the United States. *Higher Engineering Education,* (3), 35–56.

Part XI

Examples of ADC Impact Research

All academic professional development centers (ADCs) are called upon to evaluate the effectiveness of their programs and activities. Each ADC in this section was selected for inclusion here because they differ from each other. My own institution has already implemented some of the examples of impact research outlined in these case studies.

Chapters in Part XI

Chapter 38: *Change in Practice: Achieving a Cultural Shift in Teaching and Learning Through a Theory of Change.* Grahame T. Bilbow, Centre for the Enhancement of Teaching and Learning, University of Hong Kong, Pok Fu Lam, Hong Kong.

This chapter describes how, in order to begin an impact analysis of one ADC, the team set impact goals as part of the change management process. The impact data originate from stakeholder interviews and program output statistics.

Chapter 39: *Developing Beginner University Teachers' Pedagogical Competencies Through a Professional Development Program.* Roman Švaříček, Ingrid Procházková, Jeffrey A. Vanderziel, and Klára Šeďová, Masaryk University, Brno, Czech Republic.

588 Examples of ADC Impact Research

This chapter describes how staff at an ADC compared data collected through semi-structured, in-depth faculty interviews to published findings about what constitutes best practices in higher education teaching and learning. This research provided the foundation goals and principles for the design of their programs.

Chapter 40: *From Workshops to Impact Evaluation: The Case of a Chilean Center for Teaching Development and Innovation.* Ricardo García, Héctor Turra and Beatriz Moya, Universidad Católica de Temuco, Temuco, Chile.

In this chapter, the ADC team developed an evaluation model to document the impact on teaching when the center moved from workshops to a strategic, integrated model of faculty development. The authors provide a matrix detailing the levels and categories of the change data being collected and analyzed.

Chapter 41: *Extending International Collaboration to Certify High-Quality Online Teaching in Higher Education.* Yan Ding, Center for Faculty Development / Research Institute for Higher Education, Fudan University, Shanghai, China, and Yaping Gao, Quality Matters, Annapolis, MD, USA.

This chapter showcases how collaborative research between an ADC and an education quality assurance organization enabled the development of a Chinese rubric for the design of online or hybrid courses. It also encouraged the ADC to take on an influential leadership role to improve teaching competence and curriculum quality, promote scholarship of teaching and learning, create a learning community, and encourage instructional innovation, especially with regards to new models of technology-integrated teaching.

Other Relevant Chapters

Chapter 13: *Mission-Aligned Teaching Center Initiative.* Annie Soisson, Center for the Enhancement of Learning and Teaching, Tufts University, Somerville, MA, USA.

This chapter details how research conducted by an ADC found a positive correlation between participation in ADC programs and course evaluation scores.

Chapter 14: *At the Heart of the Campus: A Faculty-Led Teaching and Learning Center.* Gwendolyn Mettetal and Carolyn A. Schult, Indiana University South Bend, South Bend, IN, USA.

Examples of ADC Impact Research 589

This ADC has begun collecting impact data defined by faculty participation and satisfaction, along with rubric scoring of various elements of ADC operations and programs. New data collection is focusing on resultant instructional change.

Chapter 15: *A Member-Driven, Donor-Supported Academic Professional Development Center: The New Mexico State University Teaching Academy.* Tara Gray, Teaching Academy, New Mexico State University, Las Cruces, NM, Laura Madson, Department of Psychology, New Mexico State University, Las Cruces, NM, and Morgan Iommi, Center for Teaching and Learning Excellence, Nevada State College, Henderson, NV, USA (formerly of New Mexico State University).

In this chapter, one ADC reports how impact data allowed them to determine that 92% of its members have made positive changes to their teaching and 80% have observed improvements in student learning. However, this is self-reported survey data as opposed to evidence of student learning which many accrediting agencies are requesting.

Chapter 20: *Creating through International Partnership: A Faculty Development Center at a Pakistani University.* Asif Khan, Karakoram International University, Gilgit, Pakistan, Michele A. Parker, University of North Carolina, Wilmington, NC, and Patricia Pashby, University of Oregon, Eugene, OR, USA.

This chapter reports findings from a three-year impact study based on Stufflebeam's Context, Input, Process, and Product model.

Chapter 24: *The Making of the Learning, Teaching, and Innovative Technologies Center: Building Upon an Internal Partnership.* Barbara Draude, Thomas Brinthaupt, and Sheila Otto, Middle Tennessee State University, Murfreesboro, TN, USA.

This chapter provides details and findings from needs assessment and impact evaluation research.

Chapter 27: *Promoting a Culture of Teaching Excellence in a Chinese Research University.* Yihong Qiu, Center for Teaching and Learning Development, Shanghai Jiao Tong University, Shanghai, China.

This chapter includes data from recent surveys of the impact on teaching and learning related to ADC programming.

38

Change in Practice: Achieving a Cultural Shift in Teaching and Learning Through a Theory of Change

Grahame T. Bilbow

Introduction

Established in 1912, the University of Hong Kong (HKU) is Hong Kong's longest established university—an English-medium, research-led, comprehensive university currently ranked 26th globally according to the Quacquarelli Symonds (QS) World University Rankings (QS Top Universities, 2018). HKU is publicly funded by the Government of Hong Kong through the University Grants Committee (UGC). A center for supporting teaching and learning has existed at HKU since 1994. Initially called the Centre for the Advancement of University Teaching, its name changed in 2009 to the Centre for the Enhancement of Teaching and Learning (CETL) (CETL, n.d.-a). CETL is resourced centrally from the block grant awarded to the university by the UGC, as well as from the UGC's Teaching Development and Language Enhancement Grant.

CETL consists of a total of nine academic and academic-related staff, seven administrative/technical staff, and approximately 15 research staff and research students. The center is located in purpose-built premises on the HKU centennial campus on Hong Kong Island. The center also contains a

G. T. Bilbow (✉)
Centre for the Enhancement of Teaching and Learning, University of Hong Kong, Pok Fu Lam, Hong Kong
e-mail: grahame.bilbow@grange-education.org

© The Author(s), under exclusive license to Springer Nature Switzerland AG 2023
O. J. Neisler (ed.), *The Palgrave Handbook of Academic Professional Development Centers*,
Palgrave Studies on Leadership and Learning in Teacher Education,
https://doi.org/10.1007/978-3-030-80967-6_38

591

small E-learning and Pedagogical Support Unit, which provides support for e-learning. CETL is led by a director and supported by two assistant directors, one of whom is responsible for academic programs and the other for innovation and support. The center is overseen by the university's vice president for teaching and learning, who also serves as a member of the senior management team of the university.

Broadly speaking, the mission of CETL has, since its inception, been to identify, share, and embed internationally recognized, evidence-informed, good practices across HKU's teaching and learning. The center addresses this mission by undertaking a wide range of activities, including: mandatory professional development programs for all academic staff and research postgraduate students new to the university whose work includes teaching and learning support; a weekly lunchtime program of voluntary workshops and seminars and other events to support staff from across the university's 10 faculties; formal and informal interaction with faculties in support of curriculum design, assessment, and pedagogy; and a range of scholarly activities, including research, scholarship, and the organization of periodic teaching and learning conferences that attract both local and international participants.

CETL's Early Contributions

In the first decade of the new millennium, CETL's activities were significantly shaped by broad educational reforms taking place in Hong Kong. The two most influential of such reforms were the territory-wide implementation of outcome-based education (OBE) at the tertiary level, which began in the early 2000s, and the so-called 3-3-4 educational reform initiated in 2009, which resulted in the lengthening of standard university curricula from three to four years' duration across the higher education sector in Hong Kong.

OBE

In the early part of the decade, HKU, along with all other publicly-funded, degree-awarding institutions in Hong Kong, sought to embed outcomes-based approaches to student learning in all of its academic programs. In supporting this initiative, CETL was active in preparing academic program teams to write learning outcomes, achieve constructive alignment between outcomes and assessment, and, most recently, use evidence of student learning to demonstrate the students' achievement of program- and course-level learning outcomes (CETL n.d.-b).

3-3-4 Educational Reform

Later in the decade, the Hong Kong Government introduced the 3-3-4 educational reform for lower secondary, senior secondary, and tertiary education across the Special Administrative Region. As a result of this reform, senior secondary schooling was to be cut by a year to three years, and the normal duration of HKU's undergraduate degree programs was to be increased from three to four years.

At HKU, the opportunity was grasped to rebuild the undergraduate curriculum from the ground up, incorporating new components intended to make the curriculum more suited to the demands of the 21st century. These new components included a large interdisciplinary Common Core component, integrated overseas and mainland Chinese experiential learning opportunities for all undergraduates, greatly expanded online and mobile learning opportunities, and a greater emphasis on students' generic skills and attributes, such as critical and creative thinking, tackling uncertainty, communication skills, leadership and entrepreneurship skills, and so on (HKU, n.d.). During the curriculum design process, CETL provided a great deal of expert guidance to program teams that were responsible for rethinking their curricula and integrating the new components in creative ways. Several faculties found the process of redesigning their curricula somewhat challenging, and CETL was instrumental in providing them with the required expert support.

CETL's More Recent Contributions

Immediately following the introduction of the new four-year curriculum in 2012, CETL was called upon to provide pedagogic support for faculties as they implemented their new curricula. Students were coming to the university at a younger age than in previous years and had a range of different needs. Courses had been redesigned, new components had been introduced, and assumptions about student engagement had changed. All in all, CETL provided a valuable enabling service by listening to teachers, collaborating with them, and helping them to thrive in the changed circumstances. It was during this time that HKU set to work developing a new teaching and learning strategy, called the '3+1 I's' teaching and learning strategy, which would support the new curriculum and become an integral part of the university's vision to become "Asia's Global University", as detailed in the institution's 2016–2025 strategic plan (HKU, 2016).

594   G. T. Bilbow

The components of the '3+1 I's' strategy—standing for *internationalization*, *innovation*, and *interdisciplinarity*, converging on *impact*—were intended to reinforce the principal novel elements of the new four-year curriculum and ensure that the university's teaching and learning practices supported students' development of, alongside disciplinary knowledge, a range of attributes befitting the 21st century, including a global outlook, creative mindset, and a more nuanced, multifaceted perspective on studies and the world beyond. It was no coincidence that the launch of the strategy in 2016 coincided with the first graduating cohort of the new four-year curriculum.

With the launch of the '3+1 I's' teaching and learning strategy, CETL was called upon to support the operationalization of the strategy across the university. This time too, the support provided by CETL was not so much instructional as facilitative, listening to and collaborating with teachers and helping them to identify and share ways in which their curricula, assessment, and pedagogy embraced identified characteristics of internationalization, innovation, and interdisciplinarity and exercised a significant, positive impact on student learning.

Changing the 'what' and 'how' of CETL

It is clear from the above description of HKU's academic development over the past two decades that a substantial transition took place roughly midway through that period, precipitated by the task of creating the new four-year curriculum that began in 2010. Prior to this transition, HKU had enthusiastically adopted educational reforms, such as the move toward OBE, in an effort to remain at the forefront of undergraduate education globally; however, the university had tended neither to initiate change nor to systematically embed change at the faculty and departmental levels. Up to this point, CETL had primarily been called upon to provide standardized training interventions to support the process of reform across faculties—a process that, frankly, had met with varying degrees of success over time.

This situation was to start to change in 2010, however, when the university embarked on a new type of reform process when it began to design the new four-year curriculum, led by the then-vice president for teaching and learning, Prof. Amy Tsui Bik May, and subsequently developed the '3+1 I's' teaching and learning strategy under the leadership of her successor, Prof. Ian Holliday. Reform was no longer to reflect the previous reform processes outlined above; it was to be a far more distributed and engaged process, based on the involvement of a range of stakeholders from across the university.

As a part of this reform, the *what* and *how* of CETL were to be revisited. In terms of the *what*, the center was to go beyond simply offering a list of capacity-building, instructional activities repeated annually, and start to get involved in activities related to *advocacy*, *facilitation*, and *rapid response*, all requiring a close and supportive relationship with faculties. As for the *how* of the center, CETL was to become an important vehicle for ensuring that the change process across the university was concerted, harmonious, and avoided some of the patchiness and lack of clarity that had previously impeded reform in the past. In short, the center would not only change its range of activities, it would also change *how* it engaged in these activities. Our relationship with faculties would in future become far more collegial, collaborative, and facilitative.

Toward a Theory of Change

The CETL's transition into its new, expanded set of roles was to be underpinned by a theory of change, a well-established methodology for planning, undertaking, and evaluating systemic change in organizations. Being highly sensitive to the context in which complex change is planned, the theory of change methodology is suited to the planning of change in not-for-profit, government, or educational organizations, such as HKU.

It is perhaps surprising how many universities have traditionally been more engrossed in describing their activities than in describing their impact. In essence, theory of change methodology involves the reverse. It begins with the specification of the desired impact, and then works backward to planning activities and their outputs and outcomes. This results in what is known as a 'results chain', consisting of the following four 'links'.

Activities

These refer to the following: the repertoire of professional development programs designed and delivered; the range of seminars, workshops, and other events run throughout the year; the regular meetings (both formal and informal) held with faculties, departments, and program teams; the research projects conducted by CETL staff, individually and collaboratively; the conferences organized, and so on.

Outputs

These refer to the immediate effects and deliverables of program and policy activities, including, for example: the number of staff attending CETL programs, workshops, and events; the number of meetings held in collaboration with faculties; the number of scholarly contributions by CETL staff, individually and collaboratively, and so on.

Outcomes

These refer to the actual or anticipated effects of program and policy activities in the short and medium term, including: curriculum and assessment changes; changes in teachers' classroom behaviors; changes in local and international understanding of good curriculum, assessment, and pedagogic practices, and so on.

Impact

This refers to the long-term effects of program and policy activities, both intended and unintended, direct and indirect, and positive and negative. Impact includes "the higher-order effects and broader changes to which an intervention may be contributing" (Organization for Economic Co-operation and Development/Development Assistance Committee Network on Development Evaluation, 2019).

All theories of change, including our own, start with situational and problem analyses, which take account of the contributions and views of a wide range of interconnected stakeholders, and they all result in the creation of a results chain involving multiple critical pathways of change that both reflect and challenge prevailing cultural habits. While some of these pathways can be identified and planned relatively straightforwardly, others—especially where change involves sensitive issues and a range of stakeholders—can only be identified and planned more tentatively and may evolve more gradually.

CETL's Decision-Making Model

As mentioned previously, the theory of change methodology is highly suited to planning change in complex, not-for-profit organizations, such as universities. Part of the complexity of such organizations is that the work they undertake is typically not simple and straightforward but requires expert knowledge and the ability to cope with ambiguity and uncertainty. In the process of developing a theory of change in such organizations, it is helpful to adopt a sophisticated, context-sensitive decision-making model.

The Cynefin Network

According to literature in the area of decision-making, a Cynefin network (originating from the Welsh word *cynefin* signifying a habitat or place of multiple belonging) is a "decision-making framework that recognizes the causal differences that exist between system types ... and proposes new approaches to decision-making in complex social environments" (Snowden, 2010). A Cynefin network, as can be seen in Fig. 38.1, identifies four types of situations: *simple* (or 'obvious'), *complicated*, *complex*, and *chaotic*.

Simple (or 'Obvious') Decision-Making Situations

A *simple* situation is a decision-making context in which the solutions to problems are known, formulaic, and sometimes automated. An example of a simple decision-making situation would be office filing, where fairly simple and straightforward rules regulate decisions. In such simple situations, the

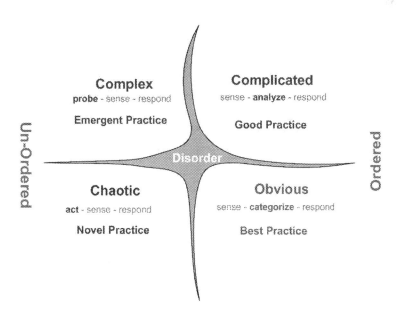

Fig. 38.1 Cynefin network (Figure reproduced with permission from Kurtz and Snowden, 2003)

G. T. Bilbow

response sequence is SENSE-CATEGORIZE-RESPOND, where problems are identified and classified into pre-established categories and standardized responses are applied. Generally, it is possible to talk of 'best practice' in simple situations, such as with office filing.

Complicated Decision-Making Situations

In contrast to a simple situation, a *complicated* situation is one in which the solution to a problem is known or knowable, but requires specialist knowledge to understand. An example of a complicated situation would be meteorology, where a high degree of knowledge is required in order to respond reliably to weather patterns. In complicated situations, the response sequence is SENSE-ANALYSE-RESPOND, where reference is made to established knowledge in order to analyze a problem prior to responding. However, even an expert with considerable knowledge and experience can be wrong-footed; so, at best, we can likely only talk about 'good (or wise) practice', rather than best practice, in more complicated situations like weather forecasting.

Complex Decision-Making Situations

A situation in which the solution to a problem is unknowable, but can be discerned in retrospect, is termed a *complex* situation. Decision-making situations in the area of genetic research, for example, tend to be complex and draw upon analyses that may be contested and not entirely reliable, and may substantially vary from one observer to another. In complex situations, the response sequence is PROBE-SENSE-RESPOND, where exploratory research is essential before a response is possible, but even then, the response needs to be tentative. The term 'emergent practice' is used to describe practices that arise as exploratory research bears fruit, such as in genetic research.

Chaotic Decision-Making Situations

In *chaotic* decision-making situations, it is impossible to reliably identify cause-and-effect relationships, as events occur haphazardly. Examples of chaotic situations are natural disasters, where random events occur concurrently and entirely unpredictably. In such situations, the response sequence is ACT-SENSE-RESPOND, whereby 'novel' decision-making practices spring up in response to rapidly changing circumstances, driven by the need to act quickly, and in some cases to save lives, as in disaster scenarios.

A Combined Cynefin and Standard+Case Approach

Research in service management has led to a more refined version of the Cynefin network, referred to as the Cynefin and Standard+Case case-based approach, which has been applied primarily in the field of information technology service management (England, 2013). This approach works when traditional approaches "struggle when it comes to addressing lower volume, unpredictable and sometimes highly complex requests" (Kofax Inc., 2012). As demonstrated in Fig. 38.2, the Cynefin and Standard+Case approach is a combination of a standard process-based approach to decision-making (employing the Cynefin network) and a case management approach typically used in sectors such as health, social work, and law. In such contexts, only a limited number of problems are standard and require formulaic resolution, and even fewer can be handled in an automated fashion. In many cases, situations are so complicated, complex, and occasionally chaotic, that responses need to be tailored on a case-by-case basis, using expertise, experience, and professional intuition.[1]

The Cynefin and Standard+Case model demonstrates that while standardization is appropriate for addressing simple situations, it tends to be ill-suited

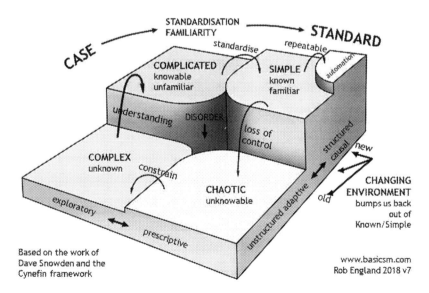

Fig. 38.2 The Cynefin and Standard+Case approach (Figure reproduced with permission from England, 2013)

600 G. T. Bilbow

to making decisions in complicated, complex, and chaotic situations. Thus, in universities such as HKU, which are extremely complex entities, the standardized instructional programs of the type traditionally offered by CETL and other teaching and learning centers around the world may only serve a limited function in achieving cultural change.

In recognition of this, the center's role in recent years has expanded to encompass a far broader range of activities to address problems that vary in their complexity and call for distinct decision-making responses. We have found that the Cynefin and Standard+Case approach—which advocates a range of less prescriptive and more exploratory responses in order to make the complex less unfamiliar and more knowable through increased understanding—has helped us to achieve significant progress in the following areas.

Instruction

This takes place in a relatively simple decision-making situation requiring a SENSE-CATEGORIZE-RESPOND sequence and a high level of standardization. The mandatory professional development programs designed by CETL and delivered to new academic staff and graduate teaching assistants (GTAs) across HKU, are examples of how the center has responded to a simple decision-making situation requiring a standardized response referenced to internationally recognized best practice.

Advocacy

This takes place in a relatively complicated decision-making situation requiring a SENSE-ANALYSE-RESPOND sequence, bringing specialist knowledge and experience to bear. The advocacy provided by CETL on a broad range of good (or wise) curriculum, assessment, and pedagogic practices is an example of how the center has responded to complex decision-making situations that require reliable knowledge supported by scholarly research in the area, some of which is generated by CETL staff themselves through their personal scholarship.

Facilitation

This takes place in complex decision-making situations requiring a PROBE-SENSE-RESPOND sequence and an exploratory approach involving dialogue across faculties, departments, and programs that is sensitive to individual needs, preferences, and practices (Bilbow et al., 2017). The cross-faculty surfacing and celebrating of emergent practices across the university are examples of how CETL has used its expertise to respond to the highly complex differences that exist across HKU.

Rapid Response

This takes place in (mercifully rare) chaotic decision-making situations requiring an ACT-SENSE-RESPOND sequence to take rapid action to address unforeseen circumstances. CETL's rapid response to the issue of end-of-term assessment during the recent political unrest in Hong Kong and during the global coronavirus pandemic, when all classes were canceled, are examples of CETL's capacity to provide a rapid response and to adapt to uncertain circumstances.

Our adapted version of the Cynefin and Standard+Case approach in Fig. 38.3 illustrates how CETL's decision-making practices have been applied across the center's expanded set of roles since 2010 as part of our theory of change.

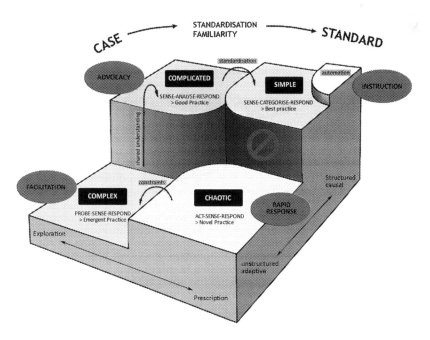

Fig. 38.3 CETL's decision-making model based on the combined Cynefin network and Standard+Case model (Figure reproduced with permission from England, 2013)

CETL's Results Chain and Logframe

As mentioned in the preceding section, an important part of planning change in CETL involved creating a results chain that identified the activities, outputs, outcomes, and intended impact of planned changes. This results chain can also be represented as a 'logframe'—a systematic visual representation of the logical flow of outputs and outcomes that link the achievement of activity targets and the delivery of intended impact. The benefit of a logframe is that it enables planners to establish and communicate changes in the form of a clear development pathway.

The results chain of CETL in relation to its *activities*, *outputs*, *outcomes*, and *impact* over the past seven years is described below with reference to each of CETL's roles (*instruction*, *advocacy*, *facilitation*, and *rapid response*). The completed logframe appears in Table 38.1.

Stage 1: Activities

Relative to its other activities, CETL's *instruction-related activities* have not grown substantially over the past decade. In the past year, CETL has successfully achieved accredited status for its three-program HKU-AdvanceHE Fellowship Scheme. All of the center's continuing professional development programs are now linked to different levels of AdvanceHE fellowship (i.e., associate fellowship, fellowship, and senior fellowship) and are scaffolded with quality-assured mentoring for those who elect to seek fellowship. Although rather less instructional than exploratory, the center's principal continuing professional development and leadership program, the three-day full-time Professional Certificate in Teaching and Learning in Higher Education (PCTLHE), is now mandatory, and the scale of this operation has grown considerably as a consequence. The aim of the program is to help senior academic managers across the university address teaching and learning management issues in their faculties and provide guidance as AdvanceHE fellowship mentors. CETL has also designed and launched a new teaching and learning massive open online course (MOOC) for an international audience of teachers new to higher education. Interestingly, this program has had a measure of washback into the center's one-month, full-time Certificate in Teaching and Learning in Higher Education (CTLHE) program for research postgraduate students who serve as GTAs at HKU.

In contrast to CETL's purely instructional activities, its *advocacy-related activities* have grown considerably over the past six or seven years. For

Table 38.1 CETL's logframe for change

	INSTRUCTION Simple SENSE-CATEGORISE-RESPOND		ADVOCACY Complicated SENSE-ANALYSE-RESPOND		FACILITATION Complex PROBE-SENSE-RESPOND	RAPID RESPONSE Chaotic ACT-SENSE-RESPOND
ACTIVITIES	3-day FT PCTLHE introductory programme for new academic staff One-month FT CLTLHE programme for RPg GTAs	3-day FT PCITLHE leadership programme for academic managers Training for HKU-AdvanceHE mentors CETL T&L MOOC programme	Theme-led workshops & seminars CETL research & scholarship Stewardship of the HKU-AdvanceHE Fellowship Scheme CETL-organised T&L conferences	CETL participation in faculty committees CETL involvement in Teaching Award mentorship and selection Feedback/ discussion on student learning experience feedback	Identifying/ sharing emergent practices (JTCs) Regular collaborative T&L e-newsletters Mentoring AdvanceHE fellow applicants Joint pedagogic research with faculties	Cross-faculty brainstorming
OUTPUTS	Approx. 200 new academic staff trained annually Approx. 500 new RPg GTAs trained annually	Approx. 25 academic managers trained annually Approx. 25 AdvanceHE fellowship mentors trained annually Approx. 2500 international teachers exposed to good practice annually	~1000 non-unique academic staff exposed to good practices in six key areas 3 CPD programme-Scheme accredited by AdvanceHE ~20 T&L research papers published annually	CETL staff participation in T&L committees in all 10 faculties ~15 HKU TAs awarded annually T&L feedback/discussions held in all 10 faculties	~15 cross-faculty panel-led sharing sessions held annually on emergent practices ~100 staff mentored for and receive AdvanceHE fellowship ~20 CETL T&L research projects annually and joint publications	Viable responses to the need for rapid action, eg a viable secure online assessment alternative to proctored end-of-term examinations when classes were cancelled during student protests
OUTCOMES (Short-term)	Threshold teaching and learning competence among new staff Basic T&L competence among RPg GTAs	Critical mass of effective academic managers across HKU Adequate supply of AdvanceHE fellowship mentors	Common understanding of good T&L practices across the University	Greater respect for the relevance of CETL in faculty processes	Joint scholarly activities with staff in faculties Increased scholarly reflection in faculties Greater attendance to emergent practices in faculties	Continued teaching and learning, even in difficult circumstances
OUTCOMES (Long-term)	Critical mass of competent, open-minded and proactive teaching staff across HKU	A robust and sustainable HKU-AdvanceHE Fellowship Scheme	Enhanced international esteem for T&L at HKU achieved through scholarly activity	High level of pro-active ownership of T&L issues in faculties	Symbiotic collaborative relationship between CETL and faculties, based on mutual respect	A robust teaching and learning environment less prone to disruption
IMPACT (Individual)	Better, more informed teaching practices (including cutting edge practices). Improved and more scaffolded career pathway and prospects (even for GTAs). Enhanced promotion opportunities. Greater opportunities to conduct T&L research and share emergent practices. Greater sense of teaching and learning community. Greater job satisfaction.					
IMPACT (Institutional)	Enhanced student learning. Better and more informed coordination of T&L across the institution and more principled decision-making, even in chaotic situations. More informed T&L management. More communication pathways and better sharing of T&L practices. More consistent and principled treatment of T&L in comparison with research. Better T&L funding opportunities and better use of T&L funding. Enhanced T&L reputation locally and internationally.					

GLOSSARY

AdvanceHE: Former Higher Education Academy UK (HEA)
FT: Full-time/ PT: Part-time
GTA: Graduate Teaching Assistant

JTC: Join-the-Conversation event
MOOC: Massive Open Online Course
RPg: Research postgraduate student

PCLTLHE: Professional Certificate in Leading Teaching and Learning in Higher Education
PCTLHE: Professional Certificate in Teaching and Learning in Higher Education
PCTLHE: Certificate in Teaching and Learning in Higher Education

T&L: Teaching and Learning
TA: Teaching Award

604   G. T. Bilbow

example, the center's regular voluntary workshops and seminars for academic staff across faculties (approximately 40 events annually) now focus on topics where the university advocates the use of specific good practices in areas of strategic development (e.g., internationalization, interdisciplinarity, pedagogic innovation, treating students as partners, embedding research in the undergraduate curriculum, and staff mentorship). These workshops draw upon CETL's research, as well as expertise sourced from outside of the university. Advocacy is also a key function of the regular international and local teaching and learning conferences organized by CETL approximately every two years, to which all HKU academic staff are invited to present papers drawing upon their own scholarly activities. A particularly key initiative advocated for by CETL over the past two years is the HKU-AdvanceHE Fellowship Scheme, as the university sees this as an important element of its staff development planning for the coming decade.

CETL's *facilitation-related activities* have also grown in recent years. They inevitably overlap to some extent with advocacy-related activities, especially when they are connected with so-called meso and faculty-level change. The aim of facilitation is to assist individuals and groups of staff in faculties with their own personal development agendas. For example, CETL staff regularly contribute to teaching and learning research projects led by academic staff in a range of faculties, mentor academic staff for the HKU-AdvanceHE Fellowship Scheme, and work with academic staff to surface and share their emergent practices through the 15 or so 'Join-the-Conversation' events conducted annually, so that these practices can be appreciated by others. These emergent practices are often written up as case studies that appear in the center's quarterly e-newsletter, *Teaching and Learning Connections* (Carless, 2016; Chan, 2016).

It is important to point out that all of the center's advocacy and facilitation-related activities are underpinned by a desire not to impose change on faculties, but to work in a collegial and facilitative way with groups of academic staff in faculties to enhance student learning. CETL staff now collaborate with faculties not only through representation on their formal committees; they also contribute to regular informal discussions in faculties about teaching enhancement as well.

A relatively recent addition to the activities of CETL is *rapid response activities*. These involve a consultative process conducted with faculties to brainstorm alternative solutions to quickly emerging teaching and learning problems and find viable and rapidly implementable solutions. During the recent widespread student protests at HKU, for example, all class teaching was suspended, and along with it, proctored end-of-term examinations. A viable and quickly implementable solution was urgently required, and the one that emerged in consultation with faculties took the form of secure online end-of-term assessment—an initiative developed in the space of four weeks and delivered to large groups of students, the largest being a group of 900 students from the Faculty of Business and Economics. During the coronavirus pandemic, a similar consultative process was conducted with faculties, involving brainstorming solutions to the pedagogic challenges faced by the university.

Stage 2: Outputs

The outputs of the center's *instruction-related activities* include approximately 200 new academic staff annually who receive PCTLHE training and approximately 500 new research postgraduate GTAs who receive CTLHE training annually. Each year, around 25 AdvanceHE fellowship mentors are also trained. Although of a different nature, the center's teaching and learning MOOC attracts about 2,500 students from around the world every year (of which about 11% qualify for certification).

As for the center's *advocacy-related activities*, outputs from the workshops and seminars conducted by CETL throughout the year include the approximately 1,000 non-unique academic staff from across HKU who have been exposed to good practices in a variety of strategically important areas. CETL staff's research in the form of approximately 20 research papers in high-impact factor journals each year supports these events. Although difficult to quantify, the many meetings between CETL staff and groups of academic staff in faculties in relation to teaching and learning also contribute to the center's advocacy-related activities. Finally, the recent successful accreditation of CETL's continuing professional development programs was an important output that reflected the university's advocacy for an internationally benchmarked, standards-based framework for recognizing and rewarding quality in teaching.

Next, the outputs from CETL's *facilitation-related activities* include the approximately 100 faculty staff that are mentored for, and receive, their AdvanceHE fellowship; the approximately 50 academic staff that serve on panel-led 'Join-the-Conversation' events every year; as well as the approximately 500 non-unique academic staff that attend them. CETL's joint research activities with staff in other faculties also generate research publications annually, as well as 20–30 articles that appear in CETL's quarterly e-newsletter every year. These articles are, in turn, read by approximately 1,000 non-unique individuals, including both HKU staff and international readers.

606   G. T. Bilbow

Lastly, the output from CETL's *rapid response-related activities* in the past year was growth in the use of effective online teaching and learning and a viable, large-scale, secure online assessment alternative to proctored end-of-term examinations when classes were canceled.

Stage 3: Outcomes

The short-term outcome of the center's *instruction-related activities* has been a regular flow of new academic staff and research postgraduate GTAs who possess threshold teaching and learning competence and basic teaching and learning competence, respectively, and teaching and learning managers with enhanced management skills and skills in mentoring more junior staff. Longer term, we have started to build a critical mass of highly professional, competent, and proactive academic staff across HKU whose teaching and learning prowess matches or exceeds their research prowess, and a robust HKU-AdvanceHE Fellowship Scheme, which provides staff with a clearer career pathway and the means for promotion.

The short-term outcome of the center's *advocacy-related activities* has been growth in a common understanding of good teaching and learning practices across the university, and increased scholarly activity to underpin these good practices, which, in the longer term, has further enhanced the teaching and learning reputation of HKU and CETL.

The short-term outcome of the center's *facilitation-related activities* has been an increase in scholarly reflection in faculties, fueled partly by an interest in AdvanceHE fellowship, greater attendance to emergent practices in faculties brought about through joint scholarly activities with staff in faculties, and regular scholarly sharing. Longer term, we have observed a higher level of proactive ownership of teaching and learning in faculties and a greater respect for the relevance of CETL in supporting faculties.

Lastly, the short-term outcome of CETL's *rapid response-related activity* this year was a relatively uninterrupted teaching, learning, and assessment operation, even in the difficult circumstances faced by the university. The longer-term outcome will be a more robust teaching and learning environment that is less prone to disruption by unforeseen circumstances. Interestingly, secure online assessment, which was initially considered a 'novel' practice for HKU, has since become an 'emergent' practice, and in time, may come to be seen as a 'good' (or wise) practice.

Stage 4: Impact

This is the most challenging aspect of the results chain to evidence. However, the qualitative, interview-based evidence we have gathered from a range of stakeholders suggests that much of the impact predicted in our theory of change has been achieved or is currently in progress. At the individual level, our combination of instruction, advocacy, and facilitation appears to have led to better and more informed teaching practices across HKU. This comment from an academic staff member in the Faculty of Arts suggests that CETL resources and activities that share good practices are found useful in supporting effective teaching:

> We can access valuable online resource repositories about best practices of teaching and learning. One example is the types of assessment in Common Core courses at HKU. The research findings from CETL have facilitated us as coordinators to strengthen the curriculum of [course name], a course for year 1 undergraduate students. (Member of Staff 1, HKU)

Other comments, including this one, also from an academic staff member in the Faculty of Arts, refer to the perceived value of scholarly reflection:

> It does come to mind as I am going about my day-to-day work sometimes. So, it is a form of noticing things that maybe I haven't noticed before … previously I would just do them from my instinct. (Member of Staff 2, HKU)

Such reflection has also helped the growth of a common language for talking about teaching and learning, as this comment from an academic staff member from the Faculty of Law suggests: "It is the first time and the only time to talk about what we truly feel about teaching and learning."

The HKU-AdvanceHE Fellowship Scheme also shows encouraging signs of enhancing career pathways and prospects for academic staff and GTAs and providing the opportunity for a teaching community to grow, leading to greater job satisfaction. This comment from an academic staff member in the Faculty of Architecture suggests that staff, especially new staff, appreciate the teaching community that has started to grow at HKU:

> I was completely new to the academic world. I knew very little about assessment or internationalization or any of this stuff … I think I need to learn from others what all this is about. I like to talk to people who also care about teaching and learning. (Member of Staff 3, HKU)

608   G. T. Bilbow

Another comment from a member of academic staff from the Faculty of Social Sciences illustrates other perceived benefits of the HKU-AdvanceHE Fellowship Scheme:

> I just finished the round of PRSD [Performance Review and Staff Development], a performance review on non-academic staff. I used some of the materials from this program when I did the performance review, so I was more able to mentor my colleagues, giving comments and suggesting specific ways they can improve. (Member of Staff 4, HKU)

At the institutional level, the evidence we have collected suggests that CETL's combination of instruction, advocacy, and facilitation activities has also supported more informed teaching and learning management and better coordination of teaching and learning across the institution, along with more principled decision-making, even in chaotic situations. This comment from an academic staff member from the Faculty of Arts supports this conclusion:

> The institution itself doesn't normally train its managers at all, just assumes that they are capable of being given the opportunity to do it. And I think, to some extent, it is a problem. And we seldom have an opportunity or a platform that is so exclusive, just teaching and learning, and nothing else. (Member of Staff 5, HKU)

Another comment from an academic staff member in the Faculty of Architecture indicates that CETL's support has strengthened their ability to coordinate teaching and learning in a larger context:

> Now I am being drawn to a wider department, a bigger teaching unit, the Dean asked me to look at how I take these teaching techniques across the entire faculty. This is going to be a big challenge. I am very grateful for your support which provided me with different perspectives to ponder over and plan my work strategically. (Member of Staff 6, HKU)

Finally, there is some evidence to suggest that HKU is now making more productive use of its teaching and learning research project funding, and that this is enhancing the university's reputation in the area of teaching and learning, both locally and internationally. This may, in turn, lead to a higher level of respect being shown for teaching and learning across faculties, along with more consistent and principled treatment of teaching activities in comparison with research activities. As an academic member of staff in the Faculty of Science put it:

I think the community for research is pretty well established ... it is systematic. But really, there has not been enough for teaching. I think more opportunities to have more discussions about teaching will be better. Perhaps you can have information sharing. I just ... think research develops very fast, but teaching does not change so much. (Member of Staff 7, HKU)

Conclusion

Trowler et al. (2005) identify and discuss the three levels of engagement in change in higher education. The first is the micro-level reflective practitioner, who has the potential to be a lone change agent. The second is the macro-level institution, a learning organization in which change "stems from alterations in organizational routines, practices and values" (427). The third is the intermediate or meso level, which refers to social practices at a departmental or subdepartmental level. It is this level which, according to Trowler et al. (2005), is essential for diffusion of innovations and culture changes and which is missing in many teaching and learning enhancement initiatives in higher education. As the authors state, the meso level is where "changes actually take place" (435).

Analysis of the impact of the change process that CETL has undergone over the past six or seven years reveals that a number of enhancements have come about, partly as a result of the theory of change that has been planned and implemented, especially at the meso level. First, there has been encouraging growth in a quality-oriented teaching and learning community of practice encompassing pockets of academics in most, if not all, HKU faculties. Within faculties, communication about teaching and learning in these groups has been enhanced, and there is now far greater bottom-up sharing of emerging teaching and learning practices, which have resulted in enhanced teaching practices and student learning. Secondly, there is now far better teaching and learning coordination at an institutional, strategic level, accompanied by more committed teaching and learning management at the faculty level. Again, this has been an impressive achievement; however, it is not universal. Thirdly, with the help of the HKU-AdvanceHE Fellowship Scheme, progress has been made in creating improved teaching career pathways and promotion prospects, especially for academic-related teaching staff. Finally, HKU's reputation for high-quality teaching and learning has been enhanced as the new teaching and learning culture has become more established; this, in turn, has resulted in the emergence of a healthier and more balanced view regarding the respective roles of teaching and research at the university.

610 G. T. Bilbow

Many challenges have arisen during this process of change and not all of them have been successfully resolved. First, not all faculties have embraced change to the same extent. In response, we have recognized the value of working in collaboration with faculties and respecting faculty priorities and practices, again especially at the meso level (e.g., with program and course teams). This has necessitated an understanding of the value of dialogue rather than monologue (Stensaker et al., 2017). Secondly, faculties tend to develop at their own pace, so we have come to appreciate that change inevitably takes time and varies in speed from one context to another and one person to another. Thirdly, we have realized that, in the past, CETL occasionally fell into the trap of not listening to academics in faculties, but instead preaching to them. Therefore, we have learnt to be less prescriptive in our views about 'best' practices and now fully recognize the value of identifying, surfacing, and celebrating locally emerging 'good' practices at the meso level. Lastly, while we understand that teaching and learning enhancement requires leadership, we have also come to realize the importance of developing collegial and productive relationships with faculties, and identifying those groups of reflective academics who acknowledge the need for change and are willing to take action to achieve and then advocate to others. As we look to the future, there is far more we can and should accomplish with these groups at the meso level within the university.

Note

1. The stop sign ($\oslash$) at the interface between simple and chaotic situations in Fig. 38.2 indicates that, while both simple and chaotic situations benefit from quick responses, the standardized responses adopted in simple situations do not usually prove effective in chaotic situations. Indeed, in such situations, a standardized response may exacerbate a chaotic situation. An example would be the use of a standardized form-filling process to respond in the case of a natural disaster.

References

Bilbow, G. T., Hounsell, D., & Zou, T. (2017). Fostering dialogue about practices. In B. Stensaker, G. T. Bilbow, L. Breslow, & R. Van Der Vaart (Eds.), *Strengthening teaching and learning in research-intensive universities* (pp. 161–185). Palgrave Macmillan.

Carless, D. (2016). Scaling up assessment for learning, *Teaching and Learning Connections, 2.* https://www.cetl.hku.hk/teaching-learning-cop/scaling-up-assessment-for-learning/

Centre for the Enhancement of Teaching and Learning (CETL). (n.d.-a). *HKU centre for the enhancement of teaching and learning.* HKU. https://www.cetl.hku.hk/

CETL (n.d.-b). *Outcomes-based approaches to student learning.* HKU. https://www.cetl.hku.hk/obasl/

Chan, K. (2016). Learning to be a better teacher: What can a novice teacher educator learn from his students through engaging in formative assessment practices? *Teaching and Learning Connections, 2.* https://www.cetl.hku.hk/teaching-learning-cop/learning-to-be-a-better-teacher/

England, R. (2013). Standard+case and Cynefin. In *Plus! The standard+case approach.* Two Hills Ltd. http://www.basicsm.com/public/standard_plus_case_and_cynefin_v1.pdf

University of Hong Kong (HKU). (2016). *Asia's global university: The next decade – Our vision for 2016–2025.* HKU. https://www.sppoweb.hku.hk/vision2016-2025.pdf

University of Hong Kong (HKU). (n.d.). *A transformative undergraduate curriculum.* HKU. https://tl.hku.hk/flexible-curriculum-structure/

Kofax Inc. (2012). *Using case management to empower employees and transform customer service* (White paper). Kofax Inc.

Kurtz, C. F., & Snowden, D. J. (2003). The new dynamics of strategy in a complex and complicated world. *IBM Systems Journal, 42*(3), 462–483.

Organization for Economic Co-operation and Development/Development Assistance Committee Network on Development Evaluation. (2019). *Better criteria for better evaluation.* Organisation for Economic Co-operation and Development. http://www.oecd.org/dac/evaluation/

Quacquarelli Symonds (QS) Top Universities. (2018). *QS world university rankings 2018.* QS Ltd. https://www.topuniversities.com/university-rankings/world-university-rankings/2018

Snowden, D. J. (2010). *The Cynefin framework* (Video). Uploaded by Cognitive Edge Network. YouTube. https://www.youtube.com/watch?time_continue=101&v=N7oz366X0-8&feature=emb_title

Stensaker, B., Bilbow, G. T., Breslow, L., & Van Der Vaart, R. (Eds.). (2017). *Strengthening teaching and learning in research-intensive universities.* Palgrave Macmillan.

Trowler, P., Fanghanel, J., & Wareham, T. (2005). Freeing the Chi of change: The Higher Education Academy and enhancing teaching and learning in higher education. *Studies in Higher Education, 30*(4), 427–444.

39

Developing Beginner University Teachers' Pedagogical Competencies Through a Professional Development Program

Roman Švaříček, Ingrid Procházková, Jeffrey A. Vanderziel, and Klára Šeďová

Introduction

This chapter focuses on improving the pedagogical competencies of university teachers through participation in a professional development program. Firstly, we describe our academic professional development center and its mission and structure. Secondly, we describe the objectives, methods, and findings of initial empirical research conducted on beginning university teachers and their approaches to teaching and professional self-perceptions. This research project was conducted to analyze how researchers, teachers, and teacher-researchers approach teaching. We identified three different sets of beliefs about teaching among early-career faculty members who each conceived of their roles differently: researchers emphasized the transmission of knowledge, while teachers emphasized that good teaching should include devoting time and energy to students and universalists emphasized the practical nature of knowledge and motivated students to work by themselves. The research outcomes substantially informed the professional development program that was subsequently established. Finally, we describe this four-module professional

---

R. Švaříček (✉) • I. Procházková • J. A. Vanderziel • K. Šeďová
Masaryk University, Brno, Czech Republic
e-mail: svaricek@phil.muni.cz; prochazkova@cerpek.muni.cz;
vanderziel@cerpek.muni.cz; ksedova@phil.muni.cz

© The Author(s), under exclusive license to Springer Nature Switzerland AG 2023
O. J. Neisler (ed.), *The Palgrave Handbook of Academic Professional Development Centers*,
Palgrave Studies on Leadership and Learning in Teacher Education,
https://doi.org/10.1007/978-3-030-80967-6_39

614   R. Švaříček et al.

development program in more detail, including the curriculum design process, how we teach beginner university teachers, issues with funding for training university teachers, and the feedback we have received from program participants.

About the Center

The Pedagogical Competence Development Centre (CERPEK) of Masaryk University (MUNI) in Brno, Czech Republic, was founded in 2017 as a component of the Academic Affairs Office of the Rector's Office (MUNI, n.d.). Since 2019, it has been an independent center that reports directly to the vice-rector for academic affairs. The CERPEK is a professional center that covers the needs of the entire university. Its goal is to systematically and continually improve the pedagogical competencies of university teachers based on traditional knowledge and modern trends, as well as on modern local and international educational research. Thus, the CERPEK contributes to improving and maintaining the quality and effectiveness of university teaching and improving student success rates. It is the only center of its type, not only at MUNI, but in the entire Czech Republic (Mudrak et al., 2018; Pabian et al., 2011).

The CERPEK is, at present, a relatively small center with three employees, including a director with a full-time-equivalent (FTE) workload of 1.0 and two project administrators, each with an FTE workload of 0.5, who also work on a project funded by the European Union's European Structural and Investment Fund and the Czech Republic's Ministry of Education, Youth and Sports. Additionally, around 40–50 external staff members (including lecturers, experts, mentors, and support staff) are involved in CERPEK' activities every year. In addition, the CERPEK receives limited university funding to provide workshops focused on specific topics. An advisory board ensures that CERPEK's activities and goals are in keeping with the university's strategic plans.

MUNI founded the CERPEK in response to global trends recognizing the importance of teaching excellence at universities, where teaching is considered to be an activity that is equally as important as science and research. Universities traditionally combine science and research with teaching, and there is a commonly held belief that the best researchers are also the best teachers. In reality, however, this idea is not so straightforward. Whereas young academics in the Czech Republic are well-prepared for research careers during their studies, as a rule they are not prepared at all for their teaching careers (Johannes et al., 2013).

Although Czech university teachers have excellent knowledge of the specific contents of their respective fields, they tend to lack didactic knowledge of this content.

In addition, universities often recruit teachers from the ranks of their doctoral students, who acquire pedagogical competencies in a nonsystematic manner and who often establish poor teaching habits based on a lack of reflective observation or using a trial-and-error method (Anderson & Anderson, 2012; Golde, 2008; Hativa et al., 2001; Iglesias-Martínez et al., 2014; Tůma & Knecht, 2019). This state of affairs makes it difficult to improve the quality of university teaching, and this is where the CERPEK comes in: its objective is to eliminate such problems by providing systematic pedagogical instruction to faculty.

Initial Empirical Research on Beginner University Teachers

In 2015, university leaders agreed on the need to develop a strategy for educating academic staff at MUNI that focused on developing their pedagogical competencies. Although this strategy was supposed to draw from foreign experience, examples of good practice, and empirical studies, it was to be based primarily on research conducted by MUNI researchers on early-career academics working at the university (Čejková, 2017; Šeďová et al., 2016). To collect these data, we conducted a research project on early-career faculty members' perceptions of themselves as professionals and their beliefs about teaching.

Methods, Data Collection, and Data Analysis

The empirical research was conducted between September and November 2015. We posed the following two research questions: (1) *What are beginning university teachers' approaches to teaching?* and (2) *What is the relationship between beginning university teachers' approaches to teaching and their professional self-perception?*

In the first step of our study, we defined beginner teachers at MUNI as those who had less than five years of experience (Berliner, 1986). We decided to use purposive sampling because of the qualitative research design. To choose our sample from the total population of 200 beginner teachers at MUNI, we applied further criteria that indicated how successful these

616   R. Švaříček et al.

teachers were, determined by how the teachers were evaluated in student course assessments. Applying this criterion, we selected a sample of 30 teachers distributed among all nine of MUNI's faculties. We chose only teachers who were evaluated as above average by their students in course evaluations, as well as those who actually taught at least one course. We contacted each teacher individually by e-mail and asked if they would like to take part in our study. In the end, we had 19 respondents, of which 14 were male and five female.

Given the research questions, we chose to collect data using in-depth, semi-structured interviews. We created a checklist of 13 open-ended questions that focused on the work of university teachers, including their conceptions of teaching, their self-concept, their working conditions, how they viewed support from their departments, and their educational needs. The objectives and nature of the study were explained to the respondents.

In total, we conducted interviews that were on average 80 minutes long with each of the 19 respondents. We assured the respondents that the information they supplied to us would be kept confidential, and we promised them that all data would be anonymized (including not only the respondents themselves, but all other names and specific information mentioned so that other individuals could not be identified). The interviews were recorded on a voice recorder and subsequently transcribed following the same principles.

Interview transcripts were on average 30 pages in length; our total data corpus consisted of more than 570 pages of text. We analyzed our data using ATLAS.ti 7.0 software and coded it in two steps. First, four different researchers coded four interviews using the method of inductive open-coding. The authors then compared the codes they used and defined a set of categories that included all codes.

Research Results

Based on our analysis, we identified three categories of perceptions about what constitutes "good teaching." From a theoretical standpoint, it is interesting to note that these conceptions corresponded with the professional self-concepts of early-career academics at MU. In this section, we will describe the three self-concepts we discovered (universalists, researchers, teachers) and the conceptions of good teaching associated with each group. The dividing line between these self-concepts runs down the middle of the double role performed by university-based academics—according to the common view, they should be both excellent researchers and enthusiastic teachers.

Universalists Want to Apply Knowledge in a Practical Way

Eight of our respondents were defined as universalists who straddled the line between teaching and research:

> The way I see it, is that it is roughly balanced and that [these activities] mutually benefit each other. If I was ever just a teacher, then I wouldn't have any growth, so what could I actually teach? At the same time, if I was only a researcher, well, it's nice to write papers, but what's the result? Knowledge needs to be passed on. (Respondent 1, Empirical Study on Early-career Faculty Members' Self-perceptions)

This quote clearly indicates that, in this self-concept, one role legitimatizes the other—teaching that is not based on one's own research experience is viewed as lacking in substance, whereas conducting research without teaching is seen as self-serving. This synergetic interaction between research and teaching was often considered to be ideal. The desires of universalists essentially correspond with the ideal profile of academic staff presented in Mägi and Beerkens's study (2016)—they take teaching seriously, but they slightly prefer research. Universalists in our study usually reported that they taught more than they would like, with some exceptions. They attributed this to the fact that they were at the beginning of their academic careers.

Universalists conceived of teaching as a way to apply knowledge in practice. A good teacher should have experience gained in the "real world," outside of a university setting. One respondent stated: "A teacher shouldn't be disconnected from reality, from real practice. He should somehow be in contact with that practice." Another claimed that "my main advantage is that I have clinical experience. So, I can figure out what is important and what's not. What the students will face and what they won't face and so on." These words indicate that practical experience can influence the curriculum—in teaching, the universalists viewed some information as useful and prioritized it, whereas they downplayed other information. Universalists valued examples and advice that teachers give based on their own experiences. They saw this as the ultimate form of legitimization. The concept of applied teaching can also involve preparing students for their jobs. A third respondent led a seminar focused on skills for future teachers: "The seminar is essentially structured in such a way that a major part is devoted to practical exercises in which the students have to present to the group." Teachers that led such applied courses often saw them as more valuable than the other courses they taught.

Teachers Want to Energize/Activate Students

More than half of our respondents indicated a clear preference for either research or teaching. Seven of them stated that they preferred teaching, although they recognized that research activities are monitored and evaluated more intensely than teaching activities. Early-career academics who preferred teaching spoke about research as something essential for being able to continue working at the university. For them, research was a "pass" that gained them access to students:

> I see my mission as being a teacher. Like just being with students. Now I am at a point in my life where the department head has promised management that I will defend my habilitation thesis. I spent some time at home and cobbled together some Register of R&D Results points. But I view my role as that of a teacher. (Respondent 2, Empirical Study on Early-career Faculty Members' Self-perceptions)

From this quote, it is evident that whereas teaching was viewed as a mission by the individual, the pressure to develop as a researcher came from the outside ("the department head has promised management"). Publishing is not considered an opportunity to inform peers about interesting research, but as a necessity. Those who preferred teaching were not interested in the research itself, but in how many points they received for it when it was evaluated. These respondents did not value their research activities (for instance, when speaking about them, they used terms such as "struggle" and "cobble together"); in contrast they considered themselves to be excellent teachers:

> I admit that I enjoy teaching, I enjoy discussing with these students. I like to prepare the lectures, and I am glad that students and colleagues appreciate that I am good at it. I also enjoy doing scientific research, but I'd say I'm struggling with it somehow. (Respondent 4, Empirical Study on Early-career Faculty Members' Self-perceptions)

Teachers, unlike researchers or universalists, greatly emphasized the energy they invested in their students. Teachers understood university-level teaching to be first and foremost aimed at students and their needs. This manifested in two ways. The first was found in the ability to captivate students during lectures:

A teacher should be a bit into their work so that they can transfer their energy to others. I have pretty good experience with that, when the kids are, say, tired and I have to try all the harder and they respond well to that, yeah. So, like sometimes I manage to captivate them. (Respondent 5, Empirical Study on Early-career Faculty Members' Self-perceptions)

Here, the point was to present materials with such energy and enthusiasm that this enthusiasm was transferred to the students. Another way such teachers expressed their enthusiasm was their willingness to be there for students when they needed help:

I am very accommodating to my students. Hmm ... So, you as a person, when they show some interest, or when they want help with something, so you just help, and essentially, if I can just say it, they can write me almost whenever, and I will answer their e-mail, usually immediately or with just a slight delay. For me, it's not true that I just talk to my students during office hours and otherwise they shouldn't come to see me or write to me (Respondent 6, Empirical Study on Early-career Faculty Members' Self-perceptions).

This approach to teaching was marked by the teacher's willingness to dedicate more time to students and to be available outside of the classroom and office hours. Investing energy in teaching did not mean only going above and beyond for students, but also making efforts to meet the students' needs, for example, by adjusting the pace of lectures or even modifying the curriculum.

Researchers Want to Transfer Knowledge

Four of our respondents considered themselves to be primarily researchers. These respondents mentioned not only their preference for research, but also the time they put into it. One respondent stated: "For me, research is the primary thing. I do teach, and I do like it and it seems like a good supplement." Another admitted: "I am primarily a researcher and not a teacher. Simply put, ninety percent of my time, or ninety-five percent of my time, is research." Unlike universalists, these respondents spent more time on research than on teaching. Either they worked overtime, or their department allowed them to teach less.

As mentioned previously, the respondents that preferred teaching did not value their own research activities and considered research to be one of their weak points. We observed similar uncertainties about teaching among respondents who preferred research:

620   R. Švaříček et al.

> Of course, I am aware of the fact that I am not a teacher. I don't think that I am one, and I don't think that it is my only role. But on the other hand, I realize that I am not at the academy of sciences, that I am at a university, which is a research and educational institution. So, if someone doesn't like students and doesn't like teaching, then what is that person doing at a university? But at the same time, I realize that I am not here as a teacher. I am here as a researcher, but I think that I haven't fully found the boundaries. (Respondent 7, Empirical Study on Early-career Faculty Members' Self-perceptions)

This respondent considered himself to be a high-quality researcher who also had a positive attitude toward teaching. The only prerequisites for teaching that he mentioned were *liking* students and teaching. But, according to him, having inadequate pedagogical competencies at a university was acceptable, whereas having poor research skills was not. For him, university students should *understand* and tolerate the weaknesses of teachers. Following this logic, teaching skills were not a necessary condition, but something extra without which university students should be able to manage.

Researchers emphasized that university teachers must possess expert knowledge and, ideally, should be leading figures in their fields or specializations. At the same time, they must be able to simply and coherently present this knowledge to students or create learning materials that incorporate this knowledge. For example, one respondent said the following about himself: "Students rate me highly as an expert, and on top of that, the way I transfer [my knowledge] to them is very accessible." Many of the respondents indicated that having expert knowledge is the most crucial quality of a teacher. These early-career researchers emphasized that, in terms of knowledge, teachers must "tower above their students at all times during lectures." If they do not, "students immediately recognize that [the teacher] doesn't know what they are talking about." These researchers also focused on the comprehensibility of their lectures. This approach could best be described as transmissive teaching. In this conception, the teacher is central, and the role of students is to receive the information that has been presented to them (Kember & Kwan, 2000; Trigwell & Prosser, 1996). Therefore, high-quality teaching materials that clearly present all the information that the teacher expects students to know must be produced.

Discussions of Research Results

There is a broad range of ideas about what constitutes good university-level teaching. Lowman (1995) created a two-dimensional model of effective university-level teaching. The first dimension comprises intellectual excitement; the second, the creation of interpersonal rapport with students. The intellectual dimension includes the clarity with which a teacher presents materials and the teacher's ability to stimulate and captivate students. The interpersonal element consists of the teacher's ability to communicate in a way that improves student motivation and enjoyment of learning.

Our findings indicate that there is a pronounced difference in how early-career researchers and teachers at MUNI view good teaching. Whereas academics who considered themselves to be primarily researchers wished to pass on their knowledge because universities are elite educational institutions and teachers possess the greatest expertise, those who thought of themselves primarily as teachers wanted to devote themselves to their students, take care of them, and spark their enthusiasm for the subject being taught.

This reveals new insights into academics' thought processes and behaviors; in our interviews, we discovered that different conceptions of what constitutes good teaching can have dramatically different impacts on courses taught by beginner teachers. For example, those who considered themselves to be researchers felt it was important for their lectures to be perfect, and they had the narrowest understanding of what teaching is. In contrast, universalists had the most progressive views about teaching. These academics tried to apply their knowledge in practice, but they also put effort into interacting with students. This finding is in tune with Mägi and Beerkense's (2016) claim that the ideal academic's professional identity is grounded in both teaching and research, although with a very slight preference for research. In the contemporary, international scholarly discourse, student-focused teaching is highly valued (Kember & Kwan, 2000; Trigwell & Prosser, 1996), and therefore, it seems as if the approach of the universalists is most compatible with this conception of teaching.

Our findings differ substantially from those reported at foreign universities where there is a high degree of separation between research and teaching activities and where senior faculty members tend to hold research positions (Austin, 2002; Geschwind & Broström, 2015; Smith & Smith, 2012). None of our respondents, for example, indicated that their position prevented them from conducting research. In contrast, those who considered themselves to be teachers felt pressure to conduct research. Their focus on teaching was the result of their own intrinsic interests.

622   R. Švaříček et al.

The Pedagogical Competencies Development Program

Based on an analysis of the data we collected, we defined three critical areas of educational needs expressed by beginning teachers: the *fundamentals* of university-level pedagogy and didactics, *course preparation and design*, and *communicating with and engaging students* in the classroom. Our empirical study was in large part the basis for a new professional development program—the Pedagogical Competencies Development Program—which was established in 2017 and has thus far provided training to 69 participants.

The Pedagogical Competencies Development Program was developed mainly to respond to these educational needs. The lecturers who guide participants through the development program aim to produce teachers who could be best described as reflective practitioners who respond to the educational needs of their students. This means, among other things, that teachers consciously focus on the contents of their lessons and that—thanks to a deep understanding of their field—they are able to select the most essential subject matter to teach; respond to student feedback; base their courses on the experience of students; and treat students as active contributors to course creation. They seek the roots of student success and failure in their own behavior and actions, not just in those of the students, are willing to share examples of good practice and failure with their colleagues, and boost the intrinsic motivation of their students by granting them autonomy in the learning process.

Modules

The Pedagogical Competencies Development Program is a two-semester program in which, ideally, all new faculty members should enroll during their first semester of teaching. However, this is not possible due to the center's capacity. The program consists of four modules that build upon each other: the Laboratory of Pedagogical Competencies; Video-based Reflection on Teaching; Teaching Workshop; and the Mentoring Program.

Laboratory of Pedagogical Competencies

The Laboratory of Pedagogical Competencies introduces participants to the Pedagogical Competencies Development Program and helps them to acquire and improve the competencies that are essential for effective teaching. It is an

39 Developing Beginner University Teachers' Pedagogical... 623

intensive week-long module consisting of 25 classroom hours that is led by a duo of experienced lecturers who also invite experts to discuss particular topics. The laboratory focuses on the fundamentals of university-level pedagogy and didactics. The syllabus covers the following topics: effective teaching and the role of the university teacher; lesson preparation and planning; communication skills for teachers; student engagement; evaluating students; working with feedback; reflection for teachers; and working with modern technologies. Participants who complete this module will be able to:

* Ground their conception of teaching in knowledge from the educational sciences
* Be familiar with the theory of social needs and be able to apply it to thinking about students and teaching
* Understand the connections between teaching objectives and methods
* Understand the advantages of constructivist teaching and learn to use its basic techniques
* Understand the impact grades have on students' learning performance
* Prepare lessons with a view to actively engage students
* Provide formative feedback to students
* Be familiar with the reflective cycle and understand each of its components and their order.

The laboratory focuses on three main areas: theoretical, reflective, and practical. This means that participants have room to: (1) reflect upon their own teaching; (2) acquire the latest relevant knowledge about pedagogy and didactics; and (3) plan their courses for the following semester under the guidance of the lecturers and with help from their peers. The laboratory also provides an opportunity to share examples of good practice as academics from MUNI's various faculties attend this course together. Thus, the laboratory comprises a unique space whereby participants can share their teaching-related knowledge, experience, and problems and establish working relationships with their colleagues that will last after the course has ended.

As part of the laboratory, we use a textbook that provides a systematic overview of key information and contains several assignments for participants to complete. The course also has an e-learning component in which the lecturers upload study materials and where the attendees can complete three types of assignments—reflection assignments, practical assignments, and discussion assignments—through which they can attempt to implement the knowledge they have acquired in this module in their own lessons.

624   R. Švaříček et al.

Video-Based Reflection on Teaching

This module directly follows up on the Laboratory of Pedagogical Competencies. It is based on the idea that laboratory participants will set development goals for themselves that they will attempt to meet during the course of the current semester. Each participant in this module spends 20 hours working individually with one of the lecturers to conduct video-based reflection. This collaborative effort is based on a video recording of the participant's teaching. This recording provides valuable insights into the participant's real actions in the classroom and reflecting upon them becomes a key means for teacher development.

The Teaching Workshop

The Teaching Workshop begins the second semester of the Pedagogical Competencies Development Program and is intended to help university teachers improve, especially in terms of selecting and using basic and innovative teaching methods. This practically focused, week-long intensive workshop is taught over 20 hours and is attended by all participants in the development program together. In this module, we focus on topics that the participants choose themselves in a survey. In the past, the following subject matters have been covered: engaging teaching methods; data visualization; lecture preparation; using video-based reflection for professional development; voice care; motivating students; using applications in the MUNI Information System; and working with students with specific learning needs. Many seasoned experts, both from MUNI and other institutes (e.g., Charles University, Prague), are involved in teaching this course. The Teaching Workshop is designed so that participants have as many opportunities as possible to actively test out the information they have learned.

The Mentorship Program

This is the capstone module of the year-long development program. Each participant chooses a mentor to help develop the competencies they would like to focus on. Participants can choose mentors from their own field, or they can engage in interdisciplinary cooperation. Mentors receive adequate training so that they can help develop the pedagogical competencies of their mentees. Mentors must attend three workshops focused on clarifying the mentor's role, indirect methods for guiding mentoring conversations, and offering feedback and providing advice. The mentor and mentee should work with each other for a minimum of 20 hours. The goal of the mentorship is to plan together a lesson that is then taught by the mentee, evaluate that lesson, and then plan further development. We view the relationship between the mentor and the mentee as a way for mentors to develop as well, and as a form of social support for teachers.

Feedback

As part of the Pedagogical Competencies Development Program, we also collect feedback through feedback forms, both during the course and at its end. Based on the feedback we receive, we make changes to the overall program and to the team of lecturers and experts. Program feedback is generally positive, both overall for the entire program and for specific components. The negative feedback we receive is generally aimed at specific aspects of the program, which we can easily address.

Lessons Learned and Challenges for the Future

As the CERPEK is a relatively new center, we therefore monitor its development, assess its strengths and weakness, and consider avenues for further strategic development. If we look back at the center's history, we discover two critical decisions that had a positive influence on its beginnings. Firstly, the most important decision we made was to conduct research on teachers' needs and beliefs before starting the center and its development program. This research provided us with empirical evidence specific to our own institution. These results were extremely important in the first months of the center's initiation, particularly as we were repeatedly faced with academics and university staff saying there was no need for such a center and that we should not copy every trend that comes from Western universities. In our context, the empirical findings provided the scientific evidence for why such a center was indeed necessary in our local context.

Secondly, we carried out a review of the organizational structure and everyday work of similar university centers. A dilemma we faced was how to establish the basic structure of our center: Should we connect the center with the Faculty of Education or with the whole university? Should we open the development program to all academics or only beginners? Should we mix

626   R. Švaříček et al.

participants from all nine faculties into one classroom, or should we divide them into "hard science" and "humanities" classrooms? We discovered differences between international universities and finally decided to associate the center with the whole university, prepare courses only for beginners—as we realized how different the expectations and needs of young and experienced academics could be—and to create a single, heterogenous classroom. We believe that these key decisions had a strong impact and garnered a great deal of respect for the center in the eyes of our academic colleagues over a relatively short time.

Nevertheless, despite our success in setting up the center and gaining the respect of our academic colleagues in a relative short period of time, we predict a few challenges to arise in future years. One of the largest will be to find a way to evaluate the effectiveness of the center. We need to find a method of evaluation which, on the one hand, would be rigorous enough, while remaining cost-effective on the other hand. We also need a more complex evaluation based on several sources to triangulate the quality of our data. Ideally, we need a tool in which we could use modern technologies and statistical methods to show causal relationships between the teachers' participation in our development program and the quality of their teaching.

Due to this chapter's limited space, we are unable to discuss all of our research findings, but we will mention one important discovery in conclusion. Our study of beginner teachers at MUNI revealed major differences in the development trajectories of scholarly and pedagogical competencies. Whereas scholarly competencies tend to grow as academics gain more experience, pedagogical competencies seem to stagnate at a certain point. In most cases, it seems as if academics have mastered the basic didactic techniques that enable them to conduct adequate university-level teaching. Teaching quality, however, is not as heavily monitored as research quality, which is regularly assessed. Academics are remunerated for high-quality research output, which also contributes to their career growth. Therefore, it seems that growth in academics' pedagogical competencies often hits a plateau. In order to expand our knowledge of this aspect, we are currently in the process of conducting an ongoing research project that will provide us with pertinent additional data.

References

Anderson, S., & Anderson, B. (2012). Preparation and socialization of the education professoriate: Narratives of doctoral student-instructors. *International Journal of Teaching and Learning in Higher Education, 24*(2), 239–251.

39 Developing Beginner University Teachers' Pedagogical... 627

Austin, A. E. (2002). Preparing the next generation of faculty: Graduate school as socialization to the academic career. *Journal of Higher Education, 73*(1), 94–122.

Berliner, D. C. (1986). In pursuit of the expert pedagogue. *Educational Researcher, 15*(7), 5–13.

Čejková, I. (2017). Pedagogically uneducated university teacher: A problem or a challenge? *Pedagogická Orientace, 27*(1), 159–179.

Geschwind, L., & Broström, A. (2015). Managing the teaching-research nexus: Ideals and practice in research-oriented universities. *Higher Education Research and Development, 34*(1), 60–73.

Golde, C. M. (2008). Applying lessons from professional education to the preparation of the professoriate. *New Directions for Teaching and Learning, 113*(1), 17–25.

Hativa, N., Barak, R., & Simhi, E. (2001). Exemplary university teachers: Knowledge and beliefs regarding effective teaching dimensions and strategies. *Journal of Higher Education, 72*(6), 699–729.

Iglesias-Martínez, M., Lozano-Cabezas, I., & Martinez-Ruiz, M. A. (2014). Listening to the voice of novice lectures in higher education: A qualitative study. *International Journal of Teaching and Learning in Higher Education, 26*(2), 170–181.

Johannes, C., Fendler, J., & Seidel, T. (2013). Teachers' perceptions of the learning environment and their knowledge base in a training program for novice university teachers. *International Journal for Academic Development, 18*(2), 152–165.

Kember, D., & Kwan, K. (2000). Lecturers' approaches to teaching and their relationship to conceptions of good teaching. *Instructional Science, 28*(5), 469–490.

Lowman, J. (1995). *Mastering the techniques of teaching.* Jossey-Bass.

Mägi, E., & Beerkens, M. (2016). Linking research and teaching: Are research-active staff members different teachers? *Higher Education, 72*(2), 241–258.

Mudrak, J., Zabrodska, K., Kveton, P., Jelinek, M., Blatny, M., Solcova, I., & Machovcova, K. (2018). Occupational well-being among university faculty: A job demands-resources model. *Research in Higher Education, 59*(3), 325–348.

Masaryk University (MUNI). (n.d.). *Home page.* MUNI. https://cerpek.muni.cz/en

Pabian, P., Šima, K., & Kynčilová, L. (2011). Humboldt goes to the labour market: How academic higher education fuels labour market success in the Czech Republic. *Journal of Education and Work, 24*(1), 95–118.

Šeďová, K., Švaříček, R., Sedláčková, J., Čejková, I., Šmardová, A., Novotný, P., & Zounek, J. (2016). Beginning university teachers and their approaches to teaching and professional self-perception. *Studia Paedagogica, 21*(1), 9–34.

Smith, E., & Smith, A. (2012). Buying-out teaching for research: The views of academics and their managers. *Higher Education, 63*(4), 455–472.

Trigwell, K., & Prosser, M. (1996). Changing approaches to teaching: A relational perspective. *Studies in Higher Education, 21*(3), 275–284.

Tůma, F., & Knecht, P. (2019). Academic inbreeding as an undesirable evil or a necessary good in higher education: A research review and implications for Czech higher education policy. *Studia Paedagogica, 24*(1), 9–31.

40

From Workshops to Impact Evaluation: The Case of a Chilean Center for Teaching Development and Innovation

Ricardo García, Héctor Turra, and Beatriz Moya

Introduction

Constant changes in the tertiary education scenario in Chile, as well as advances in higher education teaching and learning research, have led the Center for Teaching Development and Innovation (CeDID) at the Universidad Católica de Temuco (UC Temuco) to deepen the scope of its programs and services. This case focuses on the evolution of this academic professional development center (ADC) over a 13-year period, in which the center's services have transitioned from workshops to comprehensive and interconnected faculty development programs, and their impact evaluation.

Chilean tertiary education has gone through a major transformation process over the past few decades; student participation has increased dramatically due to several new public policies by the national government that seeks to achieve universal access to tertiary education (Consejo Nacional de Educación, 2017). This massification of higher education has diversified the socio-academic characteristics of the students (Biggs & Tang, 2011). As suggested by Pey and Chauriye (2011), this scenario has driven Chilean higher education institutions to implement new policies to address the challenges of educating a more diverse population of students. One of the outcomes of this

---

R. García (✉) • H. Turra • B. Moya
Universidad Católica de Temuco, Temuco, Chile
e-mail: rgarcia@uct.cl; hector.turra@ucalgary.ca; beatriz.moya@ucalgary.ca

© The Author(s), under exclusive license to Springer Nature Switzerland AG 2023   **629**
O. J. Neisler (ed.), *The Palgrave Handbook of Academic Professional Development Centers*,
Palgrave Studies on Leadership and Learning in Teacher Education,
https://doi.org/10.1007/978-3-030-80967-6_40

630   R. García et al.

challenge was the creation of new educational models based on the Tuning project—an initiative that promotes harmonization in the higher education sector—in most Chilean universities (Muñoz & Sobrero, 2018).

In this context, UC Temuco based its educational model on principles of competence-based education, student-centered teaching, the integration of information and communication technologies, lifelong learning, and humanistic and Christian education. With the development of this principles-led model, it was necessary to structure the curriculum to establish and sustain these changes and, at the same time, to develop aligned faculty teaching competences (UC Temuco, 2010). One of the chosen strategies was to establish an ADC to support both of these priorities (Veneros, 2012).

Overview of the CeDID

The CeDID was created in 2007 at UC Temuco with the support of funding from the Chilean Ministry of Education. Initially, the purpose of the center was to provide faculty with guidelines and information about its new educational model. Consequently, the center offered faculty development services in the form of workshops and provided discussion spaces to examine new teaching-learning and assessment strategies. It also supported the creation of institutional documents to guide curriculum development and offered pedagogical advice for syllabus design, facilitated by consultants from different disciplines. However, a formative evaluation analysis, based on faculties' perceptions and carried out after this first six-year process, showed that there were no significant changes in the teaching practices, despite the faculty understanding the new educational model. Faculty required a more discipline-based approach to teaching (UC Temuco, 2012).

This information regarding the perception of the workshops and the new institutional goals oriented to ensure the quality of the formation processes through the engagement of students in active learning, discipline-based experiences led the CeDID to a second phase in which the center was able to widen the range of programs it offered to include a deeper and more discipline-specific approach. In addition, the CeDID sought to "provide current and research informed quality teaching practices, skills and resources that empower faculty" (Chalmers, 2013). These new programs received funding from the Chilean Ministry of Education and aligned with UC Temuco goals, including the development of faculty learning communities (FLCs), a Certificate in

Teaching and Learning, online self-taught modules, and establishment of a School of Student Learning Assistants (SLAs). Fig. 40.1 shows an overview of the current programs being offered by the CeDID.

FLCs

The FLCs are based on the concept of communities of practice developed by Wenger and Snyder (2000) and are composed of faculty, faculty consultants, and SLAs. They are based on a collaborative model with the joint purpose of building up pertinent pedagogical knowledge so as to design, implement, and analyze evidence-based and discipline-specific teaching and learning strategies to improve the quality of students' learning.

One of the most relevant foci of the FLCs is course transformation. These communities follow a three-stage process: (1) characterization of the students, faculty, and SLAs and course redesign; (2) implementation of innovations;

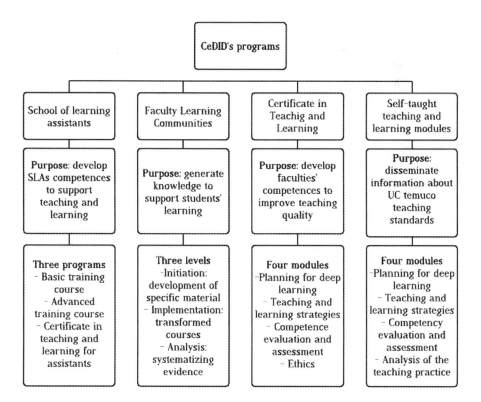

Fig. 40.1 Current faculty development programs at the CeDID

and (3) analysis of the results, particularly regarding students' perceptions of the course, evidence of students' learning, and approval/attrition rates (CeDID, 2017). This process orients the redesign of courses to help them transition from a traditional, teacher-centered approach to an active learning, student-centered one. Other foci of the FLCs include the development of teaching material, analysis of previously collected teaching and learning data, and implementation of specific teaching strategies to test them before a course transformation process.

Certificate in Teaching and Learning

The Certificate in Teaching and Learning is oriented toward the development of teacher competencies such as planning, implementing teaching and learning strategies, competence evaluation and assessment, ethical aspects of college teaching, and analysis of teaching practice. As an initial result, faculty enrolled in this program show understanding of the principles of competence-based education and a student-centered approach, allowing them to later use this information to plan and implement teaching and evaluation strategies based on these principles. All of the modules of the certificate program are mandatory to receive the final certification.

Self-Taught Modules

The purpose of these modules is to offer a flexible pathway to understand the foundational principles of the educational model, specifically in terms of planning, teaching strategies, and evaluation. Participants develop a series of online activities where they can reflect on and analyze their own teaching practices. These modules are guided by an online tutor who is also a faculty consultant from the center. Each module is certified individually as a course.

School of SLAs

The purpose of the School of SLAs program is to train outstanding undergraduate students who support teaching and learning activities in lower-level courses. The three-level training continuum (basic, advanced, and leadership) is based on a custom-made profile developed to meet UC Temuco faculty's and students' needs as well as international best practices. It is delivered in a

40 From Workshops to Impact Evaluation

blended learning format and integrates continuous advice and support in the implementation of activities guided by faculty and based on a peer learning strategy.

The complexity and interplay between each of the CeDID's programs required deeper data analysis that was not able to be obtained solely from assessment of perception and satisfaction. The CeDID needed to enhance its capacity to evaluate the effectiveness and impact of its programs (Chalmers & Gardiner, 2015). Therefore, the CeDID's main questions at this point were: *How effective are CeDID programs? What is their impact? How can the impact of faculty development programs be measured?* These questions relate to the needs of these types of centers in other contexts where the tertiary education scenario is also framed by accountability (Ahmad et al., 2018).

Conceptual Framework

Definitions for impact evaluation in the context of educational development are diverse (Garbarino & Holland, 2009); consequently, "there is no recognized evaluation standard" (Ahmad et al., 2018, 1). Some of these definitions belong to an instrumental approach to evaluation and differ from others that acknowledge aspects such as judgment, experience, and contextual knowledge (Bamber & Stefani, 2016). Impact evaluation in faculty development is a complex and contingent endeavor (Chalmers et al., 2012). Reporting participant satisfaction continues to be a dominant form of evaluation (Ahmad et al., 2018) and most evidence is largely anecdotal (Bamber, 2002). Besides, there is limited evidence in terms of effectiveness or impact regarding university teaching preparation programs and their capacity to work as quality improvement, which can be explained by a distance between academic literature regarding the impact of academic development and that assessing quality in higher education (Houston & Hood, 2017). Furthermore, academics represent only one of the many factors that impact students (Cilliers & Herman, 2010); however, student learning outcomes are the ultimate goal of professional development (Guskey, 2002, 2003).

Different impact assessment and models have been proposed as a result of a growing scholarly interest in this area (Parsons et al., 2012). Guskey's impact framework, the theory of change (Bamber & Stefani, 2016), and the Teacher Development Effectiveness Framework (Chalmers & Gardiner, 2015) all address critical characteristics of impact evaluation, such as the use of multiple sources of evidence (Theall, 2010) and the need for robustness in the model (Parsons et al., 2012).

634   R. García et al.

Guskey's impact framework provides a five-level model that helps review the effects of programs and identify where those impacts have taken place (Chalmers & Gardiner, 2015); it offers a practical analytical framework and suggests that impact from teacher development programs occurs at the level of academic reactions, conceptual change, behavioral change, development and changes in the organizational support for teacher development, and changes to student learning and performance (Parsons et al., 2012). According to Guskey (2000), the standards that need to be met in any assessment effort are fairness, credibility, and the presence of a continuous process.

In turn, the theory of change is aimed at determining *why* an initiative works (Ahmad et al., 2018) and also facilitates the evidence of value (Bamber & Stefani, 2016). The development of a theory of change for a program involves the following components: current situation, enabling factors/resources, processes/activities, desired outcomes, and long-term impact. In broad terms, it offers a roadmap toward a goal (Ahmad et al., 2018).

Finally, the focus of the Teacher Development Effectiveness Framework is to link the outcomes of ADC programs to institutionally relevant data, while also providing guidance on sources of evidence, contextual factors, and time frames (Chalmers et al., 2012). It allows universities and ADCs to identify the effectiveness and impact of their programs (Chalmers & Gardiner, 2015). There are four principles that underlie this framework—namely, relevance, rigors, context, and reliability. This framework has been complemented with both Guskey's five-level impact framework and the theory of change to determine the best levels and scale of indicators (Chalmers & Gardiner, 2015).

Methodology

The CeDID developed an impact evaluation model that was operationalized in an impact evaluation matrix. The matrix was developed through discussion so as to identify various types of indicators with corresponding evidence that could be used in the development and evaluation of each program. The main purpose of this work was to ensure that this information was useful in assisting the team to achieve a deeper understanding of the programs and their connection to UC Temuco's goal of actively engaging students in learning.

The matrix was organized using four types of indicators: input, processes, output, and outcomes. Input and output indicators are quantitative and display the scope and effects of each program in numerical terms, while processes and outcomes show the mechanisms and quality standards met by the program. The integration of both types of indicators allows for a more comprehensive analysis (Chalmers et al., 2012):

* *Input*: Shows the human, financial, and physical resources involved in the programs
* *Output*: Demonstrates the quantity of outcomes produced that are direct consequences of the programs
* *Processes*: Reveal how programs are delivered in a particular context
* *Outcomes*: Show the quality of provision, satisfaction levels, and added value of the programs.

In addition, the design of the CeDID's framework is oriented towards the center's main stakeholders:

* *Faculty*, who are interested in analyzing and reflecting on teaching practices based on a student-centered approach
* *Students*, who are the center of those teaching and learning processes
* *SLAs*, who develop new competences through a competence-based model
* *The institution*, which seeks to ensure quality teaching that it is coherent with its mission.

Table 40.1 shows some examples of different indicators, stakeholders, and levels of impact which are part of the CeDID's evaluation matrix. Another version of the matrix can be found in Moya et al. (2018).

Faculty Practices

One example of the use of this matrix has been in the application of the Approaches to Teaching Inventory (Trigwell et al., 2005) to UC Temuco faculty. Before faculty begin the course transformation process and/or participate in a learning community, CeDID consultants offer to use this instrument to set a baseline. If the faculty member accepts, the results are processed and discussed confidentially. The course transformation and/or FLC protocol is then implemented. This process can cover a full academic year, involving course design, training, and implementation. Once carried out, faculty may use the Approaches to Teaching Inventory again, using the same course as before. Results before and after the process are compared and discussed with faculty so that they may reflect on their own teaching practice.

Table 40.1 Example of the CeDID's impact evaluation framework

Stakeholder	Level of impact	Input	Processes	Output	Outcomes
Faculty	Change in practice	Academic performance survey results before course transformation Teaching before course transformation	Course transformation Protocol FLC protocol	Academic performance survey results after course transformation Approaches to teaching after course transformation	Transfer of innovation to other courses New innovation grants of faculty involved in course transformation Presentations/ conferences about pedagogical innovation
Students	Learning results	Historical pass/fail rates of FLC courses Disciplinary inventory concepts before course transformation Learning approach inventory results before course transformation	Evidence of student evaluation in transformed courses (audio-visual or written material)	Pass/fail rates of FLC courses Disciplinary inventory concepts after course transformation Learning approach inventory results after course transformation	Report with analysis of learning gains Academic studies submitted to journals by faculty in FLCs about learning gains
Institution	Changes in institutional culture	Regulations concerning academic recognition for improving teaching/learning practices before FLCs Number of collaboration agreements between UC Temuco schools and CeDID aimed at pedagogical innovation before FLCs	Presentation of faculty development policy to UC Temuco authorities Proposal for the introduction of new academic products and professional development in academic performance categorization	Regulations concerning academic recognition for improving teaching/ learning practices after FLCs Number of collaboration agreements between UC Temuco schools and CeDID aimed at pedagogical innovation after FLCs	Analysis of regulation changes

The matrix has been used to report the impact of various programs to different audiences (including institutional authorities, the Chilean Ministry of Education, and funding agencies,). Some results of the application of the matrix using different samples (students and policy changes) will be shown in the next section.

Changes in Student Learning Gains

As an illustration, a mathematics inventory test developed at UC Temuco was used as a pre/post-test in an introductory algebra course which had been redesigned using a flipped classroom approach and oriented toward mathematics problem-solving during lecture time. The course was transformed in the mathematics FLC and the application of the inventory was oriented to measure the impact of their work on students learning results (as seen in Table 40.1). The inventory was taken by the same group of 89 first-year students (comprising 24 female and 65 male students) on two separate occasions. Means obtained in the pre/post tests were compared using a Student's t-test, before Hake's (1998) formula—$(g = (post-pre)/(100-pre))$—was applied to determine the students' learning gains. Table 40.2 shows the difference in the pre-post results obtained by the students.

As can be seen, there were significant differences in the pre/post-test results. The total learning gain corresponded to 0.31. This gain is within the range reported by Hake (1998) for courses based on active learning strategies. In his study, Hake (1998) reported gains of 0.09–0.26 for courses taught using traditional strategies such as lectures, compared to gains of 0.16–0.65 for student-centered courses.

Although the results mentioned above correspond to a single sample and are framed in one semester, this framework has been continuously implemented so as to establish trends that can prove the real impact of the initiative over time. This also applies to the rest of the indicators proposed in the evaluation matrix.

Table 40.2 Difference in students' pre-post results

Student group	Mean pre-test score	Mean pre-test percentage (%)	Mean post-test score	Mean post-test percentage (%)	P value
Total	21.03	46.73	28.59	63.53	<0.001
Female	21.21	47.13	28.23	62.73	<0.001
Male	20.95	46.55	28.77	63.93	<0.001

Changes in Institutional Culture

Another example of the application of the impact evaluation model deals with the changes that the faculty development programs have made to institutional culture, specifically in the policies of teachers' evaluation. The FLC program began at UC Temuco in 2013. During the first two years, there was no formal recognition for any of the 25 teachers that were part of the four FLCs which were operating at that time. However, in late 2015, the academic provost certified the work done in the communities via a special memorandum which was used to complement the faculty's academic commitments for that year. Subsequently, in 2017, the FLC program was formally recognized in the teachers' evaluation rubric, which is used at an institutional level to evaluate a faculty member's productivity over one year. The FLC program is now recognized as an institutional entity which produces different products associated to teaching and learning. These products can be used to advance in the academic ranks. This update in institutional policy benefited over 61 faculty members participating in 15 active FLCs in 2018. It is expected that these changes in institutional culture will foster faculty participation in FLCs, thus impacting a number of students who will ultimately benefit from their initiatives.

Conclusions

In this chapter, we have described the evolution of the CeDID at UC Temuco which has resulted in the development of an impact evaluation framework based on international best practices. The development of this impact evaluation model has allowed the CeDID to continuously demonstrate the value of its different programs to various stakeholders, such as the national education and university authorities, faculty, and students, as well as to other ADC professionals. In this sense, the flexibility of the matrix and the diversity of its indicators and corresponding evidence has been well received by the institution and other entities, including the Chilean Ministry of Education. The rigor of this matrix has also become a foundation and framework to increase research experiences among university faculty. Consequently, the matrix has allowed CeDID professionals and teachers to better respond to students' learning needs by adjusting research-based teaching practices based on evidence gathered from different sources. Moreover, regular reporting of this

40 From Workshops to Impact Evaluation

evidence within the institution has helped to spread good practices and has also contributed to increased support from the institutional authorities, resulting in an update of the policies related to teachers' evaluation.

References

Ahmad, A., Fenton, N., Graystone, L., Acai, A., Matthews, K., & Chalmers, D. (2018). *Investigating impact in higher education*. Higher Education Research and Development Society of Australasia.

Bamber, V. (2002). To what extent has the Dearing policy recommendation on training new lecturers met acceptance? Where Dearing went that Robbins didn't dare. *Teacher Development, 10*(2), 433–457.

Bamber, V., & Stefani, L. (2016). Taking up the challenge of evidencing value in educational development: From theory to practice. *International Journal for Academic Development, 21*(3), 242–254.

Biggs, J., & Tang, C. (2011). *Teaching for quality learning at university. What the student does*. Open University Press.

Center for Teaching Development and Innovation (CeDID). (2017). *Course transformation protocol*. Universidad Católica de Temuco (UC Temuco).

Chalmers, D. (2013). *Report 1: CeDID's impact evaluation*. Universidad Católica de Temuco (UC Temuco).

Chalmers, D., & Gardiner, D. (2015). The measurement and impact of university teacher development programs. *Educare, 51*(a), 53–80.

Chalmers, D., Stoney, S., Goody, A., Goerke, V., & Gardiner, D. (2012). *Measuring the effectiveness of academic professional development: Identification and implementation of indicators and measures of effectiveness of teaching preparation programmes for academics in higher education (ref: SP10–1840)*. Curtin University.

Cilliers, F., & Herman, N. (2010). Impact of an educational development programme on teaching practice of academics at a research-intensive university. *International Journal for Academic Development, 15*(3), 253–267.

Consejo Nacional de Educación. (2017). *Higher education indices*. Consejo Nacional de Educación. http://www.cned.cl/indices-educacion-superior

Garbarino, S., & Holland, J. (2009). *Quantitative and qualitative methods in impact evaluation and measuring results*. Governance and Social Development Resource Center.

Guskey, T. (2000). *Evaluating professional development*. Corwin.

Guskey, T. (2003). What makes professional development effective? *Phi Delta Kappan, 84*(10), 748–750.

Guskey, T. R. (2002). Does it make a difference? Evaluating professional development. *Educational Leadership, 59*(6), 45–51.

Hake, R. R. (1998). Interactive-engagement methods in introductory mechanics courses. *Physics Education Research, 74*, 64–74.

Houston, D., & Hood, C. (2017). University teacher preparation programmes as a quality enhancement mechanism: Evaluating impact beyond individual teachers' practice. *Quality in Higher Education, 23*(1), 67–78.

Moya, B., Turra, H., & Chalmers, D. (2018). Developing and implementing a robust and flexible framework for the evaluation and impact of educational development in higher education in Chile. *International Journal for Academic Development, 24*(2), 163–177.

Muñoz, A., & Sobrero, V. (2018). Tuning project in Chile: Analysis of higher education internationalization processes. *Calidad en la Educación, 24*, 249–271.

Parsons, D., Hill, I., Holland, J., & Willis, D. (2012). *Impact of teaching development programmes in higher education.* Higher Education Academy. https://www.heacademy.ac.uk/sites/default/files/

Pey, R., & Chauriye, S. (2011). Curricular innovation in the universities of the Council of Rectors, 2000–2010. *Consejo de Rectores de Las Universidades Chilenas*, 1–91. http://sctchile.consejoderectores.cl/documentos_WEB/Innovacion_Curricular/2. Informe_INNOVACION_CURRICULAR.pdf

Universidad Católica de Temuco (UC Temuco). (2010). *Institutional development plan.* UC Temuco. https://uct.cl/archivos/pdi20102020.pdf

Universidad Católica de Temuco (UC Temuco). (2012). *Teaching needs report.* UC Temuco.

Theall, M. (2010). Evaluating teaching: From reliability to accountability. *New Directions for Teaching and Learning, 2010*(123), 85–95.

Trigwell, K., Prosser, M., & Ginns, P. (2005). Phenomenographic pedagogy and a revised approaches to teaching inventory. *Higher Education Research and Development, 24*(4), 349–360.

Veneros, D. (2012). *Teaching improvement units achievements and challenges.* Ministry of Education. http://www.mecesup.cl/usuarios/MECESUP/File/2012/seminarios/denise/2Presentacion DianaVeneros__SeminarioDeniseChalmers_3-9-12.pdf

Wenger, E. C., & Snyder, W. M. (2000). Communities of practice: The organizational frontier. *Harvard Business Review, 78*(1), 139–145.

41

Extending International Collaboration to Certify High-Quality Online Teaching in Higher Education

Yan Ding and Yaping Gao

Introduction

In the past 10 years or so, the higher education sector in China has seen a rapid, large-scale growth in the establishment of academic professional development centers (ADCs), with such centers mainly charged with addressing issues regarding the quality of teaching and learning as a result of the expansion of higher education enrollment since the end of the 1990s. Almost at the same time as the initial launch of these ADCs, massive open online courses (MOOCs) from abroad gradually entered the realm of Chinese higher education, which prompted the eager adoption of online learning modalities by Chinese college students. These changes made many education administrators realize that higher education would have to undergo fundamental reforms.

Y. Ding (✉)
Center for Faculty Development / Research Institute for Higher Education, Fudan University, Shanghai, China
e-mail: yding@fudan.edu.cn

Y. Gao
Quality Matters, Annapolis, MD, USA
e-mail: ygao@qualitymatters.org

© The Author(s), under exclusive license to Springer Nature Switzerland AG 2023
O. J. Neisler (ed.), *The Palgrave Handbook of Academic Professional Development Centers*, Palgrave Studies on Leadership and Learning in Teacher Education, https://doi.org/10.1007/978-3-030-80967-6_41

This chapter presents a case study of the ADC of Fudan University, the Center for Faculty Development (CFD), as an example to illustrate how this young entity introduced an American online course quality rubric by Quality Matters (QM)—an education quality assurance organization based in the USA—through international cooperation and promoted the local adaptation and application of these quality standards to better support the transformation of teaching and learning not only at CFD, but at numerous other higher education institutions (HEIs) across China.

Overview of Academic Development Initiatives in China

In China, the history of institutionalizing academic development (AD) for higher education is relatively short. It is closely related and largely due to the demands of society to improve the quality of higher education under the dramatic expansion of enrollment since the late 1990s. In July 2011, the Ministry of Education (MOE) issued a formal document which explicitly proposed to improve faculty members' teaching competencies as an important task in the reform of undergraduate education (MOE, 2011). This document, for the first time, required HEIs to establish ADCs, units charged with providing faculty members with professional development in teaching. In July 2012, the MOE started the selection process to identify national exemplary ADCs, with 30 centers standing out from more than 100 MOE-affiliated candidate institutions. Over the next few years, the provincial education authorities also issued relevant documents to require local colleges and universities to create ADCs, thus leading to a wave of AD institutionalization in the Chinese higher education community.

As of 2017, of all 1,171 mainstream HEIs in China, a total of 679 had established ADCs, accounting for 57.98% of all HEIs. However, the distribution of ADCs in different provinces varies. As shown in Fig. 41.1, three tiers of provinces have formed according to their respective percentages of ADCs. In first-tier provinces, more than 90% of HEIs have established ADCs; in second-tier provinces, the distribution is much lower than that of the first tier, but still exceeds 40%, while in third-tier provinces, no more than one-third of HEIs have created ADCs.

Among established ADCs, there are wide variations in the size, affiliation, and responsibilities of the centers, but some common characteristics can be

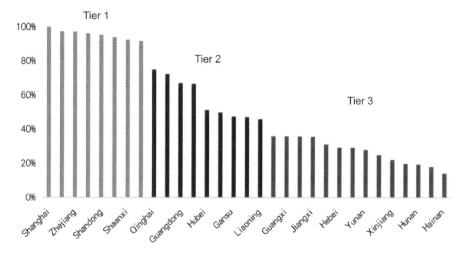

Fig. 41.1 Distribution of Chinese HEIs with established ADCs by province in 2017. Data source: *Report of the Network Training Center* (MOE, 2018)

identified. First, most units are very small, and generally do not exceed three staff members. These staff often come from other management departments of the university and devote only half of their time to AD work. Second, many ADCs are created as a subsection of larger administrative units, such as the Academic Affairs Office or Personnel Management Office, and only about 10% are created as stand-alone units. In recent years, newly emerging ADCs tend to be units under the Personnel Management Office, rather than educational management departments. This represents a new structural change in ADCs in China. Third, although the MOE has stipulated that ADCs should undertake a variety of highly specialized work and projects such as academic training in pedagogy, teaching evaluation and consulting services, and teaching research, most ADCs only engage in low-specialized transactional work, such as organizing training and teaching competitions.

Overview of the ADC at Fudan University

Fudan University, located in the metropolis of Shanghai, is one of the top research tier-one universities in China. Although the university prioritizes research, it has never overlooked teaching since its establishment in 1905. Three decades ago, when other colleges and universities still retained the former Soviet Union's educational model adapted for the planning system—that is, with narrow disciplines and majors set so as to funnel students into specific jobs after graduation—Fudan University was the first institution to propose that undergraduate education needed to lay a foundation for student, by focusing on developing their practical and comprehensive abilities and social adaptability. This proposal was subsequently implemented by reforming the undergraduate curriculum system in the following years.

Since entering the 21st century, Fudan University has launched a series of general education initiatives and has played a leading role in the reform of undergraduate education nationwide. However, these efforts mainly aim to establish strategic approaches to improving education at the institutional level, such as talent cultivation plans, curriculum settings, and admission systems, and have not yet penetrated into the classroom practices of individual faculty members and their professional development of effective teaching skills and strategies.

Fudan University set up the CFD in 2011. It is among the earliest establishments of ADCs in China and was selected as one of the 30 national exemplary ADCs in 2012. The CFD has grown over the past eight years, all the while adhering to the university's mission and philosophy of reflecting, sharing, transforming, and improving. Since its establishment, the center has become an integral support resource for Fudan University's faculty members and plays an influential leadership role for its counterparts in China. The goals of the CFD are listed as follows:

* Improve teaching competence and curriculum quality
* Encourage innovation in class teaching, especially with regard to new models of technology-integrated teaching
* Promote scholarship of teaching and learning
* Create a learning community among faculty members and a culture of teaching excellence.

The following section attempts to explain the mission and strategic work of the CFD and what the center has accomplished to develop and sustain itself in an increasingly changing higher education context. Then, the center's international collaboration with QM, the USA-based global organization leading quality assurance in online and innovative digital teaching and learning environments, will be presented to illustrate how the center has responded to the growing demand for high-quality online courses and blended teaching in China. Finally, some issues and challenges of international collaboration are discussed, as well as the future development of ADCs in China.

The Mission and Work of the CFD

Promoting Institutionalization of AD and Building a Horizontal-and-Vertical Collaborative System

Since the establishment of the CFD, with the advancement of various tasks, the organizational structure of the center and the roles and responsibilities of its staff have become gradually clear. The CFD is affiliated with the Fudan Undergraduate School, which is essentially an educational administration department. This set-up is conducive for a timely response to university teaching reforms. The unit has nine employees in total, including three part-time directors and six full-time staff members. The director is from the Department of Physics and is the former pro-vice chancellor of Fudan University. In addition, two professors from the Research Institute for Higher Education and the School of Microelectronics serve as deputy directors.

In order to improve the construction of the organization and build a broader AD support system, the CFD invited administrators, experts, and teaching enthusiasts both inside and outside of the university to establish an AD Advisory Committee (ADAC) and Invited Research Fellow (IRF) team. The ADAC provides advice, deliberation, and instruction on important policies, measures, and annual plans formulated by the CFD. The committee is composed of not only senior renowned academics and young and experienced faculty, but also leaders of relevant administrative departments and student representatives, thus representing a broader range of AD support groups. The IRF team was established to study the teaching reforms that Fudan University has focused on. Initially, its members were mainly composed of scholars with research capabilities in education. However, in recent years, more and more devoted teaching faculty have joined. Meanwhile, the research output of the team consists of not only the publication of articles, but also research and development products that greatly promote practical teaching. To date, six sub-teams have been organized to correspond to different themes of teaching research, including research related to learning-centered curriculum design, the Fudan University-QM (FD-QM) Online Course Quality Rubric (the 'FD' in the title of this initiative can refer to both Fudan University and the concept of faculty development), course ideology, and innovation and entrepreneurship education, among others.

In order to deepen the construction of systematic AD, the CFD began to provide incentives to promote the establishment of sub-centers in all academic units and faculties in 2019. The establishment of these sub-centers enables AD practices to reflect discipline-specific characteristics and provide appropriate guidance and support for disciplinary teaching. Compared with the ADAC and IRF, which are interdisciplinary, multi-sectoral groups and therefore 'horizontal', the construction of the sub-centers represents a 'vertical' effort to build an AD system. Currently, six schools at Fudan University have set up sub-centers, including the Medical School and the School of International Cultural Exchange.

Enriching Academic Programs and Activities Designed to Enhance Faculty Members' Teaching Competencies

The main responsibility of the CFD is to provide professional development programs and learning resources for all faculty members. Twice a year, the center offers one-semester-long teacher training programs. The fall semester training program is mandatory for all newly recruited faculty members who are due to start teaching, while the program of the spring semester is for experienced faculty. The former requires new faculty to understand the teaching and learning situation and characteristics, institutional policies, and regulations related to teaching, and master the necessary pedagogical knowledge and skills. The latter typically requires faculty to systematically learn course design principles and 'know-how' to implement effective teaching. Since the spring semester of 2013, 14 such training sessions have been offered with about 800 faculty members participating, accounting for 30% of the entire academic staff body.

Considering that Fudan University has multiple campuses, the CFD started to create online learning resources as early as 2014 so that all training could be conducted through a combination of online and offline modalities. The CFD became the earliest ADC to introduce blended training modalities in China. However, the shortage of quality online resources soon became apparent. Therefore, starting from 2017, the center devoted more efforts and resources to the development of faculty training programs, including the international collaboration project, namely the FD-QM Online Course Quality Rubric Training Program, explained in more detail later in this chapter.

In addition to faculty training, the CFD also supports faculty by organizing the participation of faculty members in teaching competitions and providing guidance and support. Since 2011, the center has held the Fudan Teaching Competition for Young Teachers every two years. Although the teaching competition differs from an authentic classroom, it has been proved that, if the competition is well designed and organized, the participants do benefit from the event and improve their teaching.

Encouraging Faculty to Conduct Teaching Research and Promoting Transformative Changes in Classroom Teaching Modes

The CFD greatly values the importance of the scholarship of teaching and learning. It encourages and supports IRFs and frontline faculty to carry out joint teaching research using action research methods. Faculty refer and relate to various theories to reflect on problems arising from their teaching practices and solve these practical problems by taking action while doing research. The CFD's members have successively received grants and undertaken a number of teaching research projects sponsored by the Shanghai Municipal Government as well as the MOE, covering topics such as blended teaching design, the institutionalization of AD, the internationalization of curriculum, and learning community construction.

The center also launches university-level teaching research projects annually to guide faculty to carry out teaching research under the paradigm of learner-centered teaching. Since 2012, it has funded more than 500 teaching research projects and, of these, 35 have been selected as Outstanding Undergraduate Teaching Reform Projects by the Shanghai Municipal Government.

Making Outreach Efforts and Promoting Regional and National AD

As a national exemplary center, the CFD devotes its efforts and resources to building platforms so that it can share various learning resources with its counterparts. Since 2012, the center has regularly held a Teaching and Learning Innovation Symposium in May every year, attracting hundreds of faculty, researchers, experts, leaders, and staff from different HEIs both in and beyond China. With the development of AD undertakings in China, the professionalization of faculty developers has become an urgent task. Therefore, in 2017, the CFD started to organize an Academic Developer Seminar, aiming at enhancing mutual learning and communication among professionals working at ADCs. In addition, an e-journal called *Fudan's Teaching and Learning* is published regularly by the center, encouraging cross-disciplinary dialogue on AD issues among colleagues.

Since 2012, the center has also undertaken training, instruction, and evaluation services for visiting scholars from other HEIs. Usually, these institutions are sister colleges supported by Fudan University. During their stay at Fudan

University (usually for either one semester or one academic year), the center provides the visiting scholars with open access to all online learning resources and training programs. Before the end of their visit, the center organizes experts to evaluate their learning at Fudan University. Every year, about 120 visiting scholars receive such support.

It can be seen that the central characteristic of AD in China, as represented by the CFD, is the focus on developing a strategic approach to improving teaching at the institutional level and encouraging external connection and resource-sharing, rather than on providing consultation and fostering collegiality among faculty, which is not yet a priority in China.

Collaboration with QM

The Rise of Online Courses and Blended Teaching

Shortly after the establishment of the CFD, the Chinese higher education sector faced a huge change: the rising prevalence and quick adoption of MOOCs, which subsequently spread quickly across the country. The central government regards this as both a challenge and an opportunity, and has begun to encourage domestic HEIs to build their own online courses. Stimulated by the policies of the MOE, Chinese universities have built many online courses. By 2017, the number of online courses had climbed sharply to 12,500, with a total of 200 million registered online learners, of which 65 million were HEI students who earned college credits from online courses. From the perspective of *quantity* of online education, China is a well-deserved number one in the world.

Behind the dramatic increase in online courses, the intent at the policy level to change the traditional teacher-centered teaching paradigm is also obvious. Given the rapid development of online courses, faculty members are required to take advantage of technology and adopt a blended teaching approach combining face-to-face teaching with online learning to implement student-centered teaching practices. Fudan University was one of the first universities in China to vigorously promote the development of MOOCs and blended teaching reforms. In 2013, Fudan University launched its first MOOC on the international platform Coursera. Recently, the university has increasingly been focusing on pushing online courses on national platforms as well as on campus-based platforms.

According to the target population of the courses and their specific needs, three types of online courses have emerged at Fudan University. The first type of course is mainly geared toward the general public, which is equivalent to the most prevalent MOOCs, aiming at the promotion of a lifelong learning society. The second type is for all HEI students, with the purpose of promoting the sharing of high-quality courses across institutions. Finally, the third type of online course is provided for Fudan University's own students, offered as blended learning courses. By the end of 2019, Fudan University had designed and developed more than 200 online courses in these three categories.

However, due to the fact that many faculty members have not been well trained to design courses and implement effective teaching in an online environment, the problems of many Chinese online courses include their low quality and low cost-benefit (Li & Liu, 2015; Liu, 2016). At present, only 1,291 courses have been selected as National High-Quality Online Courses, accounting for 10.3% of the total; moreover, 19.1% of the courses have fewer than 1,000 registered learners (Wang & Tian, 2019). This reflects the lack of a quality assurance process in Chinese online education, particularly the lack of quality standards to guide instructors in the design and development of high-quality online courses. These problems also existed to varying degrees at Fudan University.

Up to this point, the authoritative and widely recognized online course standards were those reflected in the *Quality Online Course Evaluation Indicators*, a document published by the MOE in 2007 (Cai & Ding, 2009). However, these standards mainly focused on evaluating input elements and were tailored for online education prior to the MOOC phenomenon. Therefore, they did do not meet the needs of the current situation. In 2015, the MOE issued a policy titled *On the Implementation and Management of Open Online Course Development among Higher Education Institutions*, which stipulated that HEIs develop online course quality standards and instruments to evaluate online teaching effectiveness, as well as a credit-hour authentication process and recognition for students taking online courses (MOE, 2015). Another policy document on the construction of high-quality courses clearly stated requirements for selecting 4,000 National First-Class Open Online Courses and 6,000 National First-Class Blended Courses within three years (MOE, 2019). Thus, there has been a strong policy shift in the development of online courses from quantitative expansion to qualitative improvement (Guo et al., 2013).

Agreement with QM

Joint development with international peers can have special advantages. It may add prestige and credibility to the research, achieve diverse perspectives, and bring multiple theoretical perspectives (Chism et al., 2010). Given the increase in the number of online and blended courses, the CFD realized the necessity of developing standards as soon as possible to guide and assist teachers in designing such courses. Thus, in May 2015, the CFD signed a five-year cooperation agreement with QM to jointly develop standards for Chinese online and blended course design. The first stage of the cooperation between the CFD and QM was to carry out collaborative research to develop a Chinese rubric based on the QM Higher Education Rubric, 5th edition (QM, 2014). Afterwards, the CFD would develop and implement a plan to disseminate these standards to other HEIs in China by providing national training and course review services.

This ambitious plan required additional supporters. Thus, in addition to six center staff members, another six IRFs were invited to join the research project. Most of the team members participated in a two-week online training program titled 'Applying the QM Rubric', which was provided by QM staff in 2015. The purpose of the workshop was to establish among colleagues at Fudan University an in-depth understanding of the QM quality assurance process, the QM Higher Education Rubric and its annotations, and the QM course review policies, procedures, and specific requirements (Ding et al., 2017).

After two years of action research, the FD-QM Online Course Quality Rubric was developed, which has been endorsed by the QM Board. Because of the great significance of this international cooperation, the CFD and QM jointly won the 2017 Global Impact Award issued by the Distance Learning Association in the USA.

FD-QM Online Course Quality Rubric and Course Review

The FD-QM Online Course Quality Rubric instrument follows a structure similar to the QM Higher Education Rubric and retains most indicators and annotations of the latter, but with some adjustments based on the unique context and characteristics of Chinese higher education. Specifically, the FD-QM Online Course Quality Rubric consists of a total of 33 specific review standards (SRSs), compared to 43 SRSs in the original QM Higher Education Rubric. These SPSs are divided into eight general standards (GSs), namely Course Review (GS1), Learning Objectives (GS2), Learning Assessment (GS3), Learning Activities (GS4), Instructional Materials (GS5), Course

Technology (GS6), Learner Support (GS7), and Course Production (GS8). Except for GS8, which replaces Accessibility and Usability in the original QM Higher Education Rubric, the names of the other GSs remain the same.

As with the original QM Higher Education Rubric, each SRS of the FD-QM Online Course Quality Rubric is accompanied by very detailed annotations which represent the core of the FD-QM rubric research project. Substantial new terminology applicable to the Chinese online environment was added into the annotations, with some of the examples in the original QM Higher Education Rubric annotations being replaced with Chinese cases. The entire set of the FD-QM Online Course Quality Rubric consists of more than 13,000 words. To a large extent, this has helped to reduce any potential ambiguity in the standards and makes application of the rubric more relevant and reliable.

Each standard is assigned different points depending on its relative importance: 19 of the 33 SRSs are considered essential and have the highest point value of 3, while nine and five are very important and important, respectively, receiving 2 and 1 points each. The maximum total of all possible points is 80, lower than the 99-point total of the original QM Higher Education Rubric. Considering that the design and development of online courses in China is still in its nascent stage, FD-QM course evaluation and certification requirements should have a lower threshold than those of QM. To this end, the research team has developed unique and appropriate course review and certification requirements. If a course is reviewed by the FD-QM reviewer team and has met the following two criteria, it will receive FD-QM Course Certification:

* Review scores of GS2, GS3, and GS5 exceed 9, 8, and 8, respectively
* The review resulted in a total overall score of at least 50 out of 80 points.

Application and Dissemination of the FD-QM Online Course Quality Rubric

In order to better disseminate the FD-QM Online Course Quality Rubric and encourage its widespread use among HEIs in China, the CFD led the establishment in 2018 of a non profit social organization called the FD-QM Online Course Quality Rubric Standard Alliance (hereafter referred to as the FD-QM Alliance) which manages the FD-QM course review and FD-QM Online Course Quality Rubric Training Program. To date, the FD-QM Alliance has attracted more than 50 institutional members. Under the framework of the alliance, member institutions can obtain FD-QM Online Course Quality Rubric training and course review services.

The research team has developed a three-day FD-QM Online Course Quality Rubric Faculty Training Program as well. It is currently the first faculty training program focusing on online course standards in China. Different from the QM professional development program, the FD-QM training program has its own characteristics in terms of training objectives, trainee recruitment, content, and form. The core feature of the FD-QM Online Course Quality Rubric Faculty Training Program is that it is outcome-based and closely integrates the peer course review practices to achieve the two-fold goals of cultivating course review professionals and certifying high-quality courses, an approach which differs from the way usual QM training separates the two objectives. Although the actual training lasts only three days, it takes about two months for participants to complete all necessary learning tasks. As shown in Fig. 41.2, before the training starts, all participants need to provide information about their own courses so they can practice peer review and 'learning by doing' during the training. After the training, participants need to complete the redesign of their own courses based on their peers' course review reports and develop exemplary courses according to the FD-QM Online Course Quality Rubric.

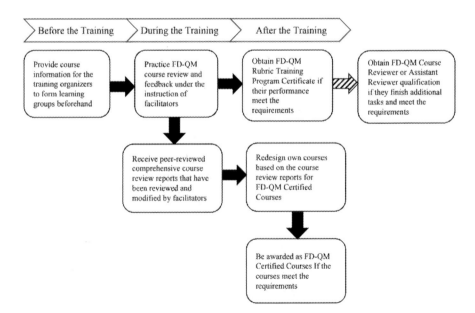

Fig. 41.2 Learning process and outcomes of the FD-QM Online Course Quality Rubric Faculty Training Program

Generally speaking, the FD-QM Online Course Quality Rubric Faculty Training Program mainly recruits faculty recommended by FD-QM Alliance member institutions to ensure that a group of outstanding instructors come to the training first, who can then in turn train other instructors at their own universities. Design of the training activities is based on the Gradual Release of Responsibility Model, consisting of mini-lectures followed by group discussions, peer evaluations, and independent learning. The model suggests that the instructor moves from assuming all responsibility for performing a task to a situation in which the learners assume all responsibility (Douglas & Frey, 2008).

To date, the CFD has conducted three training program sessions in March and November 2019 and January 2020 with 116 participants in total. After the first two training sessions, 64 out of 76 participants obtained the qualifications of FD-QM course reviewers or assistant reviewers, and 38 out of 69 courses have been awarded FD-QM Course Certification. The CFD also independently undertakes online/blended course review services for various HEIs. In May 2019, the Shanghai Municipal Education Commission issued an announcement calling for the selection of outstanding blended courses from local colleges and universities, requiring these courses to successfully meet the FD-QM Online Course Quality Rubric. In total, 50 courses were selected (Shanghai Municipal Education Commission, 2019). Thus, in addition to the 38 courses mentioned previously, a total of 88 courses nationwide have obtained FD-QM Course Certification.

Through cooperation with QM, the CFD's research team has developed the FD-QM Online Course Quality Rubric, a rubric equivalent in substance to that of the original QM Higher Education Rubric which can improve the standards of Chinese online education. With the efforts of the CFD, applications of the rubric have also expanded. Because the center has played such an active role in advancing the design and development of online courses and blended teaching, the center has achieved a greater degree of professionality and distinguishment in the eyes of other ADCs in China.

Conclusion

In general, the future of AD calls for more emphasis on organizational development and change (Sorcinelli, et al., 2006), and the same applies to the field of AD in China. It is especially important to align the work performed by ADCs and AD programs with institutional and governmental priorities. This will prompt ADCs to build additional relationships, networks, and collaborations with partners, both domestically and internationally. Gillespie (2010) once suggested two conceptual pillars for the framework of organizational development: relationship and context. Since China is a latecomer to the area of AD in higher education, there is no doubt that Chinese ADCs must improve themselves more rapidly and expand their influence by forming international collaborations. However, we must also be aware of potential issues and challenges that such collaborations might bring, such as the local adaptability and acceptance of practices and experiences from the international community, ensuring the interests of all collaborative parties are met, and the establishment of a long-term cooperation mechanism that promotes mutual interest and benefits. All of these factors need to be studied and explored as international collaborations in the field of AD in higher education continue, both within China and beyond.

Acknowledgments This research was funded by a 2018 humanities and social sciences project of the MOE entitled *Research on the Path to Improve the Quality of Blended Teaching: Scaffolding Effective Classroom Interaction and Developing Quality Standards for Online Courses.*

References

Cai, Y., & Ding, X. (2009). An analysis of the impacts of the revised excellent online course evaluation indicators on online course construction. *E-Education Research, 2009*(12), 50–53.

Chism, N. V. N., Gosling, D., & Sorcinelli, M. D. (2010). International faculty development. In K. J. Gillespie & L. R. Douglas (Eds.), *A guide to faculty development* (pp. 243–258). Jossey-Bass.

Ding, Y., Gao, Y., & Lu, F. (2017). The development of QM-Fudan adapted rubrics: Some results and analysis. *American Journal of Distance Education, 2017*(31), 198–206.

Douglas, F., & Frey, N. (2008). *Better learning through structured teaching: A framework for the gradual release of responsibility.* ASCD Publications.

Gillespie, K. J. (2010). Organizational development. In K. J. Gillespie & L. R. Douglas (Eds.), *A guide to faculty development* (pp. 379–396). Jossey-Bass.

Guo, W., Chen, L., & Chen, G. (2013). The Internet genes, the new and old online education. *Peking University Education Review, 11*(14), 173–184.

Li, Q., & Liu, N. (2015). Towards a MOOC quality assurance framework. *Open Educational Research, 21*(5), 66–73.

41 Extending International Collaboration to Certify High-Quality... 655

Liu, H. (2016). To merge online courses into higher institutional curriculum and teaching system: Obstacles and strategies. *Journal of Higher Education, 37*(5), 68–72.

Ministry of Education (MOE). (2011). *Opinions on the implementation of 'quality and teaching reform project of undergraduate education in higher education institutions (HEIs)' during the twelfth five-year plan period (2011–2015)*. MOE. http://old.moe.gov.cn/publicfiles/business/htmlfiles/moe/s5666/201109/124985.html

Ministry of Education (MOE). (2015). *Opinions of the ministry of education on strengthening the application and management of online open course construction in colleges and universities*. MOE. http://www.moe.edu.cn/publicfiles/business/htmlfiles/moe/s7056201504/186490.html

Ministry of Education (MOE). (2018). *Report of the network training center*. MOE.

Ministry of Education (MOE). (2019). *Implementation opinions on the construction of first-class undergraduate courses*. MOE. http://www.moe.gov.cn/srcsite/A08/s7056/201910/t20191031_406269.html

QM. (2014). *Quality Matters Higher Education Rubric workbook*. MarylandOnline.

Shanghai Municipal Education Commission. (2019). *On the announcement of the list of selected high-quality blended courses for Shanghai colleges and universities in 2019*. Shanghai Municipal Education Commission. http://edu.sh.gov.cn/html/xxgk/201911/418202019004.html

Sorcinelli, M. D., Austin, A. E., Eddy, P. L., & Beach, A. L. (2006). *Creating the future of faculty development: Learning from the past, understanding the present*. Anker Publishers.

Wang, W., & Tian, C. (2019). Research on the current situation of MOOC construction in Chinese universities. *Beijing Education (Higher Education), 4*, 69–72.

Appendix

Chart A.1 provides a visual overview and summary of the major themes addressed in each of the case studies as well as some demographic information about the size of the universities and the staff of their academic professional development centers (ADCs). An e-mail contact address is provided for the corresponding author of each chapter that can hopefully be used to build collaborative partnerships across institutions and ADCs.

© The Author(s), under exclusive license to Springer Nature Switzerland AG 2023
O. J. Neisler (ed.), *The Palgrave Handbook of Academic Professional Development Centers*,
Palgrave Studies on Leadership and Learning in Teacher Education,
https://doi.org/10.1007/978-3-030-80967-6

Chart A.1 Case study summary chart

Country/Region	Institution	Regional overview	Model	Mission	Structure	Theory	Governance	Funding	SaP	Student focus	Partnership	CoP	Certificate	T&L research	ADC eval	Online PD	SET	Students/programs/faculty	ADC staff	Contact e-mail
Australia		x																		denise.chalmers@uwa.edu.au
Latin America		x																		khourif@uninorte.edu.co
China		x																		fanyihong@aliyun.com
East Africa		x																		chip@kingsburyfamily.org
USA			x																	nilson@clemson.edu
USA	University of Arizona			x				State									x	45k/400/3,200	32	novod@email.arizona.edu
USA	University of San Diego			x								x						9k/89/875	na	emch@sandiego.edu
Oman	Sultan Qaboos University			x	x										x			Medical school	5	naiwardi@squ.edu.om
USA	Yale University			x	x			Endowment			x							39k/603/3,943	11	kyle.vitale@temple.edu
Australia	Monash University			x	x							x						83.5k/na/3,950	8	tammy.smith@monash.edu
Netherlands	Vriege Univeriteit Amsterdam					x							x					25k/300/2,263	na	h.a.glasbeek@vu.nl
Canada	Ontario Tech University				x								x			x		10k/90/1,550	na	bridgette.atkins@uoit.ca
USA	Tufts University				x	x		Grants			x				x			12k/150/1,500	na	Annie.Soisson@tufts.edu
USA	Indiana University South Bend						x	Grants							x			5k/na/500	7	gmetteta@iusb.edu
USA	New Mexico State University						x	Donors							x			14k/200/1,000	4	tgray@nmsu.edu

Country	University														Enrollment	Num	Email
USA	Fairfield University				x										5.3k/na/279	4	esmith@fairfield.edu
UK	University of Winchester	x	x		x	Grants	x	x		x	x				8k/50+/420	na	Tom.lowe@winchester.ac.uk
USA	University of California Merced						x							x	9k/24/657	138	asignorini@ucmerced.edu
USA	Green Mountain College (Closed)	x					x	x							NA	NA	hkeith1@radford.edu
Pakistan	Karakoram International University							x				x			5,500/17/200	3	asifbaseen@hotmail.com
Pakistan/ East Africa	Aga Khan University	x	x					x							2,500/28/500	13	tashmin.khamis@aku.edu
Turkey	Rogazici University						x	x				x		x	NA	NA	elif.bengu@agu.edu.tr, nevra.seggie@boun.edu
USA	University System of Georgia		x					x	x						na	6	jcofer@abac.edu; jordan.cofer@gcsu.edu
USA	Middle Tennessee College		x					x				x			21k+/300/980	3	Barbara.Draude@mtsu.edu
USA	University of Maryland Baltimore County			x		Grants			x						1,400/100/500	5	lhodges@umbc.edu
USA	North Central College								x						2,970/118/151	7	jlkeys@noctrl.edu
China	Shanghai Jiao Tong University					Grants			x			x			42k/143/3,236	17	yhqiu@sjtu.edu.cn
USA	State University of New York	x	x						x						18k/46/na	8	Shantih.Clemans@esc.edu
USA	Embry-Riddle Aeronautical University	x	x						x			x	x		23k/54/1,274	12	Cristina.Cottom@erau.edu

(continued)

Chart A.1 continued

Country/Region	Institution	Regional overview	Model	Mission	Structure	Theory	Governance	Funding	SaP	Student focus	Partnership	CoP	Certificate	T&L research	ADC eval	Online PD	SET	Students/programs/faculty	ADC staff	Contact e-mail
Oman	Sultan Qaboos University											x						14k/100+/1,000	5	neisler@squ.edu.om
Netherlands	Universiteit Amsterdam					x							x					22k/150/2,196	na	joyce.brouwer@vu.nl; joycebrouwerprive@gmail.com
USA	Nevada State College												x			x		5.5k/na/300	4	Christine.Draper@nsc.edu
USA	Claremont University					x							x					2,000k+/23/175	2	pff@cgu.edu ; shamini.dias@cgu.edu
Belgium	University of Liege					x							x					25k/300/3,000	na	dverpoorten@uliege.be
China	Beijing Institute of Technology													x				26k/250/2,000	na	zhangyeye@bit.edu.cn
UK	University of Leeds					x								x				39k/1,200/2,790	na	a.divan@leeds.ac.uk
China	Southwest Jiatong University										x			x				43k/na/1,100	na	fanyihong@aliyun.com
Hong Kong/China	University of Hong Kong				x	x					x				x			29k/160/1,100	31	gbilbow@hku.hk
Czech Republic	Masaryk University														x			25k+/400/2,630	10	svaricek@phil.muni.cz
Chile	Universidad Catolia de Temuco							MOE	x				x		x	x		10k+/73/867	9	rgarcia@uct.cl; richogarcia@gmail.com
China	Fudan University						x					x	x			x		30k/400/2,900+	na	yding@fudan.edu.cn

SaP Students as Partners; *CoP* Communities of Practice; *T&L* Teaching and Learning; *ADC* Academic Professional Development Center; *Eval* Evaluation; *PD* Professional Development; *SET* Student Evaluation of Teaching; *k* Thousand; *na* Not Available; *NA* Not Applicable.

Author Index

A

Abbot, S., 285
Abdel-Khalek, N., 124
Abigail, L., 413
Abuan, M., 295
Abu-Hijleh, M., 124
Acai, A., 634
Ackoff, R., 352
Adams, J. M., 511
Aelterman, G., 343
Ahmad, A., 633, 634
Al-Barwani, T., 392
Al Karusi, H., 466–467
Al Wardy N., 123, 127
Alexander, B., 389
Ali, A., 318
Allen, D., 90
Allison, T., 327
Alonso Vilches, V., 533
Al-Roomi, K., 124
Al-Sulaimani, H., 466–467
Alsup, J., 512
Altbach, P., 327, 329
Altschuld, J., 447

Ambrose, S., 104, 479
Amundsen, C., 342
Anderson, B., 615
Anderson, L., 175, 465
Anderson, M., 483
Anderson, S., 615
Anthony, P. J., 449
Appadurai, A., 511
Archer, M., 517
Argyris, C., 515, 517
Arieli, S., 521
Arif, M., 269
Armour, L., 327
Armstrong, E., 139
Arum, R., 139
Ashgar, A., 305
Astin, A. W., 111, 112, 270, 277
Astin, H. S., 110, 112
Atkins, B., 190
Atvars, T., 271
Atwell, A., 451, 452
Austen, L., 272
Austin, A. E., 359, 360, 379, 621

© The Author(s), under exclusive license to Springer Nature Switzerland AG 2023
O. J. Neisler (ed.), *The Palgrave Handbook of Academic Professional Development Centers*,
Palgrave Studies on Leadership and Learning in Teacher Education,
https://doi.org/10.1007/978-3-030-80967-6

662   Author Index

Baepler, P., 303
Baggen, Y., 345
Bain, K., 178, 465, 577, 583
Baird, M., 162
Baker, R., 305
Ballantyne, S., 497
Bamber, R., 534
Bamber, V., 633, 634
Barak, R., 615
Barker, L. R., 239
Barker, M. K., 144
Barnes, G., 271
Barnett, J. E., 410
Barr, R. B., 512
Bass, R., 399
Basu, K., 246
Bates, S., 429
Bauer, K. W., 565
Beach, A. L., 23, 24, 28, 33, 253, 254,
     333, 379, 397, 401
Beane-Katner, L., 370
Bednar, A. K., 172
Beerkens, M., 617, 621
Bekey, J., 424
Bell, M., 327
Bennett, J. S., 565
Bensimon, E., 326
Benton, S., 448
Bergquist, W., 237, 360
Berliner, D., 615
Bernstein, D., 462, 464, 465
Berret, B., 497
Berry, D. M., 562
Bérubé, M., 109
Besley, S. C., 512
Betihavas, V., 563
Bettinger, E., 305
Beuscher, L., 327
Bhutta, S. M., 345
Biggs, J., 68, 71, 103, 173, 175, 178,
     191, 336, 342, 343, 483, 629
Bilbow, G. T., 601

Billing, D., 179, 345
Binder, M., 496
Birch, A. J., 239
Birch, J., 239
Birol, G., 429
Black, B., 424
Blackmore, P., 8
Blatny, M., 614
Bless, M. M., 497
Bloom, B., 175
Bloom, L., 110
Boice, R., 410
Bok, D., 352, 359
Bolander Laksov, K., 344, 345
Boone, M. E., 515, 516
Boraiko, C., 389
Borden, V., 8, 11
Borin, P., 342
Boring, A., 354, 355
Borrego, M., 401
Borsu, O., 537
Bos, J., 484, 487, 489
Bosanquet, A., 512
Bosman, L., 472
Boutelle, K., 305
Bovill, C., 287
Boyer, E., 42–44, 56, 237, 426, 496,
     512, 518, 574, 578
     domains of scholarship, 43, 44
     multiple scholarship, 42, 43, 45, 56,
     574, 578
Bransford, J., 104, 399
Brar, R., 187, 188, 198
Braskamp, L. A., 43, 112
Bråten, H., 529
Braxton, J., 237
Breslow, L., 610
Brew, A., 8
Bridges, M., 104
Bridgman, H., 563
Brint, S., 411
Brinthaupt, T. M., 380, 383, 389
Briseño-Garzón, A., 429

Britnell, J., 81
Bronk, K. C., 111
Brookfield, S. D., 61, 517
Broström, A., 621
Brown, A., 104, 399
Brown, E. C., 365
Brown, J. S., 521
Brown, K. L., 110
Brown, M. P., 471
Brown, P. C., 104
Brown, T., 518
Brunner, J. J., 24
Brunstein, J., 558
Bryant, A. N., 111
Bryson, C., 269, 270
Buchanan, R., 514
Buckley, S., 463
Budds, K., 562
Buechner, F., 117
Bui, D., 162
Buller, J. L., 415
Bulte, J., 180
Burnett, A. N., 462
Burrow, A. L., 111
Bushney, M., 463
Byron, W. J., 113

Cai, Y., 649
Calahan, P. T., 389
Caplan, B. D., 109
Carew, A. L., 327, 329
Carfagna, A., 511
Carless, D., 604
Carr, W., 574
Carruthers, G., 124
Carson, R., 116
Cartwright, S., 517
Cash, K., 110
Cavanagh, S. R., 517
Cawyer, C. S., 370

Čejková, I., 615
Challis, D., 530
Chalmers, D., 8–10, 15, 17, 33, 429, 630, 633–635
Chambers, T. G., 110
Chan, K., 604
Chapman, M., 342
Chasteen, S. V., 144
Chauhan, S., 342
Chauriye, S., 629
Chen, G., 649
Chen, L., 649
Chen, M., 45
Chen, X., 579
Cheng, B., 285
Chermak, J., 496
Chick, N., 285
Chickering, A., 336, 342
Chism, N. V. N., 26, 239, 370, 379, 407, 650
Chitwood, E., 272
Choi, J. Y., 111
Christopher, D. F., 127
Chun, E., 415
Cilliers, F., 633
Clark, D. J., 289, 424, 531
Clarke, A., 538
Clayton, D., 531
Clayton, M. A., 389
Clegg, S., 72
Clemans, S. E., 436
Clinefelter, D. L., 448
Coaldrake, P., 9
Coates, H., 12
Cocking, R., 104
Coffman, C., 472
Cohen-Schotanus, J., 180
Cole, K. A., 239
Cole, R., 144
Collis, K., 175
Condon, W., 90, 239
Connell, G. L., 110

664 Author Index

Conway, J., 237, 242
Cook, C. E., 31, 206, 405, 422, 423, 427, 430
Cook, M. T., 517
Cook-Sather, A., 285–287, 296, 297, 328
Cordewener, B., 486
Cotter, R. J., 558
Cottom, C., 452
Cotton, K., 178
Cox, M. D., 116, 401, 410, 449, 463, 471
Cozolino, L., 157
Crawford, K., 657
Cribb, A., 110
Crisp, G., 414
Croiset, G., 178
Cross, M., 563
Cross, N., 518
Crumpton-Young, L., 352
Cruz, I., 414
Cruz, L., 328
Csikszentmihalyi, M., 521
Cunningham, D. J., 172

D

Dailey-Hebert, A., 448
Davidson, N., 511
Davis, B., 515
Davis, C. K., 448
Davis, M. H., 123
Davis, S., 370
Dawson, D., 81, 342
De Grave, W., 269
Debowski, S., 329
DeChenne-Peters, S. E., 144
Deci, E. L., 176, 177, 179
Delfosse, C., 533
Delio, I., 114
Denis, B., 537
Dennison, S., 369
Detroz, P., 533

Devyver, J., 537
Dewey, J., 517
DeWitz, S. J., 109
DeZure, D., 329
Dhamani, K., 342
Diamond, M. R., 424, 426
Didriksson, A., 24
Ding, X., 649
Ding, Y., 650
DiPietro, M., 104, 479
Divan, A., 563
Dolan, V. L., 448
Dole, S., 110
Dolmans, D., 269
Donnelli-Sallee, E., 448
Donnelly, A., 272
Donovan, D. A., 110
Dorantes, S., 295
Dörfler, V., 376
Douglas, F., 653
Draude, B. J., 380
Drea, C., 187, 188, 198
Driessen, M., 303
Du, J., 546, 549, 550
Duan, Z., 54
Duchâteau, D., 533
Duffy, T., 172
Duguid, P., 521
Dunlosky, J., 104
Dunne, E., 269, 271
Dvorakova, L. S., 285
Dykman, C. A., 448

E

Eagan, M. K. (Jr), 144
Eaton, V., 495
Eddy, P. L., 29, 81, 237, 327, 397, 653
Eddy, S. L., 498
Eden, C., 376
Edin, K., 116
Edmond, N., 534
El Din Ahmed, M. G., 124

El Hakim, Y., 270
Elbe, K., 254
Eliott, E., 472
Elliott, R. W., 90
Ellis, D. E., 379
Elman, N. S., 410
Elrod, S., 205
Elton, L., 483, 486
England, R., 62–63, 208, 599, 601
Engvik, G., 43
Entwistle, N., 5
Erickson, G., 397
Esfijani, A., 145
Eskandari, H., 352
Esson, J. M., 144
Evans, A., 415
Eynon, B., 411

F

Facione, P., 466
Falk, Barbara, 4
Fan, Y., 42, 43, 45–47, 56, 57, 573, 574
Fanghanel, J., 609
Fearn, C., 272
Feilberg, J., 43
Feldman, K. A., 496
Felten, P., 143, 285
Felton, P., 285
Feltzer, M., 178
Fendler, J., 614
Fenton, N., 537
Ferrada Hurtado, R., 24
Finelli, C. J., 424, 426
Fink, L. D., vii, 24, 71, 175, 176, 179, 180, 232, 465, 479
Finn, J. D., 269
Fischer, K. W., 517
Fishbach, A., 411
Fisher, A., 104
Fisher, L. S., 389
Flaherty, C., 82
Flavell, J. H., 515

Fletcher, J., 496
Flint, A., 286
Floden, R., 190
Forgie, S. E., 333
Forrest, L., 410
Frankham, J., 270
Franklin, J., 355, 360
Fraser, K., 4, 5, 10, 12, 15
Freeman, S., 498
Freire, P., 61, 514
Frey, N., 653
Friedman, T. L., 511
Friesen, M. D., 512
Fullan, M., 483, 485–488, 491
Furco, A., 116
Furlong, P. J., 222
Furterer, S., 352
Fyffe, J. M., 345

G

Gaillard-Kenney, S., 497
Gambino, L. M., 411
Gamson, Z., 336, 342
Gandell, T., 427
Gangloff, E., 472
Gao, X., 550
Gao, Y., 650
Gappa, J., 497
Garbarino, S., 633
Gardiner, D., 33, 429, 633, 634
Gardner, F., 110
Gardner, J. G., 389
Gastrow, M., 317
Gazzola, A. L., 24
Geertsema, J., 344, 345
Gehrke, S., 205
Geng, B., 426
George, C. F., 127
Geschwind, L., 621
Gewirtz, S., 110
Gibbs, G., 180, 333, 336, 342, 344
Gijbels, D., 239

666   **Author Index**

Gijselaers, W. H., 180
Gilbert, S., 289
Gillespie, K. J., 253, 254, 327, 407, 654
Gillian-Daniel, D. L., 326
Ginns, P., 635
Ginsberg, M., 83, 230
Giroux, H. A., 109, 514
Glasbeek, H. A., 172, 180, 483
Glassick, C. E., 237, 512
Gleadow, R., 158
Glennon, C., 517
Glover, J., 83
Glowacki-Ducka, M., 471
Goerke, V., 635
Golde, C. M., 615
Goldenberg, J., 521
Goldschmidt, A., 521
Gonzalez, A., 155
Gonzalez, D., 355
Goodburn, A., 462
Goodhew, P., 563
Goody, A., 635
Gordon, D., 192
Gordon, G., 254, 257
Gosling, D., 253, 254
Gottfried, A. C., 426
Graeff, T., 389
Graham, R., 482
Grant, A. M., 244
Gray, J., 389
Gray, K., 254
Gray, T., 237, 239, 242
Graystone, L., 634
Green, D. A., 408
Greenberg, D., 352
Greenwood, J., 517
Grooters, S., 215
Gross, N., 109
Gruber, H., 179
Grunefeld, H., 483
Guerra, C., 449

Guo, W., 649
Guskey, T., 633, 634
Gyuorko, J., 497

H

Haertel, G., 178
Hagner, P. R., 352
Hake, R. R., 637
Halcrow, C., 497
Hamdy, H., 124
Hammer, S., 110
Han, A., 429
Hande, K., 326, 327
Handstedt, P., 514, 517
Hanstedt, P., 411
Haras, C., 83, 230
Harden, R. M., 127
Hargraves, H., 5
Harrington, K., 286
Harris, C. J., 26, 239
Harris, N. L., 426
Harshman, J., 144
Harst, W., 497
Harte, K., 127
Harting, E., 484, 487, 489
Hartley III, H. V., 109
Harvey, L., 109, 336, 342
Harvey, M., 374
Hassan, G., 124
Hativa, N., 615
Hattie, J., 178–181
Haubruge, E., 537
Hausman, M., 533
Haviland, D., 410
Haynie, A., 29
Healey, M., 286
Heaton, C., 272
Heinrich, L., 158
Hénard, F., 25, 33, 35–37
Henderson, C., 401
Hendricks, M., 486

Author Index

Henkens, K., 110
Henriques, L., 410
Herman, J. H., 254, 436
Herman, L., 436
Herman, N., 633
Herrington, J., 532
Herrington, T., 532
Hershock, C., 426
Hicks, O., 8
Hill, I., 634
Hill, P. L., 111
Hinton, C., 517
Hitchcock, A., 81
Ho, A., 329
Hochschild, A., 415
Hodzi, C., 61
Hoel, T., 43
Hohnstreiter, M., 245
Holdrinet, R., 180
Holland, J., 633
Holley, M., 26, 239
Hollingsworth, H., 531
Holt, D., 530
Honeydew, M., 158
Hood, C., 9, 633
Hook, J., 153
Hooks, B., 514
Hope, A., 61
Hore, T., 5
Houston, D., 633
Howard, J., 317
Hrabowski, Freeman, Dr., 394
Huang, T., 54
Hubball, H. T., 538
Huber, M. T., 512
Huberman, M., 531
Hudson, K., 29, 31, 36
Hughes, G., 532
Humphrey, O., 277
Hunt, L., xiv
Hurney, C. A., 426
Hursh, D., 447
Hutber, L., 271
Hutchings, P., 512

Iglesias-Martínez, M., 615
Ingemarsson, I., 254
Iuzzini, J., 365
Iversen, A., 69
Iverson, E. R., 239, 467

Jackson, M., 239
Jakovljevic, M., 463
James, N., 155, 158
Jaschik, S., 416
Jay, E., 243, 245
Jayaram, K., 25
Jelinek, M., 614
Jensen, A., 69
Jensen, R., 317
Jerez, O., 34
Jérôme, F., 533, 538
Jodl, J., 497
Johannes, C., 614
Johnson, A., 449
Johnson, W. B., 410
Johnston, S., 8
Jones Taggart, H., 190
Jones, B.F., 562
Jones, S., 374
Jones-Devitt, S., 272
Jongen, H., 483
Jonsson, A., 178, 180
Jordens, J. Z., 343
Jordt, H., 498
Joshi, T., 269

Kafka, S., 414
Kahn, P., 563
Kalish, A., 422
Kallenberg, T., 483, 491
Kandlbinder, P., 5
Kanuka, H., 343
Kaplan, M., 206, 405

668 Author Index

Karagiorgi, Y., 173
Karjalainen, A., 529
Karunathilake, I., 127
Kaslow, N. J., 410
Kassab, S., 124
Kelderman, E., 109
Kember, D., 620, 621
Kemmis, S., 558, 574
Kenny, J., 484
Kent, A., 562
Keogh, B., 190
Kern, D. E., 239
Kezar, A. J., 394, 479
Kezar, A., 205
Khamis, T., 334, 341, 342
Kift, S., 13
Kimball, R., 109
King, J., 558
King, S., 270, 271
Kingsbury, C., 59, 61
Kinzie, J., 286
Kirschner, P. A., 486
Knapper, C., 343, 344
Knecht, P., 615
Knight, A. M., 239
Knight, J. K., 144
Knight, J., 327, 329
Knight, P. T., 336, 342, 345
Knorr, K., 285
Kolb, A., 352
Kolb, D., 352
Kolmos, A., 254
Kolodner, K., 239
Kornhaber, R., 562, 563
Koroluk, J., 194, 195
Kotecha, P., 495
Kotter, J., 65, 484
Kraemer, S. B., 326
Krathwohl, D., 175, 465
Krause, K., 496
Kreber, C., 495
Krogh, L., 69
Kruck, S. E., 426

Kruss, G., 317
Kuh, G. D., 178, 292, 412, 565
Kuh, G., 178, 270, 292, 412, 565
Kumar, D., 447
Kurtz, C. F., 597
Kustra, E. D. H., 559
Kusurkar, R., 177, 178
Kveton, P., 614
Kwan, K., 620, 621
Kynčilová, L., 614

L

Ladd Jr, E., 109
Lake, P., xiv, 657
Laloux, A., 254
Landinelli, J., 495
Landy K., 286
Lane, P., xiv, 657
Lankewicz, G., 447
Laski, F. A., 144
Latham, G., 272
Lave, J., 160
Lawson, E., 158
Lea, J., 277
Leach, L., 5
Leatherman, J., 317
LeBihan, J., 272
Lederman, D., 416
Leduc, L., 533, 538
Lee, A., 4, 5
Lee, C. J., 144
Lee, V., 29, 30, 317, 327, 329
Lefoe, G. E., 374
Lefoe, G., 327
Lemaitre, M. J., 342
Leslie, D., 497
Levis-Fitzgerald, M., 144
Lewis, R., 9
Li, D., 448
Li, K., 329
Li, Q., 649
Lindholm, J. A., 110, 112

Ling, P., 5, 8, 15
Linke, R. D., 6, 15
Lipset, S., 109
Liston, D., 517
Little, D., 408
Liu, H., 649
Liu, N., 649
Lizzio, A., 6
Lo, S. M., 144
Lodge, J., 512
Lohe, D., 28
Lopes, V., 563
Loughran, J., 517
Love, B. L., 514
Lovett, M., 479
Lowe, T., 270, 271, 277
Lowman, J., 620
Lozano-Cabezas, I., 615
Lu, F., 650
Luce-Kapler, R., 515
Ludwig, L., 563
Luth, R., 333
Lyman, F., 104
Lyons, R. M. K., 497

M

MacCormack, P., 339
Macfarlan, B., 153
Machovcova, K., 614
MacKenzie, J., 563
Macpherson, A., 342
Madson, L., 218, 588
Maeroff, G. I., 237, 512
Magda, A. J., 448, 497, 498
Mägi, E., 617, 621
Magruder, E., 230, 365
Malfroy, J., 428
Manathunga, C., 5
Mandell, A., 435, 436
Mandernach, B. J., 448
Mandl, H., 179
Manduca, C. A., 239, 467

Manginelli, A., 328
Mao Yisheng, 576, 579
Margolis, J., 104
Marichal, E., 533
Marie, J., 269
Marincovich, M., 427, 430
Marion, R., 486
Marks, G., 12
Marquis, E., 563
Mårtensson, K., 427
Martinez-Ruiz, M. A., 615
Martino, L., 452
Marton, F., 5
Matheus, T., 449
Matthews, K. E., 512
Matthews, K., 269
McAlpine, L., 401
McDaniel, M. A., 104
McDermott, R., 160, 368
McDonald, J., 160, 449
McDonald, R., 5
McDonnell, L. M., 144
McDonough, M., 498
McDowell, L., 179
McGrath, S., 317
McGuire, G., 228
McIntyre, G., 342
McKay, T. A., 144
McKeachie, W. J, 254, 537
McKelvey, B., 486
Mckenna, A., 449
McKinney, W., 285
McLean, J., 317
McLean, M., 317
McPherson, M., 90
McSherry, W., 110
McTighe, J., 191, 465, 518
Meadows, D. H., 515
Meadows, K. N., 342
Meena, S., 110
Meizlish, D., 317
Mercer-Mapstone, L., 285
Merriam, S., 357

670 Author Index

Merrill, D., 172
Mettetal, G., 228
Meyer, A., 191, 192
Meyer, J., 239
Mezirow, J., 61
Michele, A., 313, 328
Michelotti, N., 144
Middleton, A., 272
Miles, C. A., 495
Miller, G. E., 175
Min-Leliveld, M., 239
Miranda, D. A., 24
Miranda, X., 495
Mirshekari, C., 215
Moely, B. E., 116
Moffit, A., 25
Mohr, A., 533
Moon, J., 70
Moore, T., 157
Morgan, M., 272
Moser, D., 237
Moses, I., 5
Motley, P., 563
Moya, B., 635
Mudrak, J., 614
Mullinix, B., 81
Muñoz, A., 630
Murphy, M., 563
Murray, M. C., 109
Musgrove, A., 144
Myers, R. A., 563

N

Naidoo, K., 5
Naqvi, S., 318
Nash, R. J., 109
Nathan, M. J., 104
Navet, R., 537
Naylor, S., 190
Neal, A., 389
Neary, M., 564
Neisler, O., 466

Nelson, C., 109
Nghia Tran, L.H., 269
Nilson, L., xiv, 82, 178, 247, 465, 479, 537
Nordin, E., 449
Norman, M., 479
Norris, V. R., 448
Notta, F., 345
Novotný, P., 615
Nuhfer, E., 82

O

O'Banion, T., 56, 574
O'Brien, M., 8, 9
O'Connor, K., 500
O'Malley, K., 124
O'Neal, C., 426
Oliver, D. E., 90
Olsen, K., 342
Olsen, M., 11
Olson, M. R., 497
Olsson, T., 427
Ombres, S., 452
Omingo, M., 59, 66, 68, 70
Orchard, A., 155
Ortiz, A. M., 410
Ortquist-Ahrens, L., 379
Ory, J., 43
Ott, M., 426
Otter, R., 389
Otto, S., 314, 589
Ottoboni, K., 355
Ouellett, M., 222, 376
Owen, D., 269

P

Paas, F., 486
Pabian, P., 614
Paddison, A., 271
Palmer, M. S., 144
Palmer, P. J., 515

Palmer, S., 530
Pan, M., 47
Panadero, E., 178, 180
Panakkal, G., 295
Pang, H., 546, 549
Parker, D., 305
Parker, M., 328
Parkin, H., 272
Parks, S., 109
Parlascino, E., 537
Parsons, D., 633, 634
Parsons, J., 352
Patricio, J., 26, 33, 37
Patrick, S., 496
Patton, M., 515, 518
Paul, R., 174
Paulsen, M. B., 496
Paulsen, M., 496
Pedersen, A., 69
Perry, J., 172
Peseta, T., 296
Peters, F., 487, 488
Peters, G., 9
Petersen, I., 317
Petersen, K., 389
Pey, R., 629
Phillippi, J., 327
Phillips, S., 237, 360, 369
Piaget, J., 517
Pimmel, R., 449
Pinder-Grover, T., 424
Pingree, A., 143
Pinter, M., 380, 383, 389
Pintrich, P. R., 517
Plank, K. M., 422
Plank, K., 143
Pohan, C., 286, 295
Polovina-Cukovic, D., 495
Poole, G., 536
Potter, M. K., 559
Poulin, R., 448, 498
Powell-Coffman, J., 472
Prawatt, R., 190

Prebble, T., 5
Preckel, F., 178–180, 483
Price, C., 158
Prins, S. C. B., 426
Probert, B., 17
Prosser, M., 620, 621
Pyrko, I., 367, 376

Q

Qualters, D., 207, 208

R

Raaheim, A., 529
Rabelo, L., 352
Radloff, A., 254
Rae, B., 334
Raffo, D. M, 389
Raj, G. A., 124
Raker, J., 472
Ramsden, P., 6, 539
Rao, G. M., 124
Rathbun, G., 317
Rawat, S., 110
Rawson, K. A., 104
Ray, J., 414
Raza, S., 318
Ream, T. C., 237
Reason, R., 472
Reder, M., 406, 408
Redmond, M. V., 289, 424
Reigeluth, C. M., 172
Renkl, A., 179
Reynolds, M., 558, 561, 563–565
Rice, R., 495
Richlin, L., 428
Richman, J., 155
Rickli, S., 178
Rittel, H., 514
Rizvi, N., 342
Robertson, D. L., 253, 254, 327
Robson, S., 530

672 Author Index

Rocio, C., 449
Rockequemore, K., 410
Rodrigues, S., 337, 342
Roe, E., 5
Roediger III, H. L., 104
Rose, D., 192
Roseveare, D., 25, 33, 35–37
Roxå, T., xiin5
Rump, C., 254
Rutz, C., 467
Ryan, R. M., 177, 179
Ryan, R., 176, 177, 179
Ryan, Y., 4, 5, 9, 12
Ryan-Harshman, M., 190
Ryland, K., 374

S

Sadler, K., 389
Sagiv, L., 521
Sala-Diakanda, S., 352
Salim, Z., 94
Sambell, K., 179
Samuel, A., 448
Santangelo, T., 303
Sargeant, A., 243, 245
Sarma, M., 449
Saroyan, A., 342
Savory, P., 462
Sawyer, K., 487
Schliephake, K., 162
Schmidt, H. G., 180
Schneider, M., 178–180, 483
Schön, D. A., 515, 517
Schroeder, C. M., 204, 205, 393
Schuh, J., 178
Schwartz, B., 29
Scott, D., 334, 336
Scott, G., 480, 483, 485, 487, 488, 491
Scott, I., 11
Scott, S., 334, 336
Scully, S., 342

Sedláčková, J., 615
Šeďová, K., 615
Seelig, T., 518
Seidel, T., 614
Seipel, S., 389
Selvester, P., 496
Senge, P., 42, 56, 394, 395, 486, 488, 574, 576, 577
Senreich, E., 110
Serdyukov, P., 486
Shaefer, H. L., 116
Shammas, R., 285
Shaw, C., 271, 276
Sheikh, K., 124
Shulman, J., 512
Shulman, L. S., 399, 512
Sievers, J., 254
Signorini, A., 286, 294, 295
Šima, K., 614
Simhi, E., 615
Simmons, S., 109
Simonds, C., 370
Simpson, C., 180
Sims, S., 270, 271
Singer, S., 353
Sjoer, E., 345
Skipper, Y., 562
Skloot, R., 115
Slaughter, S., 109
Šmardová, A., 615
Smith, A., 621
Smith, B., 496
Smith, C., 29, 31, 36
Smith, E., 621
Smith, K., 289, 353
Smith, M. K., 498
Smith, T., 155
Snowden, D. J., 515–517, 597
Snyder, W., 631
Sobrero, V., 630
Soisson, A., 207, 208
Solcova, I., 614
Solomonides, I., 14

Author Index   673

Song, W., 546
Sorcinelli, M. D., 23–25, 29, 81, 237, 239, 253, 254, 257, 327, 352, 360, 379, 397, 407, 411, 653
Splinter, T. A., 180
Stains, M., 144
Stalmeijer, R., 269
Star, C., 110
Stark, P. B., 355
Stedman, L., 9
Stefani, L., 633, 634
Stein, R., 172
Stensaker, B., 610
Stes, A., 239
Stevens, M., 139
Stewart, C., 155
Stiller, J., 176
Stoney, S., 635
Strahlman, H., 328
Stranach, M., 195
Stufflebeam, D., 318
Suddaby, G., 5
Sui, Y., 551, 553
Sumara, D., 515
Supiano, B., 295
Suskie, L., 98
Sutherland, K., 333
Švaříček, R., 615
Svingby, G., 180
Svinicki, M., 537
Swail, W., 496
Swaim, K., 285
Symeou, L., 173
Szala-Meneok, K., 537

Tagg, J., 512
Takayama, K., 207
Tan, M., 42, 43, 56, 574
Tang, C., 68, 71, 103, 173, 178, 336, 342, 483, 629

Tang, L., 447
Tariq, R. H., 318
Tatzel, M., 436
Taylor, K. L., 536
Taylor, L., 352
Taylor, S. C., 83
Telmisani, A., 124
Ten Cate, T. J., 178
Thacher, J., 496
Theall, M., 355, 360, 633
Thedwall, K., 399
Thomas, L., 269, 277
Thompson, J., 536
Tian, C., 649
Timmel, S., 61
Timperley, H., 178, 180
Tinto, V., 277, 304
Tjedvoll, A., 43
Tom, M., 69
Tomlinson, C., 303
Tomljenovic-Berube, A., 563
Topping, K. J., 318
Tran, T., 270
Travis, J., 447
Trigwell, K., 620, 621, 635
Trow, M., 47
Trowler, P., 534, 609
Tůma, F., 615
Turra, H., 266, 476, 587–588

Uhl-Bien, M., 486
Uttl, B., 355
Uzzi, B., 562

Van Dalen, H., 110
Van de Poël, J.F., 533, 537, 538
Van der Drift, K., 180
van der Molen, H. T., 180
van der Rijst, R., 344, 345

674 Author Index

Van Der Vaart, R., 610
Van der Zwaan, B., 479
Van Manen, M., 517
Van Pategem, P., 239
van Rossum, H. J., 180
van Tartwijk, J., 483
Vander Ven, T., 222
Vanwyk, J., 317
Vella, J., 61
Veneros, D., 630
Verloop, N., 180
Vermunt, J., 178, 180
Verpoorten, D., 533, 538
Vince, R., 558, 561, 563–565
Vine, M., 563
Vinther, O., 254
Visser, K., 180, 483
Vithal, R., 420, 428
Voglewede, P., 472
Von Glasersfeld, E., 173
Vos, C. M. P., 180
Vos, P., 180
Vroeijenstijn, A., 341
Vygotsky, L. S., 517

W

Walker, J. D., 303
Walkington, H., 565
Walsh, L., 563
Walsh, W. B., 109
Walvoord, B., 98, 99, 102
Wang, J., 54
Wang, M., 178
Wang, W., 649
Ward, H., 496
Ward, T., 557
Wareham, T., 609
Webber, M., 514
Weggeman, M., 486
Weiner, T., 415
Wenderoth, W. P., 498

Wenger, É., 160, 366–368, 464, 631
Wenger-Trayner, B., 366
Wenger-Trayner, É., 366
West, L., 5
West, M., 487
Westers, P., 178
Weston, C., 401
Whitchurch, C., 153
Whitehead, L., 429
Whittingham, J., 269
Wieman, C., 298
Wiggens, G., 191
Wiggins, G., 465, 518
Willett, G., 239
Williams, H. L., 158
Williams, I., 158
Williams, K., 158
Willingham, D. T., 104
Willis, D., 634
Willis, J., 173
Willis, K., 428
Wilson, K., 6
Winn, J., 564
Wisdom, J., 500
Witham, K., 204
Woodard, J. B., 389
Woods, J., 496
Woolley, K., 411
Woolsey, M. L., 109
Wopereis, I., 486
Wright, D. L., 496
Wright, G., 68
Wright, M. C., 422
Wright, M., 28
Wubbels, T., 483
Wuchty, S., 562

Y

Yasuno, M., 111
Yeh, S., 326
Yoder, B., 449

Yonge, O., 333
Young, A. M., 144
Yu, Q., 426
Yu, X., 426

Z

Zabalza, M., 25, 32
Zakrajsek, T., 83, 230

Zeichner, K., 517
Zepke, N., 343, 565
Zhang, J., 296
Zhang, Y., 552
Zhao, J., 575
Zhu, Y., 47
Zimmer, K. S., 269
Zou, T., 601
Zounek, J., 615

Subject Index

A

Academic advising, 81, 130, 300, 304–306, 310, 357
Academic coaching, 104, 105, 173, 300, 305
Academic credentials, 5
Academic excellence, 110–112, 251–253, 255–257, 260
Academic Master Plan, 380, 388
Academic practice, 67
Academic Program Review (APR), 100–102, 105
Academic quality, 343–344, 437
  See also Quality assurance
Academics Without Borders (AWB), 342, 346
Accountability, 6, 33, 99, 336, 341, 633
Accreditation, xvi, 13, 14, 98, 123, 127, 130, 134, 136, 214, 274, 284, 293, 338, 346, 387, 398, 458, 468, 527, 605
Active learning, ix, 104, 159, 193, 194, 227, 277, 289–291, 293, 303, 340, 373, 458, 460, 471, 472, 496, 498, 501, 513, 517, 534, 576, 630, 632, 637

active construction of knowledge, 173
modes of teaching, 458, 472
Active teaching and learning methods, 358, 359
ADC facilities
  building, 162, 223, 307, 335
  faculty development space, 365
ADC faculty incentive(s), 35
  badge(s), 500
  course release, 222
  events award ceremony, 213
  events luncheon(s), 244, 422
  faculty grant(s), 221
  financial incentive(s), 221
  reward(s), 296
  salary increase, 500
  stipend(s), 114, 228, 253, 255
ADC faculty relationship(s)
  faculty-centered initiative(s), 413
  faculty delegate(s), 381, 383
  faculty-driven philosophy, 385
  faculty engagement, 262, 449
  faculty incentive(s), xvii, 56
  faculty involvement, 255, 385
  faculty ownership, 254, 257

© The Author(s), under exclusive license to Springer Nature Switzerland AG 2023
O. J. Neisler (ed.), *The Palgrave Handbook of Academic Professional Development Centers*,
Palgrave Studies on Leadership and Learning in Teacher Education,
https://doi.org/10.1007/978-3-030-80967-6

677

678   Subject Index

ADC faculty relationship(s) (*cont.*)
  faculty reassignment(s), 439
  liaison, 112, 253, 255, 413
  voting representative(s), 363, 364
ADC functional tasks, 50
ADC funding, xvi, 89
  budget, 236, 406, 408, 572
  contributions, 14, 227
  donor-supported, 235
  endowment, 82, 141
  external fund(s)/funding, 213,
    215, 529
  foundation, 227
  funding, 7, 9–14, 16, 24, 48, 65,
    88, 143, 217, 222, 223, 225,
    226, 229, 241, 296, 383,
    420, 630
    source(s), x
  fundraising, 241
  grants, 8, 11, 16–17, 30, 143, 205,
    213, 218, 222, 223, 236, 241,
    252, 294, 300, 307, 337, 344,
    406, 591
  internal grant funding, 401
  operating costs, 529
  operating fund, 54
  payroll deduction, xvi, 218,
    241, 243
  planned (future estate) gift(s),
    218, 235
  planned giving, 241
  seed money, 7
  state funding, 398
  student technology fee(s), 219
  teaching development grant(s), 427
ADC management
  Academic Council, 258, 271, 339
  advisory board, 83, 221, 223, 226,
    230, 239, 614
  advisory group, 439
  co-director, 381
  collaborative leadership, 255
  consolidation, 97

director, ix, 12–14, 29, 80–82, 89,
    223, 224, 253
  distributed leadership, 8
  executive directors, 141, 142
  faculty directors, 221, 223, 255
  faculty-directed, 255, 438
  fault line(s), 155–157
  hierarchy, 80, 217
  member-driven, 235, 236
  merger, 3, 139
  model ADC, 79–81, 84, 88, 481
  shared ownership, 484, 490
  strategic advisor, 529
  three-director model, 252, 256
  working group(s), 325, 563
ADC module(s), 54
ADC network(s), 31, 361
  serving all faculty (over large areas
    and distances), 365
ADC programming components, 53
  analytical framework, 634
  annual conference, 4, 428
  book discussion(s), 115, 232,
    237, 469
  breakout group(s), 195, 197
  business meeting(s), 368
  check in session(s), 368
  Colloquium, 411
  conference(s), 80, 337, 344, 420,
    535, 604
  consultations, 83, 143, 146,
    223, 464
  departmental workshop(s), 360
  dinner discussion(s), 114
  faculty retreat(s), 214, 260, 387
  handbook(s), 52, 88
  institutes, 143, 226, 228, 232
  integrated resources, 49
  listserv, 333, 368, 369, 372, 375
  local expert(s), 133
  luncheon, 244, 245, 411, 422, 425
  Lunch Series, 146
  Marshmallow Challenge, 325

new faculty orientation, 30, 192, 207, 213, 223, 227, 296, 303, 310, 365, 367, 368, 409, 419, 422, 423, 464
new initiative(s), 28, 55, 149, 333, 386, 397
newsletter(s), 88, 304, 435
observations, 143, 500, 502
podcast, 442
portfolio, 64, 70, 500, 576
remediation, 5, 406
repository of resources, 369
retreats, 148, 223, 383, 384
seminar(s), 415, 422
Shared Dropbox, 367
Summer Institute, 145
summer research immnersion, 214
summer residency, 441
Symposium, 415, 647
10 functions and services, 88
train-the-trainer, 126, 412
videoconferencing, 437, 438, 440
video format, 195
website, 12, 29, 52, 79, 83, 88, 89
weekly videoconferencing meeting, 440
workshop(s), 67, 129, 143, 196, 207, 237, 305, 337, 414, 422, 438, 464, 592, 624
ADC programs for colleges and programs
arts, 79, 255, 284
biomedical, 124
business, 80
education, 144, 458, 499
engineering, 4, 6, 79, 283, 354, 420, 552
Honor's College, 579
humanities, 284, 420
informatics department, 93, 123, 124
language, 232, 560
liberal arts, 79, 90, 142, 255, 499
medical education, 123, 128, 135, 560
medicine, 79, 123, 141, 161, 420
nursing, 124, 161, 499
sciences, 206, 283
social sciences, 283
STEM, 202, 205, 213, 289, 398, 560, 562
student service(s), 512
ADC structure, 93
centralization, 29, 340
centralized office(s), 81, 153
centrally based, 5
decentralized, 303, 304
distributed model, 8
hub-and-spoke model, 8
national center(s), 46, 48
umbrella structure, 141, 143
Adjunct instructors, 497, 500
Advance HE fellowship, 337, 346, 602, 605
continuous professional development, 134, 337
HEA fellowship, 338, 339, 346
Higher Education Academy UK, 62, 268–269
TEACH fellowship, 337, 343
Africa, 24, 59–72, 331–347
Alignment, 29, 68, 103, 141, 159, 160, 173–174, 178–180, 186, 190–192, 194, 198, 205–206, 215, 276, 297, 402, 459, 464, 465, 506, 514, 534, 592
Alignment of assessment and learning, 465
American Council on Education (ACE), 82, 83, 374
American Council on Education Faculty Development Matrix, 221, 230
AmeriCorps Volunteer, 412
Apprenticeship, 575
model, 288

680 Subject Index

Asia, 24, 333, 347, 465
Assessment, 79, 81, 159, 225, 501,
  504, 592, 607, 630, 633
  of ADC
    assessment plan, 100, 102, 104,
      107, 400
    assessment report(s), 83, 98,
      100–102, 105, 106
    evaluation questionnaire(s), 354
    event evaluation(s), 387
    faculty satisfaction survey(s), 231,
      253, 339
    feedback, 10, 17, 88, 159, 161,
      179–180, 194, 195, 222–224,
      229, 239, 278, 284, 575,
      583, 625
    feedback form(s), 422, 625
    feedback questionnaire(s),
      538, 539
    focus group(s), 70, 289, 293,
      304, 356, 357
    follow-up survey(s), 425
    impact, xii
    instructor survey(s), 426
    measuring impact, 33
    results chain, 595, 596, 602, 607
    task force, 103, 236, 240, 259
    teaching observation(s), 319,
      401, 502, 503
  approaches, 290
  committee(s), 12, 98, 224, 252,
    262, 271, 272, 278, 406, 407
  of learning, 64, 132, 134, 340,
    343, 353
    cross-check evaluation(s), 361
    evidence-based assessment(s), 129
    formative assessment, 159,
      424, 518
    formative evaluation(s), 360,
      518, 630
    learning assessment(s), 132, 534
    learning outcomes assessment(s),
      97, 98, 100, 191, 194, 303

  learning portfolio, 534
  mid-semester feedback,
    292, 502
  mid-term assessment
    feedback, 292
  mid-term evaluation, 579
  multiple-choice exam, 174
  online end-of-term
    assessment(s), 605
  performance-based
    assessment(s), 534
  student evaluation(s), 5, 6, 10,
    12, 78, 357
  summative assessment(s), 536
  measures for digital education, 145
  methods, 81, 98, 129, 134, 191,
    195, 196, 424, 502
  of student learning, 87, 98, 99, 101,
    103, 105, 106, 114, 228, 297,
    398, 400–402, 459
  of teaching, 64, 70, 130, 132, 134,
    194, 222, 343, 353
    appraisal, 127
    classroom observation(s), 104,
      196, 229, 319, 500, 575
    course evaluation
      questionnaire(s), 354
    end of semester student
      evaluations of teaching
      (SET), 355
    external review(s), 374
    faculty evaluation(s), 258–259,
      262, 414
    midterm student feedback, 419,
      424–426, 552
    peer evaluation(s), 6
    peer observation(s), 196, 472
    peer review, 229, 503, 535, 575
    self-assessment, 83, 230, 345
    student bias(es), 355
    student course assessment(s), 616
    student course evaluation(s), 208,
      258, 575

Subject Index **681**

student evaluation(s), 6, 10, 12, 78, 357
student experience survey(s), 6, 15, 293
student rating of teaching, 424
teaching evaluation(s), 32, 79
teaching portfolio, 69, 465
video evaluation(s), 575
Association for Faculty Enrichment in Learning and Teaching (AFELT), 65, 67, 71–72, 347
Association of American Colleges and Universities (AAC&U), 204, 371, 512
Association of College and University Educators (ACUE), 471, 501
ATLAS.ti 7.0, 616
Attendance, 67, 83, 156, 208, 231, 291, 340, 341, 386, 387, 410, 500, 502, 535, 538, 606
Attrition, 365–366
teacher/faculty, 365–366
teacher/faculty turnover, 370
Australian Council for Educational Research, 270
Australian Universities Quality Agency (AQUA), 10, 12, 13
Autonomy, 25, 37, 47, 176, 177, 181, 367, 442, 531, 622
Awards for university teaching, 11, 16, 56

B

Backward design approach, 194, 406
Belief system(s), 329
Belonging, 161, 240, 247, 269, 272, 277, 311, 439, 445, 449, 583, 597
Benefits, vii, xi, 52, 102, 106, 110, 147, 148, 155, 196, 210, 226, 261, 270, 277, 294, 295, 301, 302, 308–311, 320, 324,

327–328, 334, 368, 370–372, 412, 413, 445, 497, 503, 536, 562, 567, 602, 608, 610, 617, 638, 646, 654
Blended and flipped learning opportunities, 154
Blended courses, 413, 649, 650, 653
Blended education, 653
Blended teaching, 644, 647–649, 653
Blended and Digital Learning, 332
blended learning, 152, 158, 163, 296, 337, 341, 559, 576–578, 633, 649
digital badge, 228
digital education, 143
e-assessment, 129
e-learning, 126, 129, 132
flipped classroom, 326, 513, 535, 551, 637
hybrid format, 292
online learning, 325, 413, 648
Blogs, 147, 536
Board of advisors, 203
Boyer's Domains of Scholarship, 43–45, 56, 574, 578
British Conference of Undergraduate Research (BCUR), 565, 566
British Council, 62, 63
Building community, xvii, 195, 209, 210, 393–403, 433–443, 562
See also Community(ies) of practice
Business meeting(s), 368
Business plan(s), 155

C

California Critical Thinking Skills Test, 466
Capacity building, 62, 595
Career-long pedagogical development, 531
Career pathways, 606, 607, 609
Career planning, 227, 299, 300, 549

682   Subject Index

Center for Mentoring, Learning, and Academic Innovation (CMLAI), 434–443
Center impact, 401–402
Certificate in University Teaching (CUT), 168, 186, 192, 194–197
Certificate of higher education teaching and learning
  Bok Teaching Certificate, 501
  certificate(s), 66, 274, 602
  Certificate Course in Health Professions Education (CHPE), 132
  Certificate in Teaching and Learning in Higher Education (CTLHE), 602, 605, 631, 632
  certificate of tertiary teaching, 5
  certificate online, 501
  content of teaching certificate program, 465
  graduate certificate in university teaching, 10, 186
  Preparing Future Faculty (PFF) Certificate, 511, 513, 519–521
  qualification certificate, 545
  Teaching Academy certificate, 501, 504, 506
  teaching certificate(s), 27, 458, 465, 495, 497, 498, 500–501, 575
  teaching competence(s), 630
Certification, xvii, 457, 458, 475–477, 479–491, 500–503, 505, 506, 552, 605, 632, 651, 653
Challenge(s), 385–387, 396
  to faculty change, 32–34, 134, 212, 428, 625–626
    fear of facing new things, 34
    teaching load, 261, 326, 412
    time challenge, 212
    workload, 17, 326

of/for higher education, 24, 46, 55–57, 65, 360, 629
  accurate understanding of learning, 559
  communication, 559
  enrollment, 46, 394
  macro-changes, xv
  socioeconomic development, 317
of/for teaching and learning centers or ADCs, 33–34, 201, 204
  audience confusion, 141
  coping with demand, 339
  credibility, 251, 254, 261, 262
  disparities of resources, 365
  faculty resistance, 25, 334, 340, 355
  hiring freeze, 236
  release time, 439
  remediation stigma, 406
  reputation of center/ADC, 401
  resource dedication to center/ADC, 79
  seat at the table, 80
  stability and sustainability, 375–376
  sustainability, 34
  sustainable organizational structure(s), 411
  timeline, 260
  transparent/transparency, 261
  trust, 35
  visibility, 215, 259
Change and transition
  behavioral change, 634
  change culture, 36
  change management, 340
  change strategy, 486
  continuous development, 34
  continuous improvement, 35
  faculty champions, 335, 343
  key allies, 212
  key multiplier(s), 64
  learning transition (LT) team, 163

paradigm shift(s), 56, 67, 575, 576
reform pioneer(s), 575
restructuring, 437
systematic development(s), 56
systemic analysis, 486
systemic change(s), 572
systems change(s), 398
theory of change, 591–610,
633, 634
transition, 161, 595
Chat group, 466
Checklist, 616
Civic responsibility, 574
*Classroom Observation Protocol for
Undergraduate STEM*
(COPUS), 289, 292
Clinical skills, 126, 130
Clinical Skills Laboratory, 125, 126,
129–130, 132
Cognitive processes, 69
Cognitive psychology, 80
Collaboration, xvii, 8, 11, 16, 27, 31,
33, 53, 56–57, 62–63, 77, 81,
114, 115, 117, 118, 134, 140,
145–146, 149, 160, 190, 195,
197, 232, 236, 259, 260, 288,
307–310, 313–316, 322, 327,
333, 353, 361, 374, 379, 383,
386, 389, 397–399, 406, 413,
441, 446, 449, 450, 452, 462,
466, 471, 485, 513, 553, 562,
566, 569, 571–584, 596, 610
challenges of, 364–366, 644, 654
collaborative environment, 143
collaborative faculty development,
361, 363–376, 442
network, 361
collaborative learning, 345
collaborative model, 373, 631
collaborative writing group(s),
562–564, 568
communication and, 158, 159
cross-institutional, 562

cultivation of relationships, 157
international, 129, 327–328,
565, 641–654
methods of, 368–371
of communication, 357
partner(s), 81, 252, 285,
313–316, 654
peer, 465
programmatic bridges, 146
thinking together, 367
three-center collaborative
approach, 299
Communication gap, 285
effective dialogue, 207
Community(ies) of practice (CoP),
xvii, 160–161, 209, 210, 333,
334, 344, 365–368, 370–372,
391, 399, 413, 428, 445, 463,
466–467, 472, 497, 501, 552,
561, 562, 609, 631
building community, 210, 438
of learning, 9, 30, 79, 192, 205,
213, 409
faculty and professional learning,
116–117, 384
faculty learning community(ies)
(FLCs), 26, 30, 83, 116, 117,
203, 207, 208, 213, 367, 373,
385–389, 401, 445, 449, 451,
471, 472, 500, 502, 630–632,
635, 636, 638, 644
*Framework for virtual faculty learning
community(ies)
(V-FLC)*, 451–452
inter-university collaboration(s), 452
key characteristics of CoPs, 366
networking, 16, 18, 67, 368
Vince's model, 561
Virtual faculty learning community
(V-FLC), 445, 446, 449–455
Conceptual framework, 237,
389, 633–634
Conceptual underpinnings, 574, 584

684 Subject Index

Consortium on Teaching and Learning (GA-CTL), 363–376
Continuum of pedagogical development, 527, 530, 531
Council of Australian Directors of Academic Development (CADAD), 13–14, 16, 18
Council of Australasian Leaders in Learning and Teaching, 18
Council of Graduate Schools (CGS), 512
Council of Higher Education (CoHE) Strategic, 351, 361
Counseling, 63, 81, 124, 125, 130–132, 223, 307, 386, 538
Countries
  Argentina, 26–28
  Australia, x, xiv, 4, 5, 8, 9, 14, 18, 24, 152, 374, 457, 500
  Belgium, 527
  Bolivia, 26
  Brazil, 26
  Canada, x, 79, 167, 339, 457, 476
  Chile, 26–28, 30–32, 34–36, 629
  China, xiv, 41–57, 419, 420, 427, 545, 546, 553, 572, 578, 641–644, 646–648, 650–654
  Colombia, 26, 27, 32, 34, 36
  Costa Rica, 26
  Cuba, 26
  Czech Republic, 614
  Denmark, 24, 500
  Dominican Republic, 26
  Ecuador, 26
  El Salvador, 26
  Finland, 24
  Guatemala, 26
  Honduras, 26
  Hong Kong (Administrative district of China), 591, 592, 601
  Kenya, 59–63, 65, 66, 68, 71, 72, 331, 335, 347
  Lithuania, 47
  Mexico, 26, 33, 35
  Netherlands, 24, 479–491
  New Zealand, x, 24
  Nicaragua, 26
  Norway, 24, 47
  Oman, xiii, 124, 457–472
  Pakistan, 318, 324, 327, 328, 331–347
  Panama, 26
  Paraguay, 26
  Peru, 26–28, 30, 32
  Puerto Rico, 26
  Russia
  South Africa, x, 24
  Sri Lanka, x, 24, 500
  Sweden, 24, 500
  Tanzania, 71, 331
  Turkey, 351–361
  Uganda, 71, 331, 336
  United Arab Emirates, 127, 246
  United Kingdom (UK), xiv, 6, 24, 62, 64, 65, 67, 72, 269–271, 331, 338, 457, 558, 559, 561, 562, 565
  United States of America (USA), 61, 65, 201, 270, 379, 383, 457, 464, 465, 471, 495, 497, 498, 500, 650
  Uruguay, 26
  Venezuela, 26
Course Experience Questionnaire (CEQ), 6, 15
Course Review, 650–653
Courses for the certificate program, 513
Course Technology, 650–651
Credibility, 5, 81, 224, 251, 254–257, 260–262, 408, 430, 634, 650
Critical thinking, viii, 68, 72, 288, 326, 345, 412, 463–466, 471, 485, 573
Culture, xi, xiii, 28, 36, 79, 110, 139, 140, 144, 145, 148, 150, 160, 171, 173, 188, 198, 223, 244,

245, 296, 320, 324, 326–328, 332, 333, 336, 360, 364, 383, 396, 400, 408, 409, 416, 419–430, 437, 457, 472, 480, 560, 564, 609, 636, 638, 644
  of teaching excellence, 28, 333, 419–430, 644
  See also Diversity
Curriculum design and development
  backward design, 168, 186, 190, 191
  course design/development programming, 203, 384
  Course Design Institute (s), 228, 260
  course effectiveness, 303
  course review(s), 650–653
  course syllabus(i), 69, 321
  curriculum development, 15, 17, 29, 80, 124, 127, 131, 255, 256, 325, 479, 630
  curriculum map, 100, 239
  lab work, 534
  learning task(s), 68, 179, 579, 652
  syllabus design, 514, 534, 630
  universal design for learning (UDL), 186, 191–192
Curriculum reform, 123, 125–127
CUT program, 186, 192, 194–196

D

Database, 83, 154, 225, 239, 276, 308
Davis Educational Foundation/The Davis Foundation, 205, 252
Decision-making, xiv, xv, xxx, 17, 60, 136, 252, 271, 286, 398, 413, 429, 430, 487, 490, 596–601, 608
  consensus, 60
  model, 596–597, 601
Deep learning, 56, 68, 71, 171–181, 190, 551, 572
Democratic etiquette, 561

Department chairs roundtable, 203
Design thinking, 513
Digital education, 140, 142, 143, 145
  See also Blended education
Distance Learning Association, 650
Diversity, xiv, 30, 32, 37, 69, 80–82, 114, 115, 141, 161, 179, 204–207, 210, 212–214, 237, 242, 254, 305, 376, 415, 434, 435, 462, 479, 511, 514, 516–518, 527–539, 559, 638
  Council on Diversity, 204, 206
  cross-cultural understanding, 427
  cultural competence, 204, 207
  and inclusion, 80, 114, 141, 204, 205, 213, 214, 415
  inclusive excellence, 168, 204
  inclusive pedagogy, 169
  inclusive teaching, 203, 215, 517
  intercultural, 328
  LGBTQ, 206
  LGBTQ+ community, 115
  officer, 204, 206, 207, 212, 214
  of programs, 30, 462
  of services, 365
  statements, 514
  training, 82
Divisional partnership, 380, 383
Donor funding, 143, 241
Dual professionals, 66, 413

E

Early Researcher Grant, 448
East African Higher Education Quality Assurance Network, 347
Education, vii, xiii, 3, 23, 41, 60, 80, 103, 109, 123–136, 139–151, 171, 185, 201, 221, 241, 253, 269, 300, 317, 332, 351, 370, 381, 395, 407, 420, 435, 445, 459, 479, 495–506, 511, 527, 545, 557, 572, 592, 629, 641–654

686 **Subject Index**

Educational designer, 152–163, 172, 181

Educational development, 23, 26, 78, 80, 112, 136, 152, 188, 254, 285, 329, 332–336, 338–340, 370, 419, 422, 429, 430, 491, 496, 498, 633

Educational reform, 45, 318, 549, 580, 592, 593

See also Change

Educational technology(ies), 131, 143, 146, 187, 193, 256, 258, 353, 411, 421, 422, 537, 545

See also Technology-enhanced teaching and learning

Effective teaching and learning, 144, 148, 190, 374, 584

See also Theoretical foundations

Emerging trend(s), 48, 55–57, 146

Emotional labor, 415

Engaged, 15–17, 64, 70, 142, 149, 155, 186, 202, 208, 255, 257, 260–262, 271, 274–276, 278, 291, 294, 302, 303, 342, 343, 345, 406, 407, 410, 412–414, 426, 438, 450, 498, 506, 512, 564, 565, 577, 580, 594, 595

Engagement/participation, ix, xvii, 9, 66, 81, 109–118, 144, 152, 190, 203, 255, 269–279, 286, 301, 323, 336, 367, 386, 423, 429, 434, 449, 464, 498, 516, 527, 561, 593, 623, 630

Astin's *Student Involvement Developmental Theory*, 270

Australian Survey of Student Engagement, 268, 270

community-engaged learning (CEL), 412

levels of participation, Wenger's, 368

mandatory training, 533–535

models of engagement, 155, 162, 156, 154

participation, compulsory, 339

participation, volunteer, 104, 334, 342, 346, 381, 383, 435, 461, 567

participation, voluntary, 126, 128, 202, 436, 448, 592

student engagement, ix, xvii, 144, 152, 190, 191, 265, 269–279, 286, 290, 291, 343, 446, 464, 503, 593, 623

student participation, 3, 285, 629

survey of student engagement, 268

United Kingdom Survey of Student Engagement, 268, 270

ePortfolio, 387

Evaluation and quality assessment (EQA), 576, 578

Evaluation of learning, xviii, 29, 239, 467

evaluate student learning, 530, 549

evaluation rubric, 638

evaluation system, 56

ongoing constructive feedback, 359

See also Assessment, of learning

Evidence-based discipline, 80

Evidence-based teaching practices, 104, 503

Examinations, 14, 46, 63, 69–71, 118, 127, 129, 131, 132, 174, 400, 459, 545, 604, 606

Excellence in university learning and teaching, 11

Executive committee, 83, 226, 364, 368, 375

F

Faculty advisors, 192, 304–306, 310, 414

Faculty awards, 413

Faculty development space, 365

Faculty enhancement, 155
Faculty fellows, xvii, 202, 253, 384–386, 388, 461–472
  eligibility criteria, 462
  fellowships, 16, 307
  fellows program, 381, 386, 421, 457–472
  teaching fellows, 142, 144, 225
Faculty of color, 203
Faculty participation, x, xv, xvii, 387, 448, 638
Faculty profile, 24, 31
Faculty Senate, 380, 395
Faculty-student interaction, 414
FD-QM Online Course Quality Rubric Training Program, 646, 650, 651
First-generation students, 285
First-year seminars, 83, 300, 303, 306, 307, 398
Focus group discussions (FGDs), 66, 70, 71, 319, 327
The Foundations of Teaching and the Advanced Certificate, 476
Full-Scale SoTL, 537
Full-time equivalent (FTE), 82, 97, 222, 254, 480, 614
Future of center

G

Global Impact Award, 650
Governance, xvi, 217, 221, 257, 259, 260, 263, 325, 393, 413, 566
Government(s), xvi, 3, 4, 6, 7, 9–18, 27, 41, 47, 48, 59, 65, 71, 72, 317, 336, 400, 595, 629, 648
  policy(ies), 25, 36, 48, 54, 65, 72, 272, 483, 629, 637, 638
  government regulation(s), 9
  national oversight, 9
  regulation(s), 14
  umbrella organization, 4

Grades/grading, 52, 89, 228, 290, 291, 354, 355, 389, 442, 470, 498, 567, 623
  See also Evaluation of learning
Graduate assistant (GA) support program, 359
  Graduate Certificate of University Teaching, 10
  graduate intern(s), 276
  graduate teaching assistant(s) (GTA), 80, 89, 397, 602, 605
  teaching assistant (TA) development, 51
  training component(s), 52
  training manual, 52
Graduate employment, 6
Grant funding, 143, 398, 400, 445
Group work, 275, 325, 464, 537
Guidebook, 305

H

Healey's Conceptual Model, 284, 286
  See also Theoretical foundations
Hierarchy, 34, 80, 569
Higher Education Academy of China, 578
Higher Education Academy UK, 62, 271, 338
Higher Education Research and Development Society of Australasia (HERDSA), 4, 13, 16, 18
High-impact practices (HIPs), 292, 299, 303, 311, 373, 411, 565
Hispanic-serving institution, 283
Historically Black Colleges and Universities Faculty Development Network, 333
Honors university, 394, 398
Hybrid learning, 303, 535
  See also Blended teaching, blended learning

688   Subject Index

Impact, xv, 5, 26, 44, 60, 83, 104, 115, 133, 148, 155, 175, 202, 223, 239, 272, 285, 303, 331, 354, 365, 387–389, 401–402, 406, 426, 449–450, 458, 483, 502, 521–522, 533, 551, 562, 565, 571–584, 594, 621, 629–639
  on teaching, 232, 239
Impact of ADC, xviii, 64, 83, 90, 133, 149, 213–214, 239, 240, 242, 278, 294, 594, 633, 637
  data, 387–389, 589
  data analysis, 208
  evaluation matrix(s), 634
  evaluation model(s), 638
  evaluation(s), 633
  post-workshop evaluation(s), 339
  research, 354, 587–589
  retreat(s), 148
  review(s), 337, 346
  survey(s), 240, 246
Individual consultations, 83, 146, 362, 365
Informatics, 123, 124, 128, 129, 131
Information technology, vii, xv, 124–126, 128, 129, 131, 314, 332, 379–381, 383–385, 389, 529, 565, 599
  See also Technology-enhanced teaching
Infrastructure, 35, 230, 405–416
Innovation, xvi, 9, 24, 42, 140, 153, 155, 201, 221, 252, 324, 332, 374, 393–403, 407, 422, 449, 479–491, 512, 536, 551, 561, 571–584, 592, 594, 629–639, 644
  academic, 49, 436, 513
  bottom-up, 481–482
  digital, 140
  guide(s), 484
  initiative(s), 415

innovative instructional approaches, 462
innovative nation, 41, 42, 47
innovative teaching, 28, 52–54, 56, 224, 251, 374, 421, 463, 467, 546, 559, 576, 577, 580, 581, 624
learning, 24, 57, 410
pedagogical, 35, 36, 56, 393–403, 407, 536, 574
program innovation principles, 30, 520–521
project(s), 483–487, 490, 574
teaching and learning, 24, 26, 52–54, 56, 201, 578, 580–581, 644, 647
Teaching Innovation Contest(s), 548, 551
teaching innovation design report(s), 551
In-person residency, 441
Institutional and national pressure(s), 395, 398–400
Institutional audits, 6–7
Institutional continuity, 366
Institutional guideline(s), 33
Institutional interrelationships, xvii, 395–400
Institutional priorities, 364, 384, 394, 402
Institutional Review Board, 288, 441
Institutional support, 34, 35, 563
Instructional design and activities, 80, 194
  classroom management strategies, 193
  debate(s), 174
  differentiated instruction, 303
  experiential learning, 537
  group discussion(s), 194
  independent learning, 142
  knowledge sharing, 410
  laboratory, 622–623

Subject Index   689

plan-act-observe-reflect, 574
PowerPoint, 319, 321, 359
problem-based learning, 537
problem-posing pedagogy, 61
project(s), 359
project-based learning, 534, 576
rapid response activity, 604
Instructional technology, ix, 77, 81, 82,
  141, 144, 223, 225, 227, 253,
  302, 303, 332, 381, 383–385,
  387, 389, 397, 499
  See also Technology-enhanced
  teaching and learning
Integration of information and
  communication
  technologies, 630
Interactive pedagogy
  interactive learning, 197
  interactive teaching, 66, 154
Interdisciplinarity, 594, 604
  interdisciplinary courses, 51, 53,
  576–581, 583, 584
  interdisciplinary teams, 30, 579–581
Interfaculty Certificate of Pedagogical
  Development in Higher
  Education (CIDePES), 535,
  536, 538
Internal grant program, 401
International academic
  partnership, 322
International Consortium for
  Educational Development,
  370, 496, 547
International Databases for Enhanced
  Assessments and Learning
  (IDEAL), 126
Internationalization, 329, 427, 479,
  594, 604, 607, 647
  global focus, 206
  globally dispersed faculty,
  445, 446
  global university, 331

international students, 205, 379
International Network of Quality
  Assurance Agencies in Higher
  Education, 347
International Society for the
  Scholarship of Teaching and
  Learning, 547
Internship(s), 288, 307, 308, 310, 322,
  353, 415, 565
Inter-University Council for East Africa
  (IUCEA), 336

J

Journals
  *Higher Education Research and
  Development*, 4
  *Journal of the Scholarship of Teaching
  and Learning*
  *Journal on Teaching and
  Learning*, 52, 53

K

*Key to University Quality Assurance:
  Faculty/Staff Development in
  Global Context*, 47

L

Language Study, 141
Latin America, x, 23–37
Leadership, xvi, 9, 12, 13, 17, 18, 30,
  34–36, 50, 51, 54, 77, 80–81,
  89, 101, 102, 118, 141, 148,
  149, 158, 162, 179, 186, 203,
  210, 224, 232, 237, 238, 247,
  251–263, 277, 278, 300, 303,
  304, 310, 318, 324, 325, 327,
  334, 343, 345, 346, 368, 372,
  374–376, 398, 407, 410,
  413–415, 439, 462, 468,

690   Subject Index

479–491, 497, 500, 512, 549, 552, 593, 594, 602, 610, 632, 644
concept of, 325
core, 260
development, 80, 203, 251, 261, 278, 334, 483, 488, 489
distributed, 374
executive leadership team, 500
faculty leader(s), 202, 224, 237, 251–263, 450
model(s), 149, 251, 253, 255, 374
skills, 254, 485, 487
Learning activities, 68, 159, 180, 191, 192, 194, 196, 256, 285, 290, 351–361, 424, 466, 532, 632, 650
Learning assessment, 99, 534, 650
Learning culture, 148, 171, 457, 480, 609
Learning management system (LMS), 82, 89, 98, 143, 144, 147, 158, 185, 187, 193–195, 224, 311, 384, 437, 449–451, 453, 513, 514, 519
Learning objectives, 175, 239, 459, 464, 471, 498, 650
Learning outcomes, 25, 27, 63, 68, 70, 83, 97–104, 107, 114, 154, 159, 177, 191, 194, 196, 256, 259, 291, 293, 297, 303, 345, 360, 372, 398, 400–402, 410, 422, 424, 465, 483, 496, 498, 501, 504, 506, 518, 576, 579, 592, 633
Learning Outcomes Assessment Committee, 207, 214
Learning paradigm, 28, 512
Learning Technologies Center, 97
Learning theory and philosophy, 251
constructive alignment, 160, 534
constructivism, 190
constructivist pedagogy, 64–65

teaching philosophy, 196, 423, 429, 502, 514
Learning transformation (LT) team, 163
Lectureship, 66
Leeds Institute for Medical Education, 561
Liaison, 112, 157, 226, 253, 255, 271, 364, 368, 375, 413, 503
Liberal Education and America's Promise (LEAP), 371
Life-long learning, 180, 185, 237, 345, 630, 649
Listserv, 333, 368, 369, 372, 375

M

Marketing, 77, 88, 230, 560
Masters in Higher Education Pedagogy, 536
Master's in Student Engagement in Higher Education, 275
Medical Education and Informatics Department (MEID), 123–136
Membership, xi, 80, 238–241, 246, 247, 338, 363, 368, 375, 449
Mentor/mentorship, 320, 433, 440, 562, 602, 624–625
mentor(s), 18, 45, 64, 65, 214, 225, 227, 228, 311, 323, 326, 328, 338, 343, 346, 367, 370, 376, 406, 410, 416, 433–443, 538, 567, 568, 575, 602, 604, 605, 608, 614, 624, 625
mentoring, 61, 89, 116, 117, 124, 131, 203, 222, 224, 225, 232, 237, 238, 240, 255, 256, 288, 300, 304, 308–311, 338, 342–344, 364, 369, 370, 375, 383, 384, 410, 413–415, 422, 433–442, 464, 522, 532, 566–569, 602, 606, 625

Subject Index   691

mentor-mentee relationship, 567
volunteer mentor(s), 346
Micro-course teaching, 575
Micro-course videos, 551
Microteaching, 52, 325, 423, 535
Mission, xii–xvi, 29, 36, 41–44, 48, 50,
51, 77–80, 83, 93, 97, 98,
105, 110–115, 118, 124, 127,
130–132, 134, 139–150, 171,
185–188, 198, 201–215, 222,
223, 226, 236–237, 252, 257,
272, 286, 295, 301–304, 307,
311, 331, 352–353, 364, 375,
381, 383, 386–388, 394, 395,
399, 401, 402, 406, 408–409,
419–421, 427, 434, 438, 442,
443, 446, 459, 469, 480,
498–499, 512, 528, 530, 533,
547, 554, 572, 592, 613, 618,
635, 644–648
Motivation, intrinsic, 53, 176, 177,
305, 580, 622
motivates me, 359
student motivation, 176, 534, 537

N

Names of centers, 77–79
National Council for Accreditation of
Teacher Education
(NCATE), 459
National Education Association
(NEA), 42, 43
National Science Foundation (NSF),
241, 242, 289
National Student Survey, 272
National Survey of Student
Engagement, 270
Needs assessment(s), 136, 319–322,
388, 394, 447, 464, 548
needs analysis survey(s), 136, 343
needs and specific interests, 532

needs assessment survey(s), 83, 126,
127, 223, 343, 448, 461,
464, 548
student needs analysis,
318, 356–357
Network, 7, 14, 16–18, 27, 29, 31, 60,
67, 212, 215, 270, 306, 307,
326, 327, 329, 332, 334–336,
338–342, 344, 346, 347, 361,
370, 371, 420, 464, 488, 505,
560, 564, 566–569, 597,
599, 654
New Mentor Orientation,
436, 440–441
Nursing, 118, 124, 127, 332, 499

O

One-Button studio, 372, 409
Online
course(s), 79, 82, 132, 185, 186,
226, 229, 230, 293, 413, 501,
535, 576, 641, 642,
644, 648–653
course development, 535
discussion forum(s), 195
and hybrid faculty development,
168, 185–198, 259
learning, 81, 82, 89, 147, 158, 163,
224, 229, 325, 365, 413, 452,
641, 646, 648
program(s), 83, 434, 549
survey(s), 290, 428, 429
teaching and learning, 13, 194, 207,
237, 389, 448, 449, 606
Open Classrooms initiative, 384, 386
Optimal skill set(s), 254
Organizational change, 8, 18, 56, 201,
205, 212, 214, 215, 576
See also Change
Organizational development, 42, 44, 80,
237, 252, 394, 407, 653, 654

692 Subject Index

Organization for Economic
Co-operation and
Development (OECD), 596
Outcome-based education (OBE), 126,
551, 552, 592, 594
  alignment of learning outcomes and
    activities, 68, 196, 465
  graduate attribute(s), 10, 13, 344
  graduation outcomes, 100
  learning objectives, 239
  learning outcomes, 27, 70, 102,
    159, 400, 576, 579, 592, 633
  outcomes assessment, 102
  outcomes-based approaches,
    155, 592
Outcomes, xv, 7, 15–17, 25, 27, 60,
  63, 68–70, 83, 90, 97–105,
  107, 111, 114, 133, 135, 149,
  154, 157, 159, 160, 177–180,
  191, 194, 196, 205, 212, 213,
  256, 259, 275, 278, 286, 291,
  293, 297, 303, 309, 337, 342,
  345, 355, 357, 360, 371–375,
  389, 398, 400–402, 410, 415,
  422, 424, 465, 467, 468,
  483–485, 490, 496, 498, 501,
  504, 506, 514, 518, 576, 579,
  582, 592, 595, 596, 602, 606,
  613, 629, 633–635, 652

Partnership(s), xvii, 31, 59, 62–64,
  112, 206, 207, 215, 266,
  269–271, 276, 283–297, 303,
  307–309, 313–329, 344–345,
  379–389, 488, 500, 502,
  503, 522
  Aga Khan Development Network
    (AKDN), 332
  consortium, 131
  cross-divisional partnership(s),
    380, 383

England-Africa Partnership(s), 62
partner universities, xvii, 342
pooled resources, 372
strengths of partnerships,
  210, 385
Pedagogical academy, xi
Pedagogy, xvii, 24, 31, 54, 61–63, 65,
  68, 110, 117, 186, 188, 203,
  227, 251, 253, 256, 287, 290,
  292, 300, 302, 332, 337, 340,
  344, 373, 383, 385, 402, 411,
  412, 415, 422, 423, 427, 463,
  472, 498, 511–515, 518, 522,
  527, 528, 530, 533–537, 539,
  553, 559, 560, 566, 568, 572,
  592, 594, 622, 623, 643
  pedagogical competencies, 50, 51,
    530, 537, 613–626
  pedagogical research, 146, 394, 399,
    400, 569
Peer learning, 345, 633
Performance indicators, xviii,
  6, 15, 18
  See also Quality of higher education
Performance review, 17, 608
Persistence, 242, 289, 292, 300–302,
  304–306, 309, 414, 485,
  497, 519
Positive image of faculty, 31
  prestige, 240
  professional self-perception(s), 615
Postgraduate Certificate, 62, 68
Postgraduate Certificate in Student
  Engagement, 265,
  272, 274–276
Proactive approach, 415
Professional and Organizational
  Development (POD)
  Network, xiii, 31, 246, 294,
  295, 333, 370, 371, 373, 374,
  376, 448, 496, 547
  POD Network's Center for Teaching
    and Learning Matrix, 374

Subject Index **693**

Professional Certificate in Higher
Education Teaching
(PCHET), 62
Professional development strategies,
37, 109–118
Professional ethics, 549, 550, 573, 574
Professional portfolio, 307, 536
Professional standards
Program evaluation, 83, 447
Program review
  program assessment(s), 141,
    203, 275
  program outcomes, 194
Project-based management, 484
Project management, 153–154, 156,
    158, 485, 566
  project design, 485, 489, 490
  project manager(s), 154–158
Promotion, x, 12, 17, 18, 54, 134, 221,
    225, 228, 231, 237, 240, 293,
    375, 376, 406, 410, 423, 429,
    458, 471, 501, 505, 531, 536,
    539, 567, 574, 606, 609, 649
  committee(s), 17, 18
  review(s), 17, 221, 501
  teaching review portfolio, 501
  and tenure evaluation(s), 501
Proposals, xiii, xv, 62, 88, 103, 228,
    259, 369, 380, 400, 402, 412,
    415, 427, 428, 460, 462, 500,
    562, 644
Publication output(s), 562
Publicizing services, 425

Q

Quality assurance, 4–10, 13–15, 24,
    56, 72, 127, 134, 267, 270,
    315, 329, 332, 351, 353, 460,
    468, 552, 588, 642, 644,
    649, 650
Quality Assurance Agency for Higher
    Education (UK), 268–272

Quality initiative, 6
Quality of higher education, 6, 45,
    553, 642
  Academic Quality Framework, 336,
    337, 342
  "an active process within the
    present", 558
  audit(s), 10, 12, 72
  key performance indicators
    (KPIs), 559
  *key to university quality assurance:
    Faculty/Staff Development in
    Global Context*, 47
  QM Higher Education Rubric, 650
  qualification, 126
  quality assurance, 6, 8–10, 13–15,
    24, 56, 72, 127, 134, 272,
    328, 351, 353, 552, 644, 650
  quality control, 334
  quality enhancement plan (QEP),
    365, 387, 388
  quality evaluation, 50, 76
  quality improvement, 633
  Quality Matters, 229, 642
  quality of student learning, 28
  quality of teaching, 6, 420, 641
  quality report, 6
  quality rubric, 642
  teaching qualification(s), 338, 482
  teaching quality, 8, 9, 24, 155

R

R. Menges Outstanding Research for
    Educational Development
    Award, 295
Ramsden, Paul, 6, 539
Reassignment(s), 438, 439
Reflection, 61, 70, 195, 196, 222, 223,
    345, 401, 501, 531, 606, 624
  collective public, 558
  collective reflection on pedagogy,
    539, 558

694   Subject Index

Reflection (*cont.*)
  critical, 61, 142, 406, 412,
      499, 557–569
  culture of, 36
  organization of, 558
  productive, 558, 564–566, 569
  public, 558, 562–564
  reflection-on-action, 530
  reflective essay(s), 208, 502, 503
  reflective observation(s), 615
  reflective practitioner(s), xi, 262,
      345, 470, 476, 609, 622
  reflective thought, 68–70
  reflexive practice, 513, 517–518
  reflexive space(s), 558
  report(s), 535, 579, 581, 582
  self-critical, 562
  students as reflective agents, 564, 566
Reform, 41, 45–47, 105, 123,
      125–127, 317, 430, 549, 551,
      553, 575, 577–579, 592–595,
      642, 644, 645, 648
Reform in China, 45
Repository of resources, 369
Research, 318, 411, 552, 592
  action, 29, 37, 51, 54, 293, 574,
      576, 578, 579, 584, 647, 650
  case-study(ies), 193, 482, 537, 604
  classroom, xvi, 29, 37, 374, 538, 551
  constant comparative method, 357
  content analysis, 319
  data, 149, 246, 289, 319,
      351–361, 565
    entry, 354
    sources, 230
  document review, 319
  educational, 141, 144, 400, 563,
      581, 614
  empirical, 613, 615
  experiment, 35
  inductive open coding, 616
  internet search(es), 325
  interview(s), 26, 27, 208, 236, 319,
      356, 616

  item analysis, 129
  qualitative data, 355
    analysis, 471
  quantitative results, 354
  questionnaire, 467
  reliability and validity, 355
  research methodology,
      318–320, 566
  survey(s), 26, 28, 83, 240, 333, 353,
      401, 575
  undergraduate, 89, 296,
      410, 564–565
  video interview(s), 154
  website analysis, 29
Resistance, 25, 37, 106, 113, 118, 334,
      340, 343, 355
Resource-sharing outcomes, 372
Resources include, 87
Retention, 15, 18, 90, 162, 289, 292,
      293, 300–302, 304–306, 309,
      371, 410, 416, 497
Retreats, 89, 148, 210, 214, 223, 260, 274,
      275, 369, 373, 374, 383,
      384, 386, 387, 412, 520,
      562, 563
Risk Management Office (RMO),
      462, 467
Role of students, 37, 620
  See also Students as partners (SaP)
Rubric design
  rubric(s), 100, 180, 353
  Rubric training, 651

S

Scholarship, xi, xv, 9, 41–57, 72, 110,
      113, 114, 135, 188, 228, 252,
      270, 274, 311, 334, 336, 338,
      365, 370, 374, 383, 410, 414,
      438, 459, 503, 512, 520, 522,
      559–562, 566–568, 574,
      576–579, 584, 592, 600,
      644, 647
  shared, 374

Subject Index   **695**

Scholarship of teaching and learning (SoTL), xi, xv, xvii, xviii, 17, 18, 29, 37, 42, 43, 56, 72, 79, 89, 168, 221, 225, 227–228, 231, 285, 289, 293, 295, 296, 334, 337, 338, 343, 344, 365, 373, 384, 389, 399, 402, 415, 419, 426–428, 465, 472, 496, 536–539, 547, 552, 557–569, 644, 647

   classroom action-research, 29, 37

Self-directed learners, 576

Self-reflection, 110, 291, 406, 505, 575

Self-Study Reports, 100

Senge, Peter, 42, 56, 394, 395, 486, 488, 574, 576, 577

Senge's model of learning organizations, 395

Serving all faculty (over large areas and distances), 365

Shared Dropbox, 367

Shared ownership, 484, 490

Size of the centers, 30

Social learning, 193

Society for Teaching and Learning in Higher Education, 333

Solutions, viii, xviii, 15, 161, 173, 306, 327, 345, 490–491, 537, 597–599, 604, 605

   for ADCs, xii, 490–491

Soviet Union's educational model, 643

Space, xv, 31, 35, 54, 56, 69, 70, 88, 89, 113, 116, 140, 163, 181, 207, 223, 230, 274, 276, 277, 300–303, 307, 309–311, 335–337, 341, 343–346, 365, 376, 381, 384, 396, 406, 409, 440, 441, 446, 515–517, 520, 558, 560–563, 583, 605, 623, 626, 630

Stability and sustainability, 375–376

Standards, xvi, 6, 12, 17, 35, 115, 124, 125, 127, 130, 136, 153, 254, 296, 320, 338, 343, 398, 399, 406, 457, 458, 483, 557, 592, 599, 605, 634, 635, 642, 649–653

Australian Qualification Framework (AQF), 14

Tertiary Education Quality and Standards Agency (TEQSA), 14

UK Professional Standard Framework (UKPSF), 338

Standards-based, 605

Strategic goals, xvi, 29, 222

   initiatives, 371, 374

   partners, 207

   planning, 47, 65, 79, 204, 239, 337, 342, 351, 497

Strengths, 141, 245, 256, 291, 304, 308, 325, 385–387, 411, 415, 424, 485, 489, 503, 625

Student-centered, 23, 25, 28, 51, 53, 55, 56, 62, 63, 65–67, 110, 203, 286, 302, 323, 333, 337, 360, 380, 423, 442, 458, 514, 551, 552, 571–584, 630, 632, 635, 637, 648

Student counselor(s), 130

Student Engagement Partnership, xvii, 270

Student feedback, 161, 278, 284, 290, 293, 296, 424, 552, 622

Student learning, viii, ix, xvii, xviii, 24, 27–28, 33, 34, 67, 78, 80, 83, 90, 98, 99, 101–107, 110, 114, 140, 145, 158, 171–181, 188, 222, 223, 228, 285, 286, 290, 297, 299, 326, 332, 383, 398–402, 405, 406, 415, 416, 458, 459, 462, 463, 467, 471, 472, 495, 496, 498, 499, 504, 530, 534, 537, 549, 551, 592, 594, 604, 609, 633, 634, 637

   learner-centered, 284

696   Subject Index

Student learning (*cont.*)
  student-centered constructivist
    approaches, 66, 67
  student-centered learning, 23, 25,
    28, 53, 63, 65, 337, 380,
    575–577, 584
  student-centered pedagogy, 110, 203
  student-centered teaching and
    learning, 51, 110, 571–584,
    630, 648
  teacher-centered, 53, 326
Students as partners (SaP), xxii, 270,
    278, 285, 287, 296, 346,
    559, 604
  codevelopers, co-learners, and
    co-inquirers, 286
  intern(s), 283, 288
  student employee(s), 82, 223
  Student Fellow(s), 271
  student learning assistant(s), 98,
    103, 632
  student rights movement, 23
  Students Assessing Teaching and
    Learning (SATAL), 284,
    287, 296
  student-staff partnership(s), 269,
    276, 284
  students take control, 69
Student satisfaction, 10, 18, 352, 354
  course evaluation(s), 284, 354
  course survey(s), 10, 447
  student course evaluation(s), 575
  student evaluations of teaching
    (SET), 267, 294, 354
  Student Experience Survey(s), 6, 15
  student questionnaire(s), 426
  student success, 300
    data, 389
  student survey(s), 291, 353, 425, 426
Students learning, 5, 55, 68–71, 174,
    246, 289, 292, 327, 336, 470,
    480, 506, 536, 576, 579, 623,
    631, 632, 636, 638

Study behavior(s), 178, 179
Sultan Qaboos University, 517
Survival kit(s), 534

T

Taskstream by Watermark, 101
Teacher appreciation, 423
Teacher education, 332, 335
Teaching Academy Certification, 498,
    501–503, 505, 506
Teaching assistant (TA), 51–52, 89,
    144, 192, 202, 239, 303, 310,
    358, 361, 397, 422, 528, 530,
    534, 548, 600
  development, 51
  preparation, 358
  training components, 52
  training manual, 52
Teaching awards, 7, 51–52, 80, 240,
    338, 353, 369, 410
Teaching Certificate content, 511
Teaching culture, 140, 144, 320, 324,
    419, 428, 429, 457
  perceptions of, 429
Teaching Enhancement Accredited
    Certification of the Higher
    Education Academy (TEACH)
    fellowships, 337, 343
Teaching evaluation(s), 32, 36, 79,
    207, 429, 643
  See also Assessment, of teaching
Teaching Excellence Framework (TEF),
    557, 559, 562
Teaching fellow, 142, 144, 225, 226,
    338, 344, 567
  See also Faculty fellows
Teaching inventory, 635
Teaching methods, 45, 54, 142,
    172–174, 180, 321, 322, 341,
    344, 426, 470, 501, 537, 546,
    549, 551, 553, 624
  See also Instructional design

Subject Index 697

Teaching observations, 319, 502, 503
Teaching philosophy, 196, 423, 429,
  502, 514
  See also Theoretical foundations
Teaching portfolio, 69, 465, 500, 502,
  513, 514, 520
Teaching standards, 457, 557
Technology-enhanced teaching and
  learning, 342, 413
  e-Learning platform, 529
  gamification, 500, 535
  instructional technology, 225, 381, 397
  integrated networks, 334
  integration of technology, 15, 185,
    360, 413
  learning management system (LMS),
    144, 224, 384, 437, 449
  learning technologies, 15, 17, 251, 256
  massive open online course
    (MOOC), 143, 641
  multimedia studio, 529
  One Button studio, 409
  simulators, 130
  social media, 88, 230, 300, 303
  synchronous and asynchronous
    digital resources, 369
  teaching technology, 194, 225
  technology(ies), 81, 163, 185, 222
  technology-enabled learning, 15
Technology products
  Adobe Connect, 196, 453
  Blackboard, 453
  collaborate, 366, 421, 453
  DropBox, 367
  Google Docs, 195
  Moodle, 337, 437
  One-Button Studio, 372
  Padlets, 195
  PowerPoint, 144, 319, 321, 359
  Skype, 437, 438, 440, 441, 453
  Voicethread, 453
  Yellowdig, 453
  Zoom, 453

Theological, xvi, 61, 113
  Catholic, 114
  faith-based, 113
  Jesuit, 255
Theoretical foundations of
  ADCs, 167–169
  Context, Input, Process and Product
    model (CIPP), 318
  critical management education, 558
  Cynefin and Standard+Case,
    599–600, 604
  Cynefin framework, 515, 517
  Cynefin network, 597, 599, 601
  design thinking, 513
  ethical education, x, 513, 522
  five elements of a learning
    organization, 577
  five-phase FD scheme, 577
  four-dimensional faculty
    development, 44
  Systemic Innovation in Education
    (SIE) model, 168
Theoretical foundations of teaching and
  learning, 186
  competence-based, 630, 632
  constructive alignment, 103, 167,
    173, 186, 190, 191
  constructivism, 172–173
  constructivist learning theory, 167
  differentiated instruction, 303
  Functional education
  good teacher/good teaching,
    32, 606
  Healey's Conceptual Model, 286
  integrative pedagogy, 411
  logic model, 286
  mastery learning, 303
  models of teaching, 5
  science of learning, 144
  self-determination theory (SDT),
    167, 176
  social constructivism, 168, 186, 190
  social justice, 206

698   **Subject Index**

Theoretical foundations of teaching and
learning (*cont.*)
  spirituality, 110
  taxonomy of significant learning,
    Fink's, 167, 175
  theoretical, 52, 71, 197
Theory to practice, 579
  shared practice, 367
Title III grant, 301, 302, 304, 309, 311
Transferable skills, 308
Transformation, 25, 33, 36, 59–72,
    153–162, 395, 401, 458, 514,
    522, 539, 629, 631, 632,
    635, 642
  curriculum, 25, 635
  model(s), 153–155
  process(es), 33, 629, 632, 635
  skills, 179, 308
  See also Change and transition
*Transformation, Innovation, Knowledge
    Creation*, 72
Transparent/transparency, 232, 260,
    261, 373, 412, 413, 517
Trust, 33, 35, 72, 81, 147, 157, 161,
    344, 371, 374

U

UK Higher Education Academy, 62,
    268–269, 271, 338, 578
Undergraduate Curriculum
    Committee, 105, 258
United Nations Educational, Scientific
    and Cultural Organization
    (UNESCO), 24, 495–496
United States Department of
    Education, 300, 302, 496
United States National Center for
    Educational Statistics, 496
Unit enhancement (UE), 157, 159–162
Universities and colleges
  Abdullah Gul University (AGU),
    266, 314, 544

Aga Khan University (AKU),
    331–339, 342–347
Beijing Institute of Technology
    (BIT), 545–548, 551–554
Bogazici University, 266, 314, 544
California State University, 278
Charles University, 624
Chinese University of Hong
    Kong, 547
Claremont University, 168,
    476, 512
Clemson University, 78, 247
Daystar University, 62
DePaul University, 500
Embry-Riddle Aeronautical
    University-Worldwide
    (ERAU-W), 446, 448,
    449, 455
Empire State College,
    433–438, 442
Fairfield University, 251, 252,
    255, 257
Florida State University, 61
Frostburg State University, 78
Fudan University, 52–53,
    553, 642–650
Green Mountain College (GMC),
    299–302, 304, 305, 307, 308,
    310, 311
Harvard University, 501
Hong Kong Baptist University, 427
Hong Kong Polytechnic
    University, 547
Hong Kong University of Science
    and Technology, 427
Howard Hughes Medical
    Institute, 213
Indiana University (IU) South Bend,
    221–223, 229
Karakoram International
    University, 318
Kaunas University of Technology, 47
Keele University, 168, 543

Subject Index

Lund University, xi, xix
Macau University, 547
Mansfield Hall, 266, 315
Masaryk University (MUNI), 614, 615, 621, 624, 626
Middle Tennessee State University (MTSU), 379–381, 387, 388
Monash University, 5, 151–153, 161, 163
Nankai University, 553
New Mexico State University (NMSU), 78, 235–247
North Central College (NCC), 405, 406, 412, 415
Norwegian University of Science and Technology (NTNU), 43, 47
Ocean University, 47, 553
Ohio State University, 553
Oklahoma City University, 500
Peking University, 553
Prescot College, 266, 315
Renmin University, 49, 50
Russell Group universities, 559
Shanghai Jiao Tong University (SJTU), 51, 52, 419–421, 423, 424, 428–430
Southwest Jiaotong University (SWJTU), 47, 53, 55, 56, 553, 571–584
State University of New York (SUNY), 246, 433–435
Strathmore University, 66–72
Sultan Qaboos University (SQU), 123, 124, 127, 133, 134, 457–472
Swinburne University of Technology
Syracuse University, 94, 313
Taiwan University, 547
Temple University, 94, 314
Tsinghua University, 47, 553
Tuffs University

Universidad Católica de Temuco (UC Temuco), 629, 630, 632, 634–637
Universidad del Norte, 26
University of Alabama, 500
University of Arizona (UArizona), 97, 98, 100, 103, 105–107
University of Calgary, 278
University of California, Los Angeles, 78, 547
University of California, Merced (UCM), 283–287, 290–294, 296
University of Georgia, 78, 83
University of Hong Kong (HKU), 427, 547, 591–595, 600–602, 604–609
University of Kansas, 78, 79, 462
University of Leeds, 557–559, 561–563, 565, 566
University of Liège, 527, 528, 534, 535, 538
University of Maryland, Baltimore County (UMBC), 393–395
University of Maryland, Eastern Shore, 94, 314
University of Melbourne, 4, 6
University of Michigan, 78, 405, 421, 547
University of New South Wales, 5
University of North Dakota, 78
University of Ontario Institute of Technology (UOIT, Ontario Tech University), 185–188, 197, 198
University of Oregon (UO), 318, 322
University of Queensland, 5
University of San Diego (USD), 111–114, 116
University of Sydney, 5
University of Twente, 482
University of Utah, 325

700   **Subject Index**

Universities and colleges (*cont.*)
  University of Western Australia
  University of Winchester, 269–279
  University System of Georgia
      (USG), 94, 314, 363–365,
      368, 369, 371–376, 392
  Valencia College, 500
  Vanderbilt University, 78
  Vrije Universiteit Amsterdam
      (VUA), 167, 168, 475, 476,
      480–482, 491
  Xiamen University, 47
  York Saint John University, 62
  Yunnan University, 53, 54
University System of Georgia (USG),
      363–365, 368, 369, 371–376
U.S. National Center for Education
    Statistics, 496

V

Values, xvi, 33, 66, 70, 78, 79, 81, 89,
      103, 109–118, 142–145, 149,
      176, 177, 185, 186, 188, 190,
      206, 211, 227, 236, 237, 272,
      277, 279, 287, 288, 297, 311,
      327, 329, 339, 341, 353, 366,
      381, 393, 394, 401, 409, 415,
      429, 433, 435, 447, 462, 465,
      472, 504, 515, 517, 535, 536,
      539, 559, 607, 609, 610, 618,
      619, 634, 635, 638, 647, 651
  ethical conduct, 112

  ethical education, x, xvi, 522
  holistic educator(s), 57, 572
  values-based education, 111,
      116, 118
Video conferencing, 185, 308,
    368, 373
Video format, 195
Virtual center(s), 381, 446
Virtual faculty learning community(ies)
      (V-FLC), 445–455
Volunteer staff, 334, 342
  Vista volunteer(s)
Voting representative, 363

W

Web-conferencing, 193–196, 446
Wellness services, 89
Workshops, ix, xv, 5, 26, 51, 61, 83,
      101, 114, 126, 143, 152,
      186, 203, 222, 235, 258,
      288, 300, 319, 353, 365,
      373, 380, 400, 409, 419,
      435, 446, 458, 485, 498,
      513, 533, 547, 552, 568,
      575, 592, 614, 629–639, 650
Writing group(s), 384, 415, 562, 563
Writing retreat(s), 89, 384, 386,
    562, 563

Y

Yale University, 139–150

Printed in the United States
by Baker & Taylor Publisher Services